SCHAUM'S®
outlines

# Principles Of Economics

## Second Edition

**Dominick Salvatore, Ph.D.**
*Professor of Economics*
*Fordham University*

**Eugene A. Diulio, Ph.D.**
*Associate Professor of Economics*
*Fordham University*

**Schaum's Outline Series**

Mc
Graw
Hill

New York   Chicago   San Francisco   Lisbon   London   Madrid
Mexico City   Milan   New Delhi   San Juan   Seoul
Singapore   Sydney   Toronto

**DOMINICK SALVATORE** received his Ph.D. in 1971 and is currently professor of Economics at Fordham University in New York. He is the author of the textbooks *International Economics*, 5th Ed. (1995), *Microeconomic Theory*, 2nd Ed. (1994), and *Managerial Economics in a Global Economy*, 3rd Ed. (1996). He has also written Schaum's Outlines in *Microeconomic Theory, Managerial Economics, Statistics and Econometrics*, and *International Economics*, and coauthored *Development Economics*. His research has been published in numerous leading scholarly journals and presented at national and international conferences.

**EUGENE A. DIULIO**, currently associate professor of Economics at Fordham University, received his Ph.D. from Columbia University. He is the author of *Schaum's Outline of Macroeconomic Theory*. His research has been in the area of financial institutions and financial markets. He is an educational consultant to numerous banks and is an adjunct professor at Columbia University Graduate School of Business.

Appendix A is jointly copyrighted © 1996 by The McGraw-Hill Companies, Inc. and MathSoft, Inc.

3 4 5 6 7 8 9 10   CUS/CUS   1 9 8 7 6 5 4 3

ISBN      978-0-07-176253-3
MHID      0-07-176253-1

# Preface

Most students find the introductory course in economics interesting but difficult. This book is designed to enhance comprehension of introductory economics by presenting the core material in an easily understood format. Students can use this book as a supplement to an introductory textbook or as an independent text for self-study. Also, when combined with a series of readings, this book can serve as the required course text.

To make learning the subject matter easier, a summary and a list of key terms with definitions are placed at the beginning rather than at the end of each chapter. The analytical content is then presented in a clear and systematic way, followed by a series of solved problems. The solved problems illustrate and amplify the analytical content, bring into sharp focus those points which the student often feels unsure of, and provide the application and reinforcement so vital to effective learning. Throughout, both descriptive text and solved problems are further clarified by reference to carefully constructed graphs. Because a facility with graphs is essential for the mastery of economics, Chapter 1 contains a section on drafting and interpreting graphs. Each chapter ends with a set of multiple choice and true or false review questions with answers.

The topics are arranged in the order in which they are presented in most introductory texts. A one-semester course in introductory economics usually covers Chapters 1–6, 8, 10, 15–16, and 19–20. In a one-year macroeconomics/microeconomics sequence, Chapters 1–13 are normally covered in the first semester and Chapters 1–2 and 14–23 in the second semester. A microeconomics/macroeconomics sequence reverses the chapter coverage without loss of continuity.

The methodology of this book and its contents are derived from our classroom teaching at Fordham University and lectures we have given at a number of other institutions during the past twenty years. We would like to thank our good friend and colleague, Joseph R. Cammarosano, for his careful reading and constructuve comments. The patient assistance of the Schaum staff at McGraw-Hill is greatly appreciated as is the continuous encouragement and support of our wives, Lucia and Rosemary.

Dominick Salvatore
Eugene A. Diulio

# Contents

# Problems and Examples Also Found in the Companion SCHAUM'S INTERACTIVE OUTLINE

Some of the problems and examples in this book have software components in the companion *Schaum's Interactive Outline*. The Mathcad Engine, which "drives" the Interactive Outline, allows every number, formula, and graph chosen to be completely live and interactive. To identify those items that are available in the Interactive Outline software, please look for the Mathcad icons, 🖩 Mathcad, placed under the problem number or adjacent to a numbered item. A complete list of these Mathcad entries follows below. For more information about the software, including the sample screens, see Appendix A on page 379.

| | | | |
|---|---|---|---|
| Problem 2.5 | Example 7.8 | Problem 14.16 | Example 18.4 |
| Problem 2.6 | Example 7.10 | Problem 14.18 | Example 18.6 |
| Problem 3.15 | Example 8.1 | Problem 15.2 | Problem 18.11 |
| Problem 3.16 | Example 8.2 | Example 16.3 | Problem 18.15 |
| Problem 3.17 | Example 8.4 | Example 16.4 | Problem 19.3 |
| Problem 3.18 | Example 8.5 | Example 16.5 | Problem 19.4 |
| Example 4.5 | Example 8.6 | Example 16.6 | Problem 19.7 |
| Example 4.6 | Example 8.8 | Problem 16.10 | Problem 19.14 |
| Example 4.7 | Example 9.3 | Problem 16.12 | Problem 19.15 |
| Example 4.9 | Example 9.10 | Problem 16.13 | Problem 19.16 |
| Example 5.5 | Example 9.11 | Example 17.2 | Problem 20.4 |
| Example 5.6 | Table 9-2 | Example 17.3 | Problem 20.6 |
| Problem 5.5 | Example 10.1 | Example 17.4 | Problem 20.7 |
| Problem 5.8 | Example 10.5 | Example 17.5 | Problem 20.8 |
| Problem 5.10 | Example 11.1 | Example 17.6 | Problem 21.2 |
| Example 6.2 | Example 11.2 | Example 17.8 | Problem 21.6 |
| Problem 6.6 | Example 11.5 | Problem 17.5 | Problem 21.8 |
| Problem 6.9 | Example 11.6 | Problem 17.7 | Problem 21.13 |
| Example 7.3 | Problem 12.8 | Problem 17.8 | Problem 23.3 |
| Example 7.4 | Problem 12.10 | Problem 17.9 | Problem 23.5 |
| Example 7.5 | Example 14.2 | Problem 17.13 | Problem 23.6 |
| Example 7.7 | Example 14.3 | Example 18.3 | |

# Chapter 1

# Introduction to Economics

## *Chapter Summary*

1. Economics is a discipline which studies how scarce economic resources are used to maximize production for a society. Microeconomics studies the economic behavior of individual units; macroeconomics studies the behavior of aggregates.
2. Economic theories and models are developed to facilitate the understanding of complex economic phenomena. Models of economic behavior relate a dependent variable to a limited number of independent variables. The term *ceteris paribus* is used when the value of all but one of the independent variables is held constant.
3. Economists use tables, graphs, and equations to present modeled behavior. Graphs are useful in that they provide visualization of the relationship between two variables. An equation is a more concise presentation of a relationship and is essential for the forecasting of economic behavior.

## *Important Terms*

**Ceteris paribus.** A Latin phrase meaning "other things being equal." This assumption is used in modeling to indicate that the value of other independent variables are held constant.

**Dependent variable.** A variable whose value depends upon another economic event. For example, spending by an individual is dependent upon the receipt of income.

**Economics.** A social science that studies how individuals and organizations in society engage in the production, distribution, and consumption of goods and services.

**Economic theory or model.** A generalization and abstraction of reality that seeks to isolate a few of the most important determinants (causes) of an economic event in order to provide a better understanding of that event. Such models are used to develop policies that might prevent, correct, or alleviate economic problems.

**Independent variable.** A variable whose value determines the value of another (dependent) variable. For example, an individual's income largely determines the amount that an individual can spend.

**Macroeconomics.** The study of aggregate economic activity, such as the economy's level of output, level of national income, level of employment, and general price level.

**Microeconomics.** The study of economic behavior of individual decision-making units, such as consumers, resource owners, and business firms in a free-enterprise economy.

## Outline of Chapter 1: Introduction to Economics

1

## 1.1  THE SUBJECT MATTER OF ECONOMICS

Economics is a social science which studies individuals and organizations engaged in the production, distribution, and consumption of goods and services. The discipline of economics has developed principles, theories, and models which isolate a few of the most important determinants or causes of economic events. The goal is to predict economic occurrences and to develop policies that might prevent or correct such problems as unemployment, inflation, and waste in the economy.

Economics is subdivided into macroeconomics and microeconomics. Macroeconomics studies aggregate output and employment, the general price level, and the balance of payments. Microeconomics studies the economic behavior of individual decision-making units such as consumers, resource owners, and business firms in a free-enterprise economy.

**EXAMPLE 1.1.**  Economic conditions greatly affect all of us throughout our lives. They determine where we live, what we eat, what school we attend, whether we go to work or to college, what job we get, and how much we earn. Economic conditions affect the peace and stability in our cities and in the world. Problems of unemployment and inflation fill the front pages of our newspapers and news programs. It is practically impossible in today's complex world to be a responsible citizen without having some grasp of economic issues and principles. Economics seeks to give us a better understanding of how our economy operates and what can be done to avoid, correct, or alleviate unemployment, inflation, and waste.

## 1.2  THE METHODOLOGY OF ECONOMICS

Because economic phenomena are complex, economists have found it useful to model economic behavior. In constructing a model, economists make assumptions which cut away unnecessary detail and reduce the complexity of economic behavior. Once modeled, economic behavior may be presented as a relationship between a dependent variable and a few independent variables. The behavior being explained is the dependent variable; the variables explaining that economic behavior are the independent variables. Frequently, the dependent variable is presented as depending upon one independent variable, with the influence of the other independent variables held constant. Thus, $y$ depends upon $x$, *ceteris paribus* (*ceteris paribus* means that other independent variables are held constant).

**EXAMPLE 1.2.**  A manufacturer of compact discs must anticipate the quantity of compact discs that individuals will buy. Purchases, and therefore demand, are probably influenced by a large number of variables: (1) the price of each compact disc; (2) the price of compact disc players; (3) the price of tapes; (4) the price of tape decks; (5) people's income; (6) the desire to listen to music rather than watch videos; (7) and other nonspecified variables. Forecasting the demand for compact discs becomes a formidable task if we attempt to take into account all the variables that could affect demand. If one variable is largely responsible for demand, a manageable forecasting task exists. It is reasonable to assume that price is the most important variable influencing the purchase of compact discs; the demand for compact discs is therefore presented as $Q_{d_{\text{compact discs}}} = f(P_{\text{compact discs}})$, *ceteris paribus;* the quantity of compact discs demanded ($Q_d$) depends upon the price ($P$) of a compact disc, with the influence of other independent variables held constant. $Q_{d_{\text{compact discs}}}$ is the dependent variable which is determined by the price of compact discs, the independent variable.

An economic model will also specify whether the dependent and independent variables are positively or negatively related. The relationship is positive when the dependent variable moves in the same direction as the independent variable; the relationship is negative when the value of the dependent variable increases when the value of the independent variable decreases. In the model of the demand for compact discs, we expect a negative relationship—the more compact discs are purchased, the lower the price of each compact disc.

## 1.3  THE USE OF TABLES, GRAPHS, AND EQUATIONS

Models which simplify economic reality provide the framework for organizing data, empirically testing economic hypotheses, and forecasting economic behavior. In Examples 3 through 6, we model consumer spending, present data on consumer spending for a hypothetical economy, graph the data, establish an equation for consumer spending, and then use the equation to forecast consumer spending.

**EXAMPLE 1.3.** We shall assume that the amount a consumer spends ($C$) is positively related to the receipt of disposable income ($Y_d$), i.e., $C = f(Y_d)$. Table 1-1 presents data on consumer spending for five individuals with different levels of disposable income. As we can see from the table, consumption and disposable income display a positive relationship.

**Table 1-1**
**(in $)**

| Individual | Disposable Income ($Y_d$) | Consumption ($C$) |
|------------|---------------------------|-------------------|
| A | 20,000 | 20,000 |
| B | 21,000 | 20,750 |
| C | 22,000 | 21,500 |
| D | 24,000 | 23,000 |
| E | 27,000 | 25,250 |

**EXAMPLE 1.4.** The data from Table 1-1 are plotted in Fig. 1-1 and labeled $C_1$. Consumer spending is plotted on the vertical axis and disposable income is plotted on the horizontal axis. (The dependent variable normally appears on the vertical axis and the independent variable on the horizontal axis.) Graphs visually present data and the positive or negative relationship of the dependent and independent variable.

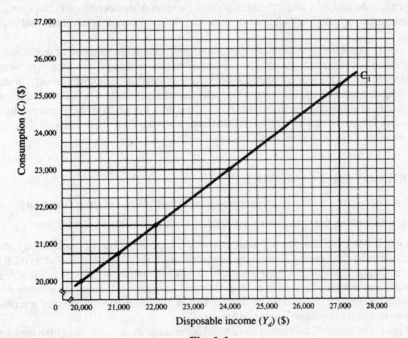

**Fig. 1-1**

**EXAMPLE 1.5.** Although Fig. 1-1 is visually informative, it does not provide us with sufficient information to predict the amount an individual with a $30,000 income will spend. Since the relation between consumption and disposable income is linear in Fig. 1-1, consumer spending behavior can be presented by the linear equation $C = \$5000 + 0.75Y_d$. Substituting $Y_d = \$20,000$ into the equation, we find that $C = \$20,000$ when $Y_d$ is $20,000, which is consistent with the consumption and disposable income of Individual A in Table 1-1. ($C = \$5000 + 0.75(\$20,000)$; $C = \$5000 + \$15,000$; $C = \$20,000$.) We use the consumer spending equation to forecast that a consumer with a $30,000 income will spend $27,500.

# Solved Problems

## THE SUBJECT MATTER OF ECONOMICS

**1.1.**    (a)    Explain the statement "Economics is a social science."

        (b)    Why is the study of economics important?

        (a)    The social sciences study how society is organized and functions. Economics, sociology, anthropology, psychology, and political science are all social sciences. Each studies the organization and functioning of society from a particular point of view. Economics studies how individuals and organizations in society engage in the production, distribution, and consumption of goods and services.

        (b)    An understanding of basic economic issues and principles is essential for a well-informed and responsible citizen. Our newspapers and news programs are filled with information about unemployment, inflation, price controls, taxes, energy, imports, monopoly power of large corporations, and other problems. Without some knowledge of economics, it is practically impossible to understand the issues involved and form sensible opinions on these important matters. Economics can also help individuals to operate their businesses and control their personal finances by providing a basis for understanding how to protect or reduce the impact of inflation, how tax reforms and energy conservation programs affect them, and so on.

**1.2.**    Distinguish between macroeconomics and microeconomics.

           *Macroeconomics* studies the economy as a whole or its major components such as households, business, and government. It deals with the price level and with the level of total output, employment, and national income. It also analyzes total private expenditures, total investments, total government expenditures, and total imports and exports of goods and services. It seeks to explain the causes of unemployment, inflation, and balance-of-payments deficits in order to formulate and implement economic policy.

           *Microeconomics,* on the other hand, studies the economic behavior of individual decision-making units such as consumers, resource owners, and business firms in a free-enterprise system (an economic system in which the government does not directly control economic activity). It deals with how an individual consumer spends income to maximize satisfaction, how a business firm combines resources or factors of production to maximize profits, and how the price of each commodity and each type of resource is determined by supply and demand. It studies how these individual decisions are affected by different forms of market organization.

## THE METHODOLOGY OF ECONOMICS

**1.3.**    (a)    How are economic models and theories developed? What is their function?

        (b)    What are some of the difficulties associated with the study of economics?

        (a)    Economic models and theories are abstractions and generalizations of reality. They seek to cut through the many details surrounding an economic event to arrive at and isolate a few of its most important causes or determinants. For example, there are many causes of inflation, but if we can identify a few of the most important ones we may be able to reduce or largely eliminate inflation. Thus, economic models help us understand economic phenomena so that we can explain and possibly predict a recession, a period of inflation, and other important economic events.

        (b)    There are a number of difficulties associated with the study of economics. (1) We may have preconceived notions about the cause and cure of an economic problem which are not supported by actual economic behavior. (2) Generalizing from individual experiences often leads to wrong conclusions (this is called *the fallacy of composition*). For example, when an individual increases his or her savings, that individual becomes richer, but when society as a whole saves more by demanding fewer goods and services it may become poorer by putting people out of work. (3) The fact that one economic event precedes another does not necessarily imply cause and effect. For example, the collapse of the U.S. stock market in 1929 did not cause the worldwide Great Depression of the 1930s. (4) Since economics is a social science and laboratory experiments cannot be conducted, economic theories can only describe expected behavior. Thus, economic theories are not as precise or reliable as the natural laws established in the pure sciences.

**1.4.** (*a*) Why are models used in economics?

(*b*) Suppose we are analyzing an individual's demand for videos. Identify whether the following variables are dependent or independent variables: quantity of videos demanded ($Q_{d_{videos}}$), the individual's disposable income ($Y$), the price of each video ($P_{videos}$), the cost of renting a video ($P_{rental}$).

(*c*) Use part (*b*) to present the dependent variable as a function of the independent variables.

(*d*) Would you expect the dependent variable to have a negative or positive relation to the independent variables?

(*a*) A model simplifies reality. In abstracting from reality, a dependent variable is explained by a limited number of independent variables.

(*b*) Quantity of videos demanded is the dependent variable since this is what we are trying to explain. The other variables are independent variables which help explain how many videos an individual wants to buy. For example, disposable income is one of the variables that influences the number of videos a person can afford. The price of a video is important, as is the cost of renting a video rather than purchasing one.

(*c*) The quantity of videos demanded is dependent upon (is a function of) an individual's disposable income, the price of each video, and the cost of renting videos. Using notation, the relationship between the dependent and independent variables can be presented as $Q_{d_{videos}} = f(Y, P_{videos}, P_{rental})$, where $Y$ represents an individual's disposable income.

(*d*) We would expect the quantity of videos demanded to be positively related to disposable income, i.e., the more spendable income a person has, the more videos this person can afford. The quantity of videos demanded would be negatively related to price since an individual is more likely to purchase a video when each video is priced at, say, \$15 rather than \$30. The quantity of videos demanded is positively related to the cost of renting a video since more videos would be purchased the higher the cost of renting a video.

**1.5.** (*a*) The demand for videos might be presented as a function of the video's purchase price. Does this mean that income and the cost of renting a video are unimportant?

(*b*) What is the meaning of and the economist's use of the term *ceteris paribus*?

(*a*) To further simplify the demand-for-videos function—$Q_{d_{videos}} = f(Y, P_{videos}, P_{rental})$—we could assume that the individual's disposable income and cost of renting videos are unchanged. Thus, while income and rental cost influence the demand for videos, more videos are purchased only because of a lower price for videos since the individual's disposable income and the cost of renting a video are unchanged.

(*b*) The term *ceteris paribus* means that other independent variables affecting the dependent variable are held constant, or are unchanged. When other independent variables that influence the quantity of videos purchased are held constant, the demand for videos can be presented as $Q_{d_{videos}} = f(P_{videos})$, *ceteris paribus*.

## THE USE OF TABLES, GRAPHS, AND EQUATIONS

**1.6.** What is a graph?

A graph is a visual presentation of the behavior of a variable over time (a *time series graph*) or of the relationship between two variables. A time series graph shows, for example, the level of interest rates over successive months or years. In the graphic presentation of the relationship between two variables, one variable is plotted on the horizontal axis and the other on the vertical axis. Graphs are useful in that they help establish relationships. Whereas a verbal explanation may be misinterpreted, a graph provides a visual presentation which is easily recalled.

**1.7.** Why is there extensive use of graphs in economics?

Economic relationships can be enhanced by a graph. For example, suppose a market researcher polls college-age students in metropolitan Boston to find the number of them that are interested in purchasing a travel package to Florida. Suppose the polltakers find that 100 would purchase a six-day package at $900, 200 at $800, 400 at $700, and 800 at $600. Obviously, more students are interested in purchasing the travel package at a lower price. The relationship between package price and positive responses is illustrated in Fig. 1-2 by demand curve D where the price ($P$) of the travel package is plotted on the vertical axis and the number of positive responses (quantity, $Q$) is plotted on the horizontal axis. In studying these responses, we find that the number of positive responses doubles for each $100 decrease in the price of the travel package.

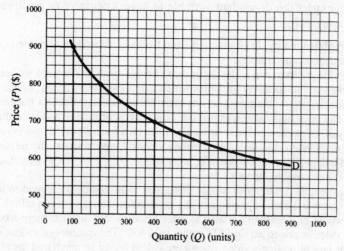

**Fig. 1-2**

**1.8.** Table 1-2 presents the number of 19-inch color TVs individuals are willing to purchase at various prices in City A and in City B.

(a) Plot these data, with price ($P$) on the vertical axis and quantity ($Q$) on the horizontal axis; set price increments at $25 and quantity increments at 25 units. For City A, connect the points which represent the price and quantity demanded and label the line $D_1$. Do the same thing for the points for City B and label the line $D_2$.

(b) Find the increase in the quantity of TV units purchased in City A and City B when the price of TVs is lowered from $300 to $275.

(c) The slope of a straight line is the change in the vertical axis (in this example $\Delta P$) divided by a change in the horizontal axis (here $\Delta Q$). Find the slope of demand lines $D_1$ and $D_2$ in Fig. 1-3 when the price is lowered from $300 to $275. Which demand line is more steeply sloped?

(d) What does the difference in the slope of demand lines $D_1$ and $D_2$ indicate?

**Table 1-2**

| Price | Quantity Demanded in | |
|---|---|---|
| | City A | City B |
| $350 | 100 | 75 |
| $325 | 150 | 100 |
| $300 | 200 | 125 |
| $275 | 250 | 150 |
| $250 | 300 | 175 |

(a) See Fig. 1-3.

(b) The quantity of TVs purchased in City A increases 50 units when the price of TVs is lowered $25; the quantity of TVs purchased in City B increases 25 units when the price is lowered $25.

(c) The slope of demand line $D_1$ is 0.50 ($\Delta P/\Delta Q = \$25/50 = 0.50$), while the slope of $D_2$ is 1.00. The slope of demand line $D_2$ is greater, indicating that it is more steeply sloped.

(d) A more steeply sloped demand line indicates that a change in price is associated with a smaller change in quantity demanded.

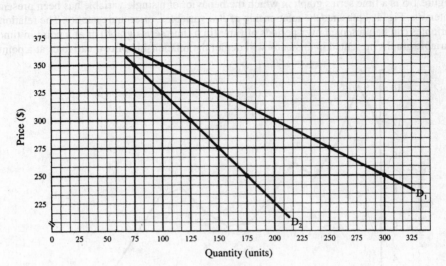

Fig. 1-3

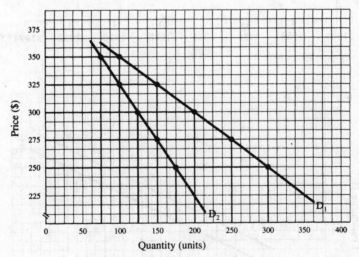

Fig. 1-4

**1.9.** Replot the data from Table 1-2. Again plot price on the vertical axis in increments of $25, but this time plot quantity demanded on the horizontal axis in increments of 50 rather than 25.

(a) Visually compare the demand lines in Figs. 1-3 and 1-4. Does it appear that the steepness of the demand lines has changed? Has the slope of either demand line changed?

(b) Can one misinterpret the strength of the relationship of two variables by visual inspection of the data?

(a) It appears that demand lines $D_1$ and $D_2$ are more steeply sloped in Fig. 1-4 than in Fig. 1-3. However, the slope of the demand lines has not changed since $\Delta P/\Delta Q$ is unchanged.

(b) One cannot reach conclusions about the sensitivity of one variable to another from visual inspection of a graph since the choice of scale affects the steepness of the relationship. For example, the demand lines in Fig. 1-4 appear steeper because the unit interval along the quantity axis is 50 while the unit interval is 25 in Fig. 1-3.

**1.10.** Figure 1-5 plots the average yield on 3-month Treasury bills from 1980 through 1993. In what way does this graph differ from the graph in Fig. 1-4?

Figure 1-5 is a time series graph in which the behavior of a single variable has been presented at various time intervals. Fig. 1-4 presents the relationship of *two* variables, price and quantity. The relationship between two variables can be presented over periods of time (in a time series graph) or at a point in time. Most of the two-variable graphs presented in this book will depict the relationship of two variables at a point in time.

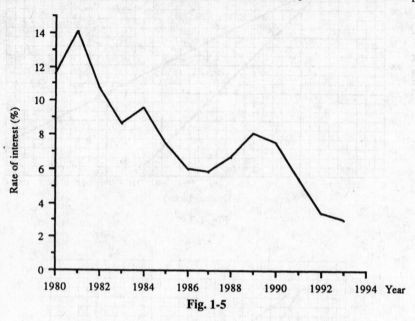

**Fig. 1-5**

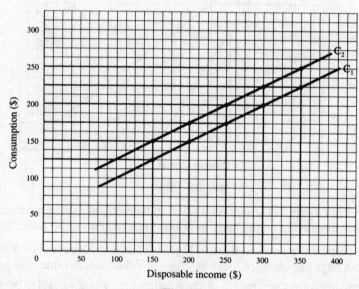

**Fig. 1-6**

**1.11.** Suppose consumption spending is presented as $C = \$50 + 0.50Y_d$, where $C$ represents the amount consumed and $Y_d$ represents disposable income.

(a) Create a table that shows the amount consumed when disposable income is \$150, \$200, \$250, \$300, and \$350.

(b) Graph the data from the table and label the line $C_1$.

(c)  Suppose the consumption spending equation changes from $C = \$50 + 0.50Y_d$ to $C = \$75 + 0.50Y_d$. Plot the new consumption equation on the same graph and label it $C_2$. What happens to the consumption line when the constant of the consumption equation increases from \$50 to \$75?

(a)

**Table 1-3**

| Disposable Income | Consumption |
|---|---|
| \$150 | \$125 |
| \$200 | \$150 |
| \$250 | \$175 |
| \$300 | \$200 |
| \$350 | \$225 |

(b)  See Fig. 1-6.

(c)  See Fig. 1-6. The consumption line shifts upward by \$25 when the constant of the consumption equation increases \$25.

## *Multiple Choice Questions*

1.  Economics studies individuals and organizations in society engaged in the
    (a)  production of goods and services,
    (b)  distribution of goods and services,
    (c)  consumption of goods and services,
    (d)  all of the above,
    (e)  none of the above.

2.  Economic principles, theories or models
    (a)  seek to explain and predict economic events in the hope of developing policies to correct economic problems,
    (b)  identify all of the numerous detailed causes of an economic event,
    (c)  develop rules of individual behavior in order to generalize and predict society's economic behavior,
    (d)  all of the above.

3.  Which of the following does *not* refer to macroeconomics?
    (a)  The study of aggregate economic activity,
    (b)  The study of the economic behavior of individual decision-making units such as consumers, resource owners, and business firms,
    (c)  The study of the causes of and policies to remedy unemployment,
    (d)  The study of the causes of inflation.

4.  Which of the following is a correct statement?
    (a)  The value of an independent variable depends upon the value of a dependent variable.
    (b)  The term *ceteris paribus* is used when the value of a dependent variable is held constant.
    (c)  The term *ceteris paribus* is used when the value of a dependent variable is changing.
    (d)  The term *ceteris paribus* is used when the value of an independent variable is held constant.

5.  When the value of an independent variable increases, the value of the dependent variable
    (a)  also increases when there is a positive relationship,
    (b)  also increases when there is a negative relationship,

    (c)   decreases when there is a positive relationship,

    (d)   decreases when there is no relationship between the two variables.

**6.**   In the statement "Quantity demanded is a function of price,"

    (a)   quantity demanded is the dependent variable and price is the independent variable,

    (b)   price is the dependent variable and quantity is the independent variable,

    (c)   quantity demanded and price have no relationship.

**7.**   *Ceteris paribus* is used in economics when

    (a)   two variables are positively related,

    (b)   two variables are negatively related,

    (c)   the value of an independent variable affecting the dependent variable is held constant,

    (d)   the value of a dependent variable affecting the independent variable is held constant.

**8.**   In the equation $C = \$10 + 0.90Y_d$,

    (a)   $C$ (consumption) is \$90 when $Y_d$ (disposable income) is \$100,

    (b)   $C$ (consumption) is \$190 when $Y_d$ (disposable income) is \$200,

    (c)   $C$ (consumption) is \$270 when $Y_d$ (disposable income) is \$300,

    (d)   $C$ (consumption) is \$390 when $Y_d$ (disposable income) is \$400.

# True or False Questions

**9.** _____   Economic models and theories are accurate statements of reality.

**10.** _____   Microeconomics deals with concerns such as the price level and the level of employment.

**11.** _____   In the statement "Consumption is a function of disposable income," consumption is the dependent variable.

**12.** _____   Two variables are positively related when their values move in the same direction.

**13.** _____   The value of the independent variable is determined by the value of the dependent variable.

**14.** _____   Graphs provide a visual representation of the relationship between two variables.

**15.** _____   In the equation $Q_d = 100 - 5P$, $Q_d$ is 50 when $P$ is 10.

### Answers to Multiple Choice and True or False Questions

| | | | |
|---|---|---|---|
| **1.** (d) | **5.** (a) | **9.** (F) | **13.** (F) |
| **2.** (a) | **6.** (a) | **10.** (F) | **14.** (T) |
| **3.** (b) | **7.** (c) | **11.** (T) | **15.** (T) |
| **4.** (d) | **8.** (b) | **12.** (T) | |

# Chapter 2

# The Economic Problem

## Chapter Summary

1. Scarcity exists in every society because human material wants are unlimited, whereas the economic resources necessary to produce the goods and services to satisfy these wants are limited. All economies therefore have an economic problem: deciding what to produce, how to produce, and who shall receive the goods and services produced.
2. This economic problem of limited production can be presented as a production-possibility frontier—the maximum alternative combinations of goods and services that can be produced at a point in time.
3. Economic growth occurs when the economy's productive capabilities increase; this growth in productive capability is depicted as an outward shift of the economy's production-possibility frontier.
4. When production is at its maximum, increased output of Good A requires reduced production of other goods, i.e., there is an opportunity cost to the increased production of Good A. The principle of increasing costs states that continuous expansion in the production of Good A is secured only by sacrificing increasing amounts of other goods.
5. Decisions on what goods and services to produce are made by government command or through a market mechanism. With a market system, decisions are determined by potential buyers' ability and willingness to pay for the goods and services produced.

## Important Terms

**Capital.** Goods such as tools, machines, factories, and transportation networks which are used in and/or facilitate the production of goods and services that satisfy human wants. The terms *capital* and *capital resources* are interchangeable.

**Command economy.** An economy in which the government directs the allocation of resources, the output of goods and services, and the distribution of the resulting output.

**Economic efficiency.** A state in which it is impossible to produce additional output of a particular good or service without decreasing the output of other goods or services.

**Economic growth.** An increase in the economy's productive capabilities due to an increase in the quantity or quality of economic resources and/or a change in technology.

**Economic problem.** Because of limited productive capabilities, there is a need to make decisions about what to produce, how to produce, and the distribution of output.

**Factors of production.** The inputs—land, labor, and capital—necessary for the production of goods and services. The terms *factors of production* and *economic resources* are interchangeable.

**Labor.** The mental and physical skills of individuals which are used to produce goods and services. The terms *labor* and *human resources* are interchangeable.

**Land.** The economy's natural resources—land, trees, oil, minerals—which can be used to produce goods and services. The terms *land* and *natural resources* are interchangeable.

**Market economy.** An economy in which individuals and businesses freely decide where to employ economic resources, freely decide which goods and services to produce, and freely distribute the resulting output.

11

**Opportunity cost.**    What must be sacrificed in order to implement an alternative action. In terms of producing goods and services it is the output that will no longer be produced in order to increase the output of a specific good or service.

**Principle of increasing costs.**    More units of one good are given up to produce an additional unit of an alternative good.

**Production possibility.**    The maximum amount of goods and services which can be produced at a point in time with existing resources and a given state of technology.

**Scarcity.**    Exists because economic resources are unable to supply (produce) all the goods and services demanded.

## Outline of Chapter 2: The Economic Problem

## 2.1    THE PROBLEM OF SCARCITY

Economics is the study of scarcity—the study of the allocation of scarce resources to satisfy human wants. People's material wants, for the most part, are unlimited: it seems that the more people have, the more they want. Output, on the other hand, is limited by the state of technology and the quantity and quality of the economy's resources, i.e., by the quantity and quality of human, capital, and natural resources. Because economic resources and the output of goods and services are limited, the production of each good and service involves a cost. Thus, each good and service produced is supplied at a price greater than zero.

Scarcity is a fundamental problem for every society. Decisions must be made regarding *what to produce, how to produce,* and *for whom to produce. What* to produce involves decisions about the kinds and quantities of goods and services to produce. *How* to produce requires decisions about what techniques to use and how the economic resources (labor, capital, and land) are to be combined in producing output. And *for whom* to produce involves decisions on the distribution of output—how what has been produced is to be distributed among the members of a society.

**EXAMPLE 2.1.**    *What to produce:* Every society must somehow decide how many luxurious mansions and how many low-cost apartments to construct, how many full-size and compact cars to build, how many schools to erect and teachers to train, how much food and medical services to supply, and how many civilian and defense goods and services to provide. *How to produce:* Since goods such as houses and cars and services such as education and medical treatments can usually be produced with many different techniques and combinations of labor, capital, and land, it is crucial to determine which of the many techniques and available factor combinations should be used. *For whom to produce:* Payment of income to individuals in the society, the price of each good and service, and the personal preferences of each individual will determine the distribution of goods and services (output) among the members of society.

Decisions on what to produce and how to produce involve opportunity costs. An *opportunity cost* is what is sacrificed to implement an alternative action, i.e., what is given up to produce or obtain a particular good or service. For example, the opportunity cost of expanding a country's military arsenal in a full-employment economy is the decreased production of nonmilitary goods and services. Opportunity costs are found in every situation in which scarcity necessitates decision making.

**EXAMPLE 2.2.**    Opportunity costs exist for society as a whole. The greater the number of people trained to provide medical services, the fewer are available to be lawyers, teachers, or accountants. Therefore, the opportunity cost of training more people to provide medical services is the amount of legal, educational, and accounting services that will not exist. As more of a society's capital equipment is used to produce cars, less capital is available to produce washing machines, motorboats, or bicycles. The opportunity cost of increased capital in the automobile industry is the amount of capital no longer available to produce washing machines, motorboats, or bicycles. Similarly, when more land is used to produce wheat, less is available to produce corn. The opportunity cost of expanded wheat production is the decreased amount of corn production.

Opportunity costs also exist for an individual. Time is a scarce resource. The more time one devotes to studying, the less time one has for leisure activities such as sports, TV, and socializing. And, of course, there is an opportunity cost in last-minute cramming for examinations—the time that otherwise would have been allocated to sleeping the night before the examination.

## 2.2    THE PRODUCTION-POSSIBILITY FRONTIER

A production-possibility frontier shows the maximum amount of alternative combinations of goods and services that a society can produce at a given time when there is full utilization of economic resources and technology. Table 2-1 presents alternative combinations of guns and butter output for a hypothetical economy. (Guns represent the output of military goods, while butter represents the production of nonmilitary goods and services.) In choosing what to produce, decision makers have a choice of producing, for example, alternative C—5000 guns and 14 million units of butter—or any of the other alternatives. This production-possibility schedule is plotted in Fig. 2-1. The curve, labeled PP, is called the production-possibility frontier. Point C on the production-possibility curve represents a position of full employment of the economy's resources and full use of its technology; at point C, 5000 guns and 14 million units of butter are produced. Point D is another possible alternative, one in which more guns and fewer units of butter are produced.

The production-possibility frontier depicts not only limited productive capability and therefore the problem of scarcity, but also the concept of opportunity cost. When an economy is on the production-possibility curve, such as at point C, gun production can be increased only by decreasing butter output. Thus, to move from alternative C (5000 guns and 14 million units of butter) to alternative D (9000 guns and 6 million units of butter), 8 million fewer units of butter are produced in order to increase gun production 4000 units. The opportunity cost of the additional 4000 units of gun production is 8 million units of butter.

The production-possibility frontier shifts outward over time as more resources become available and/or technology is improved. Growth in the economy's productive capability is depicted in Fig. 2-1 by the outward shift of the production-possibility frontier from PP to P′P′. Suppose the economy is at point C, producing 5000 guns and 14 million units of butter. When the production-possibility frontier shifts upward from PP to P′P′, 4000 additional guns can be produced without sacrificing any butter production. This example of growth in productive capacity should not be construed as a refutation of the law of opportunity cost. Fewer sacrifices may be made when growth occurs. However, when there is efficient utilization of resources and an absence of growth, additional gun production is possible only when the output of butter is decreased.

Points *on* a production-possibility frontier are efficient; points within the frontier are inefficient and points outside the frontier are unattainable. Points C and D on production-possibility frontier PP are efficient because all available resources are utilized and there is full use of existing technology. Positions outside the production-possibility frontier PP are unattainable since the production-possibility frontier defines the maximum amount that can be produced at a given time. Positions within a production-possibility frontier are inefficient because some resources are either unemployed or underemployed, i.e., either not employed at all or employed at tasks that do not fully utilize the production capability of the resource.

**EXAMPLE 2.3.**    On production-possibility frontier PP in Fig. 2-1, point C represents full and efficient utilization of resources. For curve PP, alternative C′ is unattainable since output cannot exceed the economy's productive capabilities, i.e., output cannot extend beyond the limits depicted by the production-possibility frontier PP. Once the production-possibility frontier has shifted outward to P′P′, alternative C then represents inefficient utilization of resources—resources are either unemployed or underemployed since alternative C is inside production-possibility frontier P′P′.

**Table 2-1**

| Alternative Outputs | Guns (thousand units) | Butter (million units) |
|---|---|---|
| A | 0 | 20 |
| B | 2 | 18 |
| C | 5 | 14 |
| D | 9 | 6 |
| E | 10 | 0 |

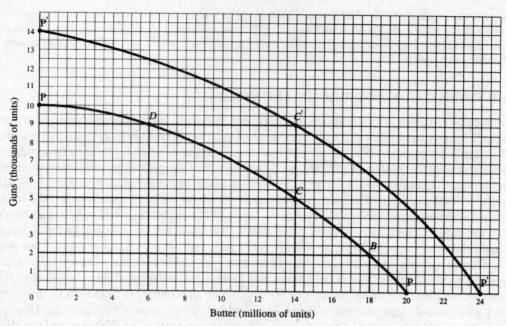

**Fig. 2-1**

## 2.3   THE PRINCIPLE OF INCREASING COSTS

Resources are not equally efficient in the production of goods and services, i.e., they are not equally productive when used to produce an alternative good. This imperfect substitutability of resources is due to differences in the skills of labor and to the specialized function of most machinery and many buildings. Thus, when the decision is made to produce more guns and less butter, the resources reallocated to the production of guns are usually less productive. It therefore follows that as larger amounts of resources are transferred from the production of butter to the production of guns, increasing units of butter are given up for fewer incremental units of guns. This increasing opportunity cost of gun production illustrates the principle of increasing costs.

**EXAMPLE 2.4.**   An economy's production-possibility schedule for food and clothing is presented in Table 2-2. In moving from alternative $A$ to alternative $B$ we find that by reducing clothing production from 10 to 9 units, enough resources are released to produce the first unit of food. Thus, the cost to produce this first unit of food is the 1 unit of clothing that is given up. (Cost here is represented in terms of units of goods, not as a money cost.) A movement from $B$ to $C$ shows that we must give up 2 units of clothing (from 9 to 7) to produce the second unit of food. Thus, the cost of this second unit of food equals the 2 units of clothing that are given up. To get the third unit of food, 3 units of clothing must be given up (a movement from $C$ to $D$). Finally, the cost of getting the fourth unit of food is 4 units of clothing. Thus, as we produce more food, we incur higher and higher costs in terms of units of clothing forgone. There is an increasing cost of food production because we are employing more resources in the production of food which are best suited to clothing production and increasingly less productive when employed in the production of food.

**Table 2-2**

| Alternative or Point | Units of Food (millions) | Units of Clothing (thousands) | Cost of Additional Units of Food |
|---|---|---|---|
| $A$ | 0 | 10 | |
| $B$ | 1 | 9 | 1 |
| $C$ | 2 | 7 | 2 |
| $D$ | 3 | 4 | 3 |
| $E$ | 4 | 0 | 4 |

## 2.4  SCARCITY AND THE MARKET SYSTEM

As we have seen, two of the most important economic decisions faced by a society are deciding what goods and services to produce and how to allocate resources among their competing uses. The combination of goods and services produced can be resolved by government command or through a market system. In a *command economy,* a central planning board determines the mix of output. The experience with central planning, however, has not been very successful, as evidenced by the changing economic and political events in the 1990s in the command economies of Eastern Europe and the former U.S.S.R. In a *market economy,* economic decisions are decentralized and are made by the collective wisdom of the marketplace, i.e., prices resolve the three fundamental economic questions of *what, how,* and *for whom.* The only goods and services produced are those which individuals are willing to purchase at a price sufficient to cover the cost of producing them. Because resources are scarce, goods and services are produced using the technique and resource combination which minimizes the cost of production. And the goods and services produced are sold (distributed) to those who are willing and have the money income to pay their prices. What develops is a circular flow which is directed by the collective wants of the employable individuals in the society (see Example 2.5).

**EXAMPLE 2.5.**   The circular flow integral to a market system is presented in Fig. 2-2. (1) Business firms purchase or hire the economic resources owned by individuals in order to produce goods and services. (2) Business firms make a monetary payment to individuals for the use of these resources. (3) Individuals use the income received for the use of their resources to purchase the goods and services produced by business firms. (4) Individuals receive the goods and services produced by business firms.

*What* goods and services are produced is determined by the spending preferences of individuals; *how* these goods and services are produced depends upon the relative scarcity of the resources needed for production and the state of technology; to *whom* the output is distributed is determined by the income received by individuals in supplying resources to business firms.

In a mixed economy such as that of the United States, this process is modified by government action. The production of items such as roads, government services, and elementary education is commanded by government; government pays for these goods and services by taxing those who own natural resources and by taxing personal and business income.

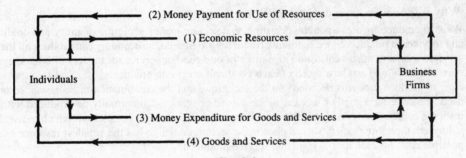

Fig. 2-2

# Solved Problems

## THE PROBLEM OF SCARCITY

**2.1.**   (*a*)   What are economic resources?

   (*b*)   Explain the meaning of (1) land, (2) capital, and (3) labor as used in economics.

   (*a*)   *Economic resources* consist of land (natural resources), capital (human-made resources), and labor (human resources). These resources are not free; they command a price because they are scarce and are essential to the production of goods and services.

   (*b*)   (1) *Land* consists of an economy's natural resources, "gifts of nature" such as minerals, forests, rivers, and agricultural land. Owners of land receive rental income when it is used to produce goods or services. (2) *Capital* is human-made resources and consists of tools, equipment, machinery, buildings, and transportation networks which are used in and/or facilitate the production of goods and services. *Financial capital* consists of financial instruments, such as savings accounts, bonds, and stocks, which come into being when individuals save and then lend this saving for the creation of tools, equipment, machinery, and so on. Capital resources are classified as *real capital* to differentiate them from financial capital. Owners of real capital receive an interest return.

(3) *Labor* consists of human beings who possess a wide array of skills which are needed to produce goods and services. The skills of labor vary, ranging from the relatively lower-skilled talents of a supermarket checkout clerk to the skills of a highly trained surgeon. Since some labor skills are scarcer and more productive than others, individuals who posses specialized skills which are in high demand receive greater compensation. *Entrepreneurial ability* is a very special labor skill. An entrepreneur is a person who forms a firm, hires economic resources, and produces goods or services that society wants. While labor resources receive wages, an entrepreneur's payment consists of profits earned by forming and managing a profitable firm.

**2.2.**  (*a*)  Why is there limited output?

      (*b*)  Why does the problem of scarcity exist?

      (*c*)  Explain the statement "Economics is the study of scarcity."

      (*a*)  Goods and services are not abundant and available for the asking; they must be produced by employing human, capital, and natural resources. A car is manufactured, for example, by employing labor, by utilizing machines, and by using natural resources such as oil (plastics) and iron and coal (steel). Wheat is grown by farmers who sow seeds in agricultural land with the use of tractors and tillers. A society's production of goods and services is thereby limited by the quantity and quality of its economic resources.

      (*b*)  Scarcity exists worldwide because people want more goods and services than can be produced by each economy's limited supply of economic resources.

      (*c*)  Since an economy cannot produce all the goods and services it wants, there are competing and therefore conflicting uses for scarce economic resources. Decisions must be made regarding the use of resources and therefore the production of goods and services. Economics is thus the study of the allocation of scarce resources among competing uses—i.e., the study of scarcity.

**2.3.**  (*a*)  Why is *what* to produce a problem for every society?

      (*b*)  Why is *how* to produce a problem?

      (*c*)  Why is *for whom* to produce a problem?

      (*a*)  *What* to produce focuses upon the decisions that society makes about the quantity and quality of goods and services to produce. Since economic resources are limited, no economy can produce all the goods and services a society may want. And since more of one good or service means less of others, every society must choose which and how much of each good and service to produce.

      (*b*)  *How* to produce concerns decisions on the technique and the combination of economic resources to be used in producing a good or service. Since a good or service can normally be produced with numerous resource combinations and by different techniques, decisions must be made on which to use. Production is limited; therefore, society should choose the technique which has the smallest resource use (the least possible cost) for each unit of good and service produced.

      (*c*)  *For whom* to produce focuses upon the distribution of the economy's output. A difficult problem of choice arises regarding the quantity of output that will flow to each member of society.

**2.4.**  (*a*)  What is meant by the term *opportunity cost?*

      (*b*)  How does opportunity cost relate to the problem of scarcity?

      (*a*)  The economist uses the term *opportunity cost* to indicate the benefits forgone when a specific decision is made. Where there are two options and one is chosen, the opportunity cost of the option chosen is the opportunity (option) forgone. For example, the opportunity cost of studying economics is the time one could have spent on alternative activities. In taking this approach, the economist makes no judgment about the decisions made since it is assumed that the options selected provide the greatest anticipated benefits.

      (*b*)  The problem of scarcity exists because of limited production. Thus, each society must make choices about what to produce and how to produce. The opportunity cost of what to produce consists of the goods and services which are sacrificed in order to produce the selected combination of goods and services. For example, the opportunity cost of producing military goods is the quantity of consumer goods that is not available because of the decision to produce military goods.

## THE PRODUCTION-POSSIBILITY FRONTIER

**2.5.** Table 2-3(a) presents a production-possibility schedule for a hypothetical economy which produces only food and clothing.

(*a*)　What does this production-possibility schedule show?

(*b*)　Suppose production is currently set at 3 million units of food and 5 thousand units of clothing. How can this economy increase food production by 1 million units when there is no change in technology or the quantity of economic resources?

(*c*)　What is the opportunity cost of increasing food production 1 million units?

(*d*)　Use the data from Table 2-3(a) to establish the opportunity cost of producing additional units of food in 1 million increments when food production is initially zero.

(*e*)　Why are food costs rising?

**Table 2-3(a)**

| Alternative or Point | Units of Food (millions) | Units of Clothing (thousands) |
|---|---|---|
| A | 0 | 8.0 |
| B | 1 | 7.5 |
| C | 2 | 6.5 |
| D | 3 | 5.0 |
| E | 4 | 3.0 |
| F | 5 | 0.0 |

(*a*)　A production-possibility schedule presents the alternative combinations of two goods that society can produce, assuming that all its resources and the best technology available are used. Table 2-3(a) shows that this economy can produce either no food and 8 thousand units of clothing, 1 million units of food and 7.5 thousand units of clothing, 2 million units of food and 6.5 thousand units of clothing, 3 million units of food and 5 thousand units of clothing, 4 million units of food and 3 thousand units of clothing, *or* 5 million units of food and no clothing. Since we assume that society is utilizing all its resources and the best technology, this society can produce more units of food only by releasing economic resources from clothing production and thereby producing less clothing.

(*b*)　This economy can increase food production only by decreasing clothing production. Increasing food production 1 million units necessitates moving from alternative *D* to alternative *E*. Society's production changes from 3 million units of food and 5 thousand units of clothing to 4 million units of food and 3 thousand units of clothing. Thus, 2 thousand units of clothing must be given up to increase food production 1 million units.

(*c*)　The opportunity cost of producing the additional 1 million units of food is the 2 thousand units of clothing that society no longer produces.

(*d*)　The opportunity cost of producing additional units of food is presented in Table 2-3(b). From Table 2-3(b), we see that the opportunity cost of 1 million units of food is 0.5 thousand units of clothing when alternative *B* rather than *A* is selected, i.e., when moving from no food production to 1 million units of food. The opportunity cost of an additional 1 million units of food, i.e., selecting alternative *C* rather than *B*, is 1 thousand units of clothing. The opportunity cost of additional food production is 1.5, 2.0, and 3.0 thousand units of clothing. Note that the cost of additional food production is rising. Economists classify this rising cost as the principle of increasing cost.

(*e*)　The cost of producing additional food rises because resources are not homogeneous. That is, the economic resources of a nation are not equally efficient in the production of food and clothing. In producing the first 1 million units of food (alternative *B*), the economy uses those resources which are most efficient in food production and least efficient in clothing production. Thus, the amount of clothing given up to produce the first 1 million units of food is very little. But as we continue to expand food production by decreasing clothing production, the economic resources that must be utilized to produce food are less and less productive in food production and more and more productive in clothing production. As a result, the cost of expanding food production in terms of reduced clothing production increases.

**Table 2-3(b)**

| Alternative or Point | Units of Food (millions) | Units of Clothing (thousands) | Cost of Additional Units of Food |
|---|---|---|---|
| A | 0 | 8.0 | 0.5 |
| B | 1 | 7.5 | 1.0 |
| C | 2 | 6.5 | 1.5 |
| D | 3 | 5.0 | 2.0 |
| E | 4 | 3.0 | 3.0 |
| F | 5 | 0.0 | |

**2.6.** (a)  Use the data from Table 2-3(a) to draw a production-possibility frontier. Plot clothing production on the vertical axis and food production on the horizontal axis. Label the production alternatives A, B, C, D, E, and F on the curve.

(b)  On the same figure, label as point U the production of 3 thousand units of clothing and 3 million units of food and as point H the production of 6 thousand units of clothing and 3.5 million units of food. What do points U and H indicate?

(c)  What is the difference between unemployed and underemployed economic resources?

(d)  When is production efficient?

(a)  The production-possibility frontier drawn from the data in Table 2-3(a) is shown in Fig. 2-3.

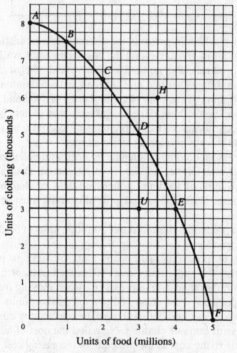

Units of food (millions)

**Fig. 2-3**

(b)  Since point U is inside the production-possibility frontier, the economy is producing below its potential, indicating that economic resources are not fully employed and/or the best technology available is not being utilized. Economic resources are therefore unemployed or underemployed. By fully employing its resources and using the best technology available, this society can move from point U to point E on the production-possibility frontier. In doing so, 3 thousand units of clothing continue to be produced while food production increases from 3 to 4 million units. Point *H* is unattainable. It is outside the production-possibility frontier and consists of a combination of food and clothing which this economy cannot produce with its currently available resources and technology.

(*c*) There is *full employment* of labor resources when those who are willing and able to work are employed. Unemployment exists when labor resources willing and able to work are not employed. *Underemployment* exists when resources are employed but are not producing the maximum amount of goods and services which they could produce.

(*d*) Efficient production exists when economic resources are fully employed and output is at its maximum level. Thus, points on the production-possibility frontier are efficient. Points within the production-possibility frontier are inefficient.

**2.7.** What is meant by the term *economic growth?* What are the sources of economic growth?

Economic growth occurs when the productive capabilities of an economy increase. It is indicated by an outward shift of the production-possibility frontier, indicating that the economy can expand the output of a good in a full-employment economy without decreasing the output of other goods and services. Increases in resources and improved resource skills and technological progress are the sources of economic growth.

**2.8.** Suppose an economy has the production-possibility frontier depicted in Fig. 2.-4.

(*a*) What implication does the selection of point *A* or *C* have regarding the economy's current and future production of consumer goods and services?

(*b*) What linkage is there between saving and economic growth?

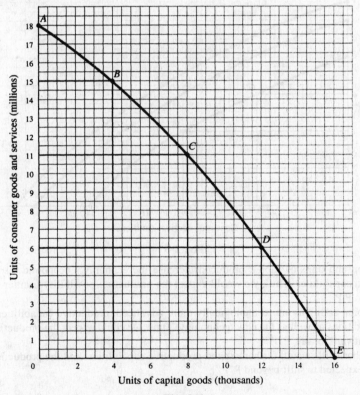

**Fig. 2-4**

(*a*) At point *A*, society has more consumer goods and services in the current period. Point *C*, however, provides the possibility of a larger quantity of consumer goods and services in the future because of additions to the economy's stock of capital resources. In producing at point *C* and thereby increasing the economy's supply of capital resources, the economy's productive capabilities expand and thereby provide an increased output of consumer goods and services in a future period. In fact, if society maintains such a mix of capital and consumer goods output over time, consumer goods and services production will exceed the 18 million units of consumer goods and services produced in the current period in selecting point A.

(b)    As discussed in (a), society must forgo purchases of consumer goods and services now if it is to increase its supply of capital and thereby expand production capabilities. Thus, people must be willing to have fewer goods and services now, that is, they must be willing to save, so that resources can be used in the current period to produce capital goods.

**2.9.**    We continue the analysis presented in Problem 2.8, where the selection of point C in Fig. 2-4 results in the production of 11 million units of consumer goods and services. Figure 2-5 depicts a production-possibility frontier for the resources available to produce the 11 million units of consumer goods and services. In Fig. 2-5 production is set at point G. At G the economy is producing 6 million units of consumer goods and 5 million units of consumer services.

(a)    What eventually happens to production-possibility frontier FGHIJ as a result of the production of 8 thousand units of capital in Problem 2.8?

(b)    What eventually happens to production-possibility frontier FGHIJ as a result of the production of 8 thousand units of capital in Problem 2.8 when this capital is technologically more advanced and therefore more productive?

(c)    Would your answer to (b) differ if, while new capital is being built, employee training programs enhance the skills of the labor force?

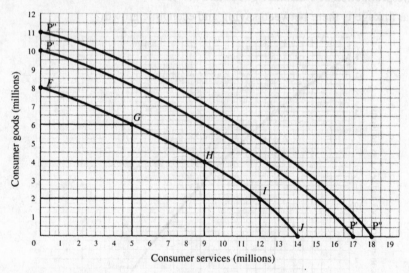

**Fig. 2-5**

(a)    The 8 thousand units of capital produced increase the economy's economic resources and expand its production capabilities. Thus, we would expect the production-possibility frontier to shift outward, from FGHIJ to P'P'.

(b)    When capital additions are technologically more advanced, productive capabilities are enhanced by the capital additions as well as the new technology. Thus, we could expect the production-possibility frontier to shift outward to, say, P''P''.

(c)    Greater labor skills would further expand productive capabilities, and the production-possibility frontier could be expected to shift beyond P''P''.

## THE PRINCIPLE OF INCREASING COSTS

**2.10.**    Table 2-4 presents a production-possibility schedule for the production of food and clothing.

(a)    Using the table, find the opportunity cost of increasing food production in increments of 1 million units.

(b)    Would you expect the opportunity cost of increasing food production to be constant? Why?

**Table 2-4**

| Alternative | Units of Food (millions) | Units of Clothing (thousands) |
|:-----------:|:------------------------:|:-----------------------------:|
| A | 0 | 8 |
| B | 1 | 6 |
| C | 2 | 4 |
| D | 3 | 2 |
| E | 4 | 0 |

(a)   The opportunity cost of increasing food production from 0 units (alternative A) to 1 million units (alternative B) is 2 thousand units of clothing (clothing production is reduced from 8 thousand units in alternative A to 6 thousand units in alternative B). Further 1 million unit increases in food production also necessitate a 2 thousand unit decrease in clothing production. Thus, in this schedule, the opportunity cost of 1 million units increments of food production is a constant 2 thousand unit decrease in food production.

(b)   The production-possibility schedule in Table 2-4 is unrealistic. All economic resources are not equally efficient when employed in the production of food and the production of clothing. For example, a farmer may be skilled in planting and harvesting food but not in the manufacture of clothing, and capital resources, such as a tractor, may increase the production of food but are of little use in manufacturing clothing. Because economic resources are not equally efficient in the production of alternative goods, the opportunity cost of expanding the production of an alternative good is likely to increase rather than be constant.

**2.11.**   Fig. 2-6 presents a production-possibility curve for food and clothing.

(a)   What is the opportunity cost of increasing food production from 0 to 2 thousand units, from 2 thousand to 4 thousand units, and from 4 thousand to 6 thousand units?

(b)   What is happening to the opportunity cost of increasing food production from 0 to 6 thousand units?

(c)   Explain how the slope of the production-possibility frontier implies increasing costs for the production of clothing and increasing costs in the production of food.

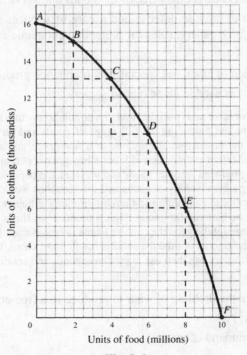

**Fig. 2-6**

(a) In increasing food production from 0 to 2 million units, production of clothing decreases from 16 million units to 15 million units; thus, the opportunity cost of producing the first 2 million units of food is 1 thousand units of clothing. The opportunity cost of a second and third additional 2 million units is 2 thousand units of clothing and 3 thousand units of clothing.

(b) The opportunity cost of increasing food production is increasing from 1 thousand units of clothing to 2 to 3 thousand units of clothing.

(c) Increasing clothing and food costs are reflected in a concave (outward-sloping) production-possibility curve. Moving down the production-possibility curve from point $A$ to points $B, C, D, E$, and $F$ shows that to produce 2 million incremental units of food (the 2-million-unit-length horizontal dashed lines in Fig. 2-6), we must give up more and more units of clothing (the vertical dashed lines of increasing length). The increasing cost of clothing production can be found by moving up the production-possibility curve from point $F$ to points $E, D, C, B$, and $A$. The opportunity cost of producing the first 6 thousand units of clothing (alternative $F$ to alternative $E$) is 2 million units of food. The opportunity cost of producing an additional 4 thousand units of clothing is 2 million units of food. The opportunity cost of producing a third increment of 2 thousand units of clothing is 2 million units of food.

## SCARCITY AND THE MARKET SYSTEM

**2.12.** What are the distinguishing characteristics of a capitalist market economy?

(1) In a capitalist market economy (also referred to as a free-enterprise or *laissez-faire* system), most economic resources are owned directly or indirectly by individuals rather than by the government.

(2) Individuals are free to rent out the resources they own for the highest price they can obtain. Individuals are also free to spend their income to buy goods and services that maximize their satisfaction. Entrepreneurs have the freedom to set up new business enterprises; to run them by hiring resources in whatever combination they deem most efficient; to use technology which minimizes production costs; and to sell their output in markets where profits can be maximized.

(3) There is competition—the existence in the marketplace of many sellers and buyers with each participant too small to affect the price of the goods and services produced.

(4) Government exists to provide defense and a core of services which otherwise might not be supplied and to enforce general rules for protecting economic and political freedom.

**2.13.** (a) Explain how division of labor and specialization enhance production in an advanced society.

(b) Explain why money is used in an advanced society.

(a) Through the division of labor and specialization, the population within a given geographic region, instead of being self-sufficient and producing the full range of goods and services wanted, can concentrate its energies and time in the production of only one or a few goods and services in which its efficiency is greatest. Thus, specialization and division of labor allow greater output. By then exchanging some of the goods and services so produced for other goods and services, the population as a whole ends up consuming a larger number and greater diversity of goods and services than would otherwise be the case.

(b) The use of money facilitates exchange and thereby promotes efficient use of resources. When money is not used, goods must be bartered for goods. Thus a producer of shoes would have to find someone who wants shoes in exchange for the good the cobbler wants to buy. Barter is very time-consuming and in this example can reduce the amount of time the cobbler has to make shoes. In using money, all parties receive a money income, which they can then use to purchase goods and services.

**2.14.** (a) How does one solve the problem of *what* to produce in a free-enterprise, capitalist economy?

(b) in a mixed economy?

(c) in a centralized, command economy?

(a) In a *free-enterprise economy*, the only goods and services produced are those whose price in the market is at least equal to the producer's cost of producing output. When a price greater than the cost of producing that good or service prevails, producers are induced to increase production. If the product's price falls below the cost of production, producers reduce supply. What to produce is thereby determined by the market price of each good and service in relation to the cost of producing each good and service.

(b) In a *mixed economy*, government replaces, regulates, or modifies the price mechanism. For example, in the United States, government produces some goods itself (police protection, roads, etc.) and finances these expenditures by taxing the income of individuals and businesses. It also influences what to produce by imposing direct regulations on producers and/or by imposing taxes on specific goods and services.

(c) In a *centralized, command economy*, a planning committee determines the economy's output of goods and services. The inability of the command economies of the former Soviet Union and Eastern Europe in the post–World War II period to expand production as rapidly as did the market economies of the United States, Japan, and Germany has resulted in a movement away from centralized planning and toward a market system in the 1990s.

**2.15.** (a)  How does the price-mechanism solve the problem of *how* to produce in a capitalist economy?

  (b)  How does the price-mechanism solve the problem of *for whom* to produce in a capitalist economy?

  (a) Because producers need to cover at least their production costs in supplying a product to the market, they choose the production technique that has the lowest cost of production. Thus, when a product can be produced by using various combinations of labor and capital, the producer selects that combination which has the lowest per unit cost. Should the price of labor increase and that of capital remain unchanged, it follows that a producer would alter the production technique and use less labor and more capital.

  (b) Goods and services are produced for those who have the money to pay for them. The higher the income of an individual, the more the economy will be geared to produce the commodities he or she wants and is willing to purchase.

**2.16.** Figure 2-7 presents the circular flow of economic resources, income, and goods and services for a capitalist market economy.

  (a)  Explain the top loop where there is a flow of economic resources and money between individuals and business firms. Explain the bottom loop where there is a flow of money and goods and services.

  (b)  Explain why a cost to business firms represents income for individuals, and vice versa.

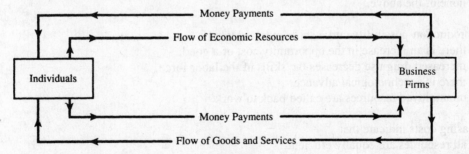

**Fig. 2-7**

  (a) In a capitalist market economy, resources are privately owned, i.e., they are owned by individuals. The top loop shows that business firms can produce only by purchasing the use of economic resources from individuals; individuals receive money payments for the use of these resources. The bottom loop shows that individuals use their money income to purchase goods and services from business firms.

  (b) The top loop in Fig. 2-7 shows that business firms purchase the use of economic resources from individuals. Thus, the cost of production for business firms is the money income of individuals. The bottom loop shows individuals purchasing output from business firms. The cost of purchasing these goods and services to individuals is the money income (the money receipts) of business firms.

## Multiple Choice Questions

1.  Scarcity exists in every society because there are
    (a) limited wants and abundant resources,
    (b) limited resources and unlimited production capabilities,
    (c) limited resources and unlimited wants,
    (d) limited production capabilities and an unlimited quantity of economic resources.

2.  The word *economic* refers to something that
    (a) is scarce,
    (b) is limited,
    (c) commands a price,
    (d) all of the above.

3.  In economics the term *opportunity cost* refers to
    (a) the monetary cost of a good or service,
    (b) the money cost of hiring an economic resource,
    (c) the value of a good or service forgone,
    (d) the money cost of providing a good or service.

4.  The production-possibility frontier depicts
    (a) the maximum amount of alternative combinations of two goods that an economy can produce at
        a point in time,
    (b) the limited amount of resources that an economy has at a point in time,
    (c) the alternative combination of capital and labor inputs used in producing goods and services over
        time,
    (d) the economy's employment level at a point in time.

5.  A point inside the production-possibility curve indicates
    (a) inefficiency,
    (b) unemployed resources,
    (c) that existing resources can produce at a higher level of output,
    (d) all of the above,
    (e) none of the above.

6.  The production-possibility curve shifts outward when
    (a) there is an increase in the opportunity cost of a good,
    (b) increased drug use decreases the skills of the labor force,
    (c) there is a technological advance,
    (d) unemployed resources are called back to work.

7.  Increasing costs indicate that
    (a) all resources are equally efficient,
    (b) all resources are equally inefficient,
    (c) the output of a good can be increased only by giving up larger and larger quantities of alternative
        goods,
    (d) the output of a good can be increased only by using more economic resources.

8.  The economic problem of *what* to produce refers to the decision of
    (a) which goods and services and how much of each are to be produced,
    (b) which goods are good for society,

(c) which goods and services to produce to maximize the rate of economic growth,
(d) what combination of resources and production techniques to use.

9. The economic problem of *how* to produce refers to the decision of
   (a) who should be given the authority to produce goods and services,
   (b) how many people in the population are to be employed,
   (c) how much of current production should go toward consumption rather than saving,
   (d) which of the production techniques is to be used.

10. The economic problem of *for whom* to produce refers to the decision of
    (a) how to allocate economic resources,
    (b) how many of the wants of various members of society are to be satisfied,
    (c) how much to produce for import or export,
    (d) how much saving should go on in the economy.

## *True or False Questions*

11. _____ Scarcity is the fundamental economic problem for every society.

12. _____ A production-possibility frontier depicts the unlimited wants of a society.

13. _____ There is no problem deciding *what* to produce when the economy's resources increase over time.

14. _____ When there is full employment, the decision to produce more of one good necessitates decreased production of another good.

15. _____ Unemployment or underemployment exists when output is at a point inside the production-possibility curve.

16. _____ In an economy with technological advance and increased economic resources, the decision to produce more of one good necessitates decreased production of another good.

17. _____ There are increasing costs of production because economic resources are not equally efficient in the production of all goods and services.

18. _____ Economic resources are able to produce more goods and services at a point in time when exchange is effected through the use of money rather than through a system of barter.

19. _____ The circular flow depicts the alternative combinations of goods and services an economy can produce at a point in time.

20. _____ The market system resolves the problem of what to produce by considering the prices that individuals are willing to pay for goods and services and the costs associated with producing them.

## Answers to Multiple Choice and True or False Questions

| | | | |
|---|---|---|---|
| 1. (c) | 6. (c) | 11. (T) | 16. (F) |
| 2. (d) | 7. (c) | 12. (F) | 17. (T) |
| 3. (c) | 8. (a) | 13. (F) | 18. (T) |
| 4. (a) | 9. (d) | 14. (T) | 19. (F) |
| 5. (d) | 10. (b) | 15. (T) | 20. (T) |

# Chapter 3

# Demand, Supply, and Equilibrium

## *Chapter Summary*

1. In a market economy, output is distributed through a system of prices. Each good and service produced is sold to those who are *willing* and *able* to pay the market price. A commodity market's price is determined by market demand and market supply.

2. The market demand for a good or service is presented as a schedule which relates the number of units (quantity) that will be purchased at alternative prices, holding constant other variables that influence the purchase decision. Presented graphically, a demand curve shows an inverse relationship between the price of the item and the quantity demanded, i.e., more units are demanded at lower prices than at higher prices.

3. A demand curve shifts when variables other than the price of the commodity change. A shift of the demand curve is classified as a change in demand. A change in the commodity's price results in a movement along an existing demand curve and therefore a change in quantity demanded.

4. The market supply of a good or service is presented as a schedule which relates the quantity that producers are willing and able to supply at alternative prices. Presented graphically, a supply curve shows a direct relationship between price and the quantity supplied, i.e., more units are supplied at higher prices than at lower prices.

5. A supply curve shifts when variables other than the price of the commodity change. A shift of the supply curve is classified as a change in supply. A change in the the commodity's price results in a movement along an existing supply curve and therefore a change in quantity supplied.

6. Market demand and market supply determine equilibrium price. A commodity's equilibrium price is the price which clears the market; it is the price at which quantity supplied is equal to quantity demanded. The equilibrium price exists at the point where the demand and the supply curves intersect.

7. A change in demand (shift of the demand curve) and/or a change in supply (shift of the supply curve) may change equilibrium price and quantity. An increase in demand, for example, results in an increase in equilibrium price and quantity, assuming no change (shift) in a positively sloped supply curve.

8. Government can mandate price ceilings (a maximum price) or price floors (a minimum price). Such mandated prices normally result in market disequilibrium, and quantity supplied is either greater or less than quantity demanded. Government can influence the equilibrium price by measures such as subsidies, taxes, and rationing. When a good is subsidized, government assumes some of the costs of production, supply is increased (supply shifts downward), and equilibrium price is lowered.

## *Important Terms*

**Change in market demand.**  A shift of the market demand curve that results from a change in the number of consumers in the market, consumer preferences, consumer money income, the price of a substitute commodity, or the price of a complementary commodity.

**Change in market supply.**  A shift of the market supply curve that results from a change in the number and/or size of producers, a change in technology, a change in the price of a factor of production, or a change in the price of other commodities used in production.

**Change in the quantity demanded.** A movement along a given demand curve due to a change in the commodity's price.

**Change in the quantity supplied.** A movement along a given supply curve due to a change in the commodity's price.

**Equilibrium.** The market condition where the quantity of a commodity that consumers are willing to purchase exactly equals the quantity producers are willing to supply. Geometrically, equilibrium occurs at the intersection of the commodity's market demand and market supply curves. The price and quantity at which equilibrium exists are known, respectively, as the equilibrium price and the equilibrium quantity.

**Income effect.** The increase in quantity purchased when the price of a normal good falls and there is an increase in the purchasing power of a given money income.

**Market demand curve.** A graphic presentation of a market demand schedule, which shows the quantities of a commodity that consumers are willing and able to purchase during a period of time at various alternative prices, while holding constant everything else that affects demand. The market demand curve for a commodity is negatively sloped, indicating that more of the commodity is purchased at a lower price.

**Market supply curve.** A graphic presentation of a market supply schedule, which relates the quantities of a commodity that producers are willing to supply during a period of time at various alternative prices, while holding constant everything else that affects supply. The market supply curve for a commodity is usually positively sloped, indicating that producers must be paid a higher price to supply more units of the commodity.

**Price ceiling.** A government-instituted maximum price for a commodity in the market. A price ceiling is below the market's equilibrium price.

**Price floor.** A government-instituted minimum price for a commodity in the market. A price floor is above the market's equilibrium price.

**Price-mechanism.** The forces of market demand and market supply which determine commodity and factor prices in a free-enterprise economy.

**Shortage.** The condition that occurs when the commodity's price is below the equilibrium price and quantity demanded exceeds quantity supplied.

**Substitution effect.** The increase in the quantity purchased of a commodity when its price falls and consumers substitute this commodity for others whose prices are unchanged.

**Surplus.** The condition that occurs when the commodity's price is above the equilibrium price and quantity supplied exceeds quantity demanded.

# Outline of Chapter 3: Demand, Supply, and Equilibrium

## 3.1 DEMAND

The demand schedule for an individual specifies the units of a good or service that the individual is willing and able to purchase at alternative prices during a given period of time. The relationship between price and quantity demanded is inverse; more units are purchased at lower prices because of a substitution effect and an income effect. As a commodity's price falls, an individual normally purchases more of this good since he or she is likely to substitute it for other goods whose price has remained unchanged. For example, when coffee prices fall and the price of tea is unchanged, more coffee and less tea is purchased. Also, when a commodity's price falls, the purchasing power of an individual with a given income increases, allowing for greater purchases of the commodity. When graphed, the inverse relationship between price and quantity demanded appears as a negatively sloped demand curve.

A market demand schedule specifies the units of a good or service all individuals in the market are willing and able to purchase. The market demand schedule reflects the collective wants of people in a market area and is the sum of the quantities demanded ($Q_d$) by these individuals at alternative prices ($P$), i.e., $Q_d = f(P)$.

**EXAMPLE 3.1.**    Table 3-1 gives an individual's demand and the market demand for a commodity. Column 2 shows one individual's demand for corn—the bushels of corn that one individual is willing and able to buy per month at alternative prices (column 1). From columns 1 and 2 we find that the individual buys 3.5 bushels of corn each month when the price is $5 a bushel; 4.5 when the price is $4; 6.0 when the price is $3; 8.0 when the price is $2; and 11.0 when the price is $1. If there are 1000 individuals in the market and each person has the same ability and willingness to buy corn, the market demand for corn is the sum of the quantities the 1000 individuals will buy at each price. Thus, while each individual is willing to purchase 3.5 bushels of corn each month at $5 a bushel, 1000 individuals collectively are willing to purchase 3500 bushels of corn each month at $5 a bushel. The quantity of corn demanded by 1000 individuals is presented in column 3. Column 3 shows the typical relationship between quantity demanded and price, i.e., more units of a commodity are demanded at lower prices.

**Table 3-1**

| Price ($P$) ($ per bu) | Quantity Demanded ($q$) by One Individual (bu per month) | Quantity Demanded ($Q$) in the Market (1000 individuals) (bu per month) |
|---|---|---|
| 5 | 3.5 | 3500 |
| 4 | 4.5 | 4500 |
| 3 | 6.0 | 6000 |
| 2 | 8.0 | 8000 |
| 1 | 11.0 | 11,000 |

**EXAMPLE 3.2.**    From Table 3-1, the demand for corn by one individual is plotted in Fig. 3-1 and the curve is labeled d: the market demand for corn is plotted in Fig. 3-2 and the curve is labeled D. The price per bushel is on the vertical axis and the quantity of bushels demanded is on the horizontal axis. Note that both demand curves are negatively sloped, i.e., the curve is downward-sloping since more units are demanded at lower prices.

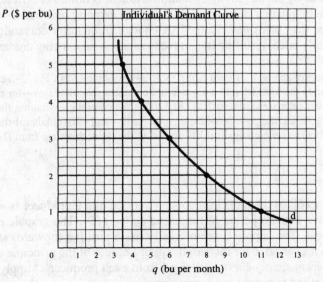

**Fig. 3-1**

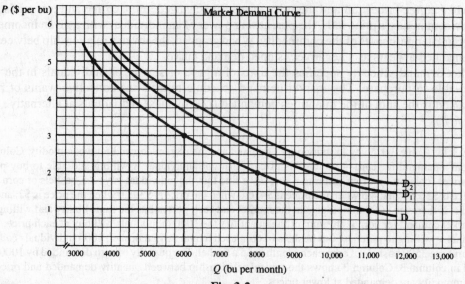

**Fig. 3-2**

## 3.2   SHIFTING OF A MARKET DEMAND CURVE

The market demand for a good or service is influenced not only by the commodity's price but also by the price of other goods and services, spendable income, wealth, tastes, and the size of the market. In presenting the demand for a good or service as a schedule relating price and quantity demanded, variables other than the commodity's price are held constant. Thus, the market demand for corn presented in Table 3-1 and Fig. 3-2 relates the quantity of corn demanded to the price per bushel, holding constant the price of wheat and other commodities, consumer preferences, income, wealth, and the size of market. This relationship is presented as $Q_d = f(P_{corn})$, *ceteris paribus*, where *ceteris paribus* indicates that variables other than the price of corn are unchanged. When one or more of these variables change, there is a change in demand and therefore a shift of the demand curve. For example, the market demand curve shifts up and to the right when the number of individuals in the market increases. More people in a market area indicates that more units are demanded at each price. The market demand curve also shifts up and to the right when there is an increased preference for the commodity, when nominal income increases, and when the price of a substitute commodity rises and/or the price of a complementary good declines.

A common error made by the beginning economics student is failure to differentiate between a change in demand and a change in quantity demanded. A change in demand refers to a shift of the demand curve because a variable other than price has changed. A change in quantity demanded occurs when there is change in the commodity's price, resulting in a movement along an existing demand curve.

**EXAMPLE 3.3.**   The market demand for corn from Table 3-1 was plotted in Fig. 3-2 and labeled D. The market demand curve shifts up and to the right from D to $D_1$ when the market size increases—for example, when the number of individuals in this market increases from to 1000 to 1200. (We continue to assume that each individual has the same preferences for corn.) Should the price of wheat then increase—and individuals substitute corn for wheat in their diets—the market demand curve for corn again shifts up and to the right, this time from $D_1$ to $D_2$.

## 3.3   SUPPLY

A supply schedule specifies the units of a good or service that a producer is willing to supply ($Q_s$) at alternative prices ($P$) over a given period of time, i.e., $Q_s = f(P)$. The graphic presentation of a supply schedule is a supply curve. The supply curve normally has a positive (upward) slope, indicating that the producer must receive a higher price for increased output because of the principle of increasing costs. (Review Section 2.3.) A market supply curve is derived from each producer's supply curve by summing the units each producer is willing to supply at alternative prices.

**EXAMPLE 3.4.** Table 3-2 relates the number of bushels of corn supplied by an individual producer at alternative prices and the number of bushels of corn supplied by all corn producers in a market area. From columns 1 and 2 we find that the producer supplies 75 bushels of corn each month at $5 a bushel. At $1 a bushel, the producer supplies 10 bushels per month. This producer's supply schedule is plotted in Fig. 3-3 and the curve is labeled s.

We have assumed that there are 100 corn producers in the market area and that each producer is willing to supply the same quantities. A market supply schedule for these 100 producers is presented in column 3. When the price of corn is $5 a bushel, 7500 bushels are supplied; smaller amounts are supplied at lower prices. The market supply schedule is plotted in Fig. 3-4 and the curve is labeled S.

**Table 3-2**

| Price (P) ($ per bu) | Quantity Supplied by One Producer (bu per month) | Quantity Supplied by All Producers in the 100 producers market (Q) (bu per month) |
|---|---|---|
| 5 | 75 | 7500 |
| 4 | 70 | 7000 |
| 3 | 60 | 6000 |
| 2 | 40 | 4000 |
| 1 | 10 | 1000 |

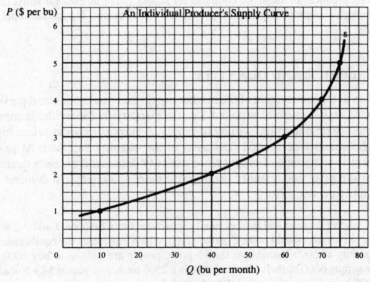

**Fig. 3-3**

## 3.4 SHIFTING OF A MARKET SUPPLY CURVE

The market supply curve shifts when the number and/or size of producers changes, factor prices (wages, interest, and/or rent paid to economic resources) change, the cost of materials changes, technological progress occurs, and/or the government subsidizes or taxes output. The market supply curve shifts down and to the right when more producers enter the market and a greater quantity of that commodity is available at each price. Other factors causing the market supply curve to shift down and to the right are decreases in factor or materials prices, improvement in technology, and government subsidization. A change in supply thereby denotes a shift of the supply curve. A change in quantity supplied indicates a change in the commodity's price and therefore a movement along an existing supply curve.

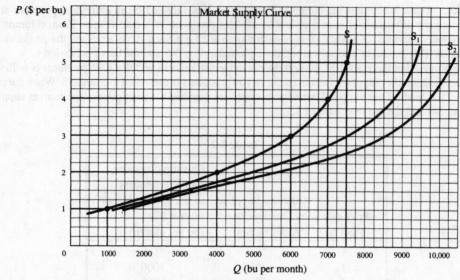

**Fig. 3-4**

**EXAMPLE 3.5.** The market supply for corn from Table 3-2 was plotted in Fig. 3-4 and labeled S. When the number of producers of corn increases from 100 to 125 (assuming that each producer has the same willingness to supply corn as the one producer in Table 3-2), the market supply curve in Fig. 3-4 shifts down and to the right, from S to $S_1$. If a technological improvement in corn production also develops, the market supply curve shifts further downward from $S_1$ to $S_2$.

## 3.5   EQUILIBRIUM PRICE AND QUANTITY

Equilibrium occurs at the intersection of the market supply and market demand curves. At this intersection, quantity demanded equals quantity supplied, i.e., the quantity that individuals are willing to purchase exactly equals the quantity producers are willing to supply. A surplus exists at prices higher than the equilibrium price since the quantity demanded falls short of the quantity supplied. At prices lower than the equilibrium price, there is a shortage of output since quantity demanded exceeds quantity supplied. Once achieved, the equilibrium price and quantity persist until there is a change in demand and/or supply, i.e., the demand and/or supply curves shift.

**EXAMPLE 3.6.**   The market demand and market supply schedules from Tables 3-1 and 3-2 are plotted in Fig. 3-5. The demand and supply curves intersect at point E on the graph, which represents the equilibrium price of $3 a bushel and the equilibrium quantity of 6000 bushels. At the $3 price, people are willing to buy 6000 bushels of corn and producers are willing to supply 6000 bushels of corn. There is a 2500 bushel surplus at $4 a bushel, since 4500 bushels are demanded while 7000 bushels are supplied. A 4000 bushel shortage exists at $2, since quantity demanded is 8000 bushels while quantity supplied is 4000 bushels.

**EXAMPLE 3.7.**   Market demand and market supply can be presented as schedules (Tables 3-1 and 3-2), in graphs (Fig. 3-5), or by equations. In equation form, the market demand can be specified as $Q_d = 100 - 10P$, and market supply in as $Q_s = 40 + 20P$. Equilibrium price is then found by equating quantity demanded ($Q_d$) and quantity supplied ($Q_s$). (Recall that an equilibrium price exists where $Q_d = Q_s$.) Equilibrium price is $2 when $Q_d = 100 - 10P$ and $Q_s = 40 + 20P$.

$$Q_d = Q_s$$
$$100 - 10P = 40 + 20P$$
$$30P = 60$$
$$P = \$2$$

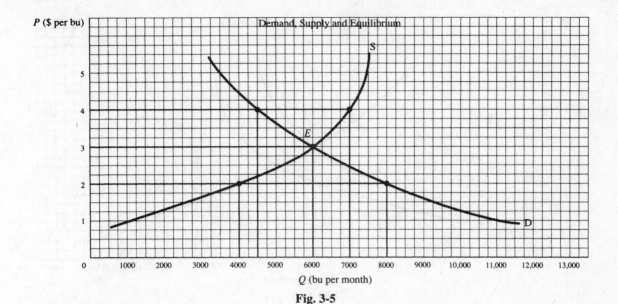

**Fig. 3-5**

## 3.6 EQUILIBRIUM WHEN MARKET DEMAND AND/OR MARKET SUPPLY CURVES SHIFT

Equilibrium price and/or equilibrium quantity change when the market demand and/or market supply curves shift. Equilibrium price and equilibrium quantity both rise when there is an increase in market demand, i.e., the market demand curve shifts up and to the right, with no change in location of the market supply curve. (See Example 3.8.) Equilibrium price falls while equilibrium quantity increases when market supply increases—the market supply curve shifts down and to the right and demand is unchanged. (See Example 3.8.) An increase in both market demand and market supply—shifts to the right by both supply and demand curves—results in a higher equilibrium quantity; the change in equilibrium price is indeterminate, however, when the magnitude of the demand and supply shift is unspecified. (See Example 3.9.)

**EXAMPLE 3.8.** The market demand and market supply schedules from Tables 3-1 and 3-2 are plotted in Figs. 3-6(a) and 3-6(b) and labeled D and S; equilibrium price is $3 and equilibrium quantity is 6000 bushels. An increase

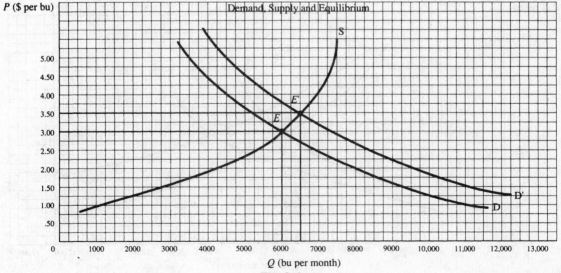

**Fig. 3-6a**

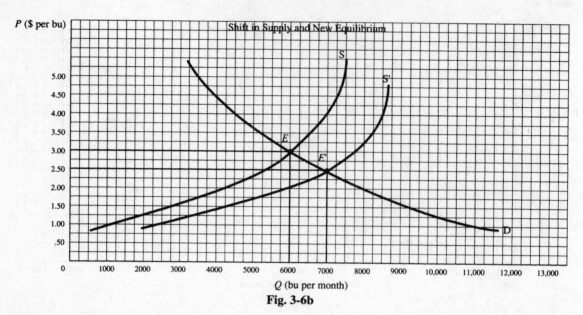

**Fig. 3-6b**

in the price of wheat, a substitute grain, shifts the demand for corn outward form D to D′ in Fig. 3-6(a). The equilibrium price of corn rises from $3.00 to $3.50, and equilibrium quantity increases from 6000 bushels to 6500 bushels. Suppose in the absence of any change in demand, a larger-than-expected corn harvest shifts supply down and to the right, from S to S′ in Fig. 3-6(b); the price of corn falls from $3.00 to $2.50, while equilibrium quantity rises from 6000 to 7000 bushels.

**EXAMPLE 3.9.**    The market demand and market supply schedules from Tables 3-1 and 3-2 are plotted in Fig. 3-7 and labeled D and S; equilibrium price is initially $3, and equilibrium quantity is 6000. Suppose increases in the demand and supply for corn shift the curves to the right, from D to D′ and from S to S′. Equilibrium price remains at $3, while equilibrium quantity increases to 8000 bushels. Equilibrium price is greater then $3 when the demand increase is greater than the increase in supply; for example, the demand shift is greater than D′ while the supply shift is from S to S′. On the other hand, equilibrium price falls below $3 when the increase in demand is less than the D to D′ while the increase in supply is from S to S′. Thus, when market demand and market supply are shifting in the same direction, the resulting equilibrium price depends upon the magnitude of the increase in demand relative to the increase in supply.

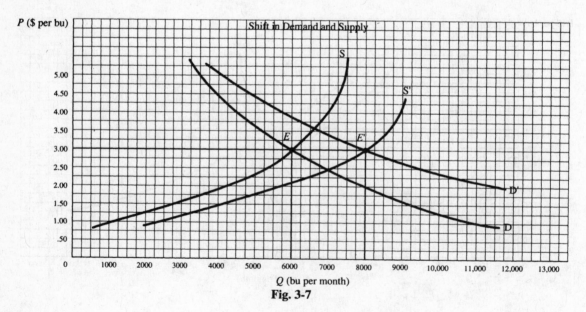

**Fig. 3-7**

## 3.7  GOVERNMENT AND PRICE DETERMINATION

The government may intervene in the market and mandate a maximum price (price ceiling) or minimum price (price floor) for a good or service. For example, some city governments in the United States legislate the maximum price that a landlord can charge a tenant for rent. Such rent-control policies, though well-intentioned, result in a disequilibrium in the housing market since, at the government-mandated price ceiling, the quantity of housing supplied falls short of the quantity of housing demanded. An example of minimum prices (price floors) in the United States is the minimum wage, which specifies the lowest hourly wage an employer can pay an employee. Price floors result in market disequilibrium in that quantity supplied at the mandated price exceeds quantity demanded.

**EXAMPLE 3.10.**  Suppose the market equilibrium price is $P_e$ in Fig. 3-8. If the government mandates a price floor at $P_f$, which is above equilibrium price $P_e$, quantity supplied will be $Q_3$, which is greater than the $Q_1$ demanded at the $P_f$ price. A mandated price ceiling of $P_c$, on the other hand, causes quantity demanded $Q_4$ to exceed the $Q_2$ quantity supplied.

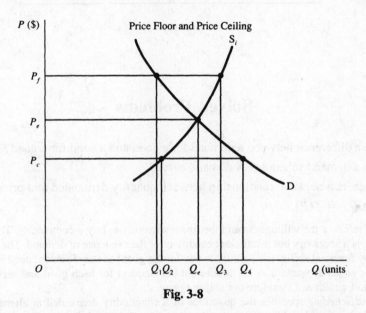

**Fig. 3-8**

The government can alter an equilibrium price by changing market demand and/or market supply. The government can restrict demand by rationing a good, i.e., by shifting the demand schedule down and to the left. When a good is rationed, an individual not only must be willing and financially able to buy a commodity but also must possess a government-issued coupon which permits purchase. The United States rationed certain clothing and food items during World War II to assure that the short supply of these goods was fairly distributed among the civilian population at a fair price. Equilibrium price can be altered by shifting the market supply curve. A tax on a good raises its supply price—shifts the market supply curve up and to the left—and causes the equilibrium price to increase and the equilibrium quantity to fall. A subsidy to the producer lowers the commodity's supply price, shifts market supply down and to the right, and results in a lower equilibrium price and larger equilibrium quantity.

**EXAMPLE 3.11.**  A market supply S and demand D for gasoline is presented in Fig. 3-9. Equilibrium price is initially $P_0$ while equilibrium quantity is $Q_0$. Suppose the government seeks to reduce gasoline consumption, i.e., decrease the quantity demanded. A tax of 50 cents on each gallon sold would decrease market supply, shift the market supply curve to the left to $S'$, and raise the equilibrium price to $P_1$; equilibrium quantity falls from $Q_0$ to $Q_1$ gallons.

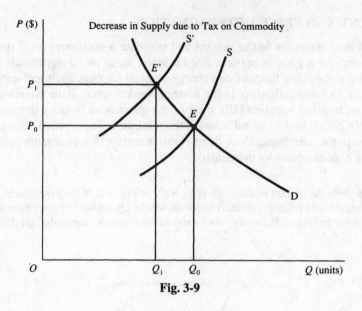

**Fig. 3-9**

# Solved Problems

## DEMAND

**3.1.** (*a*)  Is there a difference between a demand for a good and a need for a good?

(*b*)  What is a demand schedule? A demand curve?

(*c*)  Why is there a negative relationship between quantity demanded and price?

(*d*)  Explain $Q_d = f(P)$.

(*a*)  *Demand* refers to the willingness and the financial ability to buy a commodity. The existence of a *need* or a want is a necessary but insufficient condition for the existence of demand. The need or want must be backed by financial ability (i.e., ability to pay for the good) to transform the need into effective demand. Thus, our needs or wants may be infinite but our demand for each good and service is limited by our income and wealth and therefore our ability to pay.

(*b*)  A *demand schedule* specifies the quantities of a commodity demanded at alternative prices during a specified time period, holding constant other variables that may influence demand. A *demand curve* is a graphic presentation of a demand schedule.

(*c*)  The negative slope of the demand curve shows that price and quantity are inversely related. That is, larger quantities are demanded at lower prices. This conforms to our everyday experience as consumers and is the result of substitution and income effects. The *substitution effect* says that as the price of a specified commodity falls, we substitute this commodity for similar commodities whose prices are unchanged. For example, when the price of chicken falls and the price of beef is unchanged, consumers buy more chicken and less beef. The *income effect* indicates that as the price of a commodity falls, a given money income has greater purchasing power which allows the consumer to buy more of this and other commodities.

(*d*)  The quantity demanded ($Q_d$) of an item depends upon (is a function of) the price ($P$) of an item.

**3.2.**  Suppose there are only three individuals in a market area who demand brussels sprouts; the demand schedule for each individual appears in Table 3-3.

(*a*)  From the data in Table 3-3, derive a market demand schedule for brussels sprouts.

(*b*)  Plot this market demand schedule and label the curve $D_1$.

**Table 3-3**

| Price ($ per lb) | Quantity Demanded by Individual 1 (lb per month) | Quantity Demanded by Individual 2 (lb per month) | Quantity Demanded by Individual 3 (lb per month) |
|---|---|---|---|
| 2.50 | 2.25 | 0.75 | 0.25 |
| 2.00 | 2.50 | 1.00 | 0.50 |
| 1.50 | 3.00 | 1.50 | 1.00 |
| 1.00 | 4.00 | 2.25 | 1.75 |
| 0.50 | 5.50 | 3.50 | 2.75 |

(*a*)  The market demand schedule, shown in Table 3-4, is obtained by adding the quantities demanded by all individuals in the market at each price.

**Table 3-4**

| Price ($ per lb) | Quantity Demanded by Individuals 1, 2, & 3 (lb per month) | Quantity Demanded in the Market (lb per month) |
|---|---|---|
| 2.50 | (2.25 + 0.75 + 0.25) | 3.25 |
| 2.00 | (2.50 + 1.00 + 0.50) | 4.00 |
| 1.50 | (3.00 + 1.50 + 1.00) | 5.50 |
| 1.00 | (4.00 + 2.25 + 1.75) | 8.00 |
| 0.50 | (5.50 + 3.50 + 2.75) | 11.75 |

(*b*)  Market demand from Table 3-4 is plotted in Fig. 3-10, and the curve is labeled $D_1$.

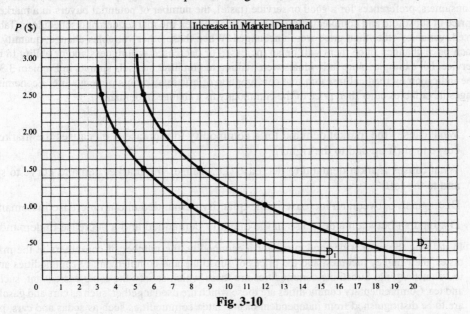

**Fig. 3-10**

**3.3.**  Suppose medical research indicates that consumption of brussels sprouts prolongs life. Assume that four rather than three individuals now demand brussels sprouts and that this additional individual has the same demand schedule as Individual 1 in Table 3-3.

(*a*)  Present the new market demand schedule for brussels sprouts.

(*b*)  Plot this new market demand schedule and label it $D_2$.

(c) What happens to a market demand schedule when more individuals in a market area demand a commodity?

**Table 3-5**

| Price ($ per lb) | Quantity Demanded by Individual 4 (lb per month) | Quantity Demanded in the Market (lb per month) |
|---|---|---|
| 2.50 | 2.25 | 5.50 |
| 2.00 | 2.50 | 6.50 |
| 1.50 | 3.00 | 8.50 |
| 1.00 | 4.00 | 12.00 |
| 0.50 | 5.50 | 17.25 |

(a) Table 3-5 presents the price per pound in column 1; the quantity demanded by Individual 4 appears in column 2; market demand appears in column 3.

(b) Market demand from Table 3-5 is plotted in Fig. 3-10 and labeled $D_2$.

(c) When more individuals in a market area demand a commodity, the market demand schedule shifts outward.

## SHIFTING OF A MARKET DEMAND CURVE

**3.4.** Is price the only variable influencing the demand for a good or service?

Recall that demand indicates a willingness and the financial ability to buy a good or service. Willingness and ability to buy a commodity are influenced not only by the commodity's price but also by the income earned by consumers, preferences for a good or service (taste), the number of potential buyers in a market area, and the price of substitute and complementary commodities. When the market demand schedule in Table 3-5 was derived, variables other than price were unchanged. When these other variables change, quantity demanded at each price changes since there will be an increased or decreased willingness and/or ability to buy a good or service. For example, more individuals were willing to purchase brussels sprouts in Problem 3.3 as a result of the indication by medical research that consumption of brussels sprouts prolongs life. Economists classify changes in variables other than price of the commodity as a change in demand.

**3.5.** (a) What causes the market demand for a commodity to increase (i.e., causes the market demand curve to shift up and to the right)?

(b) What causes market demand to decrease (i.e., causes the market demand curve to shift down and to the left)?

(c) Distinguish between an increase in the quantity demanded and an increase in demand.

(d) Distinguish between a decrease in the quantity demanded and a decrease in demand.

(a) In defining the market demand curve for a commodity, the number of consumers in the market, their tastes, their money incomes, and the prices of substitute and complementary commodities are assumed to be unchanging. Substitute commodities are those which satisfy the same basic want, such as coffee and tea. Complementary commodities are those which are used together, such as cars and gasoline. These are to be distinguished from independent or unrelated commodities such as sodas and cars, pencils and refrigerators. Market demand for a commodity increases (the market demand curve shifts up and to the right) when (1) the number of individuals buying the commodity increases (which would occur as a result of population growth), (2) consumers' preference for the commodity increases (increased concern about weight would induce more people to drink diet soda), (3) consumers' incomes rise (occurs during an economic expansion), (4) the price of a substitute commodity increases (more potatoes are demanded when the price of rice increases), or (5) the price of a complementary commodity falls (individuals purchase more fuel-efficient cars when gasoline prices rise). An increase in demand means that at each price, more units of the commodity are demanded per unit of time.

(b)   Market demand decreases (the market demand curve shifts down and to the left) when (1) the number of individuals buying the commodity decreases, (2) consumers' preference for the commodity decreases, (3) consumers' incomes fall, (4) the price of a substitute commodity decreases, or (5) the price of a complementary commodity rises. A decrease in demand means that at each price, individuals demand fewer units of the commodity per unit of time.

(c)   An increase in quantity demanded indicates that there is a decrease in price and therefore a movement down a given demand curve, while holding constant other variables that influence demand. An increase in demand refers to a shift to the right by the entire demand curve and indicates that at each price, individuals are willing to purchase more units of the commodity per unit of time.

(d)   A decrease in quantity demanded indicates an increase in price and therefore a movement up a given demand curve, while holding constant variables other than price. A decrease in demand refers to a shift to the left by the demand curve and indicates that less of the commodity is purchased at each price per unit of time.

**3.6.**   Explain what happens to the demand curve for air transportation between New York City and Washington, D.C., as a result of the following events:

(a)   The income of households in Metropolitan New York and Washington, D.C., increases 20%;

(b)   the U.S. government subsidizes Amtrak, and the cost of a train ticket between New York City and Washington, D.C., is reduced 50%;

(c)   the number of businesses with offices in both New York City and Washington, D.C., doubles;

(d)   the price of an airline ticket decreases 20%.

(a)   Individuals will travel more since they have more disposable income. The demand for air transportation between NYC and Washington increases; the demand curve shifts up and to the right.

(b)   The cost of an alternative mode of transportation between NYC and Washington has decreased; thus, more individuals will travel by train between NYC and Washington. The demand for air transportation decreases; the demand curve shifts down and to the left.

(c)   There should be increased business travel between NYC and Washington. This increased demand for air transportation shifts the demand curve up and to the right.

(d)   There is no shift but there is a movement down the existing demand curve; the lower price for an airline ticket results in an increase in the number of people traveling by air between NYC and Washington.

## SUPPLY

**3.7.**   (a)   What is a supply schedule? A supply curve?

(b)   What is the usual shape of a supply curve? Why?

(c)   Explain $Q_s = f(P)$.

(a)   A *supply schedule* presents the units of a commodity that will be supplied at alternative prices during a given period of time. A *supply curve* is a graphic presentation of a supply schedule.

(b)   A supply curve is usually positively sloped, i.e., it slopes upward and to the right. Producers normally are willing to supply additional units of a commodity at higher prices since higher production costs are associated with producing larger quantities in the short run. Although the supply curve is normally positively sloped, a supply curve can be vertical. When vertical, the same quantity is supplied regardless of its price. This occurs when the period of analysis is so short that more of the commodity cannot be produced, or when, as in the case of original works of art, the quantity supplied is fixed forever.

(c)   The quantity supplied ($Q_s$) depends upon the price ($P$) of an item.

**3.8.**   Table 3-6 presents the supply schedules of the three producers of potatoes for a market area.

(a)   Derive a market supply schedule for potatoes.

(b)   Plot this market supply schedule and label the curve S.

**Table 3-6**

| Price ($ per bu) | Quantity Supplied by Producer 1, $q_1$ (bu per month) | Quantity Supplied by Producer 2, $q_2$ (bu per month) | Quantity Supplied by Producer 3, $q_3$ (bu per month) |
|---|---|---|---|
| 5 | 37.5 | 22.5 | 17.5 |
| 4 | 35.0 | 20.0 | 15.0 |
| 3 | 30.0 | 15.0 | 10.0 |
| 2 | 20.0 | 10.0 | 5.0 |
| 1 | 5.0 | 2.5 | 0.0 |

(a)   The market supply schedule is obtained by adding the quantities of each supplier at each price (Table 3-7).

**Table 3-7**

| Price ($ per bu) | Market Supply ($Q$) $Q = q_1 + q_2 + q_3$ (bu per month) |
|---|---|
| 5 | 77.5 |
| 4 | 70.0 |
| 3 | 55.0 |
| 2 | 35.0 |
| 1 | 7.5 |

(b)   The market supply curve appears in Fig. 3-11 and is labeled S.

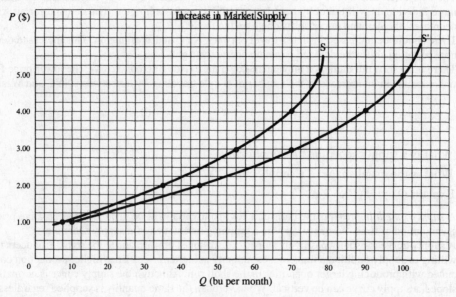

**Fig. 3-11**

**3.9.**   Suppose that high profits from growing potatoes attracts three additional producers whose combined willingness to produce potatoes is as follows: 22.5 bushels per month at price of $5 per bushel; 20 bushels per month at a price of $4; 15 bushels per month at a price of $3; 10 bushels per month at $2; and 2.5 bushels per month at a price of $1 per bushel.

(a)   How many bushels per month are supplied to the market at prices ranging from $5 per bushel to $1 per bushel?

(b) Plot the new market supply schedule and label it $S'$. What happens to the market supply curve when additional suppliers enter the market?

(a) Three additional producers of potatoes increase market supply as follows: at $5 per bushel, market supply increases from 77.5 bushels per month to 100 bushels per month; at $4, from 70.0 to 90; at $3, from 55.0 to 70; at $2, from 35.0 to 45.0; at $1, from 7.5 to 10.

(b) The new market supply schedule is plotted in Fig. 3-11 and is labeled S'. The entrance of additional suppliers shifts the market supply curve down and to the right.

## SHIFTING OF A MARKET SUPPLY CURVE

**3.10.** What variables influence a producer's willingness to supply a commodity?

A producer's willingness to supply a commodity is directly related to its production cost. A commodity's production cost is determined by the principle of increasing costs, the prices of the factors of production, the cost of materials, and technology. In a full-employment economy, the principle of increasing costs states that rising costs are associated with increased output of a commodity since economic resources are not equally efficient when producing a different combination of goods and services. (Recall that increased production of a good results in productive inefficiencies and therefore a higher per-unit cost of production, holding constant technology; the compensation of labor, land, and capital; and the prices of other commodities used in producing this good or service.) Per-unit production cost decreases and willingness to supply a commodity increases when there is a change in technology, when factor costs decline, and/or when the cost of materials falls.

**3.11.** (a) What causes an increase in market supply (a shift of the market supply curve down and to the right)?

(b) What causes a decrease in market supply (a shift up and to the left)?

(c) Distinguish between an increase in the quantity supplied and an increase in supply.

(d) Distinguish between a decrease in the quantity supplied and a decrease in supply.

(a) In defining the market supply for a commodity, it is assumed that technology, factor prices, the prices of other commodities related in production, and the number and size of producers of the commodity are unchanged. An increase in supply means that at any given price, producers supply more of the commodity per unit of time. The market supply curve for a commodity shifts down and to the right when (1) the number and/or size of producers increases, (2) technology in the production of the commodity improves, (3) the prices of factors used in the production of the commodity fall, and/or (4) the prices of commodities related in production fall. An improvement in technology or a reduction in factor prices reduces the per-unit cost of production and leads to in an increase in the supply of the commodity. Commodities related in production are those which generally use the same factors of production; thus, any change in the price of a related commodity affects its resource use and therefore resource availability for the commodity in question. A decrease in the price of a related commodity makes its resource use less profitable and therefore increases the resources available for the commodity under consideration and therefore its supply.

(b) A decrease in market supply means that at any given commodity price, producers will supply less per unit of time. The market supply curve decreases (shifts up and to the left) when (1) there are fewer producers of the commodity, (2) factor prices rise, and/or (3) the price of materials used in production rise. Note that technology cannot decrease supply since technology once learned is not unlearned.

(c) An increase in quantity supplied refers to a movement upward along a given supply curve as a result of an increase in the commodity's price, while holding constant everything else that affects supply. An increase in supply refers to a shift down and to the right by the supply curve, indicating that producers supply more of the commodity at each price per unit of time.

(d) A decrease in quantity supplied refers to a movement downward along a given supply curve due to a decrease in the commodity's price, holding constant all other variables that affect supply. A decrease in supply refers to a shift up and to the left of the supply curve where at each price producers now supply less of the commodity per unit of time.

**3.12.** What happens to the airline industry's market supply curve as a result of the following events:

(a)   There is an increase in the price of oil;

(b)   airline workers demand and receive a 20% increase in their wage;

(c)   Pratt & Whitney develops an airplane engine which is 50% more fuel-efficient;

(d)   U.S. manufacturers of airplanes are subsidized by the U.S. government.

(a)   With an increase in the price of oil, the cost of providing air transportation increases; the market supply schedule shifts up and to the left.

(b)   Higher wage contracts cause an increase in the per unit cost of supplying air transportation; the market supply schedule shifts up and to the left.

(c)   With more fuel-efficient engines, the cost of providing air transportation decreases; the market supply curve shifts down and to the right.

(d)   The U.S. government subsidy lowers the cost of airplanes to the airline industry, reducing their cost of providing air transportation; the market supply curve shifts down and to the right.

## EQUILIBRIUM PRICE AND QUANTITY

**3.13.** Market demand and market supply schedules for wheat appear in Table 3-8.

(a)   What is the relationship of quantity demanded and quantity supplied at prices per bushel of $5, $4, $3, $2, and $1? Is there a market surplus or shortage at these prices?

(b)   What effect does a surplus of wheat have upon the price of wheat?

(c)   What effect does a shortage of wheat have upon the price of wheat?

**Table 3-8**

| Price ($ per bu) | $Q_d$ (million bu per month) | $Q_s$ (million bu per month) |
|---|---|---|
| 5 | 2.25 | 3.75 |
| 4 | 2.50 | 3.50 |
| 3 | 3.00 | 3.00 |
| 2 | 4.00 | 2.00 |
| 1 | 5.50 | 0.50 |

(a)   When the price of wheat is $5 per bushel, 2.25 million bushels per month are demanded and 3.75 bushels are supplied. There is a wheat surplus since quantity supplied is greater than quantity demanded. At a $4 price, the quantity of wheat demanded is 2.5 million bushels per month, while the quantity of wheat supplied is 3.5 million, giving a 1 million bushel surplus. The quantity of wheat supplied and demanded is 3 million bushels when the price of wheat is $3 per bushel, and there is neither a surplus nor a shortage of wheat. When the price of wheat is $2 or $1, there is a shortage of wheat production since the quantity of wheat demanded exceeds that which is being supplied.

(b)   There is downward pressure on the price of wheat when a surplus exists. In order to sell this excess production, producers must lower price to induce consumers to purchase the excess production.

(c)   When a shortage exists, there is upward pressure on the price of wheat since consumers want to buy more wheat than is being supplied. Higher wheat prices induce consumers to substitute other grains for wheat, and eventually there is a balancing of quantity supplied and quantity demanded.

**3.14.** Market supply and demand schedules for wheat are plotted in Fig. 3-12. With reference to Fig. 3-12, explain

(a)   why prices of $5 and $4 per bushel are not equilibrium prices and how the price is pushed down toward an equilibrium level,

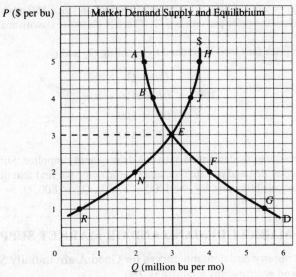

**Fig. 3-12**

(b) why prices of $1 and $2 per bushel are not equilibrium prices and how the price is pulled up toward equilibrium, and

(c) why the equilibrium price of wheat is $3 per bushel.

(a) Figure 3-12 shows that at a price of $5 per bushel, the quantity of wheat demanded falls short of the quantity supplied (from point *A* to point *H*). This surplus of unsold wheat drives the price down. As the price falls, the quantity demanded rises (a movement down the market demand curve) and the quantity supplied falls (a movement down the market supply curve). At the price of $4 per bushel, there is still a surplus (*BJ*) and a downward pressure on price. The price of wheat continues to fall until the wheat surplus is completely eliminated at the price of $3 per bushel (point *E*).

(b) At the price of $1 per bushel, the quantity of wheat demanded exceeds the quantity supplied (point *R* to *G*). Because of this unsatisfied demand, consumers bid wheat prices up. As the price rises, the quantity demanded falls (a movement upward on the demand curve) and the quantity supplied rises (a movement upward on the supply curve). At the price of $2 per bushel, there is still a shortage (*NF*) and upward pressure on the price of wheat. As the price of wheat continues to rise, the quantity demanded continues to fall and the quantity supplied continues to rise until the wheat shortage is completely eliminated at the price of $3 per bushel (point *E*).

(c) The equilibrium price of wheat is $3 per bushel; only at this price is the quantity of wheat that consumers are willing to purchase per month exactly equal to the quantity that producers are willing to supply per month. Note that at any other price, the willingness of consumers is not matched by the willingness of producers, even though the quantity bought may equal the quantity sold. For example, at the price of $2 per bushel, producers supply only 2 million bushels per month; consumers buy this entire 2 million but this is not an equilibrium point since consumers are willing to purchase more at this $2 price.

**3.15.** Suppose the market demand for Good X is given by the equation $Q_d = 1000 - 20P$, and market supply is given by the equation $Q_s = 500 + 30P$.

(a) Find quantity demanded and quantity supplied when the price of Good X is $12. Is there a surplus or shortage in the production of Good X? What should happen to the price of Good X?

(b) Find the equilibrium price for Good X by equating $Q_d$ and $Q_s$.

(c) Prove that the price found in part (b) is an equilibrium price.

(a) Quantity demanded is found by letting *P* equal $12 in the demand equation $Q_d = 1000 - 20P$. Thus, $Q_d = 1000 - 20(12)$; quantity demanded is 760. Quantity supplied is 860 when price is $12 [$Q_s =$

$500 + 30(12)$; $Q_s = 860$]. There is a surplus of production since 860 units are supplied while 760 units are demanded when the price per unit is \$12. There is therefore downward pressure on the \$12 price for Good X.

(b)   The equilibrium price for Good X is found by equating $Q_d$ and $Q_s$.

$$Q_d = Q_s$$
$$1000 - 20P = 500 + 30P$$
$$50P = 500$$
$$P = \$10$$

(c)   At equilibrium, the quantity demanded must equal the quantity supplied. Substituting the \$10 equilibrium price into the market demand and market supply equations, we find that quantity supplied and quantity demanded each equals 800 units. [$Q_d = 1000 - 20(10)$; $Q_d = 800$. $Q_s = 500 + 30(10)$; $Q_s = 800$.]

## EQUILIBRIUM WHEN MARKET DEMAND AND/OR MARKET SUPPLY CURVES SHIFT

**3.16.**  Suppose the market supply and demand curves for Good A are initially S and D in Fig. 3-13; equilibrium price is \$3 and equilibrium quantity is 280.

(a)   When the price of a substitute good increases 20%, the demand for Good A shifts up and to the right, from D to D′. After the demand shift what is the relationship between quantity demanded and quantity supplied at the initial \$3 equilibrium price? What must happen to the price of Good A in a market economy?

(b)   What is the new equilibrium price and quantity for Good A after the increase in demand?

(c)   What happens to a commodity's equilibrium price and quantity when there is an increase in demand, *ceteris paribus*?

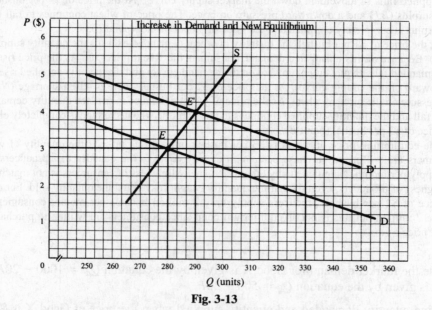

**Fig. 3-13**

(a)   Quantity demanded for market schedule D′ is 330 when the price is \$3, while market supply is 280. There is a shortage of Good A at the initial \$3 equilibrium price which puts upward pressure on the price of Good A.

(b)   The new equilibrium price for market demand curve D′ and market supply curve S is \$4; the equilibrium quantity is now 290.

(c)   Holding other variables constant, equilibrium price increases when there is an increase in demand. Equilibrium quantity also increases as long as the market supply curve is not vertical.

**3.17.** Suppose the market supply and demand curves for Good A are initially S and D in Fig. 3-14; equilibrium price is $3 and equilibrium quantity is 280.

(a)   Suppose improved technology in the production of Good A shifts the market supply curve from S to S', *ceteris paribus*. After the supply shift, what is the relationship between quantity demanded and quantity supplied at the initial $3 equilibrium price? What must happen to the price of Good A in a market economy?

(b)   What is the new equilibrium price and quantity after the technological advance has increased the supply of Good A?

(c)   What happens to a commodity's equilibrium price and quantity when there is an increase in market supply, *ceteris paribus?*

(a)   Quantity demanded for market schedule D is 280 when the price is $3, while market supply is 330. There is a surplus of Good A at the initial $3 equilibrium price which puts downward pressure on the price of Good A.

(b)   Equilibrium price falls from $3 to $2 as a result of the increase in market supply; equilibrium quantity increases from 280 to 320.

(c)   Equilibrium price falls and equilibrium quantity increases when there is an increase in market supply, *ceteris paribus.*

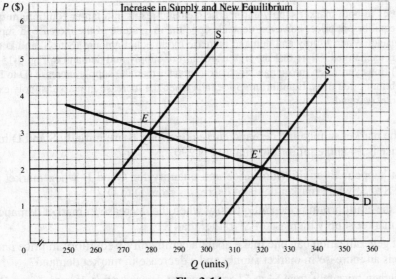

**Fig. 3-14**

**3.18.** Suppose the market supply and demand curves for Good A are initially S and D in Fig. 3-15; equilibrium price is $3 and equilibrium quantity is 280.

(a)   What happens to equilibrium price and quantity for Good A when market supply increases from S to S' and market demand increases from D to D'?

(b)   What would be the new equilibrium price and quantity had market demand increased from D to D'' instead of from D to D' while market supply increased to S'?

(c)   What generalizations can you make about the change in a commodity's equilibrium price and quantity when there are increases in both market supply and market demand?

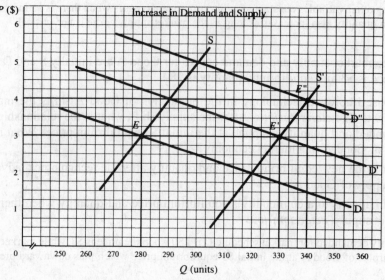

**Fig. 3-15**

(a) The equilibrium price for market supply and demand curves S and D as well as S' and D' is $3. Equilibrium quantity is 280 for curves S and D, and it increases to 330 for curves S' and D'.

(b) Equilibrium price for market supply and demand curves S' and D'' is $4, while equilibrium quantity is 340.

(c) Increases in both market supply and market demand result in a larger equilibrium quantity. The effect upon equilibrium price, however, depends upon the magnitude of the increase in supply relative to that of demand. When supply and demand increase by an equal amount (S to S' and D to D'), equilibrium price is unchanged. (Note that the rightward shift of supply and demand in Fig. 3-15 is 50 units at each price.) However, when the demand increase is greater than the supply increase (D to D'' and S to S'), the equilibrium price rises. Equilibrium price falls when the increase in market supply exceeds the increase in market demand.

**3.19.** Suppose the market supply and demand curves for Good B are initially S and D in Fig. 3-16; equilibrium price is $4 and equilibrium quantity is 290.

(a) What happens to equilibrium price and quantity for Good B when market supply increases from S to S' while market demand decreases from D to D'?

(b) Find the equilibrium price and quantity when the decrease in market demand is accompanied by a market supply increase of S'' rather than S'.

(c) What generalization can one make about a commodity's equilibrium price and quantity where there is an increase in market supply and a decrease in market demand?

(a) Equilibrium price falls from $4 to $3 as the market demand curve decreases from D to D' and market supply increases from S to S'. Equilibrium quantity is unchanged at 290 units.

(b) Equilibrium price falls from $4 (curves S and D) to $2 (curves D' and S''). Equilibrium quantity increases from 290 units to 320 units.

(c) When market supply increases and market demand decreases, equilibrium price falls. The direction of change in equilibrium quantity cannot be established without specifying the magnitude of change in supply and demand.

**3.20.** Suppose the demand for Good C shifts up and to the right as a result of higher household income. What can one establish about the shift of market supply when, as a result of the demand increase,

(a) equilibrium price remains unchanged and equilibrium quantity increases;

(b) equilibrium price falls while equilibrium quantity increases;

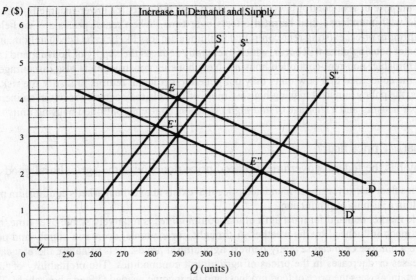

**Fig. 3-16**

(c)   equilibrium price increases while equilibrium quantity decreases.

(a)   An increase in market demand should raise equilibrium price. Since equilibrium price is unchanged, the market supply and demand curves must have shifted to the right by an equal amount, resulting in an increase in equilibrium quantity and no change in equilibrium price.

(b)   There must have been a greater increase in market supply than market demand for equilibrium price to fall.

(c)   The decrease in equilibrium quantity and increase in equilibrium price indicate that market supply is decreasing while market demand is increasing.

**3.21.**   What effect will the following events have upon equilibrium price and quantity?

(a)   There is an increase in market demand; market supply is unchanged.

(b)   Market supply decreases; market demand is unchanged.

(c)   Both market supply and market demand decrease.

(d)   There is a decrease in market demand and an increase in market supply.

(a)   The increase in market demand results in a movement up a fixed supply curve; equilibrium price and equilibrium quantity increase.

(b)   Decreased market supply results in a movement up a fixed demand curve; equilibrium price increases while equilibrium quantity decreases.

(c)   The decrease in both market demand and market supply results in a decrease in equilibrium quantity; the change in equilibrium price is undetermined since it depends upon the magnitude of the shift to the left of both curves.

(d)   The decrease in market demand and increase in market supply cause equilibrium price to fall; the change in equilibrium quantity is undetermined since it depends upon the shift to the left by market demand relative to the shift to the right by market supply.

## GOVERNMENT AND PRICE DETERMINATION

**3.22.**   (a)   What is a price ceiling?

(b)   Why did some local government units impose rent-control laws which placed ceilings on housing rentals?

(a)   A price ceiling is a government-mandated price that exists below the market's equilibrium price; price ceilings result in shortages.

(b) The purpose of rent-control laws was to reduce housing costs for lower-income households. Such laws, while well-intentioned, had harmful effects over time. When rental prices are set below the market's equilibrium price, existing rent-controlled buildings are less likely to be adequately maintained. Deterioration of housing units will occur, which eventually reduces the supply of housing and creates a shortage of affordable, non-rent-controlled housing. New housing construction is also discouraged since builders become concerned that new units may not generate sufficient returns to justify the risk of construction. Thus, the policy aimed at making housing more affordable may actually result in an increasing supply of subpar housing and a shortage of and high prices for non-rent-controlled housing units.

**3.23.** (a) What is a price floor?

(b) Why has the federal government placed price floors on some agricultural goods?

(a) A price floor is a government-mandated price that exists above the market's equilibrium price; price floors result in a surplus of production.

(b) While market demand for most agricultural commodities is relatively stable over time, market supply is very much influenced by the weather. A drought, for example, decreases supply and pushes up prices, while a bumper crop can severely depress agricultural prices. Acts of nature thereby can result in large increases or decreases in the prices of agricultural commodities. The profitability of farming becomes uncertain, as does the price of food products and the income needed to feed a household. Thus, the reasons for agricultural price supports (price floors) are: (1) to stabilize farmer incomes and encourage farmers to continue farming whether there are bumper crops or droughts; (2) to provide a more steady flow of agricultural products at relatively stable prices; and (3) to stabilize the amount of income that households need to spend on food.

**3.24.** Market supply and demand curves for Good A determine equilibrium price $P_0$ and equilibrium quantity $Q_0$ in Fig. 3-17.

(a) What actions can government take to lower the market price below $P_0$?

(b) What actions can government take to raise the market price above $P_0$?

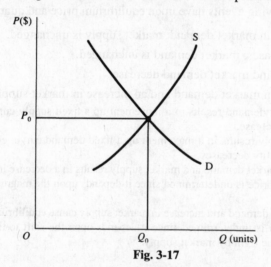

**Fig. 3-17**

(a) The market price of Good A can be lowered by decreasing market demand (a shift down and to the left by curve D) or by increasing market supply (a shift down and to the right by curve S). Market demand can be decreased by imposing a system of government rationing. When Good A is rationed, the government controls consumers' ability to buy it by requiring that each consumer have not only the financial ability to purchase Good A but a government-authorizing coupon as well. Market supply can be increased through a government subsidy. A government subsidy to the industry producing Good A can lower each firm's per-unit cost of production, which increases the number of units each producer is willing to supply at each price. Whether the government elects to ration or subsidize depends upon the policy's objective. When the intent is to fairly distribute a reduced output (i.e., decrease equilibrium quantity), rationing is called for. However, when the intent is to make the good more available to more consumers (i.e., increase equilibrium quantity), then a government subsidy is mandated.

(b) The government can increase Good A's equilibrium price by increasing market demand or decreasing market supply. In a free market economy, market demand can be increased by government purchase of Good A. For example, with government price supports, the government purchases surplus output and stockpiles these agricultural commodities. Supply can be reduced by paying producers not to produce. In agriculture, this occurs through acreage set-asides where government pays farmers to voluntarily reduce crop acreage.

## *Multiple Choice Questions*

1.  A demand schedule shows the relationship between the quantity demanded of a commodity over a given period of time and
    (a)  the price of the commodity,
    (b)  the tastes of the consumers,
    (c)  the income of the consumers,
    (d)  the price of related commodities.

2.  More of a commodity will be purchased at lower prices because
    (a)  consumers substitute this commodity for others whose price has not changed,
    (b)  at lower prices, consumers can purchase more of this commodity with a given money income,
    (c)  more consumers will buy the commodity at lower prices than at higher prices,
    (d)  all of the above.

3.  A supply schedule shows the relationship between the quantity supplied over a given period of time and
    (a)  factor prices,
    (b)  the price of the commodity,
    (c)  technology,
    (d)  the prices of other commodities related in production.

4.  The intersection of a market demand curve and a market supply curve for a commodity determines
    (a)  the equilibrium price for the commodity,
    (b)  the equilibrium quantity for the commodity,
    (c)  the point of neither surplus nor shortage for the commodity,
    (d)  all of the above.

5.  Which of the following statements is *not* true when price is above the equilibrium price?
    (a)  There is a shortage of the commodity.
    (b)  The quantity supplied exceeds the quantity demanded of the commodity.
    (c)  The pressure on the commodity price is downward.
    (d)  There is a surplus of the commodity.

6.  An increase in demand results in which of the following changes in the commodity's equilibrium price and quantity?
    (a)  Price rises and quantity falls.
    (b)  Price falls and quantity rises.

    (c)   Price and quantity both rise.
    (d)   Price and quantity both fall.

**7.** Which of the following does *not* cause an increase in demand?
    (a)   An increase in consumers' incomes,
    (b)   An increase in consumers' preference for the commodity,
    (c)   A reduction in the commodity's price,
    (d)   A reduction in the price of a complementary good.

**8.** An increase in market supply and a decrease in market demand will result in
    (a)   a decrease in equilibrium price and an increase in equilibrium quantity,
    (b)   a decrease in equilibrium price—the change in equilibrium quantity is indeterminate,
    (c)   an increase in equilibrium quantity—the change in equilibrium price is indeterminate,
    (d)   a decrease in equilibrium price and quantity.

**9.** Which of the following does *not* cause an increase in supply?
    (a)   An increase in the commodity's price,
    (b)   An improvement in technology,
    (c)   A reduction in factor prices,
    (d)   A decrease in the cost of materials.

**10.** An increase in market supply results in which of the following changes in the commodity's equilibrium price and quantity?
    (a)   Price rises and quantity falls.
    (b)   Price falls and quantity rises.
    (c)   Price and quantity both rise.
    (d)   Price and quantity both fall.

## True or False Questions

**11.** _____ As used in economics, the word *demand* is synonymous with *need*.

**12.** _____ There is a decrease in the demand for a commodity when the price of a substitute commodity increases.

**13.** _____ Taxing a commodity at the production level decreases its supply.

**14.** _____ A government-imposed price ceiling will exist above the equilibrium price and cause a shortage of the commodity.

**15.** _____ Quantity demanded falls when the government imposes a price floor.

**16.** _____ When the supply curve is positively sloped, an increase in demand will result in a larger quantity supplied.

**17.** _____ An increase in market supply and in market demand always results in an increase in equilibrium price and quantity.

**18.** _____ A surplus exists when the market price is above the equilibrium price.

**19.** _____ Government subsidization of firms producing Good A results in an increase in the demand for Good A.

**20.** _____ An increase in the supply of Good B results in an increase in the quantity of B demanded.

### Answers to Multiple Choice and True or False Questions

| | | | | | |
|---|---|---|---|---|---|
| **1.** (a) | **6.** (c) | **11.** (F) | **16.** (T) | | |
| **2.** (d) | **7.** (c) | **12.** (F) | **17.** (T) | | |
| **3.** (b) | **8.** (b) | **13.** (T) | **18.** (T) | | |
| **4.** (d) | **9.** (a) | **14.** (F) | **19.** (F) | | |
| **5.** (a) | **10.** (b) | **15.** (T) | **20.** (T) | | |

# Chapter 4

# Introduction to Macroeconomics

## *Chapter Summary*

1. Macroeconomics analyzes the economy as a whole, while microeconomics analyzes individual components of the economy. Topics in macroeconomics include the economy's level of output and employment, the price level, and the balance of payments. Topics in microeconomics include decision making by an individual, the theory of the firm, the allocation of economic resources, market structures, and price determination.

2. Three frequently used measures of aggregate output are nominal GDP, real GDP, and potential GDP. Nominal GDP measures the market value of all final goods and services produced in the domestic economy at current prices. Real GDP also measures the value of all final output in the domestic economy but with prices held constant. Potential GDP is the maximum output that can be produced in the domestic economy without putting upward pressure on the price level.

3. The GDP gap is the difference between potential GDP and real GDP. A positive GDP gap exists when real GDP falls below potential GDP. A negative GDP gap exists when real GDP exceeds potential GDP.

4. Aggregate demand represents the collective spending of individuals, businesses, government, and net exports. The aggregate demand curve is inversely related to the price level, indicating that there is less aggregate spending at a higher price level. The aggregate demand curve shifts when variables other than the price level change.

5. Aggregate supply is the collective quantity supplied by all producers. Three aggregate supply curves are presented: (1) a curve which is positively sloped, indicating that larger quantities are supplied at a higher price level; (2) a Keynesian aggregate supply curve, on which increasing quantities are supplied at a fixed price level until full-employment output is reached, at which time aggregate supply is positively sloped; and (3) a classical aggregate supply curve, which is vertical at the full-employment level of output and quantity supplied has no relationship to the price level. The aggregate supply curve shifts when the quantity or price of economic resources changes or when there is a technological advance.

6. The equilibrium level of output exists at the point of intersection of aggregate supply and aggregate demand. Equilibrium changes whenever aggregate supply or aggregate demand shifts.

7. Economic activity is subject to economic fluctuations because of periodic decreases in aggregate demand. A business cycle is a cumulative fluctuation in aggregate output that lasts for two or more years. A peak marks the point at which economic activity stops increasing, and a trough marks the point at which economic activity stops decreasing.

## *Important Terms*

**Aggregate demand.**  A schedule or curve which depicts the total quantity of output that is demanded at various price levels.

**Aggregate supply.**  A schedule or curve which depicts the total quantity of output that is supplied at various price levels.

**Business cycles.**   Fluctuations in real GDP which recur and last for periods of two years or more.

**Classical aggregate supply curve.**   An aggregate supply curve which is vertical at the full-employment level of output.

**GDP gap.**   Potential GDP less real GDP.

**Keynesian aggregate supply curve.**   An aggregate supply curve which is horizontal until the full-employment level of output, at which point it becomes positively sloped.

**Macroeconomics.**   The study of the economy as a whole; individual units in the economy are combined and analyzed as an aggregate.

**Microeconomics.**   The study of individual components of the economy, such as a household, a firm, and the price of a good or service.

**Nominal GDP.**   The market value of all final goods and services produced in the domestic economy during a one-year period measured at current prices.

**Peak.**   The point at which economic activity stops expanding and begins to decline.

**Potential GDP.**   The maximum output a domestic economy can produce without putting upward pressure on the price level.

**Real GDP.**   The market value of all final goods and services produced in the domestic economy during a one-year period measured with constant prices; real GDP is nominal GDP corrected for inflation.

**Recession.**   A period of time in which real GDP is declining.

**Trough.**   The point at which economic activity stops declining and begins to increase.

# Outline of Chapter 4: Introduction to Macroeconomics

    **4.1   Macroeconomics and Microeconomics**

    **4.2   Gross Domestic Product**

    **4.3   Aggregate Demand, Aggregate Supply, and Equilibrium Output**

    **4.4   Changes in Aggregate Output**

    **4.5   Business Cycles**

## 4.1   MACROECONOMICS AND MICROECONOMICS

The study of economics is divided into two general fields: macroeconomics and microeconomics. *Macroeconomics* analyzes the economic behavior of the entire economy and major spending sectors: household consumption, business investment, government expenditures, and net exports (gross exports less gross imports). Macroeconomics focuses primarily on the level of output for the entire economy, the general level of prices, the rate of unemployment, and the economy's balance of payments. *Microeconomics* is concerned with the economic behavior of individual decision-making units in a free-enterprise market system, analyzing how an individual consumer spends income to maximize satisfaction, how a business firm combines economic resources to maximize profits, how the price of each resource is determined, and how price is determined in diverse market structures.

## 4.2   GROSS DOMESTIC PRODUCT

Gross domestic product (GDP) measures total output in the domestic economy. Nominal GDP, real GDP, and potential GDP are three different measures of aggregate output. *Nominal GDP* is the market value of all final goods and services produced in the domestic economy in a one-year period *at current prices*. By this definition, (1) only output exchanged in a market is included (do-it-yourself services such as cleaning your own room are not included); (2) output is valued in its final form (output is in its final form when no further alteration is made to the good which would change its market value); and (3) output is measured using current-year prices. Because nominal GDP values are inflated by prices that change over time, aggregate output is also measured holding the prices of all goods and services constant over time. This valuation of GDP *at constant prices* is called *real GDP*. The third measure of aggregate output is *potential GDP* (trend GDP), the maximum production that can take place in the domestic economy without putting upward pressure on the general level of prices. Conceptually, potential GDP represents a point on a given production-possibility frontier.

Real GDP and potential GDP for the U.S. economy are plotted in Fig. 4-1 for the period 1960 through 1992. Note that the U.S. economy's potential output increases at a fairly steady rate each year while actual real GDP fluctuates around potential GDP. These fluctuations of real GDP are identified as business cycles and are discussed in Section 4.5. The GDP gap is the difference between potential GDP and real GDP; it is positive when potential GDP exceeds real GDP and negative when real GDP exceeds potential GDP. A positive gap indicates that there are unemployed resources and the economy is operating inefficiently within its production-possibility frontier. It therefore follows that an economy's rate of unemployment rises as its GDP gap increases, and falls when the gap declines. An economy is operating above its normal productive capacity when there is a negative gap. The economy's price level rises when a negative gap develops.

**EXAMPLE 4.1.** Figure 4-1 presents real and potential GDP for the U.S. economy from 1960 through 1992. Potential GDP increases annually, reflecting greater productive capability and therefore outward shifts of the economy's production-possibility frontier. Although real GDP usually increases each year, there are years when it actually decreases. For example, from 1981 to 1982, real GDP decreased from $3843.1 billion to $3760.3 billion, while potential GDP increased from $3971.8 billion to $4062.3 billion. The GDP gap is $128.7 billion in 1981 (real GDP is already below potential GDP), and it increases to $302.0 billion in 1982 as aggregate economic output in the U.S. economy decreases and potential output increases. Real GDP increases more rapidly than potential GDP beginning in 1983, and it exceeds potential GDP by 1988. The resulting negative GDP gap in 1988 causes upward pressure on the U.S. price level; the U.S. inflation rate increases from 1.9% in 1986 to 4.8% in 1989. The U.S. economy slips into a recession in 1990; real GDP falls below potential GDP during 1991.

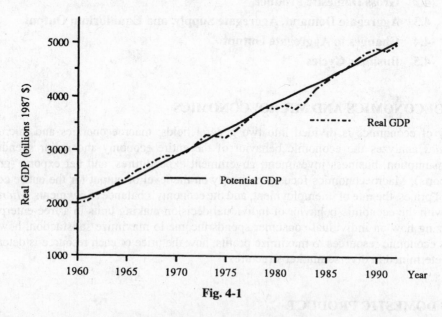

**Fig. 4-1**

**EXAMPLE 4.2.** The GDP gap and the unemployment rate for the United States are plotted in Fig. 4-2 for the period 1960 through 1992. Note how well the unemployment rate relates to the GDP gap. For example, the rise in the GDP gap from $128.7 billion in 1981 to $302.0 billion in 1982 is associated with an increase in the unemployment rate, from 7.6% to 9.7%. The unemployment rate declines after 1982 as the GDP gap narrows and reaches zero in 1987. This close relationship of the GDP gap and unemployment rate is not surprising, since increases in the GDP gap indicate that the economy is moving away from full employment, and decreases in the GDP gap indicate that the economy is moving toward its production-possibility frontier and efficient use of its resources.

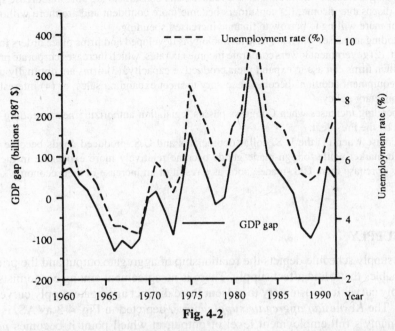

**Fig. 4-2**

## 4.3  AGGREGATE DEMAND, AGGREGATE SUPPLY, AND EQUILIBRIUM OUTPUT

The economy's equilibrium level of output occurs at the point of intersection of aggregate supply and aggregate demand. The concept of equilibrium developed in Chapter 3 is used in both macroeconomics and microeconomics. In microeconomics, equilibrium price exists where quantity demanded equals quantity supplied. The supply and demand schedules in macroeconomics differ from those in Chapter 3 in that they relate the aggregate quantity supplied and the aggregate quantity demanded to the price level.

### AGGREGATE DEMAND

An aggregate demand curve represents the collective spending of consumers, businesses, and government, as well as net foreign purchases of goods and services, at different price levels. An aggregate demand curve, like the demand curve in microeconomics, is negatively related to price, holding constant other factors that influence aggregate spending decisions. Price, presented as the *price level* in macroeconomics, affects aggregate spending because of an interest rate effect, a wealth effect, and an international purchasing power effect. The *interest rate effect* traces the effect that interest rate levels have upon aggregate spending. The nominal rate of interest is directly related to the price level, *ceteris paribus*. Increases in the price level push up the nominal rate of interest. Rising interest rates usually will depress interest-sensitive spending. The *wealth effect* relates changes in wealth to changes in aggregate spending. The market value of many financial assets falls as the price level and interest rates increase. A higher price level will decrease the household sector's net wealth, lower consumer spending, and cause a lower level of aggregate spending. A country's imports and exports are also affected by a changing price level, i.e., by an *international purchasing power effect*. When the price level increases in the home country and is unchanged in foreign countries, foreign-made commodities become relatively less expensive, the home country's exports fall, its imports increase, and there is less aggregate spending on the home country's output.

An aggregate demand curve shifts when there is a change in a variable (other than price) that affects aggregate spending decisions. Outward shifts (shifts outward to the right) occur when consumers become more willing to spend or there are increases in investment spending, government expenditures, and net exports.

**EXAMPLE 4.3.** Aggregate demand increases (the aggregate demand curve shifts outward) as a result of the following events:

Consumer spending increases when (1) taxes are reduced and consumers are able to increase spending as a result of a higher level of disposable income; (2) consumers become more confident and are more willing to spend current disposable income or more willing to borrow to finance increased spending.

Investment spending increases when (1) new technology is developed and firms place orders for more technically advanced equipment; (2) government lowers corporate income tax rates, which increases corporate profits and generates larger cash flows which firms can use to expand their productive capacity; (3) firms are optimally using their existing plant capacity, and equipment additions become necessary to meet expanding sales; or (4) interest rates decline as a result of an easier monetary policy.

Government spending increases when Congress passes legislation authorizing new spending programs and this legislation is signed by the President.

Net exports increase when (1) the U.S. dollar depreciates and U.S.-produced goods become relatively less expensive in the world market while foreign-made goods become relatively more expensive in the United States; or (2) foreign countries purchase more U.S.-made goods as a result of an increase in their economy's level of economic activity.

## AGGREGATE SUPPLY

An aggregate supply schedule depicts the relationship of aggregate output and the price level, holding constant other variables that could affect supply. There is no agreement among economists on the shape of the aggregate supply curve. It is customary to present three distinct aggregate supply curves to characterize this disagreement. The *Keynesian aggregate supply curve,* depicted in Fig. 4-3 as AS, is *horizontal* until it reaches the economy's full-employment level of output, at which point it becomes *positively sloped.* Figure 4-4 presents a positively sloped aggregate supply curve. Note for curve AS' that as aggregate output approaches the full-employment level $y_f$, increased output is associated with larger and larger increases in the price level. The *classical aggregate supply curve*, presented in Fig.4-5, is *vertical*, indicating that there is no relationship between aggregate output and the price level.

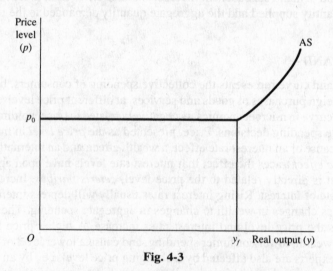

**Fig. 4-3**

**EXAMPLE 4.4.** Changes in resource availability, resource cost, and technology shift the aggregate supply curve. Aggregate supply curve AS' shifts rightward to AS'' in Fig. 4-4 when (1) improved technology increases the potential output of a given quantity of resources; (2) the quantity of economic resources increases; or (3) the cost of resources declines.

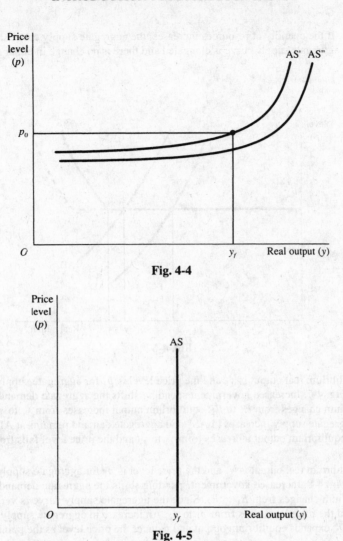

Fig. 4-4

Fig. 4-5

## 4.4 CHANGES IN AGGREGATE OUTPUT

The effect of changes in aggregate demand and/or aggregate supply upon equilibrium output and the price level depends upon the shape of the aggregate supply curve. With a *Keynesian aggregate supply curve*, an increase in aggregate demand affects only output as long as the economy is below full-employment output, whereas an increase in aggregate supply has no effect upon either the price level or output when aggregate demand intersects aggregate supply in the horizontal portion of the curve (see Example 4.5). Increases in aggregate demand and/or aggregate supply affect both the price level and real output when aggregate supply is *positively sloped*. An increase in aggregate demand increases both the price level and real output for a positively sloped aggregate supply curve, while output increases and the price level falls when there is an increase in aggregate supply (see Example 4.6). For a *classical aggregate supply curve*, increases in aggregate demand result in only a higher price level, whereas increases in aggregate supply result in a higher level of output and a lower price level (Example 4.7).

**EXAMPLE 4.5.** Equilibrium real output is $y_1$ and the price level is $p_1$ for aggregate supply and aggregate demand curves AS′ and AD′ in Fig. 4-6. Increased government spending shifts the aggregate demand curve outward to AD″, and the point of equilibrium changes from $E_1$ to $E_2$. Since the intersection of aggregate supply and aggregate demand remains in the horizontal portion of the aggregate supply curve, equilibrium output increases from $y_1$ to $y_2$ with no

change in price level $p_1$. If the quantity of resources increases, the aggregate supply curve shifts outward to AS''; the horizontal portion of the aggregate supply curve is elongated and there is no change in either equilibrium output or the price level.

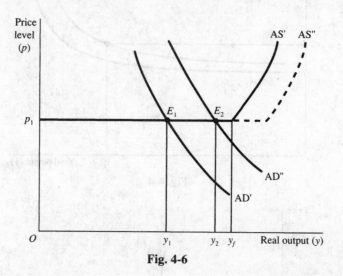

**Fig. 4-6**

**EXAMPLE 4.6.** Equilibrium real output is $y_1$ and the price level is $p_1$ for aggregate supply and aggregate demand curves AS' and AD' in Fig. 4-7. Increased government spending shifts the aggregate demand curve outward to AD'', and the point of equilibrium changes from $E_1$ to $E_2$; equilibrium output increases from $y_1$ to $y_2$ as the price level rises from $p_1$ to $p_2$. When aggregate supply increases to AS'' and aggregate demand remains at AD', the equilibrium point changes from $E_1$ to $E_3$; equilibrium output increases from $y_1$ to $y_2$ and the price level falls from $p_1$ to $p_0$.

**EXAMPLE 4.7.** Equilibrium real output is $y_1$ and the price level is $p_1$ for aggregate supply and aggregate demand curves AS' and AD' in Fig. 4-8. Increased government spending shifts the aggregate demand curve outward to AD'', and the point of equilibrium changes from $E_1$ to $E_2$. Since the aggregate supply curve is vertical, there is no change in equilibrium output and the price level rises from $p_1$ to $p_2$. An increase in aggregate supply to AS'', with no change in aggregate demand AD', expands equilibrium output and reduces the price level as the point of equilibrium changes from $E_1$ to $E_3$.

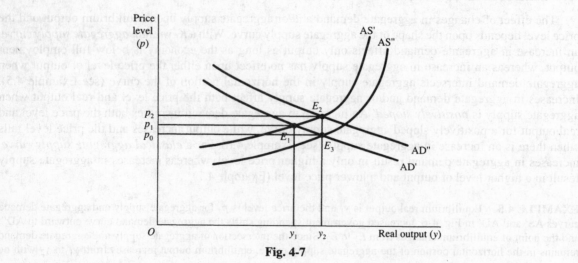

**Fig. 4-7**

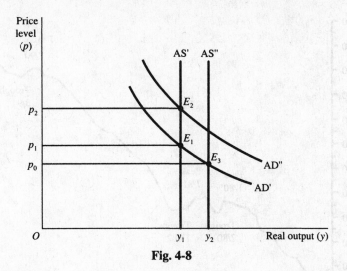

**Fig. 4-8**

## 4.5  BUSINESS CYCLES

A business cycle is a cumulative fluctuation in aggregate output that lasts for several years. Although recurrent, the duration and intensity of each fluctuation varies, and the impact of each cycle is widely diffused among a wide array of businesses. Points at which aggregate output changes direction are marked by peaks and troughs. A *peak* is a point which marks the end of economic expansion (rising aggregate output) and the beginning of a recession (decline in economic activity). A *trough* marks the end of a recession and the beginning of economic recovery. The time span between troughs and peaks is classified as an expansionary period (trough to peak) or a contractionary period (peak to trough). Peaks and troughs for the U.S. economy are presented in Table 4-1 along with the length of each expansionary and contractionary period.

**Table 4-1   Peaks and Troughs for the U.S. Economy, 1961–1991**

| Trough | Peak | Trough | Expansionary Period (Trough to Peak) | Contractionary Period (Peak to Trough) |
|--------|------|--------|--------------------------------------|----------------------------------------|
| 2/61   | 12/69 | 11/70 | 94 months  | 11 months |
| 11/70  | 11/73 | 3/75  | 36 months  | 16 months |
| 3/75   | 1/80  | 7/80  | 58 months  | 6 months  |
| 7/80   | 7/81  | 11/82 | 12 months  | 16 months |
| 11/82  | 7/90  | 3/91  | 93 months  | 9 months  |

SOURCE: *Survey of Current Business*

**EXAMPLE 4.8.**   The cyclical behavior of the U.S. economy from 1974 through 1993 is presented in Fig. 4-9. A recession began in November 1973 and continued until the March 1975 trough. Note that during this period real GDP was declining. An expansionary period followed and real GDP expanded through 1979. Note that during the expansionary period, real GDP increases fairly rapidly after the end of the recession and increases at a much slower rate in the latter phase of the expansionary period. A short six-month recession occurs in 1980 and is followed by a weak expansionary period which ends in July 1981. The 1981–1982 recession displays an uneven but decidedly downward movement of real GDP, followed by economic recovery after November 1982. The 1990–1991 recession began in July 1990 and ended in March 1991.

There are a number of explanations for the cyclical behavior of aggregate output. The central focus of many of these theories is investment spending and consumer purchase of durable goods (goods such as automobiles). No one theory of investment spending or consumer purchase of durable goods is able to

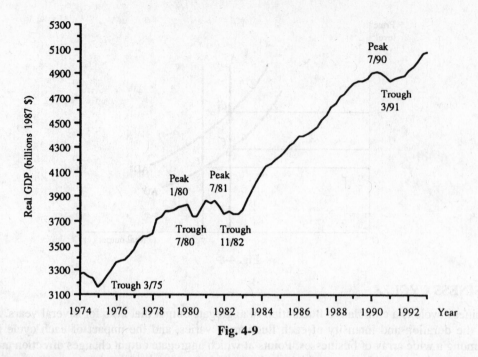

**Fig. 4-9**

explain why some business cycles are more severe than others. This suggests that there are numerous causes and that the importance of each cause varies over time.

**EXAMPLE 4.9.** Decreases in investment spending or consumer durable spending are viewed as the major cause of a decline in aggregate output. Suppose an economy's initial aggregate supply and aggregate demand curves are AS' and AD' in Fig. 4-10, and output is at the full-employment level $y_f$. A decrease in consumption and investment spending shifts aggregate demand to AD''; the equilibrium position changes from $E_1$ to $E_2$; output falls to $y_1$; and the economy is in a recession. *Consumer durable expenditures decline when* (1) government imposes higher taxes upon consumers; (2) consumers are less willing to spend because of a loss of confidence; (3) heavily indebted consumers are unable to borrow additional sums to purchase big-ticket items. *Business investment declines when* (1) government imposes higher taxes on businesses; (2) interest rates rise or businesses are less able to borrow to finance investment projects; (3) lenders are less willing to lend to businesses; (4) businesses no longer view capital additions as profitable.

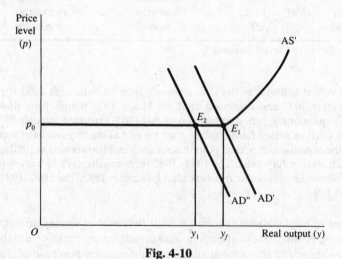

**Fig. 4-10**

# Solved Problems

## MACROECONOMICS AND MICROECONOMICS

**4.1.** Establish whether the following is a topic in macroeconomics or microeconomics.

    (a)  A consumer must decide how to reallocate spending as a result of a 10% increase in the price of food and no change in disposable income.

    (b)  Purchases of durable goods fall as a result of deteriorating consumer confidence.

    (c)  Investment spending declines as a result of rising interest rates.

    (d)  A firm contemplates the purchase of more technologically efficient equipment as a result of a 20% increase in wages.

    (e)  A cut in federal income taxes is expected to increase consumer spending.

    (a)  This is a topic in microeconomics since an individual consumer must restructure expenditures because of higher food prices.

    (b)  This is a topic in macroeconomics because consumers, as a spending sector, decrease spending on durable goods as a result of increasing pessimism. This would be a topic in microeconomics if we analyzed how Individual A's pessimism affects her spending on various goods and services.

    (c)  This is a topic in macroeconomics since we are considering the effect that rising interest rates have on total investment spending. This would be a topic in microeconomics if Corporation A was postponing capital spending plans because of rising interest rates.

    (d)  This is a topic in microeconomics since it concerns one firm's decision about adding technologically efficient equipment.

    (e)  This is a topic in macroeconomics since it considers the effect of lower taxes upon total consumer spending.

## GROSS DOMESTIC PRODUCT

**4.2.** Does gross domestic product (GDP) measure the domestic output of all final goods and services?

    There are a number of productive activities that do not involve a market transaction (e.g., do-it-yourself home repairs and the productive services of a homemaker). Since GDP includes only domestic output that involves a market exchange, such productive activities are not included; their exclusion results in an understatement of the total value of final output.

**4.3.** (a)  Distinguish between a final good and an intermediate good.

    (b)  Is a loaf of bread a final or an intermediate good? What about a bag of flour?

    (c)  Why would inclusion of final and intermediate goods in measuring GDP involve double counting?

    (a)  A *final good* is one that involves no further processing and is purchased for final use. An *intermediate good* is one that (1) involves further processing during the year, (2) is being purchased, modified, and then resold by the purchaser, or (3) is resold during the year for a profit.

    (b)  Bread and flour could be either final or intermediate goods, depending upon the purchaser's use of the goods. For example, a loaf of bread is a final good when purchased by a household for consumption; it is an intermediate good when purchased by a luncheonette which resells the bread as part of a sandwich. Similarly, a bag of flour is a final good when purchased by a household for family use but an intermediate good when purchased by a baker.

    (c)  Intermediate goods are components of final goods. If the value of intermediate and final goods were included in the measurement of the value of final output, there would be a double counting of value and an overstatement of GDP.

**4.4.** (*a*) What is the difference between nominal GDP, real GDP, and potential GDP?

(*b*) Establish whether the following involve a change in nominal GDP, real GDP, or potential GDP:
(1) More individuals who are 16 years of age or older want to work; (2) An increase in the price of oil results in an increase in the prices of a variety of goods and services whose production is energy-dependent; (3) An increase in consumer spending results in greater utilization of the economy's economic resources.

(*a*) *Nominal GDP* (current dollar GDP) is the market value of final output measured at current prices, whereas *real GDP* (constant dollar GDP) measures final output with prices that prevailed in a specific year. *Potential GDP* measures the economy's capacity to produce at a point in time; potential GDP is a point on an economy's production-possibility frontier.

(*b*) (1) Having greater economic resources (e.g., a larger number of people over age 16 who want to work) translates into greater productive capacity. There is an increase in the economy's potential GDP and therefore an outward shift of the economy's production-possibility frontier. (2) The increase in the price of oil and oil-dependent goods and services results in an increase in the price level and therefore an increase in nominal GDP. (3) Increased consumer spending results in more output and therefore an increase in real GDP. Nominal GDP is also higher as a result of the increase in real GDP.

**4.5.** An economy's potential output is depicted by the production-possibility frontier in Fig. 4-11.

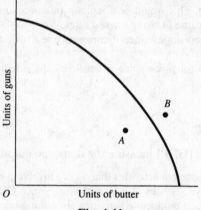

**Fig. 4-11**

(*a*) Explain the relationship between potential GDP and real GDP when output is at point *A*.

(*b*) What is a GDP gap?

(*c*) Is there a GDP gap for the situation described in part (*a*)?

(*d*) Can a GDP gap be negative?

(*a*) Point *A* is within the economy's production-possibility frontier. Thus, actual output is less than the economy's ability to produce, i.e., real GDP is less than potential GDP.

(*b*) A GDP gap exists when real GDP does not equal potential GDP. The GDP gap is measured by subtracting real GDP from potential GDP.

(*c*) There is a positive GDP gap at point *A* since the economy's production of goods and services is below its ability to produce.

(*d*) The production-possibility frontier and therefore potential GDP measures the economy's ability to produce goods and services *without* putting upward pressure on factor and output prices. The production-possibility frontier can therefore be exceeded, but in doing so there are increases in both output and the price level. Thus, a negative GDP gap can exist—real GDP can exceed potential GDP—when real GDP is, for example, at point *B* in Fig. 4-11 and the economy is producing beyond its natural full-employment level of output.

**4.6.** Potential GDP, real GDP, and the GDP gap are presented in Table 4-2 for a hypothetical economy for period 1:1 (year 1, quarter 1) through period 3:4.

(a) Is this economy ever on its production-possibility frontier?

(b) What is happening to labor's unemployment rate between periods 1:1 and 1:4? Between periods 3:1 and 3:4?

(c) What is happening to the price level between periods 2:1 and 2:4?

**Table 4-2**
**(in Billions of Constant Dollars)**

| Period | Potential GDP | Real GDP | GDP Gap |
|--------|---------------|----------|---------|
| 1:1 | 408.0 | 395.6 | 9.4 |
| 1:2 | 412.1 | 403.7 | 8.4 |
| 1:3 | 416.2 | 412.0 | 4.2 |
| 1:4 | 420.4 | 420.0 | 0.4 |
| 2:1 | 424.6 | 424.6 | 0.0 |
| 2:2 | 428.8 | 430.0 | −1.2 |
| 2:3 | 433.1 | 436.1 | −3.0 |
| 2:4 | 437.5 | 440.5 | −3.0 |
| 3:1 | 441.8 | 440.5 | 1.3 |
| 3:2 | 446.2 | 436.1 | 10.1 |
| 3:3 | 450.7 | 433.9 | 16.8 |
| 3:4 | 455.2 | 433.4 | 21.8 |

(a) Real GDP equals potential GDP during period 2:1. The economy is on its production-possibility frontier and there is full employment of economic resources.

(b) There are unemployed labor resources from period 1:1 through period 1:4—real GDP is less than potential GDP. The declining GDP gap from period 1:1 to period 1:4 indicates that labor's unemployment rate is declining during these periods. Real GDP is again below potential GDP during periods 3:1 and 3:4. The rising GDP gap from period 3:1 through period 3:4 indicates an increasing unemployment rate.

(c) Real GDP exceeds the economy's normal full-employment level of output from period 2:1 through period 2:4; the economy's price level is rising during these periods.

## AGGREGATE DEMAND, AGGREGATE SUPPLY, AND EQUILIBRIUM OUTPUT

**4.7.** Aggregate demand and aggregate supply curves for a hypothetical economy are presented in Fig. 4-12. Full employment output exists at output $y*$.

(a) Find the economy's equilibrium level of output.

(b) Is this economy producing on its production-possibility frontier? Is there a GDP gap?

(a) The equilibrium level of output exists at $y_1$ where aggregate demand equals aggregate supply.

(b) An economy is on its production-possibility frontier when there is full employment and real GDP equals potential GDP. This economy is producing within its production-possibility frontier since real GDP ($y_1$) is less than full-employment output ($y*$). The GDP gap is the distance from $y_1$ to $y*$, the amount by which potential GDP exceeds real GDP.

**4.8.** Aggregate demand is the sum of spending by individuals, businesses, and government, plus the net export of goods and services.

(a) Explain why aggregate demand is inversely related to the price level, i.e., why aggregate spending decreases as the price level increases.

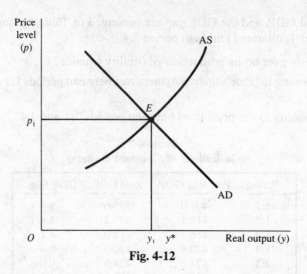

**Fig. 4-12**

(b)   What variables other than the price level can affect aggregate demand?

(c)   What happens to an aggregate demand curve when variables other than the price level change?

(a)   Consumer and business spending as well as net exports are inversely related to the price level. An increase in the price level, *ceteris paribus,* pushes up the nominal rate of interest. Because a higher interest rate negatively affects consumer purchases of durable goods (cars, etc.) and housing units and negatively affects business purchases of producers' durable goods and nonresidential structures, consumer and investment spending declines as the price level and the rate of interest increase. Higher interest rates, *ceteris paribus,* depress the market value of many financial assets and therefore the market value of consumer wealth; individuals therefore can be expected to spend less when a rising price level decreases consumer wealth. Also, an increase in the domestic price level, *ceteris paribus,* will depress net exports; a country will import more and export less when domestically produced commodities become more expensive relative to commodities produced in other countries.

(b)   Aggregate demand is affected by variables which influence spending units' ability and willingness to purchase goods and services. Ability is altered when the government changes the tax rate or the monetary authority changes the rate of interest. For example, a decrease in the personal or corporate income tax rate increases the ability of individuals or business units to consume and invest. An easing of monetary policy increases bank lending, lowers the rate of interest, and induces a higher level of consumption and investment. Willingness to purchase goods and services is affected by perceptions of job security, expectations about the future, and utilization of existing capacity. For example, individuals are less willing to consume when they become increasingly concerned about being laid off and/or they become increasingly uncertain about their future level of real disposable income. Businesses are less willing to add to their existing plant capacity when there is decreasing use of existing plant capacity and/or they expect a decrease in consumer spending.

(c)   Changes in individuals' and businesses' ability and/or willingness to spend shift the aggregate demand curve. An increased ability and/or willingness to spend shifts aggregate demand outward, whereas a decrease shifts aggregate demand inward.

**4.9.**   (a)   What is the difference between a Keynesian aggregate supply curve and a classical aggregate supply curve? Is the aggregate supply curve AS presented in Fig. 4-13 Keynesian or classical?

(b)   What happens to the economy's production-possibility frontier and the aggregate supply curve in Fig. 4-13 when there is a technological advance or an increase in the labor supply?

(a)   A *classical aggregate supply curve* is a vertical line at the full-employment level of output. A *Keynesian aggregate supply curve* has output increasing without any change in the price level until the economy reaches full employment, at which time aggregate supply becomes positively sloped. According to a Keynesian aggregate supply curve, output can be increased from a point within the production-possibility frontier to a point on the production-possibility frontier without any increase in the price level. Output beyond the normal full-employment level (outside the production-possibility frontier) is achieved only by increases in the price level. A classical aggregate supply curve appears in Fig. 4-13.

(*b*) A technological advance or an increase in the labor supply shifts the production-possibility frontier outward. Such an increase in the economy's productive capability is depicted by a parallel rightward shift of the classical aggregate supply curve in Fig. 4-13, from AS to AS′.

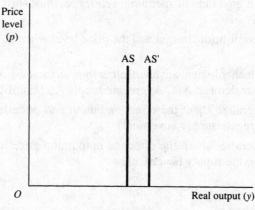

**Fig. 4-13**

**4.10.** A positively sloped aggregate supply curve appears in Fig. 4-14. Full employment exists at $y^*$.

(*a*) How does this positively sloped aggregate supply curve differ from a Keynesian aggregate supply curve?

(*b*) What happens to the aggregate supply curve in Fig. 4-14 when (1) there is a substantial increase in the cost of raw materials, and (2) there is an increase in labor productivity?

(*a*) The positively sloped aggregate supply curve in Fig. 4-14 shows that there are some increases in the price level as the economy moves from a point *within* the production-possibility frontier to a point *on* the production-possibility frontier, whereas a Keynesian aggregate supply curve shows a constant price level for such a movement. The Keynesian and positively sloped aggregate supply curves are both positively sloped for output levels beyond the full-employment level of output, $y^*$.

(*b*) (1) The cost of supplying output increases when raw material costs rise; consequently, there is an inward shift of aggregate supply curve AS in Fig. 4-14. (2) Increases in labor productivity lower production costs and result in an outward shift of aggregate supply curve AS.

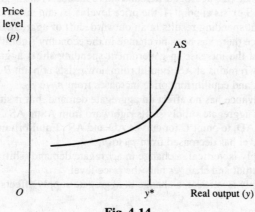

**Fig. 4-14**

## CHANGES IN AGGREGATE OUTPUT

**4.11.** Use aggregate demand and aggregate supply curves AD and AS in Fig. 4-15 to answer the following questions.

    (*a*)   Is the aggregate supply curve Keynesian or classical?

    (*b*)   Find the economy's equilibrium level of output and price level.

    (*c*)   Does an increase in government spending, *ceteris paribus*, shift aggregate demand AD or aggregate supply AS?

    (*d*)   What happens to equilibrium output and the price level when government spending increases, *ceteris paribus?*

    (*e*)   Suppose there is a technological advance rather than an increase in government spending. What happens to aggregate demand AD? Aggregate supply AS? Equilibrium output? The price level?

    (*f*)   What can one generalize about the effect on output and price level of a change in aggregate demand when aggregate supply is vertical?

    (*g*)   What can one generalize about the effect on output and price level of a change in aggregate supply when aggregate supply is vertical?

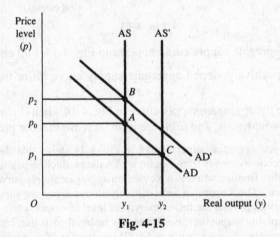

**Fig. 4-15**

    (*a*)   Figure 4-15 depicts a classical aggregate supply curve since it shows no relationship between aggregate output and the price level.

    (*b*)   Equilibrium exists where the aggregate demand curve intersects the aggregate supply curve. Equilibrium for curves AD and AS exists at point $A$; the price level is $p_0$ and output is $y_1$.

    (*c*)   Increased government spending results in an outward shift of aggregate demand. There is no change in aggregate supply since there has been no change in the economy's ability to produce goods and services.

    (*d*)   We shall assume that the increase in government spending shifts aggregate demand from AD to AD' and aggregate supply remains at AS. Equilibrium now exists at point $B$ rather than point $A$. Equilibrium output remains at $y_1$, and equilibrium price increases from $p_0$ to $p_2$.

    (*e*)   The technological advance has no effect on aggregate demand, but it shifts aggregate supply rightward. We shall assume that aggregate supply shifts rightward from AS to AS'. Equilibrium changes from point $A$ for curves AS and AD, to point $C$ for curves AD and AS'. Equilibrium output has increased from $y_1$ to $y_2$, while the price level has decreased from $p_0$ to $p_1$.

    (*f*)   When aggregate supply is vertical, a change in aggregate demand (shift of the aggregate demand curve) has no effect upon output and changes only the price level.

    (*g*)   When aggregate supply is vertical, a change in aggregate supply affects both equilibrium output and the price level.

**4.12.** Use aggregate demand and aggregate supply curves AD and AS in Fig. 4-16 to answer the following questions. (Full-employment output is $y^*$.)

    (a)   Is the aggregate supply curve in Fig. 4-16 Keynesian or classical?

    (b)   Find the economy's equilibrium level of output and price level.

    (c)   Does an increase in investment demand, *ceteris paribus*, shift aggregate demand or aggregate supply?

    (d)   What happens to equilibrium output and the price level when investment demand increases?

    (e)   What can one generalize about the effect on output and the price level when aggregate demand shifts and there is a Keynesian aggregate supply curve?

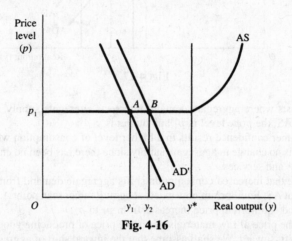

**Fig. 4-16**

    (a)   Figure 4-16 depicts a Keynesian aggregate supply curve since there can be continual increases in output without a change in the price level until full-employment output $y^*$ is reached.

    (b)   Equilibrium exists where aggregate demand intersects aggregate supply. Equilibrium output is at point $A$ for curves AD and AS; the price level is $p_1$ and output is $y_1$.

    (c)   An increase in investment demand shifts aggregate demand outward. There is no change in aggregate supply since there has been no change in the economy's ability to produce goods and services.

    (d)   We shall assume that the increase in investment demand shifts aggregate demand from AD to AD' while aggregate supply remains at AS. Equilibrium now exists at point $B$ rather than point $A$. Equilibrium output increases from $y_1$ to $y_2$ while equilibrium price remains at $p_1$.

    (e)   A change in aggregate demand increases output and has no effect upon the price level as long as the economy is below full-employment output—in this example, below $y^*$. Intersections of aggregate demand and aggregate supply beyond $y^*$ result in changes in both output and the price level.

**4.13.** Use aggregate demand and aggregate supply curves AD and AS in Fig. 4-17 to answer the following questions. (Full-employment output is $y^*$.)

    (a)   Find the economy's equilibrium level of output and price level.

    (b)   Does an increase in consumer confidence, *ceteris paribus*, shift aggregate demand or aggregate supply?

    (c)   What happens to equilibrium output and the price level when consumers become more confident?

    (d)   Suppose there is no change in consumer confidence but there is an increase in the price of raw materials. What effect will an increase in the price of raw materials have on output and the price level?

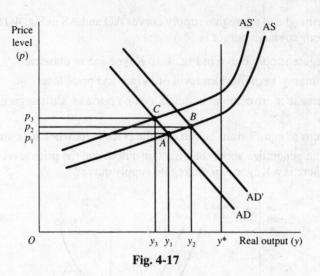

**Fig. 4-17**

(a) Equilibrium exists where aggregate demand intersects aggregate supply. Equilibrium is at point *A* for curves AD and AS; the price level is $p_1$ and output is $y_1$.

(b) Increased consumer confidence results in a higher level of consumption which shifts aggregate demand outward. There is no change in aggregate supply since there has been no change in the economy's ability to produce goods and services.

(c) We shall assume that increased consumption shifts aggregate demand from AD to AD′ while aggregate supply remains at AS. Equilibrium now exists at point *B* rather than point *A*. Equilibrium output increases from $y_1$ to $y_2$, and equilibrium price increases from $p_1$ to $p_2$.

(d) An increase in the price of raw materials raises the price of producing goods and services; the aggregate supply curve shifts inward. We shall assume that the inward shift of aggregate supply is from AS to AS′ in Fig. 4-17. AS′ and AD curves intersect at point *C*; equilibrium output falls from $y_1$ to $y_3$, and the price level increases from $p_1$ to $p_3$.

## BUSINESS CYCLES

**4.14.** (a)  What is the normal relationship of real GDP and potential GDP during a period of economic contraction? A period of economic expansion?

(b)  What is a peak? A trough?

(a)  During an economic contraction, real GDP is normally falling due to decreased spending levels, while potential GDP continues to increase since the economy's resources normally increase from quarter to quarter and technological advance is a continuous process. Potential GDP and real GDP both increase during an expansionary period. Potential GDP is usually greater than real GDP during an economic expansion until the later segment of the expansionary period, at which time real GDP exceeds potential GDP and there are increases in the economy's price level.

(b)  A *peak* is the point at which real GDP stops expanding and begins to decline. A *trough* is the point at which real GDP stops contracting and begins expanding.

**4.15.** Figure 4-18 presents quarterly data on real GDP for a hypothetical economy.

(a)  Identify periods of economic contraction, economic recovery, and economic expansion.

(b)  Identify peaks and troughs.

(a)  Economic activity is contracting during periods 1:1 through 1:3 and during periods 3:3 through 4:2. Real GDP is increasing from period 1:3 through period 3:3 and from 4:2 through 4:4. Periods of economic contraction are usually identified as recessions. Periods of economic expansion consist of the time of economic recovery, as real GDP returns to the level reached before the recession, and further expansion of real GDP.

(b) Troughs occur during periods 1:3 and 4:2, when economic activity stops declining and begins to increase. Economic activity peaks during period 3:3.

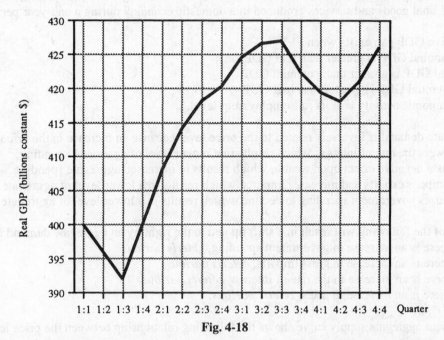

**Fig. 4-18**

**4.16.** Suppose a negatively sloped aggregate demand and a positively sloped aggregate supply curve determine a $400 billion level of real GDP for period 1:1. The economy's potential GDP during period 1:1 is $410 billion. What is the economy's GDP gap during this period?

The economy's GDP gap is +$10 billion since potential GDP exceeds real GDP by $10 billion.

**4.17.** Explain why investment spending and consumer spending on durable goods are probably the principal cause of the business cycle.

Consumer durable goods expenditures and investment spending consist of large-ticketed items whose purchase, in most cases, can be postponed. For example, an individual can repair an existing car rather than purchase a new one; a firm can produce more through greater use of existing capacity (e.g., overtime) than by adding new capacity. Thus, purchases of such big-ticketed items occur when credit (borrowing) is more readily available or less costly, individuals are more optimistic about the future, and/or cash flows are more certain. Such purchases tend to cluster and tend to be closely related to current and expected levels of real GDP.

## Multiple Choice Questions

1. Which of the following does not refer to macroeconomics?
   (a) The study of the aggregate level of economic activity,
   (b) The study of the economic behavior of individual decision-making units such as consumers, resource owners, and business firms,
   (c) The study of the cause of unemployment,
   (d) The study of the cause of inflation.

**2.** Gross domestic product is the market value of
  (*a*)   all transactions in an economy during a one-year period,
  (*b*)   all goods and services exchanged in an economy during a one-year period,
  (*c*)   all final goods and services exchanged in an economy during a one-year period,
  (*d*)   all final goods and services produced in a domestic economy during a one-year period.

**3.** A positive GDP gap exists when
  (*a*)   nominal GDP is greater than real GDP,
  (*b*)   real GDP is greater than potential GDP,
  (*c*)   potential GDP is greater than real GDP,
  (*d*)   economic activity is at its full-employment level.

**4.** Aggregate demand is inversely related to the price level because an increase in the price level
  (*a*)   lowers the rate of interest, which results in a higher level of aggregate spending,
  (*b*)   has a negative effect upon wealth, which results in increased aggregate spending,
  (*c*)   dampens exports and increases imports, which results in a lower level of aggregate spending,
  (*d*)   causes government spending to decline, which results in a lower level of aggregate spending.

**5.** Which of the following will result in a shift up and to the right by an aggregate demand curve?
  (*a*)   There is an increase in government spending, *ceteris paribus*.
  (*b*)   There is an increase in gross imports, *ceteris paribus*.
  (*c*)   There is an increase in the rate of interest, *ceteris paribus*.
  (*d*)   There is an increase in taxes, *ceteris paribus*.

**6.** A classical aggregate supply curve shows the following relationship between the price level and real output.
  (*a*)   Aggregate supply is positively related to real output.
  (*b*)   Aggregate supply is negatively related to real output.
  (*c*)   Aggregate supply is unrelated to the price level.
  (*d*)   Aggregate supply is horizontal.

**7.** Suppose equilibrium output is $y_0$ and the price level is $p_0$ for an aggregate demand and a classical aggregate supply curve. A technological advance will result in
  (*a*)   an increase in the equilibrium level of output and the price level,
  (*b*)   an increase in the equilibrium level of output and a decrease in the price level,
  (*c*)   an increase in the price level and no change in equilibrium output,
  (*d*)   an increase in the equilibrium level of output and no change in the price level.

**8.** Suppose equilibrium output is $y_0$, which is below the full-employment level, and the price level is $p_0$ for an aggregate demand and a Keynesian aggregate supply curve. An increase in government spending will result in
  (*a*)   an increase in the equilibrium level of output and the price level,
  (*b*)   an increase in the equilibrium level of output and a decrease in the price level,
  (*c*)   an increase in the price level and no change in equilibrium output,
  (*d*)   an increase in the equilibrium level of output and no change in the price level.

**9.** Which of the following statements is true?
  (*a*)   A peak occurs at the start of an economic recovery.
  (*b*)   A trough occurs at the start of an economic decline.
  (*c*)   A peak occurs when ecomomic activity starts decreasing.
  (*d*)   A trough occurs when economic activity starts decreasing.

**10.** Which of the following statements is true?
    (*a*) During a recession the economy is inside its production-possibility frontier.
    (*b*) During a recession the GDP gap is positive.
    (*c*) During a recession the unemployment rate is increasing.
    (*d*) All of the above.

# *True or False Questions*

**11.** _____ Increases in nominal GDP always result in increases in real GDP.

**12.** _____ Increases in potential GDP always result in increases in real GDP.

**13.** _____ The GDP gap is negative when real GDP exceeds potential GDP.

**14.** _____ Increases in a positive GDP gap are associated with increases in the unemployment rate.

**15.** _____ Aggregate demand shifts upward to the right when government reduces income taxes.

**16.** _____ A depreciation of the U.S. dollar causes the aggregate demand curve for the United States to shift downward to the left.

**17.** _____ All economists agree that an increase in aggregate demand will result in an increase in both the price level and real output.

**18.** _____ When aggregate supply is positively sloped, an increase in the cost of raw materials or economic resources, *ceteris paribus*, results in an increase in the price level and a decrease in real output.

**19.** _____ A business cycle occurs every two years.

**20.** _____ Economic recessions (periods of declining economic activity) are shorter than periods of economic expansion.

### *Answers to Multiple Choice and True or False Questions*

| | | | |
|---|---|---|---|
| **1.** (*b*) | **6.** (*c*) | **11.** (F) | **16.** (F) |
| **2.** (*d*) | **7.** (*b*) | **12.** (F) | **17.** (F) |
| **3.** (*c*) | **8.** (*d*) | **13.** (T) | **18.** (T) |
| **4.** (*c*) | **9.** (*c*) | **14.** (T) | **19.** (F) |
| **5.** (*a*) | **10.** (*d*) | **15.** (T) | **20.** (T) |

# Chapter 5

# Unemployment, Inflation, and National Income

## *Chapter Summary*

1. Individuals may be unemployed because of frictional, structural, or cyclical causes. A frictionally unemployed person is one who is temporarily laid off or has resigned, while a structurally unemployed person is one who has lost a job because of a change in the structure of demand or because of technological advance. Cyclical unemployment is caused by the business cycle and is due to insufficient aggregate spending.

2. Cyclical unemployment imposes a cost upon both society and the individual. Society's cost is the output lost in the current production period. Okun's law specifies that 1% of the labor force is cyclically unemployed for each 2% that real GDP falls below potential GDP. Personal losses resulting from cyclical unemployment include loss of income, loss of skills, and loss of self-esteem.

3. A price index relates the average price of a basket of goods in a specific period to the average price of the same goods during a reference period. The consumer price index (CPI), producer price index (PPI), and GDP deflator are three price indexes that measure the price level. The CPI measures the price level for urban consumers; the PPI measures the price level at wholesale for intermediate and crude materials and finished goods; the GDP deflator is a price index for all the components of GDP.

4. Inflation is the annual rate of increase in a price index. Disinflation exists when there is a decrease in the annual rate of inflation; deflation occurs when there is an annual rate of decrease in a price index. Inflation can be demand or supply induced. An excessive increase in aggregate spending is the cause of demand-pull inflation and is generally characterized by increases in both the price level and real output. Cost-push inflation is supply induced; excessive increases in production costs occur and result in increases in the price level and decreases in real output.

5. Unanticipated inflation has an uneven impact on individuals, causes a decrease in economic activity, and discourages capital formation. The cost of unanticipated inflation to an individual consists of decreases in real compensation, in real wealth, and in the purchasing power of retirement income. Economic activity declines as a result of reduced aggregate spending, and there is a slowdown in the rate of economic growth as a result of a low level of net investment.

6. Gross national product (GNP), net national product (NNP), gross domestic product (GDP), and national income (NI) are various measures of national output. NNP equals GNP less the allowance made for capital which has worn out during the year. NI consists of payments made to the factors of production owned by residents of that economy; NI plus indirect business taxes equals NNP. GDP includes only that output which is produced within an economy's geographical borders; in contrast, GNP consists of the output produced either inside or outside the country by economic resources owned by residents of that country.

7. Personal income and personal disposable income are measures of income received by individuals. Personal disposable income is the amount of income individuals have to spend, whereas personal income is the income received, some of which is paid to the government as taxes. Personal disposable income equals personal income less personal income taxes.

## *Important Terms*

**Consumer price index (CPI).**   A price index for goods and services purchased by urban consumers.

**Cost-push inflation.**   Inflation caused by large increases in the cost of producing output.

**Cyclical unemployment.**   Unemployment that exists when real output is below an economy's potential output due to an inadequate level of aggregate spending.

**Deflation.**   The annual rate of decrease in the price level.

**Demand-pull inflation.**   Inflation caused by excessive aggregate spending.

**Depreciation.**   The amount of capital used up in producing current GDP.

**Disinflation.**   A decrease in the annual rate of inflation.

**Frictional unemployment.**   Temporary unemployment of members of the labor force who are between jobs because of temporary layoffs or because they quit previous jobs and are looking for new ones.

**GDP deflator.**   The price index for the output included in GDP.

**Inflation.**   The annual rate of increase in a price index.

**Labor force.**   As measured in the United States, the number of persons 16 years of age or older who are employed (working for pay) or are unemployed and looking for paid work.

**National income (NI).**   Income earned by the factors of production.

**Natural rate of unemployment.**   The unemployment rate that exists when real GDP equals potential GDP and the GDP gap is zero.

**Net national product (NNP).**   GNP less allowance for the depreciation of the economy's stock of capital.

**Okun's law.**   A 1% unemployment rate exists for each 2% that real GDP falls below the economy's potential GDP.

**Personal disposable income.**   Personal income less income taxes; the income which individuals have available for spending.

**Price index.**   An index that relates the average price of a bundle of commodities in a specific period to the average price of these commodities during a reference period.

**Producer price index (PPI).**   A price index for goods at the wholesale level, specifically finished goods, intermediate goods, and crude materials.

**Replacement investment.**   The amount of capital needed to replace capital that depreciated (was used up) in producing current GDP.

**Structural unemployment.**   Unemployment in which members of the labor force are out of work because their skills are no longer demanded due to a change in the structure of demand or technological improvements.

**Unemployment rate.**   The percent of the total labor force which is unemployed.

# Outline of Chapter 5: Unemployment, Inflation, and National Income

## 5.1  UNEMPLOYMENT AND THE LABOR FORCE

The U.S. labor force does not include the entire population but only those who are 16 years of age or older, employed, or unemployed and looking for work. In 1990, 49.6% of the U.S. population was in the labor force; 23.0% of the U.S. population was under 16 years of age, while 27.4% of the U.S. population was retired, in school, homemakers, in the armed services, or institutionalized. Note that a working-age person who is not looking for work is considered voluntarily unemployed and is not included in the labor force. It therefore follows that the size of the labor force and the number of people unemployed can be understated when a significant number of workers, after a prolonged search, become discouraged and stop looking for work.

The unemployment rate is the percent of the total labor force which is unemployed. Individuals can become unemployed due to frictional, structural, or cyclical causes. *Frictional unemployment* is temporary and occurs when a person (1) quits a current job before securing a new one, (2) is not immediately hired when first entering the labor force, or (3) is let go by a dissatisfied employer. Workers who lose their jobs because of a change in the demand for a particular commodity or because of technological advance are *structurally unemployed;* their unemployment normally lasts for a longer period since they usually possess specialized skills which are not demanded by other employers. *Cyclical unemployment* is the result of insufficient aggregate demand. Workers have the necessary skills and are available to work, but there are insufficient jobs because of inadequate aggregate spending. Cyclical unemployment occurs when real GDP falls below potential GDP, i.e., there is a positive GDP gap. Full employment exists when there is no cyclical unemployment but normal amounts of frictional and structural unemployment; thus, full employment exists at an unemployment rate greater than zero. Economists refer to the full-employment rate of unemployment as the *natural rate of unemployment.* The natural rate of unemployment may change when there is a change in the normal amount of frictional and structural unemployment.

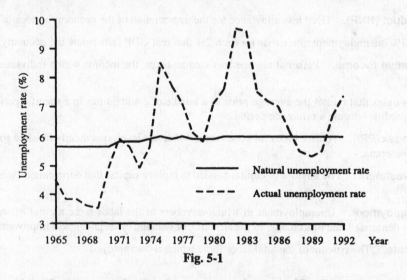

**Fig. 5-1**

**EXAMPLE 5.1.**   Figure 5-1 presents the U.S. unemployment rate and its natural rate of unemployment from 1965 through 1988. Note that the natural rate of unemployment, while relatively constant during this period, increases from 5.6% in 1965 to 6.0% in 1980. The difference between the natural rate of unemployment and the actual unemployment rate reflects cyclical unemployment. Cyclical unemployment is positive when potential GDP exceeds real GDP and negative when real GDP is greater than potential GDP. The cyclical unemployment rate increases when economic activity contracts and the economy enters a recession (1970, 1974, 1980, 1982, 1990). Note that cyclical unemployment is negative between 1965 and 1970 (the Vietnam War period) when real GDP exceeds potential GDP and the U.S. economy is producing beyond its normal full-employment level. A negative cyclical unemployment rate indicates that the normal job search period for those who are frictionally and structurally unemployed is shortened because of an abnormally large number of job openings.

## 5.2   COST OF UNEMPLOYMENT

Cyclical unemployment imposes costs upon both society and the person unemployed. Society's cost is an opportunity cost—the amount of output which is not produced and therefore is lost forever. *Okun's law,* formulated by the late Yale economist Arthur Okun, states that the unemployment rate is 1% above the natural rate for each 2% that real GDP falls below potential GDP. For example, an economy that has a\ potential output of $100 billion but actually produces only $98 billion has an unemployment rate 1% above the natural rate; the opportunity cost of this 1% cyclical unemployment rate is the $2 billion output that is not produced. In addition to this macroeconomic cost, unemployed workers bear a personal cost: loss of income, loss of skills when unemployed over an extended period of time, and loss of self-esteem. These personal costs that occur during an economic downturn are unevenly distributed between white-collar and blue-collar workers, men and women, blacks and whites, and young and middle-aged workers.

**EXAMPLE 5.2.**   Table 5-1 presents the unemployment rate by sex, age, and race in 1992, when U.S. real output was considerably below potential output, and in 1987, when U.S. real GDP equaled potential GDP. Note that the unemployment rate is always higher for 16- to 19-year-olds than for those 20 and older, and higher for blacks and others than for whites. Also note that when the economy is below its potential, the incidence of unemployment is dramatically higher for 16- to 19-year-olds than for those 20 and older, and dramatically higher for blacks and others than for whites.

**Table 5-1   U.S. Unemployment Rates, 1992 and 1987**

| Demographic Group | 1992 | 1987 |
|---|---|---|
| All civilian workers | 7.4 | 6.2 |
| By age: | | |
| 16–19 | 20.0 | 16.9 |
| All males 16–19 | 21.5 | 17.8 |
| All females 16–19 | 18.5 | 15.9 |
| Males 20 and older | 6.9 | 5.4 |
| Females 20 and older | 6.3 | 5.4 |
| By race: | | |
| White | 6.5 | 5.3 |
| Black and other | 12.7 | 11.6 |
| By sex: | | |
| Female | 6.9 | 6.2 |
| Male | 7.8 | 6.2 |

SOURCE: *Economic Report of the President, 1994*

## 5.3   THE PRICE LEVEL

A price index relates prices in a specific year (month or quarter) to prices during a reference period. For example, the *consumer price index (CPI),* the most frequently quoted price index, relates the prices that urban consumers paid for a fixed basket of approximately 400 goods and services in a given month to the prices that existed during a reference period. Column 2 in Table 5-2 presents the annual CPI for 1975 through 1993. The reference period for all consumer prices in Table 5-2 is 1982–1984. The 109.6 index for consumer prices in 1986 relative to the 100 index for 1982–1984 indicates that prices in 1986 are 9.6% higher in 1986 than they were during the 1982–1984 reference period. [The difference in the index (9.6) relative to the base year index (100) is 9.6/100 = 0.096 = 9.6%.]

The producer price index (PPI) and GDP deflator are the other two major price indexes. The *PPI* measures the prices for finished goods, intermediate materials, and crude materials at the wholesale level. Because wholesale prices are eventually translated into retail prices, changes in the PPI for consumer goods are usually a good predictor of changes in the CPI. The *GDP deflator* is the most comprehensive measure of the price level since it measures prices for net exports, investment, and government expenditures, as well as for consumer spending. Because GDP dates are only available quarterly, the CPI, which is published monthly, is used more frequently than the GDP deflator to measure inflation in the United States.

**Table 5-2    CPI and Inflation, U.S. 1975–1993**

| Year | CPI | Change in CPI from Previous Year (%) |
|------|------|------|
| 1975 | 53.8 | 9.1 |
| 1976 | 56.9 | 5.8 |
| 1977 | 60.6 | 6.5 |
| 1978 | 65.2 | 7.6 |
| 1979 | 72.6 | 11.3 |
| 1980 | 82.4 | 13.5 |
| 1981 | 90.9 | 10.3 |
| 1982 | 96.5 | 6.2 |
| 1983 | 99.6 | 3.2 |
| 1984 | 103.9 | 4.3 |
| 1985 | 107.6 | 3.6 |
| 1986 | 109.6 | 1.9 |
| 1987 | 113.6 | 3.6 |
| 1988 | 118.3 | 4.1 |
| 1989 | 124.0 | 4.8 |
| 1990 | 130.7 | 5.4 |
| 1991 | 136.2 | 4.2 |
| 1992 | 140.3 | 3.0 |
| 1993 | 144.5 | 3.0 |

SOURCE: *Economic Report of the President, 1994*

**EXAMPLE 5.3.** The CPI for 1975 through 1993 is presented in column 2 of Table 5-2. The reference period, 1982–1984, has a value of 100. [The average of the indexes for 1982, 1983, and 1984 is 100: (96.5 + 99.6 + 103.9)/3 = 100.] Prices in earlier and later years can be related to prices in the base period to establish the relative change in prices. For example, the CPI for 1987 is 113.6, indicating that prices in 1987 are 113.6% of what existed in the 1982–1984 period, i.e., prices increased 13.6% between 1982–1984 and 1987. The CPI in 1979 is 72.6, indicating that consumer prices in 1979 are 72.6% of their 1982–1984 level.

## 5.4  INFLATION

*Inflation* is the annual rate of increase in the price level. *Disinflation* is a term used by economists to denote a slowdown in the rate of inflation; *deflation* exists when there is an annual rate of decrease in the price level. U.S. inflation rates, measured by changes in the CPI, are presented in column 3 of Table 5-2. The U.S. inflation rate has varied from 13.5% in 1980 to 1.9% in 1986. Disinflation existed in the United States from 1980 through 1983 as the rate of inflation declined from 13.5% in 1980 to 3.2% in 1983. While there have been some monthly decreases in the price level, the U.S. economy has not experienced deflation, an annual rate of decrease in the price level, since the 1930s.

**EXAMPLE 5.4.** Column 3 of Table 5-2 presents annual rates of change in the CPI. The annual rate of change in the CPI is the change in an index between two years relative to the value of the index in the first of these two years. For example, the rate of inflation in 1990 is 5.4% which is the change in the CPI between 1990 and 1989 (6.7 = 130.7 − 124.0) divided by the 1989 index (124.0) and then stated as a percent (6.7/124.0 = 0.0540 = 5.40%). Consumer prices increased 5.4% between 1989 and 1990 and are 30.7% higher in 1990 than they were during the 1982–1984 base period.

Economists identify two distinct causes of inflation: demand-induced inflation and supply-induced inflation. *Demand-pull (demand-induced) inflation* is inflation that occurs when aggregate spending exceeds the economy's normal full-employment level of output. Demand-pull inflation is normally characterized by both a rising price and rising output level. It generally results in a negative GDP gap and therefore an unemployment rate lower than the natural rate. *Cost-push (supply-push) inflation* originates from increases in the cost of producing goods and services. It is usually associated with increases in the price level, decreases in aggregate output, and an increase in unemployment. When inflation is caused by supply forces, the real GDP gap is positive and the unemployment rate rises above the natural rate.

**EXAMPLE 5.5.** Aggregate output is $y_0$ and the price level is $p_0$ for aggregate supply and aggregate demand curves AS' and AD' in Fig. 5-2. We shall assume that output $y_0$ is the economy's full-employment level of output, i.e., the actual unemployment rate equals the economy's natural rate of unemployment. An increase in aggregate demand shifts the aggregate demand curve outward from AD' to AD'', which moves the equilibrium point from $E_0$ to $E_1$; the price level increases from $p_0$ to $p_1$, and real output increases from $y_0$ to $y_1$. The AD' to AD'' increase in aggregate spending is an example of demand-pull inflation: increased aggregate spending has "pulled up" the price level.

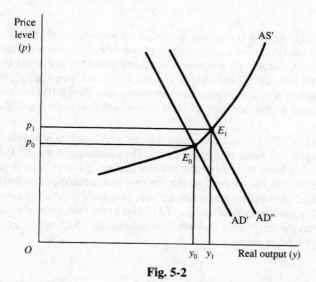

**Fig. 5-2**

**EXAMPLE 5.6.** Aggregate output is $y_0$ and the price level is $p_0$ for aggregate supply and aggregate demand curves AS' and AD' in Fig. 5-3. We shall assume that output $y_0$ is the economy's full-employment level of output. A substantial increase in the price of a basic raw material, such as oil, shifts the aggregate supply curve inward from AS' to AS'' and changes the equilibrium point from $E_0$ to $E_1$; the price level increases from $p_0$ to $p_1$, and aggregate output falls from $y_0$ to $y_1$. The substantial increase in production costs, *ceteris paribus,* pushes up the price level; inflation is induced by a decrease in aggregate supply.

## 5.5  COST OF INFLATION

Inflation can slow economic growth, redistribute income and wealth, and cause economic activity to contract. Inflation impairs decision making since it creates uncertainty about future prices and/or costs and distorts economic values. For example, an individual may postpone the purchase of a condominium or a business may postpone the purchase of equipment because of increasing uncertainty about the purchasing power of future monetary streams (Example 5.7). Such postponed capital outlays slow capital formation and economic growth. Incorrectly anticipated inflation will lower the real income and wealth of individuals and result in less consumer spending and a lower level of real GDP (Example 5.8).

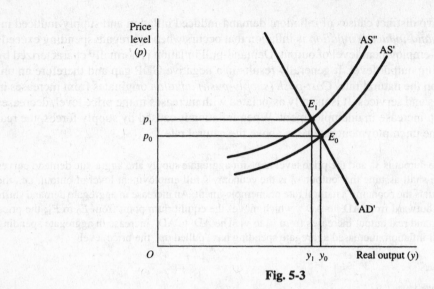

**Fig. 5-3**

**EXAMPLE 5.7.** Suppose Corporation A is planning to expand the productive capacity of one of its manufacturing facilities in Ohio; completion of the expanded facility will take three years. Corporation A might postpone the project as the rate of inflation accelerates because of increased uncertainty about (1) the actual cost of the expansion, (2) the actual profitability of the project, and (3) the adequacy of the firm's cash flow during the next three years to pay for the expansion. The firm's willingness to expand capacity improves once there is less inflation, less uncertainty about the profitability of the project, and greater certainty about the firm's cash flow and the actual cost of the project.

**EXAMPLE 5.8.** An actual rate of inflation greater than the one anticipated may adversely affect those currently employed, those who have saved, and those who have retired. The purchasing power of Individual A's income will decline when the price level rises faster than his or her nominal income. Saver B, who deposits $1000 in a savings account that pays a 5% rate of interest, has less real wealth one year later when the price level unexpectedly increases 10% since the $1050 of principal plus interest that B has one year later has a purchasing power of only $954. And the purchasing power of Retiree C's fixed retirement income of $15,000 a year falls as the price level increases. Unanticipated inflation, therefore, lowers the real income and wealth of individuals, which results in a lower level of consumer spending and therefore a lower level of output.

## 5.6   MEASURING DOMESTIC OUTPUT

There are two approaches to measuring domestic output: an *expenditure approach,* which measures the value of final sales, and a *cost approach,* which measures the value added in producing final output. The expenditure or final sales approach consists of summing the consumption spending of individuals ($C$), investment spending by businesses ($I$), government expenditures ($G$), and the net export of U.S.-made goods and services ($X_n$). [GDP $= C + I + G + X_n$]. The cost approach consists of summing the value added to final output at each stage of production.

In 1992, the U.S. government replaced gross national product with *gross domestic product* (GDP) as the primary measure of the economy's national output. Gross domestic product consists of all output produced within the boundaries of the United States, whereas GNP includes all output produced by U.S. economic resources regardless of their location, i.e., whether the resources are located inside or outside the United States. These two output measures are essentially of the same magnitude and behave similarly over time; during the past 30 years, the difference between GNP and GDP has not exceeded 1.3%, and both have displayed similar cyclical and trend patterns.

Gross national product and net national product measure national output but differ because of the treatment of investment spending. Gross investment consists of replacement investment (depreciation) and net investment. *Replacement investment* consists of capital goods that replace existing, worn-out capital, while *net investment* includes additions to the economy's stock of capital. *Gross national product* (GNP) is the expenditure measure which includes both replacement and net investment, while *net national product* (NNP) is the expenditure measure which excludes replacement investment and includes only net investment. Thus, GNP = $C + I$ (gross investment) $+ G + X_n$, while NNP = $C + I_n$ (net investment) $+ G + X_n$.

Because government taxes many goods and services before they are sold to the final purchaser, net national product and national income are two cost measures of national output. *National income (NI)* is the value added and therefore equals the sum of the payments made to the factors of production, i.e., the wages, rent, interest, and profits paid to labor, land, capital, and entrepreneurs. The full cost of *net national product* includes payments to the factors of production (national income) and the taxes imposed by government at the production or final sale level. Production and sales taxes include taxes imposed upon tobacco products and liquor in packaging the product, sales taxes, and business property taxes.

**EXAMPLE 5.9.**   Measures of output for the U.S. economy in 1993 appear in Table 5-3. National income, which consists of payments to the factors of production, appears in columns 1 and 2 and totals $5140.2 billion. Adding indirect taxes to national income generates the output measure NNP, and adding depreciation to NNP results in a GNP level of $6378.0 billion. Adjustments for factor payments to and from the rest of the world results in a GDP of $6378.1 billion. GDP also appears in columns 3 and 4 and is found by summing the final expenditures of consumers, businesses, government, and net exports. Note that compensation of employees is the major cost of producing GDP and that personal consumption expenditures is the major expenditure category.

**Table 5-3    Gross Domestic Product, 1993**
**(Billions of Dollars)**

| (1) | (2) | (3) | | (4) |
|---|---|---|---|---|
| Compensation of employees | 3772.2 | Personal consumption expenditures | | 4391.8 |
| Rents | 12.6 | Gross private domestic investment | | 891.7 |
| Interest | 445.6 | Government expenditures | | 1158.1 |
| Profit: | | Net exports of goods and services | | −63.5 |
|    Proprietors' income | 443.2 |    Gross exports | 660.1 | |
|    Corporate | 466.6 |    Gross imports | 723.6 | |
| National income | 5140.2 | Gross domestic product (GDP) | | 6378.1 |
| Indirect business taxes | 566.6 | | | |
| Net national product (NNP) | 5706.8 | | | |
| Capital consumption allowances | 671.2 | | | |
| Gross national product (GNP) | 6378.0 | | | |
| Plus: Payments of factor income to rest of the world | 131.7 | | | |
| Less: Receipts of factor income from rest of the world | −131.6 | | | |
| Gross domestic product (GDP) | 6378.1 | | | |

SOURCE: *Economic Report of the President, 1994*

## 5.7   MEASURING PERSONAL DISPOSABLE INCOME

*Personal disposable income* is the amount of income individuals receive and have available for spending. All income paid to the factors of production is not received by individuals and available for consumer spending. Corporations, which receive and retain some factor payments, and government, with its multilevel system of taxation, are recipients of approximately 26% of the value of GDP. Table 5-4 presents the adjustments made to national income to derive personal disposable income—the amount of income individuals have available for spending.

**EXAMPLE 5.10.**   Personal income is the amount of national income received by individuals. Table 5-4 presents the adjustments that are made to national income to derive personal income when there is the corporate form of organization and government has in place a system of social security and welfare. The difference between personal income and personal disposable income is primarily due to income taxes paid by individuals to government.

**Table 5-4   Personal Disposable Income, 1993**
**(Billions of Dollars)**

| | |
|---|---|
| National Income | 5140.2 |
| Less: | |
| Corporate profits | 466.6 |
| Contributions to social security | 585.3 |
| Plus: | |
| Government & business transfers to individuals | 912.1 |
| Net interest paid to individuals | 228.6 |
| Dividends paid by corporations to individuals | 159.3 |
| Personal Income | 5388.3 |
| Less: Personal income taxes | 681.6 |
| Personal disposable income | 4706.7 |

SOURCE: *Economic Report of the President, 1994*

# Solved Problems

## UNEMPLOYMENT AND THE LABOR FORCE

**5.1.** Table 5-5 presents the U.S. civilian noninstitutionalized working-age population and the total civilian labor force for 1960, 1970, 1980, and 1990.

(a)  Why is the civilian labor force smaller than the civilian noninstitutionalized working-age population?

(b)  Calculate from the data in Table 5-5 the U.S. labor participation rate (percent of the working-age population included in the labor force) for 1960, 1970, 1980, and 1990. What explanations can you offer for a change in the labor participation rate?

**Table 5-5   U.S. Civilian Labor Force, 1960, 1970, 1980, 1990**
**(in Thousands)**

| Year | Civilian Noninstitutionalized Working-age Population | Civilian Labor Force |
|---|---|---|
| 1960 | 117,245 | 69,628 |
| 1970 | 137,085 | 82,771 |
| 1980 | 167,745 | 106,940 |
| 1990 | 188,049 | 124,787 |

SOURCE: *Economic Report of the President, 1994*

(a)  The civilian noninstitutionalized working-age population includes those who are of working age (16 years of age or older), are not in institutions (e.g., mental, penal), and are not in the armed forces. Many of those who are in the working-age population are voluntarily unemployed—they are not looking for work, having left or never having entered the labor force. The voluntarily unemployed include full-time homemakers, retired people, and those in school. Because some working-age individuals do not seek work, the civilian labor force is smaller than the civilian noninstitutionalized working-age population.

(b)  The labor participation rate is 59.4% in 1960 (69,628/117,245 = 0.594), 60.4% in 1970, 63.8% in 1980, and 66.4% in 1990. There are various reasons for change in an economy's labor participation rate: changes in the length of time individuals remain in school past age 16, laws and attitudes about the age to retire, and attitudes of couples about a spouse staying home to raise children. The U.S. labor participation rate has been increasing during this 30-year period, in part because of more women in the labor force and since the 1980s because of the elimination of mandatory retirement laws.

**5.2.** The civilian labor force includes all persons 16 years of age and older who either are employed or are unemployed and looking for work.

   (*a*)   Are full-time college students included in the labor force?

   (*b*)   Suppose a person graduates from college at age 22, obtains a job upon graduation, quits working at age 24 to pursue full-time graduate study, graduates at age 26, and begins looking for a full-time position. When is this person a member of the labor force?

   (*c*)   Is a discouraged worker a member of the labor force?

   (*a*)   College-age students who do not work during the school year are not included in the labor force; they are not counted as unemployed members of the labor force since they are not looking for work.

   (*b*)   This person is a member of the labor force while employed from ages 22 through 24. This person leaves the labor force upon returning to full-time graduate study and reenters the labor force upon graduation and the start of a job search.

   (*c*)   A discouraged worker is one who stops looking for work. Such a person is not included in the labor force since that person is no longer looking for work.

**5.3.** What are frictional unemployment, structural unemployment, and cyclical unemployment?

   *Frictional unemployment* exists in a free society when workers are temporarily laid off or are between jobs and expect to find employment soon. For example, automobile workers are seasonally unemployed during model changeover periods; so are some construction workers during periods of bad weather. New entrants into the labor force are counted as unemployed (while they look for their first jobs), as are some workers who become dissatisfied with their current jobs and quit prior to finding new ones.

   A participant in the labor force is *structurally unemployed* when that person's job is lost because there is a change in demand or a technological advance, and the individual lacks the skills needed to qualify for other jobs which are available. Changing demand and technology are the principle causes of structural unemployment. A major reduction in the demand for a product will reduce the demand for labor within an industry, and the introduction of new technology makes some labor skills obsolete. If workers displaced by structural changes lack the skills required for other jobs, they become structurally unemployed and usually require retraining to be reemployed.

   *Cyclical unemployment* exists when real GDP falls below potential GDP. The economy is not producing on its production-possibility frontier, and therefore some of its resources, e.g., labor, are unemployed.

**5.4.** (*a*)   Should the federal government implement economic policies to eliminate frictional, structural, and cyclical unemployment?

   (*b*)   What is an economy's natural rate of unemployment?

   (*a*)   Economic policy should be used to promote maximum employment, i.e., employment levels which would place the economy on its production-possibility frontier. Points on the production-possibility frontier allow for the existence of frictional and structural unemployment, which are essential for a changing, free society. Since individuals may want to reject a job offer or be free to change jobs, some of them will be frictionally unemployed at any point in time. Likewise, businesses may not be able to retain employees during slack periods of demand. Structural unemployment may also be inevitable in an economy experiencing technological advance.

   While frictional and structural unemployment must exist, government can institute programs to minimize the number of labor force participants in those categories. It can facilitate the dissemination of information on job availability to expedite the employment of those who are looking for their first jobs and the reemployment of those who have left previous jobs. Government can also provide job retraining programs to facilitate the reemployment of those who are structurally unemployed. The government should not, however, use economic policies to increase aggregate spending to reduce frictional and structural unemployment since insufficient aggregate demand is not the cause of these workers being unemployed. Economic policies to increase aggregate spending should, however, be implemented when cyclical unemployment develops, at which point the economy is producing below its production-possibility curve, imposing costs upon both society and unemployed individuals.

(b)   An economy's natural rate of unemployment is the rate of unemployment that exists when there is no cyclical unemployment and there is only frictional and structural unemployment. The economy's natural rate of unemployment changes over time since the incidence of frictional and structural unemployment is not constant in a dynamic economic environment.

**5.5.**   Table 5-6 presents the number employed and the size of the U.S. labor force for 1984 through 1993.

(a)   From the data in Table 5-6, calculate the number unemployed and the unemployment rate from 1984 through 1993.

(b)   Find the annual change in the size of the labor force and the annual change in the number employed.

(c)   What happens to the unemployment rate when the change in the number employed does not equal the change in the size of the labor force?

**Table 5-6   Number Employed and Size of Labor Force, U.S., 1984–1993**
**(in Thousands)**

| Year | Size of Labor Force | Number Employed |
|------|---------------------|-----------------|
| 1984 | 113,544 | 105,005 |
| 1985 | 115,461 | 107,150 |
| 1986 | 117,834 | 109,597 |
| 1987 | 119,865 | 112,440 |
| 1988 | 121,669 | 114,968 |
| 1989 | 123,869 | 117,342 |
| 1990 | 124,787 | 117,914 |
| 1991 | 125,303 | 116,877 |
| 1992 | 126,982 | 117,598 |
| 1993 | 128,040 | 119,306 |

SOURCE: *Economic Report of the President, 1994*

(a)   The number unemployed is the difference between the size of the labor force and the number employed. This difference is presented in column 2 of Table 5-7. The unemployment rate is the percent of the total labor force which is unemployed, found by dividing the number unemployed by the size of the labor force. The unemployment rate is found in column 3 of Table 5-7.

**Table 5-7**

| (1) | (2) | (3) | (4) | (5) |
|-----|-----|-----|-----|-----|
|  |  |  | Change in | |
|  |  |  | Size of | Number |
|  | Number Unemployed | Unemployment | Labor Force | Employed |
| Year | (thousands) | Rate (%) | (thousands) | |
| 1984 | 8539 | 7.5 |  |  |
| 1985 | 8311 | 7.2 | 1917 | 2145 |
| 1986 | 8237 | 7.0 | 2373 | 2447 |
| 1987 | 7425 | 6.2 | 2031 | 2843 |
| 1988 | 6701 | 5.5 | 1804 | 2528 |
| 1989 | 6527 | 5.3 | 2200 | 2374 |
| 1990 | 6873 | 5.5 | 918 | 572 |
| 1991 | 8426 | 6.7 | 516 | −1037 |
| 1992 | 9384 | 7.4 | 1679 | 721 |
| 1993 | 8734 | 6.8 | 1058 | 1708 |

(b)  The annual change in the size of the labor force and in the number employed is calculated from the data in Table 5-6 and is presented in columns 4 and 5 of Table 5-7. In 1985, the size of the labor force increases 1,917,000, the difference between the size of the labor force in 1985 and 1984. Also in 1985, employment increases 2,145,000, the difference between the number employed in 1984 and 1985.

(c)  The unemployment rate decreases when the annual increase in the number employed is greater than the annual increase in the size of the labor force. For example, the unemployment rate falls from 7.5% in 1984 to 5.3% in 1989; in each of these years increases in the number employed are greater than increases in the size of the labor force. In 1990, the unemployment rate increases from 5.3% to 5.5% since the labor supply increased by 918,000 while the number employed increased by only 572,000. A decrease in the number employed in 1991 dramatically increased the unemployment rate. The unemployment rate does not decrease until 1993 when the increase in the number employed exceeds the increase in the size of the labor force.

## COST OF UNEMPLOYMENT

**5.6.**  (a)  What is Okun's law?

(b)  What is the cost of cyclical unemployment?

(a)  Cyclical unemployment occurs whenever real GDP falls below potential GDP. Arthur Okun discovered an empirical relationship between GDP and rate of unemployment which is now known as Okun's law. Specifically, he found that a 1% cyclical unemployment rate exists for each 2% that real GDP falls short of potential GDP.

(b)  Cyclical unemployment results in lost output, slower economic growth, and a decrease in labor productivity. Output is lost forever when labor is cyclically unemployed. For example, a 2% decrease in real GDP, *ceteris paribus,* results in a 1% increase in the rate of cyclical unemployment. Economic growth is slowed because businesses are less willing to invest in new equipment during periods of underutilization of existing facilities. A lower level of net investment results in fewer capital additions and therefore less growth of productive capacity. Those who are cyclically unemployed for a prolonged period of time lose skills, self-esteem, and motivation; there is damage to their productive capability which, in some cases, is not recoverable once jobs become available.

**5.7.**  Is the cost of cyclical unemployment borne equally by each member of society?

Each member of the labor force does not have the same likelihood of becoming unemployed when the economy enters a recession. Individuals employed in the production of consumer and producer durable goods and in residential and nonresidential construction usually have a greater likelihood of losing their jobs than those who are employed in service industries or by government. Individuals without skills are more likely to lose their jobs than those with skills. And, unfortunately, the existence of discrimination makes it more difficult for minorities than whites to find a job when there is considerable cyclical unemployment.

## THE PRICE LEVEL

**5.8.**  (a)  What is a price index?

(b)  Suppose the price of Good A is $11, $11.55, $12.24, $13.46, and $14.14 in years 1 through 5, respectively. Construct a price index for Good A using year 1 as the reference (base) year.

(c)  What has happened to the price of Good A between year 1 and year 5?

(d)  What is the annual percentage change in the price of Good A?

(a)  A price index relates the price of an item in a specific year to the price in a reference year.

(b)  A price index is calculated by dividing each year by the reference year and multiplying by 100. The price index for year 1 is 100 since year 1 is the reference year [($11.00/$11.00) × 100 = 100]. The price index for year 2 is 105 [($11.55/$11.00) × 100 = 105]; it is 111 for year 3; 122 for year 4; and 129 for year 5.

(c)  The price of Good A has increased 29% between year 1 and year 5; this percentage increase is found by dividing the change in the price index between year 1 and year 5 by the price index in year 1 (29/100 = 0.29 = 29%).

(d)  The annual percentage change in the price of Good A is found by dividing the change in the price index between two years and dividing by the price index of the first of these two years. The percentage change in the price of Good A between year 1 and year 2 is 5% (5/100 = .05 = 5%). The percentage change in the price of Good A between year 2 and year 3 is 5.7% (6/105 = .057 = 5.7%); it is 9.9% between year 3 and year 4, and 5.7% between year 4 and year 5.

**5.9.**  What is the consumer price index (CPI) and the producer price index (PPI)?

The CPI relates the prices that urban consumers pay for a fixed basket of approximately 400 goods and services in a specific year to the prices that existed in a reference period. The U.S. Bureau of Labor Statistics has divided the basket of consumer commodities into seven categories: food and beverages, housing, apparel and upkeep, transportation, medical care, entertainment, and other. Weights are applied to each of these seven spending classifications on the basis of their relative importance in the typical household budget. Because food and energy prices can be volatile due to weather patterns and/or supply shortages or surpluses, the Bureau of Labor Statistics publishes two CPI figures, one inclusive of and one exclusive of prices for food and energy.

The PPI measures the prices at the wholesale level for finished goods; for intermediate materials, supplies, and components; and for crude materials available for further processing. Because wholesale prices are eventually translated into retail prices, changes in the PPI for consumer goods are usually a good predictor of changes in the CPI. Fluctuations in the PPI, however, normally exceed those of the CPI because the CPI includes prices of goods and services, whereas the PPI only indexes the prices for goods which tend to fluctuate more.

**5.10.**  Columns 2 and 3 of Table 5-8 present nominal and real GDP from 1984 through 1990.

(a)  Calculate the GDP deflator for 1984 through 1990.

(b)  Find the annual rate of change in the GDP deflator. What does this measure?

**Table 5-8  Nominal and Real GDP, U.S. 1984–1990**
**(Billions of Dollars)**

| (1) Year | (2) Nominal GDP | (3) Real GDP | (4) GDP Deflator |
|---|---|---|---|
| 1986 | 4268.6 | 4404.5 | 96.9 |
| 1987 | 4539.9 | 4539.9 | 100.0 |
| 1988 | 4900.4 | 4718.6 | 103.9 |
| 1989 | 5250.8 | 4838.0 | 108.5 |
| 1990 | 5546.1 | 4897.3 | 113.3 |
| 1991 | 5722.9 | 4861.4 | 117.7 |
| 1992 | 6038.5 | 4986.3 | 121.1 |
| 1993 | 6374.0 | 5132.7 | 124.2 |

SOURCE: *Economic Report of the President, 1994*

(a)  The GDP deflator is found by dividing nominal GDP by real GDP and then multiplying by 100. For example, in 1988 the GDP deflator is 103.9 since (4900.4/4718.6) × 100 = 103.9. The GDP deflators for 1986 through 1993 appear in column 4 of Table 5-8.

(b)  The annual rate of change in the GDP deflator is found by dividing the difference between the GDP deflator for the selected years and then dividing by the first of these two years. The change in the GDP deflator for 1987 is the difference between the GDP deflators for 1987 and 1986 divided by the 1986 GDP deflator, stated as a percent. The annual percentage change in the GDP deflator is 3.2% for 1987, 3.9% for 1988, 4.4% for 1989, 4.4% for 1990, 3.9% for 1991, 2.9% for 1992, and 2.6% for 1993. These annual percentage changes in the GDP deflator are a measure of inflation for all components of GDP.

**5.11.** Table 5-9 presents U.S. consumer price indexes for five of the seven categories of consumer spending for 1986 and 1993.

(a)  Find the percentage increase in the CPI and these five categories between 1986 and 1993.

(b)  Have each of these five spending categories experienced the same rate of increase between 1986 and 1993?

**Table 5-9   Index of CPI and Five Expenditure Categories of the CPI, U.S., 1986 and 1993**

|                    | 1986  | 1990  | Percentage Change |
|--------------------|-------|-------|-------------------|
| CPI                | 109.6 | 144.5 | 31.8              |
| Food & beverages   | 109.1 | 141.6 | 29.8              |
| Housing            | 110.9 | 141.2 | 27.3              |
| Apparel and upkeep | 105.2 | 133.7 | 27.1              |
| Transportation     | 102.3 | 130.4 | 27.5              |
| Medical care       | 122.0 | 201.4 | 65.1              |

SOURCE: *Economic Report of the President, 1994*

(a)  The percentage increase in these various indexes appears in column 4 of Table 5-9.

(b)  There are considerable differences in the percentage increase in the CPI and five of the major expenditure categories. The cost of medical care increased 65.1% between 1986 and 1993, while the cost of transportation increased 27.5%. Since the CPI is a weighted index of seven expenditure categories, it follows that all individuals may not experience the same increase in their cost of living when their expenditures patterns differ greatly from the weights used in calculating the CPI.

## INFLATION

**5.12.** The CPI for a hypothetical economy appears in Table 5-10.

(a)  Calculate the percentage change in the CPI between year 1 and year 6.

(b)  Calculate the year-to-year percentage change in the CPI from year 1 through year 6.

(c)  What is the difference between disinflation and deflation?

(d)  From your calculations in part (b), establish the year(s) in which this economy is experiencing disinflation and deflation.

(a)  The CPI has increased 13.5% from year 1 to year 6.

(b)  The annual percentage change in the CPI is as follows: 3.5% from year 1 to year 2; 5.9% from year 2 to year 3; 3.7% from year 3 to year 4; 2.0% from year 4 to year 5; and −2.0% from year 5 to year 6.

(c)  Disinflation exists when the rate of inflation is decreasing over successive years. Deflation occurs when prices are falling and the annual percentage change in the price level is negative.

(d)  This hypothetical economy experiences disinflation from year 3 to year 4 and from year 4 to year 5 as the rate of inflation declines from 5.9% in year 3 to 2% in year 5. Deflation occurs between year 5 and year 6 since there is a 2% decline in the price level.

**Table 5-10   CPI for a Hypothetical Economy**

| Year | 1     | 2     | 3     | 4     | 5     | 6     |
|------|-------|-------|-------|-------|-------|-------|
| CPI  | 115.0 | 119.0 | 126.0 | 130.6 | 133.2 | 130.5 |

**5.13.** (*a*)    What is demand-pull inflation?

(*b*)    What is cost-push inflation?

(*a*)    *Demand-pull inflation* is inflation that originates from excessive aggregate spending such that the desire to purchase goods and services exceeds the economy's productive capabilities. Price increases selectively reduce aggregate spending to bring about an equating of aggregate demand and aggregate supply.

(*b*)    *Cost-push inflation* originates from the supply side and is usually the result of increases in the price of raw materials, the market power of labor or business, or new government taxes or regulations. Production costs increase when raw material costs, labor costs, or tax increases result in higher production costs and these cost increases are passed on to buyers through higher prices.

## COST OF INFLATION

**5.14.** (*a*)    What effect does unanticipated inflation have upon (1) individuals who are retired and living on a fixed income, (2) debtors, and (3) creditors?

(*b*)    How does indexation protect one from the redistribution effect of inflation?

(*a*)    (1) Unanticipated inflation lowers the real income of those on a fixed nominal income. An increase in the price level reduces the purchasing power of a fixed nominal income; the result is the purchase of fewer goods and services. (2) Debtors benefit from unanticipated inflation since the dollars they pay back have less purchasing power. (3) Creditors (lenders), on the other hand, lose from unanticipated inflation since the dollars they are repaid purchase fewer goods and services.

(*b*)    Indexation ties money payments to a price level so that the sum of money payments rises proportionally with the price level. For example, a $20,000 salary would increase to $22,000 when the monetary payment of $20,000 is indexed and there is a 10% increase in the price level.

**5.15.**    Why does inflation affect economic activity?

When unanticipated inflation occurs, money, money-denominated assets, and money flows lose their purchasing power, leading to a redistribution of current wealth and income flows. Such redistribution usually results in a decrease in aggregate spending. Inflation also makes money prices a poor measure of value. With no dependable system for measuring current and future values, there are greater risks associated with construction of residential and nonresidential structures and with purchases of equipment. Thus, inflation can result in the cancellation of many investment plans; the decrease in investment spending that occurs affects not only the current level of output but also the growth of the economy's productive capability.

## MEASURING DOMESTIC OUTPUT

**5.16.**    What is the difference between gross national product (GNP) and gross domestic product (GDP)?

GNP is the market value of all final goods and services produced in an economy by the factors of production owned by residents of that country. GDP also measures the market value of goods and services produced in an economy but includes only that output produced by economic resources located within that country. Hence, a country's GNP could be $100 billion, $2 billion of which may be produced by capital which is owned by residents of that country but is located outside that country. The output of resources located within the country would be $98 billion, which is the economy's GDP. GDP is therefore the same as GNP when all resources owned by residents of that country are producing output in that country. GNP is greater than GDP when residents of that country employ their resources to produce output outside that country.

**5.17.** (*a*)    Explain the terms *gross investment* and *net investment*.

(*b*)    Explain the difference between gross national product (GNP) and net national product (NNP).

(*a*)    *Gross investment* is the sum spent on the construction of new residential and nonresidential buildings; on new machinery, equipment, and tools; and on changes in inventories during a one-year period. *Net investment* equals gross investment less capital consumption allowances (depreciation, *D*)—the amount of capital goods (buildings, machinery, equipment, and tools) which were used up in producing the current year's national output. Net investment adds to the economy's stock of capital, whereas gross investment includes capital additions (net investment) and capital replacement (capital consumption allowances).

(b)   GNP and NNP are gross and net measures of the total market value of final goods and services produced by the resources of a country during a one-year period. GNP includes the market value of all final output, whereas NNP excludes the final output which represents capital replacement. Thus, $GNP - D = NNP$.

**5.18.**   (a)   What are indirect business taxes?

(b)   Why are indirect business taxes added to national income to obtain NNP?

(a)   Indirect business taxes are taxes levied on goods and services during output or at final sale which are passed on to the final buyer through higher prices. Examples of indirect business taxes are excise taxes, sales taxes, business property taxes, import duties, and license fees.

(b)   Since indirect business taxes are included in the price of final output, the factor cost of producing output (wages + interest + rent + profit) is less than the market value of final output by the amount of indirect business taxes collected by government. Thus, national income plus indirect business taxes equal NNP.

## MEASURING PERSONAL DISPOSABLE INCOME

**5.19.**   Explain why in the calculation of personal income, corporate profits and contributions for social security are deducted from national income, while government and business transfers, dividends and interest payments of government and consumers are added to national income.

*Personal income* is the aggregate income received by households during a one-year period. *National income* consists of payments made to the factors of production. In a free-enterprise economy, economic resources are owned by individuals; government and corporations intercept some of the payments made to the owners of economic resources (i.e., individuals), as government mandates that individuals make payments for social insurance, and corporations retain profits. Some payments diverted to government and corporations are returned to individuals through transfer payments, interest, and corporate dividends. In deriving personal income, additions and subtractions must be made to national income since government and corporations have altered the payments made to the owners of the factors of production.

# *Multiple Choice Questions*

1.   Frictional unemployment exists when
     (a)   there is a fall in aggregate demand,
     (b)   workers are seasonally unemployed,
     (c)   workers lack the skills necessary to be employed,
     (d)   potential GDP exceeds real GDP.

2.   Inflation is a situation in which
     (a)   there is a decrease in the purchasing power of the monetary unit,
     (b)   there is a decrease in the price level,
     (c)   a given quantity of money purchases a larger quantity of goods and services,
     (d)   increases in the price level exceed increases in the nominal wage.

3.   Cost-push inflation exists when
     (a)   consumers use their market power to push up prices,
     (b)   resource owners use their market power to push up prices,
     (c)   potential output is growing faster than real GDP,
     (d)   real GDP is increasing faster than potential GDP.

**4.** Personal income
   (*a*)   is income received by individuals during a given year,
   (*b*)   is the income individuals have available for spending during a given year,
   (*c*)   equals national income less indirect taxes,
   (*d*)   is the sum of wages plus interest received by individuals during a given year.

**5.** The natural rate of unemployment is the rate of unemployment that exists when there is only
   (*a*)   frictional and structural unemployment,
   (*b*)   frictional and cyclical unemployment,
   (*c*)   structural and cyclical unemployment,
   (*d*)   frictional unemployment.

**6.** Okun's law specifies that for each 2% that real GDP falls short of potential GDP, there is a
   (*a*)   1% rate of cyclical unemployment below the natural rate,
   (*b*)   1% rate of cyclical unemployment above the natural rate,
   (*c*)   1% rate of structural unemployment above the natural rate,
   (*d*)   1% rate of structural unemployment below the natural rate.

**7.** An increase in the price level from 200 in year 5 to 210 in year 6 indicates a
   (*a*)   10% rate of inflation between years 5 and 6,
   (*b*)   5% rate of inflation between years 5 and 6,
   (*c*)   110% rate of inflation between years 5 and 6,
   (*d*)   105% rate of inflation between years 5 and 6.

**8.** Unanticipated inflation is harmful to
   (*a*)   retirees whose retirement income is indexed,
   (*b*)   debtors,
   (*c*)   creditors,
   (*d*)   economic growth but has no effect upon individual members of the economy.

**9.** Net national product equals
   (*a*)   national income plus indirect business taxes,
   (*b*)   national income less depreciation,
   (*c*)   national income plus depreciation,
   (*d*)   gross domestic product less indirect business taxes.

**10.** Which of the following statements is false?
   (*a*)   GDP is greater than personal income.
   (*b*)   Personal disposable income is greater than personal income.
   (*c*)   GDP is greater than national income.
   (*d*)   National income is greater than personal disposable income.

## *True or False Questions*

**11.** _____   The labor force consists of the working-age population.

**12.** _____   Economic policy is directed toward reducing frictional, structural, and cyclical unemployment.

**13.** _____ Okun's law specifies that there is cyclical unemployment of 2% when real GDP is 4% below potential GDP.

**14.** _____ The GDP deflator is the best and most frequently used measure of inflation in the United States.

**15.** _____ Unemployment only imposes a cost upon those who are unemployed.

**16.** _____ A discouraged worker is an individual who has been unable to find a job, stops looking for work, and is no longer included in the labor force.

**17.** _____ Cyclical unemployment is unevenly distributed among members of the labor force.

**18.** _____ GDP is always greater than personal income.

**19.** _____ Personal income is the amount of national income received by individuals.

**20.** _____ Personal income taxes are subtracted from personal income to get personal disposable income.

### Answers to Multiple Choice and True or False Questions

| | | | |
|---|---|---|---|
| **1.** (b) | **6.** (b) | **11.** (F) | **16.** (T) |
| **2.** (a) | **7.** (b) | **12.** (F) | **17.** (T) |
| **3.** (b) | **8.** (c) | **13.** (T) | **18.** (T) |
| **4.** (a) | **9.** (a) | **14.** (F) | **19.** (T) |
| **5.** (a) | **10.** (b) | **15.** (F) | **20.** (T) |

# Chapter 6

# Consumption, Investment, and Net Exports

## *Chapter Summary*

1.  Two-thirds of total output in the United States consists of consumer goods and services. Over time, the level of consumer spending is primarily explained by the level of disposable income.
2.  The consumption function is presented as a positive, linear relationship between consumption and disposable income, holding variables other than income constant. The linear consumption function shifts when nonincome determinants of consumption change.
3.  Saving at a specific level of disposable income is derived from the consumption function by subtracting consumption from disposable income.
4.  The average propensity to consume (APC) is the ratio of consumption to disposable income at a specific level of income. Since disposable income is either consumed or saved, the average propensity to save equals $1 - $ APC.
5.  The marginal propensity to consume (MPC) is the ratio of the change in consumption associated with a change in disposable income. The ratio $\Delta C / \Delta Y d$ is not only the marginal propensity to consume but also the slope of a linear consumption function. The marginal propensity to save equals $1 - $ MPC.
6.  Gross investment consists of residential construction, nonresidential construction, purchases of producers' durable equipment, and the net change in business inventories. Gross investment is the least stable sector of aggregate spending and a major cause of the business cycle.
7.  Although numerous variables influence investment decisions, it is customary to present gross investment as being inversely related to the rate of interest, holding other variables constant. The inverse relationship between the rate of interest and investment spending, when presented graphically, is the investment demand curve. The investment demand curve shifts when noninterest variables that influence investment decisions change.
8.  Net exports, which is the value of gross exports minus gross imports, represents the net addition of exports and imports to spending on domestic output. When there is a positive net export balance (gross exports exceed gross imports), there is a net addition to spending on domestic output. Net exports for the United States have been negative in recent years; international trade has had a negative effect on spending for U.S.-produced goods and services.
9.  The exchange rate between the U.S. dollar and the currencies of foreign countries affects U.S. exports and U.S. imports. An appreciation of the U.S. dollar has a negative effect on net U.S. exports since a stronger dollar discourages U.S. exports and encourages U.S. residents to import more foreign-made goods.

## *Important Terms*

**Appreciation of the U.S. dollar.**   An increase in the value of the dollar relative to the unit currency of another nation; one U.S. dollar then buys more units of a foreign currency.

**Autonomous consumption.**   Consumer spending which is unrelated to the receipt of income.

**Average propensity to consume (APC).**   The ratio of consumption to disposable income at a given level of income. (APC = $C/Y_d$)

**Average propensity to save (APS).**   The ratio of saving to disposable income at a given level of income. (APS = $S/Y_d$)

**Consumption function.**   The relationship between consumption and disposable income.

**Gross exports.**   The value of domestic production that is sold to other countries.

**Gross imports.**   The value of foreign production that is purchased by the domestic economy.

**Gross investment.**   The sum of residential construction, nonresidential construction, the purchase of producers' durable equipment by businesses, and the net change in business inventories.

**Induced consumption.**   An increase in consumer spending that results from an increase in income.

**Investment demand curve.**   A curve that shows the relationship between gross investment and the rate of interest, holding constant other variables that affect investment spending.

**Marginal propensity to consume (MPC).**   The ratio of the change in consumption to the change in disposable income. (MPC = $\Delta C/\Delta Y_d$)

**Marginal propensity to save (MPS).**   The ratio of the change in saving to the change in disposable income. (MPS = $\Delta S/\Delta Y_d$)

**Net exports.**   Gross exports minus gross imports.

**Saving function.**   The relationship between saving and disposable income.

# Outline of Chapter 6: Consumption, Investments, and Net Exports

## 6.1   CONSUMPTION

Because consumption represents two-thirds of total aggregate spending in the United States, understanding the determinants of consumer spending is central to any analysis of the U.S. economy's level of output. Consumer spending is largely determined by personal income, income taxes, consumer expectations, consumer indebtedness, wealth, and the price level. Since consumption is impossible for most individuals without income earned from employment or through transfers from business or government, personal income is by far the most important of these variables. Personal income taxes are also central in that one's ability to spend depends not upon the income received but on the income available for spending. Figure 6-1 displays the dependency of consumer spending upon disposable income. Consumption, however, does not have a perfect linear relationship to disposable income in Fig. 6-1, indicating that other variables influence the decision to consume. Although less important, consumer confidence, consumer indebtedness, wealth, and the price level also affect consumer spending in the short run.

**EXAMPLE 6.1.**   Annual levels of consumption and disposable income for the United States are plotted in Fig. 6-1 for 1975 through 1993. A line fitted to the data shows the dependency of consumption on disposable income. Note that consumption is sometimes above the regression line (1976, 1977, 1987, 1988, 1989) and other times below (1980, 1981, 1982, 1984, 1985, 1986, 1992). Consumption is likely to move above the regression line when the economy is expanding rapidly and consumer optimism results in consumers spending a larger than normal percent of their disposable income. Consumption usually falls below the regression line when the economy is in a recession as output is considerably below full employment. As economic activity peaks, consumer indebtedness is usually high, consumers become less confident, and individuals tend to be less willing and/or able to continue spending as large a percent of their disposable income.

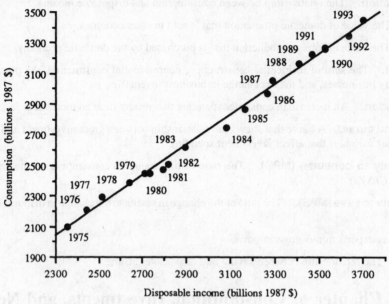

**Fig. 6-1**

## 6.2   THE CONSUMPTION FUNCTION

A consumption function is the relationship of *consumption* to *disposable income,* holding nonincome determinants of consumption constant. Table 6-1 presents a consumption function for a hypothetical economy. The data from Table 6-1 are plotted in Fig. 6-2 and the consumption function is labeled C'. A change in a nonincome determinant of consumption alters the relationship of consumption to disposable income. Such changes are depicted graphically by upward or downward shifts of the consumption function. Shifts of the consumption function affect the level of consumption and saving. Should consumers expect an increase in the price level, they are likely to spend more in the current period before prices rise. An upward shift of consumption function C' to C'' results in more consumption and less saving at each income level.

**Table 6-1**
**(in Billions of Dollars)**

| Disposable Income ($Y_d$) | Consumption ($C$) | Saving ($S = Y_d - C$) |
|---|---|---|
| 500 | 500 | 0 |
| 550 | 540 | 10 |
| 600 | 580 | 20 |
| 650 | 620 | 30 |
| 700 | 660 | 40 |
| 750 | 700 | 50 |
| 800 | 740 | 60 |

**EXAMPLE 6.2.**   The consumption function for a hypothetical economy is presented in schedule form in Table 6-1 and graphically in Fig. 6-2. From columns 1 and 2 of Table 6-1 we find that consumers spend their entire disposable income when $Y_d$ is $500 billion and spend less than their disposable income at income levels greater than $500 billion. Since disposable income is either consumed or saved, consumer saving (column 3) is found by deducting consumption

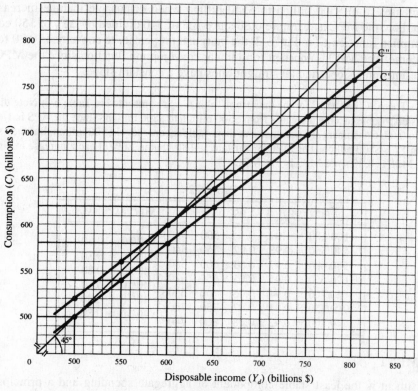

**Fig. 6-2**

from disposable income. Consumption and disposable income from Table 6-1 are plotted in Fig. 6-2, and the resulting line is labeled $C'$. (The 45° line in Fig. 6-2 is equidistant from both the consumption and disposable income axes. As drawn, $C = Y_d$ at each point on this 45° line.) For linear consumption function $C'$, there is only one level of disposable income at which consumer spending equals disposable income, and that is the point of intersection of the consumption line and the 45° line. Since the consumption line is below the 45° line at disposable income levels above $500 billion, it follows that consumers are not consuming their entire income and therefore are saving. Thus, consumer saving is the distance between the consumption line and the 45° line at each level of disposable income.

**EXAMPLE 6.3.**    Suppose consumers become more optimistic and are more willing to spend their disposable income. Such a trend would shift consumption function $C'$ in Fig. 6-2 upward to $C''$. We now find that at disposable income $500 billion, consumption exceeds disposable income, i.e., consumers are dissaving. (Consumers can dissave—consume more than their disposable incomes—by borrowing or by spending accumulated savings.) Consumption now equals disposable income when $Y_d$ is $600 billion; for consumption function $C''$ there is less saving at each level of disposable income than there is for consumption function $C'$.

## 6.3.   THE AVERAGE AND MARGINAL PROPENSITY TO CONSUME AND SAVE

The relationship between consumption and disposable income can be presented by several ratios. The *average propensity to consume* is the ratio of consumption to disposable income at a specific level of income (APC $= C/Y_d$) while the *average propensity to save* is the ratio of saving to disposable income (APS $= S/Y_d$). Obviously, at each income level, APC + APS equals 1. For the consumption function in Table 6-2, the APC is 1 and the APS is 0 when disposable income is $500 billion, indicating that consumers are spending 100% of their disposable income. At disposable income levels greater than $500 billion, the APC is less than 1; consumers are now saving and the APS is greater than 0. The *marginal propensity to consume* is the ratio of the change in consumption relative to the change in disposable income between two levels of disposable income (MPC $= \Delta C/\Delta Y_d$), while the *marginal propensity to save* is the ratio of the change in saving relative to the change in disposable income (MPS $= \Delta S/\Delta Y_d$). From Table 6-2, consumption increases from \$500 billion to \$540 billion when disposable income increases from \$500 billion to \$550 billion; the MPC is therefore 0.80 since $\Delta C$ of \$40 divided by $\Delta Y_d$ of \$50 equals 0.80. For the linear consumption function $C'$ in Fig. 6-2, the marginal propensity to consume is 0.80 for each change in disposable income. The MPC is constant for a linear consumption function since the MPC $(\Delta C/\Delta Y_d)$ is the consumption function's slope, and all straight lines have a constant slope.

**EXAMPLE 6.4.** The APC and MPC for the data from Table 6-1 are presented in Table 6-2. Note that the APC falls from 1.0 to 0.92 as disposable income increases from \$500 billion to \$800 billion. Since the APS is $1 - \text{APC}$, the APS increases from 0 to 0.08. Consumers are not saving at disposable income level \$500 billion, but they save 8% of their income level when $Y_d$ is \$800 billion. The MPC is constant at 0.80, that is, 80% of each increase in disposable income is consumed. The MPS is 0.20 since MPS is $1 - \text{MPC}$.

**Table 6-2**

| APC ($C/Y_d$) | APS | $Y_d$ | $C$ | MPC ($\Delta C/\Delta Y_d$) |
|---|---|---|---|---|
| 500/500 = 1.0 | 0 | 500 | 500 | |
| 540/550 = 0.98 | 0.02 | 550 | 540 | 40/50 = 0.80 |
| 580/600 = 0.97 | 0.03 | 600 | 580 | 40/50 = 0.80 |
| 620/650 = 0.95 | 0.05 | 650 | 620 | 40/50 = 0.80 |
| 660/700 = 0.94 | 0.06 | 700 | 660 | 40/50 = 0.80 |
| 700/750 = 0.93 | 0.07 | 750 | 700 | 40/50 = 0.80 |
| 740/800 = 0.92 | 0.08 | 800 | 740 | 40/50 = 0.80 |

## 6.4   INVESTMENT

Gross investment is the least stable component of aggregate spending and a principal cause of the business cycle (see Example 6.5). In the national income accounts, investment consists of residential construction (single-family and multifamily units); nonresidential construction (offices, hotels, and other commercial real estate); producers' durable equipment (equipment purchases by businesses); and changes in business inventories. Numerous variables affect these categories of gross investment. (See Example 6.6.) While the rate of interest is one of many variables that influence investment decisions, it is customary to present investment demand as a negative function of the rate of interest, holding constant the other variables which influence the decision to invest.

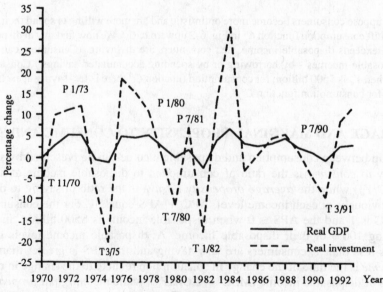

**Fig. 6-3**

**EXAMPLE 6.5.** Figure 6-3 presents the annual percentage change in real GDP, real gross investment, and the peaks and troughs in economic activity in the United States between 1970 and 1993. Both real GDP and real investment display a cyclical movement, rising after a business cycle trough and falling after a business cycle peak. Investment spending, however, displays larger and more dramatic changes. It is because of this that investment is considered the principal cause of economic fluctuations. Monetary policy seeks to dampen economic fluctuations by moderating the growth of investment spending during an economic expansion and slowing the decline in investment spending during a recession.

**EXAMPLE 6.6.** While it is customary to link investment to the rate of interest, there are numerous noninterest variables which influence the decision to invest.

*Residential construction* depends upon the willingness and ability of individuals to purchase housing units. This demand is influenced by (1) demographics (the size of the house-buying population); (2) the indebtedness of potential house-buying individuals; (3) the wealth of such individuals (and therefore their ability to come up with the down payment); (4) their current and expected income level; (5) consumer confidence and willingness to incur new debt; (6) the ability of potential home buyers to obtain a loan from a financial institution; (7) the cost of housing units; and (8) the mortgage rate of interest which determines the monthly cost of carrying a mortgage.

*Nonresidential construction* is dependent upon the willingness and ability of business units to buy commercial property. Their demand depends upon (1) the rate of interest, (2) the vacancy rate of existing units, (3) the needs of business units for additional commercial space, and (4) the ability of business units to meet increased rental costs which are directly linked to their current and expected costs and sales.

Orders for *producers' durable equipment* are linked to (1) borrowing costs, since many of these large-ticketed items must be financed, (2) the utilization of existing productive capacity, (3) the availability of advanced, more efficient technology, (4) current and expected sales, and (5) existing and future competition.

*Changes in business inventories* are linked to the rate of interest because there is an interest cost associated with carrying larger inventories. Inventory levels are also linked to current and expected sales, current and expected inventory prices, and certainty of inventory deliveries.

## 6.5  THE INVESTMENT DEMAND CURVE

An investment demand curve shows the relationship between gross investment and the rate of interest, holding constant other variables that affect investment spending. In Fig. 6-4, investment spending is

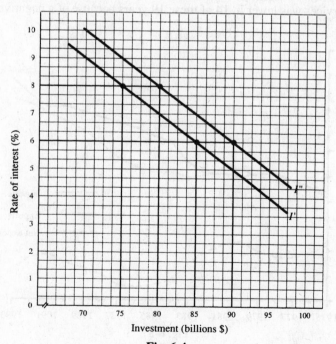

**Fig. 6-4**

inversely related to the rate of interest, i.e., a lower rate of interest is associated with a higher level of investment, while a higher rate of interest is associated with a lower level of investment. This relationship is reasonable for the categories of investment enumerated in Section 6.4. Holding other variables constant, we would expect that at a lower rate of interest (1) more households are financially able and willing to carry a mortgage, and a greater number of housing units will be demanded; (2) businesses are more willing and able to purchase durable equipment and to carry larger inventories; and (3) real estate developers find that there are a larger number of purchasers for newly constructed commercial real estate.

**EXAMPLE 6.7.**    Figure 6-4 presents investment demand line $I'$ for a hypothetical economy where the level of investment is $75 billion when the rate of interest is 8% and $85 billion when the rate of interest is 6%, holding constant other variables that influence investment spending. Should more households become more willing to purchase residential units at each rate of interest, more businesses elect to expand plant capacity at each rate of interest, and more business units demand nonresidential units, investment line $I'$ would shift outward to $I''$. Investment spending for investment demand line $I''$ would now be $80 billion at an 8% rate of interest and $90 billion at a 6% rate of interest.

## 6.6   GROSS EXPORTS AND GROSS IMPORTS

*Gross exports* are the value of goods and services produced in a home country (e.g., the United States) and sold abroad; i.e., gross exports are the value of foreign spending on U.S.-produced goods and services. *Gross imports* are the value of U.S. purchases of goods and services produced in other countries. When commodities are imported, some of the consumption and gross investment spending discussed earlier is for foreign-produced rather than U.S.-produced goods. Imports thereby lower aggregate spending on domestically produced goods.

*Net exports* are the value of gross exports less gross imports, i.e., the net addition to domestic aggregate spending that results from importing and exporting goods and services. Net exports are positive when the home country exports more than it imports, and negative when the home country imports more than it exports. Figure 6-5 presents U.S. gross exports, gross imports, and net exports in 1987 dollars from 1975 through 1993. Note the substantial growth of gross exports and gross imports in the 1980s. Also note that the United States had a negative net export balance in 14 of these 19 years—aggregate spending on U.S.-produced goods and services was lower in 14 of these 19 years because of a negative net export balance.

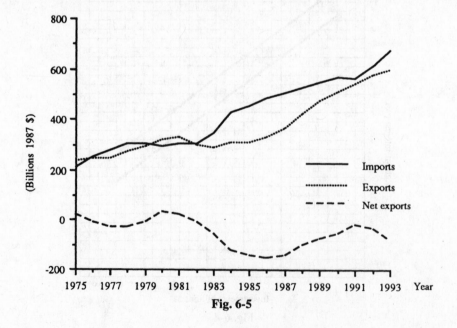

Fig. 6-5

Numerous variables affect a country's imports and exports. A country's *imports* are related to its level of income, foreign exchange rate, domestic prices relative to prices in foreign countries, import tariffs, and restrictions on imported goods. *Exports* are influenced by the same variables, except that the income levels of foreign countries rather than that of the home country affect the amount exported. Because these variables change with time, it is reasonable to expect a country's net export balance to change over time.

**EXAMPLE 6.8.**  The *gross exports* of a home country (e.g., the United States) *increase* when (1) economic activity in a foreign country increases and more goods are purchased from U.S. producers; (2) the U.S. dollar depreciates (the international value of the U.S. dollar falls) and foreigners buy more U.S.-produced commodities because they have become relatively less expensive; (3) prices in a foreign country rise but are unchanged in the United States, making U.S.-produced goods relatively less expensive than those produced in the foreign country; (4) a foreign country lowers the tariff on goods imported from the United States; and (5) a foreign country no longer prohibits the importation of certain goods produced in the United States. U.S. (home country) *gross imports increase* when (1) U.S. production levels rise, (2) the U.S. dollar appreciates in value; (3) the U.S. inflation rate exceeds that of foreign countries; and (4) the United States lowers tariffs on imports.

# Solved Problems

## CONSUMPTION

**6.1.**  Data on consumption and real GDP for the United States are presented in Table 6-3.

(*a*)  Consumption is what percent of real GDP in 1970, 1975, 1980, 1985, and 1990?

(*b*)  What explanation might one offer for the relative importance of consumer spending in the United States?

**Table 6-3  Consumption, Personal Disposable Income, and GDP for the United States**

**(Billions of 1987 Dollars)**

|  | 1970 | 1975 | 1980 | 1985 | 1990 |
|---|---|---|---|---|---|
| Consumption | 1813.5 | 2097.5 | 2447.1 | 2865.8 | 3272.6 |
| Durable goods | 183.7 | 226.8 | 262.7 | 370.1 | 443.1 |
| Nondurable goods | 717.2 | 767.1 | 860.5 | 958.7 | 1060.7 |
| Services | 912.5 | 1103.6 | 1323.9 | 1537.0 | 1768.8 |
| Personal disposable income | 2025.3 | 2355.4 | 2733.6 | 3162.1 | 3524.5 |
| Gross domestic product | 2873.9 | 3221.7 | 3776.3 | 4279.8 | 4897.3 |

SOURCE: *Economic Report of the President, 1994*

(*a*)  Consumer spending was 63% of real GDP in 1970 (*C*/GDP = $1813.5/$2873.9 = 0.63 = 0.63%); it was 65% in 1975, 65% in 1980, 67% in 1985, and 67% in 1990.

(*b*)  Individuals own the factors of production in the United States. Thus, we would expect that individuals would use most of their income for the purchase of goods and services. All production does not flow to individuals since (1) various levels of government impose taxes to finance government expenditures, and (2) individuals save some of their current income, which is loaned to businesses to finance the purchase of durable equipment and commercial real estate.

**6.2.**  (*a*)  From the data in Table 6-3, calculate consumption as a percent of disposable income.

(*b*)  Is the relationship of consumption to disposable income stable? What does this suggest?

(*c*)  Table 6-3 also presents the major components of consumption. Calculate each of these components as a percent of disposable income.

(d)  Has the relative importance of each consumption component changed during the twenty-year period?

(a)  Consumption as a percent of disposable income appears in Table 6-4.

(b)  The relationship of consumption to disposable income is relatively stable for these selected years; this suggests that consumer spending is largely dependent upon the receipt of disposable income.

(c)  Durable goods, nondurable goods, and services as a percent of disposable income are presented in Table 6-4.

(d)  Nondurable goods expenditures are of decreasing relative importance, while expenditures on services have become the major component of consumer spending by 1990. Note the increasing relative importance of durable goods expenditures: while it is the least important component of consumer spending, its relative importance has increased between 1970 and 1990.

Table 6-4   Relationship of Consumer Spending to Disposable Income

|  | 1970 | 1975 | 1980 | 1985 | 1990 |
|---|---|---|---|---|---|
| Consumption/disposable income | 89.5% | 89.1% | 89.5% | 90.6% | 92.9% |
| Durable goods/disposable income | 9.1% | 9.6% | 9.6% | 11.7% | 12.6% |
| Nondurables/disposable income | 35.4% | 32.6% | 31.5% | 30.3% | 30.1% |
| Services/disposable income | 45.1% | 46.9% | 48.4% | 48.6% | 50.2% |

**6.3.**  In Figure 6-6, annual percentage changes in the three major components of consumption are plotted for the United States from 1975 through 1993. Which component has the most and the least cyclical behavior?

Service expenditures are the least cyclical since they demonstrate the most stable year-to-year percentage change. Durable goods purchases are the least stable and therefore the most cyclical spending category. The behavior of durable goods purchases is not surprising since these are large-ticketed purchases which can usually be postponed during periods when consumers become pessimistic about the future.

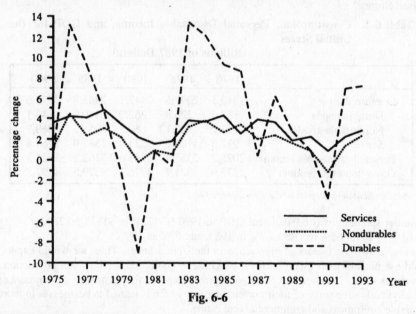

**Fig. 6-6**

## THE CONSUMPTION FUNCTION

**6.4.**  Suppose a household has the consumption function $C$ presented in Fig. 6-7.

(a)  Find consumption when disposable income is $12,000 and $14,000.

(b)  Find consumption when disposable income is $10,000. How can a household consume more than its disposable income?

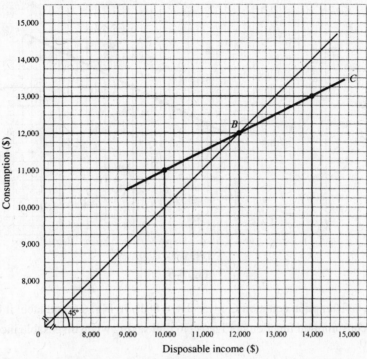

Fig. 6-7

(c)   What is true of every point on the 45° line?

(a)   When disposable income is $12,000, consumption is $12,000. When disposable income is $14,000, consumption is $13,000.

(b)   This household consumes $11,000 when its disposable income is $10,000. A household can consume more than its income (dissave) by drawing accumulated savings from earlier periods or by borrowing.

(c)   Any point on the 45° line is equidistant from the consumption and disposable income axes when the same scales of measurement are used on both axes. Thus, at point B in Fig. 6-7, $C = Y_d$.

6.5.   (a)   What is the relationship between consumption, saving, and disposable income?

(b)   Using Fig. 6-7, find saving when disposable income is $10,000, $12,000, and $14,000, and

(c)   identify the dissaving and saving areas.

(d)   Use the information in Fig. 6-7 to present in Fig. 6-8 a saving function. Put saving on the vertical axis and disposable income on the horizontal axis.

(a)   Disposable income is either consumed or saved. Thus, $Y_d = C + S$, or $S = Y_d - C$.

(b)   Since $S = Y_d - C$, saving is 0 when disposable income is $12,000, −$1000 when disposable income is $10,000, and +$1000 when disposable income is $14,000. The amount saved is the vertical distance between the consumption function and the 45° line at each level of disposable income.

(c)   The saving area is the vertical distance between the consumption line and the 45° line to the right of point B. The dissaving area is the vertical distance between the consumption line and the 45° line to the left of point B.

(d)   The saving levels found in part (b) are plotted in Fig. 6-8, and the resulting line, labeled S, is the saving function.

6.6.   Suppose the economy's consumption function is specified by the equation $C = \$50 + 0.80Y_d$.

(a)   Find consumption when disposable income ($Y_d$) is $400, $500, and $600.

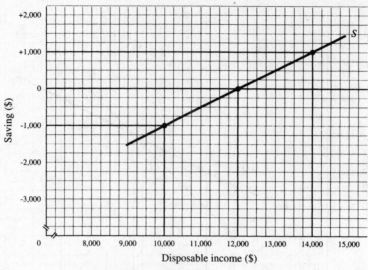

**Fig. 6-8**

(b)   Plot this consumption equation $C = \$50 + 0.80Y_d$ in Fig. 6-9 and label it $C'$.

(c)   Use the consumption function in Fig. 6-9 to find saving when disposable income is $400, $500, and $600.

(a)   Consumption for each level of disposable income is found by substituting the specified disposable income level into the consumption equation. Thus, for $Y_d = \$400$, $C = \$50 + 0.80(\$400)$; $C = \$50 + \$320$; $C = \$370$. $C$ is $450 when $Y_d$ is $500, and $530 when $Y_d$ is $600.

(b)   The linear consumption equation $C = \$50 + 0.80Y_d$ is plotted and labeled $C'$ in Fig. 6-9 for the consumption and disposable income levels found in part (a).

(c)   Saving is the difference between disposable income and consumption. Using the calculation from part (a), we find that saving is $30 when $Y_d$ is $400 ($Y_d - C = S$; $400 - \$370 = \$30$), $50 when $Y_d$ is $500, and $70 when $Y_d$ is $600. Saving in Fig. 6-9 is the difference between the consumption line and the 45° line at each level of disposable income. Thus, reading up from the $400 income level, we find that $C$ is $370 for consumption function $C'$; the distance from consumption function $C'$ to the 45° line at the $400 income level is $30—the amount of saving.

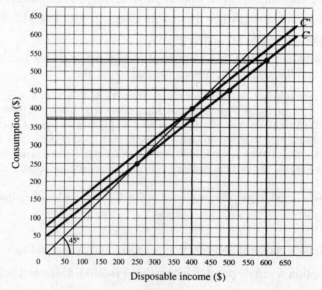

**Fig. 6-9**

**6.7.** Autonomous consumption is the amount of consumption spending which is unrelated to income. Induced consumption is that consumption which is dependent upon the receipt of income.

    (a)    What amount of consumption for consumption function $C'$ in Fig. 6-9 is autonomous, and what amount is induced when disposable income is $400? $500? $600?

    (b)    Find autonomous consumption and induced consumption from the consumption equation $C = \$50 + 0.80Y_d$ when $Y_d$ is $500.

    (a)    *Autonomous consumption* is the amount consumed when disposable income is 0. In Fig. 6-9, autonomous consumption is $50, the amount consumed when the consumption line $C'$ intersects the vertical axis and disposable income is 0. Since autonomous consumption is unrelated to income, autonomous consumption is $50 for all levels of income for consumption function $C'$ in Fig. 6-9. *Induced consumption* is the amount of consumption that depends upon the receipt of income. Consumption is $370 when disposable income is $400; since $50 is consumed regardless of the income level, $320 of the $370 level of consumption is induced by disposable income. Induced consumption is $400 when disposable income is $500, and $480 when disposable income is $600.

    (b)    *Autonomous consumption* is $50, the constant of the consumption equation. *Induced consumption* is the amount of consumption attributable to disposable income. Thus, when disposable income is $500, 0.80 of $Y_d$ ($400) is induced consumption.

**6.8.** What should happen to consumption function $C'$ in Fig. 6-9 when

    (a)    consumers consider their job secure and therefore become more confident about the future level of disposable income?

    (b)    credit card issuers implement tighter credit standards and consumers are less able to buy goods and services on credit?

    (c)    consumers expect the price level to increase 10% by the end of the year?

    (a)    Consumers become more willing to consume their current disposable income. Consumption function $C'$ in Fig. 6-9 shifts upward, and consumption is greater for each level of disposable income.

    (b)    Some consumers are no longer able to borrow to purchase goods and services in the current period. Consumption function $C'$ in Fig. 6-9 shifts downward. Consumption is lower for each level of disposable income.

    (c)    Consumers reschedule future purchases to the current period because of the expected rise in prices for goods and services. Consumption function $C'$ in Fig. 6-9 shifts upward. Consumption is higher for each level of disposable income.

## THE AVERAGE AND MARGINAL PROPENSITY TO CONSUME AND SAVE

**6.9.**    (a)    Use the consumption function $C'$ in Fig. 6-9 to find the average propensity to consume (APC) and the average propensity to save (APS) when the level of disposable income is $250, $300, and $400.

    (b)    What does the marginal propensity to consume (MPC) measure?

    (c)    From Fig. 6-9, find the MPC when income increases from $250 to $300 and from $300 to $400.

    (d)    What is the relationship between the APC and the APS? The MPC and the MPS?

    (a)    The APC $= C/Y_d$ and the APS $= S/Y_d$. When disposable income is $250, consumption is $250; the APC equals $250/250 = 1$ and the APS equals $0/\$250 = 0$. When disposable income is $300, consumption is $290; the APC $= \$290/\$300 = 0.97$ and the APS $= 0.03$. The APC $= 0.925$ when disposable income is $400 and consumption is $370; the APS $= 0.075$.

    (b)    The marginal propensity to consume (MPC) is the ratio of the change in consumption to the change in disposable income, i.e., the fraction of each change in disposable income that is consumed. The MPC is the slope of a linear consumption function.

    (c)    Consumption increases $40 (from $250 to $290) when disposable income increases $50 (from $250 to $300). Thus, the MPC is 0.80 (MPC $= \Delta C/\Delta Y_d$; MPC $= \$40/\$50 = 0.80$). Consumption increases

$80 (from $290 to $370) when disposable income increases $100 (from $300 to $400); the MPC is not unexpectedly 0.80 since the MPC is constant for a linear consumption function.

(d) Since disposable income is either consumed or saved, the average propensity to consume plus the average propensity to save must equal 1 (i.e., APC + APS = $C/Y_d + S/Y_d$ = 1). Similarly, MPC + MPS = 1.

**6.10.** Suppose an increase in household sector wealth shifts consumption function $C'$ upward to $C''$ in Fig. 6-9.

    (a) Find the APC at the $400 income level. What has happened to the average propensity to consume at the $400 income level as a result of this upward shift of the consumption function?

    (b) Find the MPC when income increases from $400 to $500. What happens to the MPC when there is a parallel shift of the consumption function?

    (a) The APC is 1.0 ($400/$400) at the $400 income level for consumption function $C''$. The APC has increased from 0.925 at the $400 income level for consumption function $C'$ to 1.0 for consumption function $C''$. The upward shift of the consumption function has resulted in consumers spending a larger percent of their current income.

    (b) The MPC is 0.80. Parallel shifts of a consumption function do not change the marginal propensity to consume since the slope of the consumption line has not changed.

**6.11.** Suppose consumption is $9000 when disposable income is $10,000.

    (a) Find consumption when disposable income is $11,000 and $12,000 when the marginal propensity to consume is 0.60.

    (b) Find saving when disposable income is $10,000, $11,000, and $12,000.

    (c) Find the APC and the APS when disposable income is $10,000, $11,000, and $12,000.

    (d) What is the marginal propensity to save?

    (a) Since 0.60 of every change in income is consumed, consumption increases $600 for each $1000 increase in disposable income. Since consumption is $9000 when income is $10,000, consumption is $9600 when income is $11,000 and $10,200 when income is $12,000.

    (b) Saving is the difference between disposable income and consumption. Thus, saving is $1000 when income is $10,000, $1400 when income is $11,000, and $1800 when income is $12,000.

    (c) The APC is 0.90 when income is $10,000 (APC = $9000/$10,000 = 0.90), 0.87 when income is $11,000, and 0.85 when income is $12,000. Since the APS = 1 − APC, the APS is respectively 0.10, 0.13, and 0.15.

    (d) The MPS = 1 − MPC. The MPS is 0.40 when the MPC is 0.60.

## INVESTMENT

**6.12.** Table 6-5 presents real GDP, gross investment, and the components of gross investment for the United States from 1973 through 1979. The U.S. economy was in a recession from November 1973 through March 1975.

    (a) Explain the major components of gross investment: residential construction, nonresidential construction, and producers' durable equipment.

    (b) Find the annual percentage change in real GDP, gross investment, and the components of gross investment.

    (c) What pattern, if any, is there in the annual percentage change of each type of investment?

    (a) Residential construction consists of the building of single-family and multifamily housing. Nonresidential construction includes the building of shopping malls, offices, hotels, and other buildings which are used for commercial purposes. Producers' durable investment consists of equipment purchases by businesses.

    (b) Annual percentage changes in real GDP, gross investment, and the components of investment appear in Table 6-6.

**Table 6-5   Gross Investment in the U.S., 1973–1979**
**(Billions of 1987 Dollars)**

|                              | 1973 | 1974 | 1975 | 1976 | 1977 | 1978 | 1979 |
|------------------------------|------|------|------|------|------|------|------|
| Real GDP                     | 3269 | 3248 | 3222 | 3381 | 3533 | 3704 | 3797 |
| Gross fixed investment       | 554  | 512  | 452  | 495  | 566  | 627  | 656  |
| Residential construction     | 197  | 156  | 135  | 166  | 202  | 215  | 207  |
| Nonresidential construction  | 135  | 132  | 118  | 121  | 126  | 144  | 163  |
| Producers' durable equipment | 222  | 224  | 199  | 208  | 238  | 269  | 286  |

SOURCE: *Economic Report of the President, 1994*

**Table 6-6**

|                              | 1974  | 1975  | 1976 | 1977 | 1978 | 1979 |
|------------------------------|-------|-------|------|------|------|------|
| Real GDP                     | −0.6  | −0.8  | 4.9  | 4.5  | 4.8  | 2.5  |
| Gross investment             | −7.6  | −11.7 | 9.5  | 14.3 | 10.8 | 4.6  |
| Residential construction     | −20.8 | −13.5 | 23.0 | 21.7 | 6.4  | −3.7 |
| Nonresidential construction  | −2.2  | −10.6 | 2.5  | 4.1  | 14.3 | 13.2 |
| Producers' durable goods     | 0.9   | −11.2 | 4.5  | 14.4 | 13.0 | 6.3  |

(c)  The annual percentage change in gross investment and in the components of investment is greater than that of real GDP. Of the various investment components, residential construction had the greatest volatility during this period. Note the rapid increase in residential construction during the initial year of the expansion (1976). Many economists view expansion of residential construction as a precondition for recovery from a recession.

## THE INVESTMENT DEMAND CURVE

**6.13.**  Why would one expect the various categories of investment to be inversely related to the rate of interest?

All components of gross investment are large expenditures. Since few potential purchasers have sufficient cash available to meet these costs, a vast majority of these purchases are financed by borrowing. It therefore follows that there is greater investment spending the lower the rate of interest. (The borrowing cost associated with these purchases is, of course, less at a lower interest rate.)

**6.14.**  (a)  Suppose an economy's investment demand curve is $I'$ in Fig. 6-10. Find gross investment when the rate of interest is 10% and 6%.

(b)  Find gross investment when the investment demand curve shifts upward to $I''$ and the rate of interest is 10% and 6%.

(a)  For investment demand curve $I'$, gross investment is $80 when the rate of interest is 10% and $100 when the rate of interest is 6%.

(b)  For investment demand curve $I''$, gross investment is $90 when the rate of interest is 10% and $110 when the rate of interest is 6%.

**6.15.**  Variables other than the rate of interest affect gross investment. Changes in these other variables cause the investment demand curve to shift inward or upward. What should happen to the economy's investment demand curve when there is a change in the following variables?

(a)  There is an increase in consumer confidence.

(b)  Manufacturers' utilization of existing capacity declines.

(c)  There is an increase in vacancy rates in commercial buildings.

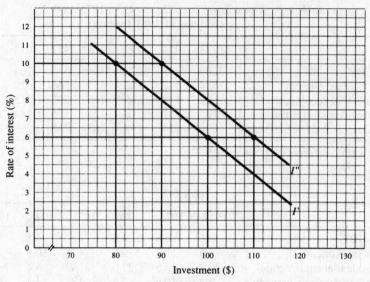

**Fig. 6-10**

(a) The investment demand curve should shift upward. Housing sales should increase as consumers become more confident; builders would construct more new housing to meet this increased demand.

(b) The investment demand curve should shift inward. Businesses' purchases of durable equipment should fall since such purchases would expand productive capacity and there is no need to expand productive capacity when utilization of existing capacity is declining.

(c) The investment demand curve should shift inward. Increased vacancy rates for existing commercial buildings indicate that there will be difficulty selling newly constructed commercial real estate. Thus, commercial real estate construction will decline.

## GROSS EXPORTS AND GROSS IMPORTS

**6.16.** (a) Explain the terms *gross exports* and *gross imports.*

(b) What is meant by the term *net exports?*

(a) *Gross exports* are the value of goods and services produced in a home country (e.g., the United States) and sold to foreigners. *Gross imports* are the value of goods and services produced by countries other than the home country and purchased by residents of the home country.

(b) *Net exports* are the value of gross exports less gross imports. Net exports are positive when gross exports exceed gross imports.

**6.17.** Table 6-7 presents real GDP, consumption plus gross investment, gross imports, and gross exports for the United States in 1970 and 1990.

**Table 6-7   Gross Imports and Gross Exports for the U.S.,
1970 and 1990**

**(Billions of 1987 Dollars)**

|  | 1970 | 1990 |
|---|---|---|
| Real GDP | 2873.9 | 4897.3 |
| Consumption plus gross investment | 2243.2 | 4019.4 |
| Gross imports | 196.4 | 565.1 |
| Gross exports | 161.3 | 510.5 |

SOURCE: *Economic Report of the President, 1994*

(a) Find net exports for the United States in 1970 and 1990.

(b) Find the percentage change in real GDP, consumption plus gross investment, gross imports, and gross exports between 1970 and 1990.

(c) What do the percentage changes calculated in part (b) suggest about the importance of imports and exports for the U.S. economy?

(a) Net exports equal gross exports less gross imports. Net exports are −$35.1 billion in 1970 and −$54.6 billion in 1990.

(b) From 1970 to 1990, real GDP increased 70%, while consumption plus gross investment increased 79%, gross imports increased 188%, and gross exports increased 216%.

(c) U.S. purchase of foreign-made goods is increasing more rapidly than private sector (consumption plus gross investment) spending. This indicates that U.S. private-sector demand is increasingly being met by producers in foreign countries. The rapid growth of U.S. exports indicates that an increasing proportion of U.S. production is being sold outside the United States.

**6.18.** (a) What is meant by an appreciation and depreciation of the U.S. dollar?

(b) What effect does an appreciation or depreciation of the U.S. dollar have upon U.S. gross exports and U.S. gross imports?

(a) An appreciation of the U.S. dollar means that one U.S. dollar purchases more units of a foreign currency, e.g., the U.S. dollar appreciates when the number of yen purchased by one dollar increases from 120 to 130. The U.S. dollar depreciates when one U.S. dollar purchases fewer units of a foreign currency, e.g., one dollar purchases 110 rather than 120 yen.

(b) U.S. gross exports decrease and gross imports increase when the U.S. dollar appreciates. When the dollar purchases more units of a foreign currency, foreign-produced goods become less expensive in the United States and U.S.-produced goods become more expensive in foreign countries. Depreciation of the U.S. dollar causes gross imports to decline, since foreign-produced commodities become more expensive in the United States; U.S. exports increase since U.S.-produced goods are less expensive in foreign countries.

## Multiple Choice Questions

1. The consumption function specifies that consumption spending is
   (a) negatively related to the level of disposable income,
   (b) positively related to the level of disposable income,
   (c) negatively related to the rate of interest,
   (d) positively related to the rate of interest.

2. Suppose consumption is $10.0 million when disposable income is $10.5 million, and consumption is $10.5 million when disposable income is $11.5 million, the marginal propensity to consume is
   (a) 0.50,
   (b) 0.75,
   (c) 0.80,
   (d) 0.90.

3. The average propensity to consume is the ratio of
   (a) a change in consumption to a change in disposable income,
   (b) a change in consumption to total disposable income at a specific income level,
   (c) total consumption to total disposable income at a specific income level,
   (d) total consumption to a change in disposable income.

**4.** A marginal propensity to consume of 0.80 indicates that
   (a)   $\Delta C$ to $\Delta Y_d$ is 0.80,
   (b)   $C/Y_d$ is 0.80,
   (c)   $\Delta Y_d$ to $\Delta C$ is 0.80,
   (d)   $Y_d/C$ is 0.80.

**5.** The saving function is
   (a)   the level of planned saving for every change in disposable income,
   (b)   the level of planned saving at different levels of disposable income,
   (c)   the ratio of total saving to total disposable income,
   (d)   the ratio of a change in planned saving to a change in disposable income.

**6.** When the MPC is 0.80 and the APC is 0.95, the MPS is
   (a)   0.20 and the APS is 0.05,
   (b)   0.05 and the APS is 0.20,
   (c)   0.20 and the APS is 0.20,
   (d)   0.05 and the APS is 0.05.

**7.** Gross investment in the national income accounts includes
   (a)   residential and nonresidential construction,
   (b)   spending on producers' durable goods,
   (c)   changes in business inventories,
   (d)   all of the above,
   (e)   none of the above.

**8.** Which of the following statements is true?
   (a)   Gross investment is solely determined by the rate of interest.
   (b)   Gross investment is negatively related to the rate of interest, *ceteris paribus*.
   (c)   Gross investment is positively related to the rate of interest, *ceteris paribus*.
   (d)   None of the above.

**9.** Which of the following statements is true?
   (a)   Imports lower aggregate spending on domestically produced goods and services.
   (b)   Exports lower aggregate spending on domestically produced goods and services.
   (c)   An increase in net exports lowers aggregate spending on domestically produced goods and services.
   (d)   Imports and exports have no effect upon aggregate spending on domestically produced goods and services.

**10.** Which of the following statements is false?
   (a)   A country's exports increase when the economic activity of its major trading partners increases, *ceteris paribus*.
   (b)   A country's exports increase when its currency depreciates, *ceteris paribus*.
   (c)   A country's exports increase when it imports less, *ceteris paribus*.
   (d)   A country's exports increase when the price level of its major trading partners rises, *ceteris paribus*.

## True or False Questions

**11.** _____ An increase in consumer confidence, *ceteris paribus*, shifts the consumption function upward.

**12.** _____    Disposable income is the only variable that determines consumption.

**13.** _____    A change in disposable income causes an equal change in consumption.

**14.** _____    The distance from the consumption line to the 45° line is the level of saving at each level of disposable income.

**15.** _____    The APC is constant along a linear consumption line.

**16.** _____    Investment spending is positively related to the rate of interest, *ceteris paribus*.

**17.** _____    Investment spending is the most unstable component of aggregate spending.

**18.** _____    The investment demand curve shifts outward when households become more willing to purchase residential units.

**19.** _____    Consumption and investment spending in the national income accounts is solely for domestically produced goods and services.

**20.** _____    Imports by a country are unrelated to its level of GDP.

### Answers to Multiple Choice and True or False Questions

| | | | |
|---|---|---|---|
| **1.** (*b*) | **6.** (*a*) | **11.** (T) | **16.** (F) |
| **2.** (*a*) | **7.** (*d*) | **12.** (F) | **17.** (T) |
| **3.** (*c*) | **8.** (*b*) | **13.** (F) | **18.** (T) |
| **4.** (*a*) | **9.** (*a*) | **14.** (T) | **19.** (F) |
| **5.** (*b*) | **10.** (*c*) | **15.** (F) | **20.** (F) |

# Chapter 7

# Traditional Keynesian Approach to Equilibrium Output

## *Chapter Summary*

1. An economy's equilibrium level of output exists when aggregate supply equals aggregate demand. A Keynesian aggregate supply curve is initially used in this chapter to analyze output changes—increasing amounts of output are supplied at a constant price level until the economy reaches its full-employment level of output. A recessionary gap is the amount of output needed to bring the economy to its full-employment level. An inflationary gap is the amount of spending which exceeds the economy's full-employment level of output and which puts upward pressure on the price level.
2. The circular flow of output and income shows the interrelatedness of production, income, and spending. Production generates income for individuals, which is used to purchase output. Equilibrium exists when there are no breaks in the circular flow, and output flows equal spending flows.
3. The economy's equilibrium level of output can be expressed graphically as the point of intersection of a positively sloped aggregate spending line ($C + I + X_n$) and a 45° line which is equidistant from both axes. An output shortage exists at points to the left of this intersection; an output surplus exists at points to the right.
4. To maintain an equilibrium level of output, the sum of leakages must equal the sum of injections. Both saving and gross imports are leakages from the circular flow since they represent sums that are not spent on domestically produced output. Investment spending and gross exports are injections in that they augment spending on domestic output. When the sum of leakages exceeds the sum of injections, output falls; when injections exceed leakages, output increases.
5. The paradox of thrift shows that attempts by consumers to increase or decrease their level of saving, holding other variables constant, affect output and have no effect upon the level of saving. Attempts to save more reduce output, while attempts to save less increase output.
6. Increases or decreases in spending have a multiplier effect upon the equilibrium level of output. This multiplier effect exists because consumer spending is dependent upon the receipt of disposable income. The value of the multiplier ($k$) is found by relating the eventual change in income to the initial change in aggregate spending ($k = \Delta Y/\Delta I$) or through the equation $k = 1/(1 - \text{MPC})$.
7. When the price level is unchanged, a change in the equilibrium level of output is specified by the equation $\Delta Y = k(\Delta E)$, where $\Delta E$ is the initial change in aggregate spending. The equilibrium level of output does not change by $k(\Delta E)$, however, when spending increases raise the price level. A higher price level reduces some price-sensitive aggregate spending because of a wealth, interest rate, or international purchasing power effect.

## *Important Terms*

**Circular flow.** The flow of money income from businesses to individuals for the services of economic resources and from individuals to businesses for the purchase of the goods and services which were produced.

**Equilibrium level of output.**   The output level determined by the equating of aggregate demand and aggregate supply.

**Inflationary gap.**   The amount by which aggregate spending exceeds the full-employment level of output.

**Injections.**   The addition of investment spending and gross exports to aggregate spending and therefore to the circular flow.

**Leakages.**   A withdrawal of aggregate spending from the circular flow when people (1) save or (2) purchase imported rather than domestically produced goods.

**Multiplier.**   The ratio of the change in the equilibrium level of output to an initial change in aggregate spending.

**Paradox of thrift.**   The attempt by society to alter its saving level results in an unchanged level of saving and a change in the equilibrium level of output.

**Production shortage.**   Occurs when aggregate spending exceeds output.

**Production surplus.**   Exists when aggregate spending is less than output.

**Recessionary gap.**   The amount of additional output that is needed to bring the economy to its full-employment level of output.

# Outline of Chapter 7: Traditional Keynesian Approach to Equilibrium Output

**7.1   The Keynesian Constant Price Level Model of Equilibrium Output**
**7.2   The Income-Output Approach to Equilibrium Output**
**7.3   The Leakage-Injection Approach to Equilibrium Output**
**7.4   The Paradox of Thrift**
**7.5   The Multiplier**
**7.6   Changes in Equilibrium Output When Aggregate Supply Is Positively Sloped**

## 7.1   THE KEYNESIAN CONSTANT PRICE LEVEL MODEL OF EQUILIBRIUM OUTPUT

John Maynard Keynes developed the framework for modern-day macroeconomics in the 1930s. Because there was considerable unemployment at that time, he assumed that changes in aggregate demand have no effect upon the price level as long as output is below the full-employment level. A constant price level analysis of economic activity is presented in Fig. 7-1, where the shift of aggregate demand from $AD_1$ to $AD_2$ raises output from $y_1$ to $y^*$ while the price level remains constant at $p_0$. A positive GDP gap—one where real GDP is below potential GDP—is now identified as a recessionary gap. The distance $y_1 - y^*$ in Fig. 7-1 is a recessionary gap when $y^*$ is specified as the full-employment level of output and aggregate demand is $AD_1$. An inflationary gap exists when there is excessive aggregate spending. In Fig. 7-1, aggregate spending is $y_3$ at price level $p_0$ for aggregate demand curve $AD_3$. Since the economy cannot supply $y_3$ at price level $p_0$, aggregate demand curve $AD_3$ results in an increase in the price level. For curve $AD_3$, there is an inflationary gap of $y^* - y_3$ at price level $p_0$.

**EXAMPLE 7.1.**   Refer to Fig. 7-2. Suppose full employment exists at the $650 output level. When equilibrium output is $500, the economy has a $150 recessionary gap, which is the difference between the $650 full-employment level of output and the $500 output level determined by the intersection of curves $AD_1$ and $AS_1$ at point $E_1$. An increase in aggregate demand which shifts the aggregate demand curve from $AD_1$ to $AD_2$ raises the equilibrium level of output to $650 and eliminates the economy's recessionary gap without any change in the $p_0$ price level. A further increase in aggregate demand, one which shifts the aggregate demand curve from $AD_2$ to $AD_3$, would result in an output level of $750 if the price level remained at $p_0$. Thus, there is a $100 inflationary gap for curve $AD_3$ at price level $p_0$ since the economy cannot produce output of $750 at price level $p_0$.

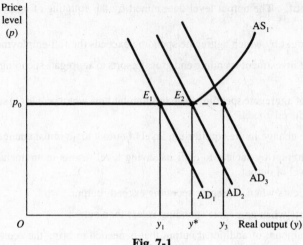

**Fig. 7-1**

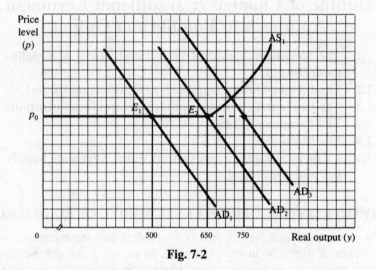

**Fig. 7-2**

## 7.2   THE INCOME-OUTPUT APPROACH TO EQUILIBRIUM OUTPUT

The Keynesian constant price level model of output is presented in Fig. 7-3 as a circular flow of income and output between businesses and individuals. In a capitalist, free-market economy, individuals own, directly or indirectly, the economy's economic resources (land, labor, capital). Businesses hire resources to produce output and pay individuals a money income for the services of these resources; individuals in turn spend their money income and purchase output. Assuming no supply constraints, which is the case when aggregate supply is horizontal, it is reasonable to expect businesses to supply output as long as the receipts from selling output (the sum of expenditures) equal the payments made by businesses to the owners of economic resources and the owners of the business firms.

**EXAMPLE 7.2.**   Fig. 7-3 illustrates the circular flow of resource services, money income, money expenditures, and goods and services between businesses and individuals in an economy where there are no government taxes or government spending. The upper portion of the flow depicts the payments made in hiring resource services. Businesses hire resources in order to produce goods and services; wages, rent, interest, and profits are paid to the owners of the resources and the owners of the businesses. The lower portion of the flow depicts expenditures and payments for the resulting flow of goods and services produced. The income that individuals receive results in a flow of spending that equals the money payments made by the businesses which produced these goods and services.

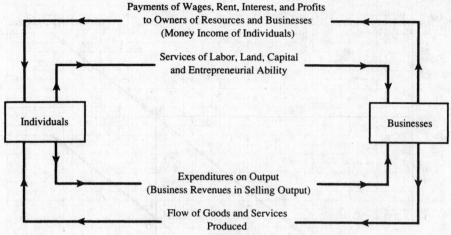

**Fig. 7-3**

The circular flow of income and expenditure can be used to establish the economy's equilibrium level of output. The market value of final output for a hypothetical economy appears in column 1 of Table 7-1. Assuming a capitalist system where there are no government taxes or spending, the value of output in column 1 is also the disposable income of individuals since individuals receive all the payments made to the factors of production. Aggregate spending in column 5 is the sum of consumer spending (column 2), investment spending (column 3), and net exports (column 4). Note that consumer spending (column 2) increases with the level of output (column 1) and therefore the level of personal disposable income. This behavior is consistent with the dependency of consumer spending upon consumer disposable income discussed in Chapter 6. Investment and net exports are assumed to be unrelated to the output level and remain at $100 billion and $10 billion, respectively. The equilibrium level of output is $800 billion since this is the only level of production at which output ($Y$) equals aggregate spending ($C + I + X_n$). This equilibrium condition is depicted in column 6 by the absence of production shortages or surpluses. At output levels below $800 billion there is a shortage of output (aggregate spending is greater than production), while at output levels greater than $800 billion there is surplus production. There is neither a production surplus nor a production shortage when output is $800 billion, since aggregate output ($Y$) equals aggregate spending ($C + I + X_n$).

**Table 7-1**
**(in Billions of $)**

| (1) Output ($Y$) | (2) Consumer Spending ($C$) | (3) Investment Spending ($I$) | (4) Net Exports ($X_n$) | (5) Aggregate Spending ($C + I + X_n$) | (6) Surplus (+)/Shortage (−) $Y - (C + I + X_n)$ |
|---|---|---|---|---|---|
| 650 | 570 | 100 | 10 | 680 | −30 |
| 700 | 610 | 100 | 10 | 720 | −20 |
| 750 | 650 | 100 | 10 | 760 | −10 |
| 800 | 690 | 100 | 10 | 800 | 0 |
| 850 | 730 | 100 | 10 | 840 | +10 |
| 900 | 770 | 100 | 10 | 880 | +20 |
| 950 | 810 | 100 | 10 | 920 | +30 |

The income-expenditure approach to output is presented graphically in Fig. 7-4 using the data from Table 7-1. Consumption's direct relationship to income is depicted in the figure by the linear consumption function $C$. Adding investment of $100 billion and net exports of $10 billion to consumption shifts the linear consumption function line $C$ upward $110 billion, to ($C + I + X_n$). The 45° line is equidistant from both the horizontal and vertical axes. Aggregate spending, which is the sum ($C + I + X_n$), equals output ($Y$) at only one level of output, determined by the intersection, at point $A$, of the ($C + I + X_n$) line and the 45° line. At

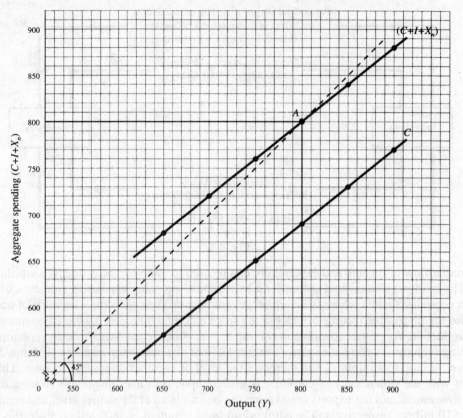

**Fig. 7-4**

this point of intersection, the $800 level of output equals the $800 sum of consumption, investment, and net export spending. We can establish from Fig. 7-4 that increases (upward shifts) or decreases (downward shifts) of aggregate spending [shifts of the $(C + I + X_n)$ line] increase or decrease the economy's equilibrium level of output. This income-expenditure approach is a demand theory of output, which is consistent with the Keynesian constant price level model of output described in Section 7.1; changes in aggregate demand and therefore aggregate spending alter the level of output without any change in the price level as long as the economy is below the full-employment level of output.

**EXAMPLE 7.3.**   Suppose consumer spending is depicted by consumption function $C'$ in Fig. 7-5, net exports equal 0, and gross investment is $120. This aggregate spending line $(C + I + X_n)$ is derived by adding investment of $120 to the $C'$ consumption line. From the $(C + I + X_n)$ aggregate spending line we find that aggregate spending is $830 when output $(Y)$ is $800, $950 when $Y$ is $950, and $1030 when $Y$ is $1050. There is a $30 shortage of output when $Y = $800 since aggregate spending exceeds output. At the $1050 output level, there is a $20 surplus since aggregate spending is $1030 when output is $1050. When output is $950, aggregate spending equals output and there is equilibrium between production and spending. Equilibrium, therefore, exists at the point of intersection of the aggregate spending line $(C + I + X_n)$ and the 45° line.

**EXAMPLE 7.4.**   The equilibrium level of output is found algebraically by equating output $(Y)$ and aggregate spending $(C + I + X_n)$. The equation for the linear consumption line in Fig. 7-5 is $C = $70 + 0.8Y$; $I$ is $120 and $X_n = 0$. The $950 equilibrium level of output is found by solving the equation $Y = C + I + X_n$ for $Y$.

$$\text{Output} = \text{aggregate spending}$$
$$Y = C + I + X_n$$
$$Y = \$70 + 0.8Y + \$120 + 0$$
$$Y - 0.8Y = \$70 + \$120 + 0$$
$$0.2Y = \$190$$
$$Y = \$190/0.20 = \$950$$

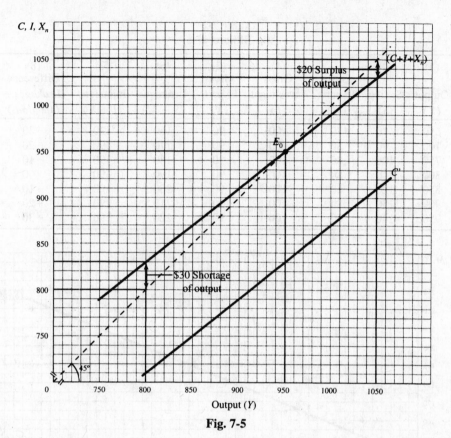

**Fig. 7-5**

## 7.3   THE LEAKAGE-INJECTION APPROACH TO EQUILIBRIUM OUTPUT

The leakage-injection approach to equilibrium output focuses on saving and gross imports as leakages from the circular flow and on investment and gross exports as spending injections. Leakages depress aggregate spending, while injections increase aggregate spending. For example, spending on domestic output declines when individuals buy more imported rather than domestically produced commodities and when individuals seek to save more of their current income. Spending on domestic output increases when foreigners buy more domestically produced commodities, and an equilibrium level of output exists in the leakage-injection approach when the sum of leakages equals the sum of injections.

**EXAMPLE 7.5.**   Table 7-2 presents saving, gross imports, gross investment, and gross exports for a hypothetical economy. We continue to assume that there are no government taxes or expenditures and that individuals receive the income from production. Various output (income) levels appear in column 1. Column 2 lists income saved at the different income levels specified in column 1. Columns 3, 4, and 5 list gross imports, gross investment, and gross exports, which are assumed to be unrelated to the level of income. Column 6 presents the sum of leakages (saving plus gross imports) and column 7 presents the sum of injections (investment plus gross exports). Column 8 displays the difference between gross leakages and gross injections. Injections equal leakages when output is $800 billion, which is the economy's equilibrium level of output.

**EXAMPLE 7.6.**   The leakage-injection approach is presented graphically in Fig. 7-6 using the data from Table 7-2. The amount saved at the various income levels is plotted and the saving function is labeled S. Line $(S + M)$ illustrates an $80 billion upward shift to the savings line when a gross import leakage of $80 billion is added to the saving function. This $(S + M)$ line measures the leakages that occur at various levels of output. Injection line $(I + X)$ is derived by adding $90 billion in gross exports to injection line $I$. Injections equal leakages when output is $800 billion.

**Table 7-2**
**(in Billions of $)**

| (1) Output (Y) | (2) Saving (S) | (3) Gross Imports (M) | (4) Gross Investment (I) | (5) Gross Exports (X) | (6) Leakages (S + M) | (7) Injections (I + X) | (8) Difference (Leakages − Injections) |
|---|---|---|---|---|---|---|---|
| 650 | 80 | 80 | 100 | 90 | 160 | 190 | −30 |
| 700 | 90 | 80 | 100 | 90 | 170 | 190 | −20 |
| 750 | 100 | 80 | 100 | 90 | 180 | 190 | −10 |
| 800 | 110 | 80 | 100 | 90 | 190 | 190 | 0 |
| 850 | 120 | 80 | 100 | 90 | 200 | 190 | +10 |
| 900 | 130 | 80 | 100 | 90 | 210 | 190 | +20 |
| 950 | 140 | 80 | 100 | 90 | 220 | 190 | +30 |

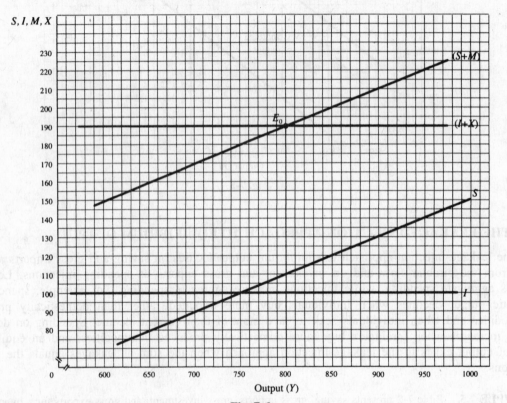

**Fig. 7-6**

## 7.4 THE PARADOX OF THRIFT

The paradox of thrift demonstrates that increases and decreases in consumers' desire to save, *ceteris paribus*, affect the economy's output level but not its saving level. Figure 7-7 presents saving function $S'$ and investment line $I'$ for an economy where there are no exports or imports and government neither taxes nor spends. Leakages equal injections at point $E'$ when output is $700 billion; saving at this equilibrium level is $80 billion, which is also the sum of investment spending. Saving function $S'$ shifts upward to $S''$ when individuals in this economy collectively try to save more. Leakages now equal injections when output is $650 billion. The desire to increase saving has lowered the equilibrium level of income from $700 billion to $650 billion; note, though, that saving remains at $80 billion when investment spending is unchanged at $80 billion. Thus, any change in the desire to save, with no change in other leakages or injections, affects the output level but has no effect upon the level of saving.

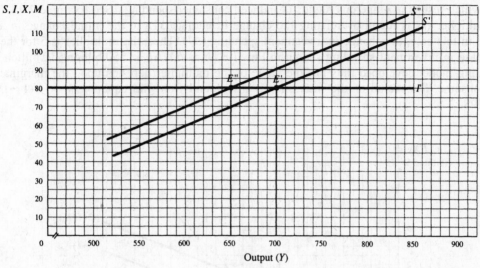

Fig. 7-7

**EXAMPLE 7.7.**   The paradox of thrift is demonstrated algebraically by equating leakages and injections. Suppose the saving function is specified as $S = -\$10$ billion $+ 0.2Y$, gross imports equal \$70 billion, gross investment is \$100 billion, and gross exports equal \$70 billion. The economy's equilibrium level of output is \$550 billion, found by equating the sum of leakages (saving plus gross imports) and the sum of injections (gross investment plus gross exports).

$$S + M = I + X$$
$$-\$10 + 0.2Y + \$70 = \$100 + \$70$$
$$0.2Y = \$110$$
$$Y = \$110/0.2 = \$550$$

In this example, saving is \$100 billion when output is \$550 billion $[S = -\$10 + 0.2Y; S = -\$10 + 0.2(\$550); S = \$100]$. A leakage of \$170 billion ($S$ of \$100 billion plus $M$ of \$70 billion) equals an injection of \$170 billion ($I$ of \$100 billion plus $X$ of \$70 billion).

Now suppose consumers decide to spend more and therefore save less; such a change is depicted by a change in the saving function from $S = -\$10$ billion $+ 0.2Y$ to $S = -\$20$ billion $+ 0.2Y$. Leakages now equal injections at an output level of \$600 billion. Increased consumer spending and therefore decreased saving has increased the equilibrium level of output from \$550 billion to \$600 billion; saving, however, has remained at \$100 billion.

$$-\$20 + 0.2Y + \$70 = \$100 + \$70$$
$$0.2Y = \$120$$
$$Y = \$120/0.2 = \$600$$

When $Y = \$600$ billion is substituted into the new saving equation $S = -\$20$ billion $+ 0.2y$, saving is found to be \$100 billion $[S = -\$20$ billion $+ 0.2(\$600$ billion); $S = \$100$ billion]. The level of saving is unchanged—the same amount is saved although individuals collectively have decided to spend more and save less.

## 7.5   THE MULTIPLIER

Shifts of the aggregate spending curve result in a change in the equilibrium level of output that is several times larger than the initial shift of the curve. For example, equilibrium output is initially \$800 billion in Fig. 7-8 for aggregate spending line $(C + I + X_n)'$. A \$10 billion increase in investment spending shifts the aggregate spending line upward, to $(C + I + X_n)''$, and increases equilibrium output from \$800 billion to \$850 billion. Any change in aggregate spending has a multiplied effect upon output because of consumption's positive relationship to income. An increase in investment spending raises consumers' income, which results in numerous rounds of induced consumer spending. (See Example 7.9.) The value of the multiplier ($k$) is found by relating the change in output ($\Delta Y$) to the initial change in aggregate spending, in this case, the change in investment spending ($\Delta I$). Thus, the multiplier is 5 for the $10 billion increase in investment spending shown in Fig. 7-8 [$k = \Delta Y/\Delta I = $50$ billion/$10 billion = 5]. In the spending model developed thus far, the value of the multiplier depends upon the marginal propensity to consume. The value of the multiplier is also found from the equation $k = 1/(1 - \text{MPC})$ or $k = 1/\text{MPS}$.

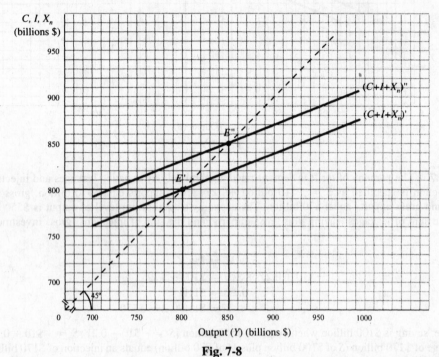

Fig. 7-8

**EXAMPLE 7.8.** When the marginal propensity to consume is 0.80, a $10 billion increase in investment spending raises equilibrium output $50 billion. This change in equilibrium output can also be found algebraically by the formula $\Delta Y = k(\Delta I)$, where $k = 1/(1 - \text{MPC})$. The multiplier is 5 when the MPC is 0.80 [$k = 1/(1 - 0.80); k = 5$]. Thus, a $10 billion increase in investment spending increases equilibrium output $50 billion: $\Delta Y = k(\Delta I); \Delta Y = 5($10$ billion); \Delta Y = $50$ billion.

**EXAMPLE 7.9.** Suppose investment spending increases $10 billion and the marginal propensity to consume is 0.80. The $10 billion increase in output raises the disposable income of individuals $10 billion, which induces consumer spending and further increases in output and disposable income. The multiplied effect of the $10 billion increase in investment spending is demonstrated below by the induced consumption that occurs over successive rounds. As shown above, the eventual increase in output is $50 billion.

Round 1: The $10 billion increase in investment spending raises output and the disposable income of individuals $10 billion.

Round 2: With $10 billion more income, individuals consume 0.80 of the $10 billion increase in their disposable income; consumption increases $8 billion, raising output and disposable income $8 billion.

Round 3: With $8 billion more income, individuals consume 0.80 of the $8 billion increase; consumption increases $6.40 billion, raising output and disposable income of individuals $6.40 billion.

Successive rounds: There are successive rounds of induced consumption, with each round of diminishing magnitude. Consumption in successive rounds totals $25.60 billion since we know that the eventual increase in output is $50 billion.

Table 7-3 summarizes this information.

**Table 7-3**
**(in Billions)**

|                   | $\Delta I$ | $\Delta C$ | $\Delta Y$ |
|-------------------|-----------|-----------|-----------|
| Round 1           | $10.00    |           | $10.00    |
| Round 2           |           | $8.00     | 8.00      |
| Round 3           |           | 6.40      | 6.40      |
| Successive rounds |           | 25.60     | 25.60     |
| Sums              | $10.00    | $40.00    | $50.00    |

## 7.6 CHANGES IN EQUILIBRIUM OUTPUT WHEN AGGREGATE SUPPLY IS POSITIVELY SLOPED

When the aggregate supply curve is positively sloped, increases in aggregate demand raise both equilibrium output and the price level, even though output may be below its full-employment level. The $50 billion outward shift of aggregate demand from AD' to AD'' in Fig. 7-9 raises equilibrium output $40 billion rather than $50 billion because of a positively sloped aggregate supply curve. If the aggregate supply curve had been horizontal in this range and the price level had remained at $p_1$, equilibrium output would have increased $50 billion, an amount equal to the shift in the aggregate demand line. It therefore follows that an increase in aggregate spending, when aggregate supply is positively sloped, has a smaller multiplier effect since the increase in the price level (1) decreases wealth (which limits the expansion of induced consumer spending), (2) causes higher interest rates (which slow investment spending), and (3) reduces the purchasing power of the home currency (which increases imports, and decreases exports).

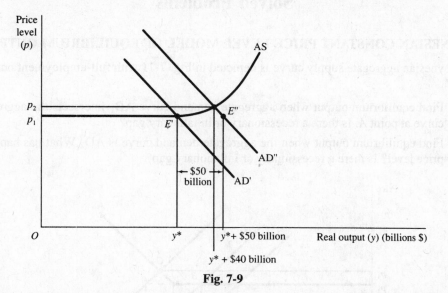

**Fig. 7-9**

**EXAMPLE 7.10.** Figure 7-10 shows an equilibrium level of output of $850 billion for aggregate spending line $(C + I + X_n)_1$. A $10 billion increase in investment spending shifts the aggregate spending line upward to $(C + I + X_n)_3$ and increases equilibrium output $50 billion when the multiplier is 5 and there is no change in the price level. When the aggregate supply curve is positively sloped, however, increased spending raises the price level, which decreases consumption, investment, and net export spending because of a wealth, interest rate, and international purchasing power effect. Thus, the $10 billion increase in investment spending results in an upward shift of aggregate spending line $(C + I + X_n)_1$ to $(C + I - X_n)_2$ rather than $(C + I + X_n)_3$, and the equilibrium level of output increases from $850 billion to $880 billion rather than $900 billion.

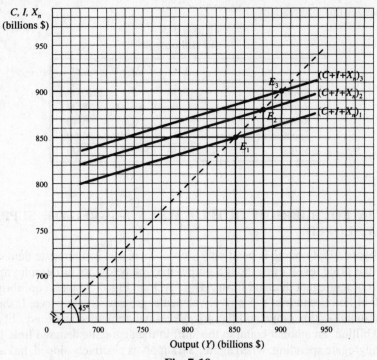

**Fig. 7-10**

# Solved Problems

## THE KEYNESIAN CONSTANT PRICE LEVEL MODEL OF EQUILIBRIUM OUTPUT

**7.1.** A Keynesian aggregate supply curve is depicted in Fig. 7-11 with full-employment output denoted by $y^*$.

   (a) Find equilibrium output when aggregate demand curve $AD_1$ intersects the aggregate supply curve at point $A$. Is there a recessionary or inflationary gap?

   (b) Find equilibrium output when the aggregate demand curve is $AD_2$. What has happened to the price level? Is there a recessionary or inflationary gap?

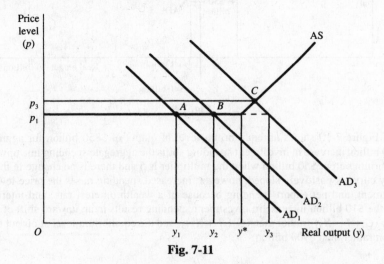

**Fig. 7-11**

(c)  Why is $y^* - y_3$ identified as an inflationary gap for aggregate demand curve $AD_3$?

(a)  Equilibrium exists at point $A$; equilibrium output is $y_1$. There is a recessionary gap of $y_1 - y^*$.

(b)  Equilibrium exists at point $B$; equilibrium output is $y_2$. The price level has remained at $p_1$. There is a recessionary gap of $y_2 - y^*$.

(c)  Equilibrium exists at point $C$. Equilibrium output is below $y_3$ since the price level has increased to $p_3$. For aggregate demand curve $AD_3$, there is an inflationary gap of $y^* - y_3$ since output cannot be increased beyond $y^*$ without an increase in the price level.

**7.2.**  A production-possibility frontier is depicted in Fig. 7-12.

(a)  What is true of points $A$, $B$, and $C$ in the figure? Assuming a Keynesian aggregate supply curve, what should happen to the price level when output increases from point $A$ to $B$ to $C$?

(b)  What is happening to the price level at point $D$?

(a)  Points $A$ and $B$ are within the production-possibility frontier, indicating that there are unemployed resources. Point $C$ is on the production-possibility frontier; in this case, economic resources are fully employed. According to traditional Keynesian analysis, there is no change in the price level as the economy moves from an output level with unemployed resources (point $A$) to an output level where there is full employment (point $C$).

(b)  The price level has increased in moving from point $C$ to point $D$ since output exceeds the economy's normal full-employment level of output.

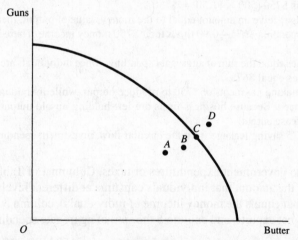

**Fig. 7-12**

## THE INCOME-OUTPUT APPROACH TO EQUILIBRIUM OUTPUT

**7.3.**  (a)  Draw a diagram which shows the direction of the flow of resource services, money income, money expenditures, and output between businesses and individuals.

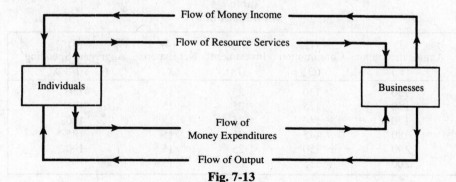

**Fig. 7-13**

(b)  Explain why a cost to business firms represents income to individuals, and vice versa.

(a)  Figure 7-13 shows a simple schematic model of the circular flow of resource services, money income, and money expenditures.

(b)  The top loop in Fig. 7-13 shows that businesses purchase the services of economic resources, which are owned by individuals. Thus, a cost of production for business firms represents money income for individuals. The bottom loop shows that individuals purchase goods and services from businesses. Such purchases represent a cost to individuals and money receipts (money income) to businesses.

**7.4.**  Suppose individuals own all businesses and economic resources, government does not tax or spend, and the business sector produces 500 units at an average price of $1.50 a unit.

(a)  What is the money value of output?

(b)  What is the money income of individuals?

(c)  Find consumer spending when individuals spend 90% of their income.

(d)  What money revenues are received by the business sector from consumer spending?

(e)  What is the relationship of the cost of producing output and the money receipts of businesses when there are only consumer expenditures? What should happen to the level of output?

(f)  What volume of investment spending is needed to stabilize output at 500 units?

(a)  The money value of output equals the quantity of output times the average price per unit. The money value of output is $750 (500 × $1.50 = $750).

(b)  Since individuals receive an amount equal to the money value of output, their money income is $750.

(c)  Individuals are spending $675—0.90 times their $750 money income. There is a $75 saving leakage from the circular flow.

(d)  Business revenues equal the sum of aggregate spending. Since individuals are the only source of spending, business revenues equal $675.

(e)  Businesses are making payments of $750 to produce output, while individuals are purchasing only $675 of what is produced. Because business firms are left holding unsold output valued at $75, they can be expected to decrease output.

(f)  To replace the $75 saving leakage from the circular flow, investment spending must equal $75.

**7.5.**  Suppose there are no government expenditures or taxes. Column 1 of Table 7-4 lists possible levels of output, column 2 the amount that individuals consume at different levels of output (recall that the money value of output equals the money income of individuals), column 3 the amount of investment spending, column 4 net exports, and column 5 the sum of aggregate spending at each level of output.

(a)  Is there a surplus or shortage of output when output is $150 billion? $160 billion? $170 billion? $180 billion? $190 billion? $200 billion?

(b)  What is the equilibrium level of output?

(c)  What is meant by an equilibrium level of output?

### Table 7-4
### (in Billions of $)

| (1) Aggregate Output ($Y$) | (2) Consumption ($C$) | (3) Investment ($I$) | (4) Net Exports ($X_n$) | (5) Aggregate Spending ($C + I + X_n$) |
|---|---|---|---|---|
| 150 | 130 | 25 | 15 | 170 |
| 160 | 135 | 25 | 15 | 175 |
| 170 | 140 | 25 | 15 | 180 |
| 180 | 145 | 25 | 15 | 185 |
| 190 | 150 | 25 | 15 | 190 |
| 200 | 155 | 25 | 15 | 195 |

(a) There is a production shortage at output levels below $190 billion. When output is $150 billion, aggregate spending is $170 and there is an output shortage of $20 billion. When output is $160 billion, there is an output shortage of $15 billion. There is a shortage of $10 billion when output is $170 billion; a shortage of $5 billion when output is $180 billion; and a production surplus of $5 billion when output is $200 billion.

(b) The equilibrium level of output is $190 billion. At this level there is neither an output surplus or shortage since aggregate spending of $190 billion equals output of $190 billion.

(c) An equilibrium level of output is one that is sustained over time as long as there are no changes in aggregate spending or in the willingness of businesses to produce.

**7.6.** (a) Refer to Fig. 7-14. Suppose output is currently $600 billion. Will production continue at the $600 billion level in successive periods?

(b) Establish from Fig. 7-14 whether there is a production surplus or shortage when output is $700 billion, $800 billion, and $900 billion.

(c) What is the equilibrium level of output?

(a) There is a production shortage at the $600 billion output level since aggregate spending of $700 billion exceeds production of $600 billion. Businesses can be expected to increase output during the next production period.

(b) There is a $50 billion production shortage when output is $700 billion, and a $50 billion production surplus when output is $900 billion.

(c) The equilibrium level of output is $800 billion since at that level aggregate spending equals output.

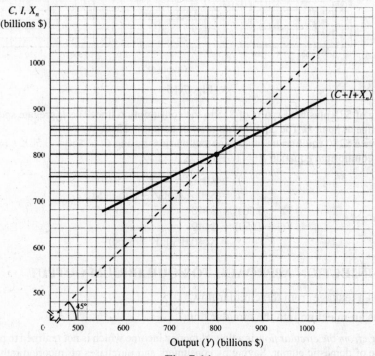

Fig. 7-14

**7.7.** Suppose consumer spending is specified as $C = \$50 + 0.50Y$, investment spending is $75, and net exports total $15.

(a) Plot in Fig. 7-15 a line representing consumer spending and label it $C'$. Also plot a line representing consumer, investment, and net export spending and label it $(C + I + X_n)$. Draw a 45° line through the origin. Find the equilibrium level of output.

(b) Find the equilibrium level of output algebraically by equating output and aggregate spending.

(a) Consumption is $50 when $Y = 0$ and $100 when $Y = \$100$; plotting these points in Fig. 7-15, we derive the linear consumption line $C'$. The aggregate spending line $(C + I + X_n)'$ is derived by adding investment

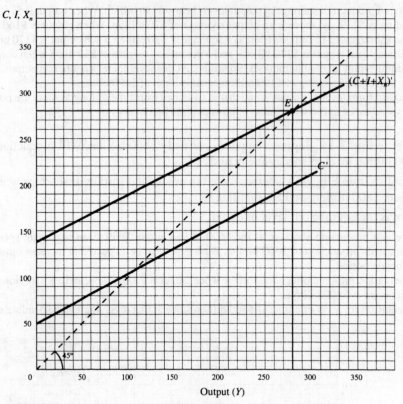

**Fig. 7-15**

spending of $75 plus net exports of $15 to the consumption line. The aggregate spending line intersects the 45° line at point $E$. The equilibrium level of output is $280.

(b) We derive a $280 equilibrium level of output by substituting $C = \$50 + 0.50Y$, $I = \$75$, and $X_n = \$15$ into the equilibrium equation $Y = C + I + X_n$.

$$Y = C + I + X_n$$
$$Y = \$50 + 0.50Y + \$75 + \$15$$
$$Y - 0.50Y = \$140$$
$$Y(1 - 0.50) = \$140$$
$$Y = \$140/0.50; Y = \$280$$

## THE LEAKAGE-INJECTION APPROACH TO EQUILIBRIUM OUTPUT

**7.8.** (a) What is a leakage from the circular flow?

(b) What is an injection into the circular flow?

(a) *A leakage from the circular flow* is a flow of money income which is not returned to producers through the purchase of domestic output. Saving by consumers and purchases of imported rather than domestically produced goods are examples of leakages from the circular flow.

(b) *An injection into the circular flow* is an expenditure that is unrelated to the flow of money income. Exporting goods to other countries is an injection, as is investment spending.

**7.9.** Suppose there are no gross imports, gross exports, government taxes, or government expenditures.

(a) What is the equilibrium level of output in Fig. 7-16?

(b) What is the level of saving and investment when output is $400, $500, and $600?

(c) There being no gross imports or exports, what is the relationship of saving leakages and investment injections when output is above and below the equilibrium level of output?

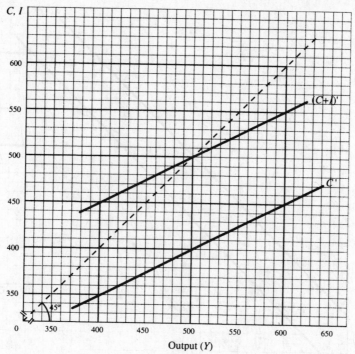

**Fig. 7-16**

(a) The equilibrium level of output is $500, determined by the point of intersection of the aggregate spending line $(C + I)'$ and the 45° line.

(b) Saving at each level of output is the difference between the income received and the amount consumed; in the graph, it is the difference between the consumption line $C'$ and the 45° line. Consumption is $350 and saving is $50 when $Y = \$400$. Saving is $100 when $Y = \$500$, and $150 when $Y = \$600$. Investment spending is $100, the distance between consumption line $C'$ and aggregate spending line $(C + I)'$.

(c) When output is below the equilibrium level of output, investment injections are greater than saving leakages; e.g., saving is $50 when $Y = \$400$ while $I = \$100$. When output is above the equilibrium level of output, investment injections are smaller than saving leakages; e.g., saving is $150 when $Y = \$600$ while $I = \$100$. At equilibrium, saving leakages equal investment injections.

**7.10.** Suppose consumer saving is specified as $S = -\$50 + 0.50Y$, investment spending is $75, gross exports total $50, and gross imports equal $35.

(a) In Fig. 7-17, plot the saving equation and label it S′, plot a leakage line $(S + M)'$, and plot an injection line $(I + X)'$. Find the equilibrium level of output.

(b) Find the equilibrium level of output algebraically by equating leakages and injections.

(a) Using the equation $S = -\$50 + 0.50Y$, we find that saving is $0 when $Y = \$100$, and $50 when $Y = \$200$; in plotting these points for a linear equation in Fig. 7-17, we derive the linear saving line S′. The leakage line $(S + M)'$ is derived by adding imports of $35 to the saving line. The injection line $(I + X)'$ is the sum of investment and exports. The equilibrium level of output is $280 where the sum of leakages equals the sum of injections.

(b) Substituting $S = -\$50 + 0.50Y$, $M = \$35$, $I = \$75$, and $X = \$50$ into the equilibrium equation, we establish that the equilibrium level of output is $280.

$$\text{Leakages} = \text{injections}$$
$$S + M = I + X$$
$$(-\$50 + 0.50Y) + \$35 = \$75 + \$50$$
$$0.50Y = \$140$$
$$Y = \$140/0.50; Y = \$280$$

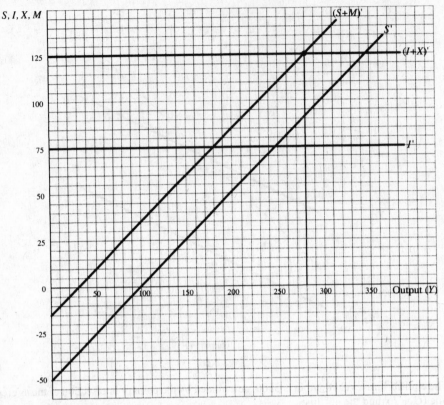

**Fig. 7-17**

## THE PARADOX OF THRIFT

**7.11.** Figure 7-18 shows an equilibrium level of output of $700 for aggregate spending line $(C + I + X_n)'$. A decrease in consumption (consumers seek to spend less and save more) shifts the consumption line downward from $C'$ to $C''$; the aggregate spending line likewise shifts downward from $(C + I + X_n)'$ to $(C + I + X_n)''$.

(a) What is the relationship of aggregate spending and output at the $700 output level after consumers decide to save more and spend less?

(b) What happens to the equilibrium level of output when consumers collectively seek to save more?

(a) Aggregate spending has decreased from $700 to $660; thus, there is now a production surplus at the $700 output level.

(b) The equilibrium level of output falls from $700 to $600 as a result of consumers' desire to save more.

**7.12.** Suppose there are no exports and no imports, and saving and investment are the only leakages and injections.

(a) What is the equilibrium level of output for saving function $S'$ and the investment spending line $I'$ in Fig. 7-19? What is the relationship of saving and investment at this equilibrium level of output?

(b) What is the relationship of saving and investment at the $600 output level after the saving function shifts upward to $S''$?

(c) What is the equilibrium level of output for saving function $S''$ and $I'$? Has the collective desire to save more affected the amount of saving in this economy?

(d) Can a society increase its saving level without any change in the quantity of injections?

(e) Why is there a paradox of thrift?

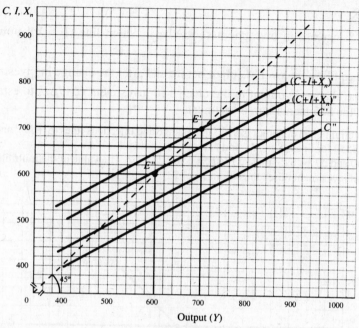

Fig. 7-18

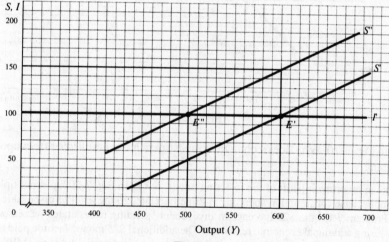

Fig. 7-19

(a)    The equilibrium level of output is $600. Saving leakages of $100 equal investment injections of $100 at this equilibrium level of output.

(b)    Saving is $150 at the $600 output level for saving function $S''$; saving leakages of $150 exceed investment injections of $100.

(c)    The equilibrium level of output for $S''$ and $I'$ is $500. Saving leakages are $100, the same level that existed for saving function $S'$.

(d)    When investment injections remain constant, a society cannot save more by decreasing consumption. In collectively attempting to save more, consumers move the economy to a lower level of output.

(e)    Thrift (saving) is necessary for investment (additions to the economy's stock of capital). Thus, saving is a necessary condition for capital expansion. An increase in saving in the absence of an increase in investment, however, is not beneficial to society since it will result in a decrease in output and therefore employment. Similarly, while increased saving is beneficial to each member of society, it is detrimental in the aggregate when it is not met by an increase in investment.

## THE MULTIPLIER

**7.13.** Suppose a \$25 increase in investment shifts the injection line $(I + X)'$ upward to $(I + X)''$ in Fig. 7-20.

    (*a*)   Find the equilibrium level of output before and after the change in investment.

    (*b*)   Relate the change in output to the change in investment ($\Delta Y/\Delta I$) to establish the multiplier effect of the \$25 increase in investment.

    (*a*)   The equilibrium level of output is \$500 for leakage and injections lines $(S + M)'$ and $(I + X)'$; equilibrium output is \$550 for lines $(S + M)'$ and $(I + X)''$.

    (*b*)   $\Delta Y = \$50$ and $\Delta I = \$25$; thus, $\Delta Y/\Delta I = \$50/\$25 = 2$. The value of the multiplier is 2 where every \$1 increase in investment raises the output level \$2.

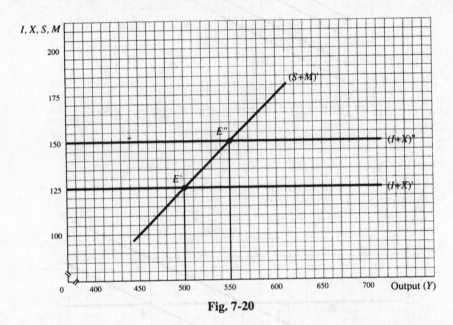

**Fig. 7-20**

**7.14.** Refer back to Fig. 7-20. Why does a change in investment have a multiple effect upon the equilibrium level of output?

    A change in investment [shift of the injection line $(I + X)'$] in Fig. 7-20 has a multiple effect upon equilibrium output because consumption spending is directly related to the level of disposable income. Using the situation in Problem 7.13, the \$25 increase in investment spending necessitates increased output. Output is increased by hiring additional economic resources. The additional \$25 money income paid to individuals (owners of economic resources) is partially consumed (MPC $\times \Delta Y$) and partially saved (MPS $\times \Delta Y$). (The MPC in Problem 7.13 is 0.50.) Increased consumption further expands output, the money income of individuals, and consumer spending. Thus, the initial increase in investment spending results in successive rounds of induced consumption. The interactions between increased spending and income are presented in Table 7-5. Note that the change in investment injections equals the change in saving leakages.

**Table 7-5**

| Round | $\Delta I$ | $\Delta Y$ | $\Delta C$ | $\Delta S$ |
|---|---|---|---|---|
| 1 | \$25.00 | \$25.00 | \$12.50 | \$12.50 |
| 2 | | 12.50 | 6.25 | 6.25 |
| 3 | | 6.25 | 3.12 | 3.12 |
| 4 | | 3.12 | 1.56 | 1.56 |
| Successive rounds | | 3.13 | 1.57 | 1.57 |
| Sum | \$25.00 | \$50.00 | \$25.00 | \$25.00 |

**7.15.** The value of the multiplier ($k$) associated with changes in aggregate spending (e.g., a change in investment spending) equals $1/(1 - \text{MPC})$ or $1/\text{MPS}$. (Recall that $\text{MPC} + \text{MPS} = 1$.)

    (*a*)   Find the value of the multiplier when MPC = 0.50, 0.75, and 0.80.

    (*b*)   What is the relationship between the value of the multiplier and the MPC?

    (*c*)   Find the change in the equilibrium level of output when there is a $10 increase in investment spending and the MPC = 0.50, 0.75, and 0.80.

    (*a*)   When the marginal propensity to consume is 0.50, the value of the multiplier is 2 $[k = 1/(1 - 0.50) = 2]$. The multiplier is 4 when the MPC is 0.75, and 5 when it is 0.80.

    (*b*)   The value of the multiplier is directly related to the magnitude of MPC, i.e., the greater the MPC, the larger the value of the multiplier.

    (*c*)   The change in the equilibrium level of output is found by solving the equation $\Delta Y = k(\Delta I)$ for $\Delta Y$. When the MPC is 0.50, the change in the equilibrium level of output is $+$20 $[\Delta Y = k(\Delta I); \Delta Y = 2(\$10); \Delta Y = \$20]$. The change in equilibrium level of output is $+$40 when the MPC is 0.75, and $+$50 when the MPC is 0.80.

## CHANGES IN EQUILIBRIUM OUTPUT WHEN AGGREGATE SUPPLY IS POSITIVELY SLOPED

**7.16.** Figure 7-21 presents the traditional Keynesian aggregate supply curve, which is horizontal until output reaches the full-employment level, at which time it slopes upward.

    (*a*)   When aggregate demand is AD', equilibrium output is at its full-employment level $y^*$. What happens to the equilibrium level of output and the price level when aggregate demand increases from AD' to AD''?

    (*b*)   Why doesn't the equilibrium level of output increase from $y^*$ to $y_2$?

    (*a*)   The equilibrium level of output increases from $y^*$ to $y_1$, and the price level increases from $p_0$ to $p_1$.

    (*b*)   The equilibrium level of output does not increase to $y_2$—an amount equal to the shift in aggregate demand—because of the increase in the price level from $p_0$ to $p_1$. The increase in the price level has negatively impacted consumption, investment, and net exports because of a decrease in consumer wealth, an increase in the rate of interest, and a decrease in the economy's ability to sell domestically produced goods in other countries.

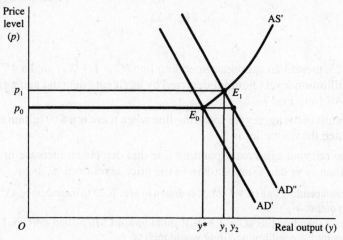

**Fig. 7-21**

**7.17.** The full-employment level of output is $y^*$ in Fig. 7-22.

    (*a*)   Find the equilibrium level of output for aggregate demand and aggregate supply curves AD' and AS in Fig. 7-22.

(b)    Find the equilibrium level of output when increased aggregate spending shifts the aggregate demand curve rightward by $50 billion.

(c)    Why hasn't the equilibrium level of output increased $50 billion—an amount equal to the shift of aggregate demand—since output is below the $y^*$ full-employment level? Under what condition would it have increased $50 billion?

(a)    The equilibrium level of output is $y_1$.

(b)    The equilibrium level of output increases from $y_1$ to $y_2$.

(c)    The equilibrium level of output has not increased $50 billion—from $y_1$ to $y_3$—because of the increase in the price level from $p_0$ to $p_1$. The aggregate supply curve is upward-sloping prior to the $y^*$ full-employment level of output. Thus, some of the stimulative effect of increased spending is dissipated through an increase in the price level. If the aggregate supply curve was horizontal at the $p_0$ price level until output level $y^*$, output would have increased $50 billion as a result of the $50 billion rightward shift of the aggregate demand curve.

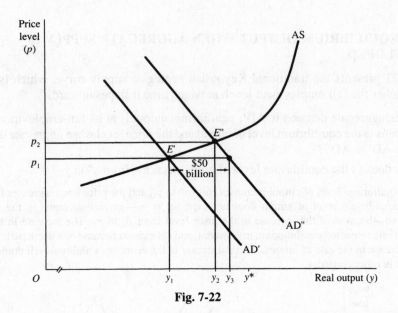

**Fig. 7-22**

**7.18.** (a)    In Fig. 7-23, present an aggregate spending line $(C + I + X_n)'$ and a 45° line which represent the $y_1$ equilibrium level of output depicted by aggregate demand and aggregate supply curves $AD'$ and AS from Fig. 7-22.

(b)    Show the shift of the aggregate spending line when there is a $10 billion increase in investment spending and the multiplier is 5.

(c)    Present the relevant aggregate spending line that depicts an increase in equilibrium output to $y_2$ rather than to $y_3$ due to an increase in the price level from $p_0$ to $p_1$.

(a)    The aggregate spending line $(C + I + X_n)'$ is drawn in Fig. 7-23 to intersect the 45° at point $E_1$ to determine equilibrium output $y_1$.

(b)    The aggregate spending line $(C + I + X_n)'$ shifts upward $10 billion to $(C + I + X_n)'''$ to intersect the 45° line at point $E_2$; equilibrium output would then be $y_3$.

(c)    The $p_0$ to $p_1$ increase in the price level reduces some consumption, investment, and net export spending such that the aggregate spending line shifts only to $(C + I + X_n)''$ and equilibrium output is $y_2$ rather than $y_3$.

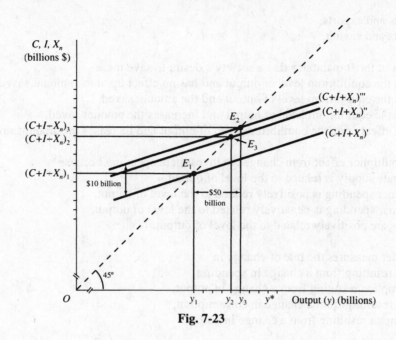

**Fig. 7-23**

# Multiple Choice Questions

1. A recessionary gap exists when
   (a)  aggregate supply exceeds aggregate demand,
   (b)  the aggregate spending line intersects the 45° line at an output level to the right of the full-employment level of output,
   (c)  the aggregate spending line intersects the 45° line at an output level to the left of the full-employment level of output,
   (d)  the aggregate spending line intersects the aggregate supply curve at a lower price level.

2. Businesses will continue producing at the current level of output when
   (a)  they receive a sum of money equal to that paid out for the services of economic resources,
   (b)  leakages equal injections,
   (c)  they are able to sell what has been offered for sale,
   (d)  all of the above,
   (e)  none of the above.

3. When actual output is to the right of the intersection of the 45° line and the aggregate spending line,
   (a)  there is a production surplus,
   (b)  output is not at the equilibrium level,
   (c)  leakages exceed injections,
   (d)  all of the above,
   (e)  none of the above.

4. Which of the following are leakages from the circular flow?
   (a)  Consumption and saving,
   (b)  Saving and imports,

  (*c*) Imports and exports,

  (*d*) Exports and saving.

**5.** The paradox of thrift maintains that a society's desire to save more

  (*a*) lowers the equilibrium level of output and has no effect upon the amount saved,

  (*b*) lowers the equilibrium level of output and the amount saved,

  (*c*) lowers the equilibrium level of output and increases the amount saved,

  (*d*) has no effect upon the equilibrium level of output and increases the amount saved.

**6.** There is a multiplier effect from changes in investment spending because

  (*a*) aggregate supply is related to the level of output,

  (*b*) consumer spending is positively related to the level of output,

  (*c*) consumer spending is negatively related to the level of output,

  (*d*) exports are positively related to the level of output.

**7.** The multiplier measures the rate of change in

  (*a*) output resulting from a change in spending,

  (*b*) consumption resulting from a change in output,

  (*c*) output resulting from a change in consumption,

  (*d*) investment resulting from a change in output.

**8.** When the marginal propensity to consume is 0.80, the value of the multiplier is

  (*a*) 2,

  (*b*) 3,

  (*c*) 4,

  (*d*) 5.

**9.** When aggregate supply is horizontal and the marginal propensity to consume is 0.50, a $10 increase in investment spending will result in

  (*a*) a $10 increase in the equilibrium level of output,

  (*b*) a $20 increase in the equilibrium level of output,

  (*c*) a $50 increase in the equilibrium level of output,

  (*d*) no change in the equilibrium level of output.

**10.** When aggregate supply is positively sloped and the marginal propensity to consume is 0.80, a $10 increase in investment spending will result in

  (*a*) a $10 increase in the equilibrium level of output,

  (*b*) a $50 increase in the equilibrium level of output,

  (*c*) an increase in the equilibrium level of output less than $50,

  (*d*) an increase in the equilibrium level of output greater than $50.

## *True or False Questions*

**11.** _____ A recessionary gap exists when equilibrium output is below the full-employment level of output.

**12.** _____ An inflationary gap exists when output is above the economy's equilibrium level of output.

**13.** _____ There is a break in the circular flow when individuals save and the amount saved is not loaned to businesses to invest.

**14.** _____ A production shortage exists when the output level is to the right of the point of intersection of the aggregate spending line and the 45° line.

**15.** _____ A production shortage exists when leakages exceed injections.

**16.** _____ A decrease in saving, *ceteris paribus*, results in a decrease in the equilibrium level of output.

**17.** _____ The multiplier is 5 when the marginal propensity to save is 0.20.

**18.** _____ A $5 billion increase in investment spending results in a $50 billion increase in the equilibrium level of output when the MPC is 0.90 and aggregate supply is horizontal.

**19.** _____ A $10 billion increase in investment spending results in less than a $40 billion increase in the equilibrium level of output when the MPC is 0.75 and aggregate supply is positively sloped.

**20.** _____ An equilibrium level of output exists when output is $550 billion, investment spending is $70 billion, net exports equal $30 billion, and the consumption function is $C = \$10$ billion $+ 0.80Y$.

### Answers to Multiple Choice and True or False Questions

| | | | |
|---|---|---|---|
| **1.** (c) | **6.** (b) | **11.** (T) | **16.** (F) |
| **2.** (d) | **7.** (a) | **12.** (F) | **17.** (T) |
| **3.** (d) | **8.** (d) | **13.** (T) | **18.** (T) |
| **4.** (b) | **9.** (b) | **14.** (F) | **19.** (T) |
| **5.** (a) | **10.** (c) | **15.** (F) | **20.** (T) |

# Chapter 8

# Fiscal Policy

## *Chapter Summary*

1. The imposition of taxes on consumers shifts the consumption line downward since a tax increase causes less consumer spending at each level of output.
2. Government transfers to individuals are viewed as a negative tax. Thus, an increase in government transfers shifts the consumption line upward since there is more consumer spending at each level of output.
3. Government spending and taxes affect the location of the aggregate spending line $(C + I + X_n + G)$. An increase in government spending shifts the aggregate spending line upward by the increase in government spending. An increase in taxes shifts the aggregate spending line downward by the increase in taxes times the MPC.
4. When an inflationary or recessionary gap occurs, government can initiate changes in government spending and/or taxes—classified as a discretionary fiscal policy—and thereby alter the location of the aggregate spending line.
5. A change in government spending has the same multiplier effect upon equilibrium output as does a similar change in investment spending. A change in lump-sum taxes has a smaller multiplier effect upon equilibrium output than does a similar change in government spending. The lump-sum tax multiplier is $-\text{MPC}/(1 - \text{MPC})$ or $-\text{MPC}(k)$.
6. An income tax $(t)$ affects the value of the expenditure $(k)$ and the lump-sum tax multipliers $(k_t)$. When there is an income tax, the expenditure multiplier is $1/[1 - \text{MPC} + t(\text{MPC})]$ and the lump-sum tax multiplier is $-\text{MPC}/[1 - \text{MPC} + t(\text{MPC})]$.
7. When output falls, government transfers (such as unemployment insurance) increase and government tax receipts from income taxes decrease. Such automatic changes in net tax revenues lessen economic fluctuations and are classified as built-in stabilizers.

## *Important Terms*

**Action lag.**   Government does not respond quickly to a recessionary or inflationary gap.

**Built-in stabilizers.**   Automatic changes in net tax revenues that result from a change in the level of output; built-in stabilizers moderate changes in aggregate spending during an expansion or recession and thereby help stabilize output.

**Discretionary fiscal policy.**   Government implements a change in government spending and/or taxes to eliminate a recessionary or inflationary gap.

**Income tax.**   A tax imposed upon the amount of income received.

**Lump-sum tax.**   A fixed-sum tax imposed on individuals which is unrelated to the amount of income received.

**Net tax revenues.**   The net tax receipts of government, which equals gross tax receipts less government transfers.

**Tax multiplier.**   The multiplier effect on output of a change in lump-sum taxes. The lump-sum tax multiplier is $-\text{MPC}/(1 - \text{MPC})$ or $-\text{MPC}(k)$ when there is no income tax.

# Outline of Chapter 8: Fiscal Policy

## 8.1 GOVERNMENT NET TAX REVENUES AND THE CONSUMPTION FUNCTION

Tax revenues finance government expenditures and government transfer payments to the private sector. Government transfer payments can be viewed as a government outlay or as a negative tax. (The latter view can be seen when we look at net tax revenues as equal to the sum of gross tax revenues less transfer payments.) In the model of economic activity presented here, (1) tax collections and transfer payments occur between the government and individuals, and (2) net tax revenues consist of income taxes plus lump-sum taxes less transfer payments. We shall assume that lump-sum taxes and transfer payments are legislated; thus, they are unrelated to the level of output. Net tax revenues fall when transfer payments increase, and rise when greater per capita taxes are imposed. With respect to income tax receipts, net tax revenues increase when output increases and more taxes are collected or when government imposes a higher income tax rate. In Fig. 8-1, a decrease in transfer payments, *ceteris paribus*, increases net tax revenues and shifts consumption line $C_1$ downward to $C_2$; the downward shift from $C_1$ to $C_2$ equals the increase in transfer payments times the marginal propensity to consume. An increase in the income tax rate shifts consumption line $C_1$ downward to $C_3$ and reduces its slope.

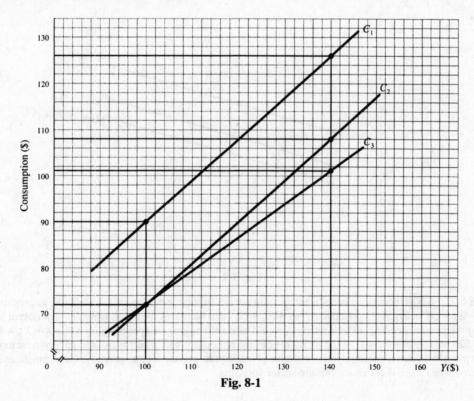

**Fig. 8-1**

**EXAMPLE 8.1.** Suppose $C = 0.90Y_d$ (individuals consume 0.90 of their disposable income). When there are no taxes and individuals receive an income equal to the value of output ($Y_d = Y$, since taxes equal 0), consumption is $90 and $126 when output is $100 and $140, respectively. Consumption line $C_1$ in Fig. 8-1 represents the relationship of consumption and output in a no-tax economy. When a lump-sum tax of $20 is introduced into this economy ($Y_d = Y - \$20$), consumption is $72 when output is $100 [$C = 0.90(\$100 - \$20) = \$72$], and $108 when output is $140 [$C = 0.90(\$140 - \$20) = \$108$]. Consumption line $C_2$ indicates the amount consumed at each level of output when there is a $20 lump-sum tax. Note that the distance between consumption line $C_1$ and $C_2$ is $18, which equals the $20 lump-sum tax times the 0.90 marginal propensity to consume. An increase or decrease in lump-sum tax revenues shifts the consumption function by the MPC times the change in lump-sum tax revenues. When there is a 20% income tax rate, no lump-sum taxes, and $C = 0.90Y_d$ ($Y_d = Y - 0.20Y$), consumption is $72 when output is $100 [$C = 0.90(\$100 - 0.2\{\$100\}) = \$72$], and $100.80 when output is $140. $C_3$ is the consumption line when there is a 20% income tax rate. Note that consumption line $C_3$ is less steeply sloped than consumption lines $C_1$ and $C_2$, for which there is no income tax.

## 8.2  GOVERNMENT EXPENDITURES, TAXES, AND THE LEVEL OF OUTPUT

Taxes reduce personal disposable income and therefore consumption and aggregate spending, whereas government expenditures increase aggregate spending. The influence of taxes and government expenditures upon aggregate spending is shown in Fig. 8-2 in the shift of aggregate spending line ($C + I + X_n + G$). An increase in net lump-sum tax revenues, *ceteris paribus*, shifts aggregate spending line ($C + I + X_n + G$) downward to ($C + I + X_n + G$)', since higher taxes reduce consumer disposable income and therefore consumer spending at each level of output. An increase in government spending, *ceteris paribus*, shifts aggregate spending line ($C + I + X_n + G$) upward to ($C + I + X_n + G$)''. It therefore follows that the government can alter the economy's equilibrium level of output by changing its expenditures or net tax revenues. Such governmental actions are classified as *discretionary fiscal policy*.

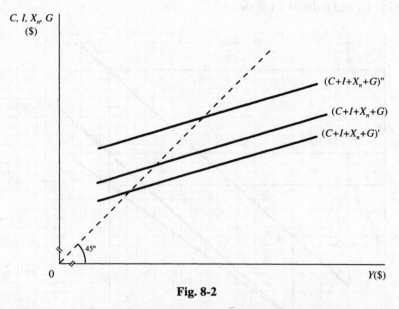

**Fig. 8-2**

**EXAMPLE 8.2.** A $20 increase in investment spending or net exports, *ceteris paribus*, shifts the aggregate spending line ($C + I + X_n + G$)' in Fig. 8-3 upward to ($C + I + X_n + G$)'' and increases the equilibrium level of output $40. A $20 increase in government spending, *ceteris paribus*, would also shift aggregate spending line ($C + I + X_n + G$)' in Fig. 8-3 upward $20 to ($C + I + X_n + G$)'' and increase equilibrium output $40. Thus, increased government expenditures can raise output when there is unemployment because of inadequate private sector spending. Government expenditures can be lowered when there is excessive private-sector spending.

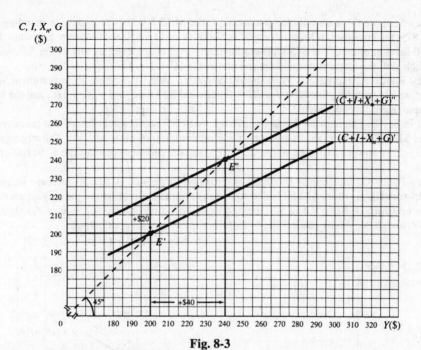

**Fig. 8-3**

**EXAMPLE 8.3.** Government expenditures inject spending into the circular flow, whereas taxes represent a leakage from the circular flow. An increase in government spending in Fig. 8-4 shifts injection line $(I + X + G)$ upward to $(I + X + G)'$, and the equilibrium level of output increases from $Y_0$ to $Y_1$. An increase in taxes shifts leakage line $(S + M + T)$ upward to $(S + M + T)'$, where it intersects injection line $(I + X + G)$ at $Y_2$, which is below the initial $Y_0$ level of output.

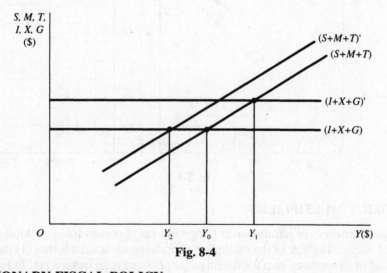

**Fig. 8-4**

## 8.3  DISCRETIONARY FISCAL POLICY

Discretionary fiscal policy involves intentional changes in government spending and/or net tax revenues in order to alter the level of aggregate spending. We have already found that an increase in government spending and/or a decrease in lump-sum taxes shifts the aggregate spending line upward and raises the equilibrium level of output, while a decrease in government spending and/or an increase in lump-sum taxes shifts the aggregate spending line downward and lowers the equilibrium level of output. The government can use discretionary fiscal actions to eliminate an inflationary or recessionary gap.

**EXAMPLE 8.4.**   Suppose there are only lump-sum taxes; the MPC is 0.80; the aggregate spending line is $(C + I + X_n + G)$ in Fig. 8-5; the equilibrium level of output is \$700; there is a \$50 recessionary gap since full employment exists at the \$750 level of output. The \$750 full-employment level is achieved by any of the following discretionary fiscal actions which shift the aggregate spending line upward to $(C + I + X_n + G)'$.

Discretionary Policy A: *Increase in Government Spending.* A \$10 increase in government spending, *ceteris paribus*, shifts aggregate spending line $(C + I + X_n + G)$ upward \$10 to $(C + I + X_n + G)'$, and the economy reaches the \$750 full-employment level of output.

Discretional Policy B: *Decrease in Lump-Sum Taxes.* A \$12.50 decrease in lump-sum taxes reduces net lump-sum tax revenues \$12.50 and shifts the consumption line upward \$10 (0.80 × \$12.50). The aggregate spending line $(C + I + X_n + G)$ shifts upward \$10 to $(C + I + X_n + G)'$, and the economy reaches the \$750 full-employment level of output.

Discretionary Policy C: *Increase in Government Transfer Payments.* A \$12.50 increase in government transfers reduces lump-sum tax revenues \$12.50 (since some tax receipts are returned to the private sector) and shifts the consumption line upward \$10 (0.80 × \$12.50); the aggregate spending line $(C + I + X_n + G)$ shifts upward \$10 to $C + I + X_n + G)'$, and the economy reaches the \$750 full-employment level of output.

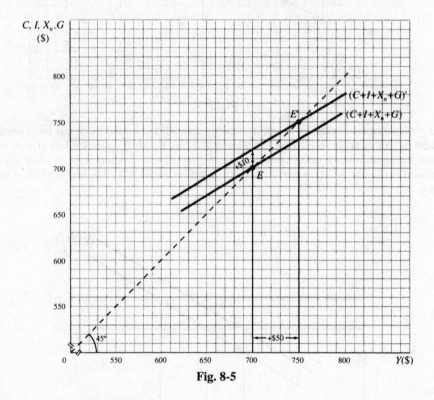

**Fig. 8-5**

## 8.4   FISCAL POLICY MULTIPLIERS

A change in government expenditures or in lump-sum tax revenues has a multiplier effect upon the equilibrium level of output. The size of the multiplier effect depends upon whether (1) there is a change in government spending or in net lump-sum tax revenues, or (2) there is an income tax. In Example 8.4, a \$10 increase in government spending or a \$12.50 decrease in net lump-sum tax revenues raises the equilibrium level of output \$50 for an economy in which there are no income taxes. The value of the multiplier for the increase in government spending is 5 ($\Delta Y/\Delta G$ = \$50/\$10 = 5), while the value of the multiplier for the \$12.50 decrease in net lump-sum tax revenues is −4 ($\Delta Y/\Delta T$ = +\$50/ − \$12.50 = −4). When there is no income tax, a change in government spending has the same multiplier effect [$k = 1/(1 − \text{MPC})$] as does a similar change in investment spending or net exports. The value of the multiplier is smaller for changes in net lump-sum tax revenues; the tax multiplier ($k_t$) is −MPC($k$) or −MPC/(1 − MPC) for an economy with no income tax.

**EXAMPLE 8.5.**    Suppose (1) there is a $60 recessionary gap since the equilibrium level of output is $700 and the full-employment level of output is $760; (2) the government expenditure multiplier is 4 since the MPC is 0.75 and there is no income tax $[k = 1/(1 - MPC); k = 1/(1 - 0.75); k = 4]$; and (3) the value of the net lump-sum tax revenue multiplier is $-3$ since the MPC is 0.75 and there is no income tax $[k_t = -MPC(k); k_t = -0.75(4); k_t = -3]$.

The $60 recessionary gap is eliminated and full-employment output is reached by increasing aggregate spending $60. This is achieved by raising government expenditures $15 or by decreasing net lump-sum tax revenues $20. The required $15 increase in government spending is found by substituting $\Delta Y = +\$60$ and $k = 4$ into the equation $\Delta Y = k(\Delta G)$. The required $20 decrease in net lump-sum tax revenues is found by substituting $\Delta Y = +\$60$ and $k_t = -3$ into the equation $\Delta Y = k_t(\Delta T)$.

An income tax reduces the value of both the expenditure and the lump-sum tax revenue multiplier since the amount of taxes paid to government is directly related to income earned. For example, when the income tax rate is 20% and personal income increases $10, tax payments to the government rise $2 and personal disposable income increases $8 rather than $10. Thus, an increase in personal income results in smaller increments in induced consumption, and therefore results in a smaller multiplier effect. When there is an income tax, the equation for the expenditure multiplier is $k = 1/[1 - MPC + MPC(t)]$, where $t$ is the income tax rate. The equation for the lump-sum tax multiplier is $k_t = -MPC(k)$ or $-MPC/[1 - MPC + MPC(t)]$.

**EXAMPLE 8.6.**    The expenditure multiplier is 4 when the MPC is 0.75 and there is no income tax: $k = 1/(1 - MPC); k = 1/(1 - 0.75); k = 4$. The expenditure multiplier is 2.5 when the MPC is 0.75 and the income tax rate $(t)$ is 0.20: $k = 1/[1 - MPC + MPC(t)]; k = 1/[1 - 0.75 + 0.75(0.20)]; k = 2.5$. The tax multiplier is $-3$ when the MPC is 0.75 and there is no income tax $[k_t = -MPC(k); k_t = -0.75(4); k_t = -3]$, and $-1.875$ when the MPC is 0.75 and the income tax rate is 0.20 $[k_t = -MPC(k); k_t = -0.75(2.5); k_t = -1.875]$.

A discretionary fiscal action has a smaller effect upon equilibrium output when there is an income tax since an income tax reduces the value of the expenditure and the lump-sum tax multiplier. In Example 8.5, aggregate spending must increase $60 to reach the full-employment level of output. This is achieved by a $15 increase in government expenditures or a $20 decrease in net lump-sum tax revenues when there is no income tax. However, when there is a 20% income tax rate, the expenditure multiplier is 2.5, while the tax multiplier is $-1.875$. With an income tax rate of 20%, government expenditures must increase $24 rather than $15 or net lump-sum tax revenues must decrease $32 rather than $20 to raise aggregate spending $60.

## 8.5    BUILT-IN STABILIZERS

Personal income taxes and various government transfers automatically change the level of net tax revenues when the economy moves away from (or toward) the full-employment level of output. For example, government collects smaller revenues from income taxes when output decreases; lump-sum tax revenues also fall when output decreases because of increased government transfer payments to individuals in the form of unemployment insurance benefits, food stamps, and other government assistance programs. Because of such automatic changes in net tax revenues, consumer disposable income is not completely dependent on the level of output, consumer spending is more stable over the business cycle, and the amplitude of economic fluctuations is lessened.

**EXAMPLE 8.7.**    Suppose the government guarantees that it will pay unemployed members of the labor force one-third of their weekly income up to a maximum of $150 per week for a period not to exceed six months. When economic activity falls and people lose their jobs, government automatically pays these benefits to those who have become unemployed. It therefore follows that government's net tax revenues fall during a recession because it is collecting less income tax revenue and it is making a larger number of transfer payments to more unemployed individuals. Thus, when a recession occurs, there is not as large a decline in personal disposable income as there would be if unemployment insurance benefits and other social welfare programs did not exist. During a recession, unemployment insurance payments moderate the decline in consumers' disposable income, the decline in aggregate consumption, and the depth and duration of a recession.

**EXAMPLE 8.8.**    Suppose equilibrium output is initially $500 billion and lump-sum tax revenues are $50 billion. The following situations show the effect that a $20 billion decrease in investment and net export spending has upon

equilibrium output when (1) there are no built-in stabilizers, (2) there is an income tax, and (3) there is an income tax and unemployment insurance.

Situation I: *No Built-in Stabilizer.*   Suppose the MPC is 0.75 and there are no income taxes or entitlement programs such as unemployment insurance. A $20 billion decrease in investment and net export spending decreases the equilibrium level of output by $80 billion, calculated as follows: The expenditure multiplier is 4 since $k = 1/(1 - \text{MPC})$; $k = 1/(1 - 0.75)$; $k = 4$. The change in output is $-$80 billion since $\Delta Y = k[(\Delta I + \Delta X)]$; $\Delta Y = 4(-$20 billion); $\Delta Y = -$80 billion.

Situation II: *An Income Tax as a Built-in Stabilizer.*   Suppose the MPC is 0.75, the income tax rate is 20%, and there are no entitlement programs such as unemployment insurance. Since the multiplier is now 2.5, a $20 billion decrease in investment and net export spending lowers equilibrium output $50 billion, calculated as follows: The expenditure multiplier is 2.5 since $k = 1/[1 - \text{MPC} + t(\text{MPC})]$; $k = 1/(1 - 0.75 + 0.15)$; $k = 2.5$. The change in output is $-$50 billion since $\Delta Y = k[\Delta I + \Delta X]$; $\Delta Y = 2.5(-$20 billion): $\Delta Y = -$50 billion.

Situation III: *An Income Tax and Unemployment Insurance as Built-in Stabilizers.*   Suppose the MPC is 0.75, the income tax rate is 20%, and unemployment insurance payments increase $10 billion when aggregate spending falls $30 billion. A $20 billion decrease in investment and net export spending is accompanied by a $10 billion increase in government transfers because of the decline in output. Equilibrium output falls $31.25 billion, calculated as follows: The expenditure multiplier is 2.5. $\Delta Y = k(\Delta I + \Delta X) + -\text{MPC}(k)(\Delta T)$; $\Delta Y = 2.5(-$20 billion) + -0.75(2.5)(-$10 billion); $\Delta Y = -$50 billion + $18.75 billion; $\Delta Y = -$31.25 billion.

## 8.6   IMPLEMENTING DISCRETIONAL FISCAL POLICY

Since discretionary changes in tax revenues and government expenditures have a multiplier effect upon equilibrium output, it would appear that government has the ability to maintain full-employment output by manipulating its net tax revenues and/or spending. Fiscal policy, however, is not as easily implemented or as successful as our analysis here suggests. Suppose a recessionary gap exists. Will Congress and the administration agree on an *immediate* course of action? In reality, an action lag is likely to occur because of conflicting priorities. For example, some individuals may advocate increased government expenditures on public goods, such as the rebuilding of roads, bridges, or water lines, while others may prefer government expenditures on services such as public education. Another group may advocate expanded welfare services, or reduced tax rates for middle-income workers, or a lower capital gains tax rate to encourage investment spending. And once a fiscal plan of action is reached and implemented, will Congress and the administration be prepared to scale down or eliminate any of these stimulative fiscal measures should the fiscal stimulus eventually become excessive?

Besides political priorities, we must also recognize that economic activity exists in a dynamic, changing environment, where other variables may change. Thus, while a fiscal stimulus may close a recessionary gap and bring the economy to full employment, *ceteris paribus*, it is possible that investment and/or net export spending may increase after the fiscal stimulus is implemented, which would result in an inflationary gap. (See Example 8.9.) In addition, economists are uncertain about the output level at which full employment exists and have been unable to establish precise values for multipliers for the U.S. economy. Lastly, many economists believe that aggregate supply is positively sloped rather than horizontal as output approaches its full-employment level.

**EXAMPLE 8.9.**   Suppose the equilibrium level of output is $500 billion, the expenditure multiplier is 2.5, and the full-employment level of output is $550 billion. Policymakers have agreed to increase government expenditures on the infrastructure in selected cities by $20 billion to close the recessionary gap. Equilibrium output is expected to increase $50 billion as a result of this fiscal stimulus, which would bring output to its full-employment level. Suppose, however, that shortly after the fiscal stimulus is passed by Congress and signed into law, the U.S. dollar depreciates 10% and U.S. exports rise. Aggregate spending is now excessive; government must now implement a fiscal action which reduces aggregate spending in order to avert an increase in the price level. Either taxes must be increased or government spending reduced.

# Solved Problems

## GOVERNMENT NET TAX REVENUES AND THE CONSUMPTION FUNCTION

**8.1.** Why is a government transfer payment considered a negative tax?

There are numerous sources of government revenues: personal and corporate income taxes, consumption taxes (e.g., a sales tax), import duties, inheritance taxes, etc. The majority of tax revenues come from those who have the ability to pay, i.e., taxes are imposed upon those who earn income and those who possess wealth. Some individuals in a society have little or no income and wealth. Government makes money transfers to such economically disadvantaged individuals, in the form of unemployment insurance, social security payments, and various government assistance programs. Government transfers are a negative tax since government is making payments to (transfers), rather than collecting revenues from, some individuals in the economy.

**8.2.** What is the difference between a lump-sum tax and an income tax?

A *lump-sum tax* is a fixed-sum tax that is unrelated to income. An *income tax* is related directly to earned income. In the case of a proportional income tax the government collects a fixed percent of income earned, while for a progressive income tax the rate of taxation increases with the level of income. Lump-sum taxes and proportional and progressive income taxes are illustrated in Fig. 8-6. Note that lump-sum taxes remain at $1000 as income increases from $10,000 to $11,000. When there is a 10% proportional income tax rate, tax payments increase from $1000 to $1100 as income increases from $10,000 to $11,000. When the tax rate is 10% on the first $10,000 earned and 20% on income greater than $10,000, tax payments increase from $1000 to $1200 when income increases from $10,000 to $11,000.

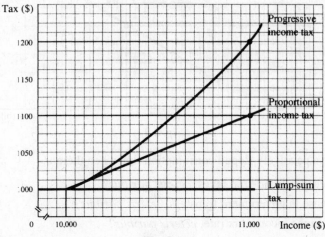

**Fig. 8-6**

**8.3.** Suppose the equation for consumer spending is $C = \$10$ billion $+ 0.75Y_d$.

    (*a*)   Find $C$ when there are no taxes or transfers and output is $800 billion and $840 billion.

    (*b*)   Find $C$ when there is a $40 billion lump-sum tax and output is $800 billion and $840 billion.

    (*c*)   Find $C$ when there is a 20% income tax and output is $800 billion and $840 billion.

    (*d*)   Plot the consumption and output levels calculated in (*a*), (*b*), and (*c*), and label them $C_1, C_2$, and $C_3$.

    (*e*)   What effect do lump-sum and income taxes have upon the consumption line?

    (*a*)   Since disposable income ($Y_d$) equals the income ($Y$) earned in producing output ($Y$) when there are no taxes and transfers, the consumption equation can be stated as $C = \$10$ billion $+ 0.75Y$. $C = \$610$ billion when $Y = \$800$ billion, and $640 billion when $Y = \$840$ billion.

(b) The consumption equation is now stated as $C = \$10$ billion $+ 0.75(Y - \$40$ billion) when there is a $40 billion lump-sum tax, since $Y_d$ now equals $Y - \$40$ billion. $C = \$580$ billion when $Y = \$800$ billion, and $610 billion when $Y = \$840$ billion.

(c) The consumption equation is now stated as $C = \$10$ billion $+ 0.75(Y - 0.20Y)$ when there is a 20% income tax, since $Y_d$ now equals $Y - t(Y)$, where the decimal value for $t$ of 20% is 0.20. Thus, $C = \$490$ billion when $Y = \$800$ billion, and $514 billion when $Y = \$840$ billion.

(d) See Fig. 8-7.

(e) Consumption line $C_1$ shifts downward $30 billion to $C_2$ when a $40 billion lump-sum tax is added. The $30 billion downward shift from $C_1$ to $C_2$ equals the 0.75 MPC times the $40 billion lump-sum tax. When a 20% income tax is added, consumption line $C_1$ shifts downward to $C_3$ and becomes less steeply sloped.

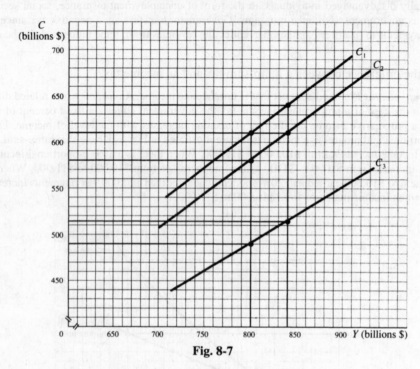

**Fig. 8-7**

**8.4.** What happens to a positively sloped consumption line when there is

(a) A $20 increase in lump-sum taxes, *ceteris paribus*?

(b) A $20 increase in government transfers, *ceteris paribus*?

(c) A decrease in the income tax rate, *ceteris paribus*?

(a) There is a parallel downward shift of the consumption line equal to the $20 increase in lump-sum taxes times the MPC.

(b) There is a parallel upward shift of the consumption line equal to the $20 increase in government transfers times the MPC.

(c) The consumption line shifts upward and becomes more steeply sloped.

## GOVERNMENT EXPENDITURES, TAXES, AND THE LEVEL OF OUTPUT

**8.5.** How do the following events affect a $(C + I + X_n + G)$ aggregate spending line?

(a) A $15 increase in government spending.

(b) A $10 decrease in investment spending.

(c) A $15 decrease in net tax revenues when the marginal propensity to consume is 0.80.

(a) The aggregate spending line shifts by $\Delta G$, the amount of the change in government spending. In this case, there is a corresponding $15 upward shift of the aggregate spending line.

(b) Changes in investment shift the aggregate spending line by $\Delta I$. Here, there is a $10 downward shift of the aggregate spending line.

(c) Changes in lump-sum taxes shift the aggregate spending line by $-MPC(\Delta T)$. Since net tax revenues decrease $15, there is a $12 upward shift of the aggregate spending line [$12 = -0.80(-\$15)$].

**8.6.** (a) What happens to a $(C + I + X_n + G)$ aggregate spending line when there is a $10 decrease in investment spending and a $10 increase in government spending, *ceteris paribus*?

(b) How can government spending be used to stabilize aggregate spending?

(a) There is no shift (change) of the aggregate spending line since the $10 decrease in investment is exactly offset by the $10 increase in government spending.

(b) Government spending can be changed to stabilize aggregate spending to offset increases or decreases in private-sector spending. For example, government expenditures could be increased when investment spending decreases as in part (a); it follows that government expenditures would need to decrease when private-sector spending increases.

**8.7.** In a closed-economy model where there are no imports or exports, the leakage-injection approach to equilibrium output requires that leakages (household saving plus taxes) equal injections (investment plus government expenditures).

(a) Why are taxes classified as a leakage and government spending as an injection?

(b) At the equilibrium level of output of $580 in Fig. 8-8, leakages $(S + T)$ of $60 equal injections $(I + G)$ of $60. When the MPC is 0.80, what effect does the following have upon the equilibrium level of output: (1) a $12 increase in government spending? (2) a $15 decrease in lump-sum taxes?

(a) When government imposes taxes and does not spend these incremental tax revenues, payments made in producing output are not returned to the business sector. That is, there is a leakage from the circular flow just as there is when individuals save some of their disposable income. Government expenditures inject spending into the circular flow in the same way that investment does.

(b) A $12 increase in government expenditures shifts the injection line $(I + G)$ in Fig. 8-8 upward $12 to $(I + G)'$; the equilibrium level of output increases $60, from $580 to $640. A $15 decrease in lump-sum taxes shifts the leakage line $(S + T)$ downward $12 to $(S + T)'$ [Lump-sum tax changes shift the leakage line by $-MPC(\Delta T)$—in this situation by $-0.80(-\$15)$]; $(I + G)$ and $(S + T)'$ intersect at the $640 output level, and the equilibrium level of output increases from $580 to $640.

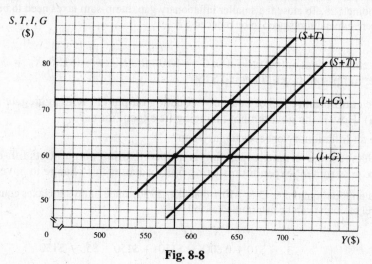

**Fig. 8-8**

## DISCRETIONARY FISCAL POLICY

**8.8.** Suppose there is full employment at the $600 level of output and the MPC is 0.80.

    (*a*)   Does the aggregate spending line ($C + I + X_n + G$) in Fig. 8-9 depict the existence of an inflationary or recessionary gap?

    (*b*)   What discretionary fiscal action can government implement to close this gap?

    (*c*)   What discretionary fiscal action is needed when investment spending decreases $5?

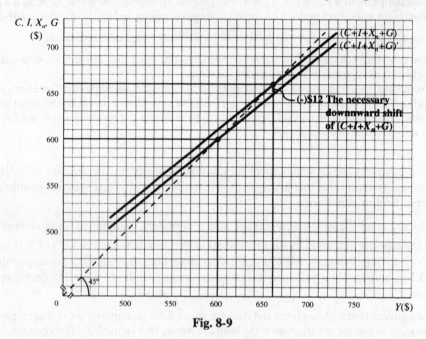

**Fig. 8-9**

    (*a*)   There is a $60 inflationary gap since the equilibrium level of output is $660 and full-employment output is $600.

    (*b*)   Government spending should be decreased $12 since the necessary decrease in aggregate spending is $60 and the multiplier is 5 [$\Delta Y = k(\Delta G)$; $-\$60 = 5(\Delta G)$; $\Delta G = -\$12$]. An alternative fiscal action is a $15 increase in lump-sum taxes since the tax multiplier is $-4$ [$\Delta Y = k_t(\Delta T)$; $-\$60 = -4(\Delta T)$; $\Delta T = +\$15$].

    (*c*)   The inflationary gap is $35 rather than $60 since the $5 decrease in investment spending lowers aggregate spending $25. To close the smaller inflationary gap, lump-sum taxes need to be increased $8.75, or government expenditures need to be reduced $7.

**8.9.** Suppose full-employment output is $1300; $C = \$10 + 0.80Y_d$; $I = \$150$; $X_n = \$50$; $G = \$150$; $Y_d = Y - T$, where lump-sum taxes ($T$) equal $150.

    (*a*)   Find the equilibrium level of output by equating output ($Y$) with aggregate spending ($C + I + X_n + G$). How is the government financing its expenditures?

    (*b*)   Is there an inflationary or recessionary gap?

    (*c*)   What change in government spending is needed to bring output to its full-employment level? How are government expenditures being financed after this change in government spending?

    (*a*)   The consumption equation is $C = \$10 + 0.80(Y - \$150)$ since lump-sum taxes equal $150. The equilibrium level of output can be determined as follows:

$$Y = C + I + X_n + G$$
$$Y = \$10 + 0.80(Y - \$150) + \$150 + \$50 + \$150$$

$$Y - 0.80Y = \$360 - \$120$$
$$0.20Y = \$240$$
$$Y = \$240/0.20 = \$1200$$

Government expenditures of $150 are being financed by the $150 collected from lump-sum taxes.

(b)    There is a recessionary gap since equilibrium output is $100 below the full-employment level of output.

(c)    Government spending should be increased $20 to bring output to its full-employment level [$\Delta Y = k(\Delta G); \$100 = 5(\Delta G); \Delta G = \$20$]. The government is now spending $170 and collecting $150 in lump-sum taxes. The $20 government deficit is financed by borrowing $20, i.e., the government is borrowing the additional $20 saved by consumers.

**8.10.** Figure 8-10 illustrates a closed economy with a full-employment level of output of $800; the MPC equals 0.80, the leakage line is $(S + T)'$, and the injection line is $(I + G)'$.

(a)    Is there an inflationary or recessionary gap?

(b)    What change in government spending is needed to bring output to its full-employment level?

(c)    What happens to the leakage and injection lines as a result of this fiscal action?

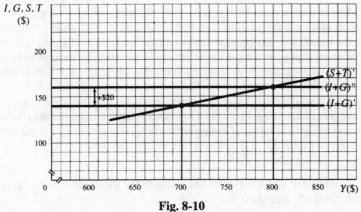

**Fig. 8-10**

(a)    There is a recessionary gap since the $700 equilibrium level of output is below the $800 full-employment level of output.

(b)    Government spending must increase $20 since $\Delta Y = k(\Delta G); \$100 = 5(\Delta G)$; and $\Delta G = \$20$. (The multiplier is 5 since the MPC is 0.80.)

(c)    There is no change in the $(S + T)'$ leakage line. The injections line $(I + G)'$ shifts upward $20 to $(I + G)''$ so that leakages equal injections at the $800 level of output.

**8.11.** What effect will each of the following events have upon the equilibrium level of output?

(a)    An increase in lump-sum taxes, *ceteris paribus*.

(b)    An increase in government spending, *ceteris paribus*,

(c)    An equal increase in government spending and lump-sum taxes, *ceteris paribus*.

(a)    An increase in lump-sum taxes reduces consumer saving and spending. A decrease in consumer spending would result in a lower level of output.

(b)    Increased government spending raises aggregate spending and therefore the level of output.

(c)    The multiplier effect of a change in taxes is less than the multiplier effect of a change in government spending. Since there is an equal increase in lump-sum taxes (which reduces spending) and government spending (which increases spending), there should be a net increase in the level of output.

## FISCAL POLICY MULTIPLIERS

**8.12.** Suppose the equilibrium level of output is $700, consumption is $570, investment is $70, government spending is $60, lump-sum taxes equal $60, and there is no income tax.

- (*a*)  Find the lump-sum tax and expenditure multipliers when the MPC is 0.80.

- (*b*)  What effect does a $10 increase in government spending have upon the equilibrium level of output?

- (*c*)  Find the change in consumption and saving as a result of the $10 increase in government spending.

- (*d*)  How is government paying for its expenditures before and after the $10 increase in government spending?

- (*e*)  Suppose lump-sum taxes are increased $10 to finance the $10 increase in government spending. What effect does an equal increase in government spending and taxes have upon the equilibrium level of output?

- (*a*)  When the MPC is 0.80 and there is no income tax, the tax multiplier is $-4$ and the expenditure multiplier is 5 $[k_t = -\text{MPC}/(1-\text{MPC}), k_t = -0.80/(1-0.80), k_t = -0.80/0.20 = -4]; [k = 1/(1-\text{MPC}), k = 1/(1-0.80), k = 1/0.20 = 5]$.

- (*b*)  The equilibrium level of output increases $50 $(\Delta Y = k(\Delta G); \Delta Y = 5(\$10) = \$50)$.

- (*c*)  Since the MPC is 0.80 and the MPS is 0.20, 80% of the increase in income is consumed, while 20% of the increase in income is saved. Thus, consumption increases $40 while saving increases $10.

- (*d*)  Government expenditures are equal to lump-sum tax revenues before the $10 increase in government spending. With no change in lump-sum tax revenues, government expenditures exceed lump-sum taxes by $10 after the $10 increase in government spending. There is a $10 deficit which is financed by borrowing the additional $10 saved by individuals.

- (*e*)  An increase in lump-sum taxes lowers aggregate spending, whereas an increase in government expenditures raises aggregate spending. Since the lump-sum multiplier is smaller than the expenditures multiplier, the $10 increase in lump-sum taxes and government spending raises the equilibrium level of output $10 $[\Delta Y = k(\Delta G) + k_t(\Delta T); \Delta Y = 5(\$10) + (-4)(\$10) = +\$10]$.

**8.13.** (*a*)  Find the expenditure and lump-sum tax multipliers when there is no income tax and the MPC is (1) 0.50, (2) 0.75, and (3) 0.90.

- (*b*)  What is the relationship of the lump-sum tax and expenditure multiplier?

- (*a*)  The equation for the expenditure multiplier is $k = 1/(1-\text{MPC})$ when there is no income tax. The expenditure multiplier is (1) 2 when the MPC is 0.50, (2) 4 when the MPC is 0.75, and (3) 10 when the MPC is 0.90. The equation for the lump-sum tax multiplier is $k_t = -\text{MPC}(k)$, or $-\text{MPC}/(1-\text{MPC})$ when there is no income tax. The lump-sum tax multiplier is (1) $-1$ when the MPC is 0.50, (2) $-3$ when the MPC is 0.75, and (3) $-9$ when the MPC is 0.90.

- (*b*)  The lump-sum tax multiplier is always smaller than the expenditure multiplier. When there is no income tax, the lump-sum tax multiplier is always negative and one less than the expenditure multiplier.

**8.14.** Suppose there is a $50 recessionary gap, the MPC is 0.80, and there is no income tax.

- (*a*)  Find the necessary change in (1) government spending or (2) lump-sum taxes to bring output to its full-employment level.

- (*b*)  Suppose tax revenues currently equal government expenditures. Can a fiscal action be initiated which brings output to its full-employment level without incurring a deficit, i.e., an action whereby there is an equal change in lump-sum taxes and government spending?

- (*c*)  Why might the fiscal measures in part (*a*) be preferable to the equal change in taxes and government spending in part (*b*)?

(d)   Which fiscal action is preferable: a change in government spending or a change in lump-sum taxes?

(a)   Output must increase $50 to close the recessionary gap.

(1)   Government spending must increase $10 since $k\Delta G = \Delta Y$; $5\Delta G = \$50$; $\Delta G = \$10$.

(2)   Lump-sum taxes must be lowered $12.50 since $k_t\Delta T = \Delta Y$; $-4\Delta T = \$50$; $\Delta T = -\$12.50$.

(b)   A $50 increase in government expenditures and a $50 increase in lump-sum taxes raise output $50: $\Delta Y = k\Delta G + k_t\Delta T$ and thus $\$50 = 5\Delta G + -4\Delta T$; and when $\Delta G$ must equal $\Delta T$, substituting $\Delta G$ for $\Delta T$ we have $\$50 = 5\Delta G + -4\Delta G$ and $\$50 = \Delta G$.

(c)   An equal change in government spending *and* taxes requires a larger expansion in government taxes and expenditures than does a change in government spending *or* taxes, which results in a budget deficit. Assuming that we wish to achieve full employment without an increase in taxes, a tax cut and/or an increase in government spending are the most viable policy alternatives.

(d)   A tax cut returns funds to the private sector and expands consumer spending, while an increase in government spending increases the size of the public sector. There should be increased government spending when there is a recognized need for increased public-sector goods.

**8.15.**  (a)   Find the value of the expenditure multiplier when the MPC is 0.80 and the income tax rate is (1) 0.10, (2) 0.25, and (3) 0.50.

(b)   What happens to the value of the expenditure multiplier when the income tax rate is increased?

(c)   Suppose there is a $100 recessionary gap. What change in government spending is needed to bring output to its full-employment level when the income tax rate is (1) 0.10, (2) 0.25, and (3) 0.50?

(a)   The equation for the expenditure multiplier is $1/[1 - \text{MPC} + (t)\text{MPC}]$ when there is an income tax. The value of the expenditure multiplier is (1) 3.57 when the income tax rate is 0.10, (2) 2.5 when the income tax rate is 0.25, and (3) 1.67 when the income tax rate is 0.50.

(b)   An increase in the income tax rate reduces the value of the expenditure multiplier.

(c)   The required increase in government expenditures is found by solving the equation $\Delta Y = k\Delta G$ for $\Delta G$, substituting $100 for $\Delta Y$. Using the multipliers determined in part (b), we find that government spending must increase (1) $28.01 when the income tax rate is 0.10, (2) $40 when the income tax rate is 0.25, and (3) $59.88 when the income tax ate is 0.50.

## BUILT-IN STABILIZERS

**8.16.**  Why are government's net tax revenues directly related to the level of output?

Net tax revenues, the sum of tax revenues less government transfers, are directly related to the level of output because of income taxes and government transfer programs. Income tax revenues increase with output since individuals and corporations have larger income flows and therefore pay more taxes to government; likewise, income tax revenues fall when there is a decrease in the level of output. Government transfer payments decline as output increases, and rise as output falls. More government assistance is provided when the level of output falls, since more individuals become eligible for unemployment insurance, food stamps, Medicaid, and other welfare payments. Such transfer payments decline as the economy recovers and more individuals obtain gainful employment. Therefore, net tax revenues decrease when output declines and increase when output rises.

**8.17.**  Suppose investment spending decreases, *ceteris paribus*.

(a)   What should happen to the levels of output and of employment?

(b)   What should happen to net tax revenues when the level of output declines and there is a federal program of unemployment insurance for unemployed members of the labor force?

(c)   What should happen to income tax revenues when the output level declines?

(d)   Why are income taxes and unemployment insurance classified as built-in stabilizers?

(a)   A decrease in investment spending shifts the aggregate spending line downward and lowers the equilibrium level of output. Since employment is tied directly to the level of output, a larger number of the labor force will be unemployed.

(b)   Unemployment compensation is paid to members of the labor force when they become unemployed and are unable to find another job. Thus, when a decrease in investment spending causes equilibrium output to fall and unemployment to increase, net tax revenues decline as a result of automatic increases in unemployment insurance transfer payments made to those who have lost their jobs.

(c)   Since output is falling, government receives less income tax revenues.

(d)   A change in output results in an automatic change in tax receipts and transfers which dampen the expanding or contracting effect of spending changes; i.e., some fiscal policy is automatic or built in. The decrease in output results in lower net tax revenues since less income taxes are collected and more transfer payments are made to a larger number of unemployed individuals. Such decreases in net tax revenues are automatic and do not require Congressional approval.

## IMPLEMENTING DISCRETIONARY FISCAL POLICY

**8.18.** (a)   Since tax revenues are impacted by built-in stabilizers, would it be advisable to support a proposal to balance the budget annually?

(b)   Would it be advisable to have a balanced budget over the business cycle?

(a)   A requirement that the federal budget balance annually would aggravate inflationary and recessionary situations. For example, tax revenues automatically fall in a recession due to built-in stabilizers. If government spending were cut at the same time as this decrease in tax revenue, the equal decreases in taxes and government spending would have a negative effect upon an already contracting economy. Similarly, tax revenue increases during an economic expansion would necessitate additional government spending to keep the budget in balance, which could result in excessive aggregate spending and therefore inflation. Given the procyclical nature of net tax revenues, an annually balanced budget would likewise be procyclical and thereby create greater fluctuations in the level of economic activity.

(b)   A proposal to balance the budget over the business cycle overcomes the disadvantages of an annually balanced budget by allowing for deficits during contractions, surpluses during expansions, and balancing the budget over the business cycle. Budget deficits during periods of rising unemployment are countercyclical because the decline in aggregate spending is offset in part by a fall in tax revenues; surpluses during an economic expansion dampen the increase in aggregate spending and thereby reduce inflationary pressures. Balancing the budget over the business cycle, while appealing, may not be practical. Recessionary and inflationary gaps are not necessarily of the same magnitude and duration, so it would be difficult to ensure that tax receipts will equal government expenditures during each complete business cycle.

## *Multiple Choice Questions*

1.   When there is an increase in lump-sum taxes, the consumption function
     (a)   shifts upward by the increase in taxes, *ceteris paribus*,
     (b)   shifts downward by the increase in taxes, *ceteris paribus*,
     (c)   shifts upward by the MPC times the increase in taxes, *ceteris paribus*,
     (d)   shifts downward by the MPC times the increase in taxes, *ceteris paribus*.

2.   Which of the following statements is true?
     (a)   An increase in lump-sum taxes increases personal disposable income, *ceteris paribus*.
     (b)   A decrease in welfare payments increases personal disposable income, *ceteris paribus*.

(c)  An increase in social security payments increases personal disposable income, *ceteris paribus*.

(d)  An increase in the income tax rate increases personal disposable income, *ceteris paribus*.

3.  An increase in government spending, *ceteris paribus*, shifts the aggregate spending line
    (a)  upward by the increase in government spending,
    (b)  downward by the increase in government spending,
    (c)  upward by the increase in government spending times the expenditure multiplier,
    (d)  downward by the increase in government spending times the expenditure multiplier.

4.  In the leakages-injection approach to income determination, an increase in lump-sum taxes, *ceteris paribus*, shifts
    (a)  the investment plus government spending line upward,
    (b)  the investment plus government spending line downward,
    (c)  the saving plus taxes line to the right,
    (d)  the saving plus taxes line to the left.

5.  An inflationary gap can be eliminated by
    (a)  equal increases in net tax revenues and government spending,
    (b)  an increase in government spending and a decrease in lump-sum taxes,
    (c)  equal decreases in net tax revenues and government spending,
    (d)  a decrease in lump-sum taxes.

6.  Suppose the full-employment level of output is $680, the equilibrium level of output is $600, the MPC is 0.80, and there is no income tax. Full-employment output can be achieved by a $16 increase in government spending *or* which of the following changes in net lump-sum tax revenues?
    (a)  A $20 decrease,
    (b)  A $20 increase,
    (c)  A $16 increase,
    (d)  A $16 decrease.

7.  Suppose the full-employment level of output is $680, the equilibrium level of output is $600, the MPC is 0.80, and there is a 0.25 income tax. Full-employment output can be achieved by a
    (a)  $20 increase in government spending,
    (b)  $25 increase in government spending,
    (c)  $30 increase in government spending,
    (d)  $32 increase in government spending.

8.  Which of the following situations results in a $50 increase in the equilibrium level of output when the MPC is 0.80 and there is no income tax?
    (a)  A $10 increase in both net lump-sum tax revenues and in government spending,
    (b)  A $12.50 increase in both net lump-sum tax revenues and in government spending,
    (c)  A $12.50 increase in net lump-sum tax revenues and a $10 increase in government spending,
    (d)  A $12.50 increase in net lump-sum tax revenues and a $20 increase in government spending.

9.  A discretionary fiscal action involves
    (a)  automatic changes in net tax revenues that result from the income tax structure,
    (b)  payment of unemployment insurance,
    (c)  a Congressionally mandated change in the level of government spending or net tax revenues,
    (d)  payment of social security to retired individuals.

10.  Built-in stabilizers are
    (a)  discretionary fiscal actions available to the President,
    (b)  increased government spending on public works projects,

(c) a change in the income tax rate,

(d) changes in net tax revenues that are the result of a change in the level of economic activity.

## *True or False Questions*

11. _____ An increase in the income tax rate shifts the consumption line downward and makes the consumption line more steeply sloped.

12. _____ Fiscal policy refers to any change in government tax revenue and/or in government spending.

13. _____ Net tax revenues fall when a decrease in economic activity results in automatic increases in tax payments.

14. _____ When there is no income tax and the MPC is 0.80, a $10 increase in transfer payments shifts the aggregate spending line upward by $8.

15. _____ When there is no income tax and the MPC is 0.75, a $10 decrease in net tax revenues results in a $30 increase in the equilibrium level of output.

16. _____ An increase in taxes, *ceteris paribus*, shifts the leakage line $(S + M + T)$ rightward, which results in an increase in the equilibrium level of output.

17. _____ A managed change in government spending and/or tax revenue is a discretionary fiscal policy.

18. _____ When the MPC is 0.75 and the income tax rate is 0.20, the lump-sum tax multiplier is $-3$.

19. _____ When the MPC is 0.75 and the income tax rate is 0.20, a $10 increase in government spending, *ceteris paribus*, increases the equilibrium level of output $30.

20. _____ The availability of food stamps is an example of a discretionary fiscal action.

### *Answers to Multiple Choice and True or False Questions*

| | | | |
|---|---|---|---|
| 1. (d) | 6. (a) | 11. (F) | 16. (F) |
| 2. (c) | 7. (d) | 12. (T) | 17. (T) |
| 3. (a) | 8. (d) | 13. (F) | 18. (F) |
| 4. (d) | 9. (c) | 14. (T) | 19. (F) |
| 5. (c) | 10. (d) | 15. (T) | 20. (F) |

# Chapter 9

# Money and Banking

## *Chapter Summary*

1. Money serves three major functions: as a medium of exchange, which allows individuals to work for a money wage rather than for receipt of a commodity; as a measure of value, which provides a common denominator for measuring prices, costs, revenues, and income; and as a store of value, which allows individuals to postpone the spending of current money income and thereby save.

2. Financial instruments other than money may serve as a store of value. The decision to hold one of these alternative financial instruments depends upon the saver's time horizon, the return on alternative financial instruments, and the willingness of savers to assume risk.

3. Depository institutions provide savers with liquid, safe financial instruments which are good stores of value for money. As a result of these substitutes, the Federal Reserve publishes three definitions of money: $M1$, which is a medium-of-exchange definition, and $M2$ and $M3$, which include $M1$ as well as liquid financial instruments issued by deposit intermediaries.

4. The Federal Reserve (the "Fed") controls the quantity of check-writing deposits in the United States by placing a reserve requirement on checking deposits and by controlling the amount of reserves held by banks.

5. The relationship between the maximum amount of check-writing deposits issued by banks ($D_{max}$) and the amount of reserves held by banks ($R$) is given by the equation $D_{max} = dR$, where $d$ equals $1/r$, and $r$ is the reserve requirement on check-writing deposits. Reserves consist of currency held by banks plus deposits at Federal Reserve Banks.

6. The $M1$ money supply depends upon the amount of reserves held by banks, the reserve requirement on check-writing deposits, and the amount of currency held outside the banking system. In equation form, $M1 = m1\ B$; $B$ (the monetary base) is the sum of currency outside banks and reserves held by banks; $m1 = (1 + c)/(r + c)$ where $c$ (the currency ratio) is $C/D$ ($C$ represents currency outside banks; $D$ represents check-writing deposits).

## *Important Terms*

**Asset.** Something which is owned by an individual, business, or government.

**Check-writing deposit.** A bank liability which is payable to the owner upon demand or is transferred to another party by the writing of a check.

**Currency ratio.** The ratio of currency outside banks ($C$) to check-writing deposits ($D$); $c = C/D$.

**Deposit multiplier.** The multiple effect that bank reserves ($R$) have upon check-writing deposits; the deposit multiplier is expressed as $d = D/R$. The maximum value of the deposit multiplier is $1/r$.

**Depository Institutions.** An institution which borrows (accepts as deposit) money and promises to repay the sum borrowed plus interest upon demand or at a specified future date. Examples include commercial banks, savings banks, savings and loan associations, and credit unions.

149

**Excess reserves.**   The amount of reserves held by banks in excess of those that are required.

**Financial instrument.**   The document issued by one party who secures funds from another party who has saved.

**Financial market.**   A market in which newly issued financial instruments transfer current saving to those who wish to borrow or in which previously issued financial instruments are exchanged.

**Liability.**   An amount owed by an individual, a business, or a government.

**Liquid financial instrument.**   An instrument which can be converted into money quickly and with little or no loss of nominal capital value.

**M1.**   The medium-of-exchange definition of money: consists of currency outside banks plus check-writing deposits issued by deposit intermediaries.

**M2.**   An expanded definition of money: consists of $M1$, savings deposits, small time deposits (up to $100,000), non-institution money-market mutual funds, and overnight Eurodollars and RPs.

**M3.**   A more inclusive definition of money: consists of $M2$, large time deposits, institution money-market mutual funds, and term RPs and Eurodollars.

**Monetary base (B).**   The sum of currency outside banks $(C)$ plus reserves held by banks $(R)$; $B = C + R$.

**Money multiplier (m1).**   The multiple effect that reserves have upon the $M1$ money supply; $M1/B = m1$.

**Net worth.**   The total assets of an individual or business less its total liabilities.

**Required reserves.**   The reserves a bank must hold relative to the amount of check-writing deposits the bank has issued.

**Reserves.**   The amount of currency held by banks and bank deposits at Federal Reserve Banks.

# Outline of Chapter 9: Money and Banking

**9.1   The Functions of Money**

**9.2   Financial Instruments and Markets**

**9.3   Depository Institutions**

**9.4   Banks, Check-Writing Deposits, and the M1 Money Supply**

**9.5   Creation and Control of the Check-Writing Deposit Component of the M1 Money Supply**

**9.6   Determinants of the M1 Money Supply**

## 9.1   THE FUNCTIONS OF MONEY

Money serves as a *medium of exchange,* a *measure of value,* and a *store of value.* As a medium of exchange, money is the payment made to economic resources for their services, which the owners of these resources use to purchase goods and services. For example, labor is paid a money wage; individuals use this money to purchase food, clothing, and shelter. Paper currency and check-writing accounts comprise the medium of exchange in most countries. While paper currency issued by the federal government has no intrinsic value, it is accepted for transactions because it has value in exchange. Check-writing deposits are liabilities of banks. Money serves as a measure of value in that it is the common denominator for measuring prices, costs, revenues, and income. For example, a newspaper costs 50¢; Corporation A reports revenues of $100 million; workers at Corporation B earn $9.85 per hour. Money functions as a store of value in that the money received today can be saved and held for expenditures at some future date.

**EXAMPLE 9.1.**   Although coins have metal content, their value as a metal is less than the face value of the coin. Paper currency has no intrinsic value in the United States since it consists of Federal Reserve notes which are non-collateralized liabilities of the Federal Reserve, i.e., the Federal Reserve holds no specified commodity to back up the paper currency that it has issued. U.S. paper currency and coins are therefore fiat (faith) money since their value as a medium of exchange exceeds their nonmonetary value. In the United States, check-writing accounts are deposits at commercial banks, savings banks, savings and loan associations, and credit unions; ownership of funds in these deposit accounts is transferred from one owner to another by the writing of a check.

## 9.2 FINANCIAL INSTRUMENTS AND MARKETS

Savings can be held in financial assets other than money. Since currency and check-writing deposits offer savers little or no interest return, many savers are willing to transfer money balances they do not intend to spend for a period of time into a higher-yielding financial instrument. A *credit* or *debt financial instrument* is one which requires that a borrower make periodic interest payments and repay the amount loaned at the end of a contract period. An *equity financial instrument* gives the saver partial ownership of a firm and a share of its profits. Many financial instruments are marketable and can be sold to another party in a secondary financial market. A financial instrument is liquid when the current owner can quickly convert it into a money balance with a minimal loss of nominal capital value. A saver therefore has a choice of holding a liquid financial instrument or money as a store of value. The portfolio decision of holding money, liquid financial instruments, or illiquid financial instruments depends upon the time horizon of the saver, the return on these alternative financial assets, and the willingness of the saver to assume risk.

**EXAMPLE 9.2.** Savers can lend a money balance to others for a specified period of time. Suppose individuals consume $90 billion of their $100 billion income. The $10 billion saved is recorded in the following T account for Savers by (1) the $10 billion increase in money assets and the $10 billion increase in net worth. Suppose that, in an effort to earn a higher interest return, Savers lend the $10 billion money balance to Borrowers for a one-year period. This $10 billion loan is recorded as (2) a $10 billion decrease in the money assets of Savers and a $10 billion increase in the financial asset "1-year note of Borrowers." Borrowers' T account entries would be (3) a $10 billion increase in money assets and a $10 billion increase in their liabilities noted as "1-year note issued to Savers."

**Savers**

| ΔAssets | | ΔLiabilities & ΔNet Worth | |
|---|---|---|---|
| (1) Money | +$10 billion | (1) Net Worth | +$10 billion |
| (2) Money | −$10 billion | | |
| (2) 1-year note of Borrowers | +$10 billion | | |

**Borrowers**

| ΔAssets | | ΔLiabilities | |
|---|---|---|---|
| (3) Money | +$10 billion | (3) 1-year note issued to Savers | +$10 billion |

**EXAMPLE 9.3.** A financial instrument's liquidity depends upon the current holder's ability to convert it into money quickly with minimal loss of nominal capital value. Suppose Saver A lends $100,000 to Corporation Z for two years; the debt contract stipulates that Corporation Z must pay an annual 6% rate of interest on the $100,000 borrowed and repay the sum borrowed at the end of the second year. Suppose that one year later, Saver A needs cash and wishes to sell Corporation Z's note in the secondary market; assume market interest rates have risen from 6% to 7%. Corporation Z's debt instrument now has one year to maturity. Investors will not pay $100,000 for this debt instrument in the secondary market since the debt contract provides only a 6% interest payment. Saver A, however, may sell this note to Saver B for $99,065.42 since the note's rate of return increases to 7% when priced at $99,065.42. [The $6000 interest payment plus the $934.58 capital gain (difference between the price paid for the note and the sum repaid at maturity) provides Saver B a 7% rate of return, since ($6000 + $934.58)/$99,065.42 = 7%.] Saver A, however, earns a return less than 6% in holding the note for only one year, because the note was sold for less than its purchase price. Although the note sold quickly in the secondary market, Saver A experienced a $934.58 capital loss (a loss of nominal value) as a result of selling the debt instrument prior to maturity. The liquidity of a financial instrument depends upon how large a capital loss a saver might incur when a financial instrument is converted back into money prior to maturity.

### 9.3 DEPOSITORY INSTITUTIONS

Depository institutions (commercial banks, savings banks, savings and loan associations, and credit unions) borrow savers' money balances and lend them to individuals, businesses, or government. By pooling the funds of many small savers and investing in a diversified portfolio of financial instruments, depository institutions reduce the transaction costs and risks associated with lending to a borrowing unit. In the United States, the Federal Deposit Insurance Corporation (FDIC) insures the liabilities of deposit intermediaries. Savers therefore readily hold the liquid, non-check-writing liabilities of these depository institutions since they normally offer a higher interest return than money. Because the liabilities of depository institutions are liquid and therefore good stores of value, the Federal Reserve presents an $M1$, $M2$, and $M3$ definition of money. The $M1$ definition is a transaction definition and consists of currency and check-writing deposits, while $M2$ and $M3$ add other liquid financial instruments to the $M1$ definition (see Example 9.4). At the end of 1993, the $M1$ money supply totaled $1128.4 billion, while the $M2$ money supply was $3564.5 billion and the $M3$ money supply was $4228.3 billion.

**EXAMPLE 9.4.**

Current measures of the money supply appear in Table 9-1. Savings deposits consist of passbook, statement, and money-market savings accounts at depository institutions. Small denomination time deposits are certificates of deposit (CDs) issued by these same financial intermediaries in amounts less than $100,000. CDs are classified as time deposits since the depositor agrees to keep these funds on deposit for a specified period of time, although the saver can convert a time deposit into an $M1$ balance by incurring an interest penalty. Noninstitution (individual) money-market mutual fund balances are share liabilities issued by investment companies; these liabilities are valued at $1 a share. Some savers keep funds in a money-market mutual fund rather than a savings deposit since this very liquid instrument normally offers a higher interest return. Overnight repurchase agreements (RPs) are large (usually $1 million or more), overnight, collateralized loans between a borrower and a lender; overnight Eurodollars are dollar-denominated deposits outside the United States owned by U.S. residents. Large-denomination time deposits are CDs in excess of $100,000. Term repurchase agreements and Eurodollars are longer than one day but still short term.

### 9.4 BANKS, CHECK-WRITING DEPOSITS, AND THE $M1$ MONEY SUPPLY

When a bank lends, it gives the borrower a check drawn upon itself. An individual receives a check rather than currency when he or she borrows money from a bank since a check is a safer medium of exchange.[1] The Federal Reserve controls the banking system's ability to issue check-writing deposits by imposing a reserve requirement on checking deposits. In the United States, bank reserves consist of currency held by banks and deposits that banks have at Federal Reserve Banks. The reserve requirement ($r$) on check-writing deposits is currently 10% ($r = 0.10$); it requires that a bank hold $1 in reserves for each $10 in checking account liability it has at the close of business. Since banks are privately owned in the United States and are managed to maximize profits, they usually expand loans and issue check-writing deposits when they have more reserves than they are required to hold (Example 9.7). Thus, the Federal Reserve can control the amount of check-writing deposits by controlling the reserves held by banks and by setting the reserve requirement on check-writing deposits.

**EXAMPLE 9.5.** When writing a check, the owner of a checking account instructs the bank to transfer a stipulated dollar amount to a designated payee. Suppose, for example, Individual E writes a check to Retailer G for $50 to pay for an item that he has purchased. When Retailer G deposits this check into her bank and the check clears, the checking deposit balance of Individual E decreases $50, while the checking deposit balance of Retailer G increases $50.

**All Banks**

| ΔAssets | | ΔLiabilities |
|---|---|---|
| | Checking deposit of Individual E | −$50 |
| | Checking deposit of Retailer G | +$50 |

---

[1]Currency is a less safe instrument in that it is a bearer instrument— the current holder of currency is the current owner. A check, on the other hand, is payee-specific; a change in ownership of a checking account balance can occur only when the current owner directs the bank to transfer a specified dollar amount to the named payee.

**Table 9-1   The U.S. M1, M2, M3 Money Supply, December 1993**
**(Billions of Dollars)**

| | |
|---|---:|
| **M1** | **1128.4** |
| Currency outside banks | 321.3 |
| Check-writing deposits | 807.1 |
| **M2** | **3564.5** |
| M1 | 1128.4 |
| Savings deposits plus money-market deposit accounts | 1215.5 |
| Small time deposits | 784.7 |
| Overnight RPs and Eurodollars | 86.0 |
| Noninstitution money-market mutual funds | 349.9 |
| **M3** | **4228.3** |
| M2 | 3564.5 |
| Large time deposits | 338.8 |
| Institution money-market mutual funds | 197.0 |
| Term RPs and Eurodollars | 128.0 |

SOURCE: *Federal Reserve Bulletin*

**EXAMPLE 9.6.** Banks issue checks when they make a loan. Suppose Corporation B applies for a $500,000 loan from First Bank. After approval of the loan, First Bank issues Corporation B a $500,000 check. These transactions are recorded in the T account below.

**First Bank**

| ΔAssets | | | ΔLiabilities |
|---|---|---|---|
| Loan to Corporation B | +$500,000 | Checking Deposit | +$500,000 |

**Corporation B**

| ΔAssets | | | ΔLiabilities |
|---|---|---|---|
| Check | +$500,000 | Amount owed to First Bank | +$500,000 |

**EXAMPLE 9.7.** Suppose Bank A has the assets, liabilities, and net worth listed in the balance sheet below. (An asset is something a bank owns; a liability is something it owes; and net worth is the sum of assets minus liabilities.) The reserves of Bank A total $10,000, which is the sum of currency plus deposits at the Federal Reserve. When the reserve requirement is 10%, Bank A must hold $8000 in reserves since its checking deposit liabilities total $80,000. Bank A has excess reserves of $2000 since it holds more reserves ($10,000) than it is required to hold ($8000). Bank A is therefore in a position to make more loans and issue additional check-writing deposits.

**Bank A**

| Assets | | Liabilities + Net Worth | |
|---|---:|---|---:|
| Currency | $ 1,000 | Check-writing Deposits | $80,000 |
| Deposits at the Fed | 9,000 | Net Worth | 10,000 |
| Loans | 80,000 | | |

**EXAMPLE 9.8.** In Example 9.7, Bank A has excess reserves of $2000 and therefore is able to lend and create additional check-writing deposits. Suppose Individual B is approved for a $500 loan by a lending officer at Bank A. In making the loan to B, Bank A's loans and check-writing deposits both increase $500 as recorded in the T account below. Bank A's required reserves increase $50 (10% of $500), and its excess reserves are now $1950 rather than $2000.

**Bank A**

| ΔAssets | | | ΔLiabilities + ΔNet Worth |
|---|---|---|---|
| Loans | +$500 | Check-writing Deposits | +$500 |

## 9.5 CREATION AND CONTROL OF THE CHECK-WRITING DEPOSIT COMPONENT OF THE $M1$ MONEY SUPPLY

Banks are privately owned, profit-seeking financial institutions which usually expand their asset portfolio and issue check-writing deposits as long as there are excess reserves in the banking system. Even when a bank has no excess reserves, it can lend and create new checking deposits if it is able to borrow the excess reserves of other banks. With banks behaving in this manner, there is a tendency for the excess reserves of the banking system to approximate zero and for the combined sum of check-writing deposits to be a multiple of the amount of reserves held by all banks. When excess reserves for the combined banking system equal zero, the relationship of check-writing deposits ($D$) and reserves ($R$) can be presented as $D_{max} = dR$, where $d$, the check-writing deposit multiplier, equals $1/r$. It therefore follows that a central bank (e.g., the Federal Reserve in the United States) can control the maximum amount of check-writing deposits by controlling the amount of reserves held by banks and by setting the reserve requirement on checking deposits.

**EXAMPLE 9.9.**   Suppose Bank Two has no excess reserves but wants to make a \$100,000 loan to Corporation Z. As shown in the following T accounts: (1) Bank Two can make the \$100,000 loan to Corporation Z if (2) it purchases reserves of \$10,000 (noted as "fed funds purchased from other banks") to meet the 10% reserve requirement for an expanded \$100,000 check-writing deposit liability.

Bank Two

| $\Delta$Assets | | | $\Delta$Liabilities + $\Delta$Net Worth | |
|---|---|---|---|---|
| (1) | Loan to Corporation Z | +\$100,000 | Checking Deposit of Corporation Z | +\$100,000 |
| (2) | Reserves | +\$10,000 | Fed funds purchased from other banks | +\$10,000 |

Other Banks

| $\Delta$Assets | | | $\Delta$Liabilities + $\Delta$Net Worth |
|---|---|---|---|
| (2) | Reserves | −\$10,000 | |
| | Fed funds sold to Bank Two | +\$10,000 | |

**EXAMPLE 9.10.**   Suppose the reserve requirement on check-writing deposits is 0.10 and reserves held by all banks total \$500,000. The maximum amount of check-writing deposits for the banking system is \$5,000,000. [$D_{max} = dR$; $d = 1/r$; $d = 1/0.10$; $d = 10$; since $R = \$500,000$, $D_{max} = (10)\$500,000 = \$5,000,000$.]

## 9.6 DETERMINANTS OF THE $M1$ MONEY SUPPLY

The $M1$ money supply consists of currency outside banks ($C$) plus check-writing deposits ($D$). The sum of $C$ and $D$ can also be presented as the product of an $m1$ money multiplier times the monetary base $B$, where $B$ is the sum of currency outside banks plus reserves held by all banks. Thus, $M1 = C + D$ or $M1 = m1(B)$. The $m1$ money multiplier equals $(1 + c)/(r + c)$, where $r$ is the reserve requirement on check-writing deposits, and $c$, the currency ratio, is the ratio of currency outside banks to check-writing deposits ($c = C/D$). The $M1$ money supply, at any point in time, depends upon the amount of reserves ($R$) held by banks, the reserve requirement set by the central bank, and the currency preferences of the private sector.

**EXAMPLE 9.11.**   Suppose currency outside banks is \$200, reserves held by banks total \$100, the currency ratio is 0.20, and the reserve requirement on check-writing deposits is 10% ($r = 0.10$). The $M1$ money supply is \$1200 when banks hold no excess reserves. This sum is found by adding $D_{max}$, where $D_{max} = 10(\$100) = \$1000$, and $C = \$200$. The \$1200 $M1$ money supply is also found by the formula $M1 = m1(B)$. The monetary base ($B$) is \$300—the sum of currency outside banks (\$200) plus reserves held by banks (\$100). The $m1$ money multiplier is 4 when the currency ratio is 0.20, since $m1 = (1 + c)/(r + c)$; $m1 = (1 + 0.20)/(0.10 + 0.20)$; $m1 = 4$. Thus, $M1 = 4(\$300)$; $M1 = \$1200$.

# Solved Problems

## THE FUNCTIONS OF MONEY

**9.1.** (a)   How does the use of money promote efficient production and help allocate good and services?

(b)   Explain the importance of money's standard of value function to an economy.

(a)   Producers use money rather than commodities to pay for the services of economic resources. Owners of economic resources are thereby free to seek employment that maximizes their money income rather than employment that provides payment in specific commodities. This promotes the efficient use of limited economic resources. The use of money also avoids the complexities and inefficiencies of barter; the worker who receives money is free to decide which goods and services to buy, whereas the worker who receives a commodity as compensation must find other individuals to barter with to obtain desired goods and services. In addition, workers paid in money have the freedom to use their money balances to buy goods or services now or at some future date.

(b)   The physical sciences require units of measurement to relate and understand physical phenomena, e.g., speeds of sound and light, the weight and size of objects, the nutrients and calories in food. Money provides a measure of the worth of economic goods and services. It also facilitates the decision of when and how much a businessperson should produce.

**9.2.** (a)   Explain money's store-of-value function.

(b)   Is money a unique store of value or can other financial assets serve as stores of value?

(c)   What is the difference between money and other financial assets as stores of value?

(a)   Money is generalized purchasing power; it is accepted as payment for goods and services. As a store of value, money allows an individual to save and therefore postpone spending; in holding money, the saver has generalized purchasing power which does not lose its nominal value. (No loss of nominal value means that the 25-cent coin you have today will still be a 25-cent coin one year from now; this should not be confused with real value, since the 25-cent coin today can lose purchasing power and have a real value less than 25 cents one year from now due to an increase in the price level.)

(b)   Financial assets, such as time and savings deposits at deposit institutions, have a fixed nominal value and also represent generalized purchasing power. Currency and check-writing deposits are therefore not unique stores of value since other financial assets also have a fixed nominal value over time.

(c)   Financial assets other than currency and check-writing deposits cannot be used for transactions, i.e., they are not a medium of exchange. To spend funds deposited in a savings deposit, an individual must convert the amount of funds wanted into currency or a checking account to make payment.

**9.3.** What is

(a)   a monetary standard?

(b)   a commodity standard?

(c)   an inconvertible paper standard?

(a)   A *monetary standard* is established by the accepted laws, practices, and customs that define money in an economy. That is, a monetary standard is what a country decides to use as money. It could be paper currency, gold, bricks, or anything else accepted as the medium of exchange.

(b)   With a *commodity standard,* the monetary unit is defined in terms of a specific commodity. In most commodity standards, paper currency usually circulates as money, but it can be converted into a specific commodity at a quoted price. For example, if the United States adopted a gold standard and defined the dollar as 24 grains of gold, holders of paper dollars could convert each paper dollar into 24 grains of gold. When a country adopts a commodity standard, the money supply depends upon the defined commodity content of the paper currency, the available quantity of that commodity, and the commercial use of the commodity.

(c)   When there is an *inconvertible paper standard,* there is no government commitment to convert the monetary unit into a specified commodity at a fixed price. An inconvertible paper standard is usually composed of promissory notes issued by the government (currency) and/or bank-issued checking accounts.

Discretionary management of the money supply is possible with an inconvertible paper standard since there is no physical (commodity) limit to the creation of money.

**9.4.**    (a)    Why are check-writing deposits included in the definition of money?

(b)    Is there backing for coins, paper currency, and check-writing deposits?

(c)    How can money have value without commodity backing?

(a)    In most cases, one can pay for the purchase of a good or service with cash or by writing a check. Since checks are accepted as payment, they are classified as money along with coins and paper currency.

(b)    In the United States, coins, paper currency, and check-writing deposits have no specific commodity backing. While coins have a metallic content, the market value of the coined metal is considerably less than the face (monetary) value of the coin. Paper currency is issued by the Federal Reserve and has no commodity backing, while check-writing deposits are noncollateralized liabilities of deposit institutions.

(c)    Anything has value when its supply is limited and demand is virtually unlimited. The basis of value for an inconvertible paper standard (coins, paper currency, and check-writing deposits) is that government can and is willing to limit its supply, economic units are willing to receive it in payment for services, and spending units can use it to obtain goods and services.

## FINANCIAL INSTRUMENTS AND MARKETS

**9.5.**    (a)    What is a financial instrument?

(b)    What are debt and equity financial instruments?

(a)    A *financial instrument* is a legally binding document issued by an individual, a business, or a government in exchange for a money balance. For example, Joe gives Larry a note (financial instrument) promising to repay the $10 that he borrowed.

(b)    A *debt financial instrument* is a contract between a borrower and a lender which specifies the amount that the borrower must repay, the interest to be paid on the sum borrowed, the dates of interest payments, and the date for repayment of principal. While also involving the transfer of funds, an *equity financial instrument* does not contractually require repayment of the amount of money transferred, nor does it require a specific interest payment. Rather, the saver receives a financial instrument which provides partial ownership and control of the firm and a promise to share in the firm's profits.

**9.6.**    Record the following transactions in T accounts for Individual A and Individual B:

(a)    Individual B borrows $100 from Individual A and issues a promissory note to A agreeing to repay the $100 borrowed plus $6 interest at the end of six months;

(b)    B pays A the sum borrowed plus interest at the end of six months.

### Individual A

| ΔAssets | | | ΔLiabilities |
|---|---|---|---|
| (a) | Money | −$100 | |
| | Promissory note | +$100 | |
| (b) | Promissory note plus interest | −$106 | |
| | Money | +$106 | |

### Individual B

| ΔAssets | | ΔLiabilities | |
|---|---|---|---|
| (a) | Money | +$100 | Promissory note | +$100 |
| (b) | Money | −$106 | Promissory note plus interest | −$106 |

**9.7.** (a)  When is a financial instrument liquid?

(b)  What are near monies?

(a)  A financial instrument is liquid when it can be quickly converted into the medium of exchange with little or no loss of original nominal value. A savings deposit is liquid since a financial institution promises to repay the depositor the sum originally deposited. An equity financial instrument (e.g., shares of AT&T) is not considered liquid; while the stock can be readily sold on the New York Stock Exchange, it is illiquid in that the investor may sell the stock at a price lower than the original purchase price—i.e., there is possible loss of nominal value.

(b)  *Near monies* are financial assets that cannot be used as a medium of exchange but are close substitutes for money since they are liquid. A savings deposit is obviously a very close substitute for money since a bank promises to repay the nominal sum deposited plus interest.

## DEPOSITORY INSTITUTIONS

**9.8.** (a)  What is a financial intermediary?

(b)  What is the difference between a depository institution and a nondeposit financial intermediary?

(a)  A *financial intermediary* is an institution that issues a financial claim to the saver upon the receipt of funds; funds received from the saver are then invested in financial instruments. Such financial institutions facilitate the flow of saving to real investment. There is a wide array of financial intermediaries, including commercial banks, savings banks, savings and loan associations, credit unions, life insurance companies, and investment companies.

(b)  A *depository institution* promises to repay the funds received on demand (checking deposits and most savings deposits) or at a future contractual date (a certificate of deposit) and to pay interest on the sum deposited. Funds at a depository institution in most instances are insured by FDIC (the Federal Deposit Insurance Corporation). A *nondeposit financial intermediary* makes the saving function ancillary to other services provided to the saver (as do life insurance companies) or provides portfolio management services and thereby passes the risk associated with financial instruments back to the saver (as do bond and stock mutual funds).

**9.9.** (a)  Using T accounts, show the transaction whereby a savings bank has an inflow of funds into savings deposits and then uses these funds to make a residential mortgage loan.

(b)  What is the importance of depository institutions to the economic process?

(a)  In the T account below, individuals deposit funds into their savings accounts. This transaction is recorded as follows: (1) individuals transfer funds from a checking deposit balance into a savings deposit account. The bank now has funds it can lend to an individual seeking a residential mortgage loan. In making the loan the savings bank (2) issues a check-writing deposit to the borrower and records the loan as an asset of the bank. Note that the net change on the savings bank T account is Residential mortgage loan, +; and Savings deposit, +.

Savings Bank

| ΔAssets | | | ΔLiabilities |
|---|---|---|---|
| | | (1) Checking deposit of individuals | − |
| | | (1) Savings deposit of individuals | + |
| (2) Residential mortgage loan | + | (2) Checking deposit issued to borrower | + |

(b)  Depository institutions supply a financial claim that is safe and highly liquid (a financial claim that can be quickly converted into money without loss of nominal value). In doing so, they increase the likelihood that savers will lend their saving to a depository institution and thereby provide funding for real investment.

**9.10.** (a)  What is a financial market?

(b)  Distinguish between a money market and a capital market.

(a) A *financial market* is a place where financial instruments are exchanged. In primary financial markets newly issued financial instruments are exchanged for money as money saved during the current period is transferred to those who wish to borrow. There are also secondary financial markets in which existing debt and equity financial instruments are exchanged for money (i.e., in which the current owner of a debt or equity instrument is able to sell the financial claim that it owns to another individual).

(b) The *money market* is a financial market that consists of financial instruments that mature in one year or less. In the *capital market*, the maturity of financial instruments issued or traded exceeds one year.

**9.11.** Why are financial intermediaries essential to the efficient operation of an economy?

An economic system is judged efficient when it achieves maximum use of economic resources and maximum satisfaction of consumer wants. Financial instruments and institutions generate efficiency in the following ways:

(1) The financial system increases consumer satisfaction by facilitating the allocation of spending over time. It allows some units to spend more than their current income (dissave) and allows other spending units to increase their future spending level by earning interest on the money they have saved.

(2) The creation of safe and liquid financial claims by financial intermediaries reduces the likelihood that some savers will hold money balances idle. By rechanneling savings into the circular flow, spending flows are stabilized. This in turn stabilizes employment and economic activity.

(3) Financial instruments encourage savers to lend their saving to those who want to spend more than their current money inflow. A large portion of the funds borrowed from savers is used by business firms to add to the economy's stock of capital. This increases productive capacity.

(4) Since the profit motive guides the operation of financial institutions, money saving is distributed to those capital uses that have the greatest productivity.

**9.12.** Federal Reserve definitions of the money supply are as follows:

$M1$ is the sum of currency outside banks plus check-writing deposits.

$M2$ is the sum of $M1$ plus savings and money-market deposits, small-denomination certificates of deposit (up to \$100,000), overnight repurchase agreements, overnight Eurodollars held by U.S. residents, and noninstitution money-market mutual funds.

$M3$ is the sum of $M2$ plus large-denomination certificates of deposit, term repurchase agreements, term Eurodollars, and institution-only money-market mutual funds.

From the data in Table 9-2, find (a) $M1$, (b) $M2$, and (c) $M3$.

(a)  $M1 = (1) + (2)$
  $M1 = \$60 + \$295.5$
  $M1 = \$355.5$
(b)  $M2 = M1 + (3) + (4) + (5) + (6)$
  $M2 = \$355.5 + \$530.0 + \$280.0 + \$38.0 + \$175.0$
  $M2 = \$1378.5$
(c)  $M3 = M2 + (7) + (8) + (9)$
  $M3 = \$1378.5 + \$340 + \$35 + \$4$
  $M3 = \$1757.5$

## BANKS, CHECK-WRITING DEPOSITS, AND THE $M1$ MONEY SUPPLY

**9.13.** (a) Explain the following terms: *asset, liability, net worth.*

(b) What is a balance sheet?

(c) Suppose a bank's assets and liabilities are as follows: currency = \$7000; loans = \$90,000; investments = \$55,000; other assets = \$19,200; check-writing deposits = \$67,000;

**Table 9-2**
**(Billions of Dollars)**

| | |
|---|---|
| (1) Currency outside banks | 60.0 |
| (2) Check-writing deposits | 295.5 |
| (3) Savings and money-market deposits | 530.0 |
| (4) Small-denomination certificates of deposit | 280.0 |
| (5) Overnight RPs and Eurodollars | 38.0 |
| (6) Noninstitution money-market mutual funds | 175.0 |
| (7) Large-denomination certificates of deposit | 340.0 |
| (8) Institution-only money-market mutual funds | 35.0 |
| (9) Term RPs and Eurodollars | 4.0 |

savings deposits = $60,000; certificates of deposit = $33,500. Which of these items are assets and which are liabilities? What is this bank's net worth?

(d)   T accounts are used in monetary economics to depict the net change in specific accounts on a balance sheet. Use a T account for a bank to depict the following transaction: depositors withdraw $500 in cash from their savings deposits.

(a)   An *asset* is something which is owned. For example, the books, clothes, VCR, etc. you own are your assets. A *liability* is what is owed. Liabilities are debts that must be repaid. For example, your liabilities increase when you take out a student loan to pay college tuition. *Net worth* is the sum of a unit's assets less its liabilities.

(b)   A *balance sheet* is a financial statement which lists the assets, liabilities and net worth for an individual, corporation, or a financial institution.

(c)   The bank's assets consist of currency, loans, investments, and other assets. The bank's liabilities consist of check-writing deposits, savings deposits, and certificates of deposits. Assets total $171,200 ($7000 + $90,000 + $55,000 + $19,200). Liabilities equal $160,500 ($67,000 + $60,000 + $33,500). Net worth equals assets less liabilities; net worth is $10,700 ($171,200 − $160,500).

(d)   The withdrawal of $500 in currency from savings deposits is recorded as follows:

**Bank**

| ΔAssets | | ΔLiabilities | |
|---|---|---|---|
| Currency | −$500 | Savings Deposits | −$500 |

**9.14.**   How does one transfer ownership of a check-writing deposit by writing a check?

In issuing a check, the owner of the check-writing deposit orders the bank to transfer a specified sum to the party named on the face of the check. The recipient of the check presents this order to the bank (with proper identification if the bank requests it) and receives either currency or a credit to its deposit account at that bank.

**9.15.**   Why is a check-writing deposit a safer medium of exchange than currency?

Currency is a bearer instrument (there is no specification of ownership on the instrument), with ownership transferred from one party to another without endorsement. Check-writing deposits are liabilities of a bank; ownership of the deposit is transferred from one party to another by an order from the original owner and endorsement by the recipient of the check. It therefore follows that a check-writing deposit is a safer medium of exchange since a check specifies the party who is to receive payment. Suppose, for example, that an envelope containing a $500 check and $500 in currency is lost. The finder of the envelope can claim ownership of the currency since there is no way of determining the ownership of these funds. But the $500 check must be endorsed by the finder in order to acquire the specified sum; this is impossible if the finder is not the person named on the face of the check.

**9.16.**   (a)   Why does a bank issue a check rather than provide currency when it makes a loan?

(b)   Use T accounts for Individual A and Bank B to record B's $1000 loan to Individual A.

(a) As noted above, a check is a safer medium of exchange than currency and provides a record of the borrower's receipt of funds. In addition, the bank may want to guarantee that the borrower uses the funds for the intended purpose of the loan. For example, when making an automobile loan, the bank normally gives the borrower a check payable to the automobile dealership for the amount of the car loan.

(b) Bank B's loan to Individual A is recorded at follows:

### Individual A

| ΔAssets | | | ΔLiabilities |
|---|---|---|---|
| Check-writing deposit with Bank B | +$1000 | Amount owed Bank B | +$1000 |

### Bank B

| ΔAssets | | | ΔLiabilities |
|---|---|---|---|
| Loan to Individual A | +$1000 | Check-writing deposit of A | +$1000 |

**9.17.** (a) What financial assets does the Federal Reserve designate as bank reserves?

(b) Explain the following: The Federal Reserve has imposed a 0.10 reserve requirement on check-writing deposits.

(c) What are excess reserves?

(d) What restricts a bank's ability to issue check-writing deposits?

(a) Bank reserves are the sum of currency held by banks plus the amount of deposits banks have with Federal Reserve Banks.

(b) A reserve requirement is the ratio of reserves a bank must hold relative to the amount of check-writing deposits it has issued. Thus, when the Fed imposes a 0.10 reserve requirement, a bank's minimum ratio of reserves to check-writing deposits is 0.10. That is, it must hold $1 in reserves for each $10 in check-writing deposit liability.

(c) A bank has excess reserves when it has more reserves than it is required to hold. For example, suppose a bank has check-writing deposit liabilities of $1200, its reserves total $150, and the reserve requirement is 0.10. The bank is required to hold reserves of $120. Since the bank's reserve holdings total $150, it has $30 in excess reserves.

(d) A bank's ability to issue check-writing deposits is limited by the amount of reserves it holds and by the amount of reserves that it can borrow from other banks.

## CREATION AND CONTROL OF THE CHECK-WRITING DEPOSIT COMPONENT OF THE $M1$ MONEY SUPPLY

**9.18.** Suppose the banking system has check-writing deposits of $95,000 and bank reserves total $10,000.

(a) What are the banking system's required reserves when the reserve requirement is 10% (i.e., the ratio is 0.10)?

(b) What is the banking system likely to do as a result of your findings in (a)? Why?

(c) What is the maximum amount of check-writing deposits supported by reserves of $10,000 when the reserve requirement is 10%?

(a) The amount of the banking system's required reserves is $9500, which is found by multiplying the reserve ratio (0.10) times the amount of check-writing deposits ($95,000).

(b) The banking system is likely to make more loans and issue more check-writing deposits. Excess reserves provide no interest return; and the only way the banking system can make this nonearning asset provide an interest return is by expanding loans and issuing more check-writing deposits.

(c) There are no excess reserves in the banking system when check-writing deposits total $100,000. Therefore, the maximum amount of check-writing deposits ($D_{max}$) is $100,000.

**9.19.** Suppose Bank Two has excess reserves of $1000. Bank Two has the option of making additional loans to its customers or selling its excess reserves in the federal funds ("fed funds") market.

    (*a*)  What is the fed funds market?

    (*b*)  Which of these two options might Bank Two pursue?

    (*a*)  The fed funds market is a financial market in which one bank lends excess reserves to another bank. Thus, a bank that has excess reserves can lend them to a bank that has a reserve deficiency.

    (*b*)  Lending to one's customers provides a bank with a higher interest return than lending excess reserves to another bank. Lending to one's customers is therefore the most profitable alternative for Bank Two. Bank Two may lend its excess reserves in the fed funds market if it has insufficient loan demand or if it expects to have excess reserves for only a short period of time.

**9.20.** (*a*)  Find the check-writing deposit multiplier ($d$) when the reserve requirement ($r$) is (1) 0.05, (2) 0.10, (3) 0.20, and (4) 0.25.

    (*b*)  Find the maximum change in check-writing deposits when reserves for the banking system increase $100 and the reserve requirement is (1) 0.05, (2) 0.10, (3) 0.20, and (4) 0.25.

    (*c*)  Reserves are often called high-powered money. How "high-powered" is a change in bank reserves?

    (*a*)  $d = 1/r$. When $r = 0.05$, $d = 1/0.05 = 20$. (2) $d = 10$ when $r = 0.10$. (3) $d = 5$ when $r = 0.20$. (4) $d = 4$ when $r = 0.25$.

    (*b*)  The maximum change in check-writing deposits is $\Delta D_{max} = d\,\Delta R$, where $d$ is the deposit multiplier and $\Delta R$ is the change in bank reserves. (1) When $r = 0.05$ and $\Delta R = \$100$, $\Delta D_{max} = 20(\$100) = \$2000$. (2) When $r = 0.10$ and $\Delta R = \$100$, $\Delta D_{max} = 10(\$100) = \$1000$. (3) When $r = 0.20$ and $\Delta R = \$100$, $\Delta D_{max} = 5(\$100) = \$500$. (4) When $r = 0.25$ and $\Delta R = \$100$, $\Delta D_{max} = 4(\$100) = \$400$.

    (*c*)  As demonstrated in part (*b*), a change in reserves is "high-powered" because it results in a multiple change in maximum check-writing deposits. Reserve changes have a greater effect upon the amount of check-writing deposits and are more high powered the lower the reserve requirement.

## DETERMINANTS OF THE *M*1 MONEY SUPPLY

**9.21.** Suppose currency outside banks is $20,000, $25,000, and $30,000 when check-writing deposits are $80,000, $100,000, and $120,000, respectively.

    (*a*)  Is there a relationship between the amount of currency held outside banks and the amount of check-writing deposits?

    (*b*)  If the currency and check-writing deposit relationship continues, what amount of currency will be held outside banks when check-writing deposits total $160,000?

    (*c*)  What is a currency ratio?

    (*a*)  Check-writing deposits have a stable 4-to-1 relationship with currency outside banks. Alternatively, we can state that there is a stable relationship of $1 in currency held for each $4 in check-writing deposits.

    (*b*)  Currency holdings should equal $40,000 when check-writing deposits increase to $160,000.

    (*c*)  A currency ratio ($c$) is the ratio of currency outside banks ($C$) to check-writing deposits ($D$); $c = C/D$. The currency ratio in this situation is 0.25.

**9.22.** The monetary base ($B$) is the sum of currency outside banks ($C$) plus the amount of reserves held by banks ($R$), i.e., $B = C + R$. Suppose $C = cD$ and $R = rD$, where $c$ is the currency ratio and $r$ is the reserve requirement on check-writing deposits. Find an equation for the *M*1 money supply.

$$B = C + R$$
since $C = cD$ and $R = rD$ $\quad B = cD + rD$
simplifying $\quad D = B/(r + c)$

$$\text{Since } M1 = C + D \quad M1 = cD + D$$
$$\text{or} \qquad\qquad\qquad M1 = D(1 + c)$$

substituting $D = B/(r + c)$ for $D$, we have

$$M1 = B[(1 + c)/(r + c)]$$

Letting $m1 = (1 + c)/(r + c)$, we have

$$M1 = m1B$$

**9.23.** The money multiplier is $m1 = (1 + c)/(r + c)$.

    (a)   Find the value for the money multiplier when (1) $r = 0.10$ and $c = 0.10$; (2) $r = 0.10$ and $c = 0.05$.

    (b)   What effect does the value of the currency ratio have upon the size of the money multiplier?

    (c)   Use the value of the money multipliers found in part (a) to find the change in the $M1$ money supply when the monetary base increases $100.

    (a)   The money multiplier is 5.5 when $r = 0.10$ and $c = 0.10$. [$m1 = (1 + 0.10)/(0.10 + 0.10)$.] The money multiplier is 7 when $r = 0.10$ and $c = 0.05$.

    (b)   As shown in the calculations in part (a), the size of the money multiplier is inversely related to the value of $c$, i.e., the value of $m1$ increases when $c$ decreases. Such a relationship exists since currency outside banks represents an alternative use of the monetary base; when increasing amounts of currency are held outside banks, less of the monetary base is available to support check-writing deposits.

    (c)   $\Delta M1 = m1\Delta B$. Thus, when $\Delta B = \$100$ and the money multiplier is 5.5, the change in the $M1$ money supply is $550. When $\Delta B = \$100$ and the money multiplier is 7, the $M1$ money supply increases $700.

## *Multiple Choice Questions*

**1.** Money as a measure of value provides
    (a)   its holder with perfect liquidity,
    (b)   a common denominator for measuring value,
    (c)   a mechanism for allocating resources and distributing output,
    (d)   a medium for exchanging final output.

**2.** In the United States, paper currency issued by the Federal Reserve
    (a)   is backed by gold but is not convertible into gold,
    (b)   has no intrinsic value but is backed by gold,
    (c)   has no intrinsic value,
    (d)   has no value in exchange.

**3.** In the United States, the $M1$ money supply consists of
    (a)   paper currency and coins,
    (b)   paper currency, coins, and check-writing deposits,
    (c)   paper currency, coins, check-writing deposits, and savings deposits,
    (d)   paper currency, coins, check-writing deposits, savings deposits, and certificates of deposit.

**4.** Reserve requirements are imposed on banks
    (a)   to control the amount of check-writing deposits in the economy,
    (b)   to regulate bank profits,
    (c)   to encourage the use of check-writing deposits,
    (d)   to discourage the use of check-writing deposits.

5. When the banking system receives $400 in additional reserves and the reserve requirement is 0.20, maximum check-writing deposit expansion is
   (a) $2000,
   (b) $1200,
   (c) $320,
   (d) $80.

6. Which of the following is not a good store of nominal value?
   (a) Checking deposit,
   (b) Savings deposit,
   (c) A 2-year bond,
   (d) A 3-month CD.

7. When a bank makes a loan to a customer, the bank's
   (a) asset account loans increases and its asset account currency decreases,
   (b) asset account loans decreases and its asset account currency increases,
   (c) asset account loans increases and its liability account checking deposit increases,
   (d) asset account loans increases and its liability account checking deposit decreases.

8. A bank's net worth is $2000 when it has
   (a) reserves of $1000, check-writing deposits of $10,000, loans of $19,000, and savings deposits of $8000,
   (b) reserves of $1000, check-writing deposits of $10,000, loans of $19,000, and savings deposits of $12,000,
   (c) reserves of $4000, check-writing deposits of $10,000, loans of $19,000, and savings deposits of $8000,
   (d) reserves of $1000, check-writing deposits of $10,000, loans of $16,000, and savings deposits of $8000.

9. When $c = 0.05$ and $r = 0.20$, a $100 increase in the monetary base will result in a maximum increase in the $M1$ money supply of
   (a) $100,
   (b) $400,
   (c) $420,
   (d) $500.

10. Which of the following financial assets is not included in the $M2$ money supply?
   (a) Savings deposits,
   (b) Large-denomination CDs,
   (c) Check-writing deposits,
   (d) Overnight repurchase agreements (RPs).

## True or False Questions

11. _____ A savings deposit is a medium of exchange.

12. _____ A debt financial instrument promises to repay the amount borrowed plus an interest return.

13. _____ A marketable financial instrument can be traded on a secondary market.

**14.** _____ A marketable financial instrument is liquid since it can be traded on a secondary market.

**15.** _____ A depository institution issues debt and equity financial instruments to its customers.

**16.** _____ The $M2$ definition of money is larger than the $M1$ definition of money.

**17.** _____ The banking system's ability to issue check-writing deposits is limited by the reserve requirement on checking deposits and the amount of reserves held by banks.

**18.** _____ A bank which has no excess reserves can lend and increase its check-writing deposits liability by selling excess reserve in the fed funds market.

**19.** _____ Liabilities of deposit intermediaries are very liquid for those who own them.

**20.** _____ A bank is just meeting its reserve requirement when the reserve requirement is 0.10, reserves total $2000, savings deposits are $10,000, and checking deposits are $10,000.

### Answers to Multiple Choice and True or False Questions

| | | | | | | | |
|---|---|---|---|---|---|---|---|
| **1.** | (b) | **6.** | (c) | **11.** | (F) | **16.** | (T) |
| **2.** | (c) | **7.** | (c) | **12.** | (T) | **17.** | (T) |
| **3.** | (b) | **8.** | (a) | **13.** | (T) | **18.** | (F) |
| **4.** | (a) | **9.** | (c) | **14.** | (F) | **19.** | (T) |
| **5.** | (a) | **10.** | (b) | **15.** | (F) | **20.** | (F) |

# Chapter 10

# The Federal Reserve and the Money Supply

## Chapter Summary

1. The Federal Reserve System consists of 12 Federal Reserve Banks, a Board of Governors, and the Federal Open Market Committee. As the monetary authority for the U.S. economy, the Federal Reserve manages the money supply to promote stable prices, full employment, and economic growth.
2. The Federal Reserve can change the money supply through open-market operations or by altering the reserve requirement on check-writing deposits. The Federal Reserve also lends to banks through the discount window; the discount rate is the rate of interest the Fed charges on such loans. The Federal Reserve relies upon open-market operations to control the supply.
3. Bank reserves increase when the Fed purchases government securities. Banks issue more check-writing accounts when they acquire more reserves; this in turn increases the $M1$ money supply. Given a demand for money, an increase in the $M1$ money supply puts downward pressure on short-term rates of interest.
4. Many large-ticketed purchases by businesses and consumers are financed by borrowing. The Federal Reserve can increase such purchases by increasing the money supply and lowering the cost of credit.
5. The equation of exchange, $MV \equiv$ GDP, is a truism which relates the $M1$ money supply and the velocity of money with the market value of gross domestic product.
6. Quantity theorists use the equation of exchange to link the money supply to the price level. In the flexible version of the quantity theory, the quantity of money is viewed as the most important determinant of spending and the price level over time.

## Important Terms

**Board of Governors of the Federal Reserve System.**  The seven-member policy-making body of the Federal Reserve System.

**Discount rate.**  The rate of interest charged by the Federal Reserve on loans to banks.

**Equation of exchange.**  A tautology specifying that the amount of money spent on goods and services times the velocity of money is equal to the market value of domestic output, i.e., $M \cdot V \equiv$ GDP.

**Federal funds ("fed funds") rate of interest.**  The rate of interest a bank receives when it lends its excess reserves to another bank.

**Federal Open Market Committee.**  The 12-member committee of the Federal Reserve System responsible for the implementation of open-market operations.

**Federal Reserve Bank.**  Twelve regionally located central banks which supervise, regulate, and provide various services to banks.

**Federal Reserve System.**  Consists of twelve Federal Reserve Banks, a Board of Governors, and a Federal Open Market Committee, which manage the money supply and supervise and regulate the banking system.

**Open-market operations.**  The purchase or sale of government securities by the Federal Reserve to increase or decrease bank reserves and therefore the money supply.

**Quantity theory of money.**  An economic theory which contends that there is a close relationship between the quantity of money and the nominal value of gross domestic product.

**Reserve-requirement variation.**   A policy tool available to the Fed to change the money supply. An increase in the reserve requirement, for example, reduces the maximum amount of check-writing accounts banks can issue and thereby decreases the $M1$ money supply.

# Outline of Chapter 10: The Federal Reserve and the Money Supply

    **10.1    The Federal Reserve System**

    **10.2    The Federal Reserve's Monetary Tools**

    **10.3    Open-Market Operations and Short-Term Interest Rates**

    **10.4    Interest Rates and Total Spending**

    **10.5    The Equation of Exchange**

    **10.6    The Quantity Theory of Money**

## 10.1   THE FEDERAL RESERVE SYSTEM

The Federal Reserve System manages the money supply for the United States in order to minimize inflationary pressures and promote economic stability. The Federal Reserve System, frequently referred to as the Fed, consists of 12 Federal Reserve Banks, a Board of Governors, and a Federal Open Market Committee. The Federal Reserve System is considered independent in that its policy directives are not directly influenced by the congressional or executive branches of the federal government.

*Federal Reserve Banks.*   Each of the 12 Federal Banks has its own president, services banks in a specific geographical area, and acts as a central bank for that region. The Federal Reserve Bank of San Francisco, for example, is the central bank for banks located in the states of Washington, Oregon, California, Arizona, Nevada, and Utah. A Federal Reserve Bank clears checks between banks, supervises and regulates banks in its region, performs bank examinations, provides currency to banks, and holds bank reserves. Private individuals and corporations do not deal directly with a Federal Reserve Bank. While each Federal Reserve Bank is owned by banks in its region, the policies of each Federal Reserve Bank are formulated within the Federal Reserve System and not by the owning banks.

*Board of Governors.*   The seven-member Board of Governors is the policy-making body of the Federal Reserve System. Each member of the Board is nominated by the President of the United States and confirmed by the Senate for a 14-year, nonrenewable term. Because appointments to the Board are terminal and last for many years, members of the Board of Governors are free of political considerations in the formulation of monetary policy.

*Federal Open Market Committee (FOMC).*   The 12-member FOMC is responsible for implementing U.S. monetary policy. It establishes directives for open-market operations (described below) which determine the $M1$ money supply. The seven-member Board of Governors and the president of the Federal Reserve Bank of New York are permanent members of the FOMC. The other four members serve for two years and rotate among the presidents of the other 11 Federal Reserve Banks.

## 10.2   THE FEDERAL RESERVE'S MONETARY TOOLS

The $M1$ money supply equation (Chapter 9) is $M1 = m1(B)$, where $B$ consists of currency outside banks ($C$) and bank reserves ($R$) and $m1$ is determined by the currency preferences ($c$) of the private sector and the reserve requirement ($r$) on check-writing deposits. The Federal Reserve supplies the private sector with whatever amount of currency it wants to hold—thus, the currency component of the $M1$ money supply is determined by the private sector. The Federal Reserve regulates the $M1$ money supply by (1) controlling the amount of reserves held by banks and (2) setting the reserve requirement on check-writing deposits. Monetary tools available to the Fed include changes in the reserve requirement, open-market operations which control the amount of reserves held by banks, and adjusting the discount rate which may influence the amount of reserves banks borrow from Federal Reserve Banks.

*Reserve-Requirement Variation.* A decrease in the reserve requirement on check-writing deposits (monetary ease) creates excess reserves and increases the amount of check-writing deposits issued by banks. Similarly, an increase in the reserve requirement (monetary tightness) decreases the check-writing component of $M1$. While reserve-requirement variation is a powerful means of changing the $M1$ money supply, it is used infrequently. Reserve-requirement variation is considered a blunt policy instrument since it equally affects all banks in the economy, which is normally undesirable. Monetary ease or tightness is usually done incrementally over successive days, weeks, and months. Weekly or monthly changes in the reserve requirement are abrupt and would create management problems for the large number of diverse banks that exist in the United States, which in turn would create considerable uncertainty in the short-run about the effect that the change in the reserve requirement would have upon the $M1$ money supply.

Mathcad

**EXAMPLE 10.1.** Suppose the reserve requirement on check-writing deposits is 12%, reserves held by the banking system total $120,000, and check-writing deposits total $1,000,000. In this situation, banks hold no excess reserves. If the Federal Reserve lowered the reserve requirement to 10%, the banking system would then have excess reserves of $20,000. [Required reserves $= r(d) = 0.10(\$1,000,000) = \$100,000$; since reserves held total $120,000, banks have $20,000 of excess reserves.] The maximum increase in check-writing deposits and therefore the $M1$ money supply from this decrease in the reserve requirement is $200,000. The $200,000 increase is found by solving the equation $\Delta D_{max} = r(E)$, where $\Delta D_{max}$ is the maximum change in check-writing deposits and $E$ is the amount of excess reserves held by the banking system as a result of a change in the reserve requirement.

*Open-Market Operations.* Open-market operations consist of the purchase and sale of government securities (debt obligations of the U.S. Treasury) by the Federal Reserve and are implemented by the Federal Reserve Bank of New York from directives issued by the FOMC. When the Federal Reserve purchases government securities, it pays for these bonds by crediting the deposit account banks have at a Federal Reserve Bank. Since reserves include bank deposit balances at the Fed, such security purchases by the Fed increase bank reserves and eventually the amount of check-writing deposits issued by banks. Federal Reserve sales of government bonds reduce bank reserves and check-writing deposits, and thereby the $M1$ money supply. When the banking system holds no excess reserves, $\Delta D_{max} = \Delta R/r$, where $\Delta R$ is the change in reserves held by banks as a result of an open-market operation.

**EXAMPLE 10.2.** Suppose the Federal Reserve Bank of New York purchases government securities valued at $100 from the banking system. The account entries for the $100 purchase are recorded below: (1) government securities owned by banks decrease $100 while government securities owned by Federal Reserve Banks increase $100; (2) Federal Reserve Banks pay for securities purchased by crediting the deposit account of the bank selling the bonds. Thus, the deposit account of banks at Federal Reserve Banks increases $100 while the deposit liability of Federal Reserve Banks to the banking system increases $100. Since $\Delta D_{max} = \Delta R/r$, the $M1$ money supply increases $1000 when the reserve requirement is 10%.

Banking System

| Δ Assets | | Δ Liabilities & Δ Net Worth |
|---|---|---|
| (1)  Government securities | −$100 | |
| (2)  Deposit at Federal Reserve | | |
|     Banks (Reserves) | +$100 | |

Federal Reserve Banks

| Δ Assets | | Δ Liabilities & Δ Net Worth | |
|---|---|---|---|
| (1)  Government securities | +$100 | (2)  Deposits of banks | +$100 |

*The Discount Rate.* A bank may borrow reserves (discount) from a Federal Reserve Bank when it has a reserve deficiency; the rate of interest it pays the Fed is the discount rate. Banks are encouraged to remedy a reserve deficiency by borrowing the excess reserves of other banks in the fed funds market rather than borrow at the Fed. Thus, banks normally correct a reserve deficiency through the fed funds market. However, since the discount rate is normally below the fed funds rate, banks increasingly borrow from the Fed when the difference between the fed funds rate and the discount rate increases. Thus, the Federal Reserve frequently changes the discount rate to keep this differential from becoming excessive. A change in the discount rate generally follows an increase or decrease in the fed funds rate. A discount rate change is newsworthy in that it confirms the direction of movement in the fed funds rate of interest and interest rates in general.

**EXAMPLE 10.3.**    Suppose Bank One is in the Federal Reserve Bank of New York District and has a $1000 reserve deficiency. Bank One can remedy this reserve deficiency by borrowing from the Federal Reserve Bank of New York. In discounting at the Fed, (1) Bank One's reserves, deposited at the Federal Reserve Bank of New York, increase $1000, while Federal Reserve Bank of New York's liabilities, deposits of Bank One, increase $1000; (2) Bank One owes $1000 to the Federal Reserve Bank of New York and Bank One's loan becomes a $1000 asset for the Federal Reserve Bank of New York.

### Bank One

| Δ Assets | | Δ Liabilities & Δ Net Worth | |
|---|---|---|---|
| (1)   Deposit at Federal Reserve | | (2)   Owed to Federal Reserve | |
| Bank of NY | +$1000 | Bank of NY | +$1000 |

### Federal Reserve Bank of NY

| Δ Assets | | Δ Liabilities & Δ Net Worth | |
|---|---|---|---|
| (2)   Discounts (loan to Bank One)  +$1000 | | (1)   Deposit of Bank One | +$1000 |

## 10.3   OPEN-MARKET OPERATIONS AND SHORT-TERM INTEREST RATES

A change in the $M1$ money supply affects the short-term rate of interest when there is no change in the private sector's demand for money. There are numerous reasons why the private sector holds money balances; these reasons can be categorized into types of demand, as follows: (1) a transaction demand, since money is needed to purchase goods and services, to pay employees, etc.; (2) a precautionary demand, since money may be held to meet emergency and unforeseen needs that may arise; (3) a portfolio (asset) demand, since some money balances are held in the expectation of opportunities in the financial markets. When there is a given demand for money, an increase in the $M1$ money supply lowers the short-term nominal rate of interest, *ceteris paribus.*

**EXAMPLE 10.4.**    $L'$ in Fig. 10-1 depicts the demand for money. The amount of money demand is inversely related to the rate of interest since the holder of money forgoes a higher interest return from an alternative financial asset.

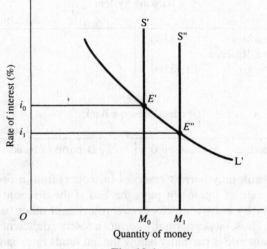

**Fig. 10-1**

When the Federal Reserve purchases government securities in the open market, bank reserves increase as does the $M1$ money supply. Thus, money supply curve S' in Fig. 10-1 shifts rightward to S'' as the $M1$ money supply increases and the short-term rate of interest falls from $i_o$ to $i_1$.

The downward pressure on short-term interest rates due to an increase in the money supply is also evident when we consider the effect that an increase in bank reserves has upon bank lending. In purchasing government securities and supplying more reserves to the banking system, the Federal Reserve increases the supply of excess reserves in the fed funds market. An increased supply of excess reserves puts downward pressure on the fed funds rate. Since lending is more profitable than selling excess reserves to other banks, many banks increase lending when additional reserves flow into the banking system. Banks can encourage more borrowers to apply for bank loans by lowering their lending rates.

## 10.4  INTEREST RATES AND TOTAL SPENDING

Consumer spending on large-ticketed items such as condominiums, houses, and cars is interest-sensitive since individuals are likely to take out loans to pay for major purchases. Business investment—purchases of new buildings and new equipment—is also interest-sensitive; many of these purchases, too, are financed by borrowing. Thus, as depicted in Fig. 10-2, a Federal Reserve increase in the money supply should lower the rate of interest, increase interest-sensitive spending, and result in a higher level of spending and gross domestic product.

$$\uparrow M \longrightarrow \downarrow i \longrightarrow \uparrow \text{total spending} \longrightarrow \uparrow \text{gross domestic product}$$

**Fig. 10-2**

## 10.5  THE EQUATION OF EXCHANGE

The importance of money as a medium of exchange is formalized in the equation of exchange $MV = \text{GDP}$, where $M$ is the $M1$ money supply, $V$ is the velocity of money (the average number of times a unit of money is used during a one-year period to purchase final goods and services), and GDP is the nominal value of final domestic output of goods and services. The nominal value of GDP can also be expressed as $PQ$ in which $P$ is a weighted average of the prices of final output and $Q$ is the quantity (units) of final output. Whether it is presented as $MV = \text{GDP}$ or $MV = PQ$, the equation of exchange is an identity and should be written $MV \equiv PQ$. (The three bars indicate that the equation is a tautology—it is true by definition.)

**EXAMPLE 10.5.**  Suppose the money supply is $312 and final output consists of the following sector spending: consumption, $1080; investment, $240; government spending, $366; and net exports, $7.

Nominal GDP must equal $1693, which is the sum of sector spending. Since the nominal money supply is $312, the velocity of money must be 5.426 since

$$MV = \text{GDP}$$
$$V = \text{GDP}/M$$
$$V = \$1693/\$312 = 5.426$$

and the equation of exchange would appear as

$$MV = \text{GDP}$$
$$\$312(5.426) = \$1693$$

## 10.6  THE QUANTITY THEORY OF MONEY

Quantity theorists have used the equation of exchange to explain price movements over time. In the rigid version of the quantity theory, $V$ and $Q$ are assumed constant; increases in the money supply, therefore, result in proportional increases in the price level (see Problem 10.21). The flexible version of the quantity theory includes the possibility of changes in $V$ and/or $Q$ over time. In a growing economy, real output ($Q$) usually increases from year to year. When velocity changes are predictable, growth in nominal GDP is closely associated with increases in the supply of money (Example 10.6). Since nominal GDP equals $PQ$, quantity theorists suggest that a relatively stable price level is achieved when growth of the money supply is closely tied to growth in the economy's ability to expand output. The flexible version of the quantity theory therefore suggests that money is an important determinant not only of the price level but of spending levels as well.

**EXAMPLE 10.6.** Suppose that the money supply is \$400, $V$ is 4, and nominal GDP is \$1600. A quantity theorist would predict that nominal GDP would increase to \$2016 over a five-year period should the Federal Reserve expand the money supply 20% over this period and should the velocity rise to 4.2 by the fifth year.

$$\text{GDP} = (M + \Delta M)V$$
$$\text{GDP} = \{\$400 + [\$400(0.20)]\}\,4.2$$
$$\text{GDP} = (\$400 + \$80)\,4.2$$
$$\text{GDP} = \$2016$$

# Solved Problems

## THE FEDERAL RESERVE SYSTEM

**10.1.** Describe the Federal Reserve System.

The Federal Reserve System consists of a Board of Governors, a Federal Open Market Committee, and 12 district Federal Reserve Banks with 24 branches throughout the United States. The seven-member Board of Governors, appointed by the President of the United States (with the consent of the Senate), oversees the various central-bank supervisory functions. The 12-member Federal Open Market Committee, which includes the Board of Governors, is responsible for open-market operations which determine the United States money supply. District Federal Reserve Banks (1) act as depositories for financial intermediaries that offer check-writing accounts (commercial banks, savings and loan associations, mutual savings banks, and credits unions), (2) lend to these deposit intermediaries during a period of adverse reserve flows, and (3) issue almost all of the U.S. paper currency.

**10.2.** Most countries have one central bank. Why did the United States create 12 Federal Reserve Banks rather than one?

Political and economic considerations were central to the passage of the 1913 Federal Reserve Act. Federal Reserve Banks were initially created to provide the economy with an elastic currency—banks could borrow currency issued by a Federal Reserve Bank once depositors lost faith in a bank and preferred to hold currency rather than to deposit their money in a bank. In addition to this lender-of-last-resort function, each Federal Reserve Bank was a vehicle for clearing checks and providing general supervision of banks who were members of the Federal Reserve System. One central bank was viewed as an inefficient way of providing such banking services since few banks had branches, and it would be difficult for a Federal Reserve Bank in the east to provide services to a bank in California. In addition, the existence of a largely decentralized government in the early twentieth century provided little support for the creation of a centralized central bank.

**10.3.** Explain the composition and principal duties of

(a) the Board of Governors of the Federal Reserve System and

(b) the Federal Open Market Committee (FOMC).

(a)   The Board of Governors of the Federal Reserve System consists of seven members appointed by the President of the United States and confirmed by the Senate for a 14-year term. No more than one board member may come from a Federal Reserve district. The chairman of the board is appointed by the President and confirmed by the Senate for a four-year term. The Board of Governors has a majority status on the FOMC (and is therefore a major voice in setting U.S. monetary policy); sets bank reserve requirements; has veto power over the discount rate which is set by each district Federal Reserve Bank; regulates international banking in the United States; regulates bank holding companies; and can set margin requirements on stock purchases.

(b)   The Federal Open Market Committee is the principal policy-making unit of the Federal Reserve System since it directs open-market purchases and sales of Treasury securities, which in turn control bank reserves and therefore the $M1$ money supply. Actual purchases and sales of securities are implemented by the Federal Reserve Bank of New York. As a result, the President of the Federal Reserve Bank of New York is a permanent member of the FOMC, as are the members of the Board of Governors. The other four members consist of presidents from the other 11 district Federal Reserve Banks; these members rotate every two years. FOMC meetings are held eight times a year and are attended by the president of each Federal Reserve Bank.

**10.4.**   Why is the Federal Reserve considered "independent"?

The Federal Reserve System was created by Congress; its mission during the second half of the twentieth century is regulation of the monetary system in the public interest. Although it is required to submit an annual report to Congress, the Fed is considered independent, since (1) it has been given a broad mandate, (2) members of the Board of Governors have a 14-year, terminal appointment, (3) the Federal Reserve System generates a profit and does not rely on Congress for its operating revenue, and (4) historically, there has been limited political interference in the Federal Reserve's performance of its public function. Friction with the executive branch of the federal government occurs occasionally since the executive branch formulates U.S. fiscal policy.

## THE FEDERAL RESERVE'S MONETARY TOOLS

**10.5.**   Suppose the banking system holds no excess reserves.

(a)   What is the maximum amount of check-writing deposits issued by the banking system when reserves total $1000 and the reserve requirement is (1) 0.20, (2) 0.16, and (3) 0.10?

(b)   Find the maximum amount of check-writing deposits when the reserve requirement is 0.20 and reserves total (1) $1000, (2) $1250, and (3) $2000.

(c)   Compare the quantity of check-writing deposits when reserves are held constant and the reserve requirement is lowered in (a) with the quantity of check-writing deposits when the amount of reserves held by banks is increased and the reserve requirement remains constant at 0.20 in (b).

(a)   The maximum amount of check-writing deposits is found by solving $D_{max} = R/r$. (1) $D_{max}$ is $5000 ($D_{max} = R/r$; $D_{max} = \$1000/0.20$; $D_{max} = \$5000$); (2) $6250; and (3) $10,000.

(b)   When the reserve requirement remains at 0.20 and bank reserves increase from $1000 to $1250 to $2000, check-writing deposits increase from (1) $5000 to (2) $6250 to (3) $10,000.

(c)   The situations in (a) and (b) show that the Federal Reserve has two alternative ways of bringing about similar increases in the amount of check-writing deposits: by lowering the reserve requirement or by increasing the amount of reserves held by the banking system.

**10.6.**   Assume that the banking system has no excess reserves.

(a)   Find the maximum amount of check-writing deposits when bank reserves total $10,000 and the reserve requirement is (1) 0.10, (2) 0.09, and (3) 0.08.

(b)   Find the change in the reserve requirement needed to increase the maximum amount of check-writing deposits from $100,000 to $102,564 when reserves total $10,000 and the reserve requirement is 0.10.

(a)   When reserves total $10,000, $D_{max}$ is (1) $100,000 when $r = 0.10$; (2) $111,111 when $r = 0.09$; and (3) $125,000 when $r = 0.08$.

(b)   When reserves are held constant, the necessary reserve requirement for a specific level of check-writing deposits is found from the equation $r = R/D_{max}$. Since $R$ is $10,000 and the desired level of $D_{max}$ is $102,564, the reserve requirement must be lowered from 0.10 to 0.0975. [$0.0975 = $10,000/$102,564.$]

**10.7.**  Why doesn't the Federal Reserve change the reserve requirement to bring about changes in the $M1$ money supply?

The Federal Reserve has taken the position that changes in the reserve requirement of less than 0.005 are administratively difficult because of the large number of banks in the United States. A change of 0.005 or more, however, results in a substantial change in excess reserves and has a potentially large, immediate effect on the $M1$ money supply. Thus, reserve-requirement variation is not used and is reserved for an economic environment in which a large change in excess reserves is deemed advisable.

**10.8.**  (a)   Use T accounts for the banking system and the Federal Reserve Banks to record the Federal Reserve's purchase of Treasury securities valued at $10,000 from the banking system.

(b)   When the Federal Reserve purchases securities valued at $10,000, what is the maximum change in the amount of check-writing deposits when the reserve requirement is 0.10?

(c)   Find the necessary open-market purchase or sale of government securities when the reserve requirement is 0.10 and the Federal Reserve wants to increase the $M1$ money supply (1) $1000 and (2) $2500.

(d)   Why are open-market operations the preferred mechanism for changing the money supply?

(e)   Are open-market operations used in all countries to change the money supply?

(a)   Federal Reserve purchase of Treasury securities valued at $10,000 are recorded in the T accounts below.

Federal Reserve Banks

| Δ Assets | | Δ Liabilities | |
|---|---|---|---|
| Treasury securities | +$10,000 | Deposit of banks | +$10,000 |

Banking System

| Δ Assets | | Δ Liabilities |
|---|---|---|
| Treasury securities | −$10,000 | |
| Deposit at Federal Reserve Banks | +$10,000 | |

(b)   $\Delta D_{max}$ is $100,000 when the Federal Reserve purchases securities valued at $10,000 since bank reserves (the banking system's deposit at Federal Reserve Banks) increase $10,000. ($\Delta D_{max} = \Delta R/r$; $\Delta D_{max} = $10,000/0.10$; $\Delta D_{max} = $100,000$.)

(c)   The Federal Reserve must purchase government securities valued at (1) $100 or (2) $250 to increase the money supply $1000 or $2500 when the reserve requirement is 0.10.

(d)   As the above calculations show, the Federal Reserve can bring about large or very small changes in the $M1$ supply by buying or selling government securities.

(e)   Open-market operations are not used by many countries as the principal tool of monetary policy. There *must* be a very large, active market in government securities to use open market operations, and such a financial market does not exist in many developing countries.

**10.9.**  What happens to bank reserves when a bank discounts (borrows) at a Federal Reserve Bank?

As shown in the T account below, a bank's deposit at a Federal Reserve Bank increases when a bank borrows from the Fed. Since reserves consist of currency held by banks and bank deposits at the Fed, reserves increase when a bank borrows from the Fed.

Banking System

| Δ Assets | | Δ Liabilities | |
|---|---|---|---|
| Deposit at Federal Reserve Bank | + | Loan from Federal Reserve Bank | + |

Federal Reserve Bank

| Δ Assets | | Δ Liabilities | |
|---|---|---|---|
| Loan to banking system | + | Deposit of banking system | + |

**10.10.** (*a*)  Explain the relationship between the discount rate and short-term rates of interest.

(*b*)  Do Federal Reserve Banks control the amount of discounting by banks?

(*c*)  Do banks have alternatives to borrowing reserves (discounting) from Federal Reserve Banks?

(*a*)  The Federal Reserve normally keeps the discount rate below short-term rates of interest. While market short-term rates change and reflect changes in the supply and demand for funds, the discount rate is changed infrequently. When the Federal Reserve does change the discount rate, it does so to bring the discount rate into conformity with market short-term rates.

(*b*)  Discounting is at the discretion of the banks. The Federal Reserve does exercise some control over the volume of discounting by its insistence that discounting is "a privilege and not a right." Thus, banks may be discouraged from borrowing from Federal Reserve Banks when they have a reserve deficiency.

(*c*)  When a bank is short of reserves, it may borrow the excess reserves of other banks, sell short-term securities that it owns, or elect not to renew loans that are maturing.

**10.11.**  What can one infer from a change in the discount rate?

Since the discount rate is normally below short-term interest rates and the availability of discounting is a privilege and not a right, changes in the discount rate should not affect a bank's willingness to borrow from the Federal Reserve. Banks are more likely to borrow from the Federal Reserve, though, when the differential between the discount rate and other short-term rates increases. Thus, the amount of discounting banks do with a Federal Reserve Bank can be influenced by a discount rate change. More important, however, is the effect that a discount rate change has upon interest rate expectations. The discount rate normally follows market short-term rates. Hence, when a discount rate change is made it confirms that rates are unlikely to reverse direction. For example, when the Federal Reserve raises the discount rate to conform to rising market rates, opinion is reinforced that interest rates will remain at the higher level.

## OPEN-MARKET OPERATIONS AND SHORT-TERM INTEREST RATES

**10.12.** (*a*)  Why is there a transaction, a precautionary, and a portfolio demand for money?

(*b*)  Why is the demand for money inversely related to the rate of interest?

(*a*)  There is a *transaction demand* for money since money expenditures frequently do not coincide with the receipt of money income. Individuals and businesses receive money balances periodically—weekly, bi-weekly, or monthly; money expenditures, on the other hand, are more continuous. Thus, money balances earned must be budgeted over extended periods of time, resulting in a transaction demand for money. There is a *precautionary demand* for money because of uncertainty about the actual receipt and expenditure of income. Hence, an individual holds a money balance to meet unexpected expenditures or to make expenditures when normal income flows are interrupted. Money may also be held in a portfolio for purposes of liquidity *(portfolio demand)*, although money balances provide no (or low) interest return. Most financial assets other than money are inferior stores of value, i.e., their capital value decreases when the rate of interest increases since the market price of debt instruments falls as the level of interest rates rises. When interest rates are expected to rise and the anticipated decrease in the price of a financial asset might exceed the instrument's interest payment, investors are likely to increase their money holdings to protect the value of their portfolios.

(*b*)  Money provides a zero or a low-interest return. Thus, as interest rates rise, the opportunity cost of holding money increases, i.e., a larger interest return is forgone by holding money rather than a nonmonetary financial asset. It therefore follows that smaller money balances are held when the rate of return on alternative financial assets is higher; i.e., the demand for money is inversely related to the rate of interest.

**10.13.** Figure 10-3 presents the supply and demand for money. Suppose the demand for money is initially L'; the supply of money is initially S'; and the rate of interest is $i_1$. Explain what happens to the rate of interest when an increase in the money supply shifts the money supply curve from S' to S".

When the money supply increases from S' to S", the quantity of money supplied at interest rate $i_1$ ($M_2$) exceeds the quantity of money demanded ($M_1$). This excess supply of money puts downward pressure upon the rate of interest, and the rate of interest falls to $i_2$, where the quantity of money supplied ($M_2$) equals the quantity of money demanded ($M_2$).

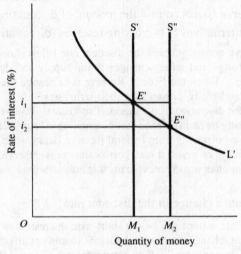

**Fig. 10-3**

**10.14.** Figure 10-4 presents the supply and demand for excess reserves. Suppose the demand for excess reserve is D'; the supply of excess reserve is S'; and the federal funds rate is $i_1$.

(a) What happens to the supply and demand for excess reserves when the Federal Reserve purchases government securities from the banking system and increases the quantity of reserves in the banking system?

(b) What happens to the federal funds rate?

(c) What should happen to bank lending rates?

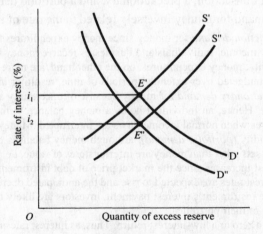

**Fig. 10-4**

(a)  There is an increased supply of excess reserves, noted by the rightward shift of the supply curve from S′ to S″. The demand for excess reserves decreases. Since the Federal Reserve supplies reserves to banks through open-market operations, fewer banks now have a demand for excess reserves and the demand for excess reserves shifts leftward, from D′ to D″.

(b)  The federal funds rate falls from $i_1$ to $i_2$.

(c)  Bank lending rates are likely to decrease. Banks that borrow reserves to lend have a lower funding cost which, in many instances, they pass on to their customers as a lower lending rate. Banks that supply excess reserves to the federal funds market now earn an even lower return in selling their excess reserves and therefore are likely to lower their lending rate in order to make more higher-yielding business and consumer loans.

## INTEREST RATES AND TOTAL SPENDING

**10.15.**  Why are some spending decisions related to the rate of interest?

Many individuals take out installment loans when they buy high-priced items such as cars. The interest rate that must be paid on an installment purchase can substantially increase the total purchase price of the good. For example, suppose Individual A borrows $10,000 for a five-year period to purchase a new car. If the rate of interest on the car loan is 15%, the purchase price of the car essentially increases to $14,273.96 since the borrower must make interest payments of $4273.96 during the five-year period of the loan. The total interest payment over five years is $2748.23 when the five-year installment loan has a 10% rate of interest. The monthly payment on a 5-year, 15%, $10,000 loan is $237.90, while it is only $212.47 when the rate of interest is 10%. Since the increased cost of loan-financed purchases decreases as interest rates decline, more individuals may be able and willing to make loan-financed purchases at lower rates of interest.

**10.16.**  Suppose interest-sensitive spending is represented by I′ in Fig. 10-5.

(a)  Find investment spending when the rate of interest is $i_1$ and $i_2$.

(b)  What happens to the level of investment spending when the Federal Reserve increases bank reserves and the rate of interest falls?

(a)  Investment spending is $I_1$ when the rate of interest is $i_1$ and $I_2$ when the rate of interest is $i_2$.

(b)  Assuming no change in the desire to purchase durable goods, investment spending increases as a result of decreases in the rate of interest.

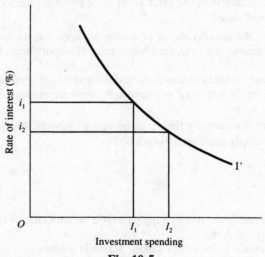

**Fig. 10-5**

## THE EQUATION OF EXCHANGE

**10.17.**  Why is the equation of exchange a tautology?

The left side of the equation ($M1V1$) is composed of the economy's supply of transaction money balances times the average use of these money balances in purchasing the economy's final output of goods and services.

The right side of the equation of exchange represents the nominal value of final domestic output of goods and services, i.e., GDP, the nominal amount received from the sale of final domestic output. Since, *ex post,* the amount spent must equal the amount received, $M1V1$ must always equal GDP.

**10.18.** (*a*)  Find velocity when the money supply is $200 and gross domestic product is $800.

(*b*)  Find nominal GDP when the money supply increases $10 and there is no change in the velocity of money (*V*).

(*c*)  Does the increase in nominal gross domestic product from (*a*) to (*b*) represent an increase in real output or an increase in the price level, i.e., *Q* or *P*?

(*a*)  *V* must equal 4 when *M* = $200 and GDP = $800 since $MV$ = GDP.

(*b*)  Nominal gross domestic product must increase from $800 to $840 when there is no change in the velocity of money (the value of *V* remains at 4) and the money supply increases from $200 to $210.

(*c*)  Nominal GDP equals *PQ*, where *P* is the average price of final output and *Q* is the quantity of output. Since the question does not provide information about the economy's ability to increase output, there is no way to ascertain whether the $40 increase in GDP represents an increase in the average price of output (*P*) and/or an increase in output (*Q*).

**10.19.** Suppose the money supply is $150, nominal GDP is $600, and the velocity of money is 4. Does a velocity of 4 mean that each unit of money is used four times during the year to purchase the economy's final output?

Velocity measures the average use of a given money supply in the same way that an academic grade measures average performance in a course. One usually obtains grades above and below the final grade for the semester. It is therefore probable that some monetary units are exchanged more than four times while others are exchanged less than four times. Velocity, therefore, measures the average use of the total money supply rather than the frequency of use for each monetary unit during the measurement period.

## THE QUANTITY THEORY OF MONEY

**10.20.** (*a*)  Why does the rigid version of the quantity theory of money conclude that there is a proportional relationship between the supply of money and the price level?

(*b*)  Would one expect changes in the price level to be proportional to changes in the money supply over long periods of time?

(*a*)  The rigid version of the quantity theory of money assumes that the velocity of money and output are constant. Given no change in *V* or *Q*, the average price of output *P* must be proportional to changes in the money supply.

(*b*)  The velocity of money is likely to change over time, and full-employment output *Q* increases annually. Therefore, it is unlikely that *M* and *P* will have a proportional relationship over extended periods of time.

**10.21.** Use the rigid version of the quantity theory of money to answer this question. What should happen to *P* when the money supply increases from $100 to

(*a*)  $150,

(*b*)  $200, and

(*c*)  $300?

(*a*)  There is a 50% increase in the money supply ($\Delta M/M$ = $50/$100 = 0.50 = 50%). The average price of output should increase 50%.

(*b*)  There is a 100% increase in the money supply; *P* should double.

(*c*)  There is a 200% increase in the money supply; *P* should triple.

**10.22.** Suppose output is at its full-employment level; government spending increases and the increase is financed by expanding the money supply from $200 to $400.

(*a*)  What should happen to the average price of output?

(b)   What is the cause(s) of increases in the price level for an economy which is at or near full-employment output?

(a)   Provided there is no change in velocity, the average price of output should double since output is at its full-employment level. $P$ would more than double should $V$ increase. $V$ is likely to increase in the short run when prices are rising or are expected to rise. In such a situation, people spend money income more quickly since they lose purchasing power when money is held for any length of time.

(b)   When $Q$ is constant, $V$ and $M$ are the only source of increases in the price level. Historically, velocity has not experienced substantial changes in the short run. Thus, increases in the money supply are the only cause of rapid increases in the price level in the short run.

**10.23.** Suppose the money supply is $250, the average price of output is $4.25, and $Q$ is 400.

(a)   Find nominal GDP and $V$.

(b)   Find $P$ and $Q$ when $V$ is constant and there is a 15% increase in output and a 20% increase in the money supply.

(c)   Find $P$ and $Q$ when $V$ increases to 7 and there is a 15% increase in output and a 20% increase in the money supply.

(d)   Could stable prices (average price of $4.25) be achieved in situations (b) and (c)?

(a)   Nominal GDP equals $PQ$. Given $P = \$4.25$ and $Q = 400$, nominal GDP $= \$1700$. $V = \text{GDP}/M$; $V = \$1700/\$250 = 6.8$.

(b)   A 15% increase in output and a 20% increase in the money supply raises $Q$ from 400 to 460 and $M$ from $250 to $300. With $V$ remaining constant at 6.8, we have

$$PQ = MV$$
$$P(460) = \$300(6.8)$$
$$460P = \$2040$$
$$P = \$4.435$$

The average price of output increases from $4.25 to $4.435.

(c)   When $Q$ increases to 460, $M$ to $300, and $V$ to 7, we have

$$PQ = MV$$
$$P(460) = \$300(7)$$
$$460P = \$2100$$
$$P = \$4.565$$

The average price of output increases from $4.25 to $4.565.

(d)   According to the flexible version of the quantity theory, a stable price level is achieved by tying growth of the money supply to projections of $V$ and $Q$. In situation (b), $V$ is expected to remain constant. $P$ would be unchanged if money supply growth matched that of $Q$, i.e., the money supply increase should be 15% rather than 20%.

In situation (c), $V$ is projected to increase to 7. Holding $P$ constant at 4.25, we find that the money supply should increase from $250 to $279.29 as $Q$ increases from 400 to 460.

$$MV = PQ$$
$$M(7) = \$4.25(460)$$
$$M = \$1955/7$$
$$M = \$279.29$$

## Multiple Choice Questions

1.   Suppose banks hold no excess reserves and reserves total $1200. When the reserve requirement is lowered from 0.12 to 0.10, check-writing deposits

(a)   increase from $1000 to $1200,

    (b)   increase from $10,000 to $12,000,

    (c)   decrease from $1200 to $1000,

    (d)   decrease from $12,000 to $10,000.

2.    When the reserve requirement is 0.10 and the Federal Open Market Committee purchases government securities valued at $1000 from banks, *ceteris paribus,* banks
    (a)   hold excess reserves of $100,
    (b)   hold excess reserve of $1000,
    (c)   increase check-writing deposits by a maximum of $1000,
    (d)   increase check-writing deposits by a maximum of $5000.

3.    A decrease in the Federal Reserve's discount rate lowers the cost of borrowing
    (a)   for banks from the Federal Reserve,
    (b)   for individuals from the Federal Reserve,
    (c)   for individuals from banks,
    (d)   for banks in the fed funds market.

4.    An increase in the discount rate usually occurs when
    (a)   the Federal Reserve no longer is willing to make loans to banks,
    (b)   short-term market rates are due to increase,
    (c)   short-term market rates, such as the fed funds rate, have risen,
    (d)   the Federal Reserve is lowering the reserve requirement.

5.    When the Federal Reserve is expanding the money supply, *ceteris paribus,*
    (a)   bank lending should increase and interest-sensitive spending should decrease,
    (b)   bank lending should decrease and interest-sensitive spending should decrease,
    (c)   bank lending should decrease and interest-sensitive spending should increase,
    (d)   bank lending should increase and interest-sensitive spending should increase.

6.    The velocity of money measures
    (a)   the use of each unit of money in purchasing final output,
    (b)   the average use of money in purchasing final output,
    (c)   the average use of money by consumers in purchasing consumer goods,
    (d)   the average use of money by the business sector.

7.    In the equation of exchange, GDP equals
    (a)   $4000 when $M1$ is $100 and the average use of money is 4,
    (b)   $1000 when $M1$ is $100 and the average use of money is 5,
    (c)   $500 when $M1$ is $100 and the average use of money is 5,
    (d)   $400 when $M1$ is $100 and the average use of money is 2.

8.    In the flexible version of the quantity theory of money,
    (a)   changes in nominal GDP are closely associated with changes in the money supply,
    (b)   changes in $V$ are closely associated with changes in the money supply,
    (c)   changes in the price level are closely associated with changes in the money supply,
    (d)   changes in nominal GDP are proportional to changes in velocity.

9.    If the $M1$ money supply is $400, velocity is 4, and there is a 10% growth in the money supply and a 25% increase in velocity, nominal GDP should increase from
    (a)   $1200 to $1600,
    (b)   $1600 to $1760,
    (c)   $1600 to $2200,
    (d)   $1760 to $2200.

**10.** In the rigid version of the quantity theory of money,
  (*a*)  changes in nominal GDP are proportional to changes in the money supply,
  (*b*)  changes in nominal GDP are proportional to changes in velocity,
  (*c*)  changes in velocity are proportional to changes in the money supply,
  (*d*)  changes in the price level are proportional to changes in the money supply.

# *True or False Questions*

**11.** _____  There are 12 Federal Reserve Banks in the United States.

**12.** _____  The Federal Open Market Committee manages the money supply by changing the reserve requirement on check-writing deposits.

**13.** _____  The Board of Governors of the Federal Reserve System is appointed by the President of the United States for a four-year term.

**14.** _____  An increase in the fed funds rate indicates that the Federal Reserve is discouraging banks from borrowing from the Federal Reserve.

**15.** _____  The maximum increase in check-writing accounts is $100,000, *ceteris paribus*, when the Federal Reserve purchases government securities valued at $10,000 and the reserve requirement is 10%.

**16.** _____  When there is stable demand-for-money curve, a decrease in the $M1$ money supply lowers the short-term nominal rate of interest.

**17.** _____  Bank reserves increase and the fed funds rate decreases when the FOMC directs the Federal Reserve Bank of New York to purchase government securities, *ceteris paribus*.

**18.** _____  A change in the money supply impacts output by affecting interest-sensitive spending.

**19.** _____  The equation of exchange is a tautology.

**20.** _____  In the rigid presentation of the quantity theory of money, an increase in the money supply results in a proportional increase in the price level.

### *Answers to Multiple Choice and True or False Questions*

| | | | |
|---|---|---|---|
| 1. (*b*) | 6. (*b*) | 11. (T) | 16. (F) |
| 2. (*b*) | 7. (*c*) | 12. (F) | 17. (T) |
| 3. (*a*) | 8. (*a*) | 13. (F) | 18. (T) |
| 4. (*c*) | 9. (*c*) | 14. (F) | 19. (T) |
| 5. (*d*) | 10. (*d*) | 15. (T) | 20. (T) |

# Chapter 11

# Monetary and Fiscal Policy

## *Chapter Summary*

1. Monetary and fiscal actions are alternative policy measures for changing the level of aggregate spending. Economists disagree, however, regarding the net effect that these policies have upon equilibrium output.
2. A fiscal stimulus may crowd out private-sector interest-sensitive spending. For example, increased government spending raises both output and the rate of interest. A higher interest rate negatively affects investment spending so that the net increase in equilibrium output is less than $k_e \Delta G$.
3. An increase in the money supply affects output through the rate of interest. The interest rate effect of an increase in the money supply depends upon the interest sensitivity of the demand for money; the effect upon aggregate spending depends upon the interest sensitivity of investment demand. The predictability of an increase in the money supply upon nominal GDP ultimately depends upon the stability of the velocity of money. Monetarists contend that velocity is predictable, whereas Keynesians contend that it is unstable.
4. The net effect of a monetary or fiscal action also depends upon the slope of the aggregate supply curve. When the aggregate supply curve is steeply sloped, an increase in aggregate demand has a larger effect upon the price level than upon real output.
5. Philosophical differences and policy lags have influenced decisions on the implementation of monetary or fiscal policy. Fiscal actions are interventionist policies and are favored by liberal economists; changes in the money supply affect spending through financial markets and are preferred by more conservative economists. While an increase in the money supply is slower in impacting spending levels, it is still the most frequently used policy tool because it can be implemented quickly.

## *Important Terms*

**Crowding out.**   Occurs when increased government spending and/or decreased taxes causes output and the rate of interest to rise, which reduces (crowds out) interest-sensitive investment spending.

**Keynesian.**   An economist who advocates the use of fiscal rather than monetary policy to change aggregate spending.

**Monetarist.**   An economist who contends that money supply changes have a more predictable effect on aggregate spending than do changes in government spending or taxes.

## Outline of Chapter 11: Monetary and Fiscal Policy

180

### 11.4 Monetary and Fiscal Policy in an Aggregate Demand and Aggregate Supply Framework

### 11.5 Monetary Policy or Fiscal Policy

## 11.1 MONETARY AND FISCAL POLICY: A RECAP

The analysis in Chapters 7 through 10 has shown that monetary and fiscal policy are alternative ways of increasing aggregate spending and closing a recessionary gap. For example, when output is below its full-employment level, an increase in the money supply, an increase in government spending, or a decrease in taxes raises aggregate spending and increases equilibrium output.

**EXAMPLE 11.1.**   Suppose $k_e$ is 5, $k_t$ is $-4$, and full-employment output exists when output is $900. Equilibrium output is $800 in Fig. 11-1 for aggregate spending line $(C + I + G + X_n)'$ . Shifting the aggregate spending line upward to $(C + I + G + X_n)''$ closes the $100 recessionary gap and brings the economy to full-employment output. This could be accomplished by a $20 increase in government spending $[\Delta Y = k_e \Delta G; \$100 = 5(\$20)]$, a $25 decrease in lump-sum taxes, or an increase in the money supply which lowers interest rates and increases investment spending $20.

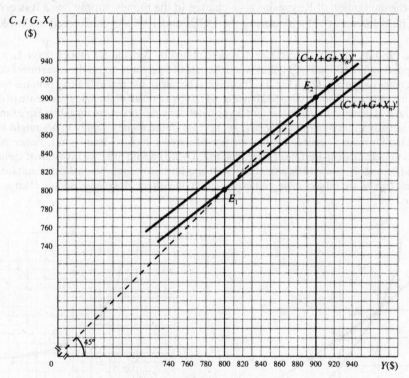

**Fig. 11-1**

## 11.2 FISCAL POLICY AND CROWDING OUT

An expansionary fiscal policy might not result in an increase in equilibrium output exactly equal to $k_e \Delta G$ because of the crowding-out effect. Government spending increases, which raise the level of output, will usually push the rate of interest higher. Private-sector interest-sensitive spending will thereby fall and be crowded out by the fiscal action. Thus, the net increase in equilibrium output due to increased government spending is usually less than $k_e \Delta G$. How much less depends upon the interest sensitivity of the demand for money and the interest sensitivity of investment spending.

**EXAMPLE 11.2.**   Suppose $k_e$ is 5, full-employment output exists when output is $900, and equilibrium output is initially $800. A $20 increase in government spending, *ceteris paribus*, should increase spending $100 and bring output to its full-employment level. But suppose the rate of interest increases as a result of the $20 increase in government

spending and investment spending declines $5. The net effect of the government's fiscal action is then $75 rather than $100, and full employment output is not reached. [The net effect equals $\Delta G(k_e) + \Delta I(k_e)$; the net effect is $75 which is $20(5) - $5(5).] Since policymakers do not know in advance the extent to which there will be crowding out, the effect of a stimulative fiscal policy upon output is uncertain.

## 11.3  PREDICTABILITY OF MONEY SUPPLY CHANGES UPON EQUILIBRIUM OUTPUT

Normally, the rate of interest falls and interest-sensitive spending and equilibrium output increase when the monetary authority increases the money supply. While most economists agree that changes in the money supply impact interest-sensitive spending, there is substantial disagreement about the predictability of the effect. Keynesians have traditionally argued that there is considerable uncertainty about the effect a money supply change has upon the rate of interest and the level of investment (see Example 11.3). Monetarists contend that a change in the money supply has a highly predictable effect upon nominal GDP. The disagreement about the predictability of a money supply change has centered around the velocity of money. In the equation of exchange, $MV$ equals nominal GDP. When the velocity of money is stable—the contention of monetarists—a change in the money supply has a relatively certain effect on nominal GDP. When velocity is variable—the contention of Keynesians—a change in the money supply has a less certain effect upon nominal GDP. The behavior of velocity during the 1970s and 1980s is considered in Problem 11.12.

**EXAMPLE 11.3.** In Fig. 11-2(a), interest rate $i_0$ is determined by demand for money curve $L_1$ and money supply $M_1$. Investment spending is $100 in Fig. 11-2(b) when the rate of interest is $i_0$ and the investment demand curve is $I'$. An increase in the money supply to $M_2$ in Fig. 11-2(a) lowers the rate of interest to $i_2$ along demand for money curve $L_1$. Investment spending increases from $100 to $120 in Fig. 11-2(b) as a result of the $i_0$ to $i_2$ decrease in the rate of interest. Keynesians contend that demand for money and/or investment demand curves are unstable. For example, although the rate of interest is initially $i_0$ for money supply $M_1$, an increase in the money supply to $M_2$ might be associated with a shift in the demand for money curve to $L_2$, and the rate of interest declines from $i_0$ to $i_1$ rather than $i_2$. Should this happen, then the $i_0$ to $i_1$ decrease in the rate of interest in Fig. 11-2(b) would increase investment spending from $100 to $105 rather than $120, and there would be a smaller rise in equilibrium output. When the demand for money and/or the investment demand curves are subject to unpredictable shifts, the effect of a money supply change upon equilibrium output is uncertain.

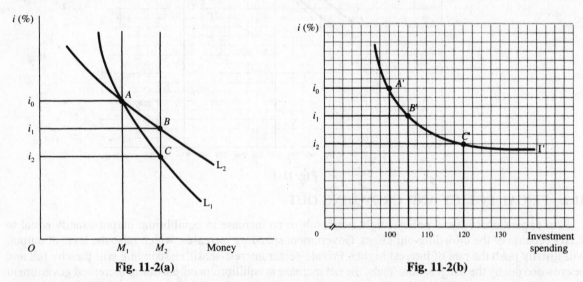

Fig. 11-2(a)                                        Fig. 11-2(b)

**EXAMPLE 11.4.** Suppose nominal GDP is $600 and the money supply is $150. The velocity of money is 4 since GDP/$M$ ($600/$150) = 4.

A monetarist would contend that a $10 increase in the money supply would raise spending $40 and increase nominal output to $640 [$(M + \Delta M)V$ = GDP; ($150 + $10)4 = $640]. [Note: In this example we assume that $V$ is constant. Monetarists recognize that $V$ may change but contend that the change in $V$ is relatively small; therefore the affect of money supply changes upon GDP is highly predictable.]

A Keynesian would maintain that a $10 increase in the money supply could have a smaller or larger effect upon nominal output. For example, a money supply increase that lowers the rate of interest might increase the quantity of money demanded and subsequently lower velocity. Thus, if the $10 increase in the money supply lowers $V$ to 3.9, nominal output would increase from $600 to $624 rather than $640. If the $10 increase in the money supply lowers $V$ to 3.85, then nominal output would increase from $600 to $616. The behavior of velocity—which reflects the interest rate effect from a change in the money supply upon interest-sensitive spending—determines the extent to which a change in the money supply affects output.

## 11.4  MONETARY AND FISCAL POLICY IN AN AGGREGATE DEMAND AND AGGREGATE SUPPLY FRAMEWORK

An aggregate demand curve shows the amount of aggregate spending at different price levels (see Chapter 5). For example, in Fig. 11-3(b), aggregate spending is $800 when the price level is $p_0$ and $900 when the price level is $p_0$ along aggregate demand curve $AD_2$. Equilibrium output is $800 in Fig. 11-3(a) when the aggregate spending line is $(C+I+G+X_n)_1$ for price level $p_0$. With the price level remaining at $p_0$, a monetary or fiscal action which shifts aggregate spending line $(C+I+G+X_n)_1$ upward to $(C+I+G+X_n)_2$ increases equilibrium output to $900. This is depicted in Fig. 11-3(b) as a $100 rightward shift of aggregate demand curve $AD_1$ to $AD_2$ at price level $p_0$. But we find in Fig. 11-3(b) that aggregate demand curve $AD_2$ and positively sloped aggregate supply curve $AS$ intersect at price level $p_1$. Thus, the stimulative monetary or fiscal policy increases equilibrium output to $875 rather than $900 because of a $p_0$ to $p_1$ increase in the price level. Aggregate spending line $(C+I+G+X_n)_2$ in Fig. 11-3(a) therefore shifts downward to $(C+I+G+X_n)_3$ since an increase in the price level reduces consumer, investment, and export spending; the change in equilibrium output is therefore $75 rather than $100.

In an aggregate demand and aggregate supply framework, an economic stimulus is constrained by a possible increase in the price level. (*Note*: Chapters 7 through 10 assumed that there would be no increase in the price level until the economy reached its full-employment level of output. Such a scenario is unlikely to exist in the real world.) It therefore follows that the effect on output of a monetary or fiscal stimulus depends on the slope of the aggregate supply curve. A steeply sloped aggregate supply curve has a smaller

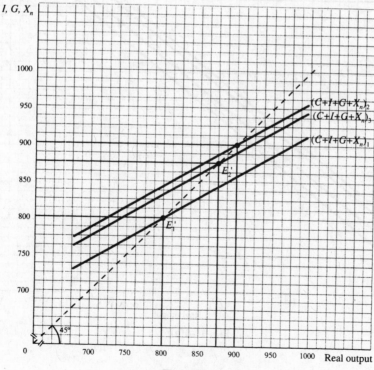

**Fig. 11-3(a)**

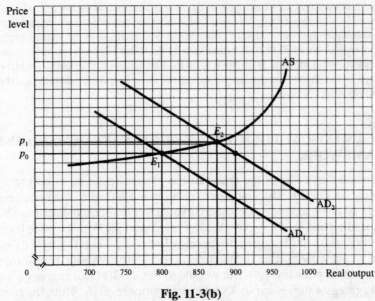

**Fig. 11-3(b)**

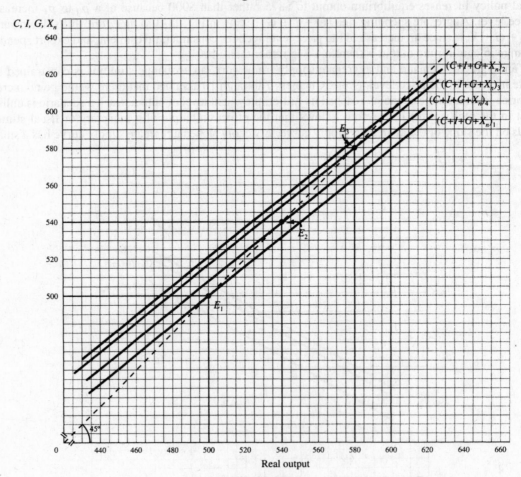

**Fig. 11-4(a)**

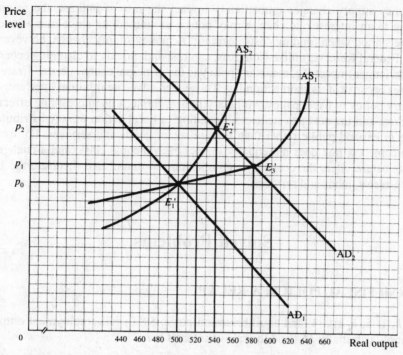

**Fig. 11-4(b)**

effect upon output than a relatively flat one. While the actual steepness of the aggregate supply curve is unknown, it is generally believed that aggregate supply is more steeply sloped the closer output is to its full-employment level.

**EXAMPLE 11.5.**   Suppose the expenditure multiplier ($k_e$) is 5, there is no crowding out, and full-employment output is $600. Equilibrium output is initially $500 in Fig.11-4(a) for aggregate spending line $(C + I + G + X_n)_1$ and in Fig. 11-4(b) for aggregate demand and aggregate supply curves $AD_1$ and $AS_1$. The recessionary gap is $100 since full-employment output is $600; the price level is initially $p_0$ in Fig. 11-4(b) for $AD_1$ and $AS_1$. Since the expenditure multiplier is 5, a $20 increase in government spending should increase output $100 and bring output to its full-employment level ($\Delta Y = k_e \Delta G$). The $20 increase in government spending shifts aggregate spending line $(C + I + G + X_n)_1$ upward to $(C + I + G + X_n)_2$, and equilibrium output increases $100 when the price level remains at $p_0$. This $100 increase in spending is presented in Fig. 11-4(b) by the shift of aggregate demand from $AD_1$ to $AD_2$. Since aggregate supply $AS_1$ is positively sloped, the price level rises from $p_0$ to $p_1$. This increase in the price level decreases private-sector spending, shifting aggregate spending line $(C + I + G + X_n)_2$ downward to $(C + I + G + X_n)_3$; equilibrium output thus increases to $580 rather than to $600. In Fig. 11-4(b), equilibrium output is $580 for curves $AD_2$ and $AS_1$; the price level is $p_1$.

**EXAMPLE 11.6.**   Suppose the aggregate supply curve for the situation in Example 11.5 is $AS_2$ rather than $AS_1$. Fig. 11-4(b) shows that the increase in aggregate demand from $AD_1$ to $AD_2$ raises the price level to $p_2$ rather than $p_1$, and equilibrium output is $540. The $p_0$ to $p_2$ increase in the price level decreases private-sector spending, and aggregate spending line $(C + I + G + X_n)_2$ shifts downward to $(C + I + G + X_n)_4$, where equilibrium output is $540. Note that there is a smaller increase in equilibrium output but a larger increase in the price level in Example 11.6 than in Example 11.5 because aggregate supply curve $AS_2$ is more steeply sloped than $AS_1$.

## 11.5   MONETARY POLICY OR FISCAL POLICY

Other factors also influence the choice of a monetary or fiscal stimulus: (1) how quickly the economic stimulus impacts economic activity and (2) how the economic stimulus affects the economy's structure of output. A change in government spending normally has the most immediate impact on economic activity since a change immediately affects spending levels. The response to money supply changes are more likely to lag. While money supply changes immediately impact the rate of interest, the response of interest-sensitive spending to an interest rate change may not be as immediate since many investment projects are not ready to be started when funding costs decrease. A money supply change, however, has a short action lag since the Federal Reserve, unlike Congress, can respond quickly to changing economic conditions. Thus, in spite of its longer impact lag, monetary policy is the principal economic stabilization measure used in the United States because of its short action lag. Those who advocate minimal interference with the market prefer monetary policy to fiscal policy. Monetary policy, through its interest rate effect, works through the financial markets and impacts private-sector spending; a fiscal action may redistribute income within the private sector or expand public rather than private-sector goods and services. For example, a change in the personal income tax rate does not equally impact each income class; and a change in government expenditure by its nature alters the economy's composition of output and therefore the balance between public and private-sector goods and services.

# Solved Problems

## MONETARY AND FISCAL POLICY: A RECAP

**11.1.** Suppose $k_e$ is 5, $k_t$ is $-4$, and equilibrium output is \$950; full-employment output is \$1000; the money supply is initially $M_1$; and the rate of interest is $i_1$.

    (a) What change in government spending is needed to bring output to its full-employment level?

    (b) What change in the money supply would also bring output to its full-employment level, given the demand for money curve $L_1$ in Fig. 11-5(a) and investment demand curve I' in Fig. 11-5(b)?

    (c) In this situation, should the government implement monetary or fiscal policy to bring output to its full-employment level?

    (a) Government spending needs to increase \$10 since the expenditure multiplier is 5. [$\Delta Y = k_e \Delta G$; \$50 = $5(\Delta G)$; $\Delta G$ = \$10.]

    (b) A \$10 increase in investment spending would also bring output to its full-employment level. This is achieved by increasing the money supply from $M_1$ to $M_2$, which lowers the rate of interest from $i_1$ to $i_2$ [Fig. 11-5(a)], thereby increasing investment spending from \$100 to \$110 (by \$10) in Fig. 11-5(b).

    (c) Monetary expansion or increased government spending are policy alternatives. Which of these alternatives is selected depends upon the perceived effectiveness of each, as well as political considerations such as the desirability of public or private-sector goods.

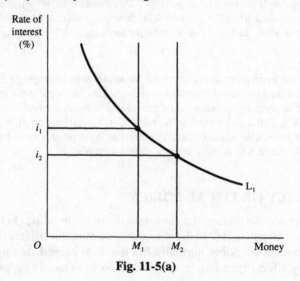

**Fig. 11-5(a)**

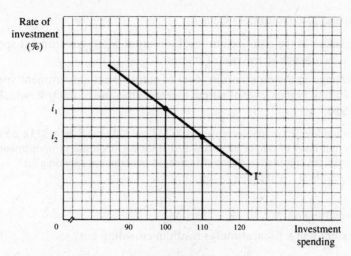

**Fig. 11-5(b)**

## FISCAL POLICY AND CROWDING OUT

**11.2.** Suppose output is below its full-employment level; the demand for money in Fig. 11-6(a) is $L_1$; the money supply is $M_1$; and the investment demand curve is I' in Fig. 11-6(b).

(a) Find the rate of interest and the level of investment when output is below full employment.

(b) Suppose government spending is increased to bring output to full employment. At full employment output, however, there is a greater demand for money and curve $L_1$ shifts upward to $L_2$. What happens to the rate of interest and the level of investment when output is at full employment?

(c) Has government spending "crowded out" private-sector investment?

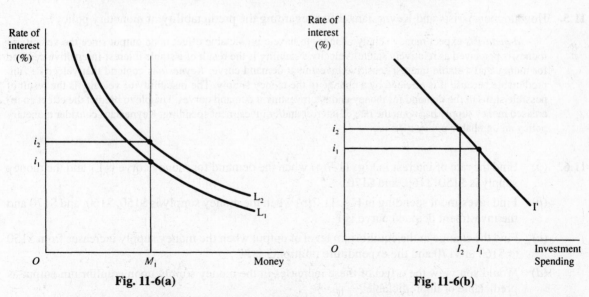

**Fig. 11-6(a)**                                                    **Fig. 11-6(b)**

(a) The rate of interest is $i_1$ when the money supply is $M_1$, output is below full employment, and the demand for money curve is $L_1$. Investment is $I_1$ when the rate of interest is $i_1$.

(b) There is a greater demand for money at full employment output; thus, the demand for money curve shifts upward to $L_2$. With an unchanged money supply, the rate of interest increases from $i_1$ to $i_2$. The increase in the rate of interest lowers investment spending from $I_1$ to $I_2$.

(c) Government spending has crowded out private-sector investment since a higher level of output has pushed up the rate of interest, thereby reducing investment spending.

**11.3.** Suppose the expenditure multiplier ($k_e$) is 4.

    (*a*)   Find the change in the equilibrium level of output when government spending increases $25 and there is no change in the rate of interest.

    (*b*)   Find the change in the equilibrium level of output when government spending increases $25 and the resulting higher level of output increases the rate of interest, which reduces investment spending $20.

    (*a*)   The equilibrium level of output increases $100 [$\Delta Y = k_e \Delta G$; $\Delta Y = 4(\$25)$; $\Delta Y = \$100$].

    (*b*)   The equilibrium level of output increases $20 since the decrease in investment spending has offset a large portion of the stimulative effect of increased government spending [$\Delta Y = k_e \Delta G + k_e \Delta I$; $\Delta Y = 4(\$25) + 4(-\$20)$; $\Delta Y = \$20$].

**11.4.** (*a*)   What is crowding out?

    (*b*)   To what extent will a fiscal stimulus result in crowding out?

    (*a*)   Crowding out occurs when a fiscal stimulus pushes up the rate of interest, which in turn results in a lower level of investment spending. The fiscal stimulus has thus crowded out investment spending.

    (*b*)   The crowding out of investment spending depends upon the resulting change in the rate of interest and the interest sensitivity of investment spending. In some instances, a higher level of government spending may result in only a small increase in the rate of interest and therefore a small decrease in investment spending; other times there might be a large increase in the rate of interest and therefore a substantial decrease in investment spending. The sensitivity of investment to changes in the rate of interest may also vary. When investment spending is highly sensitive to the rate of interest, a small increase in the rate of interest could result in substantial crowding out; when investment spending is highly insensitive to the rate of interest, large increases in the rate of interest have only a small crowding-out effect.

## PREDICTABILITY OF MONEY SUPPLY CHANGES UPON EQUILIBRIUM OUTPUT

**11.5.** How do monetarists and Keynesians differ regarding the predictability of monetary policy?

    *Monetarists* expect money supply changes to have a predictable effect upon output since the velocity of money is perceived as relatively stable. Velocity's stability is the result of a stable interest-insensitive demand for money and a stable interest-sensitive investment demand curve. *Keynesians* contend that velocity is unpredictable because it is affected by a change in the money supply. The instability of velocity is the result of possible shifts of the demand for money and the investment demand curves. Unable to predict the effect an increased money supply has upon the rate of interest and/or investment spending, Keynesians consider monetary policy an unreliable policy measure.

**11.6.** (*a*)   Find the rate of interest in Fig. 11-7(a) when the demand for money curve is $L_1$ and the money supply is $150, $160, and $170.

    (*b*)   Find investment spending in Fig. 11-7(b) when the money supply is $150, $160, and $170 and the investment demand curve is I'.

    (*c*)   Find the change in the equilibrium level of output when the money supply increases from $150 to $160 to $170 and the expenditure multiplier is 4.

    (*d*)   Would you view the effect of these increases in the money supply upon equilibrium output as predictable or unpredictable?

    (*a*)   The increase in the money supply in Fig. 11-7(a) from $150 to $160 to $170 lowers the rate of interest from 8% to 7% to 6%.

    (*b*)   Investment spending is $80 when the money supply is $150 and the rate of interest is 8%, $90 when the money supply is $160 and the rate of interest is 7%, and $100 when the money supply is $170 and the rate of interest is 6%.

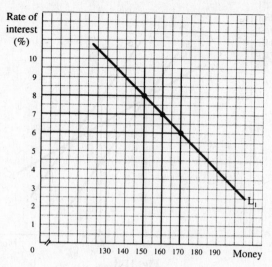

**Fig. 11-7(a)**

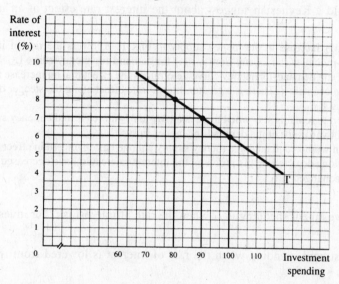

**Fig. 11-7(b)**

(c) The increase in equilibrium output for each \$10 increase in investment spending is \$40. $[\Delta Y = k_e(\Delta I);$ $\Delta Y = 4(\$10);\ \Delta Y = \$40.]$

(d) The demand for money and the investment demand curves have not shifted; thus, the increase in the money supply is having a predictable effect upon equilibrium output.

**11.7.** In Fig. 11-8, the rate of interest is $i_1$ when the money supply is $M_1$ and the demand for money is $L_1$ or $L_2$.

    (a) Find the rate of interest when the money supply increases from $M_1$ to $M_2$ and the demand for money is $L_1$ or $L_2$.

    (b) Does the slope of the demand-for-money curve affect the interest rate effect of an increase in the money supply?

    (c) Find the rate of interest when the money supply increases from $M_1$ to $M_2$ and the demand-for-money curve shifts from $L_1$ to $L_3$.

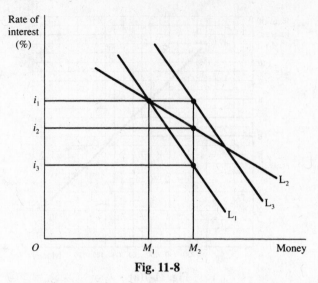

**Fig. 11-8**

(d)   What would a Keynesian suggest about the interest rate effect of an increase in the money supply?

(a)   The $M_1$ to $M_2$ increase in the money supply in Fig. 11-8 lowers the rate of interest from $i_1$ to $i_3$ for demand-for-money curve $L_1$ and from $i_1$ to $i_2$ for demand-for-money curve $L_2$.

(b)   The slope of the demand-for-money curve determines the effect that an increase in the money supply has upon the rate of interest. There is a greater interest rate effect along the steeper demand for money curve $L_1$ than along $L_2$.

(c)   The interest rate remains at $i_1$ when there is an $M_1$ to $M_2$ increase in the money supply and a proportional $L_1$ to $L_3$ rightward shift of the demand-for-money curve.

(d)   A Keynesian would contend that a money supply change has an uncertain effect upon the rate of interest. In the situations depicted in this problem, the interest rate could have decreased to $i_2$ or $i_3$ or could have remained unchanged at $i_1$.

**11.8.**   In Fig. 11-9, investment spending is $I_1$ when the rate of interest is $i_1$ for investment demand curves $I'$ and $I''$.

(a)   Find investment spending when the rate of interest is lowered from $i_1$ to $i_2$ and investment demand is $I'$ or $I''$.

(b)   Does the steepness of the investment demand curve influence the effect of a decrease in the rate of interest?

(c)   What happens to investment spending when the rate of interest is lowered from $i_1$ to $i_2$ and the investment demand curve shifts from $I'$ to $I'''$?

(d)   Does an interest rate change have a predictable effect upon investment spending?

(a)   Investment spending increases from $I_1$ to $I_2$ in Fig. 11-9 along investment demand curve $I'$ and from $I_1$ to $I_3$ along investment demand curve $I''$.

(b)   Investment spending is less sensitive to changes in the rate of interest when the investment demand curve is steeply sloped. That is, there is a smaller increase in investment spending resulting from a decrease in the rate of interest for a steeply sloped investment demand curve.

(c)   Investment spending increases from $I_1$ to $I_4$ when the investment demand curve shifts from $I'$ to $I'''$ and the rate of interest declines from $i_1$ to $i_2$. Note that even though the investment demand curve is steeply sloped, there is a large increase in investment spending as a result of the rightward shift of investment demand curve $I'''$.

(d)   This problem has shown that the effect of an interest rate change upon investment spending depends upon both the slope and the stability of the investment demand curve. When the interest sensitivity of investment demand is uncertain and the curve is subject to unexpected shifts, monetary policy has an unpredictable effect upon output.

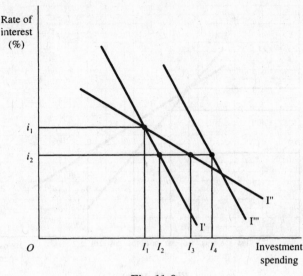

**Fig. 11-9**

**11.9.** Suppose the money supply is $400, gross domestic product is $1200, and the expenditure multiplier is 5.

(a)  Find the change in the rate of interest, the level of investment spending, and gross domestic product when the demand-for-money curve is $L_1$ in Fig. 11-10(a), the investment demand curve is $I'$ in Fig. 11-10(b), and the money supply increases from $400 to $420.

(b)  Find the change in the rate of interest, the level of investment spending, and gross domestic product when the demand for money curve is $L_2$ in Fig. 11-10(a), the investment demand curve is $I'$ in Fig. 11-10(b), and the money supply increases from $400 to $420.

(c)  Find the change in the rate of interest, the level of investment spending, and gross domestic product when the demand for money curve is $L_1$ in Fig. 11-10(a), the investment demand curve is $I''$ in Fig. 11-10(b), and the money supply increases from $400 to $420.

(a)  The rate of interest falls from $i_1$ to $i_3$, investment spending increases from $200 to $206, and output increases $30, since $\Delta Y = k_e \Delta I$.

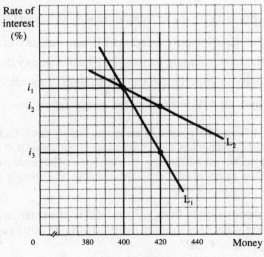

**Fig. 11-10(a)**

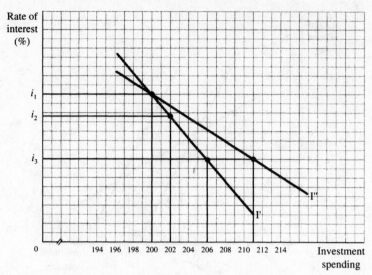

**Fig. 11-10(b)**

(b)   The rate of interest falls from $i_1$ to $i_2$, investment spending increases from \$200 to \$202, and output increases \$10.

(c)   The rate of interest falls from $i_1$ to $i_3$, investment spending increases from \$200 to \$211, and output increases \$55.

**11.10.** (a)   Find the velocity of money when the money supply is \$400 and GDP is \$1200.

(b)   Find GDP for the situations from parts (a), (b), and (c) of Problem 11.9 when the money supply increases to \$420. Find the velocity of money for these GDP levels.

(c)   In which of these situations does the \$20 increase in the money supply have the more predictable effect upon GDP?

(a)   The velocity of money is 3. [$MV$ = GDP; \$400$V$ = \$1200; $V$ = 3.]

(b)   GDP is \$1230 in part (a), \$1210 in part (b), and \$1255 in part (c). The velocity of money for each of these situations is 2.93, 2.88, and 2.99, respectively.

(c)   The situation in part (c) of Problem 11.9 has the most predictable effect since the increase in the money supply is associated with only a small change in the velocity of money.

**11.11.** Suppose the money supply is \$120, the velocity of money is 5, and GDP is \$600.

(a)   Find GDP when the money supply increases \$10 and velocity is unchanged.

(b)   Find GDP when the money supply increases \$10 and velocity declines to 4.7.

(c)   Why is stable velocity so important to the formulation of monetary policy?

(a)   When $V$ is unchanged, the \$10 increase in the money supply raises GDP to \$650. [$MV$ = GDP; \$130(5) = \$650.]

(b)   When $V$ declines to 4.7, the \$10 increase in the money supply raises GDP to \$611.

(c)   An increase in the money supply has a less predictable effect upon GDP when velocity is variable. Thus, when the change in the velocity of money is unknown, a policymaker cannot establish the increase in money supply that is necessary to raise equilibrium output by a specific amount.

**11.12.** The velocity of the $M1$ money supply from 1970 to 1993 is presented in Fig. 11-11. Has velocity been predictable in this period? What does the data for 1970 through 1993 suggest about the predictability of money supply changes upon GDP?

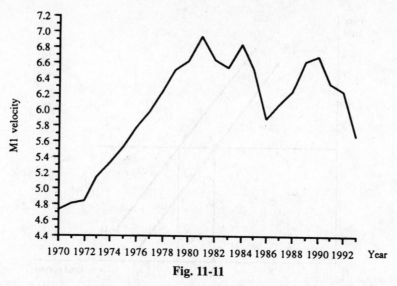

**Fig. 11-11**

The velocity of the $M1$ money supply had a relatively stable upward trend throughout the 1970s. The effect of money supply changes on nominal GDP were therefore highly predictable. The velocity of the $M1$ money supply was trendless and variable during the 1980s. Monetary policy therefore had a much less predictable effect upon nominal GDP during the 1980s.

## MONETARY AND FISCAL POLICY IN AN AGGREGATE DEMAND AND AGGREGATE SUPPLY FRAMEWORK

**11.13.** (*a*) What is the relationship between private-sector spending and the price level?

(*b*) What is an aggregate demand curve?

(*c*) Suppose equilibrium output is initially $y_1$ and the price level is $p_1$. What happens to spending equilibrium line $(C + I + G + X_n)_1$ in Fig. 11-12(a) when there is an increase in government expenditures and there is no change in the price level?

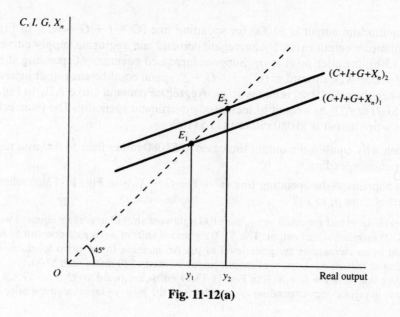

**Fig. 11-12(a)**

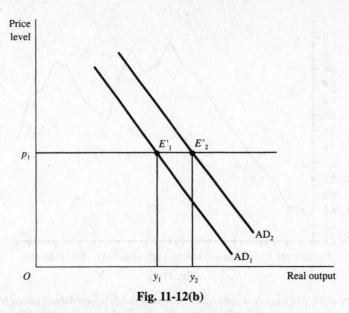

**Fig. 11-12(b)**

(*d*)   What happens to aggregate demand curve $AD_1$ in Fig. 11-12(b) as a result of the increase in government spending?

(*a*)   Private-sector spending decreases when the price level increases. A rising price level increases the nominal rate of interest, which depresses investment and consumption spending. And when the domestic price level increases and there is no change in the foreign exchange rate, foreign-made goods become relatively less expensive, which increases imports and decreases exports.

(*b*)   An aggregate demand curve presents the relationship between the price level and equilibrium output. Since a higher price level has a negative effect upon private-sector spending, the aggregate demand curve shows an inverse relationship between the price level and equilibrium output.

(*c*)   The $(C + I + G + X_n)_1$ spending line in Fig. 11-12(a) shifts upward to $(C + I + G + X_n)_2$ when there is an increase in government expenditures and no change in the price level.

(*d*)   Aggregate demand curve $AD_1$ in Fig. 11-12(b) shifts rightward to $AD_2$ by $y_1$ to $y_2$— an amount equal to the change in equilibrium output in Fig. 11-12(a) when the price level is unchanged at $p_1$.

**11.14.**   Suppose equilibrium output is \$1000 for spending line $(C + I + G + X_n)_1$ in Fig. 11-13(a); this \$1000 equilibrium output exists for aggregate demand and aggregate supply curves $AD_1$ and $AS_1$ in Fig. 11-13(b); the price level is $p_1$. Suppose increased government spending shifts the spending line $(C + I + G + X_n)_1$ upward to $(C + I + G + X_n)_2$ and equilibrium output increases from \$1000 to \$1100 when the price level remains at $p_1$. Aggregate demand curve $AD_1$ in Fig. 11-13(b) shifts rightward \$100 to $AD_2$ as a result of increased government spending. The intersection of $AD_2$ and $AS_1$ occurs when output is \$1080 rather than \$1100.

(*a*)   Explain why equilibrium output increases to \$1080 rather than \$1100 as a result of increased government spending.

(*b*)   What happens to the spending line $(C + I + G + X_n)_2$ in Fig. 11-13(a) when the price level increases from $p_1$ to $p_2$?

(*a*)   If the price level had remained at $p_1$, the \$100 rightward shift of aggregate demand would have resulted in a \$100 increase in real output. The \$100 rightward shift of aggregate demand to $AD_2$, however, has resulted in an increase in the price level to $p_2$. An increase in the price level reduces private-sector spending so that, in this case, equilibrium output increases \$80 rather than \$100.

(*b*)   Spending line $(C + I + G + X_n)_2$ in Fig. 11-13(a) shifts downward to $(C + I + G + X_n)_3$ because of the decrease in private-sector spending that results from the $p_1$ to $p_2$ increase in the price level.

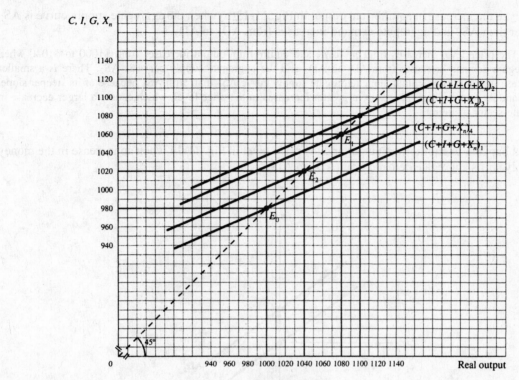

Fig. 11-13(a)

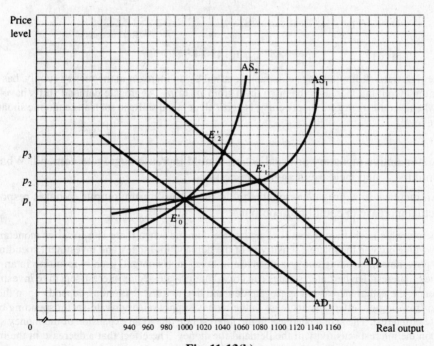

Fig. 11-13(b)

**11.15.** Analyze the increase in equilibrium output in Fig. 11-13(b) when the aggregate supply curve is $AS_2$ rather than $AS_1$ and aggregate demand increases from $AD_1$ to $AD_2$.

The price level increases from $p_1$ to $p_3$ and equilibrium output increases from \$1000 to \$1040 when aggregate demand increases from $AD_1$ to $AD_2$ and the aggregate supply curve is $AS_2$. There is a smaller increase in equilibrium output along aggregate supply curve $AS_2$ than with $AS_1$ because of its steeper slope. Demand increases along $AS_2$ result in greater increases in the price level, which causes a larger decrease in private-sector spending.

**11.16.** What happens to equilibrium output and the price level in Fig. 11-14 when an increase in the money supply shifts aggregate demand from $AD_1$ to $AD_2$?

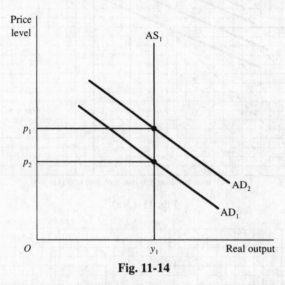

**Fig. 11-14**

The rightward shift of aggregate demand, caused by an increase in the money supply, has no effect upon equilibrium output but increases the price level from $p_1$ to $p_2$. Aggregate demand shifts have no effect upon output whenever the aggregate supply curve is vertical; demand shifts in such an economic situation only affect the price level.

**11.17.** (*a*)   A stimulative monetary or fiscal action should increase aggregate demand. What factors may limit the actual increase in aggregate demand?

(*b*)   An increase in aggregate demand should raise equilibrium output. What is responsible for the actual increase in equilibrium output?

(*a*)   Factors which constrain the shift of aggregate demand when there is a fiscal or monetary stimulus are crowding out and the interest sensitivity of the demand for money and investment spending. An increase in government spending and/or a decrease in taxes raises output, usually resulting in an increase in the rate of interest. Higher interest rates can crowd out private-sector interest-sensitive investment spending. Hence, the actual increase in aggregate demand due to a fiscal stimulus depends upon the magnitude of the crowding-out effect. An increase in the money supply raises private-sector spending by lowering the rate of interest. The actual decrease in the interest rate due to an expansion of the money supply depends upon the interest sensitivity of the demand for money. The effect that a decrease in the interest rate has upon spending in turn depends upon the interest sensitivity of investment spending. Thus, a money supply increase can cause a large or small shift of aggregate demand.

(*b*)   An increase in aggregate demand should raise equilibrium output; the actual increase in output depends upon the slope of aggregate supply. When aggregate supply is steeply sloped, demand increases have a smaller effect upon output than when aggregate supply is less steeply sloped.

## MONETARY POLICY OR FISCAL POLICY

**11.18.** (a)   Why might the magnitude and timing impact of monetary policy vary over time?

(b)   Why might a change in taxes have a variable impact upon economic activity?

(a)   The response of investment spending to a decline in the rate of interest varies over the business cycle since factors other than the rate of interest affect investment. The utilization of existing plant capacity, for example, varies over the business cycle. During a recession, capital utilization rates are generally low (there is excess capacity) for many manufacturing firms; thus, a decline in the rate of interest may have a small positive effect on investment. As the economy recovers, unused capacity rates decline, and with projections of continued economic expansion, lower interest rates are likely to have a larger stimulative effect on investment spending. Hence, monetary policy can be expected to have both a variable timing and magnitude impact on aggregate spending.

(b)   A decrease in personal income tax rates increases consumption. The magnitude of the response, however, depends upon consumers' reaction to the tax cut. If consumers believe that the tax cut will be reversed in the near future, then the incremental spending associated with the increase in disposable income will be small. There is a large spending response when the tax cut is viewed as permanent.

**11.19.** Are there philosophical differences between Keynesians and monetarists?

The majority of Keynesians are politically "liberal" and see the need for government interference to overcome the problems of social imbalance and the unequal distribution of disposable income. Fiscal policy allows policymakers to promote microeconomic policy objectives while expanding output. Most monetarists are "conservative" and view the market as the best allocator of resources and output. To them, money-supply management interferes least with the market. Philosophically, then, Keynesians, while supporting a market economy, believe in selective government intervention; monetarists prefer a market economy in which there is as little government intervention as possible.

# *Multiple Choice Questions*

1.   Crowding out occurs when
    (a)   a change in the rate of interest affects the quantity of money demanded,
    (b)   a stimulative fiscal policy pushes up the rate of interest, which lowers investment spending,
    (c)   a stimulative fiscal policy changes the velocity of money,
    (d)   a stimulative fiscal policy increases equilibrium output by $k_e \Delta G$.

2.   When $k_e$ is 4, increased government spending is \$10, and rising interest rates cause investment spending to decrease \$6, there is a net increase in equilibrium output of
    (a)   \$80,
    (b)   \$104,
    (c)   \$56,
    (d)   \$16.

3.   An increase in the money supply has a small effect upon equilibrium output when
    (a)   the demand for money and investment spending is interest-insensitive,
    (b)   the demand for money and investment spending is interest-sensitive,
    (c)   the demand for money is interest-sensitive and investment demand is interest-insensitive,
    (d)   the demand for money is interest-insensitive and investment demand is interest-sensitive.

**4.** An increase in the money supply has a small effect upon nominal GDP when
  (*a*)   government spending is also increasing,
  (*b*)   velocity is unchanged,
  (*c*)   velocity is decreasing,
  (*d*)   velocity is increasing.

**5.** Monetarists contend that an increase in the money supply has
  (*a*)   a predictable effect upon nominal GDP, as do Keynesians,
  (*b*)   a predictable effect upon nominal GDP, while Keynesians contend that the effect is uncertain,
  (*c*)   an unpredictable effect upon nominal GDP, as do Keynesians,
  (*d*)   an unpredictable effect upon nominal GDP, while Keynesians contend that the effect is certain.

**6.** Which of the following would not be consistent with a Keynesian view about the effectiveness of monetary policy?
  (*a*)   Velocity is relatively stable.
  (*b*)   The demand for money is unstable.
  (*c*)   The demand for money is interest-sensitive.
  (*d*)   Investment demand is unstable.

**7.** When $k_e$ is 5 and government spending increases \$20, aggregate demand and therefore output increase
  (*a*)   \$100 when there is no crowding out and aggregate supply is horizontal,
  (*b*)   \$100 when there is crowding out and aggregate supply is horizontal,
  (*c*)   \$100 when there is no crowding out and aggregate supply is positively sloped,
  (*d*)   \$100 when there is no crowding out and aggregate supply is vertical.

**8.** A positively sloped aggregate supply curve indicates that
  (*a*)   an increase in aggregate demand will be associated with an increase in the price level and no change in equilibrium output,
  (*b*)   an increase in aggregate demand will be associated with an increase in both the price level and equilibrium output,
  (*c*)   an increase in aggregate demand will be associated with an increase in equilibrium output and no change in the price level,
  (*d*)   none of the above.

**9.** Which statement is false?
  (*a*)   Increased government spending affects aggregate spending more quickly than does an increase in the money supply.
  (*b*)   Increased government spending affects aggregate supply less quickly than does an increase in the money supply.
  (*c*)   It takes Congress longer to authorize an increase in government spending that it takes for the Federal Reserve to increase the money supply.
  (*d*)   Monetary policy can be changed quickly by the Federal Reserve.

**10.** Which statement is false?
  (*a*)   Many Keynesians are politically liberal.
  (*b*)   Monetarists advocate policies which interfere least with the market.
  (*c*)   Monetarists contend that increased government spending has no crowding-out effect.
  (*d*)   Keynesians contend that an increase in the money supply has an unpredictable effect upon nominal GDP.

## *True or False Questions*

11. _____ An increase in government spending always crowds out an equal amount of private-sector interest-sensitive spending.

12. _____ The net increase in equilibrium output is $10 when $k_e$ is 5, government spending increases $10, and higher interest rates crowd out $8 of investment spending.

13. _____ An increase in the money supply has a predictable effect upon nominal GDP when the demand-for-money curve and the investment demand curve are unstable.

14. _____ Monetarists contend that the velocity of money is predictable.

15. _____ Keynesians contend that an increase in the money supply has an unpredictable effect upon nominal GDP since velocity is unstable.

16. _____ When the money supply is $100 and nominal GDP is $500, a $10 increase in the money supply always results in a $50 increase in nominal GDP.

17. _____ An increase in aggregate demand has no effect upon real output when aggregate supply is vertical.

18. _____ A $10 increase in the money supply increases equilibrium output $50 when $k_e$ is 5, there is no crowding out, and aggregate supply is positively sloped.

19. _____ Monetarists advocate minimal government intervention in the market.

20. _____ Monetary policy is more frequently used than fiscal policy since it more quickly impacts aggregate spending.

### *Answers to Multiple Choice and True or False Questions*

| | | | |
|---|---|---|---|
| 1. (*b*) | 6. (*a*) | 11. (F) | 16. (F) |
| 2. (*d*) | 7. (*a*) | 12. (T) | 17. (T) |
| 3. (*c*) | 8. (*b*) | 13. (F) | 18. (F) |
| 4. (*c*) | 9. (*b*) | 14. (T) | 19. (T) |
| 5. (*b*) | 10. (*c*) | 15. (T) | 20. (F) |

# Chapter 12

# Inflation, Unemployment, Deficits, and Debt

## *Chapter Summary*

1. Any event which increases the cost of supplying aggregate output shifts the aggregate supply curve to the left, causing increases in the price level and decreases in output. Inflationary pressures stemming from costs (cost-push inflation) are most often associated with increases in the costs of labor and raw materials.

2. Demand-pull inflation occurs when output is unable to meet increases in aggregate spending. Inflationary pressures can develop prior to full-employment output when increases occur in aggregate demand and the aggregate supply curve is positively sloped. Inflationary pressures from increasing aggregate demand are greater when the unemployment rate falls below its natural rate.

3. The Phillips curve shows an inverse relationship between the rate of inflation and the rate of unemployment. The unemployment rate can be pushed below the natural rate in the short run by increasing the rate of inflation. The unemployment rate will not permanently remain below the natural rate over time, however, because of eventual rightward shifts of the Phillips curve.

4. A federal deficit exists when government outlays exceed revenues. The U.S. federal budget has been in deficit almost every year since World War II. The U.S. structural deficit—the deficit that exists when output is at its full-employment level—rose during the 1980s because federal outlays increased at a faster rate than did federal revenues.

5. The public debt is the amount owed by the federal government. The U.S. public debt increased dramatically during the 1980s as a result of increasing federal deficits. The nominal public debt per capita increased from $1,799.67 in 1970 to $15,103.34 in 1993.

## *Important Terms*

**Cost-push inflation.**   Inflation caused by increases in the cost of producing output rather than by increases in aggregate demand.

**Cyclical deficit.**   The federal deficit that arises when output is below its full-employment level.

**Demand-pull inflation.**   Inflation that occurs because of increases in aggregate demand.

**Phillips curve.**   A curve depicting an inverse relationship between the rate of inflation and the rate of unemployment.

**Public debt.**   The amount owed by the federal government; that is, the sum of interest-bearing debt obligations issued by the federal government.

**Stagflation.**   A situation in which there is increasing inflation and unemployment simultaneously.

**Structural deficit.**   The federal deficit that exists when output is at its full-employment level.

# Outline of Chapter 12: Inflation, Unemployment, Deficits, and Debt

## 12.1   COST-PUSH INFLATION

Cost-push inflation results from increases in the price of supplying output, e.g., increases in the wages paid to labor, in the price of raw materials, and in the business sector's profit margin on sales. Increases in the price of supplying output shifts the aggregate supply curve upward and, given an unchanged aggregate demand curve, results in an increase in the price level and a decrease in output. Because output falls as the price level increases, periods of cost-push inflation are referred to as stagflation.

**EXAMPLE 12.1.**   In Fig. 12-1, equilibrium output is initially $y_f$ and the price level is $p_0$ for aggregate supply and aggregate demand curves $AS_1$ and $AD_1$. Suppose there are substantial increases in the price of oil, which raise the cost of supplying output and shift the aggregate supply curve upward from $AS_1$ to $AS_2$ to $AS_3$. The price level increases from $p_0$ to $p_1$ to $p_2$ as output falls from its full-employment level $y_f$ to $y_1$ to $y_2$.

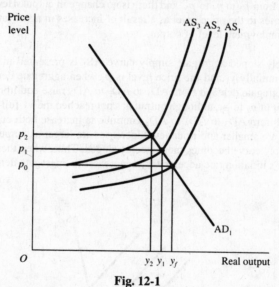

**Fig. 12-1**

## 12.2   DEMAND-PULL INFLATION

Demand-pull inflation exists when there are continuous increases in the price level due to increases in aggregate demand. With a traditional Keynesian aggregate supply curve, aggregate supply is horizontal until the full-employment level of output is reached so that demand-pull inflation occurs only after the economy has reached its full-employment level of output (Example 12.2). When the aggregate supply curve is positively sloped, increases in aggregate demand raise output and the price level as there is movement toward full employment (Example 12.3).

**EXAMPLE 12.2.**   A traditional Keynesian aggregate supply curve $AS_1$ is presented in Fig. 12-2; output $y_f$ represents the full-employment level of output. Output is initially $y_1$ and the price level is $p_1$ for aggregate demand curve $AD_1$.

Increases in aggregate spending which shift aggregate demand from AD₁ to AD₂ to AD₃ increase equilibrium output from $y_1$ to $y_2$ to $y_f$ with no change in the price level. Increases in aggregate demand from AD₃ to AD₄ to AD₅, on the

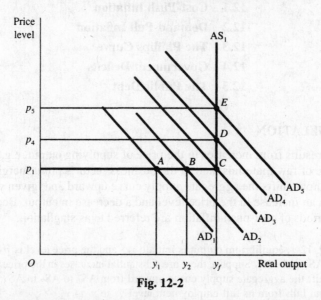

Fig. 12-2

other hand, raise the price level from $p_1$ to $p_4$ to $p_5$, and there is no change in output. Hence, for a Keynesian aggregate supply curve, continuous increases in the price level as a result of increases in aggregate demand occur only after the economy has reached its full-employment level of output.

**EXAMPLE 12.3.**    A positively sloped aggregate supply curve AS₁ is presented in Fig. 12-3; $y_f$ represents full-employment output. Output is initially $y_1$ and the price level is $p_1$ when aggregate demand is AD₁. Increases in aggregate demand which shift aggregate demand from AD₁ to AD₂ to AD₃ raise equilibrium output from $y_1$ to $y_2$ to $y_3$ and raise the price level from $p_1$ to $p_2$ to $p_3$, although output has not reached the $y_f$ full-employment level. Additional increases in aggregate demand from AD₃ to AD₄ to AD₅ continue to increase both output and the price level. Note, however, that output increases are smaller and price level increases are larger as output approaches full-employment level $y_f$ and the aggregate supply curve becomes more steeply sloped. Thus, when there is a positively sloped aggregate supply curve, an economy's inflation rate accelerates as increases in aggregate demand bring the economy closer to full-employment output.

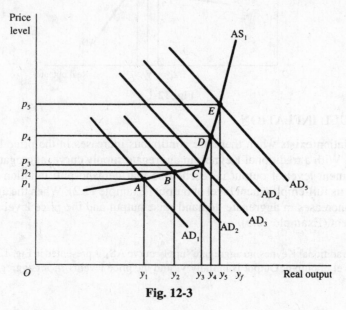

Fig. 12-3

## 12.3   THE PHILLIPS CURVE

The analysis in Section 12.2 indicates that when aggregate supply is positively sloped, increases in aggregate demand raise both output and the price level. A. W. Phillips, investigating unemployment and price/wage increases over time, found that low rates of unemployment in Great Britain were associated with high rates of price/wage rate increase, while higher levels of unemployment were associated with lower rates of price/wage rate increase. This inverse relationship between inflation and unemployment, depicted in Fig. 12-4 by curve $P_1$, was designated the Phillips curve. The negatively sloped $P_1$ Phillips curve was initially believed by some economists to represent a trade-off between inflation and unemployment. Economists have found, however, that attempts to push the unemployment rate below its natural rate result in upward shifts of a short-run Philips curve (e.g., from $P_1$ to $P_2$ to $P_3$) giving rise, over the long run, to a vertical Phillips curve $P_L$ at the economy's natural rate of unemployment.

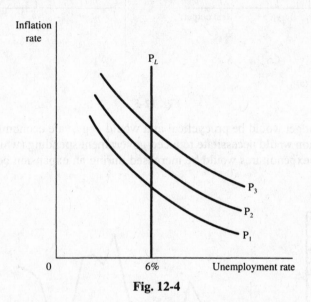

**Fig. 12-4**

**EXAMPLE 12.4.**   Suppose full-employment output is $y_f$ and the unemployment rate consistent with $y_f$ (the natural rate of unemployment) is 6%. Output is $y_f$ and the price level is $p_0$ in Fig. 12-5(a) for aggregate demand curve $AD_1$ and aggregate supply curve $AS_1$. An increase in government spending, *ceteris paribus,* shifts aggregate demand outward from $AD_1$ to $AD_2$; output increases to $y_1$ and the price level increases to $p_1$. The $y_f$ to $y_1$ increase in output is associated with a decrease in the rate of unemployment; this lower unemployment rate is depicted in Fig. 12-5(b) by a higher rate of inflation and therefore a movement up Phillips curve $P_1$ and a fall in the unemployment rate from 6% (the natural rate) to 4%. The $p_0$ to $p_1$ rise in the price level eventually results in wage increases which shift aggregate supply curve $AS_1$ to $AS_2$. Output returns to full-employment level $y_f$, and the price level increases to $p_2$. The increased price level shifts Phillips curve $P_1$ to $P_2$, and a 6% unemployment rate is now associated with a 2% rather than a 0% rate of inflation. Additional attempts to lower the unemployment rate below 6% cause further shifts of the Phillips curve to $P_3$ and $P_4$, indicating that, over the long run, the Phillips curve is a vertical line at the natural rate of unemployment.

## 12.4   GOVERNMENT DEFICITS

A federal deficit exists when government outlays exceed revenues. Fig. 12-6 presents the U.S. federal deficit for the years 1965 to 1993 by relating the deficit to GDP. Note the increases in the federal deficit that occurred in the 1980s; this has become an important issue in the 1990s.

A structural deficit is one that exists when output is at its full-employment level, which in 1989 represented approximately 2.9% of U.S. GDP. While many economists advocate a reduction in the economy's structural deficit, few would support legislation which would mandate an annually balanced budget.

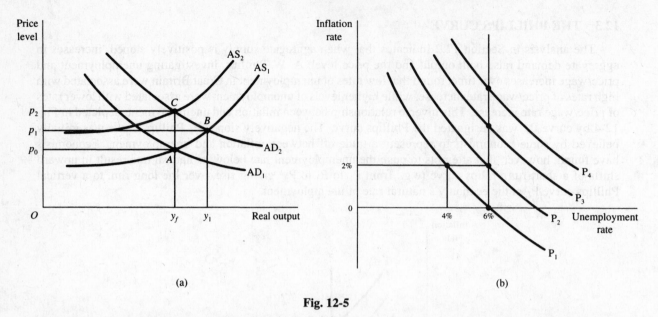

**Fig. 12-5**

An annually balanced budget would be procyclical and would aggravate economic fluctuations; lower tax revenues during a recession would necessitate reduced government spending (which could deepen a recession), while government expenditures would be increased during an expansion because of greater income tax receipts.

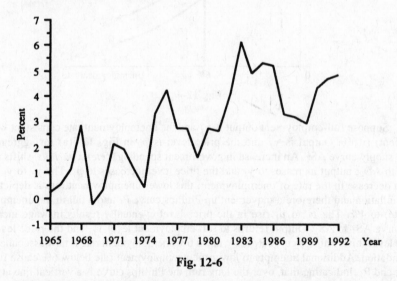

**Fig. 12-6**

**EXAMPLE 12.5.** Federal receipts and outlays as a percent of gross domestic product are presented in Fig. 12-7. Notice that since 1965, federal outlays have exceeded federal receipts each year except for 1969. Also note that the increasing relative size of the deficit during the 1980s is the result of relatively larger government outlays rather than large reductions in tax receipts.

**EXAMPLE 12.6.** The structural deficit is the deficit that exists when output is at its full-employment level; a cyclical deficit is the amount of the deficit that is attributable to output being below its full-employment level. In Fig. 12-8, $y_f$ represents full-employment output. The economy's structural deficit is $200—the deficit that exists at full-employment level $y_f$ [$500 in government spending less $300 in net tax receipts]. Note that the deficit increases to $300 when output declines to $y_1$, which is not surprising since there are smaller tax receipts and larger government transfers

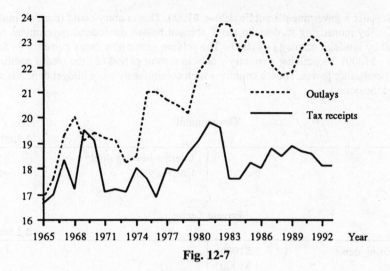

**Fig. 12-7**

at output levels below $y_f$. Thus, at output $y_1$ the $300 deficit consists of a $200 structural deficit and a $100 cyclical deficit.

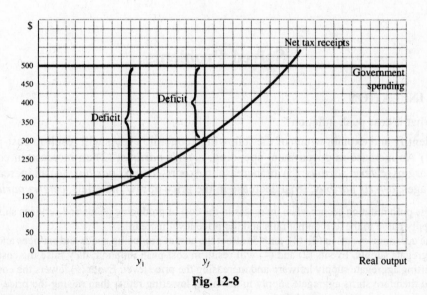

**Fig. 12-8**

## 12.5  THE PUBLIC DEBT

The public debt is the amount of interest-bearing debt issued by the federal government at a point in time. On December 31, 1993, the U.S. federal debt was $4,408.6 billion. It is frequently argued that a large public debt will result in default and federal bankruptcy. The federal government will not default, however, since it has the power to print money and the power to tax. Because the market knows that the government will not default, the federal government can always repay a maturing debt obligation by issuing a new debt obligation. However, because of possible redistribution effects, there is concern about the large increases in the U.S. federal debt. A rapidly rising federal debt necessitates larger and larger interest payments. Government must therefore increase taxes in order to pay its higher interest expense, causing a redistribution of income from those who pay taxes to those who have substantial wealth. There is also a transfer of real output from the domestic economy to foreign economies to the extent that the federal debt is foreign-owned.

**EXAMPLE 12.7.**   Suppose a government's public debt is $1000. This country could retire all interest-bearing debt by issuing currency, i.e., by monetizing its debt. In the T account below, the federal government retires its interest-bearing debt (−$1000) by issuing currency (+$1000). The private sector now owns currency (+$1000) rather than interest-bearing debt (−$1000). Monetizing a country's debt in a short period of time would result in inflation and a loss of the currency's purchasing power. Thus, a country which continuously has a budget deficit is advised to borrow rather than to monetize the deficit.

Government

| Δ Assets | | Δ Liabilities |
|---|---|---|
| | Interest-bearing debt | −$1000 |
| | Currency | +$1000 |

Private Sector

| Δ Assests | | Δ Liabilities |
|---|---|---|
| Interest-bearing debt | −$1000 | |
| Currency | +$1000 | |

# Solved Problems

## COST-PUSH INFLATION

**12.1.**   (a)   What is cost-push inflation?

(b)   Identify and explain which of the following economic events will result in cost-push inflation. (1) An increase in government spending, *ceteris paribus;* (2) an increase in corporate profit margins, *ceteris paribus;* (3) an increase in exports, *ceteris paribus;* (4) an increase in nominal wages, *ceteris paribus;* (5) a decrease in the price of raw materials, *ceteris paribus.*

(a)   Cost-push inflation occurs when increases in the cost of producing goods and services shift the aggregate supply curve to the left; output falls and the price level increases.

(b)   The economic events in (2), (4), and (5) affect the cost of producing goods and services and therefore shift aggregate supply. Events (2) and (4) will result in cost-push inflation; they raise the cost of production, shifting aggregate supply leftward and increasing the price level. Event (5) lowers the cost of production and therefore shifts aggregate supply to the right, lowering rather than raising the price level. The economic events in (1) and (3) shift the aggregate demand and not the aggregate supply curve and therefore result in demand-pull inflation.

**12.2.**   In Fig. 12-9, equilibrium output is initially $y_1$ and the price level is $p_1$ for aggregate supply and aggregate demand curves $AS_1$ and $AD_1$.

(a)   What happens to both aggregate supply and aggregate demand when there is a large increase in the price of raw materials, *ceteris paribus?*

(b)   What happens to output and the price level as a result of this event?

(a)   The increase in the price of raw materials raises the cost of producing goods and services. As a result, the aggregate supply curve $AS_1$ shifts leftward to $AS_2$, and there is movement along an unchanged aggregate demand curve.

(b)   The price level increases from $p_1$ to $p_2$ as output declines from $y_1$ to $y_2$.

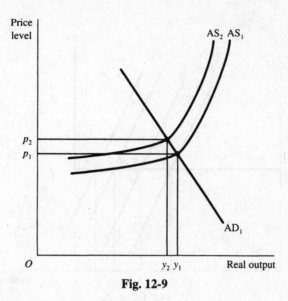

**Fig. 12-9**

**12.3.** (a) What is stagflation?

(b) What causes stagflation?

(a) Stagflation occurs when unemployment is increasing because of a stagnating economy and the price level is rising. Thus, stagflation is characterized by simultaneous increases in the rates of unemployment and inflation.

(b) Stagflation is the result of cost-push inflation. Stagflation occurred in the United States and in other industrialized countries during the 1970s and early 1980s as a result of cost-push shocks originating from large increases in the price of oil. In this case, large increases in the cost of a basic raw material caused leftward shifts of aggregate supply, increases in the price level, and decreases in output.

## DEMAND-PULL INFLATION

**12.4.** (a) What is demand-pull inflation?

(b) Which of the following events can result in demand-pull inflation? (1) An increase in investment spending, *ceteris paribus;* (2) an increase in corporate profit margins, *ceteris paribus;* (3) an increase in the income tax rate, *ceteris paribus;* (4) an increase in government transfer payments, *ceteris paribus.*

(a) Demand-pull inflation is the result of increases in aggregate demand which are not met by increases in output without a rise in the price level. Demand-pull inflation normally occurs when output is nearing the full-employment level.

(b) Events (1), (3), and (4) affect aggregate demand. Events (1) and (4) increase aggregate spending, shift aggregate demand to the right, and, with a positively sloped aggregate supply, increase the price level. Event (3) lowers aggregate spending and shifts aggregate demand to the left. Event (2) impacts aggregate supply, shifting it to the left.

**12.5.** A traditional Keynesian aggregate supply curve AS₁ is plotted in Fig. 12-10. Suppose aggregate demand is AD₁ and successive increases in government spending shift aggregate demand rightward to AD₂, AD₃, and AD₄. Have any of these increases in aggregate demand resulted in demand-pull inflation?

Each of the rightward shifts of aggregate demand in Fig. 12-10 increases output and has no effect upon the price level since the aggregate demand shifts occur over the horizontal portion of the aggregate supply curve. Thus, none of the increases in government spending result in demand-pull inflation.

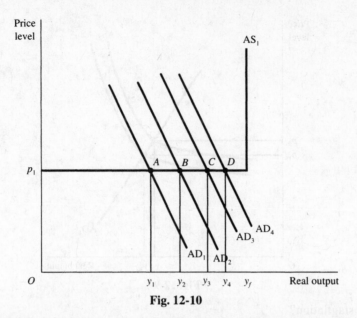

**Fig. 12-10**

**12.6.** A positively sloped aggregate supply curve $AS_1$ is plotted in Fig. 12-11. Suppose aggregate demand is $AD_1$ and successive increases in government spending shift aggregate demand rightward to $AD_2$, $AD_3$, and $AD_4$. Have any of these increases in aggregate demand in Fig. 12-11 resulted in demand-pull inflation?

    Because aggregate supply is positively sloped, each rightward shift of aggregate demand increases the price level; thus, in these circumstances each increase in government spending results in demand-pull inflation.

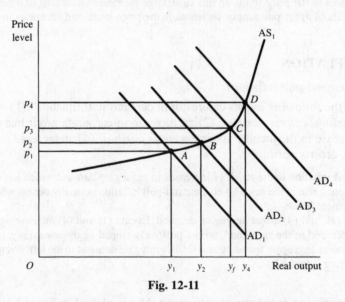

**Fig. 12-11**

**12.7.** Why might there be upward pressure on the price level prior to the economy's reaching its full-employment level of output?

    In highly industrialized economies, labor, natural, and capital resources are not homogeneous but rather are highly specialized. And in a country the size of the United States, some economic resources are also geographically immobile. Thus, there is not one market for an economic resource such as labor, but instead there are a large number of separate and distinct markets. It therefore follows that some specialized resources become fully employed before others; thus, bottlenecks or spending imbalances develop as output approaches its full-employment level. Increases in aggregate spending therefore raise output in some industries and prices in others; industries in which resources are not fully employed can expand output, whereas other industries in which resources are fully employed raise prices.

**12.8.** (*a*) Suppose an economy's final output consists of the five goods listed in Table 12-1. Find the average price of these goods and the nominal value of final output.

**Table 12-1**

| Good | Unit Price | Units of Output | Value of Output |
|------|-----------|-----------------|-----------------|
| A | $1.00 | 75 | $ 75.00 |
| B | 2.50 | 50 | 125.00 |
| C | 1.25 | 60 | 75.00 |
| D | 3.00 | 40 | 120.00 |
| E | 2.00 | 125 | 250.00 |
| | | 350 | $645.00 |

(*b*) Suppose personal income taxes are lowered to increase spending since output is below its full-employment level. The output levels after the tax cut are presented in Table 12-2. Find the average price of these goods and the nominal value of final output.

**Table 12-2**

| Good | Unit Price | Units of Output | Value of Output |
|------|-----------|-----------------|-----------------|
| A | $1.00 | 85 | $ 85.00 |
| B | 2.50 | 60 | 150.00 |
| C | 1.50 | 62 | 93.00 |
| D | 3.00 | 50 | 150.00 |
| E | 2.25 | 128 | 288.00 |
| | | 385 | $766.00 |

(*c*) Compare output in Tables 12-1 and 12-2 to establish the industries which were closest to the full-employment level prior to the tax cut.

(*a*) The nominal value of final output is the sum of the dollar value of the five goods produced, in this case $645. The average price of output is a weighted sum of the price of each good and can be found by dividing the nominal value of final output by the total units of output or by weighting each unit price by the ratio of each good's output to that of total output. The average price of output is $1.84.

(*b*) The nominal value of final output has increased to $766; the average price of output is $1.99.

(*c*) The tax cut has affected the demand for each of these five goods. Industries producing Goods A, B, and D are able to expand output without increasing prices; industries producing C and E appear to be closer to full employment prior to the tax cut since the increase in demand has a larger impact on price than on output.

## THE PHILLIPS CURVE

**12.9.** (*a*) What is a Phillips curve?

(*b*) Explain why there should be an inverse relationship between the rate of unemployment and the rate of inflation as a result of shifts in aggregate demand along a stable, positively sloped aggregate supply curve.

(a) The Phillips curve depicts an inverse relationship between the rate of unemployment and the rate of inflation. This inverse relationship is reasonable since, in the absence of cost-push inflation, increases in the price level (and therefore inflation) should occur as output nears its full-employment level (and unemployment approaches the natural rate of unemployment).

(b) Shifts of an aggregate demand curve along a positively sloped aggregate supply curve produce a positive relationship between output and the price level. Increases in aggregate demand bring output closer to full employment but put upward pressure on the price level. Decreases in aggregate demand lower output and the price level. Since output is inversely related to the rate of unemployment, it follows that increases in aggregate demand along a positively sloped aggregate supply curve lower the unemployment rate and increase the inflation rate, while decreases in aggregate demand increase the unemployment rate while lowering the inflation rate.

**12.10.** In Fig. 12-12(a), aggregate demand curve $AD_1$ and aggregate supply curve $AS_1$ intersect at full-employment output $y_f$. The natural rate of unemployment is 6% and the inflation rate is $\pi_1$ along Phillips curve $P_1$ in Fig. 12-12(b).

(a) Introduce an increase in government spending which shifts aggregate demand curve $AD_1$ to $AD_2$. What has happened to output and the price level in Fig. 12-12(a) and the unemployment rate and inflation rate in Fig. 12-12(b)?

(b) Will the unemployment and inflation rates in Fig. 12-12(b) remain at the level established in part (a) when aggregate demand remains at $AD_2$?

(a) Output in Fig. 12-12(a) increases to $y_2$ while the price level rises to $p_2$. In Fig. 12-12(b) there is movement up Phillips curve $P_1$; the unemployment rate declines to $u_1$ while the inflation rate increases to $\pi_2$.

(b) Output will not remain at $y_2$ nor will the unemployment rate stay at $u_1$. Because the inflation rate has increased from $\pi_1$ to $\pi_2$, labor demands an increase in its nominal wage, which shifts the aggregate supply curve $AS_1$ leftward to $AS_2$ in Fig. 12-12(a). Output returns to $y_f$ and the price level increases to $p_3$. Aggregate supply shifts inward as a result of this increase in the cost of producing output; the Phillips curve in Fig. 12-12(b) shifts rightward to $P_2$; and the unemployment and inflation rates are now 6% and $\pi_2$.

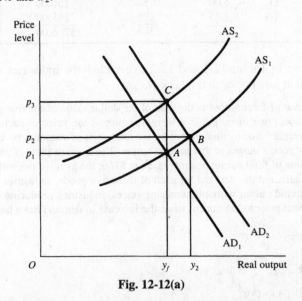

**Fig. 12-12(a)**

**12.11.** Can the unemployment rate remain below its natural rate in the long run?

An economy's unemployment rate can be below the natural rate in the short run but not in the long run. Increases in aggregate spending, which keep output above the economy's full-employment level, are eventually

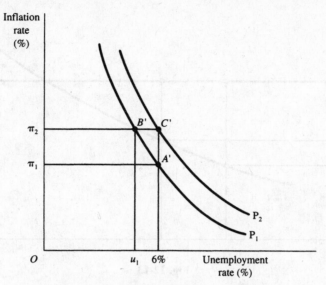

**Fig. 12-12(b)**

met by leftward shifts of the aggregate supply curve which move output back toward its full-employment level. Shifts of aggregate supply occur because an abnormally low unemployment rate results in labor shortages which increase wages and the cost of producing output.

## GOVERNMENT DEFICITS

**12.12.** (a)   What is a federal deficit?

(b)   What is the difference between a structural deficit and a cyclical deficit?

(a)   A deficit exists for the federal government when (1) its outlays (government expenditures plus transfers) exceed its gross tax revenues or (2) government expenditures exceed net tax receipts (gross tax revenues less transfers).

(b)   There is a structural deficit when government outlays exceed tax receipts at the full-employment level of output, i.e., when government revenues at their maximum under the existing tax structure are insufficient to pay for all government outlays. Net tax receipts decline as output falls, since gross tax revenues are directly related to income, and transfers (e.g., unemployment insurance) increase when there are fewer jobs and more people are unemployed. A cyclical deficit develops when government expenditures are unchanged and net tax receipts decrease because of lower output.

**12.13.** In Fig. 12-13, $T'$ represents net tax receipts, while $G'$ represents government expenditures; full-employment output is $y_f$.

(a)   Why are net tax receipts positively related to output, whereas government expenditures are constant?

(b)   Find the structural and cyclical deficit when output is $y_f$ and $y_1$.

(a)   Net tax receipts equal gross tax revenues less government transfers. Gross tax revenues are positively related to output because most federal taxes are based on private-sector income. Government transfers are negatively related to output since transfers, such as unemployment insurance, increase when fewer people are employed. Government expenditures are unrelated to income since most congressionally authorized expenditures are not tied to the receipt of tax revenue.

(b)   The structural deficit is unrelated to output; it is $BC$ at output levels $y_1$ and $y_f$. There is no cyclical deficit when output is at full-employment level $y_f$; it is $AB$ when output is $y_1$ and below full employment.

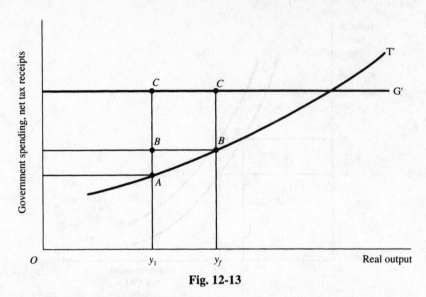

**Fig. 12-13**

**12.14.** How can the structural deficit be reduced?

In the short run, the structural deficit can be reduced by increasing tax revenues or by decreasing government outlays (transfers or expenditures). A structural deficit can also be reduced in the long run if tax revenues increase faster than government outlays. Economic growth results in higher output. Higher output produces greater tax revenues because many private-sector taxes are related to income. By restricting the growth of government outlays as tax revenues increase, the structural deficit decreases as a result of economic growth.

**12.15.** (*a*)  Should Congress try to avoid annual federal deficits by passing legislation that mandates that the budget be balanced annually?

(*b*)  Why is a cyclically balanced budget more advisable than an annually balanced budget?

(*a*)  The government should not try to balance receipts and outlays annually since an annually balanced budget will be procyclical—i.e., recessions will be deeper and expansions more inflationary. Tax revenues automatically fall with output, and thus a mandate for an annually balanced budget would require that government spending be reduced as revenues fall. Since the expenditure multiplier is larger than the tax multiplier, an equal decrease in taxes and government expenditures would cause greater reductions in aggregate spending and deepen a recession. Similarly, during an expansion increased government expenditures would further expand aggregate spending and accelerate inflation.

(*b*)  A cyclically balanced budget is one where there is no federal deficit for a complete business cycle. A cyclically balanced budget overcomes the procyclical disadvantages of an annually balanced budget by allowing for deficits during recessions, surpluses during expansions, and a balanced budget over the business cycle. While theoretically appealing, a cyclically balanced budget may be difficult to implement. Since each business cycle has unique characteristics, each recession and each expansion is usually not of the same magnitude or duration. Thus, it may be impossible to equate government receipts and outlays over each business cycle.

## THE PUBLIC DEBT

**12.16.** (*a*)  Will the federal government default or go bankrupt as a result of an increasing public debt?

(*b*)  Does a large public debt place a burden on future generations?

(*a*)  *Default* occurs when a borrower fails to meet its financial obligations. *Bankruptcy* exists when a borrower's debts far exceed its ability to meet its financial obligations. The federal government will neither default nor face bankruptcy since it has the power to tax and print money. Suppose, for example, the federal government has no tax revenue to meet interest payments. It can secure whatever funds it needs by raising taxes. Alternatively, since it is the sole issuer of paper currency, it can print paper currency and use it to meet interest payments. Thus, government has virtually unlimited sources of funds to meet the interest payments on its debt.

(b)  A public debt places a burden on future generations to the extent that taxes are imposed on later generations to pay interest on the debt and to the extent that the debt is foreign-owned. Interest payments impose a burden in that government taxes current income to make interest transfers to those who own the debt. In addition, when government borrows from foreigners, future generations must be taxed not only to make interest payments but to eventually repay the debt, which reduces the quantity of goods available in the domestic economy.

**12.17.**  Suppose the federal debt is $100,000 and is completely owned by the banking system.

(a)  Use T accounts for the Federal Reserve and for the banking system to record the Federal Reserve's purchase of the existing $100,000 interest-bearing debt owned by the banking system.

(b)  Why is a country ill-advised to monetize its interest-bearing debt?

(a)

**Banking System**

| Δ Assets | | Δ Liabilities |
|---|---|---|
| Government securities | −$100,000 | |
| Reserves | +$100,000 | |

**Federal Reserve**

| Δ Assets | | Δ Liabilities | |
|---|---|---|---|
| Government securities | +$100,000 | Bank reserves | +$100,000 |

(b)  The Federal Reserve monetizes debt by purchasing interest-bearing government securities. The banking system upon selling these debt instruments to the Federal Reserve has additional reserves which allow the banking system to increase the checking-deposit component of the money supply. Governments are ill-advised to monetize debt to eliminate interest-bearing obligations because doing so might effect too large an increase in the money supply, resulting in inflation.

## Multiple Choice Questions

**1.**  An increase in the cost of producing output, *ceteris paribus,*
(a)  increases the price level and real output,
(b)  increases the price level and decreases real output,
(c)  increases the price level and has no effect upon real output,
(d)  has no effect upon the price level or real output.

**2.**  When there is a Keynesian aggregate supply curve, an increase in aggregate demand results in proportional increases in
(a)  real output, as long as output is below its full-employment level,
(b)  the price level, as long as output is below its full-employment level,
(c)  the cost of producing real output, as long as output is below its full-employment level,
(d)  real output once output is at its full-employment level.

**3.**  An increase in aggregate demand results in an increase in output
(a)  and in the price level when there is a Keynesian aggregate supply curve,
(b)  and no change in the price level when aggregate supply is vertical,
(c)  and in the price level when aggregate supply is positively sloped,
(d)  and no change in the price level when aggregate supply is positively sloped.

**4.** The Phillips curve shows that
   (a) high unemployment rates are associated with low inflation rates,
   (b) high unemployment rates are associated with high inflation rates,
   (c) high unemployment rates are associated with a large increase in the nominal wage,
   (d) high inflation rates are associated with a small increase in the nominal wage.

**5.** In the short run, increases in the nominal wage are associated with
   (a) movement up a Phillips curve,
   (b) an outward shift of the Phillips curve,
   (c) a decrease in the rate of unemployment,
   (d) increased likelihood of demand-pull inflation.

**6.** The existence of a natural rate of unemployment suggests that
   (a) there is no inflation-unemployment trade-off in the long run,
   (b) nominal wage increases lag price increases in the long run,
   (c) nominal wage increases lead price increases in the long run,
   (d) the short-run Phillips curve is steeper than the long-run Phillips curve.

**7.** A federal deficit exists when
   (a) government expenditures are greater than gross tax revenues plus government transfers,
   (b) government expenditures plus government transfers are greater than gross tax revenues,
   (c) gross tax revenues less government transfers are greater than government expenditures,
   (d) gross tax revenues plus government transfers are greater than government expenditures.

**8.** What happens to the structural deficit and the cyclical deficit when the unemployment rate is above the natural unemployment rate?
   (a) The structural deficit increases; there is no change in the cyclical deficit.
   (b) The structural deficit and the cyclical deficit increase.
   (c) The cyclical deficit increases; there is no change in the structural deficit.
   (d) The cyclical deficit increases, while the structural deficit decreases.

**9.** The public debt imposes a burden on future generations when
   (a) the government balances the budget over the business cycle,
   (b) it is completely owed to citizens of the issuing country,
   (c) it is largely owed to foreigners,
   (d) taxes do not have to be increased in the future to cover higher interest payments on the debt.

**10.** The federal deficit increased during the 1980s because
   (a) federal outlays increased at a faster rate than federal transfers,
   (b) federal outlays increased at a faster rate than net tax receipts,
   (c) federal outlays increased at a faster rate than federal revenues,
   (d) government expenditures increased at a faster rate than federal transfers.

## True or False Questions

**11.** _____ An increase in personal income tax rates results in cost-push inflation.

**12.** _____ Output decreases and the price level increases when there is cost-push inflation.

**13.** _____ Demand-pull inflation will never occur unless output is at its full-employment level.

**14.** _____ Demand-pull inflation results in stagflation.

**15.** _____ The Phillips curve shows that there is an inverse relationship between the inflation rate and the unemployment rate in the short run.

**16.** _____ Rightward shifts of the Phillips curve are caused by leftward shifts of aggregate supply.

**17.** _____ The unemployment rate will not be below the natural rate of unemployment in the long run.

**18.** _____ The United States has had a cyclical deficit every year for the past 40 years.

**19.** _____ The structural deficit decreases over time when federal outlays increase at a slower rate than federal revenues.

**20.** _____ The Federal Reserve is monetizing the public debt when it implements open-market operations and purchases government securities from the private sector.

### Answers to Multiple Choice and True or False Questions

| | | | |
|---|---|---|---|
| **1.** (b) | **6.** (a) | **11.** (F) | **16.** (T) |
| **2.** (a) | **7.** (b) | **12.** (T) | **17.** (T) |
| **3.** (c) | **8.** (c) | **13.** (F) | **18.** (F) |
| **4.** (a) | **9.** (c) | **14.** (F) | **19.** (T) |
| **5.** (b) | **10.** (c) | **15.** (T) | **20.** (T) |

# Chapter 13

# Economic Growth and Productivity

## *Chapter Summary*

1. Economic growth exists when there is an increase in an economy's ability to produce, and/or an increase in its output per capita. An increase in output per capita means the economy is producing more goods and services per person and therefore the economy's standard of living is improving.

2. In the early nineteenth century, economists failed to realize the productivity benefits derived from technological change. They applied the law of diminishing return to population growth and projected a decline in output per capita. Malthus's predictions were most dismal; rapid population growth would reduce living standards to a subsistence level.

3. Neoclassical growth theory focuses upon capital accumulation and the attendant benefits to output per capita. Increases in the economy's ratio of capital to labor (known as capital deepening) were perceived as the source of this benefit. This theory held that capital deepening would cease—and an economy would reach a steady state—when the rate of return from capital was equal to the real rate of interest.

4. U.S. productivity growth slowed during the 1970s and 1980s, returning to the slower rate that had existed in the early twentieth century. Economists have been unable to empirically establish the cause of this productivity growth slowdown.

5. Supply-siders in the 1970s and 1980s proposed tax cuts as a way of increasing U.S. productivity growth. They contended that lower tax rates for individuals and businesses would increase saving, investment, and the incentive to work (which would improve labor productivity).

## *Important Terms*

**Capital deepening.**   An accumulation of capital that results in an increase in the ratio of capital to labor.

**Capital-output ratio.**   The ratio of the economy's stock of capital to total output.

**Capital widening.**   An increase in capital that is necessary because of increases in the labor supply; i.e., capital additions are necessary to keep the ratio of capital to labor constant.

**Economic growth.**   The increase in an economy's ability to produce, as measured by the absolute or relative increase in GDP or in per capita output over time.

**Labor productivity.**   Labor's output per hour measured by dividing real GDP by the number of hours worked by labor.

**Law of diminishing returns.**   The tendency of incremental output to fall as additional inputs of a variable resource are used with a fixed quantity of other economic sources.

**Malthusian theory of population.**   The economy's ability to grow food increases at a slower rate than the increase in population, resulting in a decreasing standard of living.

**Neoclassical model of economic growth.**   A model of growth which emphasizes the importance of capital deepening and technological change.

216

**Output per capita.**   Total output (GDP) divided by the total population.

**Steady state.**   A situation whereby capital deepening ceases and there is no further increase in the economy's standard of living.

**Supply-side economics.**   An approach to economic policy which emphasizes potential output.

# Outline of Chapter 13: Economic Growth and Productivity

## 13.1   CONCEPT OF ECONOMIC GROWTH

Economic growth is concerned with the expansion of an economy's ability to produce (potential gross domestic product) over time. Expansion of potential output $Y_p$ occurs when there is an increase in natural resources $R$, human resources $N$, or capital $K$, or when there is a technological advance. The two most common measures of economic growth are an increase in real GDP and an increase in output per capita. Of these two measures, an increase in output per capita is more meaningful since it indicates there are more goods and services available per person and hence a rise in the economy's standard of living. An increase in potential output can be conceptualized by an outward shift of an economy's production-possibility frontier (see Chapter 2). In our discussion of economic growth, we shall assume that increases in potential output are matched by equal increases in spending so that full-employment growth is assured.

**EXAMPLE 13.1.**   Suppose an economy's production-possibility frontier is curve PP' in Fig. 13-1; aggregate spending is composed of $A_1$ units of private-sector goods and $B_1$ units of public-sector goods. Assume that an increase in economic resources shifts the production-possibility frontier outward to TT'. When the increase in potential output is matched by an equal increase in aggregate spending, the output of private-sector goods could increase from $A_1$ to $A_2$, while production of public goods increases from $B_1$ to $B_2$.

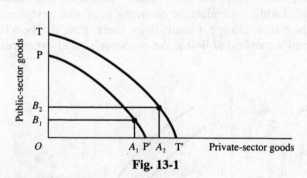

**Fig. 13-1**

## 13.2   POPULATION AND ECONOMIC GROWTH

An increase in the labor supply, *ceteris paribus,* expands potential output. The law of diminishing returns shows that the incremental output from an additional labor input decreases when other economic resources and technology are unchanged. Thus, the possibility exists that aggregate output could increase while output per capita decreases. Expecting rapid population growth, economists in the early 19th century predicted such growth would result in declining output per capita. The predictions of Thomas Malthus in particular were dismal; he held that the population would increase at a such a rapid rate that the economy would increasingly be unable to grow enough food to feed its population; eventually output per capita would fall to a subsistence level. While technology has allowed highly industrialized countries to avoid the gloomy projections of early 19th-century economists, rapid population growth is a problem for many developing countries.

**EXAMPLE 13.2.**   Suppose there is no technological change and nonlabor economic resources are unchanged; the labor supply is initially 200 units in period $t$ and increases 10% during each successive time period; output is initially $1,000,000 and increases by 5%, 4%, and 3% in successive time periods as a result of increases in the labor supply. Table 13-1 presents the labor supply and aggregate output over four successive time periods. Note that output per capita has decreased over the four periods; the labor supply is obviously increasing faster than aggregate output.

**Table 13-1**

| Time Period | Labor Inputs | Output (in constant $s$) | Output per Worker (in constant $s$) |
|:-----------:|:------------:|:------------------------:|:-----------------------------------:|
| $t$         | 200          | 1,000,000                | 5,000.00                            |
| $t + 1$     | 220          | 1,050,000                | 4,772.73                            |
| $t + 2$     | 242          | 1,092,000                | 4,512.40                            |
| $t + 3$     | 266          | 1,124,760                | 4.228.42                            |

## 13.3   CAPITAL ACCUMULATION AND ECONOMIC GROWTH

The neoclassical model of economic growth maintains that, in the absence of technological change, an economy reaches a steady state—a situation in which there are no further increases in output per capita. In the steady state, capital deepening ceases, although capital widening may still occur because of growth in the labor supply. Capital widening exists when capital additions are made to keep the ratio of capital per worker constant because of increases in the supply of labor. Capital deepening occurs when there is more capital per worker, i.e., there is an increase in the ratio of capital to labor. When there is no technological advance, capital additions which are capital widening do not change output per worker; however, capital additions which are capital deepening increase output per worker. There is no population growth in a simplified neoclassical model of growth; thus, all capital additions are capital deepening and therefore increase output per worker. When there is no change in the labor force, capital additions result in diminishing returns and have decreased rates of return. Capital additions cease—and the economy reaches a steady state—when the rate of return from capital additions equals the economy's real rate of interest. Since there is a limit to capital deepening when there is no change in technology, there must also be a limit to output per worker and therefore to the economy's standard of living. An economy's steady-state position can be pushed to a

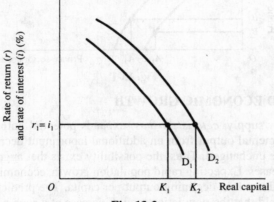

**Fig. 13-2**

higher level of output per worker by an increase in its rate of saving, by improved technology, and/or by better education of its population.

**EXAMPLE 13.3.**   Suppose technology, the labor supply, and the quantity of natural resources are unchanged; the diminishing returns associated with increases in the stock of capital are represented by curve $D_1$ in Fig. 13-2. Additions to the economy's stock of capital cease along curve $D_1$ when the capital stock reaches $K_1$ since the rate of return from capital $r_1$ is equal to the $i_1$ real rate of interest. Once capital stock $K_1$ is reached, there are no further increases in output per worker and the economy's standard of living.

**EXAMPLE 13.4.**   Suppose a technological advance shifts the return from capital curve $D_1$ in Fig. 13-2 rightward to $D_2$. At real interest rate $i_1$, the maximum capital stock is now $K_2$. Thus, an economy can continuously experience capital deepening and avoid a steady state—where output per worker no longer increases—as long as there is technological change.

## 13.4   THE PRODUCTIVITY GROWTH SLOWDOWN IN THE UNITED STATES

Productivity is measured by dividing real GDP by the total number of hours worked by labor. Over the past 20 years, the growth of labor productivity in the United States has slowed dramatically. Whereas labor productivity—labor's output per hour—increased at an average annual rate of 2.5% between 1948 and 1973, it fell to an annual rate of 0.7% between 1973 and 1991. Although economists have been unable to empirically establish the cause of this productivity growth slowdown, a number of factors appear to be responsible: (1) an increase in environmental regulations, (2) high energy costs in the 1970s, which resulted in the substitution of more labor and capital for energy, and (3) a large increase in the number of less skilled workers in the labor force during the 1970s. Many economists recommend that policies be implemented which would increase private-sector saving, increase capital accumulation, and thereby increase output per worker.

**EXAMPLE 13.5.**   A productivity growth slowdown has implications for a country's standard of living. Standard of living is measured by an economy's real GDP per capita (total output divided by population), whereas productivity is measured as real GDP per hour of labor input (output divided by the number of hours worked to produce this output). Suppose an economy's labor force is *always* 50% of its population. Increases in labor's output per hour will result in higher GDP per capita and therefore raise the economy's standard of living. When output per hour is unchanged, there will be no increase in ouput per capita and therefore no improvement in the economy's standard of living.

## 13.5   SUPPLY-SIDE ECONOMICS

Concern about the slowdown in U.S. productivity growth during the 1970s helped popularize the theory of supply-side economics. Supply-siders stressed that U.S. productivity would be enhanced by actions which promoted incentives to produce. A decrease in private-sector taxes was proposed. Proponents of this theory called for a decrease in corporate income tax rates, which would increase corporate profits and therefore business saving; this in turn would encourage business investment and capital accumulation. A reduction in the personal income tax rate would increase the reward from working and promote the work ethic, which is perceived as a way of increasing labor productivity. Decreased tax rates on interest income and corporate dividends would increase household saving, which would result in capital deepening. While not identified as supply-side economics, various measures have been promoted in the 1990s which would also increase the economy's ability to produce. Improvement of the U.S. educational system and making job retraining more readily available would enhance labor skills, increase worker productivity, and thereby promote economic growth.

**EXAMPLE 13.6.**   In Fig. 13-3, it is assumed that the labor supply and population are unchanged and that a combination of tax incentives and a better-educated population shift the aggregate supply curve $AS_1$ rightward to $AS_2$. An increase in the money supply shifts aggregate demand from $AD_1$ to $AD_2$; the price level remains constant and output increases from $y_1$ to $y_2$. Since there is no change in population, output per capita has increased with an attending rise in the economy's standard of living.

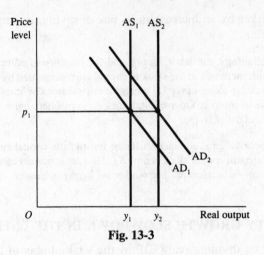

**Fig. 13-3**

# Solved Problems

## CONCEPT OF ECONOMIC GROWTH

**13.1.** Explain how the analysis of economic growth differs from the analysis of equilibirum output in Chapters 7 through 12.

The analysis of equilibrium output focuses upon spending and the economy's equilibrium level of output when potential output is unchanged. Thus, the analysis of equilibrium output is short-run; it focuses upon the necessary change in the money supply, taxes, or government spending to bring output to its full-employment level. Economic growth analyzes outward shifts of the production-possibility frontier over time. It takes a longer-term look at output and evaluates the effect of resource growth upon productive capacity and the economy's standard of living.

**13.2.** Table 13-2 presents growth in real GDP for Country A and Country B. Find each country's

    (*a*)   relative increase in output between 1984 and 1994,

    (*b*)   output per capita for 1984 and 1994, and

    (*c*)   relative increase in output per capita between 1984 and 1994.

    (*d*)   Which measure of economic growth [that which is calculated in (*a*) or (*b*)] is more useful?

**Table 13-2**

|  | 1984 | 1994 |
|---|---|---|
| **Country A** | | |
| Real GDP | $650,000,000 | $1,300,000,000 |
| Population | 166,000 | 224,000 |
| **Country B** | | |
| Real GDP | $528,614,000 | $1,295,100,000 |
| Population | 135,000 | 270,000 |

    (*a*)   The relative increase in output is found by dividing 1994 output by that for 1984. The relative increase in Country A's real GDP is 2.0 ($1,300,000,000/$650,000,000); thus, Country A's real GDP doubled between 1984 and 1994. The relative increase for Country B is 2.45 for the same period; B's real GDP more than doubled.

(b) An economy's per capita GDP is found by dividing real GDP by the economy's population. In Country A, per capita output is $3915.66 in 1984 and $5803.57 in 1994. Country B's per capita output increased from $3915.66 in 1984 to $4796.67 in 1994.

(c) The relative increase in per capita output between 1984 and 1994 is found by dividing per capita output in 1994 by that in 1984. The relative increase in per capita output is 1.48 for Country A and 1.22 for Country B.

(d) Economic growth is frequently presented as the increase in real GDP. While useful for some analysis, increases in real GDP do not measure the economic well-being of individuals in an economy, which is best measured by increases in per capita output. The calculations in parts (a) and (c) show how one might reach different conclusions about an economy's economic growth. Country B's real GDP more than doubled between 1984 and 1994, while A's only doubled; B obviously has increased its output at a faster rate than A. On a per capita basis, however, output per capita increased more rapidly in Country A than B. Which measure is more useful depends upon one's intent in measuring growth. When one is only interested in the increase in aggregate output, growth in real GDP is the relevant measure. However, when the focus is upon the standard of living in the economy, output per capita is the better measure of economic growth.

**13.3.** What is the importance of an increase in output per capita?

An increase in output per capita raises an economy's standard of living. When there is no change in output per capita, increased output of one good necessitates decreased output of other goods. Economic growth can eliminate such need for substitution since it increases the amount of goods and services produced in an economy.

**13.4.** Suppose an economy's production-possibility frontier is PP' in Fig. 13-4.

(a) Does the production of a combination of net investment and other private and public sector goods at point B rather than A affect an economy's growth?

(b) Should a society select point A or B?

(a) Net investment adds to an economy's stock of capital and its productive capacity. Thus, point B results in greater capital accumulation and is a position for more rapid economic growth.

(b) In deciding between points A and B, a society is making a decision about having (1) more private and public sector goods today (point A) or (2) less today (point B) and more sometime in the future. Point A is selected when current goods are more valuable to a society than future goods; point B is selected when a society is willing to sacrifice today for a higher standard of living in the future.

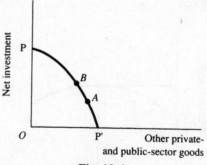

**Fig. 13-4**

**13.5.** What objections, if any, are there to economic growth?

Some economists object to maximizing economic growth because in doing so it may possibly affect the quality of life, in such ways as pollution of the environment and waste of natural resources. Maximized economic growth may also fail to resolve socioeconomic problems or may exacerbate them. Rapid economic growth through technological change in many instances increases worker obsolescence (workers no longer have skills needed in the labor markets), brings about new anxieties and insecurities because of the potential of obsolescence, and undermines family relationships as the workplace takes on greater importance than human relationships. Although attempts are being made to curb pollution, industrial waste is a by-product of increased output. It therefore can be expected that water, land, and air pollution will increase with time. Waste of economic resources may also result when least-cost methods dictate current resource use with little attention paid to the possible effect that current use may have upon future generations. And there is no guarantee that growth resolves socioeconomic problems such as poverty. Poverty in an economy is relative to the economy's standard of living. Thus, growth does not resolve the problem of relative poverty, which is only resolved by a redistribution of current income.

## POPULATION AND ECONOMIC GROWTH

**13.6.** In the early 19th century, Thomas Malthus theorized that population would increase at a rate faster than the economy's ability to produce food.

    (a)    Use the law of diminishing returns to explain Malthus's position.

    (b)    What does Malthus's theory of population suggest about living standards for an ecoonomy?

    (c)    Might it be possible to postpone Malthus's dismal predictions?

    (a)    The incremental output of food per labor input falls when additional labor units are added to a fixed amount of land, given no change in technology. With the marginal output of food declining, rapid population growth would exceed increases in the production of food, and the average output of food per worker would decline.

    (b)    When the average output of food per worker falls, each individual will have decreasing quantities of food over time. Lower-income individuals will be pushed toward a subsistence diet; starvation will eventually check the population expansion and leave lower-income individuals at the subsistence level.

    (c)    Malthus's application of the law of diminishing returns to the production of food assumes a constant state of technology and no increase in resources other than population. If farmable land increases in proportion to the growth of population, food output should increase proportionately and there should be no decrease in average farm output. On the other hand, new technology, such as crop rotation and fertilizers, would increase the productivity of land and raise the average output of food per unit of labor input. Thus, the postponement of Malthus's dismal prediction depends upon technological advance occurring more rapidly than population growth.

**13.7.** An average output-per-capita curve is presented in Fig. 13-5, holding constant technology and non-labor economic resources.

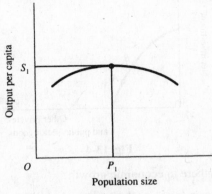

**Fig. 13-5**

    (a)    Why is $P_1$ the economy's optimum population?

    (b)    What happens to the optimum population when there is a technological advance and/or an increase in nonlabor economic resources?

    (a)   $P_1$ is the economy's optimum population: to the left of $P_1$ output per capita rises as population increases; to the right of $P_1$ output per capita falls as population increases. Thus output per capita is at its maximum—as is the economy's standard of living—when population is $P_1$.

    (b)   The output curve shifts upward and to the right when there are technological advances and/or increases in nonlabor economic resources. Thus, the optimum population occurs at a population size greater than $P_1$, and output per capita can exceed $S_1$.

**13.8.** Suppose an economy has a population of $P_2$ and the average output-per-capita curve is L′ in Fig. 13-6.

    (a)   Does this economy have an optimum population and maximum standard of living?

    (b)   Suppose there is technological advance which shifts the output per capita curve upward to L″ and the population increases to $P_4$. Has there been an increase in the economy's standard of living?

    (c)   What can this economy do to increase its standard of living?

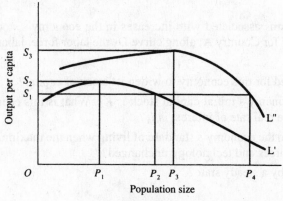

**Fig. 13-6**

    (a)   Population $P_2$ exceeds the economy's optimum population for output-per-capita curve L′. Thus, output per capita is $S_1$ rather than $S_2$, which would exist at population $P_1$ along curve L′.

    (b)   Output per capita is still $S_1$ for output curve L″ when the population is $P_4$. Although advances have been made in technology, no change has occurred in the economy's standard of living because of the large increase in the economy's population.

    (c)   There is a need to limit population growth. If the increase in population was $P_3$, output per capita would have risen to $S_3$ and the economy's standard of living would have improved.

**13.9.** Why is rapid population growth a deterrent to economic growth for a developing country?

    Many developing countries can be characterized as follows: a large percentage of their economic resources is devoted to the production of food; the labor force is largely unskilled, and illiteracy is widespread; many families are at or near a subsistence standard of living; capital is scarce; there is considerable malnutrition and disease and a high infant-mortality rate. Given these characteristics, the output-per-capita curve in Fig. 13-5 shifts upward slowly over time. But when these characteristics are combined with rapid population growth, ouput per capita may fail to rise and might even fall. Slower population growth is necessary, as are larger upward shifts of the output-per-capita curve, which can be achieved through education (increases in labor skills), better nutrition (improvement in labor productivity), capital accumulation, and adoption of modern farming techniques such as crop rotation, fertilization, and hybrid seeds.

## CAPITAL ACCUMULATION AND ECONOMIC GROWTH

**13.10.** (a)   What is meant by capital accumulation?

      (b)   When does capital accumulation result in capital widening and capital deepening?

(c)   Does capital widening or capital deepening result in an increase in the economy's standard of living?

(a)   Capital accumulation occurs when an economy adds to its stock of capital. For example, the economy has more machines and factories available to produce goods and services.

(b)   Capital widening exists when more capital is needed to support increases in the economy's labor supply. For example, suppose an economy's real capital is $100,000 and there are 100 people in the labor supply. The economy's capital-labor ratio is $1000; each worker has $1000 in capital to work with. When 20 additional people enter the labor force, capital must increase $20,000 to maintain the existing capital-labor ratio—thus, there is capital widening. Capital deepening occurs when the capital-labor ratio increases. The ratio of capital to labor is $1000 when the capital stock is $100,000 and there are 100 people in the labor supply. An increase in the stock of capital to $110,000, with no change in the labor force, increases the ratio of capital to labor to $1100—thus, there is capital deepening.

(c)   Capital widening maintains labor productivity since labor has the same amount of capital to work with and there is no change in per capita output. Capital deepening increases labor productivity since labor works with increasing amounts of capital. Thus, capital deepening, caused by increases in the capital-labor ratio, raises labor productivity and output per capita, which results in a higher standard of living.

**13.11.** The incremental returns associated with increases in the economy's stock of capital are shown by curve $D_1$ in Fig. 13-7 for Country A; along curve $D_1$ the labor force, labor skills, and technology are unchanged.

(a)   Is there any need for this economy to widen its stock of capital?

(b)   Suppose the economy's initial capital stock is $K_1$. What is this economy's maximum stock of capital when the real rate of interest is $i_1$?

(c)   What happens to the economy's standard of living when the maximum capital stock is reached, with other resources and technology unchanged?

(d)   What is meant by a steady state?

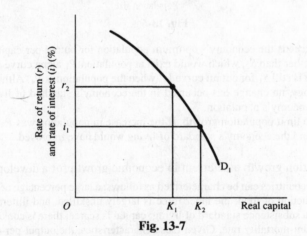

**Fig. 13-7**

(a)   There is no need for capital widening since the labor supply is unchanged.

(b)   An economy reaches its maximum capital stock when the rate of return from capital equals the real rate of interest. The rate of return from capital stock $K_1$ in Fig. 13-7 is $r_2$ which exceeds the real rate of interest $i_1$. Thus, there is capital deepening until the capital stock reaches $K_2$, which is the economy's maximun stock of capital.

(c)   Capital deepening increases labor productivity and therefore the economy's standard of living. Once the maximum capital stock is reached, there are no further increases in the economy's standard of living.

(d)   A steady state is a situation where there is no further capital deepening and therefore no improvement in an economy's standard of living.

**13.12.** What can a country do to improve its standard of living when it has reached a steady state?

There are a number of measures that a country can take to increase its standard of living. One approach would be to encourage private-sector saving. Further capital deepening will occur when increased saving lowers the economy's real rate of interest. Labor productivity is enhanced by improving labor skills; this can be achieved by training and various educational programs. Labor productivity also increases when there is greater worker motivation and technological advance. Thus, it is unlikely that an economy will reach a steady state unless technological change ceases and it becomes impossible to improve the skills of the labor supply.

## THE PRODUCTIVITY GROWTH SLOWDOWN IN THE UNITED STATES

**13.13.** (a)   How is productivity measured?

(b)   Does an increase in labor productivity mean that increased output is due to the efforts of labor?

(c)   Why are increases in labor productivity important?

(a)  Productivity is measured by relating the number of hours worked by labor to produce output. Thus, productivity measures the output per hour of labor input.

(b)  Increased labor productivity could be the result of a more highly motivated labor force or a better-educated one which produces more output per hour. Greater output per hour could also be the result of capital deepening or technological advance. Thus, while productivity is measured in terms of labor inputs, increases in productivity may be the result of factors other than the labor force.

(d)  Increases in labor productivity are the basis for increasing labor's real wage and therefore its standard of living. Productivity increases also allow for a shorter workweek and more vacation time. Thus, quality of life can be enhanced by increased productivity.

**13.14.** Increases in labor productivity in the United States over 10-year intervals are presented in Table 13-3. What has been happening to increases in U.S. productivity during the 20th century?

**Table 13-3**

| Period | Percentage Increase in Output per Hour of Labor Output |
|---|---|
| 1900–1910 | 5.9 |
| 1910–1920 | 17.7 |
| 1920–1930 | 24.3 |
| 1930–1940 | 26.0 |
| 1940–1950 | 31.9 |
| 1950–1960 | 23.7 |
| 1960–1970 | 26.7 |
| 1970–1980 | 11.8 |
| 1980–1990 | 9.2 |

Continuous increases occurred in the growth of labor productivity each decade until a peak was reached during the decade of 1940–1950. Improvements in labor productivity remained high from 1950 to 1970 but slowed in the 1970s and 1980s. Concern about increases in U.S. productivity focuses upon the 1970–1990 period because it represents one of the slowest periods of productivity growth during the 20th century.

## SUPPLY-SIDE ECONOMICS

**13.15.** What factors contribute to economic growth?

An economy's potential output depends upon its natural and human resources, stock of capital, and technological capability. An economy's natural resources are relatively fixed and not a major source of increased productive capacity over time. Since some of these natural resources, such as petroleum deposits, may be undiscovered, they are a source of economic growth when they are found. An increase in the economy's labor force and/or in the number of hours worked per week expands an economy's productive capacity as does improvement in the educational level and skills of an existing labor force. Capital accumulation, where the number of machines and factories is increased, is a key element to the growth process. Through capital accumulation an economy is able to use capital (e.g., a machine) rather than labor to manufacture goods. By substituting capital for labor, productive capacity is enhanced since labor resources are then available to produce other goods and services. Technology is the development and application of new knowledge to enhance the productive process. It may involve investment in new and more efficient machinery or more effective ways of combining existing resources.

**13.16.** What economic measures did the proponents of supply-side economics promote in the 1970s and 1980s?

Supply-siders during the 1970s and 1980s advocated cutting various private-sector tax rates; in their judgment, a burdensome tax system undermined an economy's potential output. High taxes in the United States were seen as undermining saving, and business investment, and people's desire to work and innovate. A high income tax rate was believed to discourage saving since it lowers the reward for saving. For example, a 5% return on saving is only 2.5% when an individual pays a 50% effective income tax rate to federal, state, and local governments. When high tax rates discourage saving, there is less investment and capital deepening and slower productivity growth. A high personal income tax rate and a readily available, poorly monitored welfare system can undermine personal motivation. A highly progressive income tax structure means that individuals rapidly move to higher and higher income tax brackets as a result of success in the workplace. Supply-siders viewed such a tax structure as a disincentive to succeed since, on an after-tax basis, success is not adequately compensated. And a poorly monitored but generous welfare system can act as a disincentive to less-skilled workers who may seek welfare relief rather than improve skills and become productive members of the labor force. Thus, supply-siders hoped to reverse the productivity slowdown that had taken place in the United States by cutting taxes and reversing what they believed were disincentives to work and save.

**13.17.** What economic measures are being promoted in the 1990s to increase economic growth?

The 1990s have emphasized worker training and employment, elimination of workplace discrimination, and improvement of elementary and secondary education. Worker training and employment are viewed as ways of making the labor markets become more efficient. Some workers in the labor markets are not productive because their skills are not currently sought (workers' skills may become obsolete because of changing demand patterns or technological advance) or they did not develop adequate skills while still in school. Retraining such workers provides them with marketable skills and obviously increases their productivity. Workplace discrimination slows productivity growth. When discrimination is absent, the best- and more productive-worker is hired; when discrimination exists, a less-qualified worker may be hired because of religion, gender, color, or ethnic origin, which is an obvious deterrent to productivity. Better educated workers are also more productive. They can read and follow directions, think constructively, and offer suggestions for improving production techniques; also, they have self-confidence, which is essential for high worker performance.

## *Multiple Choice Questions*

1.  There is an increase in the economy's potential output when there is
    (a)   an increase in government spending,
    (b)   a decrease in government spending,
    (c)   an increase in the economy's capital stock,
    (d)   an increase in the economy's depreciation rate.

2.  There is an increase in output per capita when a 10% increase in the population is associated with a
    (a)   10% increase in output,
    (b)   20% increase in output,
    (c)   10% increase in the capital stock,
    (d)   5% increase in output.

3.  According to the law of diminishing returns, continuous increases in population size with no change
    in other resources or technology
    (a)   eventually result in an increase in real output per capita,
    (b)   eventually result in a decrease in real output per capita,
    (c)   have no effect upon an economy's ability to produce food,
    (d)   eventually increase an economy's ability to produce food.

4.  According to Malthusian population theory, in the long run output per capita
    (a)   tends toward the subsistence level,
    (b)   increases at an increasing rate,
    (c)   increases at a decreasing rate,
    (d)   does not increase.

5.  Capital deepening occurs when there is
    (a)   an increase in the stock of capital,
    (b)   an equal increase in the stock of capital and the labor supply,
    (c)   a greater increase in the labor supply than in the stock of capital,
    (d)   a greater increase in the stock of capital than in the labor supply.

6.  Capital deepening ceases
    (a)   as a result of population growth,
    (b)   when there is no additional increase in the population,
    (c)   when the rate of return from capital is equal to the real rate of interest,
    (d)   when the real rate of interest falls, *ceteris paribus*.

7.  Labor productivity in the United States
    (a)   was unchanged during the 1970s and 1980s,
    (b)   was increasing at a faster rate in the 1980s than in the 1930s,
    (c)   increased at a slower rate in the 1970s than in the 1960s,
    (d)   increased at a faster rate in the 1970s than in the 1960s.

8.  Which of the following does not result in an increase in output per capita?
    (a)   Capital widening,
    (b)   Capital deepening,
    (c)   Technological advance,
    (d)   Better-educated workers.

9.  Which of the following proposals would not be supported by supply-side economists?
    (a)   A decrease in the personal income tax rate,
    (b)   Improved welfare benefits,
    (c)   A decrease in the capital gains tax rate,
    (d)   A decrease in the corporate income tax rate.

10. Which of the following proposals would increase labor productivity?
    (a)   Improve the educational system,
    (b)   Reduce job discrimination,

(c)  Retrain workers,
(d)  All of the above.

## True or False Questions

11. _____  An economy's standard of living is rising when real GDP is increasing 10% while population is increasing 5%.

12. _____  Assuming full employment of resources, an increase in the labor force, *ceteris paribus*, increases output.

13. _____  Assuming full employment of resources, an increase in the labor force, *ceteris paribus*, always increases output per capita.

14. _____  Malthus's theory of population maintained that population growth would eventually push the economy's living standard to the subsistence level.

15. _____  Capital deepening ceases when the real rate of return from capital equals the real rate of interest.

16. _____  Additions to the economy's stock of capital always result in capital deepening and capital widening.

17. _____  Labor productivity is found by dividing output by the number of workers in the labor force.

18. _____  Supply-siders in the 1980s advocated government-sponsored retraining programs.

19. _____  Supply-side policies aim at increasing the economy's ability to produce.

20. _____  The slowdown in U.S. productivity growth was caused by capital widening.

### Answers to Multiple Choice and True or False Questions

| | | | |
|---|---|---|---|
| 1. (c) | 6. (c) | 11. (T) | 16. (F) |
| 2. (b) | 7. (c) | 12. (T) | 17. (F) |
| 3. (b) | 8. (a) | 13. (F) | 18. (F) |
| 4. (a) | 9. (b) | 14. (T) | 19. (T) |
| 5. (d) | 10. (d) | 15. (T) | 20. (F) |

# Chapter 14

# Demand, Supply, and Elasticity

## *Chapter Summary*

1. In Chapter 3, we examined how demand and supply curves determine the equilibrium price and quantity of a commodity in a free-enterprise system. This chapter extends the discussion to the concept and measurement of demand and supply elasticities.
2. The elasticity of demand ($E_D$) measures the percentage change in the quantity demanded of a commodity as a result of a given percentage change in price. Demand is said to be elastic if $E_D > 1$, unitary elastic if $E_D = 1$, and inelastic if $E_D < 1$.
3. When the price of a commodity falls, demand is elastic, unitary elastic, or inelastic depending on whether total revenue rises, remains unchanged, or declines, respectively.
4. The elasticity of supply ($E_S$) measures the percentage change in the quantity supplied of a commodity as a result of a given percentage change in its price. Supply is said to be elastic if $E_S > 1$, unitary elastic if $E_S = 1$, and inelastic if $E_S < 1$.
5. The concept of elasticity has many useful applications. For example, the more inelastic demand is, the greater is the burden on consumers of a per-unit tax collected from producers. On the other hand, for a given demand, the more elastic the supply, the greater is the incidence of the tax on consumers.

## *Important Terms*

**Elasticity of demand ($E_D$).** The measurement of the (average) percentage change in the quantity demanded of a commodity as a result of a given (average) percentage change in its price, expressed as a positive pure number. Demand is said to be elastic, unitary elastic, or inelastic if $E_D > 1$, $E_D = 1$, or $E_D < 1$, respectively.

**Elasticity of supply ($E_S$).** The measurement of the (average) percentage change in the quantity supplied of a commodity as a result of a given (average) percentage change in its price, expressed as a positive pure number. Supply is elastic, unitary elastic, or inelastic if $E_S > 1$, $E_S = 1$, or $E_S < 1$, respectively.

**Equilibrium.** The market condition where the quantity of a commodity that consumers are willing and able to purchase equals the quantity producers are willing to supply. Geometrically, equilibrium occurs at the intersection of the market demand and supply curves of the commodity. The price and quantity at which equilibrium exists are known, respectively, as the equilibrium price and the equilibrium quantity.

**Incidence of a tax.** The burden or proportion of the tax paid. The incidence on consumers of a per-unit tax collected by the government from producers indicates the proportion of the tax burden that actually falls on consumers in the form of higher prices. The more inelastic the demand and the more elastic the supply, the greater is the incidence of the tax on consumers.

**Market demand curve.** A graphic representation showing the total quantity of a commodity that consumers are willing and able to purchase over a given period of time at various alternative commodity prices when everything else that affects demand is constant. The market demand curve of a commodity is negatively sloped, because more of the commodity will be purchased at lower commodity prices.

**Market supply curve.** A graphic representation showing the total quantity of a commodity that producers are willing to produce or sell over a given period of time at various alternative commodity prices when everything else that affects supply is constant. The market supply curve for a commodity is usually positively sloped, because higher prices must be paid to induce producers to supply more of the commodity.

**Shortage.**   An excess in the quantity demanded over the quantity supplied of a commodity over a given period of time which leads to a pressure on the commodity price to rise.

**Surplus.**   The excess in the quantity supplied over the quantity demanded of a commodity over a given period of time which leads to a pressure on the commodity price to fall.

**Total revenue (TR).**   The total amount received in exchange for goods or services, which is equal to price times quantity.

# Outline of Chapter 14: Demand, Supply, and Elasticity

## 14.1   DEMAND, SUPPLY, AND MARKET PRICE

In Section 3.1 we introduced the concepts of demand schedule and demand curve, and in Section 3.3, the supply schedule and supply curve. Then, in Section 3.5, we brought together demand and supply and showed how the equilibrium market price and quantity are determined in a free-enterprise system. After briefly reviewing these basic concepts, this chapter extends our discussion to the concept and measurement of elasticities of demand and supply and shows their usefulness with some applications.

**EXAMPLE 14.1.**   Table 14-1 gives a hypothetical market demand and supply schedule for wheat; it shows whether a surplus or shortage occurs at each price and indicates the pressure on price toward equilibrium. The market demand and supply schedules of Table 14-1 are plotted in Fig. 14-1. The figure shows that at the prices of $4 and $3, a surplus results which drives the price down. At the price of $1, a shortage results which drives the price up. Thus, the equilibrium price is $2 because the quantity demanded, 4500 bushels of wheat per month, equals the quantity supplied.

**Table 14-1**

| Price ($ per bu) | Quantity Demanded in the Market (1000 bu per month) | Quantity Supplied in the Market (1000 bu per month) | Surplus (+) or Shortage (−) | Pressure on Price |
|---|---|---|---|---|
| $4 | 2.0 | 7.0 | +5 | downward |
| 3 | 3.0 | 6.0 | +3 | downward |
| 2 | 4.5 | 4.5 | 0 | equilibrium |
| 1 | 6.5 | 2.5 | −4 | upward |

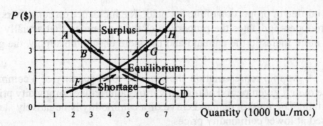

**Fig. 14-1**

## 14.2   ELASTICITY OF DEMAND

The elasticity of demand ($E_D$) measures the percentage change in the quantity demanded of a commodity as a result of a given percentage change in its price. The formula is

$$E_D = \frac{\text{percentage change in the quantity demanded}}{\text{percentage change in price}}$$

$$= \frac{\text{change in quantity demanded}}{\text{original quantity demanded}} \div \frac{\text{change in price}}{\text{original price}}$$

$E_D$ can also be calculated in terms of the new quantity and new price; however, different results would then be obtained. To avoid this problem, economists generally measure $E_D$ in terms of the average quantity and the average price, as follows:

$$E_D = \frac{\text{change in quantity demanded}}{\text{sum of quantity demanded}/2} \div \frac{\text{change in price}}{\text{sum of prices}/2}$$

$E_D$ is a pure number. As such, it is a better measurement tool than the slope, which is always expressed in terms of the units of measurement [see Problem 14.3($d$)]. Also, $E_D$ is always expressed as a positive number, even though price and quantity demanded move in opposite directions. The demand curve is said to be elastic if $E_D > 1$, unitary elastic if $E_D = 1$, and inelastic if $E_D < 1$.

**EXAMPLE 14.2.**   The elasticity between points $A$ and $B$ along the demand curve of Fig. 14-1 is calculated below, using the original, new, and average quantities and prices.

$$E_D = \frac{\text{change in quantity}}{\text{original quantity}} \div \frac{\text{change in price}}{\text{original price}} = \frac{1}{2} \div \frac{1}{4} = \frac{1}{2} \times \frac{4}{1} = \frac{4}{2} = 2$$

$$= \frac{\text{change in quantity}}{\text{new quantity}} \div \frac{\text{change in price}}{\text{new price}} = \frac{1}{3} \div \frac{1}{3} = \frac{1}{3} \times \frac{3}{1} = \frac{3}{3} = 1$$

$$= \frac{\text{change in quantity}}{\text{sum of quantities}/2} \div \frac{\text{change in price}}{\text{sum of prices}/2} = \frac{1}{(2+3)/2} \div \frac{1}{(4+3)/2} = \frac{1}{2.5} \div \frac{1}{3.5} = \frac{1}{2.5} \times \frac{3.5}{1} = \frac{3.5}{2.5} = 1.4$$

By convention, we use the last result and say that this demand curve is elastic (on the average) between points $A$ and $B$. The student should check to see that between $B$ and $E$, (average) $E_D = 1$.

## 14.3   ELASTICITY AND TOTAL REVENUE

When the price of a commodity falls, the total revenue of producers (price times quantity) increases if $E_D > 1$, remains unchanged if $E_D = 1$, and decreases if $E_D < 1$. This is because when $E_D > 1$, the percentage increase in quantity exceeds the percentage *decline* in price and so total revenue (TR) increases. When $E_D = 1$, the percentage increase in quantity equals the percentage decline in price and so TR remains unchanged. Finally, when $E_D < 1$, the percentage increase in quantity is less than the percentage decline in price, and so TR falls.

We can also say that as price falls, demand is elastic, unitary elastic, or inelastic depending on whether total revenue rises, remains unchanged, or declines, respectively.

**EXAMPLE 14.3.**   According to the total revenue rule, the market demand curve of Fig. 14-1 is shown in Table 14-2 to be elastic between points $A$ and $B$, unitary elastic between $B$ and $E$, and inelastic between $E$ and $C$ (see also Example 14.2 and Multiple Choice Question 5).

**Table 14-2**

| Point | $P$ (in $) | $QD$ (in thousands) | TR (in thousand $) | $E_D$ |
|-------|------------|---------------------|--------------------|-------|
| $A$   | $4         | 2.0                 | $8.0               | elastic |
| $B$   | 3          | 3.0                 | 9.0                | unitary |
| $E$   | 2          | 4.5                 | 9.0                | inelastic |
| $C$   | 1          | 6.5                 | 6.5                | |

The elasticity of demand is greater (1) the greater the number of good substitutes available, (2) the greater the proportion of income spent on the commodity, and (3) the longer the period of time considered.

## 14.4  ELASTICITY OF SUPPLY

The *elasticity of supply* ($E_S$) measures the percentage change in the quantity *supplied* of a commodity as a result of a given percentage change in its price. As in the case of elasticity of demand, we get different values for the elasticity of supply if we use the original or the new price and quantity. To avoid this problem, we again use the average quantity and price as follows:

$$E_s = \frac{\text{change in quantity supplied}}{\text{sum of quantities supplied}/2} \div \frac{\text{change in price}}{\text{sum of prices}/2}$$

$E_S$ is a pure number and is positive because price and quantity move in the same direction. Supply is said to be elastic if $E_S > 1$, unitary elastic if $E_S = 1$, and inelastic if $E_S < 1$.

**EXAMPLE 14.4.**   The (average) elasticity between points $F$ and $E$ along the supply curve of Fig. 14-1 is

$$E_s = \frac{2}{(2.5 + 4.5)/2} \div \frac{1}{(1 + 2)/2} = \frac{1}{3.5} \div \frac{1}{1.5} = \frac{1}{3.5} \times \frac{1.5}{1} = \frac{1.5}{3.5} \simeq 0.43.$$

The student should check to see that between $E$ and $G$, $E_S = \frac{3.75}{5.25} \simeq 0.71$. Thus, the supply curve of Fig. 14-1 is inelastic between $F$ and $G$. The supply curve becomes more elastic the longer the time period under consideration (see Problem 14.13).

## 14.5  APPLICATIONS OF ELASTICITY

The concept of elasticity has many useful applications. It tells us whether the price of a subway or taxi ride should be increased or decreased in order to increase total revenue, and it explains why farmers' income often rises in times of bad harvest (see Problem 14.14). It shows that the more inelastic the demand for a commodity, the greater the burden (or incidence) on consumers of a per-unit tax collected from producers (see Problem 14.15). On the other hand, for a given demand, the more elastic the supply, the greater the incidence of the tax on consumers (see Problem 14.16). Elasticity can also help the government determine the relative cost of various alternative farm-aid programs (see Problem 14.17).

# Solved Problems

## DEMAND, SUPPLY, AND MARKET PRICE

**14.1.**   (a)   What do a demand schedule and demand curve show?

(b)   What do a supply schedule and supply curve show?

(c)   How is the market price of a commodity determined in a free-enterprise system?

(d)   What is held constant in drawing a demand curve? What happens if there is change?

(e)   What is held constant in drawing a supply curve? What happens if there is change?

(a)   A *demand schedule* shows the quantity demanded of a commodity per unit of time at various alternative prices for the commodity, when everything else that affects demand is held constant. Plotting a demand schedule, we get a *demand curve*. This is negatively sloped because price and quantity are inversely related along a demand curve. See also Section 3.1.

(b)   A *supply schedule* shows the quantity supplied of a commodity per unit of time at various alternative prices for the commodity, when everything else that affects supply is held constant. Plotting a supply schedule, we get a *supply curve*. This is usually positively sloped because more of the commodity will be supplied at higher prices. See also Section 3.3.

(c)   In a free-enterprise system, the *market* or *equilibrium price* (and quantity) of a commodity is determined at the intersection of the market demand and supply curves for the commodity. This is the price at which the quantity of the commodity that consumers are willing to purchase over a given period of time exactly equals the quantity producers are willing to supply. At higher prices, the quantity demanded falls short of the quantity supplied and the resulting *surplus* will push the price down toward its equilibrium level. At prices below the equilibrium price, the quantity demanded exceeds the quantity supplied, and the resulting *shortage* will drive the price up toward the equilibrium level. Thus, the equilibrium market price, once achieved, tends to persist. See also Section 3.5.

(*d*) In defining the market demand curve for a commodity, it is assumed that the number of consumers, consumers' tastes, and money incomes, and the price of related commodities remain constant. The market demand curve will *increase* or *shift up* if the number of consumers increases, if their money incomes rise, if the price of substitute commodities rises, or if the price of complementary commodities falls. Opposite changes will cause a *decrease* or *downward shift* in demand. A commodity's equilibrium market price and quantity will both rise when its demand curve shifts up; both will fall when it shifts down.

(*e*) In defining the market supply curve of a commodity, technology, factor prices, and the price of other commodities related in production remain unchanged. If the number and size of producers of the commodity increase, if technology improves, or if the prices of factors or other commodities (related in production) fall, then the entire market supply curve of the commodity will increase (i.e., shift down and to the right), leading to a lower equilibrium market price and higher quantity.

**14.2.** A hypothetical market demand and supply schedule of wheat is given in Table 14.3(a).

**Table 14-3(a)**

| Price ($ per bu) | Quantity Demanded in the Market (billion bu per year) | Quantity Supplied in the Market (billion bu per year) |
|---|---|---|
| $5 | 2.5 | 5.7 |
| 4 | 3.5 | 5.5 |
| 3 | 5.0 | 5.0 |
| 2 | 7.0 | 4.0 |
| 1 | 10.0 | 2.5 |

(*a*) Prepare a table showing the market equilibrium price and quantity. Show the surplus or shortage and the pressure on price at prices other than equilibrium.

(*b*) Graph the results from part (*a*).

(*a*) See Table 14-3(b).

**Table 14-3(b)**

| Price ($/bu) | QD (billion bu/year) | QS (billion bu/year) | Surplus (+) or Shortage (−) | Pressure on Price |
|---|---|---|---|---|
| $5 | 2.5 | 5.7 | +3.2 | downward |
| 4 | 3.5 | 5.5 | +2.0 | downward |
| 3 | 5.0 | 5.0 | 0 | equilibrium |
| 2 | 7.0 | 4.0 | −3.0 | upward |
| 1 | 10.0 | 2.5 | −7.5 | upward |

(*b*) See Fig. 14-2.

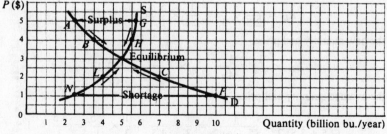

**Fig. 14-2**

## ELASTICITY OF DEMAND

**14.3.**  (a)  What happens to the quantity demanded of a commodity when its price falls? How do we measure the responsiveness in the quantity demanded of a commodity to a change in its price?

(b)  Give the formula for the elasticity of demand. How is the percentage change in quantity calculated? The percentage change in price?

(c)  How is the slope of the demand curve measured? How is this different from the elasticity of demand?

(d)  Why is the slope of demand an unsatisfactory measure of the responsiveness in the quantity demanded of a commodity to a change in its price? How does the elasticity of demand overcome these difficulties?

(a)  When the price of a commodity falls, the quantity demanded of the commodity per unit of time increases. This is indicated by a downward movement along the negatively sloped demand curve for the commodity. The responsiveness in the quantity demanded of a commodity per unit of time is measured by the elasticity of demand ($E_D$).

(b)  $E_b = \dfrac{\text{the percentage change in the quantity demanded of the commodity}}{\text{the percentage change in the commodity price}}$

The percentage change in the quantity demanded is found by dividing the change in quantity by the original quantity or by the new quantity. Because we get different results if we use the original or the new quantity, we divide the change in quantity by the *average* of the original and new quantities. Similarly, the percentage change in price is found by dividing the change in price by the original price or by the new price. But to avoid different results, we usually use the average price.

(c)  The slope between any two points on a line is found by the vertical change divided by the horizontal change. Since we plot price on the vertical axis and quantity along the horizontal axis in drawing a demand curve, the slope of the demand curve is measured by the *change in price* divided by the change in quantity. This is different from the elasticity of demand, which measures the *percentage change in quantity* divided by the percentage change in price.

(d)  The slope of the demand curve cannot adequately measure the responsiveness in the quantity demanded of a commodity to a change in its price because the slope is expressed in specific units of measurement. By simply changing the units of measurement (i.e., dollars to cents, pounds to tons, etc.), we get a different slope for the same demand curve. In addition, since the slope is expressed in specific units of measurement, it cannot be used to compare the responsiveness of the demand of different commodities to changes in their prices. The elasticity of demand avoids these difficulties by comparing percentage changes which have no units attached to them.

**14.4.**  Find the elasticity of the market demand curve in Problem 14.2, using the original, the new, and the average quantity and price between points

(a)  $A$ and $B$,

(b)  $B$ and $E$,

(c)  $E$ and $C$, and

(d)  $C$ and $F$.

(a)  The elasticity of demand between points $A$ and $B$ when the original quantity and price are used is

$$E_D = \frac{1}{2.5} \div \frac{1}{5} = \frac{1}{2.5} \times \frac{5}{1} = \frac{5}{2.5} = 2$$

Using the new quantity and price,

$$E_D = \frac{1}{3.5} \div \frac{1}{4} = \frac{1}{3.5} \times \frac{4}{1} = \frac{4}{3.5} \simeq 1.14$$

Using the average quantity and price,

$$E_D = \frac{1}{(2.5 + 3.5)/2} \div \frac{1}{(5 + 4)/2} = \frac{1}{3} \div \frac{1}{4.5} = \frac{1}{3} \times \frac{4.5}{1} = \frac{4.5}{3} = 1.5$$

(b)  Between points $B$ and $E$ when the original quantity and price are used,

$$E_D = \frac{1.5}{3.5} \div \frac{1}{4} = \frac{1.5}{3.5} \times \frac{4}{1} = \frac{6}{3.5} \approx 1.71$$

Using the new quantity and price,

$$E_D = \frac{1.5}{5} \div \frac{1}{3} = \frac{1.5}{5} \times \frac{3}{1} = \frac{4.5}{5} = 0.90$$

Using the average quantity and price,

$$E_D = \frac{1.5}{4.25} \div \frac{1}{3.5} = \frac{5.25}{4.25} \approx 1.24$$

(c)  Between points $E$ and $C$, in terms of the original quantity and price,

$$E_D = \frac{2}{5} \div \frac{1}{3} = \frac{2}{5} \times \frac{3}{1} = \frac{6}{5} = 1.20$$

Using the new quantity and price,

$$E_D = \frac{2}{7} \div \frac{1}{2} = \frac{2}{7} \times \frac{2}{1} = \frac{4}{7} \approx 0.57$$

Using the average quantity and price,

$$E_D = \frac{2}{6} \div \frac{1}{2.5} = \frac{2}{6} \times \frac{2.5}{1} = \frac{5}{6} \approx 0.83$$

(d)  Between points $C$ and $F$, using the original quantity and price,

$$E_D = \frac{3}{7} \div \frac{1}{2} = \frac{3}{7} \times \frac{2}{1} = \frac{6}{7} \approx 0.86$$

Using the new quantity and price,

$$E_D = \frac{3}{10} \div \frac{1}{1} = \frac{3}{10} \times \frac{1}{1} = 0.30$$

Using the average quantity and price,

$$E_D = \frac{3}{8.5} \div \frac{1}{1.5} = \frac{3}{8.5} \times \frac{1.5}{1} = \frac{4.5}{8.5} \approx 0.53$$

**14.5.**  From the hypothetical market demand schedule in Table 14-4, find the elasticity of market demand between points

(a)  $A'$ and $B'$,

(b)  $B'$ and $E'$,

(c)  $E'$ and $C'$, and

(d)  $C'$ and $F'$.

### Table 14-4

| Price ($ per bu) | Quantity Demanded in the Market (billion bu per year) | Alternative or Point |
|---|---|---|
| $5 | 3.5 | $A'$ |
| 4 | 4.2 | $B'$ |
| 3 | 5.0 | $E'$ |
| 2 | 6.0 | $C'$ |
| 1 | 7.5 | $F'$ |

(a)   Since nothing is specified to the contrary, we follow the convention of using the average quantity and price to measure the elasticity of the market demand schedule in Table 14-4. Thus, between $A'$ and $B'$,

$$E_D = \frac{0.7}{(3.5 + 4.2)/2} \div \frac{1}{(4 + 5)/2} = \frac{0.7}{3.85} \div \frac{1}{4.5} = \frac{0.7}{3.85} \times \frac{4.5}{1} = \frac{3.15}{3.85} \approx 0.82$$

(b)   Between $B'$ and $E'$,

$$E_D = \frac{0.8}{4.6} \div \frac{1}{3.5} = \frac{0.8}{4.6} \times \frac{3.5}{1} = \frac{2.8}{4.6} \approx 0.61$$

(c)   Between $E'$ and $C'$,

$$E_D = \frac{1}{5.5} \div \frac{1}{2.5} = \frac{1}{5.5} \times \frac{2.5}{1} = \frac{2.5}{5.5} \approx 0.45$$

(d)   Between $C'$ and $F'$,

$$E_D = \frac{1.5}{6.75} \div \frac{1}{1.5} = \frac{1.5}{6.75} \times \frac{1.5}{1} = \frac{2.25}{6.75} \approx 0.33$$

**14.6.**   If we refer to the market demand of Table 14-3 as $D_1$ and that of Table 14-4 as $D_2$,

(a)   find the slope of $D_1$ between points $A$ and $B$. How does this comapre with $E_D$ between points $A$ and $B$?

(b)   What is the relationship of $E_D$ found by using the original, the new, and the average quantity and price for $D_1$?

(c)   What happens to $E_D$ as we move down $D_1$ and $D_2$?

(d)   What is the relationship between $E_D$ of $D_1$ and $D_2$?

(e)   Plot $D_1$ and $D_2$ on the same set of axes. Can you explain the answer to part (d) by the slope of $D_1$ and $D_2$?

(a)   The slope of $D_1$ between points $A$ and $B$ is equal to the change in price over the change in quantity, or $\frac{-1}{+1} = (-)1$. This is different from $E_D$ [see the solution to Problem 14.4(a)].

(b)   For any movement along $D_1$, $E_D$ is always largest when the original quantity and price are used; $E_D$ is always smallest when the new quantity and price are used. $E_D$ when the average quantity and price are used will always lie between the $E_D$ found by using the original quantity and price and the $E_D$ found by using the new quantity and price (see Problem 14.4).

(c)   As we move down $D_1$ and $D_2$, $E_D$ falls (see Problems 14.4 and 14.5). This is usually, but not always, the case.

(d)   For corresponding changes in prices and movements along $D_1$ and $D_2$, (average) $E_D$ is always greater on $D_1$ than on $D_2$.

(e)   See Fig. 14-3.

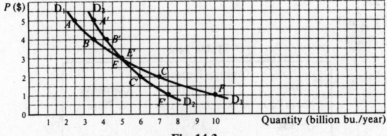

**Fig. 14-3**

Since $D_2$ is steeper or has a greater (absolute) slope than $D_1$, and $E_D$ is always less on $D_2$ than on $D_1$, we might be tempted to say that the steeper the demand curve, the smaller its elasticity. While this is true here, it is not always the case—especially if the demand curves do not cross. We cannot (and should not) generally infer much about the elasticity of a demand curve by looking at its slope.

**14.7.** Find the elasticity of the market demand curve of Fig. 14-4 between points

    (a)   *A* and *C*,

    (b)   *C* and *F*, and

    (c)   *F* and *H*.

    (d)   How do the results of parts (*a*), (*b*), and (*c*) compare with the slope of this demand curve?

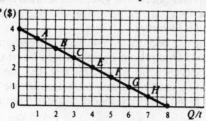

Fig. 14-4

    (a)   Between *A* and *C*, $E_D = \frac{2}{2} \div \frac{1}{3} = \frac{2}{2} \times \frac{3}{1} = \frac{6}{2} = 3$. This is equivalent to finding $E_D$ at point *B* (the midpoint between *A* and *C*) because we used the average quantity of 2 units and the average price of \$3 (point *B*).

    (b)   Between *C* and *F*, $E_D = \frac{2}{4} \div \frac{1}{2} = \frac{2}{4} \times \frac{2}{1} = \frac{4}{4} = 1$. This is equivalent to finding $E_D$ at point *E* (the midpoint between *C* and *F*).

    (c)   Between *F* and *H*, $E_D = \frac{2}{6} \div \frac{1}{1} = \frac{2}{6} \times \frac{1}{1} = \frac{2}{6} = \frac{1}{3}$. This is equivalent to finding $E_D$ at point *G*.

    (d)   Since the market demand curve of Fig. 14-4 is a straight line, its slope is constant at $(-)\frac{4}{8} = (-)\frac{1}{2}$. Thus, while the slope of a straight-line demand curve is constant, $E_D > 1$ above the midpoint (*E*), $E_D = 1$ at *E* and $E_D < 1$ below the midpoint. This is always the case for a straight-line demand curve.

**14.8.** (*a*)   On the same set of axes, draw a demand curve which is vertical ($D_1$), and one which is horizontal ($D_2$).

    (b)   What is the elasticity of $D_1$? Why?

    (c)   What is the elasticity of $D_2$? Why?

    (a)   See Fig. 14-5.

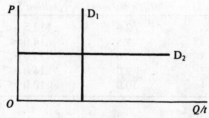

Fig. 14-5

    (b)   $E_D$ of $D_1$ is always equal to zero because there is no percentage change in quantity, regardless of the change in price. Thus, when the slope of a demand curve is infinite, its elasticity is zero. This is always the case.

    (c)   $E_D$ of $D_2$ is infinite because the percentage change in quantity is very large for an infinitesimally small percentage change in price. Thus, when the slope of D is zero, its elasticity is infinite. Note that vertical and horizontal demand curves are very rare occurrences, and it is only in these two cases that we can correctly infer the elasticity of demand by looking at the slope.

## ELASTICITY AND TOTAL REVENUE

**14.9.** What is the relationship between total revenue and elasticity

    (a)   if price declines? Why?

    (b)   if price rises? Why?

(c) What general conclusion can you reach with regard to the relationship between price, total revenue, and elasticity?

(a) If TR rises as $P$ falls, $E_D > 1$. The reason for this is that for TR to rise, the percentage increase in quantity must exceed the percentage decline in price. This is the definition of an elastic demand. If TR remains unchanged as $P$ falls, $E_D = 1$, because for TR to remain unchanged, the percentage increase in quantity must be equal to the percentage decline in price (i.e., demand is unitary elastic). Finally, if TR falls as $P$ falls, $E_D < 1$ because for TR to fall, the percentage increase in quantity must be less than the percentage fall in price (i.e., demand is inelastic).

(b) If TR rises as $P$ rises, $E_D < 1$ because for TR to rise, the percentage *decrease* in quantity (the numerator in the elasticity formula for a price increase) must be less than the percentage *increase* in price (the denominator). If TR is unchanged as $P$ rises, $E_D = 1$, because for TR to remain unchanged, the percentage decrease in quantity must equal the percentage increase in price. Finally, if TR falls as $P$ rises, $E_D > 1$, because for TR to fall, the percentage decrease in quantity must exceed the percentage increase in price.

(c) If $P$ and TR move in the same direction, $E < 1$; if $P$ and TR move in opposite directions, $E > 1$; if TR remains unchanged as $P$ rises or falls, $E_D = 1$. This is a very handy rule for the student to remember.

**14.10.** Construct a table for each of the following, showing the relationship between price, quantity, total revenue, and elasticity:

(a) $D_1$ of Table 14-3 and Fig. 14-3,

(b) $D_2$ of Table 14-4 and Fig. 14-3, and

(c) the demand of Fig. 14-4.

(a) See Table 14-5.
Between points $A$ and $E$ in Table 14-5, $D_1$ is elastic because as $P$ falls, TR rises; from $E$ to $F$, $D_1$ is inelastic because as $P$ falls, TR also falls (compare these results with those of Problem 14.4).

**Table 14-5**

| Point | $P$ (in $) | $QD$ (billion bu/year) | TR (billion $) | $E_D$ |
|-------|-----------|------------------------|----------------|-------|
| A | $5 | 2.5 | $12.5 | elastic |
| B | 4 | 3.5 | 14.0 | elastic |
| E | 3 | 5.0 | 15.0 | inelastic |
| C | 2 | 7.0 | 14.0 | inelastic |
| F | 1 | 10.0 | 10.0 | |

(b) See Table 14-6.
Since in Table 14-6, TR falls continuously as $P$ falls, $D_2$ is always inelastic (compare these elasticity results with those of Problem 14.5).

**Table 14-6**

| Point | $P$ (in $) | $QD$ (billion bu/year) | TR (billion $) | $E_D$ |
|-------|-----------|------------------------|----------------|-------|
| A' | $5 | 3.5 | $17.5 | inelastic |
| B' | 4 | 4.2 | 16.8 | inelastic |
| E' | 3 | 5.0 | 15.0 | inelastic |
| C' | 2 | 6.0 | 12.0 | inelastic |
| F' | 1 | 7.5 | 7.5 | |

(c)  See Table 14-7.

A straight-line demand curve extended to the axes is elastic above its geometric midpoint (E), inelastic below its midpoint, and unitary elastic at its midpoint (see Problem 14.7).

**Table 14-7**

| Point | $P$ (in $) | $QD$ (billion bu/year) | $TR$ (billion $) | $E_D$ |
|-------|-----------|------------------------|------------------|-------|
| A | $3.5 | 1 | $3.5 | |
| B | 3.0 | 2 | 6.0 | elastic |
| C | 2.5 | 3 | 7.5 | elastic |
| E | 2.0 | 4 | 8.0 | elastic |
| F | 1.5 | 5 | 7.5 | inelastic |
| G | 1.0 | 6 | 6.0 | inelastic |
| H | 0.5 | 7 | 3.5 | inelastic |

**14.11.** Draw a demand curve which is unitary elastic throughout.

For a demand curve to be unitary elastic throughout, TR (or the area under the demand curve) must remain constant at every point. D in Fig. 14-6 is a rectangular hyperbola with TR = 4 and $E_D = 1$ at every point.

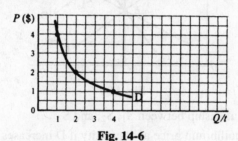

**Fig. 14-6**

**14.12.** (a)  Is the demand for table salt elastic or inelastic? Why?

(b)  Is the demand for stereos elastic or inelastic? Why?

(a)  The demand for salt is inelastic because there are no good substitutes for salt and households spend only a very small proportion of their total income on this commodity. Even if the price of salt were to rise substantially, households would reduce their purchases of salt minimally, and $E_D < 1$.

(b)  The demand for stereos is elastic because stereos are expensive and, as a luxury rather than a necessity, their purchase can be postponed or avoided when their price rises. One could also use the radio as a partial substitute for a stereo.

## ELASTICITY OF SUPPLY

**14.13.** Find the elasticity of the market supply curve in Problem 14.2 (Fig. 14-2) between points

(a)  G and H,

(b)  H and E,

(c)  E and L, and

(d)  L and N.

(a)  The elasticity of supply between points G and H is

$$E_S = \frac{\text{change in quantity supplied}}{\text{sum of quantities supplied/2}} \div \frac{\text{change in price}}{\text{sum of prices/2}}$$

$$= \frac{0.2}{(5.5 + 5.7)/2} \div \frac{1}{(5 + 4)/2} = \frac{0.2}{5.6} \div \frac{1}{4.5} = \frac{0.2}{5.6} \times \frac{4.5}{1} = \frac{0.9}{5.6} \approx 0.16$$

(b)    Between $H$ and $E$,

$$E_S = \frac{0.5}{(5.5 + 5)/2} \div \frac{1}{(4 + 3)/2} = \frac{0.5}{5.25} \div \frac{1}{3.5} = \frac{0.5}{5.25} \times \frac{3.5}{1} = \frac{1.75}{5.25} \simeq 0.33$$

(c)    Between $E$ and $L$,

$$E_S = \frac{2.5}{4.5} \simeq 0.56$$

(d)    Between $L$ and $N$,

$$E_S = \frac{2.25}{3.25} \simeq 0.69$$

Thus, this supply curve is inelastic throughout.

**14.14.** With reference to Fig. 14-7,

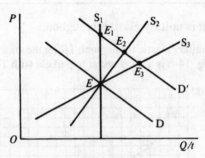

**Fig. 14-7**

(a)    explain the time relationship between $S_1$, $S_2$, and $S_3$.

(b)    What happens to equilibrium price and quantity if D increases to D′ and $S_1$, $S_2$, or $S_3$, respectively, becomes the relevant supply curve?

(a)    $S_1$ is vertical; that is, no matter what $P$ is, $Q$ remains unchanged. Thus, the elasticity of $S_1$ is zero, and supply is said to be perfectly inelastic. This is called the *market period* or the very short run. For example, on any given day, the supply of fresh milk is given and fixed regardless of its price.

$S_2$ is positively sloped and shows that producers would be willing to supply more of the commodity at higher prices. Thus, the elasticity of $S_2$ is greater than zero. For example, this may represent the supply of fresh milk over a period of a month, or the *short run*. The quantity supplied responds positively to price because producers could redirect more of their milk to consumers and less to cheese makers.

$S_3$ could refer to the supply curve of milk over a still longer time period, say, one year or more. This longer period is referred to as the *long run*. In the long run, the quantity response for a given increase in price is even greater (i.e., the supply curve is even more elastic) because over a period of one or more years, farmers could raise more cattle, build more barns, and hire more farmhands to produce more milk. Note that in the long run, $S_3$ could even be horizontal (constant costs); however, it is usually positively sloped because costs generally rise.

(b)    With D and $S_1$ or $S_2$ or $S_3$, the equilibrium price and quantity is given by point $E$ (see (Fig. 14-7). If D shifts up to D′, only $P$ rises in the market period (point $E_1$ on $S_1$). In the short run and in the long run, both price and quantity increase, but equilibrium output rises more and price less in the long run than in the short run (compare $E_3$ on $S_3$ in the long run with $E_2$ on $S_2$ in the short run).

## APPLICATIONS OF ELASTICITY

**14.15.** (a)    Should the price of a subway ride or bus ride be increased or decreased if total revenue needs to be increased?

(b)    What about the price of a taxi ride?

(c)    Why do farmers' incomes often rise when harvests are bad and fall when harvests are good?

(a) To the extent that there are no inexpensive good substitutes for public transportation in metropolitan areas, the demand for subway and bus rides is inelastic. Their prices should, therefore, be increased to increase total revenues. In addition, unless the demand for public transportation has zero elasticity, some decrease in the quantity demanded is likely to occur when its price is increased. This leads also to a reduction in operating costs. With rising total revenues and falling operating costs, municipalities can reduce their deficits in public transportation. However, this can be self-defeating. Sharply increasing the price of public transportation will encourage people to use their cars and increase congestion and pollution.

(b) For taxi rides, the case is likely to be different. Taxi rides are relatively expensive; an increase in their price may encourage people to rely much more on their cars and public transportation. To the extent that this makes the demand for taxi rides elastic, total revenue will fall when the price of taxi rides is increased. Since fewer people ride taxis when the price of taxi rides increases, total costs would also fall. What happens to the total profits (or losses) of fleet owners depends on whether total revenue or total costs fall faster. In the real world, a market study should be undertaken to estimate empirically the elasticity of demand before deciding to change prices.

(c) A bad harvest is reflected by a decrease in supply (i.e., an upward shift in the market supply curve of agricultural commodities). Given the market demand for agricultural commodities, this decrease in supply causes the equilibrium price to rise. Since the demand for agricultural commodities is usually price inelastic, the total receipts of farmers as a group increase. (When the demand for an agricultural commodity is price inelastic, the same result can be achieved by reducing the amount of land under cultivation for the commodity. This is done in some farm-aid programs.) When harvests are good, the farmers' incomes usually fall for the opposite reason.

**14.16.** Draw a figure showing that the more *inelastic* the market demand curve for a commodity, the greater the burden or incidence on the consumers of a per-unit tax collected from producers.

Mathcad

In Fig. 14-8, market demand $D_1$ is more elastic than its alternatives $D_2$ and $D_3$, while supply curve $S'$ is parallel and above S by the amount of the per-unit tax collected by the government from producers. (The supply curve shifts up by the amount of the per-unit tax in order to leave producers with the same *net* per-unit price for each quantity sold that they received before the imposition of the tax.) With either $D_1$, $D_2$, *or* $D_3$ and S (i.e., in the absence of the per-unit tax), we have equilibrium at point E. When the government imposes the per-unit tax on producers (i.e., with $S'$), the equilibrium point rises to $E_1$ with $D_1$ (the more elastic demand), to $E_2$ with $D_2$, and to $E_3$ (i.e., by the full amount of the vertical shift in $S'$ or the per-unit tax) with $D_3$. Thus, the more inelastic the market demand curve for a commodity, the more the equilibrium price will rise for a given per-unit tax collected from producers. In other words, the more inelastic the demand, the more producers are able to shift the burden or incidence of the tax to consumers in the form of higher prices.

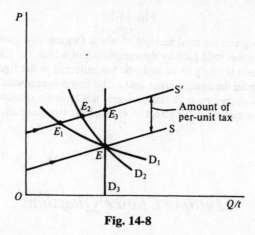

Fig. 14-8

**14.17.** Draw a figure showing that for a given demand, the more *elastic* the supply, the greater the incidence of the tax on consumers.

In Fig. 14-9, $S_2$ is more elastic than $S_1$ and equilibrium is at E without the tax. When a given per-unit tax is collected from producers, both $S_1$ and $S_2$ shift up vertically by the amount of the per-unit tax to $S_1'$ and

$S_2'$, respectively. With $S_1'$, the new equilibrium point ($E_1$) is lower than $E_2$ with $S_2'$. Thus, for a given demand, the more elastic the supply, the greater the incidence of the tax on (i.e., the greater the increase in price for) consumers and the smaller the incidence on producers or suppliers.

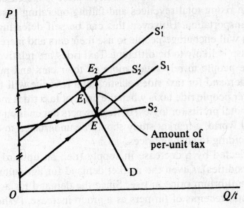

**Fig. 14-9**

**14.18.** With reference to Fig. 14-10, consider the following two aid programs for wheat farmers: (1) The government sets the price of wheat at $P_2$ per bushel and purchases the resulting surplus of wheat at $P_2$. (2) The government allows wheat to be sold at the equilibrium price of $P_1$ and grants each farmer a cash subsidy of $P_2 - P_1$ for each bushel sold. Which of the two programs is more expensive to the government?

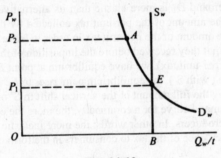

**Fig. 14-10**

Regardless of the program, the total receipts of wheat farmers as a group are the same ($OP_2$ times $OB$). The greater the fraction of this total paid by the consumers of wheat, the smaller the cost to the government. Since the demand for wheat is likely to be inelastic (as reflected in the figure), consumers' expenditures on wheat would be greater under the first program, and so the first program would cost the government less. (Note that we have assumed no storage costs in this problem, nor have we considered what the government would do with the surplus wheat and what the effect of each of the two programs would be on the welfare of the consumers.)

## Multiple Choice Questions

1. The intersection of the market demand and supply curves for a commodity determines
   (a) the equilibrium price,
   (b) the equilibrium quantity,
   (c) the price at which there is neither a surplus nor a shortage of the commodity,
   (d) all of the above.

**2.** The elasticity of demand is measured by
  (a)  the slope of the demand curve,
  (b)  the inverse of the slope of the demand curve,
  (c)  the percentage change in price for a given percentage change in quantity,
  (d)  the percentage change in quantity for a given percentage change in price.

**3.** The elasticity between points E and C along the demand curve of Fig. 14-1, using the *original* quantity and price, is
  (a)  2/4.5, or about 0.44,
  (b)  4/4.5, or about 0.89,
  (c)  4/6.5, or about 0.62,
  (d)  6/6.5, or about 0.92.

**4.** The elasticity between points E and C along the demand curve of Fig. 14-1, using the *new* quantity and price, is
  (a)  2/6.5, or about 0.31,
  (b)  2/4.5, or about 0.44,
  (c)  1/6.5, or about 0.15,
  (d)  1/4.5, or about 0.22.

**5.** The (average) elasticity between points E and C along the demand curve in Fig. 14-1 is
  (a)  3/11, or about 0.27,
  (b)  2/11, or about 0.18,
  (c)  3/5.5, or about 0.55,
  (d)  2/5.5, or about 0.36.

**6.** If total revenue remains unchanged when price changes, the demand curve is
  (a)  elastic,
  (b)  unitary elastic,
  (c)  inelastic,
  (d)  any of the above.

**7.** If total revenue rises when price falls, the demand curve is
  (a)  elastic,
  (b)  unitary elastic,
  (c)  inelastic,
  (d)  any of the above.

**8.** If total revenue rises when price rises, the demand curve is
  (a)  elastic,
  (b)  unitary elastic,
  (c)  inelastic,
  (d)  any of the above.

**9.** The demand curve for a commodity is more elastic
  (a)  the greater the number of good substitutes available,
  (b)  the greater the proportion of income spent on the commodity,
  (c)  the longer the period of time considered,
  (d)  all of the above.

**10.** The (average) elasticity between points G and H along the *supply* curve of Fig. 14-1 is
  (a)  3.5/13, or about 0.27,
  (b)  3.5/6.5, or about 0.54,

    (c)   4/13, or about 0.31,
    (d)   7/6.5, or about 1.08.

11.  When harvests are bad,
    (a)   the supply of farm products decreases,
    (b)   farm prices rise,
    (c)   farmers' incomes usually rise,
    (d)   all of the above.

12.  The burden on consumers of a per-unit tax collected from producers is greater
    (a)   the more elastic the demand curve,
    (b)   the more inelastic the demand curve,
    (c)   the more inelastic the supply curve,
    (d)   none of the above.

## True or False Questions

13.  _____  $E_D$ measures the percentage change in the quantity demanded of a commodity as a result of a given percentage change in price.

14.  _____  Demand is inelastic if $E_D < 0$.

15.  _____  Demand is inelastic if the percentage increase in quantity exceeds the percentage decrease in price.

16.  _____  Demand is elastic if the percentage decrease in price is greater than the percentage increase in quantity.

17.  _____  A decline in price leaves total revenue unchanged when $E_D = 1$.

18.  _____  Supply elasticity measures the percentage change in quantity supplied resulting from a given percentage change in price.

19.  _____  Supply is said to be elastic if $E_S < 1$, unitary elastic if $E_S = 1$, and inelastic if $E_S > 1$.

20.  _____  Demand and supply elasticities are always positive.

21.  _____  The supply curve becomes more elastic the longer the time period under consideration.

22.  _____  The concept of elasticity can be used to explain why farmers' incomes often rise during bad harvests.

23.  _____  A per-unit tax leads to a greater burden on producers the more elastic the demand for the commodity.

24.  _____  For a given demand, the more inelastic the supply, the greater the tax incidence on the consumers.

## Answers to Multiple Choice and True or False Questions

| | | | | | | | |
|---|---|---|---|---|---|---|---|
| 1. | (d) | 7. | (a) | 13. | (T) | 19. | (F) |
| 2. | (d) | 8. | (c) | 14. | (F) | 20. | (T) |
| 3. | (b) | 9. | (d) | 15. | (F) | 21. | (T) |
| 4. | (a) | 10. | (b) | 16. | (F) | 22. | (T) |
| 5. | (c) | 11. | (d) | 17. | (T) | 23. | (F) |
| 6. | (b) | 12. | (b) | 18. | (T) | 24. | (F) |

# Chapter 15

## The Theory of Consumer Demand and Utility

### *Chapter Summary*

1.  The demand curve is downward-sloping because of the substitution and income effects. These effects refer to the fact that when the price of a commodity falls, consumers use this commodity to replace similar commodities in consumption and can purchase more of this commodity and other commodities.
2.  A commodity is demanded because of the utility derived from its consumption. The law of diminishing marginal utility states that although total utility increases as more of the commodity is consumed, the marginal utility derived from each additional unit decreases.
3.  A consumer maximizes utility when the marginal utility of the last dollar spent on each commodity is the same.
4.  To derive an individual demand curve, we start at a point where the consumer is in equilibrium. At a lower price, the consumer must purchase more of the commodity to remain in equilibrium. These and other points similarly obtained define an individual downsloping demand curve.
5.  Consumer's surplus refers to the difference between what the consumer is willing to pay to purchase a given number of units of a commodity and what he or she actually pays for them. It is measured by the area under the demand curve and above the commodity price.

### *Important Terms*

**Consumer's equilibrium.**   The point at which the consumer maximizes the total utility or satisfaction from spending his or her income.

**Consumer's surplus.**   The difference between what the consumer would be willing to pay for a given amount of a commodity and what he or she actually pays.

**Diminishing marginal utility.**   A concept stating that as an individual consumes more units of a commodity per unit of time, the total utility he or she receives increases, but the extra or marginal utility decreases.

**Income effect.**   The increase in the quantity purchased of a commodity with a given money income when the commodity price falls.

**Paradox of value.**   The question of why some commodities which are essential to life cost much less than others which could be easily forgone.

**Substitution effect.**   The increase in the quantity purchased of a commodity when its price falls (as a result of switching from the purchase of other similar commodities).

**Utility.**   The property of a commodity that enables it to satisfy a want or a need.

### Outline of Chapter 15: The Theory of Consumer Demand and Utility

> 15.1   **Substitution and Income Effects and the Downsloping Demand**
> 15.2   **The Law of Diminishing Marginal Utility**

## 15.1   SUBSTITUTION AND INCOME EFFECTS AND THE DOWNSLOPING DEMAND

In Section 3.1 we saw that the market demand curve for a commodity is derived by adding the individuals' demand curves for the commodity. We also saw that each individual's (and thus the market) demand curve for a commodity is downward-sloping because of the substitution and income effects. The *substitution effect* refers to the fact that as the price of a commodity falls, consumers use it to replace similar commodities in consumption. The *income effect* refers to the fact that as the price of a commodity falls, a given money income allows the consumer to buy more of this and other commodities (because his or her purchasing power has increased).

**EXAMPLE 15.1.**   When the price of coffee falls, consumers substitute coffee for tea in consumption. In addition, when the price of coffee falls, a consumer can buy more coffee (and other commodities) with a given money income. Thus, the consumer's (and market) demand curve for coffee is downsloping because of this substitution and income effect. The better and the greater are the number of substitutes available for the commodity, the more elastic is its demand curve. A complementary explanation of the law of downward-sloping demand rests on the law of diminishing marginal utility.

## 15.2   THE LAW OF DIMINISHING MARGINAL UTILITY

An individual demands a particular commodity because of the satisfactions, or *utility*, he or she receives from consuming it. The more units of a commodity the individual consumes per unit of time, the greater is the *total utility* he receives. Although total utility increases, the extra, or *marginal*, utility received from consuming each additional unit of the commodity decreases. This is referred to as the *law of diminishing marginal utility*.

**EXAMPLE 15.2.**   For purposes of illustration, we assume in Table 15-1 that satisfaction can actually be measured in terms of units of utility called *utils*. The first two columns of Table 15-1 give an individual's hypothetical total utility (TU) schedule from consuming various quantities of commodity $X$ (say oranges) per unit of time. Note that as the individual consumes more units of $X$, $TU_x$ increases.

Columns 1 and 3 of the table give this individual's marginal utility (MU) schedule for commodity $X$. Each value of column 3 is obtained by subtracting two successive values of column 2. For example, if the individual's consumption of $X$ goes from zero units to 1, $TU_x$ goes from zero utils to 10 utils, and the MU of the first unit of $X$ is 10 utils. Similarly, if the consumption of $X$ rises from 1 unit to 2 units, $TU_x$ rises from 10 to 18, and the MU of the second unit of $X$ is 8.

**Table 15-1**

| (1) $q_x$ | (2) $TU_x$ | (3) $MU_x$ |
|---|---|---|
| 0 | 0 | |
| | | 10 |
| 1 | 10 | |
| | | 8 |
| 2 | 18 | |
| | | 6 |
| 3 | 24 | |
| | | 4 |
| 4 | 28 | |
| | | 2 |
| 5 | 30 | |

**EXAMPLE 15.3.**   The total and marginal utility schedules of Table 15-1 give the total and marginal utility curves of Fig.15-1. Since marginal utility has been defined as the *change* in total utility from a one-unit change in consumption, each value of $MU_x$ has been recorded midway between the two levels of consumption. The falling $MU_x$ curve illustrates the *law of diminishing marginal utility*.

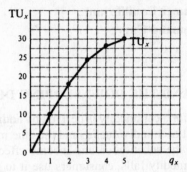 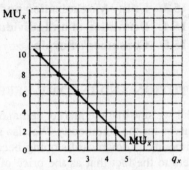

**Fig. 15-1**

## 15.3   UTILITY MAXIMIZATION AND CONSUMER EQUILIBRIUM

A consumer maximizes the total utility or satisfaction obtained from spending his or her income (and is said to be in equilibrium) when the marginal utility of the *last* dollar spent on each commodity is the same. This equilibrium condition for utility maximization can be restated as follows:

$$\frac{MU_x}{P_x} = \frac{MU_y}{P_y} = \ldots = \text{common MU of the } \textit{last } \$ \text{ spent on each commodity}$$

**EXAMPLE 15.4.**   Table 15-2 shows the marginal utility that an individual receives from consuming various units of X and Y per unit of time.

**Table 15-2**

| Units of Commodities | $MU_x$ | $MU_y$ |
|:---:|:---:|:---:|
| 1 | 10 | 6 |
| 2 | 8 | 5 |
| 3 | 6 | 4 |
| 4 | 4 | 3 |
| 5 | 2 | 2 |

Suppose that the consumer has $7 to spend on X and Y, and that $P_x$ (the price of X) = $2 and $P_y$ = $1. This consumer maximizes total utility and is in equilibrium by spending $4 of his $7 to buy 2X and the remaining $3 to purchase 3Y. At this point, $\frac{MU_x \text{ of 8 utils}}{P_x \text{ of } \$2} = \frac{MU_y \text{ of 4 utils}}{P_y \text{ of } \$1}$ = MU of 4 utils from the *last* $1 spent on X and Y. By purchasing 2X and 3Y, $TU_x$ = 18(10 + 8), $TU_y$ = 15(6 + 5 + 4), and TU from both is 33(18 + 15) utils. If this consumer spent his $7 in any other way, his TU would be less.

## 15.4   DERIVATION OF AN INDIVIDUAL'S DEMAND CURVE

Starting with a consumer in equilibrium, we get one point on his or her demand curve. At a lower commodity price, the consumer must purchase more of the commodity to be in equilibrium, and so we get another point on that demand curve. From these and other points of consumer equilibrium, we can derive a downsloping demand curve because of diminishing MU.

**EXAMPLE 15.5.**   In Example 15.4, we saw that the consumer was in equilibrium when he spent his income of $7 to purchase 2X and 3Y, at $P_x$ = $2 and $P_y$ = $1. Thus, $P_x$ = $2 and $q_x$ = 2 is one point of consumer demand for X. From Table 15-2, we see that at $P_x$ = $1; this consumer would be in equilibrium by purchasing 4X and 3Y because at that point

$$\frac{MU_x \text{ of 4 utils}}{P_x \text{ of } \$1} = \frac{MU_y \text{ of 4 utils}}{P_y \text{ of } \$1} = \text{MU of 4 utils for last } \$ \text{ spent on X and Y}$$

Table 15-3 gives two points on the consumer's demand schedule for commodity $X$. Other points could be similarly obtained. Note that because MU declines, $P_x$ must fall to induce the individual consumer to buy more of $X$. Thus, a downsloping $d_x$ can be explained in terms of diminishing $MU_x$.

**Table 15-3**

| $P_x$ | $2 | $1 |
|-------|-----|-----|
| $q_x$ | 2 | 4 |

## 15.5   CONSUMER'S SURPLUS

*Consumer's surplus* refers to the difference between what the consumer would be willing to pay to purchase a given number of units of a commodity and what he or she actually pays for them. It arises because the consumer pays for all units of the commodity the price he or she is just willing to pay for the last unit purchased, even though the MU on earlier units is greater. Consumer surplus can be measured by the area under the consumer's demand curve and above the commodity price.

**EXAMPLE 15.6.**   In Fig. 15-2, the consumer purchases $AF$ units of the commodity at price $AB$ and spends $AB$ times $AF$ (the area of the rectangle $ABCF$) on this commodity. However, this consumer would have been willing to pay a higher price for all but the last unit of this commodity purchased (as indicated by the height of her demand curve) because these previous units give her a greater MU than the last unit purchased. The difference between what she would be willing to pay for $AF$ units of the commodity (the area of $AGCF$) and what she actually pays for them (the area of $ABCF$) is an estimate of this consumer's surplus (the area of triangle $BGC$).

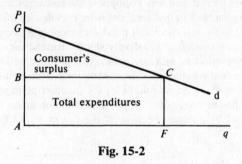

**Fig. 15-2**

# Solved Problems

## SUBSTITUTION AND INCOME EFFECTS AND THE DOWNSLOPING DEMAND

**15.1.**   (*a*)   How is the market demand for a commodity derived?

(*b*)   Why is the market demand curve for a commodity downsloping?

(*c*)   Why is the individual's demand curve for a commodity downward or negatively sloped?

(*d*)   How does the substitution effect contribute to the downward slope of the consumer's demand curve?

(*e*)   How does the income effect contribute to the downward slope of the consumer's demand curve?

(*a*)   The market demand curve for a commodity is derived by the horizontal summation of all individuals' demand curves for the commodity (see Problems 3.2 and 3.3).

(*b*)   The market demand curve for a commodity is downsloping because the consumers' demand curves for the commodity (of which the market demand is the summation) are downward or negatively sloped.

(*c*)   The individual's demand for a commodity is downsloping (indicating that at lower prices the individual demands more of the commodity per unit of time) because of the substitution and the income effects.

(d) The substitution effect refers to the fact that as the price of a commodity falls, consumers substitute this for similar commodities in consumption. For example, if the price of wine falls, we substitute wine for beer in consumption. On the other hand, if the price of wine rises, we consume less wine by substituting beer for wine.

(e) The income effect refers to the fact that a reduction in the price of a commodity increases consumers' purchasing power or real income (from given and fixed money incomes) and this allows consumers to purchase more of this (and other) commodities. For example, when the price of wine falls, a consumer can purchase more wine (and more of every other normal good) out of his or her given money income. On the other hand, if the price of wine rises, the income effect is negative.

**15.2.** Suppose that at $P_x = \$2$ and $P_y = \$1$ the consumer purchases $4X$ and $8Y$ and spends his entire income of $16. Suppose now that $P_x$ falls to $1.

**Mathcad**

(a) Explain how the income effect operates.

(b) Explain how the substitution effect operates.

(c) Explain why $d_x$ is downward or negatively sloped. How much of $X$ and $Y$ will this consumer purchase at $P_x = P_y = \$1$?

(a) When $P_x$ falls from $2 to $1, this consumer can purchase the same $4X$ and $8Y$ by spending only $12 of his fixed money income of $16. Thus, the reduction in $P_x$ increased his real income or purchasing power by $4. Suppose that he uses this $4 to buy 2 additional units of $X$ and $Y$. The additional $2X$ (and $2Y$) that the consumer is now able to purchase represents the income effect resulting from the fall in $P_x$.

(b) When $P_x$ falls from $2 to $1, commodity $X$ becomes a better buy in relation to commodity $Y$. Thus, the consumer will purchase more $X$ and less $Y$. Suppose the consumer transfers 3 units of purchases from $Y$ to $X$. The substitution effect is 3 in this case and is independent of the above income effect.

(c) When $P_x$ falls from $2 to $1, this consumer purchases more of $X$ because of the income and substitution effects. This leads to a downward or negatively sloped demand curve for commodity $X$. In part $(a)$ we assumed that the income effect is $+2X$; in part $(b)$ that the substitution effect is $+3X$. This gives a total of $+5X$ for the income and substitution effects combined. Thus, while at $P_x = \$2$ this consumer buys $4X$ (one point on $d_x$), at $P_x = \$1$ he purchases $9X$ (another point on $d_x$). Note that at the unchanged $P_y = \$1$ there is an income effect of $+2Y$ but a substitution effect of $-3Y$, for a net change of $-1Y$. Thus, $d_y$ shifts leftward by one unit because of the fall in $P_x$, so that the consumer purchases $7Y$ at $P_y = P_x = \$1$.

## THE LAW OF DIMINISHING MARGINAL UTILITY

**15.3.** (a) With what is consumer demand theory concerned? Why do we study it?

(b) What do we mean by "utility"? What does a utility schedule show?

(c) What happens to the total utility that a consumer receives from consuming increasing quantities of a commodity per unit of time?

(d) What is "marginal utility"? What happens to marginal utility as an individual consumes more units of the commodity per unit of time?

(a) Consumer demand theory is concerned with the individual's demand curve for a commodity, how it is derived, and the reasons for its location and shape. We study consumer demand theory in order to learn more about the market demand curve for a commodity (which, as shown in Section 3.1, is obtained by the horizontal summation of all individuals' demand curves for the commodity).

(b) Utility refers to the property of a commodity that enables it to satisfy a want. Without this property, there would be no demand for the commodity. For purposes of illustration, we assume that utility can be measured in terms of "utils." A utility schedule shows the number of utils that an individual receives from consuming various quantities of the commodity per unit of time. Thus, a utility schedule shows the tastes of an individual for the commodity. Different individuals usually have different tastes for the commodity and therefore have different utility schedules. When the tastes of an individual change, his or her utility schedule also changes (shifts).

(c)   As an individual consumes more units of a commodity per unit of time, the total utility (TU) he or she receives increases. However, if an individual continued to consume more and more units of a commodity, a point would be reached where the individual's total utility would stop increasing. This is called the *saturation point*. Consuming still more units of the commodity would cause his or her TU to fall (because of storage or disposal problems).

(d)   Marginal utility (MU) refers to the change in TU as an individual consumes each additional unit of the commodity. MU is positive but declining as long as TU rises. MU is zero at the saturation point (where TU is maximum and is neither rising nor falling). Past the saturation point, TU falls and MU is negative. Note that up to a point, MU may be rising. For example, the second cigarette may give more satisfaction than the first. But as the individual smokes more and more cigarettes per day, MU will eventually begin to decline.

**15.4.**   (a)   From the $TU_x$ schedule in Table 15-4, derive the $MU_x$ schedule.

   (b)   Graph the two schedules.

**Table 15-4**

| $q_x$ | 0 | 1 | 2 | 3 | 4 | 5 | 6 | 7 | 8 | 9 | 10 |
|---|---|---|---|---|---|---|---|---|---|---|---|
| $TU_x$ | 0 | 14 | 26 | 37 | 47 | 56 | 64 | 70 | 74 | 77 | 78 |

(a)   See Table 15-5.

**Table 15-5**

| $q_x$ | 0 | 1 | 2 | 3 | 4 | 5 | 6 | 7 | 8 | 9 | 10 |
|---|---|---|---|---|---|---|---|---|---|---|---|
| $TU_x$ | 0 | 14 | 26 | 37 | 47 | 56 | 64 | 70 | 74 | 77 | 78 |
| $MU_x$ | | 14 | 12 | 11 | 10 | 9 | 8 | 6 | 4 | 3 | 1 |

(b)   See Fig. 15-3. Note that $MU_x$ is plotted at the midpoints. The decline in $MU_x$ is referred to as the *law of diminishing marginal utility*.

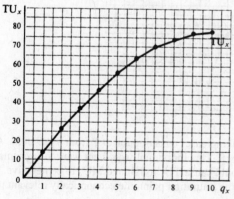 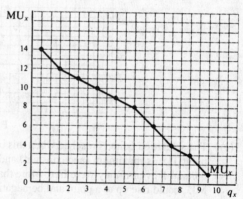

**Fig. 15-3**

**15.5.**   (a)   From the $TU_y$ schedule in Table 15-6, derive the $MU_y$ schedule.

**Table 15-6**

| $q_y$ | 0 | 1 | 2 | 3 | 4 | 5 | 6 | 7 | 8 | 9 | 10 |
|---|---|---|---|---|---|---|---|---|---|---|---|
| $TU_y$ | 0 | 13 | 24 | 34 | 42 | 49 | 55 | 58 | 60 | 60 | 55 |

   (b)   Graph the two schedules.

   (c)   Where is this individual's saturation point for commodity $Y$?

(a) In Table 15-7 note that the sum of all $MU_y$ up to a particular $q_y$ equals $TU_y$ at that $q_y$.

**Table 15-7**

| $q_y$ | 0 | 1 | 2 | 3 | 4 | 5 | 6 | 7 | 8 | 9 | 10 |
|-------|---|----|----|----|----|----|----|----|----|----|----|
| $TU_y$ | 0 | 13 | 24 | 34 | 42 | 49 | 55 | 58 | 60 | 60 | 55 |
| $MU_y$ | | 13 | 11 | 10 | 8 | 7 | 6 | 3 | 2 | 0 | −5 |

(b) See Fig. 15-4.

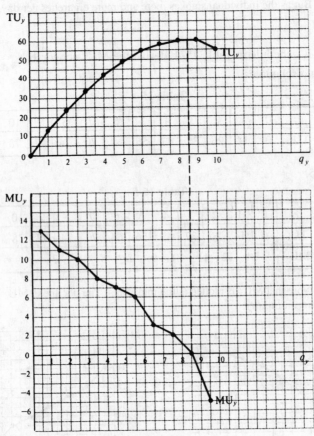

**Fig. 15-4**

(c) The saturation point is reached when this individual increases consumption of $Y$ from 8 to 9 units. At that point $TU_y$ is maximum (and constant) and $MU_y = 0$. This individual would not want to consume more units of $Y$ even if they were free. More than $9y$ would cause $TU_y$ to fall and $MU_y$ to be negative. While $MU_y$ could rise up to a point and be negative past the saturation point, the economically relevant portion of the $MU_y$ function is positive but declining.

## UTILITY MAXIMIZATION AND CONSUMER EQUILIBRIUM

**15.6.** (a) What is meant by "consumer equilibrium"?

(b) State the condition for consumer equilibrium.

(c) If $MU_x/P_x$ of the last dollar spent on commodity $X$ exceeds $MU_y/P_y$ of the last dollar spent on $Y$, how can the consumer reach equilibrium?

(a) Given his tastes (from MU schedules), his income, and commodity prices, a rational consumer is in equilibrium when he spends his income in such a way as to maximize the total utility or satisfaction that he receives from spending his income.

(b)  A consumer maximizes the total utility or satisfaction from spending his income (and is said to be in equilibrium) when the marginal utility of the *last* dollar spent on each commodity is the same. This equilibrium condition for utility maximization can be stated mathematically as follows:

$$\frac{MU_x}{P_x} = \frac{MU_y}{P_y} = \text{common MU of the } last \text{ \$ spent on each commodity}$$

where $P_x$ and $P_y$ refer to the price of $X$ and the price of $Y$, respectively. The equilibrium condition can also be restated as $\frac{MU_x}{P_x} = \frac{MU_y}{P_y}$ at the point where $(p_x)(q_x) + (p_y)(q_y) = M$ (the consumer's money income). $MU_x/P_x = MU_y/P_y = \ldots$, by itself, is a necessary but not sufficient condition for consumer equilibrium. There may be other levels of consumption at which $MU_x/P_x = MU_y/P_y = \ldots$, but only the one at which the consumer is exactly spending his total income is *the* (single) point of consumer equilibrium or utility maximization.

(c)  If $MU_x/P_x$ exceeds $MU_y/P_y$, the last dollar spent on commodity $X$ gives this consumer more utility than the last dollar spent on $Y$. This consumer would increase his total utility from his given and fixed level of expenditures by purchasing more of $X$ and less of $Y$. As he purchases *more* of $X$, the consumer moves *down* his diminishing $MU_x$ schedule. As he purchases *less* of $Y$, he moves *up* his diminishing $MU_y$ schedule. This should continue until $MU_x/P_x = MU_y/P_y$ for the last dollar spent on $X$ and $Y$. Note that the consumer can reach the equilibrium position of utility maximization because of the law of diminishing $MU_x$ and $MU_y$. The consumer should follow exactly the same process to reach equilibrium if he spends his income on more than two commodities.

**15.7.**  Suppose that a consumer has the $MU_x$ of Table 15-5 and the $MU_y$ of Table 15-7. Suppose also that her money income is \$10, $P_x = \$2$, and $P_y = \$1$.

(a)  Describe how this consumer should spend *each* of her \$10 to purchase *each unit* of $X$ and $Y$ so as to maximize her total utility or satisfaction.

(b)  Show that her TU would be less if she bought one more unit of either $X$ or $Y$.

(c)  Find the TU of this consumer if she spent all of her income (1) on $X$ and (2) on $Y$.

(a)  Because $P_x = \$2$, if this consumer spent her first \$2 to buy the first unit of $X$, she would receive a $MU_x$ of only 14, or 7 utils per dollar spent on $X$. On the other hand, if this consumer spent her first dollar to purchase the first unit of $Y$, she would receive a $MU_y$ of 13, or 13 utils per dollar. Thus, she should spend her first dollar to purchase the first unit of $Y$ and receive 13 utils of satisfaction. Similarly, this consumer should spend her second, third, and fourth dollars to purchase the second, third, and fourth units of $Y$ and receive 11, 10, and 8 utils, respectively. This consumer is indifferent between purchasing the fifth unit of $Y$ or the first unit of $X$ because she receives 7 utils *per dollar* spent on each. Suppose that she purchases both and spends her fifth, sixth, and seventh dollars to purchase the fifth $Y$ and the first $X$ (remember, $P_x = \$2$). Similarly, the consumer should spend her eighth, ninth, and tenth (or last) dollar to purchase the sixth $Y$ (and receive 6 utils) and the second $X$ (and receive 12 utils, or 6 utils per dollar—the same as for the sixth $Y$). By purchasing $2X$ and $6Y$, this consumer is receiving 81 utils ($14 + 12$ from $X$ and $13 + 11 + 8 + 7 + 6$ from $Y$). This is the maximum TU she can receive by spending her total income of \$10 on $X$ and $Y$ when $P_x = \$2$ and $P_y = \$1$. Thus, the consumer is in equilibrium by purchasing $2X$ and $6Y$.

(b)  To buy the third unit of $X$ (at $P_x = \$2$), this consumer would have had to give up the fifth and sixth units of $Y$ (at $P_y = \$1$). She would gain 11 utils by purchasing the third unit of $X$ but lose 13 utils ($7 + 6$) by giving up her sixth and fifth $Y$, with a net loss of 2 utils. The TU of this consumer would be only 79 utils if she purchased $3X$ and $4Y$ (compared with a TU of 81 utils with $2X$ and $6Y$) and she would not be maximizing the TU from spending her \$10 of income. On the other hand, by giving up her second $X$ (thus losing 12 utils), this consumer could purchase her seventh and eighth $Y$ (gaining only a total of 5 utils), with a net loss of 7 utils. Purchasing $1X$ and $8Y$, this consumer would receive a total of 74 utils ($81 - 7$) and would not be in equilibrium.

(c)  If this consumer spent her \$10 on $X$ only, she could purchase $5X$ (at $P_x = \$2$) and receive a TU = 56 utils ($14 + 12 + 11 + 10 + 9$). If, instead, she spent her \$10 on $Y$ only, she could purchase $10Y$ (at $P_y = \$1$) and receive a TU = 55 utils ($13 + 11 + 10 + 8 + 7 + 6 + 3 + 2 + 0 - 5$). From the above, we can conclude that any combination of $X$ and $Y$ (other than $2X$ and $6Y$) that this consumer could purchase with her income of \$10 would give her a smaller TU than the 81 utils she receives from purchasing $2X$ and $6Y$.

**15.8.** (a) Show that the equilibrium condition for utility maximization given in Problem 15.6(b) is satisfied when the consumer in Problem 15.7 purchases 2X and 6Y.

(b) Why is the pairing of 1X and 5Y not equilibrium?

(c) Why are 7X and 7Y or 8X and 8Y not equilibrium?

(a) With 2X and 6Y, the consumer is in equilibrium because

$$\frac{MU_x \text{ of } 12 \text{ utils}}{P_x \text{ of } \$2} = \frac{MU_y \text{ of } 6 \text{ utils}}{P_y \text{ of } \$1} = MU \text{ of } 6 \text{ utils from the last } \$ \text{ spent on } X \text{ and } Y$$

Another way of showing that this consumer is in equilibrium by purchasing 2X and 6Y is

$$\frac{MU_x}{P_x} = \frac{MU_y}{P_y} \quad \text{and} \quad (P_x)(q_x) + (P_y)(q_y) = M(\text{the consumer's money income})$$

Substituting the values of the problem into the above expression for consumer equilibrium, we get

$$\frac{12 \text{ utils}}{\$2} = \frac{6 \text{ utils}}{\$1} \quad \text{and} \quad (\$2)(2) + (\$1)(6) = \$10$$

In order to be in equilibrium, not only must the MU per dollar spent on each commodity be the same, but the consumer's income must just be exhausted.

(b) If the consumer purchases 1X and 5Y,

$$\frac{MU_x \text{ of } 14 \text{ utils}}{P_x \text{ of } \$2} = \frac{MU_y \text{ of } 7 \text{ utils}}{P_y \text{ of } \$1}$$

but the consumer spends only \$7 of her income of \$10. The consumer is not in equilibrium because she can increase her TU by spending her remaining \$3 on X and Y.

(c) With 7X and 7Y or 8X and 8Y, $MU_x/P_x = MU_y/P_y$ but the consumer does not have enough income to purchase these combinations of X and Y and is not in equilibrium. Note that if in part (a), $MU_x$ had been 11 utils instead of 12, the equilibrium condition would hold only approximately (unless X and Y were perfectly divisible, in which case the consumer should purchase a little less than 2X and a little more than 6Y, until $MU_x/P_x$ exactly equaled $MU_y/P_y$).

**15.9.** Why is water, which is essential to life, so cheap, while diamonds, which are not essential to life, so expensive?

Because water is essential to life, the TU received from water exceeds the TU received from diamonds. However, the price we are willing to pay for each unit of a commodity depends not on the TU but on the MU. We consume so much water that the MU of the last unit of water consumed is very low. Therefore, we are willing to pay only a very low price for the last unit of water consumed. Since all units of water consumed are identical we pay the same low price on all other units of water consumed.

On the other hand, we purchase so few diamonds that the MU of the last diamond purchased is very high. Therefore, we are willing to pay a high price for this last diamond and for all the other diamonds purchased. Classical economists did not distinguish TU from MU and thus they were unable to resolve this "water-diamond paradox."

## DERIVATION OF AN INDIVIDUAL'S DEMAND CURVE

**15.10.** (a) Explain, on the basis of diminishing MU, why an individual purchases more of a commodity per unit of time when the commodity price falls.

(b) How do we get one point on the consumer's demand schedule and curve for a commodity?

(c) How are other points found?

(d) Explain the process by which the consumer in Examples 15.4 and 15.5 moves from the first to the second equilibrium point as $P_x$ falls from \$2 to \$1.

(a) Because each additional unit of the commodity gives the individual less extra, or marginal, utility, he will purchase more units of the commodity only at lower commodity prices. Thus, a downsloping demand can be explained in terms of diminishing MU. This is a complementary explanation to the substitution and income effects for a downsloping demand curve.

(b)  Given an individual's MU schedules and income and the commodity prices, we can find the point of consumer equilibrium. This gives the quantity of the commodity that the individual would purchase at the given commodity price in order to maximize the TU from spending his income. This defines one point on the consumer's demand schedule and demand curve for the commodity.

(c)  In order to find other points on the consumer's demand schedule and demand curve for the commodity, we must use alternative commodity prices. At each alternative commodity price, the consumer will have to purchase a different quantity of the commodity in order to be in equilibrium. These alternative price-quantity relationships at consumer equilibrium points give other points of consumer demand for the commodity. Since the MU of the commodity falls, lower commodity prices will be associated with greater quantity purchases of the commodity (and the demand curve will be downsloping).

(d)  In Example 15-4, the individual was in equilibrium when he purchased $2X$ and $3Y$ (at $P_x = \$2$ and $P_y = \$1$, respectively) with an income of $7. When $P_x$ fell to $1 in Example 15-5, the individual's equilibrium condition was no longer satisfied by the continued purchase of $2X$ and $3Y$ because

$$\frac{MU_x \text{ of } 8 \text{ utils}}{P_x \text{ of } \$1} > \frac{MU_y \text{ of } 4 \text{ utils}}{P_y \text{ of } \$1}$$

and the individual was spending only $5 of his $7 income. In order to reach equilibrium when $P_x = \$1$, this consumer must spend his sixth and seventh dollars of income to purchase the third and fourth units of $X$ so that his $MU_x$ falls to 4 utils (the same as $MU_y$ at $P_x = P_y = \$1$) and his entire income of $7 is spent.

**15.11.**  Table 15-7 is repeated below as Table 15-8. With income of $10, $P_x = \$2$ and $P_y = \$1$, the consumer is in equilibrium by purchasing $2X$ and $6Y$.

(a)  Find the point of consumer equilibrium with $P_x = \$1$.

(b)  How is this consumer's demand schedule for commodity $X$ derived?

**Table 15-8**

| Units | 1 | 2 | 3 | 4 | 5 | 6 | 7 | 8 | 9 | 10 |
|---|---|---|---|---|---|---|---|---|---|---|
| $MU_x$ | 14 | (12) | 11 | 10 | 9 | 8 | 6 | 4 | 3 | 1 |
| $MU_y$ | 13 | 11 | 10 | 8 | 7 | (6) | 3 | 2 | 0 | -5 |

(a)  If $P_x$ falls to $1, the consumer will no longer be in equilibrium by continuing to purchase $2X$ and $6Y$ because

$$\frac{MU_x \text{ of } 12 \text{ utils}}{P_x \text{ of } \$1} > \frac{MU_y \text{ of } 6 \text{ utils}}{P_y \text{ of } \$1}$$

and he is spending only $8 of his income of $10. Compare this with Problem 15.8(a). Since the second dollar spent to purchase the second unit of $X$ (at $P_x = \$1$) gives this individual more (marginal) utility than the sixth dollar spent to purchase the sixth unit of $Y$, the individual should spend more on $X$ and less on $Y$. As he buys more $X$, the consumer moves down his diminishing $MU_x$ schedule. As he buys less of $Y$, he moves up his diminishing $MU_y$. The consumer will be in equilibrium when the MU of the last dollar spent on $X$ equals the MU of the last dollar spent on $Y$. This occurs when this consumer spends his $10 to purchase $6X$ and $4Y$ because

$$\frac{MU_x \text{ of } 8 \text{ utils}}{P_x \text{ of } \$1} = \frac{MU_y \text{ of } 8 \text{ utils}}{P_y \text{ of } \$1} = MU \text{ of } 8 \text{ utils from the last } \$ \text{ spent on } X \text{ and } Y$$

Note that as $P_x$ fell from $2 to $1 in Example 15-5, the consumer bought more $X$ *but the same amount of $Y$* to reach a new equilibrium point. Here, the consumer buys more $X$ *but less $Y$*.

(b)  When $P_x = \$2$, this consumer purchases $2X$ in order to be in equilibrium. This gives one point of his demand schedule for commodity $X$. Other points on the consumer's demand schedule for $X$ can be similarly obtained by allowing $P_x$ to change again and recording $q_x$ at equilibrium. Since the total expenditures of this consumer on commodity $X$ rise as $P_x$ falls, $d_x$ is price elastic between $P_x = \$2$ and $P_x = \$1$.

## CONSUMER'S SURPLUS

**15.12.** (*a*) How does the consumer's surplus arise? How can it be measured?

(*b*) What is the consumer's surplus in Fig. 15-5 when price is *AF*? *AC*? *AB*? How is the size of the consumer's surplus related to the commodity price?

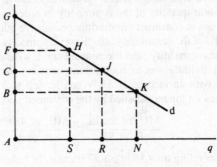

**Fig. 15-5**

(*a*) The price that a consumer is willing to pay for each unit of the commodity is given by the height of her demand curve. Since each additional unit of the commodity gives her less MU, she is willing to pay less for each additional unit (i.e., her demand curve is downsloping). The consumer ends up with a surplus because she pays for all units the price that she is willing to pay for the last unit, even though the MU on previous units is greater. When, as in Fig. 15-5, the commodity is perfectly divisible, the consumer's surplus can be measured by the area under the consumer's demand curve and above the commodity price.

(*b*) At the price of *AF*, the consumer purchases *AS* of the commodity and spends *AFHS*. Because she would be willing to pay *AGHS* for *AS* of the commodity but pays only *AFHS*, she receives a consumer surplus of *FGH*. At price of *AC*, the consumer's surplus is *CGJ*. At price *AB*, the consumer's surplus is *BGK*. Given the individual's demand curve for a commodity, the lower the commodity price, the greater the consumer's surplus.

**15.13.** Given the consumer's demand schedule for commodity *X* in Table 15-9,

(*a*) indicate how much this consumer would be willing to pay for each unit of commodity *X*.

(*b*) If the *market* demand and supply curves for commodity *X* intersect to give a market equilibrium $P_x = \$1$, what is this consumer's surplus from commodity *X*?

(*c*) How could the producer of commodity *X* extract from this consumer the entire consumer surplus?

(*d*) Draw a figure that would allow you to measure this consumer's surplus graphically.

**Table 15-9**

| $P_x$ | \$2.50 | \$2.00 | \$1.50 | \$1.00 |
|-------|--------|--------|--------|--------|
| $q_x$ | 1 | 2 | 3 | 4 |

(*a*) The demand schedule of Table 15-9 shows that this consumer would be willing to pay \$2.50 for the first unit of *X*, \$2.00 for the second, \$1.50 for the third, and \$1.00 for the fourth.

(*b*) If the market demand curve for commodity *X* intersects the market supply curve at $P_x = \$1$, this consumer will purchase 4*X* at $P_x = \$1$. Since he would be willing to pay \$7 (\$2.50 + \$2.00 + \$1.50 + \$1.00) for these 4*X*, but instead pays only \$4, he receives a surplus of \$3 (\$1.50 on the first unit of *X*, \$1.00 on the second, \$0.50 on the third, and nothing on the fourth).

(*c*) The producer of commodity *X* could extract the entire surplus from the consumer by offering to sell these 4*X* for a total price of \$7—take it or leave it. Since to the consumer, 4*X* are "worth" \$7, he will pay the \$7 and lose his entire consumer's surplus. Note that this implies that the producer has the economic and legal power to do this and knows precisely the consumer's demand schedule for commodity X. These conditions do not generally hold in the real world, and the consumer in general retains his or her surplus.

(d) In Fig. 15-6, the consumer's surplus of $3 is given by the shaded area. This figure is different from Fig. 15-5 because we are here dealing with discrete rather than perfectly divisible units of the commodity.

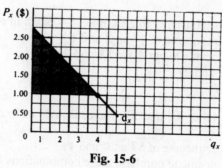

**Fig. 15-6**

# *Multiple Choice Questions*

1. The law of downward-sloping demand can be explained in terms of
   (a) the substitution effect,
   (b) the income effect,
   (c) both the substitution and income effects,
   (d) neither the substitution nor income effect.

2. A complementary explanation of the downsloping demand curve is given by
   (a) diminishing returns,
   (b) diminishing marginal utility,
   (c) decreasing costs,
   (d) decreasing returns to scale.

3. When total utility increases, marginal utility is
   (a) negative and increasing,
   (b) negative and declining,
   (c) zero,
   (d) positive and declining.

4. If the consumer in Example 15-4 spent his $7 to purchase $3X$ and $1Y$, his TU would be
   (a) 35,
   (b) 33,
   (c) 30,
   (d) 27.

5. If the consumer in Example 15-4 spent his $7 to purchase $1X$ and $5Y$, his TU would be
   (a) 35,
   (b) 33,
   (c) 30,
   (d) 27.

6.  At what combinations (other than $2X$ and $3Y$) is the condition $MU_x/P_x = MU_y/P_y$ satisfied in Table 15-2?
    (a)  $1X$ and $2Y$,
    (b)  $3X$ and $4Y$,
    (c)  $4X$ and $5Y$,
    (d)  all of the above.

7.  By purchasing $1X$ and $2Y$, the consumer in Example 15-4 is not in equilibrium because he
    (a)  is not spending his entire income of $7 on $X$ and $Y$,
    (b)  does not have enough income to purchase $1X$ and $2Y$,
    (c)  is not satisfied with $1X$ and $2Y$,
    (d)  does not know $P_x$ and $P_y$.

8.  With combinations $3X$ and $4Y$ or $4X$ and $5Y$, the consumer in Example 15-4 is not in equilibrium because he
    (a)  is not spending his entire income of $7 on $X$ and $Y$,
    (b)  does not have enough income to purchase these combinations of $X$ and $Y$,
    (c)  does not want so much $X$ and $Y$,
    (d)  does not know $P_x$ and $P_y$.

9.  $d_x$ in Table 15-3 is downsloping because $MU_x$ is
    (a)  rising,
    (b)  constant,
    (c)  falling,
    (d)  zero.

10.  $d_x$ of Table 15-3 is unitary elastic (on the average) between $P_x = \$2$ and $P_x = \$1$ because
    (a)  the consumer's total expenditure on $X$ remains constant,
    (b)  the consumer's total expenditure on $X$ rises,
    (c)  the slope of $d_x$ is constant,
    (d)  the slope of $d_x$ is negative.

11.  Consumer's surplus is defined as
    (a)  the difference between what the consumer actually pays and what he is willing to pay,
    (b)  the difference between what the consumer is willing to pay and what he actually pays,
    (c)  the sum of what the consumer pays and what he is willing to pay,
    (d)  what the consumer is willing to pay divided by what he actually pays.

12.  From Fig. 15-2, we can see that at a commodity price lower than $AB$ the consumer's surplus would
    (a)  equal area $BGC$,
    (b)  be smaller than area $BGC$,
    (c)  be larger than area $BGC$,
    (d)  any of the above.

## True or False Questions

13.  _____  The demand curve is downward-sloping because of the substitution and income effects.

14.  _____  As the price of a good declines, less of the good is bought because consumers can replace it with similar commodities in consumption.

**15.** _____ The income effect describes the situation wherein a decline in price leads to increased purchasing power for the consumer, thus allowing him or her to purchase more of the commodity.

**16.** _____ The more of a commodity is consumed, the higher is the total utility derived.

**17.** _____ The law of diminishing marginal utility states that each successive unit of the commodity consumed leads to a larger addition to total utility.

**18.** _____ The consumer is in equilibrium when he or she equalizes the marginal utilities derived from the last dollar spent on each commodity.

**19.** _____ Consumer utility maximization is satisfied by the condition that $MU_x = MU_y = MU_z$.

**20.** _____ An individual demand curve is the locus of consumer equilibrium points.

**21.** _____ The demand curve slopes downward because of the operation of the law of diminishing marginal utility.

**22.** _____ Consumer's surplus is derived from an individual's total expenditures on a certain commodity.

**23.** _____ Consumer's surplus can be measured by the area under the demand curve and below the commodity price.

**24.** _____ Commodities which are essential to life always cost more than those which could easily be forgone.

## Answers to Multiple Choice and True or False Questions

| | | | |
|---|---|---|---|
| **1.** (c) | **7.** (a) | **13.** (T) | **19.** (F) |
| **2.** (b) | **8.** (b) | **14.** (F) | **20.** (T) |
| **3.** (d) | **9.** (c) | **15.** (T) | **21.** (T) |
| **4.** (c) | **10.** (a) | **16.** (T) | **22.** (F) |
| **5.** (c) | **11.** (b) | **17.** (F) | **23.** (F) |
| **6.** (d) | **12.** (c) | **18.** (T) | **24.** (F) |

# Chapter 16

# Costs of Production

## *Chapter Summary*

1. The firm's production costs are made up of explicit and implicit costs. Explicit costs are out-of-pocket expenditures that a firm pays the factors of production it hires. Implicit costs are the costs of factors owned by the firm. The excess of revenues over both these costs is the firm's profit.

2. The law of diminishing returns states that as we use more and more units of some factors of production while keeping one or more factors fixed, we get less and less additional output from each additional factor used.

3. Total fixed costs are the costs which the firm incurs in the short run for its fixed inputs; these are constant regardless of the level of the firm's output. Total variable costs are costs incurred by the firm for the variable inputs that it uses; these vary directly with the level of output produced. Total costs equal the sum of total fixed costs and total variable costs.

4. Average fixed cost equals total fixed costs divided by output. Average variable cost equals total variable costs divided by output. Average cost equals average fixed costs plus average variable costs. Marginal cost equals the change in total cost or total variable cost per unit change in output.

5. In the long run, there are no fixed factors. The long-run average cost curve shows the minimum per-unit cost of producing each level of output.

6. If all factors of production are increased by a given proportion, returns to scale are constant, increasing, or decreasing, depending on whether output increases in the same, greater, or smaller proportion, respectively.

## *Important Terms*

**Average cost (AC).**   Total costs divided by output, or average fixed cost plus average variable cost.

**Average fixed cost (AFC).**   Total fixed costs divided by output.

**Average variable cost (AVC).**   Total variable costs divided by output.

**Constant returns to scale (or constant costs).**   The long-run situation when increasing all inputs by a given proportion results in an increase in output in the same proportion.

**Decreasing returns to scale (or increasing costs).**   The long-run situation when output increases proportionately less than inputs.

**Explicit costs.**   The actual, out-of-pocket expenditures incurred by the firm to purchase or hire the services of the factors of production it needs.

**Implicit costs.**   The estimated values (in their best alternative employment) of the factors owned by the firm and used in its own production processes.

**Increasing returns to scale (or decreasing costs).**   The long-run situation when output increases proportionately more than inputs.

**Law of diminishing returns.**   Refers to the falling marginal product resulting from using more variable factors with some fixed factor(s).

**Long run.**   The time period when all factors of production are variable.

**Long-run average cost (LAC).**   The minimum per-unit cost of producing a level of output when any desired scale of plant can be built.

**Long-run marginal cost (LMC).**   The change in total costs per unit change in output when any desired scale of plant can be built.

**Marginal cost (MC).**   The change in total costs or total variable costs per unit change in output.

**Opportunity cost.**   The amount of a commodity that society must give up in order to release just enough resources to produce one more unit of another commodity.

**Profit.**   The excess of total revenue over all explicit and implicit costs.

**Short run.**   The time period in which at least one factor of production is fixed in quantity (cannot be varied).

**Total costs (TC).**   The sum of total fixed costs and total variable costs.

**Total fixed costs (TFC).**   The costs which the firm incurs in the short run for all fixed inputs, regardless of the level of output.

**Total variable costs (TVC).**   The changing costs incurred by the firm for all variable inputs.

# Outline of Chapter 16: Costs of Production

**16.1   Explicit Costs, Implicit Costs, and Economic Profit**

**16.2   The Law of Diminishing Returns**

**16.3   Short-Run Total Costs**

**16.4   Short-Run Per-Unit Costs**

**16.5   Long-Run Production Costs**

**16.6   Constant, Increasing, and Decreasing Returns to Scale**

## 16.1   EXPLICIT COSTS, IMPLICIT COSTS, AND ECONOMIC PROFIT

In this chapter we concentrate on the firm's production costs—or what lies behind its supply curve. *Explicit costs* are the actual, out-of-pocket expenditures of the firm to purchase or hire the services of the factors of production it needs. *Implicit costs* are the costs of the factors owned by the firm and used in its own production processes. These costs should be imputed or estimated from what these factors could earn in their best alternative use or employment. In economics, costs include both explicit and implicit costs. *Profit* is the excess of revenues over these costs.

**EXAMPLE 16.1.**   The explicit costs of a firm are the wages it must pay to hire labor, the interest to borrow money capital, and the rent on land and buildings used in the production process. To these, the firm must add such implicit costs as the wage that the entrepreneur would earn working as a manager for somebody else; the interest he would get by supplying his money capital (if any) to someone else in a similarly risky business; and the rent on his owned land and buildings, if he were not using them himself. Only if the total revenue received from selling the output exceeds both its explicit and implicit costs is the firm making an economic or pure profit.

## 16.2   THE LAW OF DIMINISHING RETURNS

The law of diminishing returns is one of the most important and unchallenged laws of production. This law states that as we use more and more units of some factors of production to work with one or more fixed factors, after a point we get less and less extra or marginal output or product from each additional unit of the variable factors used. The time period when at least one factor of production is fixed in quantity (i.e., cannot be varied) is referred to as the *short run*. Thus, the law of diminishing returns is a short-run law. In the *long run*, all factors are variable.

**EXAMPLE 16.2.** Table 16-1 shows the total and marginal product of using each additional unit of labor on the same (say, one acre of) land. Note that with zero labor, TP = 0. By adding the first unit of labor, TP = 3 and MP (i.e., the change in TP) = 3. By adding the second unit of labor, TP = 8 and MP = 5. The third unit of labor leads to a TP of 12 and an MP of 4, etc. The law of diminishing returns begins to operate in this example with the addition of the third unit of labor.

**Table 16-1**

| Inputs of the Variable Factor (labor, in person-years) | Total Product (TP, in bushels per year) | Extra or Marginal Product (MP) |
|:---:|:---:|:---:|
| 0 | 0 | |
| 1 | 3 | 3 |
| 2 | 8 | 5 |
| 3 | 12 | 4 |
| 4 | 15 | 3 |
| 5 | 17 | 2 |

## 16.3. SHORT-RUN TOTAL COSTS

In the short run, there are total fixed costs, total variable costs, and total costs. *Total fixed costs* (TFC) are the costs which the firm incurs in the short run for its fixed inputs; these are constant regardless of the level of output and of whether it produces or not. An example of TFC is the rent which a producer must pay for the factory building over the life of a lease. *Total variable costs* (TVC) are costs incurred by the firm for the variable inputs it uses. These vary directly with the level of output produced. Examples of TVC are raw material costs and some labor costs. *Total costs* (TC) are equal to the sum of total fixed costs and total variable costs.

**EXAMPLE 16.3.** Table 16-2 presents hypothetical TFC, TVC, and TC schedules for various levels of output (*Q*). These schedules are graphed in Fig.16-1.

**Table 16-2**

| Q | TFC ($) | TVC ($) | TC ($) |
|:---:|:---:|:---:|:---:|
| 0 | 60 | 0 | 60 |
| 1 | 60 | 30 | 90 |
| 2 | 60 | 40 | 100 |
| 3 | 60 | 45 | 105 |
| 4 | 60 | 55 | 115 |
| 5 | 60 | 75 | 135 |
| 6 | 60 | 120 | 180 |

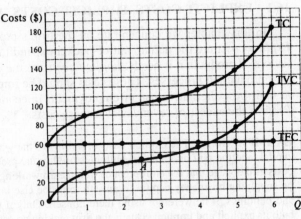

**Fig. 16-1**

From Table 16-2, we see that TFC are $60 regardless of the level of output. This is reflected in Fig. 16-1 in a TFC curve which is parallel to the quantity axis and $60 above it. TVC are zero when output is zero and rise as output rises. The particular shape of the TVC curve follows directly from the law of diminishing returns. Up to point A (about 2.5 units of output), the firm is using so few of the variable inputs together with its fixed inputs that the law of diminishing returns is not yet operating. Therefore, TVC increase at a decreasing rate and the TVC curve faces down. Past point A, the law of diminishing returns begins to operate so that TVC increase at an increasing rate and the TVC curve faces up. At every output level, TC equals TFC plus TVC. For this reason, the TC curve has the same shape as the TVC curve and, in this case, is everywhere $60 above it.

## 16.4  SHORT-RUN PER-UNIT COSTS

Though total costs are very important, per-unit or average costs are even more important in the short-run analysis of the firm. The short-run per-unit costs that we consider are the average fixed cost, the average variable cost, the average cost, and the marginal cost. *Average fixed cost* (AFC) equals total fixed costs divided by output. *Average variable cost* (AVC) equals total variable costs divided by output. *Average cost* (AC) equals total costs divided by output; AC also equals AFC plus AVC. *Marginal cost* (MC) equals the change in TC or the change in TVC per unit change in output.

**EXAMPLE 16.4.**    Table 16-3 presents the AFC, AVC, AC, and MC schedules derived from the TFC, TVC, and TC schedules of Table 16-2 (repeated in columns 1–4 of Table 16-3). The AFC schedule (column 5) is obtained by dividing TFC (column 2) by the corresponding quantities of output produced ($Q$ in column 1). The AVC schedule (column 6) is obtained by dividing TVC (column 3) by $Q$. The AC schedule (column 7) is obtained by dividing TC (column 4) by $Q$. AC at every output level also equals AFC (column 5) plus AVC (column 6). The MC schedule (column 8) is obtained by subtracting successive values of TC (column 4) or TVC (column 3). Thus, MC does not depend on the level of TFC.

**Table 16-3**

| (1) $Q$ | (2) TFC ($) | (3) TVC ($) | (4) TC ($) | (5) AFC ($) | (6) AVC ($) | (7) AC ($) | (8) MC ($) |
|---|---|---|---|---|---|---|---|
| 1 | 60 | 30 | 90 | 60 | 30 | 90 | 10 |
| 2 | 60 | 40 | 100 | 30 | 20 | 50 | 5 |
| 3 | 60 | 45 | 105 | 20 | 15 | 35 | 10 |
| 4 | 60 | 55 | 115 | 15 | 13.75 | 28.75 | 20 |
| 5 | 60 | 75 | 135 | 12 | 15 | 27 | 45 |
| 6 | 60 | 120 | 180 | 10 | 20 | 30 | |

**EXAMPLE 16.5.**    The AFC, AVC, AC, and MC schedules of Table 16-3 are graphed in Fig. 16-2. Note that the values of the MC schedule (from column 8) are plotted halfway between successive levels of output. Also note that while the AFC curve falls continuously as output is expanded, the AVC, the AC, and the MC curves are U-shaped. The MC curve reaches its lowest point at a lower level of output than either the AVC curve or the AC curve. Also, the rising portion of the MC curve intersects the AVC and AC curves at their lowest points. This is always the case (see Problem 16.11).

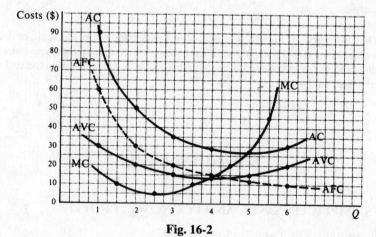

**Fig. 16-2**

## 16.5  LONG-RUN PRODUCTION COSTS

In the long run, there are no fixed factors, and the firm can build a plant of any size. Once a firm has constructed a particular plant, it operates in the short run. A plant size can be represented by its short-run average cost (SAC) curve. Larger plants can be represented by SAC curves which lie further to the right. The long-run average cost (LAC) curve shows the minimum per-unit cost of producing each level of output when any desired size of plant can be built. The LAC curve is thus formed from the relevant segment of the SAC curves.

**EXAMPLE 16.6.** Fig. 16-3 shows four hypothetical plant sizes that the firm could build in the long run. Each plant is shown by a SAC curve. To produce up to 300 units of output, the firm should build and utilize plant 1 (given by $SAC_1$). From 300 to 550 units of output, it should build the larger plant given by $SAC_2$. From 550 to 1050, it should operate on $SAC_3$, etc. Note that the firm could produce an output of 400 with plant 1, but only at a higher cost than with plant 2. The irrelevant portions of the SAC curves are dashed. The remaining (undashed) portions form the LAC curve. By drawing many more SAC curves, we would get a smoother LAC curve.

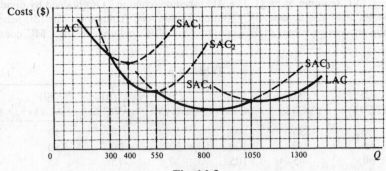

**Fig. 16-3**

## 16.6   CONSTANT, INCREASING, AND DECREASING RETURNS TO SCALE

If in the long run we increase all factors used in production by a given proportion, there are three possible outcomes: (1) output increases in the same proportion, so that there are *constant returns to scale* or constant costs; (2) output increases by a greater proportion, giving *increasing returns to scale* or decreasing costs; and (3) output increases in a smaller proportion, giving *decreasing returns to scale* or increasing costs. Increasing returns to scale or economies of mass production may result because of division of labor and specialization in production. Beyond a certain size, however, management problems resulting in decreasing returns to scale may arise.

**EXAMPLE 16.7.** The LAC curve of Fig. 16-3 at first shows increasing returns to scale or decreasing costs. Then for a small range of outputs (around 800 units), it shows constant returns to scale (constant costs). For larger outputs, we have decreasing returns to scale (increasing costs). Whether and when this occurs in the real world depend on the firm and industry under consideration.

# Solved Problems

## EXPLICIT COSTS, IMPLICIT COSTS, AND ECONOMIC PROFIT

**16.1.** (a)   Why do we study a firm's costs of production?

  (b)   Distinguish among opportunity costs, explicit costs, and implicit costs.

  (a)   We study a firm's costs of production to learn more about the firm's supply curve. It is by adding individual firms' supply curves for a commodity that we get the market supply curve of the commodity. This, together with the market demand curve, determines the equilibrium price and quantity of the commodity in a free-enterprise economy (see Sections 3.3 and 3.5).

(b)   Opportunity costs refer to the fact that as *society* uses more of its scarce resources to produce some goods and services, fewer resources are available to produce other goods and services. For example, the opportunity cost of producing each additional unit of cloth equals the amount of food that society has to give up to release just enough (scarce) resources to produce each of the additional units of cloth. Explicit costs are the actual, out-of-pocket expenditures of the *firm* to purchase or hire the services of the factors of production it needs. Implicit costs are the costs of the services of the factors owned and used by the *firm* in its own production process.

**16.2.** (a)   Distinguish between cost and profit in economics.

(b)   How do these concepts differ from the everyday usage of these terms?

(a)   In economics, costs include both explicit and implicit costs. The resources that a firm owns and uses in production are not free. They involve costs which can be estimated by what these same resources would earn in their best alternative employment. If we say that the firm is making zero profit, it must be remembered that the firm is already receiving a "normal" return on its owned factors. When we speak of profits in economics, we mean above-normal returns.

(b)   The everyday usage of the term "cost" refers only to the out-of-pocket expenditures of the firm to purchase or hire the services of factors of production (what economists call explicit costs). The person on the street calls profit all the excess of the firm's revenue over these out-of-pocket expenditures. For the economist, part or all of this revenue represents the "normal return" on the firm's owned factors or implicit costs. This normal return on owned factors must be included in order for the firm to justify the continued use of its owned factors (i.e., to bid its owned factors away from their best alternative employments).

**16.3.**   A firm pays $200,000 in wages, $50,000 in interest on borrowed money capital, and $70,000 for the yearly rental of its factory building. If the entrepreneur worked for somebody else as a manager she would earn at most $40,000 per year, and if she lent out her money capital to somebody else in a similarly risky business, she would at most receive $10,000 per year. She owns no land or building.

(a)   Calculate the entrepreneur's profit if she received $400,000 from selling her year's output.

(b)   How much profit is the entrepreneur earning from the point of view of the person on the street? To what is the difference in the results due?

(c)   What would happen if the entrepreneur's total revenue were $360,000 instead?

(a)   The explicit costs of this entrepreneur are $320,000 ($200,000 in wages plus $50,000 in interest plus $70,000 in rents). Her implicit costs are $50,000 ($40,000 in wages in her best alternative employment plus $10,000 interest on her money capital). Thus, her total costs (explicit plus implicit) are $370,000. Since the total revenue from selling the year's output is $400,000, this entrepreneur earns a (pure or economic) profit of $30,000 for the year.

(b)   The person on the street would instead say that this entrepreneur's profit is $80,000 (the total revenue of $400,000 minus the out-of-pocket expenditures, or explicit costs, of $320,000). However, $50,000 of this $80,000 represents the normal return on the entrepreneur's owned factors and is appropriately considered a cost by the economist.

(c)   If the entrepreneur's total revenue were $360,000, she would earn less than a normal return on her owned factors (her wage and interest in the best alternative employment) and it would pay for her (eventually) to go out of business and work as a manager for and lend her money to someone else. This clearly shows that implicit costs are indeed part of costs of production because they must be covered in order for the firm to remain in business and continue indefinitely to supply the goods or services it produces.

## THE LAW OF DIMINISHING RETURNS

**16.4.** (a)   Distinguish between the short run and the long run.

(b)   How long is the long run?

(a)   The short run refers to the time period during which at least one factor of production, such as plant, is fixed in size and there is not sufficient time to change it. Thus, in the short run, the firm can increase its output by hiring more labor and using more raw materials within its existing plant. The time period sufficiently long for the firm to be able to change all of its factors of production, such as enlarging its plant or building a larger plant, is defined as the long run.

   (b)   The length of the long run depends on the industry under consideration. For some firms producing services, the long run may be only a few weeks. For others in basic industries, such as steel, it may be several years. It all depends on how long it takes for the particular industry to be able to change all of its factors of production, including its plant size.

**16.5.**   (a)   State the law of diminishing returns in terms of labor and land.

   (b)   When does the law of diminishing returns begin to operate? What is its cause? Why may it start only after some quantity of labor is employed?

   (a)   As more units of labor per unit of time are used to cultivate a fixed amount of land, after a point the extra or marginal output or product (MP) will *necessarily* decline. This is one of the most important laws of production and is referred to as the law of diminishing returns. Note that to observe the law of diminishing returns, at least one factor of production or input must be fixed. Technology is also assumed to remain constant.

   (b)   The law of diminishing returns begins to operate when the marginal product resulting from an additional unit of a variable factor begins to decline. Up to that point, the variable factor(s) have been used so sparsely with the fixed factors that we (may) get increasing rather than diminishing returns. However, as we use more and more of the variable factors with some fixed factor(s), each unit of the variable factor will have less and less of the fixed factor(s) to work with, and diminishing returns will eventually result.

**16.6.**   Suppose that a tailor working alone can make 2 suits per month; 2 tailors working in the same shop can produce 5 suits; 3 tailors, 10 suits; 4 tailors, 14 suits; 5 tailors, 17 suits; and 6 tailors, 19 suits.

   (a)   Find the marginal product of labor ($MP_L$).

   (b)   When does the law of diminishing returns begin to operate? Why do you have increasing returns up to that point?

   (c)   Why do diminishing returns eventually set in?

**Table 16-4**

| Number of Tailors | Number of Suits (TP per month) | Extra or Marginal Suits per Additional Tailor ($MP_L$) |
|---|---|---|
| 0 | 0 | |
| | | 2 |
| 1 | 2 | |
| | | 3 |
| 2 | 5 | |
| | | 5 |
| 3 | 10 | |
| | | 4 |
| 4 | 14 | |
| | | 3 |
| 5 | 17 | |
| | | 2 |
| 6 | 19 | |

   (a)   See Table 16-4.

   (b)   The law of diminishing returns begins to operate with the addition of the fourth tailor. Up to that point, the shop is underutilized. Since a single tailor could either be taking measurements, cutting the fabric, or sewing the suit together, most of the equipment in the shop is idle most of the time. As we go from one to two and then to three tailors, one tailor could be taking measurements most of the time, a second cutting the fabric, and the third sewing so that the workers and equipment are in use almost constantly. In addition, each tailor can now specialize and become more productive by performing only one specific routine.

   (c)   Adding the fourth tailor to the same shop does not increase the number of suits proportionately (i.e., by one-quarter) but by less. There is now not enough equipment in the shop to keep all four tailors fully occupied all the time. The shop is also becoming "too crowded" and too much "conversation" may start going on. Diminishing returns have set in and they become even smaller as still more tailors are added to the same shop.

## SHORT-RUN TOTAL COSTS

**16.7.** (a) One the same set of axes, plot the TFC, TVC, and TC schedules given in Table 16-5.

**Table 16-5**

| Q | TFC ($) | TVC ($) | TC ($) |
|---|---------|---------|--------|
| 0 | 120 | 0 | 120 |
| 1 | 120 | 60 | 180 |
| 2 | 120 | 80 | 200 |
| 3 | 120 | 90 | 210 |
| 4 | 120 | 105 | 225 |
| 5 | 120 | 140 | 260 |
| 6 | 120 | 210 | 330 |

(b) Explain the reason for the shape of the curves.

(a) See Fig. 16-4.

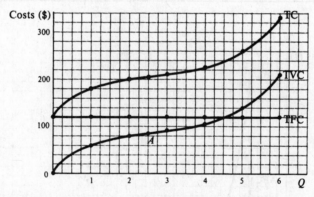

**Fig. 16-4**

(b) Since TFC are $120 per time period at all levels of output, the TFC curve is parallel to the horizontal axis and $120 above it. TVC are zero when output is zero and rise as output rises. Up to about 2.5 units of output (point $A$), the law of diminishing returns does not operate and TVC increase at a decreasing rate. Past 2.5 units of output, the law of diminishing returns operates and TVC increase at an increasing rate. Thus, the TVC curve begins at the origin and is positively sloped. It faces downward up to point $A$ and faces upward thereafter. Since TC equal TFC plus TVC, the TC curve has exactly the same shape as the TVC curve but is at all outputs $120 above it.

**16.8.** (a) Give some examples of fixed and variable factors in the short run.

(b) What is the relationship between the quantity of fixed inputs used and the short-run level of output?

(a) Fixed factors in the short run include payments for renting land and buildings, at least part of depreciation and maintenance expenditures, most kinds of insurance, property taxes, and some salaries such as those of top management, which are fixed by contract and may have to be paid over the life of the contract whether the firm produces or not. Variable factors include raw materials, fuels, most types of labor, excise taxes, and interest on short-run loans.

(b) The quantity of fixed inputs used determines the size or the *scale of plant* which the firm operates in the short run. Within the limits imposed by its scale of plant, the firm can vary its output in the short run by varying the quantity of variable inputs used per unit of time.

**SHORT-RUN PER-UNIT COSTS**

**16.9.** From Table 16-6,

    (a)  find the AFC, the AVC, and the AC schedules, and

    (b)  plot the AFC, AVC, and AC on the same set of axes.

    (c)  Why does the AFC curve fall continuously? What is the relationship between AFC, on the one hand, and the AC and AVC on the other?

    (a)  See Table 16-6. AFC equals TFC divided by output. AVC equals TVC divided by output. AC equals TC divided by output. AC also equals AFC plus AVC.

**Table 16-6**

| Q | TFC ($) | TVC ($) | TC ($) | AFC ($) | AVC ($) | AC ($) |
|---|---------|---------|--------|---------|---------|--------|
| 0 | 120 | 0 | 120 | | | |
| 1 | 120 | 60 | 180 | 120 | 60 | 180 |
| 2 | 120 | 80 | 200 | 60 | 40 | 100 |
| 3 | 120 | 90 | 210 | 40 | 30 | 70 |
| 4 | 120 | 105 | 225 | 30 | 26.25 | 56.25 |
| 5 | 120 | 140 | 260 | 24 | 28 | 52 |
| 6 | 120 | 210 | 330 | 20 | 35 | 55 |

    (b)  See Fig. 16-5.

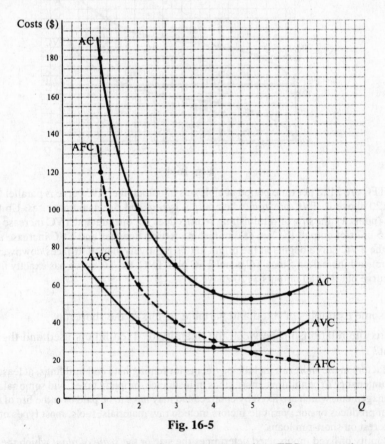

**Fig. 16-5**

    (c)  AFC in Table 16-6 declines continuously as output expands as TFC are spread over more and more units of output. This is reflected in the continuously falling AFC curve of Fig. 16-5. Since AC equals AFC plus

AVC (see Table 16-6), the vertical distance between the AC curve and the AVC curve at each level of output in Fig. 16-5 represents AFC. Thus, as output increases, the vertical distance between the AC curve and the AVC curve decreases, reflecting the continuously falling AFC. For this reason, the AFC curve will be omitted in subsequent figures and chapters (and was dashed in Figs. 16-2 and 16-5).

**16.10.** Refer to Table 16-6.

    (a)   Find the MC schedule, and

    (b)   on the same set of axes, plot the MC, AVC, and AC schedules.

    (a)   See Table 16-7. MC equals the change in either TVC or TC per unit change in output. Since TVC and TC differ only by TFC, *the changes* in TVC and TC per unit change in output (MC) are the same.

**Table 16-7**

| Q | TVC ($) | TC ($) | MC ($) |
|---|---------|--------|--------|
| 1 | 60 | 180 | |
| 2 | 80 | 200 | 20 |
| 3 | 90 | 210 | 10 |
| 4 | 105 | 225 | 15 |
| 5 | 140 | 260 | 35 |
| 6 | 210 | 330 | 70 |

    (b)   See Fig. 16-6. Note once again that MC is recorded in Table 16-7 and plotted in Fig. 16-6 *between* the various levels of output.

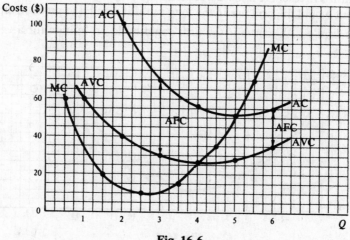

**Fig. 16-6**

**16.11.** (a)   Why are the MC, AVC, and AC curves U-shaped?

     (b)   Why does the AC curve reach its lowest point to the right of the point at which the AVC curve is lowest?

     (c)   Why does the MC curve intersect the AVC and the AC curves at their respective lowest points?

     (a)   As we start using variable factors with some fixed factors, we may first obtain increasing returns, but eventually diminishing returns will set in. As a result, the MC, AVC, and AC curves first fall but eventually rise, giving them their U shapes.

     (b)   The reason the AC curve reaches its lowest point at a higher level of output than the AVC curve is that for a while, the falling AFC (as output expands) more than counterbalances the rising AVC, and AC will continue to fall. Because the AC curve does and the AVC curve does not include this falling AFC, the AC curve falls over a larger range of outputs than does the AVC curve.

(c)   The MC curve always intersects the AVC and the AC curves at their respective lowest points because as long as MC is below AC, it pulls the average down. When MC is above AC, it pulls the average up. Only when MC equals AC is AC neither falling nor rising (i.e., AC is at its lowest point). This is logical. For example, if your grade on the next quiz is lower than your previous average, your average will fall. If your grade on the next quiz is higher than your previous average, your new average will be higher. If your grade is equal to your previous average, the average will remain unchanged.

## LONG-RUN PRODUCTION COSTS

**16.12.**   Suppose that five of the alternative scales of plant that a firm can build in the long run are shown by the SAC schedules in Table 16-8.

**Table 16-8**

| $Q$ | $SAC_1$ SAC (\$) | $Q$ | $SAC_2$ SAC (\$) | $Q$ | $SAC_3$ SAC (\$) | $Q$ | $SAC_4$ SAC (\$) | $Q$ | $SAC_5$ SAC (\$) |
|---|---|---|---|---|---|---|---|---|---|
| 1 | 15.50 | 2 | 15.50 | 5 | 10.00 | 8 | 10.00 | 9 | 12.00 |
| 2 | 13.00 | 3 | 12.00 | 6 | 8.50 | 9 | 9.50 | 10 | 11.00 |
| 3 | 12.00 | 4 | 10.00 | 7 | 8.00 | 10 | 10.00 | 11 | 11.50 |
| 4 | 11.75 | 5 | 9.50 | 8 | 8.50 | 11 | 12.00 | 12 | 13.00 |
| 5 | 13.00 | 6 | 11.00 | 9 | 10.00 | 12 | 15.00 | 13 | 16.00 |

(a)   Sketch these five SAC curves on the same graph, and

(b)   show the firm's LAC curve if these five plants are the only ones that are feasible technologically. Which plant would the firm use in the long run if it wanted to produce three units of output?

(c)   Define the firm's LAC curve if the firm could build an infinite (or a very large) number of plants.

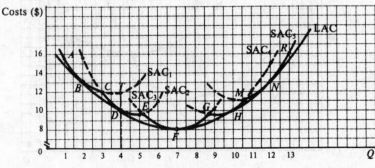

**Fig. 16-7**

(a)   See Fig. 16-7.

(b)   The firm's LAC curve is the solid portions of the SAC curves in Fig. 16-7. That is, the LAC curve for the firm is given by the solid line joining points *A, B, C, D, E, F, G, H, M, N,* and *R.* The dashed portions of the SAC curves are irrelevant since they represent higher-than-necessary AC for the firm in the long run. If the firm wanted to produce three units of output per time period, the firm would utilize either plant 1 or plant 2 and the firm would be at point *C.* In either case the SAC for the firm would be \$12.

(c)   If the firm could build an infinite (or a very large) number of alternative plants, in the long run, there would be a very large number of SAC curves. By drawing a curve tangent to all these SAC curves we get the curve labeled LAC in Fig. 16-7. This curve is the "envelope" of all the SAC curves and shows the minimum per-unit cost of producing each output when the firm can build any desired scale of plant.

**16.13.** From the LAC schedule in Table 16-9 (which corresponds to the LAC curve in Fig. 16-7),

Mathcad

**Table 16-9**

| Q | 1 | 2 | 3 | 4 | 5 | 6 | 7 | 8 | 9 | 10 | 11 | 12 |
|---|---|---|---|---|---|---|---|---|---|----|----|----|
| LAC ($) | 15 | 13 | 11.30 | 10 | 9 | 8.30 | 8 | 8.20 | 8.90 | 10 | 11.30 | 13 |

    (*a*)   find the long-run total costs (LTC) schedule, and

    (*b*)   derive the long-run marginal costs (LMC) schedule. What do these measure?

    (*c*)   What is the relationship between LAC and LMC?

**Table 16-10**

| Q | 1 | 2 | 3 | 4 | 5 | 6 | 7 | 8 | 9 | 10 | 11 | 12 |
|---|---|---|---|---|---|---|---|---|---|----|----|----|
| LAC ($) | 15 | 13 | 11.30 | 10 | 9 | 8.30 | 8 | 8.20 | 8.90 | 10 | 11.30 | 13 |
| LTC ($) | 15 | 26 | 33.90 | 40 | 45 | 49.80 | 56 | 65.60 | 80.10 | 100 | 124.30 | 156 |
| LMC ($) | | 11 | 7.90 | 6.10 | 5 | 4.80 | 6.20 | 9.40 | 14.50 | 19.90 | 24.30 | 31.70 |

    (*a*)   The LTC for any level of output can be obtained by multiplying output by the LAC at that level of output. LTC show the minimum total costs of producing various levels of output when any scale of plant can be built. LMC equals the change in LTC per unit change in output. The LTC and LMC are calculated in Table 16-10. Note that the LMC is entered *between* the various levels of output.

    (*b*)   In Fig. 16-8, the LMC values are plotted between the various levels of output.

    (*c*)   The relationship between LMC and LAC is the same as between SAC and SMC. That is, when the LAC curve is falling, the LMC curve is below it; LMC = LAC when LAC is lowest; and when the LAC curve is rising, the LMC curve is above it.

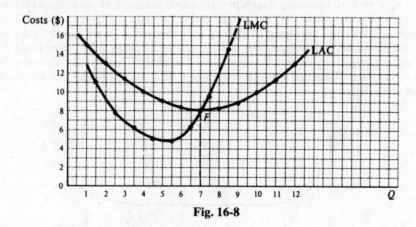

**Fig. 16-8**

## CONSTANT, INCREASING, AND DECREASING RETURNS TO SCALE

**16.14.** Explain

    (*a*)   constant returns to scale,

    (*b*)   increasing returns to scale, and

    (*c*)   decreasing returns to scale. Give examples.

    (*a*)   *Constant returns to scale* occurs when all factors of production are increased in a given proportion and the output produced increases in the *same* proportion. If, for example, the quantities of labor and capital used per unit of time are both increased by 10%, output will also increase by 10%; if labor and capital are doubled, output doubles. This makes sense: if we use two workers of the same type and two identical machines, we expect twice as much output as with one worker with one machine. Similarly, if all inputs are reduced by a given proportion, output is reduced by the same proportion. As a result, long-run average cost (LAC) is constant.

(b) *Increasing returns to scale* occurs when all factors are increased in a given proportion and output increases in a *greater* proportion. If labor and capital are increased by 10%, output rises by more than 10%; if labor and capital are doubled, output more than doubles. As a result, LAC declines. Increasing returns to scale may occur because by increasing the scale of operation, greater division of labor and specialization becomes possible. That is, each worker can specialize in performing a simple repetitive task rather than many different tasks. As a result, labor productivity increases. Time is also not wasted by workers in going from one machine to another. In addition, a larger scale of operation may permit the use of more productive, specialized machinery which was not feasible at a lower scale of operation. A great part of our high productivity and standard of living is due to these *economies of mass production*.

(c) If output increases in a *smaller* proportion than the increase in all inputs, we have decreasing returns to scale and increasing LAC. For example, an increase in the scale of operation may cause communications problems which make it more and more difficult for the entrepreneur to operate effectively. It is generally believed that at very small scales of operation, the firm encounters increasing returns to scale. As the scale of operation rises, increasing returns give way to constant returns to scale and eventually to decreasing returns to scale. Whether this is the case for a particular firm is an empirical question.

**16.15.** (a) Draw an LAC curve showing increasing returns to scale in the first small range of outputs, constant returns to scale in the ensuing "large range" of outputs, and decreasing returns to scale thereafter.

(b) What does this LAC curve imply for the sizes of the firms in the same industry?

(a) In Fig. 16-9, we have increasing returns to scale and decreasing LAC up to output $0A$; we have constant returns to scale and constant LAC between the output levels $0A$ and $0B$; past output $0B$, we have decreasing returns to scale and increasing LAC. LAC and returns to scale are opposite sides of the same coin. Note that economies and diseconomies of scale may both operate in the same range of outputs. When economies of scale overwhelm diseconomies of scale, the LAC curve falls; otherwise the LAC is either constant or rising. The actual output level at which the LAC stops falling or starts rising depends, of course, on the industry.

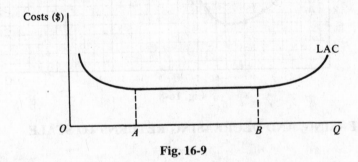

**Fig. 16-9**

(b) An LAC curve with a flat bottom, showing constant returns to scale over a wide range of outputs, implies that small firms may coexist side by side with larger firms in the same industry. If increasing returns to scale operated over a very wide range of outputs, large firms (operating large plants) would have much lower LAC than small firms and would drive the latter out of business. Many economists and business-people believe (and some empirical studies indicate) that the LAC curve in many industries has a flat bottom, as shown in Fig. 16-9. In such cases, the flat portion of the LAC curve is formed by the lowest point of a number of SAC curves.

# Multiple Choice Questions

1. The interest paid by a firm to borrow money capital represents an
   (a) explicit cost,
   (b) implicit cost,
   (c) opportunity cost,
   (d) all of the above.

2. The wage that an entrepreneur would earn if he or she worked instead as a manager for someone else in his or her best alternative employment represents a(n)
   (a) profit,
   (b) explicit cost,
   (c) implicit cost,
   (d) opportunity cost.

3. The law of diminishing returns is a
   (a) monetary relationship between inputs and output,
   (b) short-run law,
   (c) long-run law,
   (d) questionable production relationship.

4. The law of diminishing returns begins to operate when the
   (a) total product begins to rise,
   (b) total product begins to fall,
   (c) marginal product begins to rise,
   (d) marginal product begins to fall.

5. If only part of the labor force employed by a firm can be dismissed at any time and without pay, the total wages and salaries paid out by the firm must be considered
   (a) a fixed cost,
   (b) a variable cost,
   (c) partly a fixed and partly a variable cost,
   (d) any of the above.

6. When the law of diminishing returns begins to operate, the TVC curve begins to
   (a) fall at an increasing rate,
   (b) rise at a decreasing rate,
   (c) fall at a decreasing rate,
   (d) rise at an increasing rate.

7. All of the following cost curves are U-shaped except the
   (a) AVC curve,
   (b) AFC curve,
   (c) AC curve,
   (d) MC curve.

8. AFC equals the vertical distance between the
   (a) AC curve and the AVC curve,
   (b) AC curve and the MC curve,
   (c) AVC curve and the MC curve,
   (d) all of the above.

9. The MC schedule is obtained by subtracting successive values of
    (a) TC,
    (b) TVC,
    (c) either TC or TVC,
    (d) none of the above.

10. The LAC curve shows the
    (a) minimum cost of producing various levels of output within a particular plant,
    (b) minimum cost of producing various levels of output when plant size can be varied,
    (c) profit-maximizing level of output,
    (d) change in TC of producing various levels of output when all inputs can be varied.

11. A firm's declining LAC curve over some ranges of output can be explained by
    (a) diminishing returns,
    (b) decreasing returns to scale,
    (c) increasing returns to scale,
    (d) increasing costs.

12. If a firm doubles all inputs in the long run and total output less than doubles, we have a case of
    (a) diminishing returns,
    (b) constant returns to scale,
    (c) increasing returns to scale,
    (d) decreasing returns to scale.

## True or False Questions

13. _____ Implicit costs are the costs of the factors of production owned by the firm.

14. _____ The firm makes an economic profit if its revenues exceed its explicit costs.

15. _____ The law of diminishing returns states that as we use more and more units of some factors of production, while keeping one or more factors fixed, we get less and less additional output from each additional factor used.

16. _____ The law of diminishing returns holds in both the short-run and long-run periods.

17. _____ All factors are variable in the long run.

18. _____ TFCs are constant regardless of the level of firm output.

19. _____ TC are zero when the firm does not produce any output.

20. _____ AC is constant in the short run.

21. _____ In the long run, MC equals the change in the TVC per unit change in output.

22. _____ The LAC is formed from the relevant segments of the firm's various SAC curves.

23. _____ As more firms enter the industry, the industry supply curve becomes horizontal.

**24.** _____    Decreasing costs refers to the situation wherein output increases proportionately more than inputs.

## Answers to Multiple Choice and True or False Questions

| | | | | | | | |
|---|---|---|---|---|---|---|---|
| **1.** | (*a*) | **7.** | (*b*) | **13.** | (T) | **19.** | (F) |
| **2.** | (*c*) | **8.** | (*a*) | **14.** | (F) | **20.** | (F) |
| **3.** | (*b*) | **9.** | (*c*) | **15.** | (T) | **21.** | (F) |
| **4.** | (*d*) | **10.** | (*b*) | **16.** | (F) | **22.** | (T) |
| **5.** | (*c*) | **11.** | (*c*) | **17.** | (T) | **23.** | (F) |
| **6.** | (*d*) | **12.** | (*d*) | **18.** | (T) | **24.** | (T) |

# Chapter 17

# Price and Output: Perfect Competition

## *Chapter Summary*

1.  An industry is perfectly competitive if it is composed of a large number of firms selling a homogeneous product and firms can easily enter or leave the industry.
2.  A firm maximizes total profits in the short run at the point where total revenue exceeds total cost by the largest amount.
3.  Marginal revenue is the change in total revenue per unit change in the quantity sold. The perfectly competitive firm can sell any quantity at the prevailing price, so its marginal revenue equals price. Such a firm maximizes profits at the point where marginal revenue (or price) intersects the rising portion of the marginal cost curve.
4.  A firm breaks even if price equals average cost. It minimizes total losses if price is greater than average variable cost but less than average cost; and it minimizes losses by shutting down if price is less than average variable cost.
5.  The perfectly competitive firm's short-run supply curve is given by the rising portion of its marginal cost curve over and above its average variable cost curve or shutdown point.
6.  All firms in a perfectly competitive industry in long-run equilibrium produce where price equals the lowest long-run average cost.
7.  The demand for factors of production increases as industry output expands. Factor prices may remain constant, rise, or fall. This determines if the firm is in a constant-cost, increasing-cost, or decreasing-cost industry.

## *Important Terms*

**Break-even point.**   The output level at which the firm's total revenue equals its total costs, and its total profits are zero.

**Constant-cost industry.**   An industry whose long-run supply curve is horizontal because factor prices remain constant as industry output expands.

**Decreasing-cost industry.**   An industry whose long-run supply curve is negatively sloped because factor prices fall as industry output expands.

**External diseconomy.**   An upward shift in a firm's cost curves as industry output expands.

**External economy.**   The downward shift in a firm's cost curves as industry output expands.

**Increasing-cost industry.**   An industry whose long-run supply curve is positively sloped because factor prices rise as industry output expands.

**Marginal revenue (MR).**   The change in total revenue for a unit change in the quantity sold. With perfect competition, price ($P$) is constant, and $MR = P$.

276

**Perfect competition.**    An industry composed of a large number of firms selling a homogeneous product and in which firms can easily enter or leave the industry.

**Perfectly competitive firm's short-run supply curve.**    The rising portion of the firm's marginal cost curve above its average variable cost curve or shutdown point.

**Shutdown point.**    The output level at which price equals average variable cost.

# Outline of Chapter 17: Price and Output: Perfect Competition

## 17.1    PERFECT COMPETITION DEFINED

An industry is said to be *perfectly competitive* if (1) it is composed of a large number of independent sellers of a commodity, each too small to affect the commodity price; (2) all firms in the industry sell homogeneous (identical) products; and (3) there is perfect mobility of resources, and firms can enter or leave the industry in the long run without much difficulty. As a result, the perfectly competitive firm is a "price taker" and can sell any amount of the commodity at the prevailing market price.

**EXAMPLE 17.1.**    Perhaps the closest we have ever come to perfect competition is in the market for such agricultural commodities as wheat, corn, and cotton. There, we may have a large number of producers each too small to affect commodity price. The output of each farmer (say wheat of a given grade) is identical, and it is rather easy to enter or leave this industry. The perfectly competitive model is used to analyze markets, such as these, that approximate perfect competition. It is also used to evaluate the efficiency of the other forms of market organization (see Chapters 18 and 19).

## 17.2    PROFIT MAXIMIZATION IN THE SHORT RUN: TOTAL APPROACH

A firm maximizes total profits in the short run when the (positive) difference between total revenue (TR) and total costs (TC) is greatest. TR equals price times quantity. TC were examined in Section 16.3.

**EXAMPLE 17.2.**    In Table 17-1, quantity (column 1) times price (column 2) equals TR (column 3). TR minus TC (column 4) equals total profits (column 5). Total profits are maximized (at $16.90) when the firm sells 6.5 units of output (if we assume that fractional units, such as parts of a bushel of wheat, can be produced and sold).

**EXAMPLE 17.3.**    The profit-maximizing level of output for this firm can be seen graphically in Fig. 17-1 (obtained by plotting the values of columns 3 and 4 of Table 17-1). TR is a positively sloped straight line through the origin because *P* is constant at $8. At outputs smaller than 3 and larger than 8, TC exceeds TR and the firm incurs losses. At the outputs of 3 and 8 (points *A* and *B*), TR = TC and the firm breaks even. Between *A* and *B*, TR exceeds TC and the firm makes a profit. Total profits are maximized at 6.5 units of output when TR exceeds TC by the greatest amount ($16.90).

**Table 17-1**

| (1) Q | (2) P (\$) | (3) TR (\$) | (4) TC (\$) | (5) Total Profits (\$) |
|-------|-----------|------------|------------|-----------------------|
| 0 | 8 | 0 | 8 | − 8 |
| 1 | 8 | 8 | 20 | −12 |
| 2 | 8 | 16 | 23 | − 7 |
| 3 | 8 | 24 | 24 | 0 |
| 4 | 8 | 32 | 25.40 | + 6.60 |
| 5 | 8 | 40 | 28 | +12 |
| 6 | 8 | 48 | 32 | +16 |
| *6.5 | 8 | 52 | 35.10 | +16.90* |
| 7 | 8 | 56 | 40 | +16 |
| 8 | 8 | 64 | 64 | 0 |

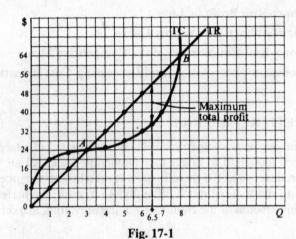

**Fig. 17-1**

## 17.3  PROFIT MAXIMIZATION IN THE SHORT RUN: MARGINAL APPROACH

In general, it is more useful to analyze the short-run behavior of the firm by using the marginal-revenue–marginal-cost approach. Marginal revenue (MR) is the change in TR per unit change in the quantity sold. Since the perfectly competitive firm can sell any quantity of the commodity at the prevailing price, its MR $=$ P, and the demand curve it faces is horizontal at that price. The perfectly competitive firm maximizes its short-run total profits at the output at which *MR or* P *equals MC* (and MC is rising).

**EXAMPLE 17.4.**   In Table 17-2, MR (column 4) is the change in TR and is recorded *between* the various quantities sold. MC (column 7) is the change in TVC and in TC and is also entered *between* the various levels of output. AVC (column 8) equals TVC/$Q$. AC (column 9) equals TC/$Q$. Profit per unit (column 10) equals $P -$ AC. Total profits (column 11) equal profits per unit times the quantities sold (and are the same as in column 5 of Table 17-1, except for rounding). Note that total profits are maximized at \$16.90 when the firm produces and sells 6.5 units of output (as in the total approach of Table 17-1). At that level of output, MR or $P =$ MC and MC is rising.

**EXAMPLE 17.5.**   The profit-maximizing (or best) level of output of this firm can also be viewed in Fig. 17-2. The MC and AC values are from Table 17-2. The demand curve facing the firm is horizontal at $P =$ \$8 $=$ MR. As long as MR exceeds MC, it pays for the firm to expand output. The firm would be adding more to its TR than to its TC and so its total profits would rise. It does not pay for the firm to produce past point $C$ since MC exceeds MR. The firm would add more to its TC than to its TR and so its total profits would fall. Thus, the firm maximizes its total profits at the output level of 6.5 units (given by point $C$ where $P$ or MR equals MC and MC is rising). The profit per unit at this level of output is $CF$, or \$2.60 (see Table 17-2), and total profit is given by the area of rectangle $CFGH$, which equals \$16.90.

**Table 17-2**

| (1) | (2) | (3) | (4) | (5) | (6) | (7) | (8) | (9) | (10) Profit per Unit ($) | (11) Total Profits ($) |
|---|---|---|---|---|---|---|---|---|---|---|
| Q | P ($) | TR ($) | MR ($) | TVC ($) | TC ($) | MC ($) | AVC ($) | AC ($) | | |
| 0 | 8 | 0 | | 0 | 8 | | — | — | — | − 8 |
| 1 | 8 | 8 | 8 | 12 | 20 | 12 | 12 | 20 | −12 | −12 |
| 2 | 8 | 16 | 8 | 15 | 23 | 3 | 7.5 | 11.50 | − 3.50 | − 7 |
| 3 | 8 | 24 | 8 | 16 | 24 | 1 | 5.33 | 8 | 0 | 0 |
| 4 | 8 | 32 | 8 | 17.40 | 25.40 | 1.40 | 4.35 | 6.35 | + 1.65 | + 6.60 |
| 5 | 8 | 40 | 8 | 20 | 28 | 2.60 | 4 | 5.60 | + 2.40 | +12 |
| 6 | 8 | 48 | 8 | 24 | 32 | 4 | 4 | 5.33 | + 2.67 | +16.02 |
| *6.5 | 8 | 52 | 8 | 27.10 | 35.10 | 8 | 4.17 | 5.40 | + 2.60 | +16.90* |
| 7 | 8 | 56 | 8 | 32 | 40 | 24 | 4.57 | 5.71 | + 2.29 | +16.03 |
| 8 | 8 | 64 | | 56 | 64 | | 7 | 8 | 0 | 0 |

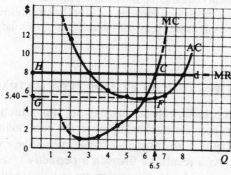

**Fig. 17-2**

## 17.4  SHORT-RUN PROFIT OR LOSS

If, at the point where MR = P = rising MC, P exceeds AC, the firm is maximizing its total profits. If P = AC, the firm is breaking even. If P is larger than AVC but smaller than AC, the firm minimizes total losses. If P is smaller than AVC, the firm minimizes its total losses by shutting down. Thus, P = AVC is the *shutdown point* for the firm.

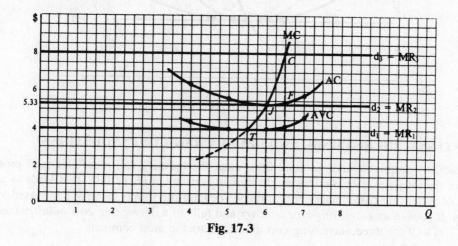

**Fig. 17-3**

**EXAMPLE 17.6.** In Fig. 17-3, the AVC curve (from column 8 of Table 17-2) and three *alternative* demand and MR curves that the firm might face are shown with the MC and AC curves of Fig. 17-2. With $d_3$, the firm produces at $C$, and $Q = 6.5$; profit per unit equals $2.60, and total profits $= $16.90 (as in Example 17.5). With $d_2$, the firm produces at $J$ and breaks even (since $P = $ AC). With $d_1$, $P = $ AVC (point $T$) and the firm incurs a loss per unit equal to its AFC and a total loss equal to its TFC, whether it produces or not. Thus, $T$ is the shutdown point. Below $P = $4, the firm minimizes its total losses (equal to its TFC) by shutting down. Between the prices of $4 and $5.33, $P$ exceeds AVC so that the firm is also covering part of its AFC. In this case, the firm minimizes its total losses by staying in business.

## 17.5   FIRM'S SHORT-RUN SUPPLY CURVE

Since the perfectly competitive firm always produces where MR $= P = $ rising MC (as long as $P$ exceeds AVC), the firm's short-run supply curve is given by the rising portion of its MC curve over and above its AVC, or shutdown point.

**EXAMPLE 17.7.** In Fig. 17-3, the short-run supply curve of the firm is the rising portion of its MC curve above $T$ (shutdown point). If factor prices remain constant, the short-run supply curve of the competitive *industry* is obtained by adding the individual firms' supply curves (see Problem 17.11). The (equilibrium) price at which all firms in this competitive industry sell their output is determined by the intersection of this industry supply curve and the market demand curve (see Problem 17.12).

## 17.6   LONG-RUN EQUILIBRIUM OF THE COMPETITIVE FIRM

If the firms in a perfectly competitive industry are making short-run profits, more firms will enter the industry in the long run. This increases the market supply of the commodity and reduces the market price until all profits are competed away and all firms just break even. The exact opposite occurs if we start with firms with short-run losses. As a result, all firms in a perfectly competitive industry with long-run equilibrium produce where $P = $ lowest LAC. Resources are utilized in the most efficient way to produce the goods and services most wanted by society, and consumers pay the lowest possible price.

**EXAMPLE 17.8.** Figure 17-4 shows that each firm in a perfectly competitive industry at long-run equilibrium produces at point $E$, where $P = $ SAC $= $ SMC $= $ lowest LAC. The forces that inevitably lead to point $E$ are explained in Problem 17.13. Some shortcomings of perfect competition are discussed in Problem 17.15.

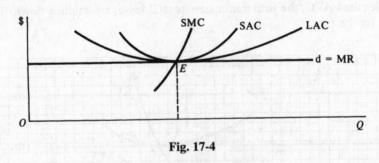

**Fig. 17-4**

## 17.7   CONSTANT-, INCREASING-, AND DECREASING-COST INDUSTRIES

When industry output expands as more firms enter the industry and more factors of production are demanded in the long run, factor prices might remain constant, rise, or fall. This leads to a constant-, increasing-, or decreasing-cost industry, respectively. The long-run supply curve of a *constant-cost industry* is horizontal. It rises in an *increasing-cost industry* and falls in a *decreasing-cost industry* (see Problems 17.16 and 17.17). Of the three, increasing-cost industries are the most common.

# Solved Problems

## PERFECT COMPETITION DEFINED

**17.1.** Explain each of the three component parts of the definition of perfect competition given in Section 17.1.

    (*1*)  There are a large number of independent sellers of the commodity, each too small in relation to the market to be able to affect the price of the commodity by its own actions. This means that a change in the output of a single firm will not *perceptibly* affect the market price of the commodity.

    (*2*)  The products of the firms in the market are homogeneous, identical, or perfectly standardized. As a result, the buyer cannot distinguish between the product of one firm and that of another and so is indifferent as to the particular firm from which he or she buys. This refers not only to the physical characteristics of the commodity but also to the "environment" (such as the location and pleasantness of the seller, etc.) in which the purchase is made.

    (*3*)  There is perfect mobility of resources. That is, workers and other inputs can easily move geographically and from one job to another and can respond very quickly to monetary incentives. In the long run, firms (entrepreneurs) can enter or leave the industry without much difficulty. That is, the products are not patented or copyrighted, vast amounts of capital are not necessary to enter the industry, and already-established firms do not have any lasting cost advantages based on experience over new entrants.

**17.2.** (*a*)  Does perfect competition, as defined above, exist in the real world?

    (*b*)  Why do we study the perfectly competitive model?

    (*a*)  Perfect competition, as defined above, has never existed. Perhaps the closest we may have come to satisfying the three assumptions is in the market for certain agricultural commodities such as wheat and corn.

    (*b*)  The fact that perfect competition has never existed in the real world does not reduce the usefulness of the perfectly competitive model. The perfectly competitive model does give us some very useful (if at times rough) explanations and predictions of many real-world economic phenomena when assumptions are only approximately (rather than exactly) satisfied. In addition, this model helps us evaluate and compare the *efficiency* with which resources are used under different forms of market organization.

**17.3.** A car manufacturer may regard his business as highly competitive because he is keenly aware of his rivalry with the few other car manufacturers in the market. Each car manufacturer undertakes vigorous advertising campaigns seeking to convince potential buyers of the superior quality and better style of his automobiles and reacts very quickly to claims of superiority by his rivals. Is this the meaning of perfect competition from the economist's point of view? Explain.

    The above market is diametrically opposed to the economist's view of perfect competition. It describes a market which stresses the rivalry among firms. The economist's view stresses the *impersonality* of a perfectly competitive market. According to the economist, in a perfectly competitive market there are so many independent sellers of the commodity, each so small in relation to the market, that no seller regards others as competitors or rivals. The products of all firms in the market are homogeneous and so there is no rivalry among firms based on advertising, quality, and style differences.

## PROFIT MAXIMIZATION IN THE SHORT RUN: TOTAL APPROACH

**17.4.** (*a*)  How can the firm increase its output in the short run?

    (*b*)  How many units of the commodity can the firm sell in the short run at the prevailing commodity price?

(c)   What is the shape of the total revenue curve of a perfectly competitive firm? Why?

(d)   What is the shape of the short-run total cost curve of the firm? Why?

(e)   When is the firm in short-run equilibrium?

(a)   Within the limitations imposed by its given scale of plant, the firm can vary the amount of the commodity produced in the short run by varying its use of the variable inputs.

(b)   The perfectly competitive firm is too small to affect market price and can sell any amount of the commodity at the prevailing market price.

(c)   The TR of a perfectly comptetitive firm is shown by a positively sloped straight line through the origin. This is the case whenever commodity price is constant.

(d)   The short-run total cost of the firm is equal to its fixed costs at zero output. It rises at a decreasing rate (faces down) as output rises, before the law of diminishing returns begins to operate, and it rises at an increasing rate (faces up) thereafter.

(e)   The firm is in short-run equilibrium when it maximizes its total profits or minimizes its total losses. It should be noted that not all firms seek to maximize total profits (or minimize total losses) at all times. However, the assumption of profit maximization is essential if we are to have a general theory of the firm. The short-run equilibrium of the firm can be looked at from a total-revenue–total-cost approach or from a marginal-revenue–marginal-cost approach.

**17.5.**   If short-run TVC and TC of a firm at various outputs are the values in Table 17-3 and $P = \$4$,

**Table 17-3**

| Q   | 0  | 10  | 20  | 30  | 40  | 50  | 60  | 65  | 70  | 75  | 80  | 85  | 90  |
|-----|----|-----|-----|-----|-----|-----|-----|-----|-----|-----|-----|-----|-----|
| TVC | 0  | 35  | 65  | 85  | 95  | 105 | 120 | 131 | 145 | 162 | 185 | 225 | 295 |
| TC  | 65 | 100 | 130 | 150 | 160 | 170 | 185 | 196 | 210 | 227 | 250 | 290 | 360 |

(a)   determine the output and dollar amount at which the firm maximizes total profits. At what two levels of output does the firm break even?

(b)   Plot the TR and TC schedules on one set of axes and indicate the point of profit maximization.

(a)   Table 17-4 shows that this firm maximizes its total profits of $73 at 75 units of output and breaks even at 40 and 90 units of output.

(b)   See Fig. 17-5.

**Table 17-4**

| (1)<br>Q | (2)<br>P($) | (3)<br>TR ($) | (4)<br>TVC ($) | (5)<br>TC ($) | (6)<br>Total Profits ($) | (7)<br>Position |
|-----|-----|-----|-----|-----|-----|-----|
| 0   | 4 | 0   | 0   | 65  | −65 | Losses |
| 10  | 4 | 40  | 35  | 100 | −60 | Losses |
| 20  | 4 | 80  | 65  | 130 | −50 | Losses |
| 30  | 4 | 120 | 85  | 150 | −30 | Losses |
| 40  | 4 | 160 | 95  | 160 | 0   | Break-even point |
| 50  | 4 | 200 | 105 | 170 | +30 | Profits |
| 60  | 4 | 240 | 120 | 185 | +55 | Profits |
| 65  | 4 | 260 | 131 | 196 | +64 | Profits |
| 70  | 4 | 280 | 145 | 210 | +70 | Profits |
| 75  | 4 | 300 | 162 | 227 | +73 | Total profits maximized |
| 80  | 4 | 320 | 185 | 250 | +70 | Profits |
| 85  | 4 | 340 | 225 | 290 | +50 | Profits |
| 90  |   | 360 | 295 | 360 | 0   | Break-even point |

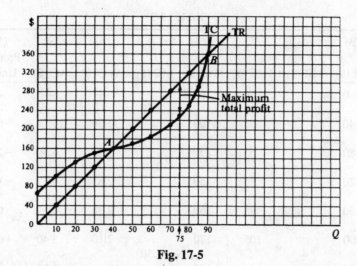

**Fig. 17-5**

## PROFIT MAXIMIZATION IN THE SHORT RUN: MARGINAL APPROACH

**17.6.** (a) Define marginal revenue. How is it calculated? Why is marginal revenue constant and equal to price under perfect competition?

(b) What is the shape and elasticity of the demand curve facing a perfectly competitive firm? Why?

(c) What is the shape of and relationship among the firm's MC, AVC, and AC curves? Why?

(d) How does the firm determine how much to produce in the short run?

(a) MR is defined as and is equal to the change in TR for a one-unit change in the quantity sold. Since the perfectly competitive firm can sell any amount of the commodity at the prevailing market price, its MR = P = constant. For example, if P = $4, TR = $4 when the firm sells one unit and TR = $8 for two units. Thus, MR = change in TR = $4 = P.

(b) Since the perfectly competitive firm can sell any amount at the prevailing market price, the demand curve it faces is *horizontal* or *infinitely elastic* at the prevailing market price. With a horizontal demand curve, an infinitely *small* fall in price causes an infinitely *large* increase in sales. As the denominator of the elasticity formula (the percentage change in price) approaches zero and the numerator (the percentage change in quantity) becomes very large, the value of the fraction and elasticity ($E_d$) approaches infinity (see Section 14.2).

(c) The MC, AVC, and AC curves of the firm are usually U-shaped. MC, AVC, and AC eventually rise because of diminishing returns. The rising portion of the MC curve intersects the AVC and AC curves at their lowest points. AC − AVC = AFC. Since AFC declines continuously as output expands, the AC curve reaches its minimum point at a higher level of output than the AVC curve.

(d) We can determine how much a firm produces in the short run by making the reasonable assumption that the firm wants to maximize its total profits or minimize its total losses. The general rule is that the firm should expand its output until MR = rising MC (as long as P exceeds AVC). Total profits are maximized when the (positive) difference between TR and TC is greatest. A firm should expand its output as long as the addition to TR from an additional unit sold (its MR) exceeds the addition to TC to produce this extra unit (its MC). As long as MR exceeds (>) MC, and up to the point where MR = MC, the firm can increase its total profits by expanding output. The firm should not produce any unit for which MC > MR. If it did, it would be adding more to its TC than to its TR and its total profits would fall.

**17.7.** From Table 17-4, construct a table similar to Table 17-2 showing MR, MC, AVC, AC, profit per unit, total profits, and the profit-maximizing level of output.

Mathcad

In Table 17-5, MR (column 4) equals the change in TR per unit change in sales. For example, as the quantity sold rises from zero to 10, TR rises from zero to $40, giving an average change in TR per additional unit sold of $40/10 = $4 = MR (entered *between* Q = 0 and Q = 10). Similarly, MC equals the change

**Table 17-5**

| (1) | (2) | (3) | (4) | (5) | (6) | (7) | (8) | (9) | (10) Profit per | (11) Total |
|---|---|---|---|---|---|---|---|---|---|---|
| Q | P ($) | TR ($) | MR ($) | TVC ($) | TC ($) | MC ($) | AVC ($) | AC ($) | Unit ($) | Profit ($) |
| 0 | 4 | 0 | | 0 | 65 | | — | — | — | −65 |
| | | | 4 | | | 3.50 | | | | |
| 10 | 4 | 40 | | 35 | 100 | | 3.50 | 10 | −6 | −60 |
| | | | 4 | | | 3 | | | | |
| 20 | 4 | 80 | | 65 | 130 | | 3.25 | 6.50 | −2.50 | −50 |
| | | | 4 | | | 2 | | | | |
| 30 | 4 | 120 | | 85 | 150 | | 2.83 | 5 | −1 | −30 |
| | | | 4 | | | 1 | | | | |
| 40 | 4 | 160 | | 95 | 160 | | 2.38 | 4 | 0 | 0 |
| | | | 4 | | | 1 | | | | |
| 50 | 4 | 200 | | 105 | 170 | | 2.10 | 3.40 | +0.60 | +30 |
| | | | 4 | | | 1.50 | | | | |
| 60 | 4 | 240 | | 120 | 185 | | 2 | 3.08 | +0.92 | +55.20 |
| 65 | 4 | 260 | 4 | 131 | 196 | 2.50 | 2.02 | 3.02 | +0.98 | +63.70 |
| 70 | 4 | 280 | | 145 | 210 | | 2.07 | 3 | +1 | +70 |
| *75 | 4 | 300 | 4 | 162 | 227 | 4 | 2.16 | 3.03 | +0.97 | +72.75 |
| 80 | 4 | 320 | | 185 | 250 | | 2.31 | 3.13 | +0.87 | +69.60 |
| 85 | 4 | 340 | 4 | 225 | 290 | 11 | 2.65 | 3.41 | +0.59 | +50.15 |
| 90 | 4 | 360 | | 295 | 360 | | 3.28 | 4 | 0 | 0 |

in TVC or TC per unit change in output. For example, as $Q$ rises from 0 to 10, TC rises from \$65 to \$100, giving an MC of \$35/10 = \$3.50 for each of the additional 10 units produced (entered *between* $Q = 0$ and $Q = 10$). Note that the MR and MC between $Q = 60$ and 70, $Q = 70$ and 80, and $Q = 80$ and 90 are entered *alongside* the midvalues of 65, 75, and 85, respectively. AVC (column 8) equals TVC/$Q$. AC (column 9) equals TC/$Q$. Profit per unit (column 10) equals $P - $ AC. Total profits (column 11) equal profit per unit times the units produced (and equal the values in Table 17-4, except for rounding). As in the case of the total approach, the marginal approach indicates that this firm maximizes its total profits when it produces and sells 75 units of output, given by the point where MR or $P = $ rising MC (and $P > $ AVC).

**17.8.** (a)  On the same set of axes, plot the firm's demand curve and its MC and AC curves from Table 17-5. Indicate the output at which the firm maximizes its total profits.

(b)  At what output level is profit per unit greatest? Why does the firm not produce at this output?

(a)  In Fig. 17-6, the best level of output is 75 units (indicated by point $C$, where MR = rising MC). Since at $C$, $P = \$4$ while AC = \$3.03, the firm is earning a profit per unit ($P - $ AC) of \$0.97 ( $CF$ in Fig. 17-6) and a total profit of \$72.75 (\$0.97 times 75 units), which equals the area of rectangle $CFGH$.

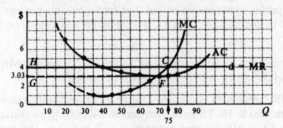

**Fig. 17-6**

(b)   Profit *per unit* is maximized at the lowest point on the AC curve, where $Q = 70$ (see Fig. 17-6 and Table 17-5). At that point AC = $3, so that a price of $4 gives a profit per unit of $1. However, total profit at that point is $70 as opposed to $73 (rounded to the nearest dollar) at point $C$, and the firm wants to maximize total profits—not profit per unit.

## SHORT-RUN PROFIT OR LOSS

**17.9.**   From Table 17-5,

(a)   plot the AC and AVC curves and the rising portion of the firm's MC curve. On the same figure, draw five alternative demand curves that the firm might face: $d_5$ at $P = \$4$, $d_4$ at $P = \$3$, $d_3$ at $P = \$2.50$, $d_2$ at $P = \$2$, and $d_1$ at $P = \$1.50$.

(b)   Set up a table indicating for each alternative demand curve, the best level of output, AC, profit per unit, total profits, whether the firm produces or not, and whether it makes profits or losses.

(a)   See Fig. 17-7.

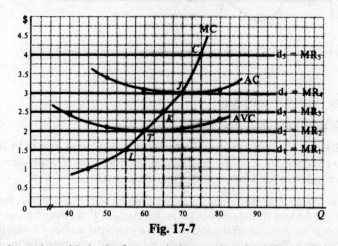

**Fig. 17-7**

(b)   Table 17-6 shows that with $d_5$, the firm maximizes total profits. With $d_4$, $P = $ AC and TR $= $ TC so that the firm breaks even. With $d_3$, the firm minimizes total losses at $33.80 by producing 65 units of output. If the firm stopped producing, it would incur losses equal to its TFC of $65. Thus, by producing, the firm recovers all of its TVC plus part of TFC. With $d_2$, the firm's total losses equal $65 (rounded to the nearest dollar) whether it produces or not. This is the shutdown point for the firm. With $d_1$, the best level of output is 55 units (at which MR = rising MC). However, at this output, the firm's total losses would equal $92.40. But by stopping production altogether and going out of business, the firm would limit its total losses to only $65 (its TFC). Thus, the firm would not produce at $P = \$1.50$.

**Table 17-6**

| Demand | $Q$ | AC ($) | Profit per Unit ($) | Total Profits ($) | Result |
|---|---|---|---|---|---|
| $d_5$ ($P = \$4$) | 75 (point $C$) | 3.03 | 0.97 | +72.75 | Total profits maximized |
| $d_4$ ($P = \$3$) | 70 (point $J$) | 3 | 0 | 0 | Break-even point |
| $d_3$ ($P = \$2.50$) | 65 (point $K$) | 3.02 | −0.52 | −33.80 | Total losses minimized |
| $d_2$ ($P = \$2$) | 60 (point $T$) | 3.08 | −1.08 | −64.80 | Shutdown point |
| $d_1$ ($P = \$1.50$) | 55 (point $L$) | 3.18 | −1.68 | −92.40 | Firm does not produce |

**17.10.**   On a set of axes, draw typical AC, AVC, and MC curves and five alternative demand curves that the perfectly competitive firm might face. Draw $d_5$ such that the firm makes a profit and indicate by point $A$ where the firm produces and by $AB$ the profit per unit. Draw $d_4$ so that the firm breaks even and indicate by point $C$ where the firm produces. Draw $d_3$ such that the firm minimizes its total losses and indicate by point $D$ where the firm produces and by $DE$ the losses per unit. Draw $d_2$ such that the firm is at its shutdown point and indicate by point $F$ where the firm would produce (if it chose to) and by $FG$ the losses per unit. Draw $d_1$ such that the firm would prefer to shut down rather than produce at point $H$.

See Fig. 17-8.

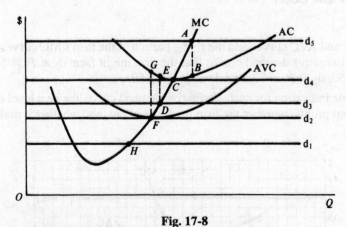

**Fig. 17-8**

## FIRM'S SHORT-RUN SUPPLY CURVE

**17.11.** (a)    What gives the firm's short-run supply curve? Why?

(b)    Draw the short-run supply curve of the perfectly competitive firm of Problem 17.9, and a short-run *industry* supply curve on the assumption that there are 100 identical firms in this perfectly competitive industry (and factor prices remain constant).

(a)    The best level of output for any firm is the output at which MR = rising MC. Since under perfect competition, MR = $P$, the firm should produce the output at which $P$ = rising MC, as long as $P$ > AVC. Given the market price, we can read off the MC curve how much the perfectly competitive firm would produce and sell at that price. This unique price-quantity relationship is nothing else than the firm's supply curve. Therefore, we can say that the firm's MC curve above its AVC or shutdown point is the competitive firm's short-run supply curve.

(b)    Panel A of Fig. 17-9 shows the short-run supply curve of the competitive firm. Note that at prices below $2, the firm supplies zero units of the commodity. Panel B shows the industry's short-run supply curve (S). Note that the quantity supplied by the industry at each price is 100 times greater than the quantity supplied by a single firm and reflects the assumption that there are 100 identical firms in the industry (the symbol $\Sigma$ stands for "the summation of"). This conclusion is based on the assumption that as the commodity price rises and each firm in the industry expands its output (and demands more factors), *factor prices* remain constant.

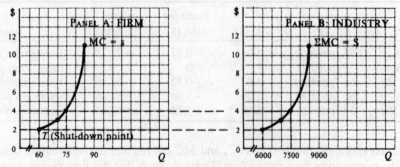

**Fig. 17-9**

**17.12.** (a) Redraw Fig. 17-9. Add to Panel B a typical market demand curve for the commodity intersecting the industry supply curve at $P = \$4$. Add to Panel A the firm's demand curve and its AC and AVC curves (from Problem 17.9).

(b) Explain the sequence of events shown by this figure.

(a) See Fig. 17-10.

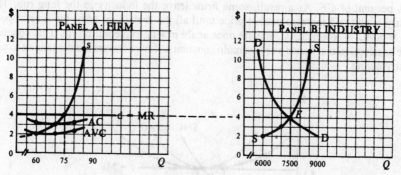

**Fig. 17-10**

(b) The sequence of events shown in Fig.17-10 is as follows. We start in Panel A with the firm's MC curve above its AVC or shutdown point. This is the competitive firm's short-run supply curve (s). By multiplying this by 100, we get the competitive industry short-run supply curve (S, in Panel B). At the intersection of the market demand (D) and supply (S) curves, we find the equilibrium market price of $4 (point $E$ in Panel B). Each competitive firm is too small to affect the commodity price (i.e., each firm is a "price taker") and can sell any quantity at that price. Thus, each firm's demand curve is horizontal or infinitely elastic at the equilibrium market price of $4. Since $P$ is constant, $P = MR$ and d = MR (in Panel A). Given the firm's MC curve, the firm produces where MR = $P$ = rising MC (75 units in Panel A). Since there are 100 identical firms in the industry, the equilibrium market quantity is 7500 units (in Panel B). At 75 units of output, each firm makes a profit per unit equal to the excess of $P$ over AC ($0.97, from Table 17-5) and maximizes its total profits at $73 (rounded to the nearest dollar) by multiplying the per-unit profit of $0.97 times $Q = 75$.

## LONG-RUN EQUILIBRIUM OF THE COMPETITIVE FIRM

**17.13.** Starting at point $E$ in Fig. 17-4, show what happens if the equilibrium market price

(a) rises and

(b) falls.

(a) Figure 17-11 shows that as the equilibrium market price rises, d shifts up, say, to d'. Each firm then produces at point $A$ in the short run, where MR or $P$ = rising MC, and makes a profit per unit of $AB$. Profits attract new firms into this industry in the long run. This will increase industry output and reduce market

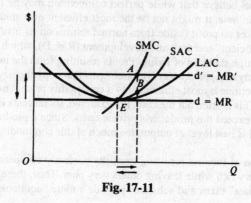

**Fig. 17-11**

price until all firms (old and new) produce at point $E$, where $P = $ SAC $= $ SMC $= $ lowest LAC and are in long-run equilibrium. Industry output is now larger because there are more firms in the industry. The market price is the same as the original long-run equilibrium price, if factor prices are assumed to remain constant.

(b)  Figure 17-12 shows that as the equilibrium market price falls, d shifts down, say, to d″. Each firm then produces at point $C$ in the short run, where MR or $P = $ rising MC (as long as $P > $ AVC) and incurs a loss per unit of $CF$. As a result, some firms leave the industry in the long run. This will lower the industry output and increase market price until all the remaining firms produce at point $E$, where $P = $ SAC $= $ SMC $= $ lowest LAC, and are once again in long-run equilibrium. This conclusion is also based on the assumption that factor prices remain constant as fewer factors are demanded to produce the smaller industry output.

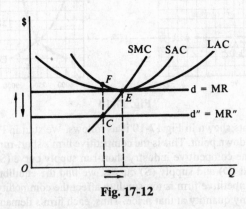

**Fig. 17-12**

**17.14.** Discuss the advantages of perfect competition.

The most important advantages of the perfectly competitive form of market organization are that resources are utilized in the most efficient way to produce the goods and services most wanted by society and that consumers pay the lowest possible prices. In long-run equilibrium, each perfectly competitive firm operates the *optimum scale of plant* at the *optimum level of output*. This is given by the lowest point of the SAC curve, which generates the lowest point of the LAC curve. Resources could not possibly be arranged more efficiently. Furthermore, since the forces of competition eliminate all profits in the long run, consumers get the good or service at $P = $ lowest LAC. Finally, since the commodity price measures the utility or satisfaction that the last unit of the commodity produced gives the consumer, and this is equated to the MC of producing this unit, there is no better use of these resources. That is, the same resources could not possibly be used to produce goods and services which give greater utility or satisfaction to consumers. As a result, perfect competition is used as the standard against which the efficiency of other forms of market organization (discussed in Chapters 18 and 19) is compared.

**17.15.** What are the major shortcomings of the perfectly competitive market organization?

*First*, some economists believe that while perfect competition may be the most efficient form of market organization *at one point in time*, it might not be the most efficient *over time*. The perfectly competitive firm is generally small and makes no profit (aside from normal returns on its investment) in the long run. It is thus not able to undertake "sufficient" research and development (R & D), which perhaps more than anything else is responsible for today's high standard of living. Profits resulting from the introduction of a new technique by a firm are easily and quickly competed away by other firms that copy the new technique.

*Second*, perfect competition is most efficient only if commodity prices and costs truly and accurately reflect social benefits and costs. This is often not the case. For example, social costs (i.e., the cost to society as a whole) when a producer pollutes exceed the producer's private costs. Since a producer equates his private MC costs to his MR in determining his best level of output, too much of this commodity is produced from society's point of view.

*Third*, the distribution of income resulting from the perfectly competitive form of market organization may leave some people very rich while leaving others very poor. Thus, there is the need for the government to step in and with "appropriate" taxes and subsidies provide a more "equitable and fair" distribution of income and try to reconcile social costs and benefits with private costs and benefits. There are also some goods and services, such as police protection, which are best provided by government rather than by the free market.

## CONSTANT-, INCREASING-, AND DECREASING-COST INDUSTRIES

**17.16.** Draw a two-panel figure showing (A) one of a large number of identical perfectly competitive firms and (B) the industry. Start with a particular industry demand curve (D) and supply curve (S) and assume that the firm is originally in long-run equilibrium. Suppose that the industry demand then increases to D'. Discuss the sequence of events whereby industry and firm achieve short-run and long-run equilibrium. (Assume that factor prices remain constant.) Draw the industry long-run supply curve.

Point $E_1$ in Panel B of Fig. 17-13 shows the original equilibrium market price at which the perfectly competitive firm is in long-run equilibrium (point $E$ in Panel A). Suppose that now, for some reason (such as a change in tastes), the industry demand curve increases to D'. A new market equilibrium price is determined at $E_2$. Each firm will be in short-run equilibrium by producing at point A, where d' = MR' = rising MC, and will have a profit per unit of AB. These profits attract more firms to the industry until the industry supply curve increases from S to S', giving the new equilibrium point $E_3$. The firm now returns to its original long-run equilibrium point $E$. Industry output is greater because new firms entered the industry in the long run. The equilibrium prices at $E_1$ and $E_3$ are the same because we have assumed that factor prices remained constant. By joining $E_1$ to $E_3$, we get this industry's horizontal long-run supply curve. This is a constant-cost industry.

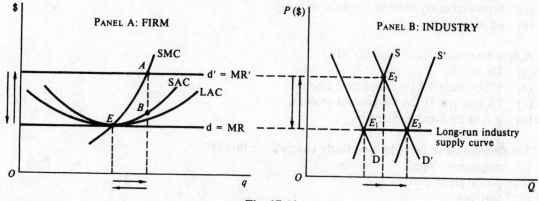

**Fig. 17-13**

**17.17.** (a) Draw two figures similar to Panel B of Fig. 17-13 that show an increasing-cost and a decreasing-cost industry.

(b) Explain, using examples, why there are increasing-cost and decreasing-cost industries.

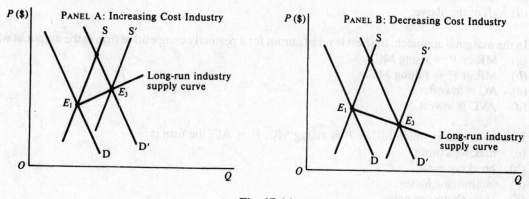

**Fig. 17-14**

(a)  See Fig. 17-14.
(b)  If an industry uses very specialized resources (rather than resources used by many other industries and widely available in the economy) it is likely to be an increasing-cost industry. That is, when the demand for these specialized resources increases in order to expand this industry's output, resource prices are likely to rise and cause an upward shift in all firms' cost curves. For example, if there is a change in tastes in favor of more beef, more single-family homes, or almost anything else, more output and higher prices usually result (see Panel A). This is often referred to as an "external diseconomy." On the other hand, in some rare instances, as industry output expands, factor prices might fall. This would lower all firms' cost curves and lead to a negatively sloped, long-run industry supply curve (see Panel B). For example, as more firms are established in a given locality, improvements in transportation may become feasible and lead to lower costs for all firms in the industry. This is referred to as an "external economy."

## Multiple Choice Questions

1.  In perfect competition,
    (a)  there are a large number of independent sellers, each too small to affect the commodity price,
    (b)  the product of all firms is homogeneous or identical,
    (c)  firms can easily enter or leave the industry,
    (d)  all of the above.

2.  A firm maximizes its total profits when
    (a)  TR = TC,
    (b)  TC exceeds TR by the greatest amount,
    (c)  TR exceeds TC by the greatest amount,
    (d)  it is at the break-even point.

3.  The demand curve faced by a perfectly competitive firm is
    (a)  negatively sloped,
    (b)  positively sloped,
    (c)  horizontal,
    (d)  any of the above.

4.  MR for the perfectly competitive firm
    (a)  is equal to the change in TR per unit change in the quantity sold,
    (b)  equals $P$,
    (c)  is constant,
    (d)  all of the above.

5.  In the marginal approach, the best level of output for a perfectly competitive firm is the output at which
    (a)  MR or $P$ = rising MC,
    (b)  MR or $P$ = falling MC,
    (c)  AC is lowest,
    (d)  AVC is lowest.

6.  If at the output at which MC or $P$ = rising MC, $P$ = AC, the firm is
    (a)  making a profit,
    (b)  breaking even,
    (c)  minimizing losses,
    (d)  at its shutdown point.

**7.** If at the best level of output, *P* is smaller than AC but higher than AVC, the firm
    (*a*)   shuts down,
    (*b*)   breaks even,
    (*c*)   minimizes total losses,
    (*d*)   maximizes total profits.

**8.** If at the best level of output, *P* is smaller than AC but higher than AVC, the firm
    (*a*)   incurs total losses greater than its TFC,
    (*b*)   incurs total losses equal to its TFC,
    (*c*)   incurs total losses smaller than its TFC,
    (*d*)   makes a profit.

**9.** The shutdown point for the firm is the output of lowest
    (*a*)   AC,
    (*b*)   AVC,
    (*c*)   MC,
    (*d*)   *P*.

**10.** The competitive firm's short-run supply curve is the rising portion of the
    (*a*)   MC curve above AVC,
    (*b*)   MC curve above AC,
    (*c*)   AC curve above AVC,
    (*d*)   AVC curve above MC.

**11.** A perfectly competitive firm in long-run equilibrium produces the output at which
    (*a*)   *P* = lowest SAC,
    (*b*)   *P* = lowest LAC,
    (*c*)   *P* = SMC,
    (*d*)   all of the above.

**12.** If factor prices rise as industry output expands in the long run, we have
    (*a*)   a constant-cost industry,
    (*b*)   a decreasing-cost industry,
    (*c*)   an increasing-cost industry,
    (*d*)   any of the above.

## True or False Questions

**13.** _____ In perfect competition, firms sell homogeneous products.

**14.** _____ In a perfectly competitive industry, each firm can affect the commodity price.

**15.** _____ The perfectly competitive firm can sell any amount of the commodity at the prevailing market price.

**16.** _____ In the short run, total profits are maximized at the point where the difference between total cost and total revenue is the greatest.

**17.** _____ The marginal revenue of a firm in perfect competition is equal to the commodity price.

**18.** _____ The perfectly competitive firm maximizes profits at the point where its marginal revenue curve or price intersects the rising portion of its marginal cost curve.

**19.** _____ The shutdown point for the firm is where price equals average cost.

**20.** _____ A firm breaks even when price equals its average variable cost.

**21.** _____ A firm's supply curve is given by its entire MC curve.

**22.** _____ All firms in perfect competition break even in the long run.

**23.** _____ The long-run supply curve of a constant-cost industry is upward-sloping.

**24.** _____ As industry output expands, the demand for factors of production rises and always bids up factor prices.

### Answers to Multiple Choice and True or False Questions

| | | | | | | | |
|---|---|---|---|---|---|---|---|
| **1.** | (d) | **7.** | (c) | **13.** | (T) | **19.** | (F) |
| **2.** | (c) | **8.** | (c) | **14.** | (F) | **20.** | (F) |
| **3.** | (c) | **9.** | (b) | **15.** | (T) | **21.** | (F) |
| **4.** | (d) | **10.** | (a) | **16.** | (F) | **22.** | (T) |
| **5.** | (a) | **11.** | (d) | **17.** | (T) | **23.** | (F) |
| **6.** | (b) | **12.** | (c) | **18.** | (T) | **24.** | (F) |

# Chapter 18

# Price and Output: Monopoly

## *Chapter Summary*

1. Pure monopoly is the form of market organization in which there is a single seller of a commodity for which there are no close substitutes.
2. The monopoly faces the negatively sloped industry demand curve, and so its marginal revenue curve lies below the demand curve.
3. The best level of output for the monopolist is the one at which marginal revenue equals marginal cost. The monopolist can earn profits, break even, or incur losses in the short run.
4. A monopolist can increase its total profits by practicing price discrimination. This involves charging different prices for different quantities purchased, to different classes of consumers, or in different markets.
5. Since price exceeds marginal revenue, the monopolist produces less and charges a higher price than the perfect competitor. Thus, pure monopoly leads to a misallocation of resources.
6. Natural monopolies are often allowed to operate subject to government regulation so as to earn only a normal rate of return on investment.

## *Important Terms*

**Natural monopoly.** A firm that experiences increasing returns to scale (i.e., falling long-run average cost) and is able to supply the entire market at a lower per-unit cost than two or more firms could.

**Price discrimination.** The practice of charging different prices for a commodity (1) for different quantities purchased, (2) to different classes of consumers, or (3) in different markets.

**Pure monopoly.** The form of market organization in which there is a single seller of a commodity for which there are no close substitutes.

## Outline of Chapter 18: Price and Output: Monopoly

## 18.1  PURE MONOPOLY DEFINED

*Pure monopoly* is the form of market organization in which there is a single seller of a commodity for which there are no close substitutes. Thus, it is at the opposite extreme from perfect competition. Pure monopoly may be the result of (1) increasing returns to scale, (2) control over the supply of raw materials, (3) patents, or (4) government franchise.

**EXAMPLE 18.1.**  Electrical companies, telephone companies, and other "public utilities" usually have increasing returns to scale (i.e., falling long-run average costs) over a sufficient range of outputs as to enable a single firm to satisfy the entire market at a lower per-unit cost than two or more firms could. These *natural monopolies* usually operate under a government franchise and are subject to government regulation. Before World War II, Alcoa (the Aluminum Corporation of America) had a virtual monopoly over the production of aluminum in the United States by controlling the entire supply of bauxite (the raw material required to produce aluminum). A monopoly may also arise because a firm may own a patent which precludes other firms from producing the same commodity.

## 18.2  DEMAND AND MARGINAL REVENUE

Under pure monopoly, the firm *is* the industry and faces the negatively sloped industry demand curve for the commodity. As a result, if the monopolist wants to sell more of the commodity, it must lower its price. Thus, for a monopolist, MR is less than *P*, and its MR curve lies below its D curve.

**EXAMPLE 18.2.**  In Table 18-1, columns 1 and 2 give the demand schedule faced by a monopolist. The TR values of column 3 are obtained by multiplying each value of column 1 by the corresponding value in column 2. The MR values of column 4 are the differences between successive TR values and are recorded between successive levels of TR and sales. The MR of $3 recorded *at* the sales level of 2.5 units is the change in TR resulting from the increase in sales from 2 to 3 units (this will be needed later to find the equilibrium level of output for the monopolist). D and MR are graphed in Fig. 18-1. Note that the MR values are plotted *between* successive levels of sales.

**Table 18-1**

| (1) P ($) | (2) Q | (3) TR ($) | (4) MR ($) |
|---|---|---|---|
| 8.00 | 0 | 0 | |
| 7.00 | 1 | 7.00 | 7 |
| 6.00 | 2 | 12.00 | 5 |
| *5.50 — | 2.5 — | 13.75 | 3 |
| 5.00 | 3 | 15.00 | 1 |
| 4.00 | 4 | 16.00 | -1 |
| 3.00 | 5 | 15.00 | -3 |
| 2.00 | 6 | 12.00 | -5 |
| 1.00 | 7 | 7.00 | -7 |
| 0 | 8 | 0 | |

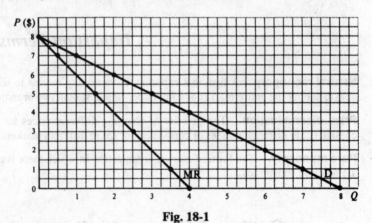

**Fig. 18-1**

## 18.3  PROFIT MAXIMIZATION

The profit-maximizing or best level of output for the monopolist is given at the output at which MR = MC. Price is then read off the demand curve. Depending on the level of AC at this output, the monopolist can have profits (see Example 18.3), break even, or minimize the short-run total losses (see Problem 18.11).

**EXAMPLE 18.3.**  In Table 18-2, the values in columns 1 through 4 come from Table 18-1. Columns 2 and 5 give a typical TC schedule. The other values in this table are derived from the values given in columns 1, 2, 3, and 5. The

monopolist maximizes total profits at $3.75 when it produces and sells 2.5 units of output at the price of $5.50. At this output, MR = MC = $3. As long as MR exceeds MC, the monopolist will expand output and sales because doing so adds more to TR than to TC (and profits rise). The opposite is true when MR is less than MC (see Table 18-2). Thus total profits are maximized where MR = MC. The same conclusion can be reached with the "total-revenue–total-cost approach" (see Problem 18.8).

**Table 18-2**

| (1)<br>P ($) | (2)<br>Q | (3)<br>TR ($) | (4)<br>MR ($) | (5)<br>TC ($) | (6)<br>MC ($) | (7)<br>AC ($) | (8)<br>Profit/Unit ($) | (9)<br>Total Profit ($) |
|---|---|---|---|---|---|---|---|---|
| 8.00 | 0 | 0 | | 6 | | ... | ... | − 6.00 |
| 7.00 | 1 | 7.00 | 7 | 8 | 2 | 8.00 | −1.00 | − 1.00 |
| 6.00 | 2 | 12.00 | 5 | 9 | 1 | 4.50 | +1.50 | + 3.00 |
| *5.50 | 2.5 | 13.75 | 3 | 10 | 3 | 4.00 | +1.50 | + 3.75* |
| 5.00 | 3 | 15.00 | | 12 | | 4.00 | +1.00 | + 3.00 |
| 4.00 | 4 | 16.00 | 1 | 20 | 8 | 5.00 | −1.00 | − 4.00 |
| 3.00 | 5 | 15.00 | −1 | 35 | 15 | 7.00 | −4.00 | −20.00 |

**EXAMPLE 18.4.** The profit-maximizing or best level of output for this monopolist can also be seen in Fig. 18-2 (obtained by plotting the value of columns 1, 2, 4, 6, and 7 of Table 18-2). In Fig. 18-2, the best level of output is at the point where MR = (rising) MC. At this best output level of 2.5 units, the monopolist makes a profit of $1.50 per unit (the vertical distance between D and AC at 2.5 units of output) and $3.75 in total (2.5 units of output times the $1.50 profit per unit). Note that since P exceeds MR where MR = MC, the rising portion of the MC above the AVC does not represent the monopolist supply curve (see Problem 18.12). In the long run, the monopolist can adjust the scale of plant, and profits may persist because of blocked or restricted entry.

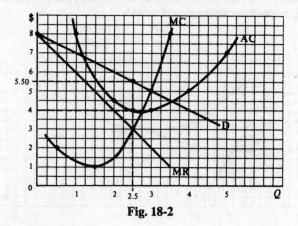

**Fig. 18-2**

## 18.4   PRICE DISCRIMINATION

A monopolist can increase TR and profits at a given level of output and TC by practicing *price discrimination*. This involves charging different prices for the commodity (1) for different quantities purchased, (2) to different classes of consumers, or (3) in different markets.

**EXAMPLE 18.5.** A telephone company may charge individuals 15 cents for each of the first 50 telephone calls made during each month, 10 cents for each of the next 100 calls, and so on. Electrical companies usually charge less per kilowatt-hour to industrial users than to households because industrial users have more substitutes available (such as generating their own electricity) and thus have a more elastic demand curve than households. The markets are kept separate or segmented by meters whereby industrial users are unable to buy more electricity than they need and undersell the monopolists to households. The monopolist reaps the maximum benefit from price discrimination when the MR of the last unit sold to different buyers or markets is the same (see Problem 18.15).

## 18.5 EFFICIENCY CONSIDERATIONS

Since the monopolist produces the output at which MR = MC and *P* exceeds MR, the monopolist produces less and charges a higher price than a perfect competitor with the same cost curves. For example, if Fig. 18-2 referred to a perfectly competitive *industry,* output would be 3 units and price $5 (given where *P* = MC), rather than *Q* = 2.5 and *P* = $5.50 for the monopolist. Thus, monopoly leads to a misallocation of resources. Monopoly profits may also persist in the long run because of blocked or restricted entry. Since corporate stocks are owned mostly by high-income groups, monopoly profits lead to greater income inequality. Finally, the monopolist may feel secure and have no great incentive to make technological advances.

## 18.6 REGULATION OF MONOPOLY

For efficiency considerations, a government (federal, state, or local) often allows natural monopolies (such as public utilities) to operate but subjects them to regulation. This usually takes the form of setting a price which allows the monopolist only the "normal or fair" return of about 8% to 10% on its investment. However, such regulation only partially corrects the more serious problem of misallocation of resources.

**EXAMPLE 18.6.** In Fig. 18-3, the unregulated monopolist would produce 400 units (shown by the point where MR = MC), sell them at *P* = $12 (on D), and receive a profit of $1 per unit (*P* − AC at *Q* = 400) and $400 in total. The government could set *P* = $9 (where *P* = AC) so that the monopolist would break even and earn only a normal or fair return at *Q* = 600 units. However, at this point, *P* still exceeds MC and there still remains some misallocation of resources. At *P* = MC (where D crosses MC), *P* exceeds AC. In this case, this monopolist would incur a loss and would not produce in the long run without a government subsidy.

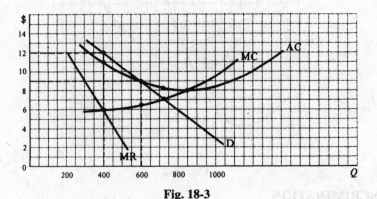

**Fig. 18-3**

# Solved Problems

## PURE MONOPOLY DEFINED

**18.1.** Define pure monopoly. What is the relationship between pure monopoly and perfect competition?

Pure monopoly occurs when (1) there is a single firm selling the commodity, (2) there are no close substitutes for the commodity, and (3) entry into the industry is very difficult or impossible (see Problem 18.2).

Pure monopoly is at the opposite extreme from perfect competition. (See Chapter 17.) Instead of an industry composed of numerous firms, in pure monopoly there is only a single firm. Instead of many firms producing a homogeneous, identical, or perfectly standardized product, there are no close substitutes or similar commodities for the monopolist's product. Instead of firms being easily able to enter or leave the industry in the long run, entry under pure monopoly is blocked or very difficult (otherwise the monopolist would not remain a monopolist in the long run).

**18.2.** What conditions might give rise to monopoly?

(*1*) Increasing returns to scale may operate over a sufficiently large range of outputs as to leave only one firm to produce the industry output. These are called "natural monopolies" and are fairly common in industries such as public utilities and transportation. What the government usually does in these cases is to allow the monopolist to operate but subjects it to government control. For example, electricity rates in New York City are set so as to leave Con Edison with only a "normal rate of return" of, say, 8% to 10% on its investment.

(*2*) A firm may control the entire supply of raw materials required to produce the commodity. For example, up to World War II, Alcoa owned or controlled almost every source of bauxite (the raw material necessary to produce aluminum) in the United States and had a complete monopoly over the production of aluminum in the United States.

(*3*) A firm may own a patent which precludes other firms from producing the same commodity. For example, when cellophane was first introduced, du Pont had monopoly power based on its patents.

(*4*) A monopoly may be established by a government franchise. In that case, the firm is set up to be the sole producer and distributor of a good or service but is subjected to governmental control in certain aspects of its operation. For efficiency considerations, this is fairly common in public utilities [see (1), above].

**18.3.** (*a*) Are cases of pure monopoly common in the United States today?

(*b*) What forces limit the pure monopolist's market power?

(*a*) Aside from regulated monopolies, cases of pure monopoly have been rare in the past and are prohibited today by antitrust laws. Even so, the pure monopoly model is often useful in explaining observed business behavior in cases approximating pure monopoly, and also gives us insights into the operation of the other types of imperfectly competitive markets discussed in Chapter 19.

(*b*) A pure monopolist does not have unlimited market power. It faces indirect competition for the consumer's dollar from all other commodities. Even though there are no *close* substitutes for the commodity sold by the monopolist, substitutes may nevertheless exist: for example, plastic for aluminum, aluminum for steel, etc. Fear of government prosecution and the threat of potential competition also act as a check on the monopolist's market power.

## DEMAND AND MARGINAL REVENUE

**18.4.** (*a*) What type of demand curve does the monopolist face? Why? How does this differ from perfect competition? Why?

(*b*) Why is MR less than *P* for the monopolist? How does this differ from perfect competition? Why?

(*a*) Since the monopolist is the only seller of a commodity for which there are no good substitutes, it *is* the industry and faces the negatively sloped industry demand curve for the commodity. The market demand curve facing a perfectly competitive *industry* is also negatively sloped. However, in a perfectly competitive industry there are a very large number of firms, each supplying only a very small fraction of the total market. As a result, each competitive firm, being so small in relation to the market, does not affect market price and faces a horizontal or infinitely elastic demand curve at the prevailing market price.

(b) Since the monopolist faces the negatively sloped industry demand curve, it must lower its price if it wants to sell more. Because it must also lower its price on *all* units sold, the MR (i.e., the change in TR from selling one more unit) is less than *P*. For example, when the monopolist of Table 18-1 sells 3 units at *P* = $5, its TR = $15. To sell 4 units, it must lower its price *on all units* to $4 each. Thus, TR = $16 and MR = $1, while *P* = $4. A perfectly competitive firm, on the other hand, can sell any quantity at the prevailing market price; thus the change in TR in selling one more unit (i.e., its MR) is constant and equals *P*.

**18.5.** For the monopolist demand schedule of Table 18-3,

    (a)   find TR and MR, and

    (b)   graph D and MR.

**Table 18-3**

| P ($) | 12 | 11 | 10 | 9 | 8 | 7 | 6 | 5 | 4 | 3 | 2 | 1 | 0 |
|---|---|---|---|---|---|---|---|---|---|---|---|---|---|
| Q | 0 | 1 | 2 | 3 | 4 | 5 | 6 | 7 | 8 | 9 | 10 | 11 | 12 |

    (a)   Note that in Table 18-4 MR is obtained by subtracting successive TR and is recorded *between* various levels of sales.

    (b)   In Fig. 18-4, MR is plotted *between* various levels of sales and lies below D.

**Table 18-4**

| P ($) | 12 | 11 | 10 | 9 | 8 | 7 | 6 | 5 | 4 | 3 | 2 | 1 | 0 |
|---|---|---|---|---|---|---|---|---|---|---|---|---|---|
| Q | 0 | 1 | 2 | 3 | 4 | 5 | 6 | 7 | 8 | 9 | 10 | 11 | 12 |
| TR ($) | 0 | 11 | 20 | 27 | 32 | 35 | 36 | 35 | 32 | 27 | 20 | 11 | 0 |
| MR ($) | | 11 | 9 | 7 | 5 | 3 | 1 | −1 | −3 | −5 | −7 | −9 | −11 |

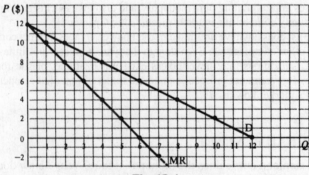

**Fig. 18-4**

**18.6.** (a) From the relationship between *P* and TR in Table 18-4, determine if and when the D of Fig. 18-4 is elastic, inelastic, and unitary elastic.

    (b)   What can you say in general about the relationship among $E_D$, TR, and MR? Why?

    (a)   In Section 14.3, we saw that when *P* falls, D is elastic if TR rises, unitary elastic if TR remains unchanged, and inelastic if TR falls. The D of Table 18-4 is elastic up to *P* = $6, inelastic at *P* lower than $6, and unitary elastic at *P* = $6.

    (b)   From Table 18-4 and Fig. 18-4, we see that as long as $E_D > 1$, a fall in *P* increases TR, and MR is positive. When $E_D < 1$, a fall in *P* reduces TR, so MR is negative. When $E_D = 1$, TR does not change (and is maximum), and MR = 0.

## PROFIT MAXIMIZATION

**18.7.**   (a)   What is the basic difference between the pure monopolist and the perfectly competitive firm, if the monopolist does not affect *factor* prices?

(b)   What basic assumption do we make in order to determine the pure monopolist's best level of output?

(a)   If the monopolist does not affect factor prices (i.e., if it is a perfect competitor in the factor markets), then its cost curves are similar to those developed in Chapter 16 and need not be different from those used in Chapter 17 for the analysis of perfect competition. Thus, the basic difference between the perfectly competitive firm and the monopolist lies on the selling or demand side rather than on the production or cost side.

(b)   In order to determine the pure monopolist's best level of output, we assume (as in the case of perfect competition) that the monopolist wants to maximize total profits. We can look at this either from the total-revenue–total-cost approach or from the marginal-revenue–marginal-cost approach.

**18.8.**   Referring to Table 18-5,

(a)   find the profit-maximizing or best level of output for this monopolist by using the TR and TC approach, and

(b)   graph the results.

**Table 18-5**

| P ($) | 12 | 11 | 10 | 9 | 8 | 7 |
|-------|----|----|----|----|----|----|
| Q | 0 | 1 | 2 | 3 | 4 | 5 |
| TC | 10 | 17 | 18 | 21 | 30 | 48 |

(a)   Table 18-6 shows that the best level of output for this monopolist is three units per time period. At this output, the monopolist charges a price of $9 and has the maximum total profit of $6 per time period.

(b)   Note that the monopolist's TR curve in Fig. 18-5 is not a (positively sloped) straight line through the origin as it was in the case of perfect competition. Total profits are maximized at Q = 3, where TR exceeds TC by the greatest amount ($27 − $21).

**Table 18-6**

| P ($) | Q | TR ($) | TC ($) | Total Profits ($) |
|-------|---|--------|--------|-------------------|
| 12 | 0 | 0 | 10 | −10 |
| 11 | 1 | 11 | 17 | − 6 |
| 10 | 2 | 20 | 18 | + 2 |
| *9 | 3 | 27 | 21 | + 6 |
| 8 | 4 | 32 | 30 | + 2 |
| 7 | 5 | 35 | 48 | −13 |

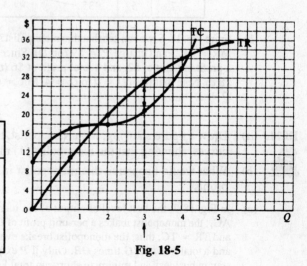

**Fig. 18-5**

**18.9.** In terms of the marginal-revenue–marginal-cost approach,

   (*a*)  state and explain the condition for profit maximization.

   (*b*)  At what price does the monopolist sell? How does this differ from perfect competition?

   (*c*)  Can the monopolist incur short-run losses?

   (*a*)  The profit-maximizing or best level of output for the monopolist is the output at which MR = MC. The reason for this is that as long as MR exceeds MC, the monopolist expands output, adding more to total revenue than to total cost, and so total profits rise. On the other hand, it does not pay for the monopolist to produce where MR is smaller than MC because it would be adding more to TC than to TR and the total profits would fall. This leaves the output at which MR = MC as the profit-maximizing or best level of output for the monopolist.

   (*b*)  The price charged is read from the demand curve facing the monopolist at the sales level at which MR = MC. Because the demand curve is negatively sloped, P exceeds MR. This differs from the perfectly competitive case where (because the demand curve facing each firm is horizontal or infinitely elastic) P = MR. Note that the monopolist neither charges the highest possible price ($12 in Table 18-5 at which the monopolist would incur a loss of $10), nor sells the output at which TR is maximum ($36 at Q = 6 in Table 18-4).

   (*c*)  The monopolist can incur losses, break even, or make a profit in the short run. If P = AC, it breaks even. If P is lower than AC (as long as P exceeds AVC), the monopolist minimizes total losses by staying in business in the short run.

**18.10.** (*a*)  Using Table 18-5, find this monopolist's MR, MC, and AC.

   (*b*)  Show graphically the profit-maximizing level of output. How much profit per unit and in total does the monopolist make?

   (*a*)  See Table 18-7.

**Table 18-7**

| P ($) | Q | TR ($) | MR ($) | TC ($) | MC ($) | AC ($) |
|---|---|---|---|---|---|---|
| 12 | 0 | 0 | | 10 | | — |
| 11 | 1 | 11 | 11 | 17 | 7 | 17 |
| 10 | 2 | 20 | 9 | 18 | 1 | 9 |
| 9 | 3 | 27 | 7 | 21 | 3 | 7 |
| 8 | 4 | 32 | 5 | 30 | 9 | 7.50 |
| 7 | 5 | 35 | 3 | 48 | 18 | 9.60 |

   (*b*)  From Fig. 18-6, we can see that this monopolist should produce 3 units of output (shown by the point where MR = MC) and charge P = $9 (on D). Since P = $9 and AC = $7 at Q = 3, the monopolist makes a profit per unit of $2, and a total profit of $6 (the same as when the total approach was used in Problem 18.8). Note that from Q = 2 to Q = 4, MR = (32 − 20)/2 = $6 and equals MC = (30 − 18)/2 = $6 at Q = 3.

**18.11.** (*a*)  Draw a figure showing, for a monopolist, the best level of output. Include three alternative AC curves, showing that the monopolist (1) makes a profit, (2) breaks even, and (3) incurs a loss.

   (*b*)  What would happen to this monopolist in the long run if it incurs short-run losses? Short-run profits?

   (*a*)  In Fig. 18-7, the best level of output of the monopolist is OB, given by point C where MR = MC. With AC₁, the monopolist makes a per-unit profit of GF and a total profit of GF times OB. With AC₂, P = AC and TR = TC; thus, the monopolist breaks even. With AC₃, the monopolist incurs a per-unit loss of HG and a total loss of HG times OB. Only if P exceeds AVC (so that TR exceeds TVC) will the monopolist stay in business and minimize short-run total losses by producing OB.

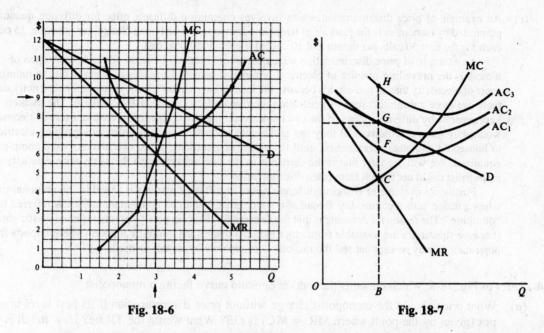

**Fig. 18-6**                                              **Fig. 18-7**

(*b*)  If the monopolist has short-run losses, it could, in the long run, build the most appropriate scale of plant
to produce the best long-run level of output. The monopolist might also advertise in an attempt to cause
an upward shift in the D curve it faces. (This, however, will also shift cost curves up.) If this monopolist
would still incur a loss after having considered all of these long-run possibilities, it will stop producing
the commodity in the long run. If the monopolist was already making short-run profits, it will still build
the most appropriate plant in the long run and increase total profits (if entry into the industry continues to
be blocked and the monopolist does not fear government action).

**18.12.** Can we derive the monopolist's supply curve from the MC curve? Why?

In Chapter 17, we saw that the perfectly competitive firm always produces where MR = *P* = rising MC
(as long as *P* exceeds AVC). As a result, given *P*, we can read from the MC curve the quantity supplied by
the firm at that price. Thus, the rising portion of the firm's MC above AVC or shutdown point is the firm's
supply curve. On the other hand, the monopolist produces where MR = MC but *P* exceeds MR. As a result,
the monopolist's MC curve does not give a unique price-quantity relationship as required along a supply curve.
All we can say is that for the monopolist, costs are related to supply but the MC curve does not itself represent
the supply curve. In the next chapter, we will see that this is the case whenever the demand curve faced by the
firm is negatively sloped, as in all forms of imperfect competition.

## PRICE DISCRIMINATION

**18.13.** (*a*)  What is price discrimination? Why does a monopolist want to practice it?

(*b*)  What are the conditions necessary for the monopolist to be able to practice price discrimination?

(*c*)  Give an example of each of the three types of price discrimination.

(*a*)  Price discrimination involves charging different prices for the commodity (1) for different quantities purchased, (2) to different classes of customers, or (3) in different markets. By practicing price discrimination,
the monopolist can increase TR and total profits from any given level of output and TC.

(*b*)  In order for the monopolist to practice and benefit from price discrimination, (1) it must have knowledge of
the demand for its commodity by different classes of customers or in different markets, (2) these demand
curves must have different elasticities, and (3) the monopolist must be able to separate (or segment) the
two or more markets and keep them separate.

(c)   An example of price discrimination which involves charging a different price for different quantities purchased by customers is the practice of telephone companies, which may charge, for example, 15 cents each for the first 50 calls per month and 10 cents for each additional call.

An example of price discrimination which involves charging different prices to each class of customers is the prevailing practice of electrical power companies. They charge a lower rate to industrial users of electricity than to households because the former have a more elastic demand for electricity since there are more substitutes, such as generating their own electricity, available to them. The markets are kept separate by different meters. If the two markets were not kept separate, industrial users of electricity would buy more electricity than they use and would undersell the monopolist in supplying electricity to household and other private users until the prices of electricity in the two markets were completely equalized. We will see later that if the demands in the two markets have the same price elasticity, the monopolist could not benefit from price discrimination.

Finally, an example of charging different prices in different markets is found in international trade when a nation sells a commodity abroad at a lower price than in its home market. This is referred to as "dumping." The reason for dumping is that the demand for the monopolist's product is more elastic abroad (because substitutes are available from other nations) than in the domestic market (where imports from other nations may be kept out and the markets kept separate by import restrictions).

**18.14.**   Refer to Fig. 18-8, which contains the market demand curve facing a monopolist.

(a)   What price should the monopolist charge without price discrimination if its best level of output (given by the point where MR = MC) is *OB*? What would the TR be? How much is the consumers' surplus?

(b)   Suppose the monopolist sold *OA* units at price *OF* and in order to induce consumers to buy *AB* additional units, it lowered its price to *OC* only on *AB* units. How much would TR be now? How much of the consumers' surplus remains? If the monopolist was already making profits without price discrimination, why would the total profits now be higher?

(c)   Could the monopolist completely take away all of the consumers' surplus?

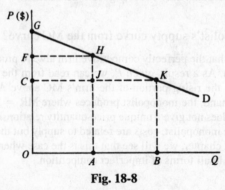

**Fig. 18-8**

(a)   The highest price the monopolist can charge (without price discrimination) to sell *OB* units is *OC*. The TR would then equal the area of rectangle *OCKB*. Consumers' surplus is *CGK* (see Section 15.5).

(b)   TR is *OFHA* (for *OA* units) plus *AJKB* (for *AB* units). Note that price discrimination has increased TR by *CFHJ* (and this is the amount by which the consumers' surplus declined). Consumers' surplus is now only *FGH* plus *HKJ*. The monopolist's total profits are now higher because TR has increased for unchanged TC (for the same *OB* units produced).

(c)   The monopolist could completely take away the consumers' surplus by demanding to sell *OB* units *as a whole* for TR = *OGKB*, take it or leave it (see Problem 15.13). This is rare in the real world.

**18.15.**   Figure 18-9 shows a monopolist selling output in market 1 (with its more inelastic $D_1$ and $MR_1$) and in market 2 (with $D_2$ and $MR_2$). The monopolist is able to keep these two markets separate.

(a)   What is this monopolist's best *total* level of output? How is it determined?

(b)   What part of total output should the monopolist sell in each market in order to maximize TR and total profits? Why?

(c) What price should the monopolist charge in each market? How is the price charged in each market related to price elasticity of demand?

(d) What price would the monopolist charge without price discrimination?

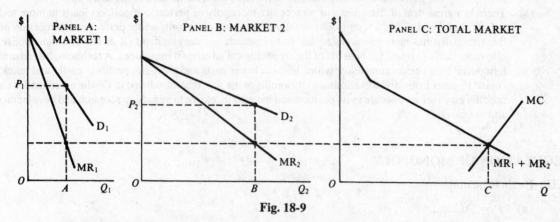

**Fig. 18-9**

(a) The profit-maximizing or best level of output for the monopolist is $OC$ in Panel C. This is at the point where the horizontal sum of $MR_1$ and $MR_2$ equals MC in Panel C.

(b) The monopolist should sell $OA$ in market 1 and $OB$ in market 2 ($OA + OB = OC$). This is at the point where $MR_1 = MR_2 = MC$ for the entire output. If MR were different in the two markets, the monopolist would not be maximizing TR for given TC. For example, if from the last unit sold, MR = $10 in market 1 and $8 in market 2, the monopolist would gain $10 and lose $8 in revenue (for a net gain of $2) by transferring one unit of sales from market 2 to market 1. The possibility of further gain would be exhausted only when $MR_1 = MR_2$.

(c) The monopolist should charge $P_1$ for $OA$ units sold in market 1 and $P_2$ for $OB$ units sold in market 2. Since $D_1$ is more inelastic than $D_2$, $P_1$ exceeds $P_2$.

(d) Without price discrimination, the monopolist would charge a price (the same in both markets) between $P_1$ and $P_2$ such that the total sold in both markets equaled $OC$ units. However, at this price, TR and total profits from $OC$ units of output would be less than with price discrimination.

## EFFICIENCY CONSIDERATIONS

**18.16.** (a) If Fig. 18-6 referred to a perfectly competitive industry instead of to a monopolist, what would the output and price be? Why? How does this compare with the monopolist's price and output?

(b) How does monopoly affect the distribution of income? Why?

(a) If Fig. 18-6 referred to a perfectly competitive industry, output would be about 3.40 units and price about $8.60 because this is where D crosses MC. MC would in this case represent the perfectly competitive industry's supply curve if factor prices are constant (see Section 17.5). Therefore, the equilibrium price and quantity would be determined where D crosses MC or S. This compares with the monopolist's $Q = 3$ and $P = $9$, determined where MR = MC. Thus, monopoly involves a misallocation (specifically, an underallocation) of resources.

(b) Since long-run profits may persist in monopoly because of blocked or restricted entry into the industry and corporate stocks are owned mostly by high-income groups, monopoly tends to increase income inequality.

**18.17.** (a) Should the government break up a monopoly into a large number of perfectly competitive firms? Why?

(b) Does monopoly lead to more technological progress than perfect competition? Why?

(a) *In industries operating under cost and technological conditions (such as constant returns to scale) that make the existence of perfect competition feasible*, the dissolution of a monopoly (by government antitrust action) into a large number of perfectly competitive firms will result in a greater long-run equilibrium output for the industry, a lower commodity price, and usually a lower LAC than under monopoly. However, because of cost and technological conditions, it is not desirable to break up a *natural* monopoly into a large number of perfectly competitive firms. In such cases, comparison of the long-run equilibrium position of the monopolist with that of the perfectly competitive industry is meaningless. In dealing with natural monopolies, the government usually chooses to regulate them rather than break them up.

(b)   There is a great deal of disagreement on whether monopoly or perfect competition leads to more technological progress. Since a monopolist usually makes long-run profits while perfect competitors do not, the monopolist has more resources to devote to research and development (R & D). The monopolist is also more likely to retain the benefits of the technological advance it introduces. A technological advance introduced by a perfect competitor which leads to lower costs and short-run profits is easily and quickly copied by other firms, and this eliminates the profits of the firm that introduced it. On the other hand, a monopolist may feel very secure in its position and have no incentive to engage in research and development and to innovate.

## REGULATION OF MONOPOLY

**18.18.** Evaluate setting

(a)   $P = AC$ and

(b)   $P = MC$ as choices that government can employ to regulate a public utility which is a natural monopoly.

(a)   By setting $P = AC$ for the monopolist's service, the government can eliminate all of the monopolist's profits so that it receives only a normal or fair return on investment. However, at $P = AC$, $P$ still exceeds MC and some misallocation of resources remains (see Fig. 18-3).

(b)   If the governmental regulatory agency set $P = MC$, the misallocation of resources would be eliminated. If the monopolist still makes a profit at $P = MC$, those profits can be completely eliminated by also imposing a flat (or lump-sum) tax on the monopolist equal to total profits (see Problem 18.19). However, at $P = MC$, $P$ may be smaller than AC (see Fig. 18-3) so that the monopolist would incur a loss and not supply the service in the long run without a government subsidy. This, together with the difficulties in estimating MC, usually leads the government to set $P = AC$ for regulated public utilities.

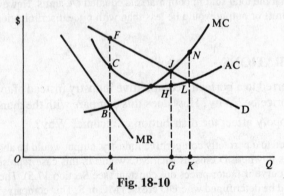

**Fig. 18-10**

**18.19.** With reference to Fig. 18-10,

(a)   determine the output, $P$, and profit for the unregulated monopolist.

(b)   What happens if the government sets $P = AC$?

(c)   What happens if the government sets $P = MC$?

(a)   The unregulated monopolist would produce $OA$ (at which MR = MC), sell at $P = AF$ (on D), receive a profit of $FC$ per unit, and $FC$ times $OA$ in total.

(b)   If the government set $P = AC$, the monopolist would produce $OK$, sell at $P = (AC =)KL$, and break even. However, $P$ is smaller than MC and resources are misallocated (too much of this product or service is produced).

(c)   If the government set $P = MC$, the monopolist would produce $OG$, sell at $P = GJ$, and obtain a profit per unit of $JH$. However, the government could also impose a flat or lump-sum tax on the monopolist equal to *JH* times *OG* and so tax away all of the monopolist's total profits. In this way there would be no misallocation of resources and no profits. However, it is often the case that at $P = MC$, $P$ is less than AC. In this case, the monopolist would incur a loss and could not continue to supply this service in the long run without a government subsidy. This, together with the fact that MC is much more difficult to estimate than AC, leads the government to set $P = $ AC for public utilities.

## *Multiple Choice Questions*

1. In pure monopoly,
   (*a*) there is a single seller of a commodity for which there are no close substitutes,
   (*b*) there is a single seller of a commodity for which there are close substitutes,
   (*c*) there are few sellers of a commodity for which there are no close substitutes,
   (*d*) firms can enter or leave the industry in the long run without much difficulty.

2. Pure monopoly may be based on
   (*a*) increasing returns to scale,
   (*b*) control over the supply of raw materials,
   (*c*) patent or government franchise,
   (*d*) all of the above.

3. The demand curve facing the pure monopolist is
   (*a*) negatively sloped,
   (*b*) horizontal,
   (*c*) positively sloped,
   (*d*) any of the above are possible.

4. The MR of the monopolist is
   (*a*) larger than *P*,
   (*b*) equal to *P*,
   (*c*) smaller than *P*,
   (*d*) any of the above is possible.

5. The best level of output for the monopolist is the output at which
   (*a*) MR equals AC,
   (*b*) MR equals MC,
   (*c*) MR exceeds MC,
   (*d*) MR is less than MC.

6. In the short run, the monopolist
   (*a*) makes a profit,
   (*b*) breaks even,
   (*c*) incurs a loss,
   (*d*) any of the above is possible.

7. The short-run supply curve of the monopolist is
   (*a*) the rising portion of the MC curve,
   (*b*) the rising portion of the MC curve above AVC,
   (*c*) the rising portion of the MC curve above AC,
   (*d*) none of the above.

**8.** In the long run, the monopolist
   (*a*)   can incur losses,
   (*b*)   breaks even because other firms enter the industry and compete away profits,
   (*c*)   can continue to make profits because entry into the industry is blocked or restricted,
   (*d*)   always produces at the lowest point on the LAC curve.

**9.** Price discrimination involves charging different prices for a commodity
   (*a*)   for different quantities purchased,
   (*b*)   to different classes of customers,
   (*c*)   in different markets,
   (*d*)   all of the above.

**10.** With respect to a perfectly competitive industry with identical cost conditions, a monopolist
   (*a*)   produces a larger quantity,
   (*b*)   produces a smaller quantity,
   (*c*)   charges the same price,
   (*d*)   charges a lower price.

**11.** Government can eliminate all monopoly profits by setting a price equal to
   (*a*)   AC,
   (*b*)   AVC,
   (*c*)   AFC,
   (*d*)   MC.

**12.** A regulated monopolist would *not* misallocate resources only if the government regulatory agency set the price equal to
   (*a*)   AC,
   (*b*)   AVC,
   (*c*)   AFC,
   (*d*)   MC.

## True or False Questions

**13.** _____   Pure monopoly is the opposite of perfect competition.

**14.** _____   Decreasing returns to scale may explain the existence of monopolies.

**15.** _____   A monopolist can sell any amount of the commodity at a constant price.

**16.** _____   The demand curve facing the monopoly lies above its MR curve.

**17.** _____   The monopoly maximizes profit at the output level where $P = $ MC.

**18.** _____   The monopolist always earns profits in the short run.

**19.** _____   The profits of a monopolist are measured by the excess of price ($P$) over MR.

**20.** _____   A monopolist can raise its profits by practicing price discrimination.

**21.** _____ A monopoly leads to a higher commodity price and less output than perfect competition.

**22.** _____ All monopoly profits disappear in the long run.

**23.** _____ Monopoly profits lead to a higher income inequality because corporate stocks are usually owned by high-income groups.

**24.** _____ Government regulation of a monopoly effectively corrects for the misallocation of resources that is created.

### Answers to Multiple Choice and True or False Questions

| | | | | | | | |
|---|---|---|---|---|---|---|---|
| **1.** | (a) | **7.** | (d) | **13.** | (T) | **19.** | (F) |
| **2.** | (d) | **8.** | (c) | **14.** | (F) | **20.** | (F) |
| **3.** | (a) | **9.** | (d) | **15.** | (F) | **21.** | (T) |
| **4.** | (c) | **10.** | (b) | **16.** | (T) | **22.** | (F) |
| **5.** | (b) | **11.** | (a) | **17.** | (F) | **23.** | (T) |
| **6.** | (d) | **12.** | (d) | **18.** | (F) | **24.** | (F) |

# Chapter 19

# Price and Output: Monopolistic Competition and Oligopoly

## Chapter Summary

1.  Monopolistic competition is the form of market organization in which there are many firms selling a differentiated product. It is a blend of competition and monopoly.
2.  The best level of output for a monopolistic competitor is the output at which marginal revenue equals marginal costs, provided that price exceeds average variable costs. In the short run, a monopolistic competitor can earn profits, break even, or incur losses. In the long run, it breaks even.
3.  The monopolistic competitor misallocates resources because it produces where price exceeds marginal cost, but the misallocation is small because demand is very elastic. The monopolistic competitor practices nonprice competition in an effort to increase market share.
4.  Oligopoly is the form of market organization in which there are few sellers of a homogeneous or differentiated product. Oligopolists are mutually interdependent and usually engage in nonprice competition.
5.  The kinked-demand-curve model seeks to explain the existence of price rigidity in oligopolistic markets by postulating that the demand curve facing each oligopolist has a "kink" (is bent) at the prevailing market price.
6.  Collusion refers to an overt or tacit agreement among oligopolists on what prices to charge and on how to divide the market. Overt collusion is illegal in the United States.
7.  Oligopolists misallocate resources and can earn profits in the long run because of restricted entry. Oligopolists usually engage in excessive advertising and product differentiation but may spend more on research and development than firms under other forms of market organization.

## Important Terms

**Antitrust laws.**   Legislation which prohibits unregulated monopoly and overt collusion, and tries to achieve "workable competition."

**Centralized cartel.**   A formal organization of oligopolists which achieves the monopoly solution and is the most extreme form of overt collusion.

**Collusion.**   A formal or informal agreement among oligopolists on what prices to charge and how to divide the market.

**Countervailing power.**   The powerful labor unions and the organizations of suppliers to and buyers from large corporations which often arise to protect themselves from and check the power of the large corporation.

**Differentiated oligopoly.**   The form of market organization in which there are few sellers of a differentiated product.

**Differentiated products.**   Similar but not identical products having real or imaginary differences which can be created by advertising.

**Kinked demand curve.**   A demand curve with a kink or bend at the prevailing market price, which is used to rationalize the price rigidity often observed in oligopolistic markets.

**Markup pricing.**   The prevalent real-world policy of setting product prices by adding a specific percentage to estimated average costs.

**Monopolistic competition.**   The form of market organization in which there are many sellers of a differentiated product.

**Mutual interdependence.**   The relationship among the few large sellers of a product in oligopoly which causes the actions of each to affect the others.

**Nonprice competition.**   The competitive techniques of advertising, sales promotion, customer service, and product differentiation often found in monopolistically competitive and oligopolistic markets.

**Oligopoly.**   The form of market organization in which there are few sellers of a homogeneous or differentiated product.

**Overt collusion.**   A *formal* agreement among oligopolists (as in a cartel) on what price to charge, what output to produce, and how to divide the market.

**Price leadership.**   A form of tacit collusion by which oligopolists achieve an orderly price change and match the price changes initiated by the dominant or most efficient firm, recognized as the price leader of the industry.

**Price rigidity.**   The inflexible or unchanging prices often observed in oligopolistic markets during relatively long periods of time and in the face of widely changing cost conditions.

**Pure oligopoly.**   The form of market organization in which there are few sellers of a homogeneous product.

**Tacit collusion.**   An informal understanding among oligopolists, even without explicitly meeting for that purpose, for setting commodity prices and/or dividing the market.

**Workable competition.**   The balancing of the efficiency requirements of large-scale production with protection from the abuses of monopoly or oligopoly power.

# Outline of Chapter 19: Price and Output: Monopolistic Competition and Oligopoly

## 19.1   MONOPOLISTIC COMPETITION DEFINED

In *monopolistic competition* there are many firms selling a *differentiated* product or service. It is a blend of competition and monopoly. The competitive elements result from the large number of firms and the easy entry. The monopoly element results from differentiated (i.e., similar but not identical) products or services. Product differentiation may be real or imaginary and can be created through advertising. However, the availability of close substitutes severely limits the "monopoly" power of each firm.

**EXAMPLE 19.1.**   Monopolistic competition is the most prevalent form of market organization in retailing. The numerous grocery stores, gasoline stations, dry cleaners, etc. within close proximity of each other are good examples. Examples of differentiated products include the numerous brands of headache remedies (e.g., aspirin, Bufferin, Anacin,

Excedrin, etc.), soaps, detergents, breakfast cereals, and cigarettes. Even if the differences are imaginary (as in the case of the various brands of aspirin), they are economically important if the consumer is willing to pay a few pennies more or walk a few blocks more for a preferred brand.

## 19.2  PROFIT MAXIMIZATION

The monopolistic competitor faces a demand curve which is negatively sloped (because of product differentiation) but highly elastic (because of the availability of close substitutes). The monopolistic competitor's profit-maximizing or best level of output is the output at which MR = MC, provided $P$ exceeds AVC. At that output, the firm can make a profit, break even, or minimize losses in the short run. In the long run, firms are either attracted into an industry by short-run profits or leave an industry if faced with long-run losses until the demand curve (d) facing each remaining firm is tangent to its AC curve, and the firm breaks even ($P = AC$).

**EXAMPLE 19.2.**    Panel A of Fig. 19-1 shows a monopolistic competitor producing 550 units of output (given where MR = MC), selling it at $10.50 (on d), and making a profit of $3.50 per unit and $1925 in total. These profits attract more firms into the industry. This causes a downward (leftward) shift in this firm's demand curve to d' (in Panel B), at which the firm sells 400 units at $8 and breaks even. Since $P$ exceeds MR where MR = MC, the rising portion of the MC curve above AVC does not represent the firm's supply curve. Because of product differentiation, our analysis is confined to the "typical" or "representative" firm and we do not have a single equilibrium price and quantity but a cluster of prices and quantities.

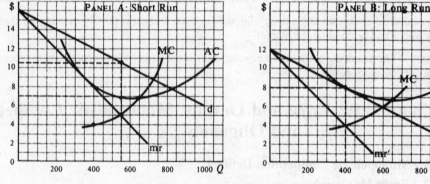

**Fig. 19-1**

## 19.3  LONG-RUN EFFICIENCY IMPLICATIONS OF MONOPOLISTIC COMPETITION

The monopolistically competitive firm misallocates resources because it produces where $P$ exceeds MC (see Fig. 19-1). It does not, in addition, produce at the lowest point on its LAC curve as a perfect competitor does. However, these inefficiencies are usually not great because of the highly elastic demand faced by monopolistic competitors.

In contrast to the perfect competitor, the monopolistic competitor engages in *nonprice competition,* which takes the form of advertising and product differentiation. Such tactics are intended to increase the firm's share of the market and shift its demand curve upward (to the right). However, they also increase the firm's costs and shift the firm's cost curves upward. While some advertising informs the consumer and product differentiation satisfies the consumers' desire for variety, both may be excessive and wasteful (see Problem 19.8).

## 19.4  OLIGOPOLY DEFINED

*Oligopoly* is the form of market organization in which there are few sellers of a product. If the product is homogeneous, there is a *pure* (or *standardized*) *oligopoly.* If the product is differentiated, there is a *differentiated oligopoly.* Since there are only a few large sellers of a product, the actions of each seller affect the others. That is, the firms are *mutually interdependent.* As a result, oligopolists usually engage in nonprice rather than price competition.

**EXAMPLE 19.3.** Pure oligopoly is found in the production of cement, steel, copper, aluminum, and many other industrial products which are sold according to precise specifications and are virtually standardized. Examples of differentiated oligopolies are industries producing automobiles, cigarettes, PCs, and most electrical appliances, where three or four large firms dominate the market. Because of mutual interdependence, if one firm lowered its price, it could take most of the sales away from the other firms. Other firms are then likely to retaliate and possibly start a price war. As a result, there is a strong compulsion for oligopolists not to change prices but, rather, to compete on the basis of quality, product design, customer service, and advertising.

## 19.5  THE KINKED DEMAND CURVE AND PRICE RIGIDITY

The kinked-demand-curve model seeks to explain the observed existence of price rigidity or inflexibility in oligopolistic markets. It postulates that the demand curve facing each oligopolist has a "kink" or is bent at the prevailing market price. The demand curve is much more elastic above the kink than below because other oligopolists will not match price increases but will match price cuts. As a result, the MR curve has a discontinuous vertical section directly below the kink. As long as the MC curve shifts within the vertical section of the MR curve, the oligopolist keeps its price unchanged, or rigid.

**EXAMPLE 19.4.** In Fig. 19-2, the demand curve facing the oligopolist is $CEJ$ and has a "kink" at the prevailing price of $4 per unit and quantity of 200. Note that demand curve $CEJ$ is much more elastic above the kink than below, illustrating the assumption that other oligopolists will not match price increases but will match price cuts. The corresponding marginal revenue curve is $CFGN$; $CF$ is the segment corresponding to the $CE$ portion of the demand curve; $GN$ corresponds to the $EJ$ portion of the demand curve. The kink at point $E$ on the demand curve causes the discontinuity between $F$ and $G$ in the marginal revenue curve. The oligopolist's marginal cost curve can rise or fall anywhere within the vertical (discontinuous) portion of the MR curve (from MC to MC', in Fig. 19-2) without inducing the oligopolist to change the sales level and the price of $4 it charges. Note that once again, $P$ exceeds MR where MR $=$ MC, and so the rising portion of the MC curve above AVC does not represent the oligopolist's supply curve.

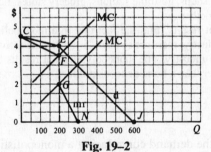

**Fig. 19–2**

## 19.6  COLLUSION

An orderly price change (i.e., one that does not start a price war) is usually accomplished by *collusion* when changed cost conditions make such a price change inevitable. Collusion can be overt or tacit. The most extreme form of *overt collusion* is the *centralized cartel,* in which the oligopolists produce the monopoly output, charge the monopoly price, and somehow allocate production and profits among the cartel members (see Problem 19.14). Antitrust laws make overt collusion illegal in the United States. In *tacit collusion,* the oligopolists, informally and without even meeting, follow a recognized *price leader* in their pricing policies or agree on how to share the market.

**EXAMPLE 19.5.** Until the 1980s, U.S. Steel (now called USX) was the recognized price leader. When rising costs required it, U.S. Steel raised the price on some of its products on the tacit understanding that other domestic steel producers would match the price within a few days. An orderly price increase was thus achieved without exposing producers to government antitrust action or the danger of a price war. In recent years the pattern has become more complex, with other steel companies also initiating price increases. If the rise in domestic steel prices encourages steel imports, domestic steel producers then lobby Congress for import restrictions.

## 19.7   LONG-RUN EFFICIENCY IMPLICATIONS OF OLIGOPOLY

While the oligopolist can make profits, break even, or incur losses in the short run, in the long run the firm will leave the industry rather than incur losses. Oligopolists underallocate resources and can earn long-run profits because of restricted entry. Usually they also engage in excessive advertising and product differentiation. However, efficiency considerations may allow only a few firms in the industry, and oligopolists may use their profits for research and development (R & D) (see Problem 19.17).

The great economic power of large oligopolistic corporations may have stimulated the growth of powerful labor unions and large organizations of buyers from and sellers to these large corporations. The function of these unions and organizations is to protect themselves from and check the power of the large corporation (that is, to be a "countervailing power"). This, and the fear of antitrust prosecution, has resulted in a degree of "workable competition" or a balancing of the efficiency requirements of large-scale production with some protection from the abuses of oligopoly power.

# Solved Problems

## MONOPOLISTIC COMPETITION DEFINED

**19.1.**   (a)   Define monopolistic competition, giving a few examples, and

(b)   identify its competitive and monopolistic elements.

(a)   Monopolistic competition is the type of market organization in which there are many sellers of a differentiated product. Monopolistic competition is common in the retail and service sectors of our economy. Examples are the barber shops, gasoline stations, grocery stores, liquor stores, drug stores, etc. located in close proximity to one another.

(b)   The competitive element results from the fact that in a monopolistically competitive industry (as in a perfectly competitive industry) there are so many firms that the activities of each have no perceptible effect on the other firms in the industry. The monopoly element results because the monopolistic competitors sell a differentiated rather than a homogeneous product.

## PROFIT MAXIMIZATION

**19.2.**   (a)   What is the shape of the demand curve facing a monopolistic competitor? Why?

(b)   How does the monopolistic competitor decide what output to produce?

(c)   Can the monopolistic competitor incur short-run losses?

(d)   Can we derive the monopolistic competitor's supply curve from its MC curve? Why?

(e)   What happens in the long run if the monopolistic competitor is making short-run profits? Incurring short-run losses?

(a)   The demand curve facing a monopolistic competitor is negatively sloped because of product differentiation, but it is highly elastic because of the availability of close substitutes.

(b)   The best level of output of the monopolistic competitor is the output at which MR = MC, provided that P exceeds AVC.

(c)   The monopolistic competitor can make a profit, break even, or incur a loss in the short run. It all depends on the level of its AC in relation to P at the output level at which MR = MC.

(d)   Because the demand curve facing the monopolistic competitor is negatively sloped, P exceeds MR at the output level at which MR = MC. As a result, the MC curve does not give the unique price-quantity relationship required along a supply curve. All we can say is that costs are related to supply, but the MC curve does not itself represent the supply curve.

(e) Short-run profits attract more firms in the long run. As more firms share the market, each competitor's demand shifts down until it is tangent to the AC curve and each firm just about breaks even. On the other hand, short-run losses cause some firms to shut down in the long run. This causes the demand curves of the remaining firms to shift up until they are tangent to their respective AC curves and each firm just breaks even.

**19.3.** Draw a figure showing, in Panel A, a monopolistic competitor making short-run profits, and, in Panel B, the same monopolistic competitor breaking even in the long run.

In Panel A of Fig 19-3, the monopolistic competitor produces 800 units (at which MR = MC) at AC = $6.25, sells them at $P = \$8$ (on d), and makes a per-unit profit of $1.75 and a total profit of $1400. In the long run, more firms are attracted into the industry and cause the firm's demand curve to shift down to d' (in Panel B), where it is tangent to the AC curve and the firm breaks even by producing 700 units and selling them at $P = \$6.50$.

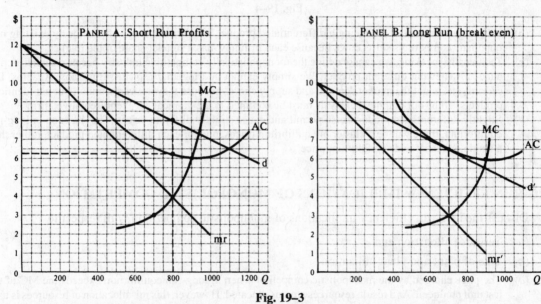

**Fig. 19-3**

**19.4.** Draw a figure showing, in Panel A, a monopolistic competitor incurring short-run losses, and, in Panel B, the same monopolistic competitor breaking even in the long run.

The AC and MC curves in Fig. 19-4 are the same as in Fig 19-3, but the demand curve facing the firm in Panel A is lower (d''). With d'', the monopolistic competitor produces 550 units at AC = $7.50, sells them at $P = \$5.25$, incurs a loss of $2.25 per unit and $1237.50 in total. In the long run, some firms shut down and cause the firm's demand curve to shift up to d' (in Panel B, the same as in Fig. 19-3), where it is tangent to the AC curve and the firm breaks even by producing 700 units and selling them at $P = \$6.50$. Note that the end result is the same as in Problem 19.3.

**19.5.** (a) Why does a prospective monopolistic competitor find it relatively easy to start production in the long run?

(b) Why does the demand curve of a monopolistic competitor shift down when more firms start production?

(c) Why is it difficult or impossible to define the industry under monopolistic competition?

(d) Why is there a cluster of prices rather than a single equilibrium price in this kind of industry?

(a) A prospective monopolistic competitor usually finds it relatively easy to start production because very little capital and no great technical know-how are required to open a small gasoline station, grocery store, country store, barber shop, etc.

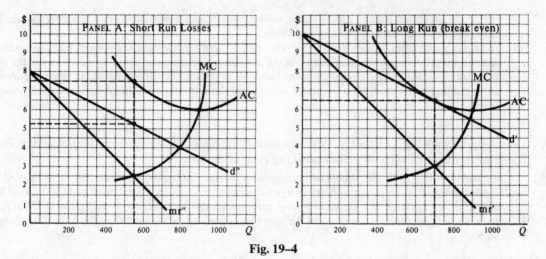

**Fig. 19-4**

(*b*)   When more firms start producing a differentiated product, the demand curve of previously existing monopolistic competitors shifts down because each firm now has a smaller share of the market.

(*c*)   Technically speaking, we cannot define the monopolistically competitive industry because each firm produces a somewhat different product. We simply cannot add together aspirins, Bufferins, Anacins, Excedrins, etc. to get the market demand and supply curves because they are very similar, but not identical, products. Thus, our graphical analysis must be confined to the "typical" or "representative" firm.

(*d*)   Slightly differentiated products also permit and cause slightly different prices. That is, even in long-run equilibrium, there will be a cluster of equilibrium prices, one for each differentiated product, rather than a single, industry-wide equilibrium price.

## LONG-RUN EFFICIENCY IMPLICATIONS OF MONOPOLISTIC COMPETITION

**19.6.**   Discuss the long-run efficiency implications of monopolistic competition with respect to

(*a*)   resource allocation and

(*b*)   size of plant and plant utilization.

(*a*)   The price charged by the monopolistic competitor when in long-run equilibrium exceeds the MC of the last unit produced. As a result, resources are misallocated. However, this misallocation of resources is usually not great because the demand curve facing the monopolistically competitive firm, though negatively sloped, is highly elastic.

(*b*)   We saw before that in long-run equilibrium the demand curve facing each firm is tangent to its AC curve and each firm breaks even. Since the demand curve is negatively sloped, the tangency point will always occur to the left of the lowest point on the firm's AC curve (see Figs. 19-3 and 19-4). Thus, the firm underutilizes a smaller-than-optimum scale of plant when in long-run equilibrium. This allows the existence of more firms in the industry than otherwise (see Problem 19.7). An example of this is the "overcrowding" of gasoline stations, barber shops, grocery stores, etc., each of which is idle some of the time.

**19.7.**   Compare the long-run equilibrium position of the firm of Problems 19.3 and 19.4 to the long-run equilibrium position of a perfectly competitive firm with the same AC curve.

In Fig. 19-5, point $E'$ is the long-run equilibrium point for the monopolistically competitive firm of Problems 19.3 and 19.4. If this had been a perfectly competitive firm with the same AC curve, it would have produced at point $E$ in long-run equilibrium. Thus, the cost of production and the price of the monopolistically competitive firm is $6.50 rather than $6 and its output is 700 rather than 900 units. As a result, the monopolistically competitive firm underallocates resources. The smaller output of each firm in monopolistic competition allows more firms to exist and results in excessive capacity and overcrowding. Sometimes, losses even persist in the long run because as soon as some firms leave, others immediately take their place because of ignorance or misplaced hope. These are sometimes referred to as "sick industries."

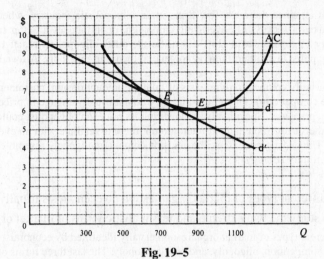

**Fig. 19–5**

**19.8.** (a) What is meant by nonprice competition? Why do monopolistic competitors engage in it while perfectly competitive firms do not?

(b) What is the effect of advertising and product differentiation on the firm's demand and cost curves?

(c) What are the benefits and costs of advertising and product differentiation?

(a) Nonprice competition refers to advertising, sales promotion, customer service, and product differentiation. A monopolistic competitor engages in it in order to convince customers that its product or service is unique and superior. The perfect competitor does not engage in nonprice competition because it can sell any quantity at the prevailing market price and the product is homogeneous or perfectly standardized.

(b) Advertising and product differentiation, when successful, can shift the demand curve of the monopolistic competitor up, allowing it to charge a slightly higher price and/or capture a bigger share of the market. However, they also add to the firm's costs and cause an upward shift in its AC and MC curves. Advertising and product differentiation should be undertaken as long as they add more to TR than TC. By doing this, the firm would increase its total profits. However, it is often difficult to anticipate the exact effect of advertising and product differentiation on the firm's TR and profits.

(c) Some advertising is useful, particularly in a dynamic world, because it educates consumers and informs them of new products and their usefulness. Some product differentiation, such as different qualities, design, color, etc., is also useful since it satisfies the different tastes of consumers and their desire for variety. However, these practices are often thought to be excessive in monopolistic competition. "Excessive" advertising adds only to costs and is passed on to consumers in the form of higher prices.


## OLIGOPOLY DEFINED

**19.9.** (a) Define oligopoly.

(b) What is the single most important characteristic of oligopolistic markets?

(c) Do oligopolists engage in price or nonprice competition? Why?

(a) Oligopoly is the form of market organization in which there are few sellers of a commodity. If there are only two sellers, we have a duopoly. If the product is homogeneous (e.g., steel, cement, copper), we have a pure oligopoly. If the product is differentiated (e.g., cars, cigarettes), we have a differentiated oligopoly. Oligopoly seems to be the most prevalent form of market organization in the manufacturing sector of modern economies and arises for the same general reasons as monopoly (i.e., economies of scale, control over the source of raw materials, patents, and government franchise).

(b) The interdependence among the firms in the industry is the single most important characteristic of oligopoly and sets it apart from other market structures. This interdependence is the natural result of fewness. That is, since there are few firms in an oligopolistic industry, when one of them lowers its price, undertakes a successful advertising campaign, or introduces a better model, the demand curve faced by other oligopolists will shift down. So the other oligopolists react. How they react will vary from one oligopolist to another; there is no general theory of oligopoly. All we have are specific cases or models.

(c)  Oligopolists usually compete on the basis of quality, product design, customer service, and advertising (i.e., nonprice competition). The reason that they do not usually engage in price competition is their fear of triggering a price war. Specifically, by lowering its price, an oligopolist could significantly reduce the sales of the other firms in the industry and prompt them to retaliate with an even greater price reduction of their own. Thus, to a great extent, the decision context in oligopoly resembles chess or poker-playing, and perhaps military strategy.

**19.10.** (a)  What four different types of market organization do economists usually identify?

(b)  Why do we study the two extreme and less realistic forms of market organization first?

(a)  The four different types of market organization usually identified by economists are perfect competition, monopolistic competition, oligopoly, and pure monopoly. The last three forms of market organization fall into the realm of imperfect competition. Economists identify these four types of market organization in order to organize their analysis.

(b)  We examined first the two extreme forms of market organization (i.e., perfect competition and pure monopoly) because historically, these are the models that were first developed. More important, these are the models that are more fully and satisfactorily developed. The monopolistic competition and oligopoly models, though more realistic in terms of actual forms of business organization in our economy (and, in general, in most other economies), are not very satisfactory and leave much to be desired from a theoretical point of view.

## THE KINKED DEMAND CURVE AND PRICE RIGIDITY

**19.11.** (a)  Draw a figure showing a kinked demand curve, its corresponding MR curve, and an MC curve that shows the oligopolist selling at the price at which the demand curve is kinked.

(b)  How can you explain the shape of a kinked demand curve? Of the corresponding MR curve? Over what range of MC will the oligopolist sell at the same price?

(a)  In Fig. 19-6, *CEJ* (with kink at *E*) is the demand curve facing the oligopolist. *CFGN* is its MR curve. The oligopolist produces 300 units (at which its MR curve crosses its MC curve) and sells them at *P* = \$6 (shown on d).

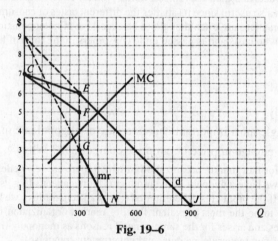

**Fig. 19–6**

(b)  The demand curve facing the oligopolist is drawn with a kink at the prevailing market price at the quantity sold. It is very elastic above the kink because if an oligopolist increases its price, others in the industry will not raise theirs and so it would lose most of its customers. On the other hand, d is much less elastic below the kink because if the oligopolist lowers its price, the others will match the price reduction and the oligopolist only retains its approximate share of the market. The *CF* portion of the MR curve is derived from the *CE* portion of d, and *GN* from *EJ*. The MR curve is discontinuous directly below (and caused by) the kink at point *E* on d. MC can vary from \$3 to \$5 and still intersect MR at $Q = 300$ with $P = \$6$.

**19.12.** (a)  What does the kinked-demand-curve model accomplish?

(b)  What would happen if a new and higher MC curve were to intersect the MR curve to the left of and above its vertical portion?

(c)  Does this rising portion of the oligopolist's MC over and above AVC represent his supply curve? Why?

(a)  The kinked-demand-curve model can *rationalize* the price rigidity in oligopolistic markets when there are widespread changes in cost conditions. It is of no use, however, in *explaining* how the prevailing prices were originally determined.

(b)  If a new and higher MC curve intersects the MR curve to the left and above its vertical portion, this and other firms would want to increase prices. An orderly price increase is then usually accomplished through collusion (see Section 19.6).

(c)  In oligopoly, as in other forms of imperfect competition where the firm faces a negatively sloped demand curve, *P* exceeds MR at the output at which MR = MC. As a result, the rising portion of the oligopolist's MC curve above AVC does not represent its supply curve. Once again, we must conclude that MC is related to supply but the MC curve is not the oligopolist's supply curve.

## COLLUSION

**19.13.** (a)  What is meant by collusion? By tacit collusion? By overt collusion?

(b)  What are the forces which lead to collusion? What are the obstacles to it?

(c)  What is a cartel? How does it operate?

(d)  What is price leadership? How does it operate?

(a)  Collusion refers to a formal or informal agreement among oligopolists on what prices to charge and/or on how to divide the market. Overt collusion refers to a formal agreement, such as a cartel, and it is illegal under U.S. antitrust laws. Tacit collusion is an informal agreement, such as price leadership, and is not illegal.

(b)  Collusion is the natural result of the mutual interdependence of firms in oligopolistic markets. It can serve to avert price wars and to increase industry profits. The greatest obstacle to collusion is antitrust laws. But the greater the number of firms and the extent of product differentiation, the more difficult collusion becomes. Poor economic conditions, as in a recession, and cheating by the member firms are other obstacles to effective collusion.

(c)  A cartel is a formal organization of producers for the purpose of setting prices and/or dividing the market so as to maximize industry profits and/or block entry into the industry. The most extreme form is the centralized cartel, which behaves as a monopolist. Cartels are illegal in the United States today, but they nevertheless help us understand some oligopolistic practices and tendencies.

(d)  Price leadership is a form of tacit collusion often practiced in oligopolistic markets. It is not illegal in the United States today. When changed cost conditions make a price change inevitable, the dominant or most efficient firm in the industry usually starts a price increase on the tacit understanding that the other firms in the industry will more or less match the price increase within a few days. This averts the danger of a price war without exposing the oligopolists to possible government antitrust action.

**19.14.** (a)  Draw a figure that shows the demand, marginal revenue, and marginal cost curves of a centralized cartel producing a homogeneous product, and use them to determine the industry output and price.

(b)  How can the cartel allocate production and profits among its members?

(a)  Since the centralized cartel behaves as a monopolist, it faces the market demand curve for the commodity (D, in Fig. 19-7) and the related marginal revenue curve (MR). ΣMC is the summation of the MC curves above AVC of all the cartel members, if factor prices remain constant. Behaving as a monopolist, the cartel produces 300 units of output (where MR = ΣMC) and sets $P$ = \$4.50 (on D). The cartel's profits depend on the AC of producing $Q$ = 300.

(b)  The cartel's total output of 300 units can then be obtained by allowing each member to produce up to the point where its MC equals \$3 (MR = ΣMC in Fig. 19-7). This may involve the shutting down of the most inefficient plants (while still sharing the profits). The cartel profits can then be shared among its members equally, according to the amount produced, or through bargaining.

**19.15.**  Suppose that there are only two identical firms in a particular *pure* oligopolistic industry (duopoly) facing a total market demand curve identical to that of Fig. 19-7. Suppose also that *each* duopolist has an MC curve identical to that of the entire cartel of Fig. 19-7. Draw a figure showing how much each duopolist would produce and what price each would charge in the absence of collusion.

Mathcad

In Fig. 19-8, D is the market demand shared equally by the duopolists. Each duopolist will produce 200 units (given where MR = MC) and charge $P$ = \$4 (on d). Thus, 400 units of output are sold to the market as a whole at $P$ = \$4 (on D).

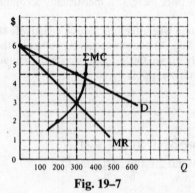

**Fig. 19-7**                                   **Fig. 19-8**

**19.16.** Suppose that in Problem 19.15, the second duopolist has a lower MC, which intersects $mr_2$ at \$1.

 (a)  Draw a figure showing how much each duopolist would like to produce and the price he would like to charge in order to maximize total profits.

Mathcad

(b)  What must the final result be without collusion? How is this related to price leadership?

(a)  In Fig. 19-9, duopolist 1 would like to produce 200 units and charge $P$ = \$4 (as in Problem 19.15 and Fig. 19-8). However, duopolist 2 would like to produce 250 units ($mr_2$ = $MC_2$) and charge $P$ = \$3.50 (on $d_2$).

(b)  Since the product is homogeneous (we assumed a pure duopoly in Problem 19.15), the more *in*efficient duopolist 1 will also be forced to sell 250 units at $P$ = \$3.50, and so will not maximize total profits (since $mr_1$ is smaller than $MC_1$ at $Q$ = 250). The larger and more efficient duopolist may then assume the natural role of price leader and set a price which will allow the other to stay in business and earn some profits even if this means not maximizing its own total profits. (If the less efficient duopolist went out of business, duopolist 2 could be prosecuted for monopolizing the market.)

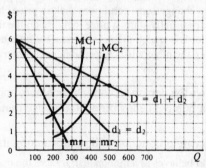

**Fig. 19-9**

## LONG-RUN EFFICIENCY IMPLICATIONS OF OLIGOPOLY

**19.17.**  (a)    What are some of the natural and artificial barriers to entry into oligopolistic industries?

   (b)    What are the possible harmful effects of oligopoly?

   (c)    What are the possible beneficial effects of oligopoly?

   (a)    The natural barriers to entry into such oligopolistic industries as the automobile, aluminum, and steel industries are the smallness of the markets in relation to efficient operation and the huge amounts of capital and specialized inputs required to start efficient operation. Some of the artificial barriers to entry are control over sources of raw materials, patents, and government franchise. When entry is blocked or at least restricted (the usual case), the firms in an oligopolistic industry can earn long-run profits.

   (b)    In the long run, oligopoly may lead to the following harmful effects: (1) $P$ exceeds MC and so there is an underallocation of the economy's resources to the firms in the oligopolistic industry, (2) price usually exceeds LAC in oligopolistic markets, (3) the oligopolist usually does not produce at the lowest point on its LAC curve, and (4) when oligopolists produce a differentiated product, too much may be spent on advertising and model changes.

   (c)    For technological reasons, many products (such as automobiles, steel, aluminum, etc.) cannot possibly be produced under conditions of perfect competition (because their cost of production would be prohibitively high). In addition, oligopolists spend a great deal of their profits on research and development, and some believe that this leads to faster technological advance and a higher standard of living than if the industry were organized along more competitive lines. Finally, some advertising is useful since it informs customers, and some product differentiation has the economic value of satisfying the different tastes of different consumers.

**19.18.**  Compare the efficiency implications in long-run equilibrium of the four different forms of market organization with respect to

   (a)    total profits,

   (b)    allocation of resources,

   (c)    LAC, and

   (d)    sales promotion.

   (a)    It is difficult to interpret and answer this question since cost curves may differ under various forms of market organization. A few generalizations can nevertheless be made, if they are interpreted with caution. First, the perfectly competitive firm and the monopolistically competitive firm break even in long-run equilibrium. Thus, consumers get the commodity at cost of production. On the other hand, the monopolist and the oligopolist can and usually do make profits in the long run. These profits, however, may lead to more research and development and to faster technological progress and a rising standard of living in the long run.

   (b)    While the perfectly competitive firm in long-run equilibrium produces the output at which $P = $ MC, the imperfectly competitive firm produces the output at which $P$ exceeds MC. Thus there is an underallocation of resources in these imperfectly competitive industries and a misallocation of resources in the economy. That is, under any form of imperfect competition, the firm is likely to produce less and charge a higher price than in perfect competition. This difference is greater in pure monopoly and oligopoly than in monopolistic competition because of the greater elasticity of demand in monopolistic competition.

   (c)    While the perfectly competitive firm produces at the lowest point on its LAC curve in long-run equilibrium, the monopolist and the oligopolist are very unlikely to do so, and the monopolistic competitor never does. However, the size of efficient operation is often so large in relation to the market that only a few firms are required in the industry. Perfect competition under such circumstances would either be impossible or lead to prohibitively high costs.

   (d)    Finally, the waste resulting from excessive sales promotion is likely to be zero in perfect competition, and greater in oligopoly and monopolistic competition.

**19.19.**  (a)    Explain the term *countervailing power*. What is its function and usefulness in modern economies?

   (b)    What is meant by "workable competition"?

(a) Countervailing power refers to the rise in powerful labor unions and large organizations of buyers from and sellers to large corporations in response to and in order to protect themselves from and check the great power of the giant corporation. Thus, the giant General Motors faces the powerful United Automobile Workers Union. The big three of the auto industry purchase steel from the big four or five of the steel industry. Large agricultural cooperatives sell their produce to large food processors. This limits the power and the possible abuses of such power in oligopolistic markets and makes the economy more competitive. However, countervailing power does not work in the same or in a sufficient degree in all oligopolistic markets. For example, GM dealers are not in a position to check the great power of GM.

(b) Workable competition refers to the balancing of the efficiency requirements of large-scale production with protection from the abuses of monopoly and oligopoly power. Those who agree that workable competition is desirable acknowledge that perfect competition is often impossible or would lead to prohibitive costs. However, they also see the need to check the great economic power often associated with large corporations. Workable competition would result in government regulation of public utilities, antitrust action against overt collusion, and the encouragement of the development of countervailing power.

**19.20.** It is often asserted that businesspeople usually set prices by adding a specific "markup" to their estimated average costs of production because they do not know the exact shape of the demand curve and cost curves that they face. Therefore, most of microeconomics is "academic" and irrelevant. How would you counter such charges?

It is true that businesspeople often do not know the shape of the demand curve and cost curves that they face. It is also true that in the real world many businesspeople in imperfectly competitive markets set prices at the level of their estimated average cost plus a certain percentage, or "markup," of costs. However, those firms which constantly set their prices at levels far different from prices consistent with the MR = MC condition are likely to go out of business in the long run. On the other hand, those firms which, by a process of trial and error, correctly estimate the "best" price to charge are more likely to make profits, to remain in business in the long run, and to expand.

The study of the general principles of demand, production, and cost can be very useful in providing guidelines in this estimation process. They are also a rational and logical way for the firm to think when selecting production and pricing policies. In addition, they will surely stimulate the alert manager to collect pertinent data. Note, however, that sometimes the firm may purposely not want to charge the price that would lead to profit maximization, even if it knew exactly what that price should be. One reason for this was given in Problem 19.16 (b). Another reason might be to limit profits voluntarily to discourage potential entry into the industry.

## Multiple Choice Questions

1. Monopolistic competition refers to the form of market organization in which there are
   - (a) many sellers of a homogeneous product,
   - (b) many sellers of a differentiated product,
   - (c) few sellers of a homogeneous product,
   - (d) few sellers of a differentiated product.

2. The demand curve facing the monopolistic competitor is
   - (a) negatively sloped and highly elastic,
   - (b) negatively sloped and highly inelastic,
   - (c) horizontal,
   - (d) infinitely elastic.

3. The best level of output for the monopolistic competitor is the output at which
   - (a) MR equals AC,
   - (b) MR equals MC,
   - (c) MR exceeds MC,
   - (d) MR is less than MC.

4. In the short run, the monopolistic competitor
   (a) breaks even,
   (b) makes a profit,
   (c) incurs a loss,
   (d) any of the above is possible.

5. In the long run, a monopolistic competitor
   (a) incurs a loss,
   (b) breaks even,
   (c) makes a profit,
   (d) any of the above is possible.

6. A monopolistic competitor, in the long run,
   (a) produces where $P$ exceeds MC,
   (b) does not produce at the lowest point on its AC curve,
   (c) engages in nonprice competition,
   (d) all of the above.

7. Which of the following most closely approximates an oligopoly?
   (a) The cigarette industry,
   (b) The barbershops in a city,
   (c) The gasoline stations in a city,
   (d) Wheat farmers in the midwest.

8. The short-run supply curve of the oligopolist is
   (a) the rising portion of the MC curve,
   (b) the rising portion of the MC curve above AVC,
   (c) the rising portion of the MC curve above AC,
   (d) none of the above.

9. The kinked demand curve is used to rationalize
   (a) collusion,
   (b) price competition,
   (c) price rigidity,
   (d) price leadership.

10. Price leadership is
    (a) a form of overt collusion,
    (b) a form of tacit collusion,
    (c) illegal in the United States,
    (d) used to explain price rigidity.

11. If an oligopolist incurs losses in the short run, then in the long run,
    (a) it will go out of business,
    (b) it will stay in business,
    (c) it will break even,
    (d) any of the above is possible.

12. The oligopolist
    (a) produces where $P$ exceeds MC,
    (b) usually produces at the lowest point on the AC curve,
    (c) breaks even in the long run,
    (d) does not engage in nonprice competition.

## *True or False Questions*

**13.** _____ A monopolistic competitor always earns a profit in the short run.

**14.** _____ The monopoly power of a monopolistic competitor is limited by the availability of close substitutes.

**15.** _____ A monopolistic competitor produces at the lowest point on its LAC curve.

**16.** _____ Monopolistic competitors engage in nonprice competition.

**17.** _____ Product differentiation is a distinguishing characteristic of monopolistic competition.

**18.** _____ Restricted entry is another characteristic of monopolistic competition.

**19.** _____ Oligopolists usually engage in price competition.

**20.** _____ According to the kinked-demand-curve model, oligopolists match price cuts and price increases.

**21.** _____ In tacit collusion, oligopolists meet and decide on a price leader to follow in their pricing policies.

**22.** _____ Pure oligopolists are mutually interdependent, whereas differentiated oligopolists are not.

**23.** _____ Overt collusion is illegal in the United States.

**24.** _____ In the long run oligopolists earn profits.

### *Answers to Multiple Choice and True or False Questions*

| | | | |
|---|---|---|---|
| **1.** (b) | **7.** (a) | **13.** (F) | **19.** (F) |
| **2.** (a) | **8.** (d) | **14.** (T) | **20.** (F) |
| **3.** (b) | **9.** (c) | **15.** (F) | **21.** (F) |
| **4.** (d) | **10.** (b) | **16.** (T) | **22.** (F) |
| **5.** (b) | **11.** (a) | **17.** (T) | **23.** (T) |
| **6.** (d) | **12.** (a) | **18.** (F) | **24.** (T) |

# Chapter 20

# Production and the Demand for Economic Resources

## *Chapter Summary*

1. Resource prices, such as wages, rents, interests, and profits, are determined by demand and supply. The demand for resources is derived from the demand for the commodities that require the resource in production. The greater the demand for the commodity and the more productive the resource, the greater the price that firms are willing to pay for the resource.

2. The marginal revenue product (MRP) measures the increase in the firm's total revenue from selling the extra product that results from employing one additional unit of the resource. As additional units of the variable resource are used with fixed inputs, the extra output, or marginal physical product (MPP), falls due to diminishing returns.

3. A firm that is a perfect competitor in the resource market maximizes profits when its marginal revenue product from the variable resource equals the resource price. Thus, the firm's marginal revenue product schedule is the firm's demand schedule for the variable resource.

4. If the firm is an imperfect competitor in the commodity market, its marginal revenue product declines both because the marginal physical product from the variable input declines and because the firm must lower the commodity price in order to sell more units of the commodity.

5. A firm's demand for a productive resource will increase if the demand for the product increases, if the productivity of the resource rises, if the price of a substitute resource rises, or if the price of a complementary resource falls.

6. If the firm is an imperfect competitor in resource markets, the firm maximizes total profits by hiring each resource until the marginal revenue product from each resource equals the marginal resource cost. The marginal resource cost is equal to the increase in the firm's total cost for hiring each additional unit of the resource.

## *Important Terms*

**Derived demand.**  The demand for productive resources which arises because resources are needed to produce final commodities that consumers demand.

**Firm's demand schedule for a resource.**  The MRP schedule of the resource (when the firm is a perfect competitor in the resource market), reflecting the profit-maximization rule that the firm should continue to hire a resource until MRP equals the resource price.

**Marginal physical product (MPP).**  The change in total product that results from employing one additional unit of a variable resource together with other fixed resources.

**Marginal revenue product (MRP).**  A measurement of the change in the firm's total revenue from selling the extra or marginal physical product that results from employing one additional unit of a resource together with other fixed resources.

323

**Perfectly competitive firm in the factor market.**    A firm that is too small to affect the price of the resource (factor) it purchases and can hire any quantity of the resource at the prevailing market price.

**Perfectly competitive firm in the product market.**    A firm that is too small to affect the price of the product (commodity) it sells and can sell any quantity of the product at the prevailing market price.

**Resource pricing.**    The manner in which wages for various kinds of labor, rents for various types of land and other natural resources, interests on capital assets, and profits on entrepreneurship are determined in a mixed economy such as that of the United States.

**Total revenue (TR).**    The product price times the total product sold.

# Outline of Chapter 20: Production and the Demand for Economic Resources

## 20.1    INTRODUCTION TO RESOURCE PRICING

We now examine how the prices of productive resources such as *wages, rents, interests,* and *profits* are determined in a mixed economy such as that of the United States. Resource prices are a major determinant of money incomes and of the allocation of resources to various uses and firms.

Broadly speaking, the price of a resource is determined by its market demand and supply. Firms demand resources in order to produce commodities. The demand for resources is a *derived demand*—derived from the demand for the commodities which require the resources in production. The greater the demand for the commodity and the more productive the resource, the greater the price that firms are willing to pay for the resource.

**EXAMPLE 20.1.**    As a result of consumers' demand for a final commodity, say, shoes, firms hire labor and other resources in order to produce shoes. The greater the demand for shoes and the more productive labor in shoe production, the greater the firms' demands for labor. In the absence of market imperfections, minimum wage laws, union power, etc., the wage rate of labor is determined exclusively by the market demand and supply of labor. The wage rate is the major determinant of the money income of labor and of how labor is allocated to various firms and users in the economy.

## 20.2    MARGINAL REVENUE PRODUCT UNDER PERFECT COMPETITION

In order to derive a firm's demand for a resource, we must first define the *marginal revenue product (MRP). MRP measures the increase in the firm's total revenue from selling the extra product that results from employing one additional unit of the resource.* If the firm is a perfect competitor in the commodity market, it can sell this extra output at the given market price for the commodity (see Section 17.3). However, as additional units of the variable resource are used together with fixed resources, after a point the extra output or *marginal physical product (MPP)* declines because of the operation of the law of diminishing returns (see Section 16.2). Because of the declining MPP, MRP also declines.

**EXAMPLE 20.2.**   In Table 20-1, column 1 refers to units of a variable resource, say, labor, employed in a given plant. Column 2 gives the total product produced. Column 3 gives the marginal physical product or the change in total product per unit change in the use of the resource.

MPP declines because of the law of diminishing returns (assumed here for simplicity to begin operating with the first unit of resource hired). Column 4 shows the commodity price. It is constant because of perfect competition in the product market. Column 5 gives the total revenue obtained by multiplying the commodity price by the total product. Column 6 gives the marginal revenue product, measured as the increase in the total revenue in column 5. MRP declines because MPP declines.

**Table 20-1**

| (1) Units of Resource | (2) Total Product | (3) MPP or Δ (2) | (4) Product Price | (5) Total Revenue (2) × (4) | (6) MRP or Δ (5) |
|---|---|---|---|---|---|
| 0 | 0 | | $10 | $ 0 | |
| 1 | 5 | 5 | 10 | 50 | $50 |
| 2 | 9 | 4 | 10 | 90 | 40 |
| 3 | 12 | 3 | 10 | 120 | 30 |
| 4 | 14 | 2 | 10 | 140 | 20 |
| 5 | 15 | 1 | 10 | 150 | 10 |

## 20.3   PROFIT MAXIMIZATION AND RESOURCE DEMAND UNDER PERFECT COMPETITION

In order to maximize total profits, a firm should hire additional units of a resource as long as each adds more to the firm's total revenue than to its total costs. The increase in total revenue was defined in Section 20.2 as the marginal revenue product (MRP). The increase in total cost gives the *marginal resource cost (MRC)* of the resource. If the firm is a perfect competitor in the resource market, it can hire any quantity of the variable resource at the given resource price, and MRC equals the resource price. Thus to maximize total profits, the firm should hire the resource until MRP equals the resource price. The declining MRP schedule then represents the firm's demand schedule for the variable resource.

**EXAMPLE 20.3.**   If the firm represented in Table 20-1 is also a perfect competitor in the resource market and the resource price is $50, the firm will hire only one unit of the resource (say one worker) given where the MRP of $50 (column 6 in Table 20-1) equals the resource price of $50. If the resource price were $40, the firm would hire two units of the resource. At the price of $30, the firm would hire three units, and so on. The declining MRP schedule (columns 6 and 1 in Table 20-1) gives the firm's demand schedule for this resource and is graphed in Fig. 20-1.

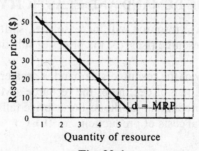

**Fig. 20-1**

## 20.4   MARGINAL PRODUCTIVITY AND RESOURCE DEMAND UNDER IMPERFECT COMPETITION

If the firm is an imperfect competitor in the commodity market, the MRP declines both because the MPP declines and because the firm must lower the commodity price in order to sell more units. If the firm remains a perfect competitor in the resource market, the firm again maximizes total profits when it hires the resource until MRP equals the resource price. The declining MRP schedule then represents the firm's demand schedule for the variable resource.

**EXAMPLE 20.4.** The first three columns of Table 20-2 are the same as in Table 20-1. Commodity price (column 4) declines because of imperfect competition in the commodity market. Total revenue (column 5) is obtained by multiplying commodity price by total product. Column 6 gives the MRP, measured as the change in total revenue in column 5. MRP declines both because MPP declines (column 3) and because the product price declines (column 4). A firm which is a perfect competitor in the resource market would maximize its total profits by employing the resource (say, workers) until their MRP equals the resource price.

Table 20-2

| (1)<br>Units of<br>Resource | (2)<br>Total<br>Product | (3)<br>MPP<br>or Δ (2) | (4)<br>Product<br>Price | (5)<br>Total Revenue<br>(2) × (4) | (6)<br>MRP<br>or Δ (5) |
|:---:|:---:|:---:|:---:|:---:|:---:|
| 0 | 0 | | $11 | $ 0 | |
| 1 | 5 | 5 | 10 | 50 | 50 |
| 2 | 9 | 4 | 9 | 81 | 31 |
| 3 | 12 | 3 | 8 | 96 | 15 |
| 4 | 14 | 2 | 7 | 98 | 2 |
| 5 | 15 | 1 | 6 | 90 | −8 |

The MRP schedule of columns 6 and 1 in Table 20-2 is the firm's demand schedule for the resource and is graphed as d′ in Fig. 20-2. At the resource price of $50, the firm will hire one unit of the resource. At the resource price of $31, the firm will hire two units of the resource, and so on. Note that d′ is less elastic than d in Fig. 20-1.

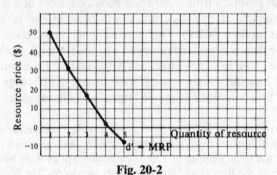

Fig. 20-2

## 20.5   CHANGES IN RESOURCE DEMAND AND ELASTICITY

A firm's demand for a productive resource will increase (i.e., shift up) if (1) the product demand increases, (2) the productivity of the resource rises, (3) the prices of substitute resources rise, or (4) the prices of complementary resources fall.

On the other hand, the elasticity of the resource's demand is greater (1) the greater the elasticity of the product demand, (2) the smaller the rate of decline of the resource's MPP, (3) the easier it is to substitute this resource for other resources in production (as the resource price falls), and (4) the larger the proportion of the cost of this resource to the total costs of production.

**EXAMPLE 20.5.** If the market demand for shoes rises and if the firm provides each worker with better but more expensive equipment, the firm's demand for labor will also rise (i.e., shift up). That is, to produce more shoes requires more labor; better equipment makes labor more productive and so the demand for labor increases; an increase in the price of capital equipment encourages the substitution of labor for capital in production. On the other hand, the firm's demand for labor is very elastic if consumers' demand for shoes is very elastic, if the MPP of labor in shoe production falls very slowly, if the firm can easily substitute labor for capital equipment when the price of labor falls, or if the cost of labor in relation to total costs is high.

## 20.6   A FIRM'S DEMAND FOR SEVERAL RESOURCES

If a firm uses more than one variable resource, say labor ($L$) and capital ($K$), the firm will maximize total profits when it uses labor and capital until the marginal revenue product of each resource equals the resource price (if the firm is a perfect competitor in the resource markets). That is, the firm will maximize total profits when $\mathrm{MRP}_L = P_L$ or wage rate, and $\mathrm{MRP}_K = P_K$ or the rate of interest. This can be rewritten as $\mathrm{MRP}_L/P_L = \mathrm{MRP}_K/P_K = 1$ and can be generalized to any number of resources. If the firm is an imperfect competitor in the resource markets, the profit maximization condition is generalized to $\mathrm{MPP}_L = \mathrm{MRC}_L$ and $\mathrm{MPP}_K = \mathrm{MRC}_K$ or $\mathrm{MPP}_L/\mathrm{MRC}_L = \mathrm{MPP}_K/\mathrm{MRC}_K = 1$ (where MRC refers to the marginal resource cost—see Sections 20.3 and 21.3).

# Solved Problems

## INTRODUCTION TO RESOURCE PRICING

**20.1.**   (*a*)   What is resource pricing?

   (*b*)   Why is it important?

   (*c*)   How is the price of resources determined in a mixed economy such as that of the United States?

   (*a*)   Resource pricing examines or studies the determination of (1) the wages of various kinds of labor, (2) the rents of various types of land and other natural resources, (3) the interest rates on capital assets, and (4) profits from various forms of entrepreneurial activity. This chapter deals with resource pricing in general. Chapter 21 deals with wage determination, and Chapter 22 covers the determination of rents, interests, and profits.

   (*b*)   Wages, rents, interests, and profits are major determinants of the money income of resource owners and of the inequality in the personal distribution of income. Thus, the prices of resources help determine the answer to the fundamental economic question of *for whom* to produce (see Section 2.1) and refer to the bottom loop in Fig. 2-2. The prices of resources also help to determine which commodities will be produced and how firms will combine various resources to minimize the costs of production and to maximize profits.

   (*c*)   Broadly speaking, the price of a resource is determined, just as the price of a final commodity is determined, by the interaction of the market supply and demand. The interaction of the forces of market demand and supply for each kind of labor time determines the wage rate of various kinds of labor. The interaction of the forces of market demand and supply for each type of land or other natural resource determines the rent of each of these natural resources. The same is true for interest on various kinds of capital and profit on various forms of entrepreneurship. However, in a mixed economy, the operation of the forces of market demand and supply is often modified by such market imperfections as union power and minimum wage legislation (see Section 21.3).

**20.2.**   (*a*)   Why do firms demand resources? In what way is a firm's demand for a resource a derived demand? How does this differ from consumers' demand for final commodities?

   (*b*)   What determines the strength of a firm's demand for a productive resource?

   (*a*)   Firms demand resources in order to produce final commodities. However, resources may first be utilized to produce capital equipment that would then facilitate the production of final commodities. It is the consumers' demand for final commodities that ultimately gives rise to the firm's demand for productive resources. Because of this, the demand for a resource is referred to as a derived demand. It is derived from the demand for the final commodities which require the resource in production. While consumers demand final commodities because of the direct utility or satisfaction that they get from consuming commodities, producers demand resources only because the resource can be used to produce the commodities that consumers demand.

(b)  The strength of a firm's demand for a resource depends on (1) the strength of the demand for the commodity that the resource is used to produce, (2) the productivity of the resource in producing the final commodity, and (3) the prices of other related (i.e., substitute and complementary) resources. The higher the demand for the final commodity, the more productive is the resource; the higher the price of substitute resources and the lower the price of complementary resources, the greater the firm's demand for the resource.

## MARGINAL REVENUE PRODUCT UNDER PERFECT COMPETITION

**20.3.**  (a)  When is a firm a perfect competitor in the product market?

(b)  When is a firm a perfect competitor in the resource market?

(a)  A firm is a perfect competitor in the product market if it is one of a large number of sellers of a homogeneous commodity and can sell any quantity of the commodity without affecting the market price. The perfectly competitive firm is a price taker. That is, it faces an infinitely elastic demand for the commodity it sells at the prevailing market price (see Sections 17.1 and 17.3).

(b)  A firm is a perfect competitor in the resource market if it is one of a large number of buyers of the resource, each too small to affect the resource price. Thus, the firm faces an infinitely elastic *supply* of the resource and can purchase any quantity of the resource at its prevailing market price.

**20.4.**  From Table 20-3,

Mathcad

**Table 20-3**

| Units of Resource | Total Product | Product Price |
|---|---|---|
| 0 | 0 | |
| 1 | 10 | $1 |
| 2 | 18 | 1 |
| 3 | 24 | 1 |
| 4 | 28 | 1 |
| 5 | 30 | 1 |

(a)  find the marginal physical product (MPP), total revenue, and the marginal revenue product (MRP) schedules.

(b)  Why does the MPP decline? Why does the MRP decline? How can you tell that this firm is a perfect competitor in the product market?

(a)  Column 3 in Table 20-4 gives the MPP. It is obtained from the change in total product per unit change in the use of the variable resource. Column 5 gives the total revenue of the firm. It is obtained by multiplying the product price (column 4) by the total product (column 2). Column 6 gives the marginal revenue product. It is obtained from the increase in the total revenue in column 5.

**Table 20-4**

| (1) Units of Resource | (2) Total Product | (3) MPP or Δ(2) | (4) Product Price | (5) Total Revenue (2) × (4) | (6) MRP or Δ(5) |
|---|---|---|---|---|---|
| 0 | 0 | | | $ 0 | |
| 1 | 10 | 10 | $1 | 10 | $10 |
| 2 | 18 | 8 | 1 | 18 | 8 |
| 3 | 24 | 6 | 1 | 24 | 6 |
| 4 | 28 | 4 | 1 | 28 | 4 |
| 5 | 30 | 2 | 1 | 30 | 2 |

(b)    The MPP that results from employing each additional unit of the variable resource (together with fixed amounts of other resources) declines because of the law of diminishing returns (see Section 16.2). For simplicity, it is here assumed that the law of diminishing returns begins to operate with the first unit of the variable resource hired. The marginal revenue product declines because MPP declines. We know that this firm is a perfect competitor in the product market because product price remains constant at $1 per unit regardless of the quantity of the product sold by the firm.

## PROFIT MAXIMIZATION AND RESOURCE DEMAND UNDER PERFECT COMPETITION

**20.5.**    (a)    What general rule should a firm follow in hiring a resource in order to maximize total profits? Explain marginal resource cost (MRC).

(b)    What is MRC when the firm is a perfect competitor in the resource market? How does this affect the rule that the firm should follow in hiring a resource in order to maximize its total profits?

(a)    In order to maximize total profits, a firm should hire additional units of a resource as long as each adds more to the firm's total revenue than to its total costs. The increase in total revenue is called the marginal revenue product (MRP). The increase in total costs (from hiring one additional unit of a resource to be used with other fixed resources) is called the marginal resource cost (MRC). Thus, to maximize total profits a firm should hire a resource as long as MRP exceeds MRC and until MRP = MRC. Note the similarity between this and the condition for profit maximization (MR = MC) in Section 17.3. The only difference is that our main focus is now the resource market rather than the product market.

(b)    If the firm is a perfect competitor in the resource market (so that it can hire any quantity of the resource at the prevailing market price of the resource), the change in its total costs in hiring one more unit of the resource (i.e., its MRC) equals the resource price. The rule for profit maximization when the firm is a perfect competitor in the resource market is to hire a resource as long as MRP exceeds the resource price and up to the point when they are equal. (The case where the firm is an imperfect competitor in the resource market is discussed in detail in Section 21.3.)

**20.6.**    (a)    Following the profit-maximization rule for the firm of Problem 20.4, how many units of the variable resource should the firm hire if the resource price is $10, $8, $6, $4, $2?

(b)    Draw this firm's demand curve for the variable resource.

(a)    Since the firm is a perfect competitor in the resource market, it will maximize its total profits by hiring the variable resource as long as MRP exceeds the resource price and until they are equal. Thus, at the resource price of $10, the firm will hire one unit of the resource. At the resource price of $8, the firm will hire two units of the resource. The firm will hire three units of the resource at the price of $6, four units at the price of $4, and five at the price of $2. Thus columns 6 and 1 of Table 20-4 give the firm's demand schedule for the variable resource.

(b)    See Fig. 20-3. Graphing the firm's demand schedule, we get the firm's demand curve (d) for the resource. Note that the MRP is plotted at the midpoint of each resource unit.

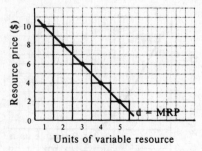

Fig. 20-3

## MARGINAL PRODUCTIVITY AND RESOURCE DEMAND UNDER IMPERFECT COMPETITION

**20.7.** Suppose that the product price in Table 20-3, instead of remaining at $1, declined to $0.90 when two units of the product sold, to $0.80 for three units sold, $0.70 for four, and to $0.60 for five units of the product sold.

    (*a*)   Find the MPP, the total revenue, and the MRP schedules.

    (*b*)   Why does the MRP decline? How can you tell that this firm is an imperfect competitor in the product market?

    (*a*)   Column 3 in Table 20-5 gives the MPP (the same as in Table 20-4). Column 5 gives the total revenue of the firm (obtained by multiplying the total product by product price). Column 6 gives the MRP, measured as the change in total revenue.

**Table 20-5**

| (1) Units of Resource | (2) Total Product | (3) MPP or $\Delta$ (2) | (4) Product Price | (5) Total Revenue (2) × (4) | (6) MRP or $\Delta$ (5) |
|---|---|---|---|---|---|
| 0 | 0 | | | $ 0.00 | |
| | | 10 | | | $10.00 |
| 1 | 10 | | $1.00 | 10.00 | |
| | | 8 | | | 6.20 |
| 2 | 18 | | 0.90 | 16.20 | |
| | | 6 | | | 3.00 |
| 3 | 24 | | 0.80 | 19.20 | |
| | | 4 | | | 0.40 |
| 4 | 28 | | 0.70 | 19.60 | |
| | | 2 | | | −1.60 |
| 5 | 30 | | 0.60 | 18.00 | |

    (*b*)   The MRP declines because both (1) MPP declines (due to the operation of the law of diminishing returns) and (2) product price declines. The firm represented in Table 20-5 is an imperfect competitor in the product market because it must lower the product price in order to sell more units of the product. (In order to distinguish it from this case, the MRP when the firm is a perfect competitor in the product market is sometimes referred to as "the value of the marginal product," or the VMP.)

**20.8.** If the firm in Problem 20.7 is a perfect competitor in the resource market,

    (*a*)   how many units of the variable resource should this firm hire at the resource price of $10, $6.20, $3.00, and $0.40? Why will the firm not hire the fifth unit of the resource even if it were free?

    (*b*)   Draw this firm's demand curve for the variable resource.

    (*a*)   The firm will hire one unit of the variable resource at the resource price of $10 (where MRP equals the resource price), two units at the resource price of $6.20, three at the price of $3, and four at the resource price of $0.40 per unit. The firm would not employ the fifth unit of the resource even if it were free because the MRP of this fifth unit is negative (−$1.60). That is, by lowering the product price in order to sell the MPP of the fifth unit of the variable resource, the total revenue of the firm will decline. Because

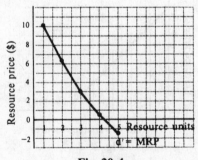

**Fig. 20-4**

the firm hires a resource up to the point where MRP equals the resource price, this is referred to as the marginal productivity theory.

(b)　Columns 6 and 1 of Table 20-5 give the firm's demand schedule for the variable resource. This is plotted as d' in Fig. 20-4. Note that d' is less elastic than d in Fig. 20-2.

## CHANGES IN RESOURCE DEMAND AND ELASTICITY

**20.9.**　Explain what can cause an increase or upward shift in a firm's demand for a productive resource.

When the market demand for a product increases, firms will purchase more resources in order to increase their output of the product. For example, when the demand for housing rises, construction firms tend to hire more electricians, plumbers, and construction workers and to purchase or rent more construction equipment and land in order to build more homes. As workers are supplied with better equipment, the productivity and demand for labor increase still further. If the price of capital equipment subsequently rose in relation to wages, firms would increase their demand for labor as they substituted labor for capital in production. On the other hand, when the wage rate of electricians falls (so that more electricians are employed), the demand for plumbers (the complementary labor to build houses) also increases.

**20.10.**　Explain what determines the elasticity of demand for a resource.

The elasticity of resource demand depends on several conditions:

(1)　The greater the elasticity of the product demand, the greater the elasticity of resource demand. When the firm is a perfect competitor in the product market and faces an infinitely elastic product demand, the firm's resource demand is more elastic than when the firm is an imperfect competitor in the product market (compare d in Fig. 20-3 to d' in Fig. 20-4).

(2)　Since a resource demand schedule is given by its MRP schedule and the MRP depends on the resource MPP schedule (and the commodity price), the smaller the rate of decline in the resource MPP schedule, the more elastic the MRP or the resource demand curve (everything else being held constant).

(3)　If a resource can easily be substituted for others as the resource's price falls, the percentage increase in the quantity demanded of the resource will be large in relation to the percentage decline in the resource's price and result in an elastic resource demand.

(4)　If the resource's cost is large in relation to the firm's total costs, an increase in the resource's price will cause a relatively large increase in costs of production, leading to a relatively large decline in production and, hence, in the quantity of the resource demanded.

**20.11.**　(a)　How do we get the total market demand for a resource?

(b)　Why is this important?

(a)　The total market demand (i.e., the demand of all firms) for a resource is obtained by summing the quantity demanded of the resource by each firm at each resource price. In a more advanced course, you will see that this is not as straightforward and simple as obtaining the market demand for a *product* by totaling *individual* demands for the product (see Section 3.1). This happens because as a resource price falls, firms will hire more of the resource and produce more of the commodities which require that resource in production. This increase in the product-market supplies will reduce product prices and cause a downward shift in the resource MRP and the demand curve.

(b)　The resource-market demand is important because, together with the resource-market supply, it determines the resource-market equilibrium price. This is the price which the perfectly competitive firm in the resource market uses to determine how much of the resource to employ (see Section 21.1).

## A FIRM'S DEMAND FOR SEVERAL RESOURCES

**20.12.**　Explain how much of each variable resource a firm should hire in order to maximize total profits, if the firm is a perfect competitor in the resource markets.

We saw in Section 20.3 that in order to maximize total profits, a firm which is a perfect competitor in the resource market should hire the variable resource as long as its MRP exceeds its price and until they are equal. In the usual case, the firm employs more than one variable resource, say labor ($L$) and capital ($K$), but the same rule applies. That is, in order to maximize total profits, the firm should hire labor and capital as long as the $MRP_L$ exceeds $P_L$ or wage rate ($W$) and until $MRP_L = P_L$ or $W$. Similarly, the firm should employ capital as long as the $MRP_K$ exceeds $P_K$ or rate of interest and until $MRP_K = P_K$. When $MRP_L = P_L$, $MRP_L/P_L = 1$. Similarly, when $MRP_K = P_K$, $MRP_K/P_K = 1$. Thus, the condition for profit maximization for a firm employing labor and capital can be rewritten as $MRP_L/P_L = MRP_K/P_K = 1$. This is a *special rule* for the firm which is a *perfect competitor* in the resource markets, and can be extended to any number of variable resources. See Problem 20.13.

**20.13.** Explain how much of each variable resource a firm should hire in order to maximize total profits, if the firm is an imperfect competitor in the resource markets.

When a firm which is an imperfect competitor in the resource markets wants to hire more of a resource, it will have to pay a higher price, not only on the additional units of the resource but also on all previous units of the resource hired. Thus, the increase in the total costs of hiring an additional unit of the resource or marginal resource cost (MRC) exceeds the resource price (see Section 21.2). The firm will maximize total profits when it hires variable resources as long as each resource MRP exceeds its MRC and until they are equal. With variable resources labor ($L$) and capital ($K$), the firm maximizes total profits when $MRP_L = MRC_L$ and $MRP_K = MRC_K$ or $MRP_L/MRC_L = MRP_K/MRC_K = 1$. This is the *general rule* of which $MRP_L/P_L = MRP_K/P_K = 1$ is the special case for the firm in a perfectly competitive resource market. Another way of stating the profit-maximization condition is to say that a firm should hire resources until the MRP per dollar spent on each resource is the same and equal to 1. Once again, this rule can be extended to any number of variable resources.

# Multiple Choice Questions

1. Wages, rents, interests, and profits are a major determinant of
   (a)   the money incomes of resource owners,
   (b)   the relative shares of national income going to various kinds of resource owners,
   (c)   how resources are allocated to various uses and firms,
   (d)   all of the above.

2. Which of the following statements is *incorrect?*
   (a)   Consumers demand final commodities because of the utility or satisfaction they get from them.
   (b)   Firms demand resources in order to produce goods and services demanded by consumers.
   (c)   Firms demand resources because of the utility or satisfaction they get from them.
   (d)   The more productive a resource in producing a commodity, the greater the resource price.

3. The extra product generated by adding one unit of a resource to the other fixed resources is called
   (a)   marginal physical product (MPP),
   (b)   marginal revenue product (MRP),
   (c)   marginal resource cost (MRC),
   (d)   marginal revenue (MR).

4. When the firm is a perfect competitor in the product market, its MRP declines because of declining
   (a)   MPP only,
   (b)   commodity price only,
   (c)   marginal revenue only,
   (d)   MPP and the commodity price.

5. Which of the following statements is *incorrect?*
   (*a*) The increase in the firm's total costs in hiring one more unit of the variable resource is called the marginal resource cost (MRC).
   (*b*) When the firm is a perfect competitor in the resource market, the marginal resource cost equals the resource price.
   (*c*) Total revenue equals product price times MPP.
   (*d*) To maximize total profits, a firm should hire the variable resource until MRP = MRC.

6. When the firm is a perfect competitor in the resource market, its demand for the variable resource is the schedule of
   (*a*) MRP,
   (*b*) MPP,
   (*c*) MRC,
   (*d*) MR.

7. When the firm is an imperfect competitor in the product market, its MRP declines because of declining
   (*a*) MPP only,
   (*b*) commodity price only,
   (*c*) marginal revenue only,
   (*d*) MPP and commodity price.

8. When the firm is an imperfect competitor rather than a perfect competitor in the product market, its demand for the variable resource (other things being equal) is
   (*a*) more elastic,
   (*b*) less elastic,
   (*c*) infinitely elastic,
   (*d*) unitary elastic.

9. A firm's demand for a productive resource increases (i.e., shifts up) when
   (*a*) the product demand increases,
   (*b*) the productivity of the resource rises,
   (*c*) the prices of substitute resources rise or the prices of complementary resources fall,
   (*d*) all of the above.

10. Which of the following is *incorrect?* A firm's demand for a resource is *more elastic,*
    (*a*) the more elastic the product demand,
    (*b*) the greater rate of decline of the resource's MPP,
    (*c*) the easier it is to substitute this for other resources in production when the price of the resource falls,
    (*d*) the larger the proportion of the resource's cost to total production costs.

11. When a perfectly competitive firm in the labor and capital markets is maximizing its total profits,
    (*a*) $MRP_L = P_L$,
    (*b*) $MRP_K = P_K$,
    (*c*) $MRP_L/P_L = MRP_K/P_K = 1$,
    (*d*) all of the above.

12. When an imperfectly competitive firm in the labor and capital markets is maximizing profits,
    (*a*) $MRP_L = P_L$, and $MRP_K = P_K$,
    (*b*) $MRP_L/P_L = MRP_K/P_K = 1$,
    (*c*) $MRP_L/MRC_L = MRP_K/MRC_K = 1$,
    (*d*) none of the above.

## True or False Questions

13. _____    The demand for resources is derived from the goods that require the resource in production.

14. _____    The price of a resource is determined by the demand for the resource.

15. _____    The marginal revenue product measures the increase in total costs in hiring each additional unit of the variable input.

16. _____    If the firm is a perfect competitor in the product market, its marginal revenue product curve is downward-sloping only because the marginal physical product curve of the resource is downward-sloping.

17. _____    A firm's marginal revenue product curve is steeper if the firm is an imperfect rather than a perfect competitor in the product market.

18. _____    Marginal resource cost refers to the increase in the firm's total costs in hiring each additional unit of the resource.

19. _____    To maximize profits, a firm should hire resources as long as each additional unit of the resource adds more to the firm's total costs than to its total revenue.

20. _____    A firm's demand for a resource is its marginal revenue product curve if the firm is a perfect competitor in the product market.

21. _____    A firm's demand for a resource shifts up if the productivity of the resource increases.

22. _____    A firm's demand for a resource shifts up if the price of a substitute resource increases.

23. _____    A firm's demand for a resource shifts down if the price of a complementary resource declines.

24. _____    To maximize profits a firm must hire a resource until the marginal revenue product from the resource is equal to the marginal resource cost.

### Answers to Multiple Choice and True or False Questions

| | | | |
|---|---|---|---|
| 1. (d) | 7. (d) | 13. (T) | 19. (F) |
| 2. (c) | 8. (b) | 14. (F) | 20. (F) |
| 3. (a) | 9. (d) | 15. (F) | 21. (T) |
| 4. (a) | 10. (b) | 16. (T) | 22. (T) |
| 5. (c) | 11. (d) | 17. (T) | 23. (F) |
| 6. (a) | 12. (c) | 18. (T) | 24. (T) |

# Chapter 21

# Wage Determination

## Chapter Summary

1. The money wage rate divided by the price index gives the real wage rate. Economics is primarily interested in real rather than money wages. The greater the productivity of labor, the higher real wages.
2. The competitive-equilibrium real wage rate is determined at the intersection of the market demand and supply curves for labor. Each firm then hires labor until the marginal revenue product or demand for labor equals the wage rate.
3. With imperfect competition in the labor market, the firm hires labor until the marginal revenue product of labor equals the marginal resource cost of labor and pays the wage indicated on the supply curve of labor.
4. Labor unions attempt to increase wages by increasing the demand for labor, restricting the supply of labor, and bargaining with employers under the threat of a strike.
5. Wage differentials arise because jobs differ in attractiveness; because of differences in skills, education, and training of workers; and because of market imperfections.

## Important Terms

**Bilateral monopoly.**   The market in which a union (a monopolist in selling labor services) faces a monopsonist (a monopolist buyer of labor services).

**Competitive equilibrium real-wage rate.**   The wage rate at which the quantity of labor demanded equals the quantity of labor supplied.

**Craft union.**   A union in which all members have a particular type of skill (e.g., printers, electricians, plumbers, etc.).

**Equalizing differences.**   The wage differences resulting from the varying attractiveness of different jobs. For the same level of capacity and training, the more unpleasant a job, the higher the wage rate.

**Industrial union.**   A union whose membership is comprised of workers (skilled and unskilled) employed in a given industry. Examples are the United Mine Workers (UMW) and the United Auto Workers (UAW) of America.

**Marginal resource cost (MRC).**   A measurement of the change in total cost of hiring an additional unit of the resource. MRC exceeds the resource price in imperfectly competitive resource markets.

**Market demand for labor.**   The total quantity of labor demanded at various alternative wage rates. It is obtained by summing all firms' demands for labor.

**Market supply of labor.**   The total quantity of labor supplied at various alternative wage rates. It depends on the population size, the proportion of the population in the labor force, and the state of the economy.

**Money wage.**   The dollar payment received for one hour, day, week, etc. of labor.

**Money-wage index.**   An economic indicator that measures the percentage change in the money-wage rate with respect to a base year taken as 100.

**Monopsony.** A market in which there is a single buyer of a resource. The monopsonist has a monopoly power in the purchase of the resource.

**Noncompeting groups.** Occupations requiring different capacities, skills, and training and, therefore, receiving different wages.

**Price index.** An indicator which measures the percentage change in the general price level with respect to a base year taken as 100.

**Real wage.** The actual purchasing power of the money wage.

**Real-wage index.** The money-wage index divided by the price index and multiplied by 100, which measures the percentage change in actual purchasing power associated with a given percentage change in money wages.

# Outline for Chapter 21: Wage Determination

## 21.1  GENERAL LEVEL OF WAGES

The *wage rate* (or money-wage rate) refers to the earnings per hour of labor. The money-wage rate divided by the price index gives the *real wage rate* or actual "purchasing power" of money wages. We are primarily concerned with real wages.

The level of real wages depends on the productivity of labor. Real wages are higher (1) the greater the amount of capital available per worker, (2) the more advanced the technology of production, and (3) the greater the availability of natural resources (fertile land, mineral deposits, etc.).

**EXAMPLE 21.1.** If the average U.S. *money-wage index* doubled (from 100 to 200) between 1970 and 1995 but the general price index rose by 60 percent (from 100 to 160), the real-wage index increased by only one-quarter, or 25 percent (i.e., $200/160 = 1\frac{1}{4}$).

Real wages are generally higher in the United States than in most other countries because (1) capital equipment per worker is higher in the United States, (2) the technology of production is more advanced, and (3) the relationship between workers and natural resources is more favorable.

## 21.2  WAGE DETERMINATION UNDER PERFECT COMPETITION

In the preceding chapter, we saw that firms demand labor (and other resources) in order to produce the products demanded by consumers. By adding each firm's demand for labor, we get the *market demand for labor.* On the other hand, the *market supply of labor* depends on the population size, the proportion of the population in the labor force, the state of the economy (such as boom or recession), and the level of real wages (see Problem 21.5).

The *competitive equilibrium real-wage rate* is determined at the intersection of the market demand and supply of labor curves. The firm then hires labor until the *marginal revenue product of labor* ($MRP_L$) or its demand for labor ($d_L$) equals the wage rate.

**EXAMPLE 21.2.** In Panel B of Fig. 21-1, the competitive equilibrium real-wage rate of $6 per hour is determined at the intersection of the market demand and supply of labor. The supply of labor to the competitive firm of Panel A ($s_L$) is horizontal at the wage rate of $6. This means that the firm is so small (say, one of 1000 identical firms in the market) that it can hire any quantity of labor at the equilibrium market wage rate without affecting that wage rate. To maximize total profits the firm hires 30 units of labor because $MRP_L = W = \$6$ at 30 units of labor (see Section 20.3).

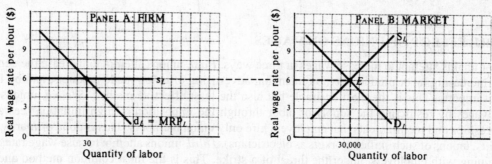

**Fig. 21-1**

## 21.3   WAGE DETERMINATION UNDER IMPERFECT COMPETITION

Workers are often not hired competitively. In a company town, a firm that is the only or dominant employer has monopoly power in the local labor market and is referred to as a *monopsonist*. A monopsonist faces the rising *market* supply curve of labor which indicates that it must pay higher wages to hire more workers. As a result, the change in the total cost of hiring an additional unit of labor or *marginal resource cost of labor* ($MRC_L$) exceeds the wage rate. To maximize total profits, the firm hires labor until $MRP_L = MRC_L$ and pays the wage indicated on the supply curve of labor for that quantity of labor.

**EXAMPLE 21.3.**   In Table 21-1, columns 1 and 2 are the market supply schedule of labor facing the monopsonist. Column 1 times column 2 gives column 3, which measures the total cost of hiring various quantities of labor. Column 4 shows the change in total costs in hiring each additional unit of labor, or $MRC_L$. Note that $MRC_L$ exceeds $W$.

**Table 21-1**

| (1) Wage Rate ($) | (2) Quantity of Labor | (3) Total Cost of Labor | (4) Marginal Cost of Labor |
|:---:|:---:|:---:|:---:|
| 1 | 1 | 1 | |
| 2 | 2 | 4 | 3 |
| 3 | 3 | 9 | 5 |
| 4 | 4 | 16 | 7 |
| 5 | 5 | 25 | 9 |

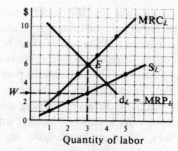

**Fig. 21-2**

Plotting columns 1 and 2 as $S_L$ and columns 2 and 4 as $MRC_L$ in Fig. 21-2 and superimposing the firm's $MRP_L$ on the same graph, we see that the monopsonist will hire 3 units of labor (given by point $E$, where $MRP_L = MRC_L$) and pay the wage of \$3 (on $S_L$ at $Q_L = 3$).

## 21.4  THE EFFECT OF UNIONS ON WAGES

Labor unions attempt to increase wages in three ways. *First,* unions attempt to increase the demand for labor by increasing labor productivity, by financing advertising of union-made products, and by lobbying to restrict imports. This is the most desirable but also the least effective method. *Second,* unions attempt to raise wages by restricting the supply of labor through the imposition of high initiation fees and long apprenticeships and requirements that employers hire only union members. This is done primarily by *craft unions* (i.e., unions of such skilled workers as electricians). *Third,* unions attempt to raise wage rates directly by bargaining with employers, under the threat of a strike. This is the most common method and is used primarily by *industrial unions* (i.e., unions of all the workers of a particular industry, such as automobile workers). Empirical studies seem to indicate that in general, unions in the United States have raised real wages for their members by only about 10 to 15%.

**EXAMPLE 21.4.**  In Panel A of Fig. 21-3, the equilibrium real-wage rate is \$4 and employment is 3000 workers (at point $E$, where $D_L$ intersects $S_L$). If the union can successfully increase $D_L$ to $D'_L$, $W = \$6$ and employment rises to 4000. Starting from the same original equilibrium point $E$ in Panel B, a craft union could instead attempt to reduce $S_L$ to $S'_L$ so that $W = \$6$ but only 2000 are employed. In Panel C, an industrial union could attempt to negotiate $W = \$6$ at which 2000 workers are employed and another 2000 workers ($E'A$) are unable to find jobs. The result would be the same without a union if the government set the minimum wage at \$6. A union or a government minimum-wage requirement could also overcome the tendency of a monopsonist to pay wages below the marginal revenue product of labor [see Problem 21.13(*a*)].

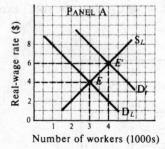 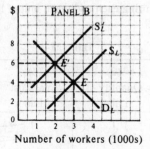 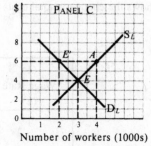

**Fig. 21-3**

## 21.5  WAGE DIFFERENTIALS

If all jobs and individuals were exactly alike and all markets perfectly competitive, there would be a single wage for all jobs and all workers. However, jobs requiring equal qualifications may differ in attractiveness, and higher wages must be paid to attract and retain workers in more unpleasant jobs. Thus, garbage collectors receive higher wages than porters. Such wage differentials are known as *equalizing differences.* Even if all jobs were equally attractive, wage differences would persist because individuals such as doctors, accountants, and clerks differ widely in capacities, skills, training, and education. Thus, labor falls into many *noncompeting groups,* each requiring different training and receiving different wages. Finally, some wage differences are the result of *imperfect markets.* Market imperfections include lack of information, unwillingness to move, union power, minimum-wage laws, and monopsony power. The wide wage differences actually observed in the real world among different categories of people and jobs are in general the result of a combination of these three factors.

# Solved Problems

## GENERAL LEVEL OF WAGES

**21.1.** (a)  In what sense is labor the "most important" resource?

(b)  What is the relationship between the discussion of resource pricing in Chapter 20 and wage determination?

(c)  Why are wage rates important?

(d)  What is the distinction between money wages and real wages?

(a)  Labor is the most important resource because, first and foremost, labor refers to human beings rather than to machines or objects. Secondly, labor receives between 75 and 80 percent of the national income.

(b)  The discussion of resource pricing in Chapter 20 was general and referred to any factor of production (labor, land, capital, and entrepreneurship). Wage determination refers particularly to the price of labor services. What we said in Chapter 20 is entirely relevant, but we now extend that discussion to those things which are unique to labor resources.

(c)  Wage rates are the most important determinant of individuals' incomes and of the distribution of incomes in society. Individuals' incomes depend for the most part on the wage rate they receive and the number of hours they work. The different wages for different types of jobs also determine to a large extent the income inequalities among different occupations and individuals.

(d)  The money wage is the *dollar* payment that a worker receives for work. This can be expressed in so many dollars per hour, day, week, or year but is most usually dollars per hour. However, the actual *real* or *purchasing power* of the money wage depends also on the general price level. The higher the price level, the lower the real wage or purchasing power of a given money wage.

**21.2.**  Explain the terms

(a)  *money-wage index,*

(b)  *price-level index,* and

(c)  *real-wage index.*

(d)  If the money-wage rate were $5 per hour in 1980 and $6.50 per hour in 1995, and the price index rose from 100 in 1980 to 120 by 1995, what is the real-wage index in 1995 in terms of 1980 prices?

(a)  The money-wage index refers to the dollar money wage in one year, say, in 1995, in terms of the money wage in a previous (base) year, say, 1980, when the money wage in 1980 = 100. This means that the money wage rose by 30% between 1980 and 1995.

(b)  The price-level index expresses the general level of prices in one year, say, in 1995, in terms of the price level in a previous (base) year, say, in 1980, when the price level in 1980 is taken as 100. When we say that the price-level index in 1995 is 120 relative to 1980 = 100, this means that the price level rose by 20% between 1980 and 1995. The government regularly publishes several price indexes. The consumer price index gives the price in terms of a "representative basket" of goods purchased by the "average" family.

(c)  The real-wage index equals the money-wage index deflated or divided by the price index and then multiplied by 100. That is,

$$\text{Real-wage index} = \frac{\text{money-wage index}}{\text{price index}} \times 100$$

The real-wage index measures the change in the purchasing power of a given change in money wages.

(d)  If we take the $5 wage per hour in 1980 as 100, we can then express the 1995 wage of $6.50 as 130. This is calculated by setting up the following proportion: $5/100 = 6.5/W$, and cross-multiplying, so that $5W = 650$ and $W = 130$.

This says that the money-wage index rose by 30% between 1980 and 1995. However, since the price index was 120 in 1995, the real-wage index in 1995 is $130/120 \times 100 = 1.0833 \times 100 = 108.33$. This means that the purchasing power of wages rose by only 8.33% between 1980 and 1995.

**21.3.** Why have real wages risen in the United States over time?

Real wages have risen historically in the United States (and in most other nations) because the productivity of labor has increased. The productivity of labor increased as labor became more skilled and better trained, as technology improved, and as more capital and natural resources were made available to each worker. Over the past century or so, labor productivity in the United States rose on the average between 2% and 2.5% per year, and doubled real wages every 30 to 35 years. The larger part of this increase resulted from an increase in the level of skills and training of the labor force and from technological progress. The growth of real wages seems to have slowed down considerably in recent years as a result of a greater social awareness of the environment (pollution control is expensive) and in the attempt to achieve greater income equality (more progressive income taxes tend to reduce the efforts of workers somewhat).

## WAGE DETERMINATION UNDER PERFECT COMPETITION

**21.4.** (a) Why do firms demand labor?

   (b) What is the firm's demand for labor? Why does it slope downward?

   (c) What determines the strength of a firm's demand for labor?

   (d) How is the market demand curve of labor determined?

   (a) Firms demand labor (and other resources) in order to produce the products demanded by consumers. Thus, the demand for labor as well as the demand for any productive resource is a derived demand—derived from the demand for *final* commodities that require labor and other resources in production.

   (b) The firm's demand for labor is its marginal revenue product (MRP) of labor schedule or curve. A perfectly competitive firm's MRP or demand for labor curve slopes downward because the returns from each additional unit of labor, when used with other fixed resources, diminish.

   (c) A firm's demand for labor is greater (1) the greater the demand for the commodity that uses labor in production, (2) the greater the productivity of labor, and (3) the higher the price of substitute resources, say, capital equipment, and the lower the price of complementary resources (say, land, used with labor and capital to produce the final commodity).

   (d) The market demand for labor is obtained by summing all firms' demands for labor. The greater the number of firms demanding labor and the greater the demand of each firm, the greater the market demand for labor.

**21.5.** (a) On what does the market supply of labor depend?

   (b) How does the state of the economy affect the market supply of labor?

   (c) What is the effect of the real-wage rate level on the quantity of labor supplied in the market?

   (a) The market supply of labor depends on the population size, the proportion of the population in the labor force, and the state of the economy. In general, the larger the population and the greater the participation rate of the population in the labor force, the greater the market supply of labor.

   (b) The state of the economy (boom or recession) affects the market supply of labor. When the economy is booming, many people not previously employed or seeking work may, attracted by the availability of high-paying jobs, decide to enter the labor force. On the other hand, a homemaker or college student who felt the need to look for a job under less prosperous conditions, may leave the labor force when the spouse or parent gets a high-paying job in a booming economy. Thus, the supply of labor may increase, decrease, or remain unchanged depending on the net effect of these two opposing forces. The opposite is true in a recession.

   (c) The level of real wages also gives rise to two opposing forces affecting the quantity of labor supplied. On the one hand, a high level of real wages induces workers to substitute work for leisure and work more hours per week to take advantage of the high real wages. On the other hand, a high real wage (and income) results in workers demanding more of every normal commodity, including leisure, and working fewer hours per week. Once again, the quantity of labor supplied may increase, decrease, or remain unchanged, depending on the net effect of these two opposing forces.

**21.6.** Suppose that the marginal revenue product schedule or demand for labor for one of 100 identical and perfectly competitive *firms* is given by columns 1 and 2 of Table 21-2, and the market supply schedule of labor is given by columns 1 and 3.

Mathcad

**Table 21-2**

| (1)<br>Wage Rate<br>($) | (2)<br>Quantity of<br>Labor Demanded<br>by One Firm | (3)<br>Total Quantity<br>of Labor Supplied |
|---|---|---|
| 12 | 40  | 12,000 |
| 10 | 60  | 10,000 |
| 8  | 80  | 8,000  |
| 6  | 100 | 6,000  |
| 4  | 120 | 4,000  |

(*a*)   Find the market demand schedule for labor and the equilibrium wage rate.

(*b*)   How much labor should the firm hire to maximize its total profits?

(*c*)   Graph the results to parts (*a*) and (*b*).

(*a*)   Since there are 100 identical firms, the market demand schedule for labor is 100 times the firm's demand schedule for labor and is given by columns 1 and 2A of Table 21-3. The competitive equilibrium wage rate is $8 per hour, at which the market quantity of labor demanded matches the market quantity supplied of 8000 hours. At higher wages, the quantity of labor supplied in the market exceeds the quantity of labor demanded. The resulting surplus of labor (involuntary unemployment) puts pressure on the wage rate to move downward toward the equilibrium level. At wages below the equilibrium wage rate, the resulting shortage of labor causes wages to rise toward the equilibrium level of $8 per hour.

**Table 21-3**

| (1)<br>Wage Rate<br>($) | (2)<br>Quantity of<br>Labor Demanded<br>by One Firm | (2A)<br>Market Demand<br>of Labor | (3)<br>Total Quantity<br>of Labor Supplied |
|---|---|---|---|
| 12 | 40  | 4,000  | 12,000 |
| 10 | 60  | 6,000  | 10,000 |
| 8  | 80  | 8,000  | 8,000  |
| 6  | 100 | 10,000 | 6,000  |
| 4  | 120 | 12,000 | 4,000  |

(*b*)   Since the firm is a perfect competitor in the labor market, it can hire any amount of labor at the $8 per hour market equilibrium wage rate. This means that the supply curve of labor to the firm ($s_L$) is horizontal or infinitely elastic at the competitive market equilibrium price [see Problem 20.3 (*b*)]. To maximize total profits, each firm should hire 80 hours of labor, at which the firm's marginal revenue product of labor equals the $8 per hour equilibrium market-wage rate.

(*c*)   The solutions to part (*a*) and (*b*) are shown graphically in Fig. 21-4.

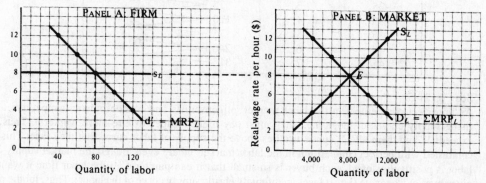

**Fig. 21-4**

## WAGE DETERMINATION UNDER IMPERFECT COMPETITION

**21.7.** (*a*)  What is monopsony?

(*b*)  How does monopsony arise?

(*c*)  What are oligopsony and monopsonistic competition?

(*a*)  Monopsony is the form of market organization where there is a single buyer of a particular resource. An example of monopsony is the "mining towns" of yesteryear in the United States, where the mining company was the sole employer of labor in town (often these mining companies even owned and operated the few stores in town).

(*b*)  Monopsony arises when a resource is specialized and is thus much more productive to a particular firm than to any other firm or use. Because of the greater resource productivity, this firm can pay a higher price for the resource and so become a monopsonist. Monopsony can also occur when resources lack geographical and occupational mobility.

(*c*)  Oligopsony and monopsonistic competition are two other forms of imperfect competition in resource markets. An oligopsonist is one of the few buyers of a homogeneous or differentiated resource. A monopsonistic competitor is one of many buyers of a differentiated resource.

**21.8.**  Given the labor market supply schedule of Table 21-4,

Mathcad

**Table 21-4**

| Wage rate per day ($) | 10 | 15 | 20 | 25 | 30 | 35 | 40 | 45 |
|---|---|---|---|---|---|---|---|---|
| Number of workers | 0 | 1 | 2 | 3 | 4 | 5 | 6 | 7 |

(*a*)  derive the monopsonist marginal resource cost of labor schedule. Why does $MRC_L$ exceed $W$?

(*b*)  Graph the labor supply and marginal resource cost schedules faced by the monopsonist.

(*c*)  How would these schedules look if we were dealing instead with an oligopsonist or monopsonistic competitor? A perfect competitor?

(*a*)  In Table 21-5, column 1 times column 2 gives column 3, which measures the total cost of hiring various numbers of workers. Column 4 shows the changes in total costs from hiring each additional worker, or $MRC_L$. $MRC_L$ exceeds $W$ because in order to hire more workers, the monopsonist must pay a higher wage not only to the additional workers hired but also to all previously hired workers.

**Table 21-5**

| (1) Wage Rate per Day ($) | (2) Number of Workers | (3) Total Cost of Labor ($) | (4) Marginal Cost of Labor ($) |
|---|---|---|---|
| 10 | 0 | 0 | |
| 15 | 1 | 15 | 15 |
| 20 | 2 | 40 | 25 |
| 25 | 3 | 75 | 35 |
| 30 | 4 | 120 | 45 |
| 35 | 5 | 175 | 55 |
| 40 | 6 | 240 | 65 |
| 45 | 7 | 315 | 75 |

(*b*)  See Fig. 21-5.

(*c*)  As imperfect competitors in the labor market, oligopsonists and monopsonistic competitors also face rising supply curves of labor (i.e., they must pay higher wages to hire more workers). Thus, $MRC_L$ exceeds $W$ and their $MRC_L$ curve also lies above the supply of labor curve that they face. This is to be contrasted with perfect competition in the labor market, where even though the market supply curve of labor is positively sloped, each buyer is so small that it can purchase all the labor time it wants at the given market wage rate (i.e., it faces an infinitely elastic supply curve of the labor). Thus, for the perfectly

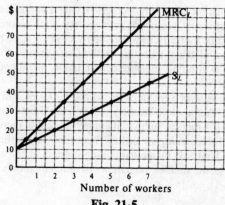

**Fig. 21-5**

competitive employer, the $MRC_L$ curve coincides with the horizontal supply curve of labor at the market equilibrium wage rate.

**21.9.** Given the $S_L$ and $MRC_L$ curves of Fig. 21-5, if labor is the monopsonist's only variable factor and $MRP_L = \$60$ at $Q_L = 2$ (i.e., with 2 workers), \$50 with 4 workers, and \$40 with 6 workers,

    (a)   draw a figure showing how many workers this monopsonist employs to maximize its total profits and what wage it pays. Why is this the profit-maximizing point?

    (b)   How many workers would have been hired and what wage would have been paid if this labor market had been perfectly competitive?

    (a)   In Fig. 21-6, the monopsonist hires 4 workers because $MRP_L = MRC_L$ at $Q_L = 4$, and pays a wage of \$30 (point $A$ on $S_L$). With 3 workers, $MRP_L$ exceeds $MRC_L$ and the monopsonist's total profits would increase by hiring more workers. However, the monopsonist would not hire the fifth worker because its $MRP_L$ is smaller than $MRC_L$ and total profits would be lower. Thus, the monopsonist maximizes its total profits when it hires 4 workers.

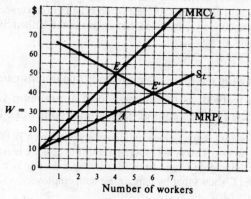

**Fig. 21-6**

    (b)   If the labor market had been perfectly competitive, all firms together would have hired a total of 6 workers and paid a wage of \$40 per worker (shown at point $E'$, where $MRP_L = S_L$). Because of its monopoly power in hiring labor, the monopsonist hires fewer workers and pays a lower wage rate than if the labor market had been perfectly competitive. The same is generally true with oligopsony and monopsonistic competition [see Problem 21-8 (c)].

## THE EFFECT OF UNIONS ON WAGES

**21.10.** (a)   What is a craft union? What is its primary method of attempting to increase wages?

    (b)   What is an industrial union? What is its primary method of attempting to increase wages?

(a) A craft union is one which includes only workers having a particular skill. For example, there are separate craft unions for electricians, plumbers, printers, etc. Such unions attempt to increase the real wages of their members primarily by restricting the supply of labor (i.e., by causing an upward and leftward shift in the supply curve of labor with this skill). Craft unions do this by forcing firms to hire only union members and then limiting the number of union members by imposing high initiation fees, long apprenticeships, etc.

(b) An industrial union is one which includes *all* workers, skilled and unskilled, of a particular industry. Examples are the United Automobile Workers (UAW), the United Steel Workers (USW), and the United Mine Workers (UMW) of America. Industrial unions attempt to increase wage rates directly by bargaining with employers and threatening to strike. The ability and willingness of such unions to negotiate wage increases is limited not only by the bargaining strength of employers but also because the larger the negotiated wage increase, the smaller the number of union members who will actually remain employed (see Panel C of Fig. 21-3).

**21.11.** (a) What is another (third) general method that unions can use to raise wages? Why is this the best method of raising wages? What is its feasibility?

(b) Have unions raised real wages in the United States?

(a) Another general method by which any union can attempt to increase wages is by increasing the (derived) demand for union labor by (1) raising the productivity of labor, (2) lobbying to restrict imports, and (3) financing such advertising campaigns for union-made products as the "look for the union label" slogan of the International Ladies' Garment Workers Union (ILGWU). This is the "best" method of increasing wages because it also increases the level of employment. However, it offers only limited possibilities because labor productivity and the derived demand for union labor are largely outside the unions' control. The most widely used method of increasing wages by unions today is by collective bargaining with employers under the threat of a strike.

(b) The ability of unions to increase wages is a controversial subject. Union labor does receive wages that are about 20 percent higher than nonunion labor wages in the United States today. However, unionized industries are generally large-scale industries that employ more skilled labor and paid higher wages before unionization. On the other hand, wage differences between unionized and nonunionized labor may underestimate the effectiveness of unions in raising wages because nonunionized firms may more or less match union wages in order to retain their workers and to keep unions out. Most economists who have studied this question tentatively concluded that unions in the United States have increased the wages of their members by about 10% to 15%.

**21.12.** (a) Sketch a graph showing the three main methods that unions can use to raise wages.

(b) To which of these methods is the imposition of a minimum wage by the government most similar? What are the pros and cons of having minimum-wage laws?

(a) Panel A of Fig. 21-7 shows that a union can increase wages from $W$ to $W'$ and employment from $OA$ to $OB$ by increasing $D_L$ to $D'_L$. This is the most desirable but also the least effective method. Panel B shows that a (craft) union can increase wages from $W$ to $W'$ by reducing $S_L$ to $S'_L$. However, employment falls from $OA$ to $OC$. Panel C shows that by bargaining with employers, a (craft) union could increase wages

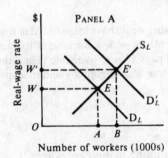
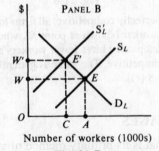
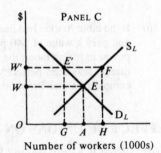

**Fig. 21-7**

from $W$ to $W'$, but this reduces employment from $OA$ to $OG$ and $GH(=E'F)$ workers are unable to find jobs. The actual loss of employment resulting from a given rise in wages depends on the elasticity of $D_L$ (see Section 20.5).

(b)  If government imposed a minimum wage of $W'$, the result would be the same as if the union had negotiated the wage of $W'$ shown in Panel C. This is particularly beneficial to previously low-paid workers near the poverty level. With higher wages and incomes, the health and vigor of these workers may increase and result in greater productivity. Imposing or raising a minimum wage can also have a "shock effect" on business and induce lethargic employers to introduce more productive techniques. However, the imposition of a minimum wage also tends to reduce the level of employment. Therefore, while those remaining employed are better off, others find themselves jobless. Training programs for the unemployed might then help them find jobs. However, this is not easy to accomplish. The United States has had a minimum wage since 1938. In 1993, its level was $4.25 per hour.

**21.13.** (a)  What would happen if a strong union forced the monopsonist of Fig. 21-6 to pay a wage of $40 per day? How does this compare with the profit-maximizing position of the monopsonist in the absence of the union?

(b)  How are the wage rate and employment level determined in the real world when a powerful labor union faces a monopsonist?

(a)  When a union forces a wage of $40 per day upon the monopsonist of Fig. 21-6 (repeated as Fig. 21-8 for ease of reference), the monopsonist will behave as a perfect competitor in the labor market and hire 6 workers (at which $MRP_L = W = \$40$) instead of 4 workers at $W = \$30$. Thus, both the wage rate and the level of employment are higher. A minimum wage set by the government at $40 per day would have exactly the same effect in curbing monopsony power.

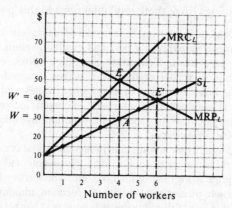

**Fig. 21-8**

(b)  When a powerful labor union (a monopoly in supplying labor) faces a monopsonist (a monopolist buyer of labor time), we have a so-called *bilateral monopoly*. With a bilateral monopoly, wages and employment are *theoretically* indeterminate. That is, economic theory cannot tell us what wage rate and level of employment will actually be established. The result depends on the relative bargaining strength of the union and the employer. In general, the final result of the bargaining process is somewhere between what the two sides originally wanted. Thus, big labor (e.g., UAW, USW, etc.) to some extent checks the power of big business (e.g., G.M., U.S. Steel, etc.), and vice versa. This is an example of countervailing power (see Section 19.7).

## WAGE DIFFERENTIALS

**21.14.** (a)  What causes wage differences?

(b)  What are equalizing differences? How do these give rise to wage differences?

(c)  What are noncompeting groups? How do they give rise to wage differences?

(d)  What are imperfect labor markets? How do they give rise to wage differences?

(a) Wages differ among different categories of people and jobs because of (1) equalizing differences, (2) the existence of noncompeting occupational groups, and (3) imperfections in labor markets.

(b) Equalizing differences are wage differences that serve to compensate workers for nonmonetary differences among jobs. That is, jobs requiring equal qualifications may differ in attractiveness, and higher wages must be paid to attract and retain workers in the more unpleasant jobs. For example, garbage collectors receive higher wages than porters.

(c) Noncompeting groups are occupations which require different capacities, skills, training, and education and, therefore, receive different wages. That is, labor is not a single productive resource but many different resources, each not in direct competition with others. Thus, doctors form one group which is not in direct competition with other groups of workers. Lawyers, accountants, electricians, bus drivers, etc. belong to other separate, noncompeting groups. There is a particular wage rate structure for each of these noncompeting groups, depending on the abilities, skills, and training required for each occupation. Note that for some jobs mobility among competing groups may be possible (for example, when an electrician becomes an electronics engineer by going to night school); however, mobility is generally limited.

(d) An imperfect labor market is one in which there is some lack of information on job opportunities and wages; in which some workers are unwilling to move to other areas and jobs in order to take advantage of higher wages; and in which union power, minimum-wage laws, and monopsony power exist. Any of these circumstances causes some differences in wages for jobs which are exactly alike and require equal capacities and skills.

**21.15.** Getting an education and training is sometimes referred to as an "investment in human capital."

(a) In what ways is this similar to any other investment?

(b) Why is treating education and training as investments in human capital useful?

(c) What are its shortcomings? Are there any objections to this point of view?

(a) Getting an education and training can be considered an investment in human capital because, as with any other investment, it involves a cost and entails a return. The cost of getting an education and training involves such explicit expenses as tuition, books, etc. and such opportunity cost as the forgone wages while in school or the lower wages received while in training. The return on education and training takes the form of the *higher* wages and salaries received over the individual's working life. By discounting all costs and extra income to the present and comparing returns to costs, we can calculate the rate of return on the investment in human capital and compare it to the returns from other investments.

(b) Viewing education and training as investments in human capital is useful in explaining many otherwise unexplainable real-world occurrences such as why we educate and train the young more than the old, why young people migrate more readily than old, etc. The answer is that young people have a longer working time over which to receive the benefits of education, training, and migration.

(c) Some shortcomings of this line of thinking are as follows: (1) Not all expenses for education and training represent costs. Some of these expenses should be regarded as consumption since they do not contribute to subsequent higher earnings (for example, when an engineering student takes a course in poetry). (2) Higher subsequent earnings may be as much the result of innate ability and greater intelligence and effort as it is of training. (3) The antipoverty programs of the 1960s to improve the health of and to train low-income people failed to reduce income inequalities.

Besides these shortcomings, there is the objection that education and training deal with human beings and should not be compared or analyzed with the same tools used to analyze investment in machinery, factories, etc.

## *Multiple Choice Questions*

1. If the money-wage index were to rise by 50% between 1990 and 1995 and the price index were to rise by 20% over the same period, then the real wage index would rise by
   (*a*)  35%,
   (*b*)  30%,
   (*c*)  25%,
   (*d*)  20%.

2. Real wages are higher,
   (*a*)  the greater the amount of capital available per worker,
   (*b*)  the more advanced the technology of production,
   (*c*)  the greater the availability of natural resources such as fertile land and mineral deposits,
   (*d*)  all of the above.

3. Which of the following statements is *incorrect?*
   (*a*)  Firms demand labor and other resources in order to produce the products demanded by consumers.
   (*b*)  A perfectly competitive firm's demand for labor is its marginal revenue product of labor schedule or curve.
   (*c*)  Another name for the marginal revenue product of labor is the marginal resource cost of labor.
   (*d*)  The market demand for labor is obtained by adding each firm's demand for labor.

4. The market supply of labor depends on
   (*a*)  the population size,
   (*b*)  the proportion of the population in the labor force,
   (*c*)  the state of the economy,
   (*d*)  all of the above.

5. Which of the following statements is *incorrect?*
   (*a*)  The competitive equilibrium wage rate is determined at the intersection of the market demand and supply curve of labor.
   (*b*)  In order to hire more labor, the perfectly competitive firm must pay a higher wage rate.
   (*c*)  The perfectly competitive firm hires labor until the marginal revenue product of labor equals the wage rate.
   (*d*)  If the market demand for labor increases, the equilibrium wage rate rises.

6. A firm which is the only buyer of or has monopoly power in the labor (or other resource) market is called a(n)
   (*a*)  monopolist,
   (*b*)  monopsonist,
   (*c*)  oligopolist,
   (*d*)  oligopsonist.

7. Which of the following statements about a monopsonist in the labor market is *incorrect?*
   (*a*)  It faces a rising market supply curve of labor.
   (*b*)  The marginal resource cost of labor is rising.
   (*c*)  The wage rate exceeds the marginal resource cost of labor.
   (*d*)  The marginal resource cost of labor curve is above the market supply curve of labor.

**8.** Which of the following statements about a monopsonist is *incorrect*?
  (*a*)   To maximize total profits, it hires labor up to the point where $MRP_L = MRC_L$.
  (*b*)   The wage that it pays is read from the labor supply curve.
  (*c*)   $W$ is smaller than $MRP_L$.
  (*d*)   $W = MRC_L$.

**9.** If a union is successful in increasing the demand for labor,
  (*a*)   the wage rate rises but employment falls,
  (*b*)   the wage rate falls but employment rises,
  (*c*)   both the wage rate and employment will rise,
  (*d*)   all of the above are possible.

**10.** The attempt of industrial unions to raise wage rates usually results in
  (*a*)   higher wages and more employment,
  (*b*)   higher wages and less employment,
  (*c*)   higher wages without affecting employment,
  (*d*)   actually lower wages but more employment.

**11.** The reason for wage differentials is
  (*a*)   the different attractiveness of different jobs,
  (*b*)   the different skills and training required for different jobs,
  (*c*)   imperfect labor markets,
  (*d*)   all of the above.

**12.** Noncompeting groups refer to workers
  (*a*)   in jobs of different attractiveness,
  (*b*)   with different capacities, skills, and training,
  (*c*)   in imperfect labor markets,
  (*d*)   all of the above.

## True or False Questions

**13.** _____ The money-wage rate gives the purchasing power of money.

**14.** _____ Wages are higher the more workers there are for a given amount of capital.

**15.** _____ In a perfectly competitive labor market, the market supply curve of labor is found by adding the individual firms' supply curves of labor.

**16.** _____ The competitive equilibrium real-wage rate is determined at the intersection of the market demand and supply curves of labor.

**17.** _____ In a perfectly competitive labor market, a firm hires labor until the marginal revenue product of labor equals the wage rate.

**18.** _____ A monopsonist must pay higher wages to hire more workers.

**19.** _____ A monopsonist hires labor until the marginal revenue product equals the marginal resource cost and the wage rate.

**20.** _____ The most common method that labor unions use to increase wages is to threaten to strike.

**21.** _____ Craft unions try to restrict labor supply through high initiation fees and long apprenticeships.

**22.** _____ Noncompeting groups receive different wages.

**23.** _____ The wage differentials observed in the real world are generally due to imperfect markets.

**24.** _____ Labor unions are an example of market imperfection.

### Answers to Multiple Choice and True or False Questions

| | | | |
|---|---|---|---|
| **1.** (c) | **7.** (c) | **13.** (F) | **19.** (F) |
| **2.** (d) | **8.** (d) | **14.** (F) | **20.** (T) |
| **3.** (c) | **9.** (c) | **15.** (T) | **21.** (T) |
| **4.** (d) | **10.** (b) | **16.** (T) | **22.** (T) |
| **5.** (b) | **11.** (d) | **17.** (T) | **23.** (F) |
| **6.** (b) | **12.** (b) | **18.** (T) | **24.** (T) |

# Chapter 22

# Rent, Interest, and Profits

## *Chapter Summary*

1. Rent is the price for the use of land and other natural resources which are given and fixed in total supply. Rent is determined at the intersection of the market demand curve and the vertical market supply curve of land.

2. Interest is the price paid for the use of money or loanable funds, expressed as a percentage of the amount borrowed. The equilibrium interest rate is determined at the intersection of the market demand and supply curves of loanable funds.

3. Profits are the excess of total revenue over total explicit and implicit costs. Profits can result from a successful innovation, as the reward for uninsurable risk-bearing or uncertainty, or from monopoly power.

4. In 1990, the breakdown of U.S. national income was as follows: wages and salaries, 74%; proprietors' incomes, 7%; corporate profits, 8%; interest, 10%; and rents 1%.

5. In a free-enterprise economy, commodity and factor prices are determined by their respective demand and supplies. Firms demand resources owned by households in order to produce the goods and services demanded by households. Households then use the income they receive to purchase the goods and services produced by firms. This circular flow of economic activity determines *what*, *how*, and *for whom* to produce.

## *Important Terms*

**Circular flow of economic activity.** The flow of resources from households to firms and goods and services from firms to households.

**Demand for loanable funds.** The demand for borrowed funds of firms, consumers, and governments.

**Entrepreneur or innovator.** An individual or firm who introduces a new product or a new production technique in hopes of making a profit.

**General equilibrium system.** The vast and interdependent system of markets of which the economy is composed and such that a change in any market affects every other market.

**Income shares.** The proportion of national income going for (1) wages and salaries, (2) proprietors' incomes, (3) corporate profits, (4) interest, and (5) rent.

**Interest.** The price for the use of money or loanable funds, expressed as a percentage of the amount borrowed.

**Liquidity-preference theory of interest.** States that the competitive equilibrium market rate of interest is determined by the market demand for money (or liquidity) and the supply of money.

**Loanable-funds theory of interest.** States that the competitive equilibrium market rate of interest is determined by the market demand and supply of loanable funds.

**Partial equilibrium analysis.** The study of one market in isolation by abstracting from all the interconnections existing between this and other markets.

**Precautionary demand for money.**    The demand for money needed to make unforeseen payments. It varies directly with national income.

**Private benefits and costs.**    The benefits and costs to the individual or household.

**Profits.**    The excess of total revenue over total explicit and implicit costs.

**Pure rate of interest.**    The rate of interest on a riskless loan (such as on a U.S. government bond).

**Rent.**    The price paid for the use of land (and other natural resources).

**Risk.**    The probability of incurring an extra cost (such as the breakdown of a machine) or a loss (such as from fire or theft) against which the firm can insure itself.

**Single-tax movement.**    A proposal introduced by Henry George in the late 1800s aimed at raising government revenue by taxing only rental incomes since the amount of land available is fixed and would not be reduced by the tax.

**Social benefits and costs.**    The benefits and costs to society as a whole.

**Social or public goods.**    Such goods and services as pubic schools, public transportation, etc., which can be used by more than one person at the same time.

**Social welfare.**    The common good or well-being of society.

**Speculative demand for money.**    The demand for money in the expectation of higher interest rates in the future. It is inversely related to the rate of interest.

**Supply of loanable funds.**    The supply of loanable funds saved by individuals and firms and available for borrowing.

**Transaction demand for money.**    The demand for money needed to make everyday payments. It depends on the level of national income.

**Uncertainty.**    The possibility of a fall in revenue or increase in costs due to cyclical and structural changes which are uninsurable.

# Outline of Chapter 22: Rent, Interest, and Profits

## 22.1   RENT

*Rent* is the price for the use of land and other natural resources which are given and fixed in total supply. If we assume for simplicity that all land is alike and has only one competitive use (say, the growing of wheat), then rent is determined at the intersection of the market demand curve and the *vertical* market supply curve of land. Regardless of the height of the market demand and the rent paid, the same amount of land remains available. As a result, rent could be taxed away entirely without affecting the supply of land. In contrast, *variable* resources of labor and capital are supplied in reduced quantities when taxed. This concept was the basis for Henry George's proposal for a *single tax* on land in the late 19th century (see Problem 22.3).

**EXAMPLE 22.1.**    With the supply of land fixed (S) in Fig. 22-1, rent is equal to $r$ when the market demand curve for land is D, and $r'$ when it is D'. If from the equilibrium rent of $r'$, the government imposed a tax of $r'r$ on rental incomes, land users would continue to pay $r'$ but landowners would retain only $r$. The quantity of land supplied, however, would

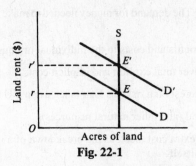

**Fig. 22-1**

remain unchanged (see Section 14.5). In the real world, we have different types and uses of land with different rental values. The supply of land can also be increased somewhat (by drainage, reclamation, etc.) or reduced (by improper use). On the other hand, the quantities of certain kinds of labor and capital resources may not be entirely variable and part of their return may thus be in the nature of a rent (see Problem 22.4).

## 22.2   INTEREST

*Interest* is the price paid for the use of money or *loanable funds*, expressed as a percentage of the amount borrowed. If the rate of interest is 8% per year, this means that for $100 borrowed today, $108 will have to be repaid a year from today. For simplicity, we will discuss the *pure rate of interest*. This is the interest on a riskless loan (as on a U.S. government bond). Other interest rates are higher depending on the risk, maturity, administrative cost, and the competitiveness of the loanable-fund, market (see Problem 22.5).

The equilibrium interest rate is determined at the intersection of the market demand and supply curves of loanable funds. The *demand for loanable funds* comes from the borrowing of firms, consumers, and government, and is negatively sloped. To maximize profits, a firm will borrow in order to invest in machinery, inventory, etc., as long as the return, or marginal productivity, of the investment exceeds the rate of interest on borrowed funds. Thus, interest rates allocate the scarce loanable funds to the most productive uses. The *supply of loanable funds* stems from the past and current savings of individuals and firms. It is upward sloped and is greatly affected by monetary policy [see Problem 22.8 (*b*)].

**EXAMPLE 22.2.**   In Fig. 22-2, the intersection of the market demand and supply curves of loanable funds determines the equilibrium interest rate of 8%. Related to this is the *liquidity-preference theory*, which states that the interest rate is determined at the intersection of the demand curve for *all money* (not just loanable funds) and the supply curve of *all money*. The demand for money, or *liquidity preference*, arises in order to carry out everyday transactions (the transactions motive), to meet unforeseen conditions (the precautionary motive), and from the expectation of higher interest rates in the future (the speculative motive). At lower interest rates, it is cheaper (in terms of the earnings forgone) to hold idle money, and thus the quantity demanded for money (or liquidity preference) is greater. The supply of money is determined or controlled by the federal government (through the Federal Reserve Banks) and is fixed at any time [see Problem 22.8 (*b*)].

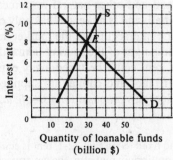

**Fig. 22-2**

## 22.3  PROFITS

*Profits* are the excess of total revenue over total costs, where total costs include both explicit and implicit costs. This differs from the everyday usage of the term profit, which refers to total revenue minus the explicit, or out-of-pocket, expenses only (see Problem 22.9).

Profits stem from the introduction of a successful innovation, as a reward for uninsurable risk-bearing or uncertainty, and as a result of monopoly power. They serve as incentives for innovation, to shift resources to the production of those commodities that society wants most, and as a reward for efficiency.

**EXAMPLE 22.3.**   Firms introduce new products and new production methods in the expectation of profits. If successful, other firms will imitate the successful innovator and compete those profits away. But in the meantime other innovations are introduced. Similarly, more risky ventures (such as petroleum exploration) require the expectation of a higher profit to induce investments. Finally, monopoly power allows a firm to restrict output artificially, keep competitors out, and charge a price that allows profits to persist.

## 22.4  INCOME SHARES

In 1990, the breakdown of U.S. national income was as follows: wages and salaries, 74%; proprietors' incomes, 7%; corporate profits, 8%; interest, 10%; and rents, 1%. However, this classification does not precisely fit the economist's definitions. For example, much of proprietors' incomes represent the implicit wages and salaries of the persons owning and running businesses (e.g., the corner drugstore).

Since 1900, wages and salaries have increased relatively and proprietors' incomes have fallen relatively. This is due to the increase in the importance of corporations relative to individual-owned businesses and, similarly, of manufacturing and services relative to agriculture. As a result, the share of wages, salaries, and proprietors' incomes combined have remained fairly stable at about 80% of national income. This has left a fairly constant share of about 20% for rent, interest, and corporate profits combined.

## 22.5  EPILOGUE ON COMMODITY AND RESOURCE PRICING

In a free-enterprise economy, commodity and factor prices are determined by their respective demands and supplies. Firms demand resources owned by households in order to produce the goods and services demanded by households. Households then use the income they receive to purchase the goods and services produced by firms. This circular flow of economic activity determines *what*, *how*, and *for whom* to produce. It is a *general equilibrium system* because a change in any part of the economy affects every other part of the economy.

When markets are perfectly competitive and are in long-run equilibrium, resources are allocated most efficiently and the economy's output of goods and services is maximized. In the real world, however, this most efficient resource allocation is interfered with by market imperfections, by the existence of social goods, and by divergencies between social and private benefits and costs (see Problem 22.16). Government may seek to overcome these complications and achieve a more equal distribution of income through a system of taxes and subsidies (see Problem 22.17).

**EXAMPLE 22.4.**   The top loop in Fig. 22-3 shows that households purchase goods and services from business firms. Thus, what is a cost or consumption expenditure from the households' point of view represents the income or the money receipts of business firms. On the other hand, the bottom loop shows that business firms purchase the services of economic resources from households. What is a cost of production from the viewpoint of business firms also represents the money income of households. This circular flow of economic activity represents a vast and interdependent general equilibrium system. The operation of this system is modified by government measures aimed at maximizing social welfare.

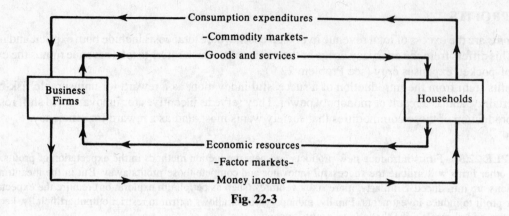

**Fig. 22-3**

# Solved Problems

## RENT

**22.1.** (*a*)  What is rent? How is it determined?

(*b*)  What determines the demand for land?

(*c*)  How is the supply of land different from the supply of other resources?

(*a*)  Rent is the price for the use of land and other natural resources which are fixed in total supply. The rent on land, as the price of any other resource, is determined by the market demand for and the market supply of land.

(*b*)  The demand for land, like the demand for any other resource, is a derived demand. It is derived from demand for the commodities that require land (and other resources) in production. The demand for land is greater: (1) the greater the demand for the commodities that use land in production, (2) the greater the productivity of land, and (3) the higher the price of substitute resources and the lower the price of complementary resources.

(*c*)  Land and other natural resources are usually taken as fixed in total supply, while the supply of other factors (labor and capital) is usually regarded as variable. Thus, while the supply curve of land is taken as vertical or having zero price elasticity, the supply of other factors is taken as upward-sloping, indicating that at higher resource prices more will be supplied to the market. However, in the real world, land and other natural resources are not completely fixed. Thus, for example, the supply of land can be increased somewhat by drainage, reclamation, and clearing and can be reduced by soil erosion and improper use. Similarly, natural resources such as mineral deposits can be depleted and new ones discovered. On the other hand, the supply of other resources may not be completely variable. For example, even with proper training, not everyone could become a heart surgeon, an electrical engineer, or an accomplished-violinist.

**22.2.** (*a*)  Draw a figure showing the level of rent with three alternative demand curves, $D_1$, $D_2$, and $D_3$.

(*b*)  How is the determination of rent different from the determination of the price of other resources?

(*a*)  See Fig. 22-4. Given the fixed supply of land (S), rent is equal to $r_1$ with $D_1$, $r_2$ with $D_2$, and $r_3$ with $D_3$.

(*b*)  In general, demand and supply are equally important in determining resource prices. But because the quantity of land available is fixed, only the height of the demand curve actively determines the rent of land.

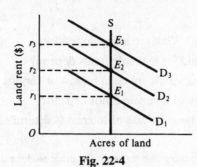

**Fig. 22-4**

**22.3.** (*a*)  What is the incidence of (i.e., who actually ends up paying) a tax on rental income? Why?

(*b*)  What is the economic significance of this?

(*c*)  How is this related to the single-tax movement?

(*d*)  What are the criticisms of the single-tax movement?

(*a*)  The incidence of a tax on rents falls entirely on landowners if the total quantity of land is fixed. The general rule stated in Section 14.5 is that for a given demand, the more inelastic supply, the greater the incidence of the tax on suppliers. Therefore, with the supply of land having zero price elasticity, all of the tax burden falls on landowners.

(*b*)  The economic significance of this is that a tax on rental income does not reduce the availability of land and other natural resources in fixed supply. On the other hand, a tax on wages, salaries, or interest income causes an upward shift in and a reduced supply of labor and capital. (With the supply curve of land vertical, an upward shift, due to the tax, leaves the supply curve of land unchanged.)

(*c*)  A tax on land and other natural resources in fixed supply is in a sense an ideal tax since the tax does not reduce the availability of land and other natural resources. This gave impetus to the single-tax movement promoted by Henry George in the late 1880s. The thrust of this movement was that since a tax on variable resources of labor and capital reduces the supply of these resources while a tax on land does not, all taxes should be raised by taxing only rental incomes.

(*d*)  There are three basic criticisms of a single tax on land. First, the rental value of land is the return to land itself as well as on costly land improvements such as drainage, reclamation, or irrigation. Therefore it may be difficult in practice to isolate the purely rental elements. Second, rents in the United States today amount to just about 1% of GNP, while taxes are above 25% of GNP. Third, the price of labor and capital also may contain some purely rental elements (see Problem 22.4) so that taxing only landowners may be an unfair and discriminatory practice.

**22.4.** (*a*)  Describe some of the different uses to which land can be put. How do these affect the rental value of land?

(*b*)  How is the large salary paid to a star baseball player similar to rent on land?

(*a*)  Land, like labor and capital, is not homogeneous. It has many different uses, each with a different productivity and each commanding a different rent. Each of the large number of rents paid on land of different quality and uses is determined by the market demand and supply of land for the particular type and location. For example, rents are high in the center of the city and they are lower in areas of urban decay and remote, barren land. Note, however, that since the same land can have many alternative uses, the supply of land for any of these uses is not fixed but can be bid away for other uses (e.g., urban renewal). Thus, while the return on land is a rent from the point of view of society as a whole, it is a cost of production from the viewpoint of a firm using the land.

(*b*)  The difference between what the star baseball player earns in playing baseball and what he would earn in the best alternative occupation (say, by being a baseball coach) is a rent in the sense that the large salary need not be paid to keep him playing baseball. Of the $1.5 million paid to the player per year, $1.2 million is a rent if he would earn only $300,000 in his best alternative occupation. The government could tax the player $1.2 million and he would probably continue to play baseball. To be sure, the $1.5 million is a cost to the team's front office because if one team does not pay, another would, but most of it ($1.2 million) is a rent from society's point of view.

## INTEREST

**22.5.** *(a)*  What is the interest rate? What are loanable funds?

   *(b)*  On what does the demand for loanable funds depend?

   *(c)*  How does a firm determine how much to borrow at various interest rates?

   *(d)*  On what does the supply of loanable funds depend?

   *(e)*  Draw a figure showing how the rate of interest is determined according to the loanable-funds theory.

   *(a)*  The interest rate (given in percentage terms) is the price paid for the use of money or loanable funds. For example, if the interest rate is 10% per year and a firm borrows $1000 today for one year, it will have to repay $1100 a year from today. Loanable funds are the total amount of money available for borrowing.

   *(b)*  The demand for loanable funds arises from (1) firms that want to invest in machinery, inventory, and buildings; (2) consumers who want to finance the purchase of homes, automobiles, washing machines, vacations, etc., and (3) government's need to finance budgets to construct highways, schools, and other public projects. In general, the quantity demanded of loanable funds is greater at lower than at higher interest rates.

   *(c)*  Firms borrow funds in order to make productive investments. The net productivity of various investments varies, and the firm seeking maximum profits first makes those investments with the highest return. A firm should continue to borrow and invest as long as the rate of return on investment exceeds the rate of interest on borrowed funds, and until they are equal. New technological advances, by opening new investment opportunities, cause the firm's investment schedule to shift upward.

   *(d)*  The supply of loanable funds stems from the past and current savings of households and businesses and from money created by commercial banks (see Section 9.4). Broadly speaking, the supply of loanable funds is greater at higher rates of interest. However, it is greatly affected by monetary policies (the control which government exerts over the nation's money supply) designed to regulate the level of business activity [see Problem 22.8 *(b)* and Chapter 10].

   *(e)*  In Fig. 22-5, the competitive equilibrium market rate of interest is 6%, at which the quantity demanded of loanable funds of $30 billion matches the quantity supplied.

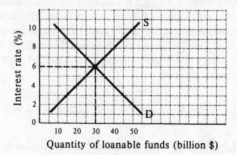

**Fig. 22-5**

**22.6.**  How many rates of interest do we have? On what do they depend?

   In the real world, we do not have a single rate of interest but rather a whole structure of many different rates of interest. Each of these rates depends on the risk, maturity, and administrative cost of the loan and on the competitiveness of the loanable-fund market. In general, the interest rate on a loan is higher, (1) the greater the risk of borrower default, (2) the longer the term of the loan, (3) the smaller the amount of the loan (i.e., administering many small loans costs much more than administering one larger loan, everything else remaining the same), and (4) the less competitive the financial system (i.e., a single financial institution in an isolated locality can charge higher interest rates on loans than if there were several such lenders).

   When we speak of the rate of interest, we usually refer to the *pure* rate of interest. This is the rate of interest on riskless loans and is roughly equal to the interest rate on long-term government bonds which will almost certainly be repaid. Other interest rates are higher and depend on the four factors listed above. Generally, when the pure rate of interest rises, the whole structure of interest rates also rises.

**22.7.** (*a*)   What are the transaction, precautionary, and speculative demands for money? On what do they depend?

     (*b*)   On what does the supply of money depend?

     (*c*)   How is the rate of interest determined according to the liquidity-preference theory of interest? What is its relationship to the loanable-funds theory of interest?

     (*a*)   The *transaction demand for money* refers to the demand of households and businesses to hold money balances rather than bonds, stocks, etc. in order to carry on their everyday purchases and payments. This does not depend on the rate of interest but varies directly with the level of national income only.

          The *precautionary demand for money* refers to the demand for money in order to make any unforeseen payments. This too depends only on the level of national income.

          The *speculative demand for money* refers to the demand for money in the expectation of higher interest rates in the future. That is, people hold larger money balances if they expect interest rates to rise in the future, rather than tying this money up in bonds now. This speculative demand for money is inversely related to the interest rate. As a result, the *total* demand curve for *money*, or liquidity, is also downward-sloped when plotted against interest rates.

     (*b*)   The total supply of money is determined or controlled by the federal government and is given and fixed at any time. That is, the U.S. government regulates the creation of demand deposits by the banking system and changes the money supply in the conduct of monetary policy.

     (*c*)   According to the liquidity-preference theory of interest, the interest rate is determined at the intersection of the demand for *all money* or the liquidity-preference curve and the supply curve of *all money*. On the other hand, according to the loanable-funds theory, the rate of interest is determined by the intersection of the market demand and supply curves of *loanable funds* only. These two theories are complementary rather than conflicting. However, their relationship is rather intricate and is discussed in more advanced courses and books.

**22.8.** (*a*)   What is the function of the rate of interest?

     (*b*)   How and why does the federal government influence the rate of interest?

     (*a*)   The function of the rate of interest, like the price of other resources, is to allocate the scarce supply of loanable funds to the most productive uses (i.e., to those uses where the net productivity or rate of return on investment is greatest). This is accomplished because firms borrow and invest as long as the rate of return on investments exceeds the interest rate and up to the level at which they are equal. However, the government directly allocates some public investments to highways, schools, hospitals, and other public projects without regard to their profitability. In addition, the greater bargaining power of larger firms may allow them to borrow at lower rates than smaller firms and thus make some investments that are less productive than those that could be made by smaller firms.

     (*b*)   The federal government influences the rate of interest or interest rate structure by changing the nation's money supply and, through it, the supply of loanable funds. The government may want to increase the money supply (i.e., conduct an easy monetary policy) in order to reduce the rate of interest and stimulate investment (which would then cause a multiple expansion in GNP) if the economy is operating at less than full employment. The opposite is true when the economy faces demand-pull inflation (see Chapter 10).

## PROFITS

**22.9.** (*a*)   Distinguish between cost and profit in economics.

     (*b*)   How do these concepts differ from the everyday usage of these terms?

     (*a*)   In economics, costs include both explicit and implicit costs. The resources that a firm owns and uses in production are not free. They involve an element of cost which can be estimated by what these same resources would earn in their best (most rewarding) alternative employment. Thus, if we say that the firm is making zero profit, it means that the firm is already receiving a "normal" return on its owned factors. When we speak of profits in economics, we mean above-normal returns (see also Chapter 16).

(b)     The everyday usage of "cost" refers only to the out-of-pocket expenditures of the firm made to hire factors of production (what economists call explicit costs). Most people call profit the excess of the firm's revenue over these out-of-pocket expenditures. However, for the economist, part or all of this revenue represents the "normal return" on the firm's owned factors (i.e., what its owned factors would earn in their best alternative employments). Thus, for the economist, profit refers to total revenue minus all explicit and implicit costs.

**22.10.**  From what do economic profits arise?

Profits can be regarded as the reward for a successful innovation, as a reward for bearing uncertainty, and as a result of monopoly power. We saw in Section 17.6 that in a long-run and perfectly competitive equilibrium, all firms make zero profits. In the short run, a firm may make profits by introducing such a successful innovation as a new product or a cost-reducing production technique. However, in the long run other firms will imitate the innovation until all profits are competed away. In the meantime, other innovations may be introduced. The expectation of higher profits is also necessary to induce investments in more uncertain ventures. For example, petroleum exploration and the introduction of new products face greater uncertainties and possibilities of losses than entering established industries to produce traditional products. Investments will flow into new ventures facing greater uncertainties only in the expectation of higher profits. Similarly, buying a stock may give a greater but more uncertain return than putting the money in a savings account. Finally, monopolists and oligopolists produce at a price which exceeds marginal cost, and by keeping competitors out, they can continue to make profits in the long run.

**22.11.**  (a)     What is meant by invention? By innovation?

(b)     What is the difference between risk and uncertainty ?

(a)     An invention refers to a new process, a new technique, or a new product. An innovation is the commercial introduction of an invention. For example, the discovery of radio waves led to the introduction of radios. Not all inventions lead to innovations. The invention may involve a new product that society does not want or a new process or technique which at present may be more costly than existing processes and techniques. Thousands of inventions patented each year in the United States are never introduced or applied commercially, giving only delusions to the inventors. Most nations allow inventions to be patented so as to stimulate inventions by offering a temporary monopoly and possibility of profit to the inventor. In this context it is important to distinguish an entrepreneur or innovator from a manager. The entrepreneur or innovator, if successful, makes profits. The manager only earns wages.

(b)     A risk refers to the probability of incurring an extra cost (such as the breakdown of a machine) or a loss (such as from a fire or theft) against which the firm can insure itself. For example, if experience indicates that 3 out of 100 machines break down in the course of production each year, the firm can include the cost of repairs and of lost production into its estimates of future production costs. Similarly, firms can buy insurance against the hazards of fire and theft. Uncertainty, on the other hand, refers to the possibility of a fall in revenue or increase in costs due to cyclical and structural changes in the economy. Against these uncertainties, firms cannot buy insurance.

**22.12.**  (a)     What are the functions of profits?

(b)     What are some objections to profits?

(a)     Profits serve as incentives for innovators to shift resources to the production of those commodities that society wants most, and as a reward for efficiency. The introduction of an innovation involves uncertainty and may result in financial loss if it is not successful. The expectation of a financial reward in the form of profits is required to induce innovations. Similarly, profit in some industries and losses in others is the indication that society wants more commodities from the former and less from the latter. This is the signal for resources to shift from the industries incurring losses into those making a profit. Related to this is the fact that more efficient firms in a given industry are rewarded with profits which they can then use to expand, while less efficient firms incur losses and have to contract operations or go out of business.

(b) Among the objections to profits are the following: (1) Profits arising from monopoly serve no socially useful purpose (except when they lead to more innovations). Therefore, such profits should be taxed away or the monopoly should be regulated (if it is not feasible to break it up). (2) Profits may lead to an excessively unequal distribution of income. This, too, can be corrected by progressive taxation.

However, a general attack on all profits is not justified, because profits, as we have seen before, do perform socially useful functions. Thus, the sharp criticism of Marxists that all profits represent exploitation of labor by the capitalist class and should therefore be entirely eliminated is invalid.

## INCOME SHARES

**22.13.** (a)  What was the distribution of 1990 U.S. national income among the owners of the various resources? What definitional problems arise?

(b)  How have these relative shares changed over time?

(a)  In 1990, U.S. national income was distributed as follows: wages and salaries, 74%; proprietors' incomes, 7%; corporate profits, 8%; interest, 10%; and rents, 1%. However, these are for the most part accounting definitions and differ somewhat from the economist's concept of wages, profit, interest, and rent. For example, most of proprietors' incomes were implicit wages and salaries, interest, and rent from owned resources rather than profits in the economist's sense. As such, most of proprietors' incomes should be added to wages and salaries, giving a combined total of 81% of U.S. national income in 1990.

(b)  Since 1900, the share of U.S. national income that was wages and salaries rose from about 55% to 74% in 1990. On the other hand, proprietors' incomes have fallen from about 24% in 1900 to 7% in 1990. The fall in proprietors' income resulted from the reduction in the number and relative importance of small businesses owned and run by individuals (unincorporated sole proprietorships and partnerships) since 1900 and the growing importance of corporations. Another reason has been the exodus of small independent farmers from agriculture and the growth in the relative importance of manufacturing and services. As the number of self-employed declined, so did the share of proprietors' incomes. However, most of proprietors' income represents their implicit wages and salaries and should thus be added to wages and salaries. As a result, the share going to labor remained fairly constant over time at about 80%. This left the relatively constant share (of about 20%) for corporate profits, interest, and rent combined. Within this 20%, interest remained fairly stable, rents declined sharply, and corporate profits, as it might well have been expected, fluctuated greatly over time, depending on the state of the economy.

## EPILOGUE ON COMMODITY AND RESOURCE PRICING

**22.14.** (a)  How are commodity prices determined in a free-enterprise economy? What are the shapes of the market demand curves and market supply curves for commodities?

(b)  How are resource prices determined in a free-enterprise economy? What are the shapes of the market demand curves and market supply curves for resources?

(c)  How does the circular flow of economic activity solve the basic economic problems in a free-enterprise economy?

(a)  In a free-enterprise economy, commodity prices (and outputs) are determined at the intersections of the market demand curve and the market supply curve for the commodity. The market demand curves are downward-sloped because of diminishing marginal utilities. The market supply curves are usually upward-sloped because of increasing marginal costs.

(b)  In a free-enterprise economy, resource prices (i.e., wages, rents, interest, and profits) are determined at the intersections of the market demand curve and the market supply curve for the resource. The market demand curves are downward-sloped because of diminishing marginal productivities. The market supply curves are usually upward-sloped (except for land, for which it is vertical) indicating that higher resource prices are usually required to make larger quantities of the resource available.

(c)  In a free-enterprise economy, households use the income received from selling the use of their resources to business firms to purchase the goods and services produced by business firms. In this circular flow of economic activity, the market demand and supply curves for commodities determine commodity prices.

These prices help determine *how* businesspeople should combine resources to minimize costs of production. In addition, resource prices together with inheritance, luck, etc. determine the distribution of income in society. This distribution in turn determines *for whom* goods and services are produced.

**22.15.** (*a*)   What is meant when we say that the economy is a general equilibrium system?

(*b*)   How can we study only one market or justify partial equilibrium analysis?

(*a*)   As indicated by the circular flow of economic activity, the economy is a vast and interdependent system of markets in which a change in any market affects every other market. It is to stress the fact that all markets in the economy are interrelated that the economy is often referred to as a general equilibrium system. For example, an increase in gasoline prices affects primarily the petroleum and automobile industries, but through them, practically every other market in the economy is also affected. The demand for large cars decreases relative to the demand for small cars and public transportation. Resources shift to the production of more small cars and public transportation. This shift affects the distribution of income and thus other commodity and factor markets.

(*b*)   In economics, we usually study one market in isolation and initially abstract from the interconnections existing between this and other markets. This is referred to as *partial equilibrium analysis*. This differs from general equilibrium analysis which studies all markets of the economy and their interconnections *simultaneously*. The justification for partial equilibrium analysis is that by focusing on a single market at a time, the analysis is more manageable and does give, in most instances, a sufficiently close first approximation to the solution sought. For example, suppose we want to study the effect of the increase in gasoline prices on the automobile industry. To do so, we might initially disregard the effect of the auto industry on related industries (steel, rubber, glass, etc.) and the repercussions which then might affect the auto industry itself. The smaller these repercussions are, the more accurate and justified is partial equilibrium analysis.

**22.16.** (*a*)   Why is a perfectly competitive system of markets the most efficient system in the long run?

(*b*)   How do market imperfections, the existence of social goods, and divergencies between social and private benefits and costs interfere with the most efficient allocation of resources?

(*a*)   A perfectly competitive system is the most efficient system in the long run because (1) consumers purchase commodities in such a way as to maximize their total utility from spending their incomes, and (2) firms produce the goods and services most wanted by consumers with the most efficient methods. That is, firms produce goods and services at the lowest possible long-run average cost and up to the point where the commodity price equals its marginal cost. Firms hire resources in quantities at which the marginal revenue product of each resource equals its price or marginal cost. As a result, there is *economic efficiency* in consumption because no transfer of commodities among consumers would make anyone better off without at the same time making someone else worse off. Similarly, there is *technical efficiency* in production because no reallocation of resources would increase the output of some commodities without reducing the output of others (i.e., society is on its production-possibility curve; see Section 2.2).

(*b*)   If we have imperfect competition in some commodity markets, the output of those commodities is artificially restricted because the firm produces where MR = MC but MC falls short of the commodity price. Similarly, in imperfectly competitive resource markets, the use of resources is artificially restricted because the firm uses resources only in the quantity at which MRP = MRC but MRP exceeds the resource price.

Even a perfectly competitive system will not allocate resources most efficiently when there are social goods and when social and private benefits and costs diverge. Without government intervention, there would be a tendency to underproduce and underconsume social or public goods (i.e., such goods and services as public schools and public transportation, which can be used by more than one individual at a time). Similarly, there might be underinvestment in education when the social benefits (i.e., the benefits to society as a whole) exceed the private benefit (i.e., the benefit to the individuals paying for their education). At the same time, there is overproduction of such goods as automobiles which pollute the air, resulting in social costs which exceed the private costs of buying and operating the car.

**22.17.** (*a*)  How does the government seek to overcome market imperfections, provide adequate social or public goods, and reconcile social and private benefits and costs?

(*b*)  Why and how does the government redistribute income from the rich to the poor? Why is it important to define objectively the maximum social welfare?

(*a*)  The government seeks to overcome the distortions resulting from market imperfections with a system of taxes and controls. For example, controls and taxes are imposed on monopolists in an attempt to overcome the artificial restrictions that they would otherwise place on production in their effort to maximize total profits. Governments use most of their tax revenues to provide such essential social or public goods as education, transportation, law and order, and defense. Similarly, they subsidize private education and basic research, and tax and control pollutants in the effort to reconcile social benefits and costs with private benefits and costs.

(*b*)  In the name of fairness and equity, the government redistributes income from the rich to the poor (through a system of progressive taxation and subsidies) in order to reduce the income inequality that results from the operation of the market mechanism. However, since it is impossible to make inter-personal comparisons of utility, governments do not generally know how far this redistribution should be pursued in order to maximize social welfare. Indeed, it is impossible even to know objectively whether social welfare increases when, in order to make someone better off, we make someone else worse off.

## Multiple Choice Questions

1.  When the amount of land is fixed,
    (*a*)  the supply curve for land is vertical and has zero elasticity,
    (*b*)  the rent on land is actively determined by the demand for land,
    (*c*)  the higher the demand for land, the greater the rent,
    (*d*)  all of the above.

2.  A tax on land falls
    (*a*)  entirely on land users,
    (*b*)  entirely on landowners,
    (*c*)  partly on land users and partly on land owners,
    (*d*)  any of the above is possible.

3.  The interest rate is
    (*a*)  the price of using money or loanable funds,
    (*b*)  expressed in percentage terms,
    (*c*)  determined by the demand for and the supply of loanable funds,
    (*d*)  all of the above.

4.  In order to maximize profits, a firm borrows until the return on investment
    (*a*)  equals the rate of interest,
    (*b*)  exceeds the rate of interest,
    (*c*)  is smaller than the rate of interest,
    (*d*)  any of the above.

5.  The interest rate serves to allocate the scarce loanable funds to
    (*a*)  the most needed uses,
    (*b*)  the most productive uses,
    (*c*)  the most liquid uses,
    (*d*)  none of the above.

**6.** The interest rate charged on a loan depends on
   (a) the risk of the loan,
   (b) the maturity of the loan,
   (c) the administrative cost and competitive conditions of the loan,
   (d) all of the above.

**7.** Profit is equal to total revenue minus
   (a) explicit costs,
   (b) implicit costs,
   (c) implicit and explicit costs,
   (d) wages and rents.

**8.** Which of the following statements is *not* true with regard to profit?
   (a) It may arise from diminishing returns.
   (b) It may arise from introducing an innovation.
   (c) It may be the reward for uncertainty.
   (d) It may arise from monopoly power.

**9.** Which is *not* a function of profit?
   (a) To encourage innovations.
   (b) To shift resources to the production of those commodities that society wants most.
   (c) To increase costs of production.
   (d) To reward efficiency.

**10.** The share of 1990 U.S. national income going for wages and salaries and for wages, salaries, and proprietors' income combined were, respectively,
   (a) 74% and 81%,
   (b) 70% and 93%,
   (c) 85% and about 93%,
   (d) 66% and about 73%.

**11.** Which of the following is *not true* with regard to the functioning of a free-enterprise economy?
   (a) It is a vast and interdependent system.
   (b) It is a partial equilibrium system.
   (c) The questions of *what*, *how*, and *for whom* to produce are answered simultaneously.
   (d) It is a general equilibrium system.

**12.** The most efficient allocation of resources is prevented in the real world by
   (a) imperfect competition,
   (b) the existence of social goods,
   (c) divergencies between social and private benefits and costs,
   (d) all of the above.

## True or False Questions

**13.** _____ The supply curve of land and natural resources is upward-sloping.

**14.** _____ A tax on land has the same general effect as a tax on variable inputs.

**15.** _____ The factors affecting interest rates are risk, maturity, administrative costs, and competitiveness of the loanable funds market.

**16.** _____ The demand for loanable funds comes from the borrowing of firms, consumers, and government.

**17.** _____ Firms borrow as long as the rate of interest is greater than the marginal productivity of the investment.

**18.** _____ According to the liquidity-preference theory, the interest rate is determined at the intersection of the demand and supply curves for loanable funds.

**19.** _____ Monetary policy has no effect on the supply of loanable funds.

**20.** _____ Only explicit costs are used in calculating profits.

**21.** _____ In order for firms to invest in higher risk ventures the expected profit must be higher.

**22.** _____ Since 1900, the share of rent, interest, and corporate profits has remained more or less constant.

**23.** _____ Government can use taxes and subsidies in correcting market imperfections.

**24.** _____ Perfect competition leads to the most efficient allocation of resources and maximum social welfare.

### Answers to Multiple Choice and True or False Questions

| | | | |
|---|---|---|---|
| **1.** (d) | **7.** (c) | **13.** (F) | **19.** (F) |
| **2.** (b) | **8.** (a) | **14.** (F) | **20.** (F) |
| **3.** (d) | **9.** (c) | **15.** (T) | **21.** (T) |
| **4.** (a) | **10.** (a) | **16.** (T) | **22.** (T) |
| **5.** (b) | **11.** (b) | **17.** (F) | **23.** (T) |
| **6.** (d) | **12.** (d) | **18.** (F) | **24.** (T) |

# Chapter 23

## International Trade and Finance

### *Chapter Summary*

1. Most nations are open economies in the sense that they are connected to the rest of the world through a network of trade and financial relationships. Even though trade is generally more important to small countries than to large countries, the welfare of both is greatly dependent on trade.

2. Each nation can gain from trade by specializing in the production of the commodity in which it has a comparative advantage and trading some of this for the commodity of its comparative disadvantage. The nation has a comparative advantage in the commodity with the relatively lower opportunity cost.

3. Tariffs and quotas are often used to restrict imports. An import tariff is a tax on the imported commodity, whereas an import quota is a quantitative restriction on imports. Most of the arguments for trade restrictions are invalid and based on misconceptions.

4. The balance of payments is a summary statement of a nation's transactions with the rest of the world during a year. Credits consist of foreign currency earned by exporting goods and services and receiving capital inflows. Debits are foreign currency expenditures for imports and capital outflows. The nation has a deficit in its balance of payments if its debits exceed its credits.

5. When foreign currencies can be freely bought and sold, the rate of exchange between the domestic currency and a foreign currency is determined at the intersection of the market demand and supply curves of the foreign currency.

6. From the end of World War II until 1971, the world operated under a fixed-exchange-rate system, and since then the system has been a managed float. The most pressing international economic problems today are the need to devise acceptable rules for intervening in foreign exchange markets, rising trade protectionism, excessive exchange rate fluctuations, and the deep poverty in many developing countries.

### *Important Terms*

**Appreciation of the domestic currency.**   A decrease in the domestic currency price of one unit of the foreign currency. (This is the same as a depreciation of the *foreign* currency.)

**Balance of payments.**   A summary statement of all the transactions of a nation with the rest of the world during a year. It includes the current, capital, and official reserve accounts.

**Bases for trade.**   The forces that give rise to trade. These are comparative advantage, increasing returns to scale or decreasing costs, product differentiation, and differences in tastes.

**Capital account.**   The balance-of-payments section that includes the flows of investments and loans between the nation and the rest of the world.

**Closed economy.**   An economy which has no trade or financial relationships with, and is completely isolated from, the rest of the world.

**Comparative advantage.**   The ability of a nation to produce a commodity at a relatively lower cost or at a lower opportunity cost than another nation.

**Complete specialization.**   The situation in which a nation produces only one of the two commodities with trade. This generally occurs under constant costs.

**Constant opportunity costs.**   The *constant* amounts of a commodity that must be given up in order to release just enough resources to produce each additional unit of a second commodity.

**Credit (+).**   A transaction that results from a payment *from* foreigners. This includes exports of goods and services, and capital inflows (i.e., investments and loans received from abroad).

**Current account.**   A balance-of-payments section that includes the flow of goods, services, and government grants between the nation and the rest of the world.

**Debit (−).**   A transaction that results in a payment *to* foreigners. This includes imports of goods and services, government grants to foreigners, and capital outflows (i.e., investments and loans made abroad).

**Deficit in balance of payments.**   The excess of debits (−) over credits (+) in the nation's current and capital accounts.

**Depreciation of the domestic currency.**   An increase in the domestic currency price of one unit of the foreign currency. (This is the same as the appreciation of the *foreign* currency.)

**Fixed-exchange-rate system.**   The system in which the rates of exchange between the domestic and foreign currencies are fixed.

**Flexible-exchange-rate system.**   A system in which the rate of exchange floats freely to find its equilibrium level at the intersection of the market demand and supply curves of the foreign currency.

**Gains from trade.**   The increases in the consumption of both commodities that result from specialization in production and trade.

**Import quota.**   A restriction on the quantity of a good that is allowed to be imported into a nation during a year.

**Import tariff.**   A tax on imports.

**Increasing opportunity costs.**   The increasing amounts of a commodity that must be given up in order to release just enough resources to produce each additional unit of a second commodity.

**Infant-industry argument for protection.**   The claim that a newly established industry requires protection until it can grow in size and efficiency and be able to face foreign competition.

**Official reserve account.**   The balance-of-payments section that shows the change in the nation's official (i.e., government) reserves and liabilities required to balance its current and capital accounts.

**Open economy.**   An economy which is connected with the rest of the world through trade and financial relationships.

**Production-possibilities or transformation curve.**   The graphic representation of the various alternative combinations of two commodities that a society can produce by fully utilizing all of its resources and the best available technology.

**Rate of exchange or exchange rate.**   The domestic currency price of one unit of the foreign currency.

**Surplus in the balance of payments.**   The excess of credits (+) over debits (−) in the nation's current and capital accounts.

**Terms of trade.**   The trade exchange ratio or the rate at which one commodity is exchanged for another.

# Outline of Chapter 23: International Trade and Finance

## 23.1   THE IMPORTANCE OF INTERNATIONAL TRADE

Thus far, we have assumed a *closed economy,* or an economy completely isolated from the rest of the world. In reality, most nations are *open economies.* That is, they are connected to other nations through a network of trade and financial relationships. These relationships have great advantages but they may also result in problems.

Even though trade is generally more important to small than to large developed nations, the welfare of the latter is also greatly dependent on trade. (See Problem 23.2.)

**EXAMPLE 23.1.**   In Table 23-1, we see that exports as a percentage of GDP for the United States in 1992 were lower than for most other industrial nations and second only to Germany's in dollar amount. Export earnings helped finance U.S. imports of automobiles, petroleum, machinery, steel, coffee, and so on.

**Table 23-1**

| Country | Exports as a Percentage of GDP | Total Value of Exports in 1992 (in Billions of Dollars) |
|---|---|---|
| Belgium | 69 | 140 |
| Netherlands | 52 | 167 |
| Germany | 38 | 681 |
| Canada | 27 | 151 |
| France | 23 | 304 |
| United Kingdom | 23 | 245 |
| United States | 11 | 636 |
| Japan | 10 | 374 |

SOURCE: *International Financial Statistics, 1993.*

## 23.2   THE BASIS AND THE GAINS FROM TRADE: COMPARATIVE ADVANTAGE

Since the availability of resources differs among nations, the opportunity cost of producing more of one commodity (in terms of the amount of a second commodity that would not be produced) also usually differs among nations. In a two-nation, two-commodity world, each nation should specialize in the production of the commodity with the lower opportunity cost; this is the commodity in which the nation has a *comparative advantage.* The nation should trade part of its output (with the other nation) for the commodity with the higher opportunity cost; this is the commodity in which the nation has a *comparative disadvantage.* Doing this results in a larger *combined* output of both commodities than would occur in the absence of specialization in production and trade.

**EXAMPLE 23.2.**   Figure 23-1 shows a hypothetical production-possibilities curve for cloth *(C)* and food *(F)* for the U.S. and U.K. under constant costs (the solid lines). It shows that the U.S. could produce 40*C* and 0*F*, 30*C* and 20*F*, 20*C* and 40*F*, 10*C* and 60*F*, or 0*C* and 80*F*. For each unit of cloth the U.S. gives up, it releases resources to produce two additional units of food. The *domestic exchange ratio* or *cost ratio* is 1*C* = 2*F*, or $\frac{1}{2}C = 1F$, and is constant in the U.S. In the U.K., 2*C* = 1*F*. Since the opportunity cost of *F* is $\frac{1}{2}C$ in the U.S. and 2*C* in the U.K., the U.S. has a comparative advantage in *F*. Similarly, the U.K. has a comparative advantage in *C*. Suppose that in the absence of trade, the U.S. and U.K. produced and consumed at points *A*(20*C* and 40*F*) and *A'*(20*C* and 20*F*), respectively. With trade, the U.S. should specialize in the production of *F* and produce at *B*(80*F* and 0*C*) and the U.K. should specialize in *C* and produce at *B'*(60*C* and 0*F*). By then exchanging, say, 30*F* for 30*C* with the U.K., the U.S. would end up consuming at *E*(30*C* and 50*F*) and the U.K. would consume at *E'* (30*C* and 30*F*). Thus, both the U.S. and the U.K. end up consuming 10*C* and 10*F* more than without specialization and trade (compare *E* with *A* and *E'* with *A'*). With increasing costs, the production-possibilities curves are concave or bulge outward, and there would be incomplete specialization in production (see Problem 23.7). Besides comparative advantage, trade could also be based on economies of scale, product differentiation, and differences in tastes (see Problem 23.8).

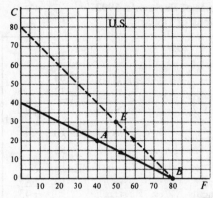 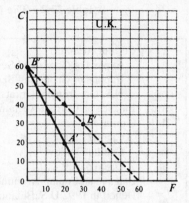

**Fig. 23-1**

## 23.3  OBSTACLES TO THE FLOW OF TRADE: TARIFFS AND QUOTAS

Even though trade can be the source of major gains, most nations restrict the free flow of trade by imposing tariffs, quotas, and other obstructions. An *import tariff* is a tax on the imported commodity. An *import quota* is a quantitative restriction on the amount of a good that may be imported during a year. Trade restrictions are advocated by labor and firms in some industries as a protection against foreign competition. These restrictions, however, generally impose a burden on society as a whole because they reduce the availability of goods and increase their prices. Some of the specific arguments advanced for trade restrictions are (1) to protect domestic labor against cheap foreign labor, (2) to reduce domestic unemployment, (3) to protect young or "infant" industries, and (4) to protect industries important for national defense. Most of the arguments are invalid and are based on misconceptions (see Problem 23.10).

**EXAMPLE 23.3.**  Protection is advocated by labor and firms in those industries in which the United States has lost or is losing its comparative advantage. Some of these industries are textiles, shoes, bicycles, and perhaps even steel and automobiles. Protection generally reduces the range of goods available and raises prices for U.S. consumers.

## 23.4  THE BALANCE OF PAYMENTS

The balance of payments is a summary statement of a nation's transactions with the rest of the world during a year. The balance of payments is divided into three major sections: I. The Current Account, which shows flows of goods and services and government grants. II. The Capital Account, which shows flows of investments and loans. (A statistical discrepancy may also be included here since it refers mostly to unreported capital transactions.) III. The Official Reserve Account, which shows the change in the nation's official (i.e., government) reserves and liabilities to balance the current and capital accounts.

The nation earns foreign currencies by exporting goods and services and receiving capital inflows (i.e., investments and loans) from abroad. All of these are credits and are entered with a plus sign. The nation spends these foreign currencies to import goods and services and to invest and lend abroad. These are *debits* and are shown with a minus sign. When the sum of all these debits (−) exceeds the sum of all the credits (+) *in the current and capital accounts*, the nation has a deficit in its balance of payments equal to the difference. The deficit is settled by a reduction in the nation's reserves of foreign currency or by an increase in the foreign monetary authorities' holdings of the deficit nation's currency. The opposite is true for a balance-of-payments surplus.

**EXAMPLE 23.4.**  Table 23-2 is a simplified version of the U.S. Balance of Payments for the year 1992.

**Table 23-2    The U.S. Balance of Payments, 1992**
**(in Billions of Dollars)**

| | | | |
|---|---|---|---|
| I. | Current Account | | |
| | Exports of Goods and Services ......................... | +730 | |
| | Imports of Goods and Services ......................... | −764 | |
| | U.S. Government Grants .............................. | −33 | |
| | Balance on Current Account ............................. | | −67 |
| II. | Capital Account | | |
| | Capital Inflow ...................................... | + 89 | |
| | Capital Outflow ..................................... | − 53 | |
| | Discrepancy ........................................ | − 12 | |
| | Balance on Capital Account ........................... | | +24 |
| | *Deficit in 1992 U.S. Balance of Payments ............... | | −43 |
| III. | Official Reserve Account | | |
| | Increase in Foreign Official Holdings of U.S. Dollars ... | | +43 |
| | | | 0 |

SOURCE: *Survey of Current Business,* June 1993.

## 23.5    THE FLEXIBLE-EXCHANGE-RATE SYSTEM OF ADJUSTMENT

A nation generates a supply of foreign currencies or monies in the process of exporting goods and services and receiving grants, investments, and loans from abroad. On the other hand, the nation uses foreign currencies to import goods and services and to make grants, investments, and loans abroad. When foreign currencies can be freely bought and sold, the rate of exchange between the domestic and a foreign currency is determined by the market demand for and the supply of the foreign currency. If the demand for the foreign currency increases, the rate of exchange rises. That is, more domestic currency is required to purchase one unit of the foreign currency (so that the domestic currency depreciates).

**EXAMPLE 23.5.**    In Fig. 23-2, D is the U.S. demand curve and S is the U.S. supply curve for pounds (£, the currency of the United Kingdom). D is downsloping because at *lower* dollar prices for pounds it is cheaper for the United States to import from, invest in, and extend loans to the U.K. S is upward-sloping because at *higher* dollar prices for pounds, it is cheaper for the U.K. to import from, invest in, and extend loans to the United States. D and S intersect at the equilibrium rate of exchange of $2 = £1 and the equilibrium quantity of £300 million. If D shifts up to D′, the rate of exchange rises to $3 = £1. If, on the other hand, the rate of exchange is not allowed to rise (as under the fixed-exchange-rate system), the United States would have a deficit (with the U.K.) of $EF = £200 = \$400$ million in its balance of payments (see Fig. 23-2). This deficit could only be corrected by reducing the level of national income, by allowing domestic prices to rise less than abroad, or by government control of trade and payments (see Problem 23.15).

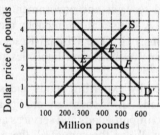

**Fig. 23-2**

## 23.6    THE INTERNATIONAL MONETARY SYSTEM AND CURRENT INTERNATIONAL ECONOMIC PROBLEMS

From the end of World War II until 1971, the world operated under a fixed-exchange-rate system known as the Bretton Woods System. Under this system, the United States faced large and chronic deficits, which it was justifiably unwilling to correct by domestic deflation or direct controls on trade and payments. The resulting lack of adjustment forced the abandonment of the fixed-exchange-rate system and the establishment of a flexible-exchange-rate system in 1973. However, the system that is in operation today is not freely flexible or completely floating because national monetary authorities intervene in foreign exchange markets to prevent erratic and unwanted fluctuations in exchange rates. This is referred to as "managed" or "dirty" floating. Today, there is a need to make such an arrangement more formal by devising acceptable rules for intervening in foreign exchange markets. Other current and related international economic problems are rising trade protectionism, excessive exchange rate fluctuations, and deep poverty in most developing countries.

# Solved Problems

## THE IMPORTANCE OF INTERNATIONAL TRADE

**23.1.** (a)  What is an "open economy"?

(b)  Why does our study of economics include international trade and finance?

(c)  How do the economic relationships among nations differ from the economic relationships among various parts or regions of a nation?

(a)  An open economy is one which is connected to other nations through a network of trade and financial relationships. Most, if not all, nations of the world are open economies to various degrees.

(b)  We want to analyze the international flow of goods, services, resources, and payments because they can greatly affect the nation's welfare.

(c)  Nations usually impose restrictions on the free international flow of goods, services, resources, and payments. Differences in language, customs, and laws also hamper these international flows. In addition, international flows involve receipts and payments in different currencies which usually change in value in relation to one another through time. In contrast, interregional flows of goods, services, resources, and payments within the same nation face no such restrictions as tariffs and quotas. Such flows are conducted in the same currency and usually in the same language, among entities having the same customs and laws.

**23.2.** (a)  How can we measure a nation's degree of economic interdependence with the rest of the world?

(b)  Why does the United States rely less on trade than most other developed nations?

(c)  What would happen to its standard of living if the United States withdrew completely from international trade?

(a)  A rough measure of the degree of interdependence of a nation with the rest of the world is given by the value of its exports as a percentage of its GDP. In 1992, for the small developed nations Belgium and the Netherlands the figures were 69% and 52%, respectively. For large developed nations such as Japan, Germany, and the United States, the figures range from 10% to 38% (see Table 23-1).

(b)  The United States is a nation of continental size with immense natural and human resources. As such, it can produce with relative efficiency most of the products it needs. In contrast, a small nation like Belgium can only specialize in the production and export of a small range of commodities and must import all the others. In general, as the figures in Table 23-1 indicate, the larger the nation, the smaller its economic interdependence with the rest of the world. The exception is Japan, which, though significantly smaller than the United States, exports a smaller percentage of its GDP than does the United States.

(c)  Even though the United States relies only to a relatively small extent on foreign trade, a *significant part* of its high standard of living depends on it. For one thing, the United States is incapable of producing such commodities as coffee, tea, cocoa, and Scotch whiskey. In addition, the United States has no known deposits of such minerals as tin and tungsten, which are important for industrial production. It also needs to import huge quantities of petroleum. In addition, there are many commodities which the United States could produce domestically but only at a relatively higher cost than the costs of some foreign countries to produce those commodities. Thus, trade is very important to the welfare of the United States.

## THE BASIS AND THE GAINS FROM TRADE: COMPARATIVE ADVANTAGE

**23.3.** (a) What is a production-possibilities or transformation curve? What does a straight-line transformation curve indicate?

(b) Plot transformation curves for the U.S. and the U.K. from the data in Table 23-3.

(c) What is the opportunity cost of food in the U.S. and the U.K.?

**Table 23-3**

| U.S. | | U.K. | |
|---|---|---|---|
| C | F | C | F |
| 40 | 0 | 60 | 0 |
| 30 | 10 | 45 | 5 |
| 20 | 20 | 30 | 10 |
| 10 | 30 | 15 | 15 |
| 0 | 40 | 0 | 20 |

(a) A production-possibilities or transformation curve shows the various alternative combinations of two commodities that a nation can produce by fully employing all of its resources and using the best technology available. Its slope indicates how much of a commodity the nation must give up in order to release just enough resources to produce more of a second commodity. A straight-line transformation curve indicates constant opportunity costs. This would occur only if all resources were equally efficient in the production of both commodities. Constant costs are assumed here only to simplify the analysis. (The more realistic increasing-cost case is discussed in Problem 23.7.)

(b) See Fig. 23-3.

(c) The opportunity cost of $F$ in the U.S. is $1C$. That is, the domestic exchange ratio or cost ratio is $1F = 1C$ and is reflected in the (absolute) slope of 1 of the U.S. transformation curve. This means that for each additional unit of food the U.S. wants to produce, it must give up $1C$. In the U.K., the opportunity cost of $1F$ is $3C$ and equals the (absolute) slope of the U.K. transformation curve. Thus, the opportunity cost of $F$ in the U.K. is three times that of the U.S.

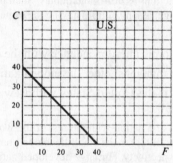
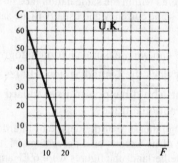

**Fig. 23-3**

**23.4.** (a) Explain comparative advantage. According to Problem 23.3, in what commodities do the U.S. and the U.K. have a comparative advantage?

(b) What combination of cloth and food do the U.S. and the U.K. produce and consume in the absence of trade?

(a) Comparative advantage refers to the commodity that a nation can produce at a *relatively* lower cost or at a lower opportunity cost than the other nation. Since the opportunity cost of $1F = 1C$ in the U.S. and $1F = 3C$ in the U.K., the U.S. has a comparative advantage in food and a comparative disadvantage in cloth with respect to the U.K. In a two-nation, two-commodity world, comparative advantage by one nation (the U.S.) in one commodity ($F$) necessarily implies that the other nation (the U.K.) has a comparative advantage in the other commodity ($C$). In Fig. 23-3, the lower absolute slope of the U.S. transformation curve indicates that the opportunity or relative cost of food (the commodity measured along the horizontal axis) is less in the U.S. than in the U.K. Therefore, the U.S. has a comparative advantage in $F$, and the U.K. in $C$.

(b) The U.S. and the U.K. can produce any combination of $C$ and $F$ indicated on their respective transformation curves. In the absence of trade, the U.S. and the U.K. can only consume what they will produce. Among the various combinations of $C$ and $F$ shown on their respective transformation curves, the U.S. and U.K. will produce that particular combination which, according to national tastes, gives them the greatest satisfaction.

**23.5.** Suppose that in Fig. 23-3 the U.S. and U.K. produce and consume at point $A$ ($30C$ and $10F$) and $A'$ ($15C$ and $15F$), respectively, in the absence of trade.

(a) Where will the U.S. and the U.K. produce with free trade? By how much does the total output of $C$ and $F$ increase with specialization in production?

(b) Draw a figure showing by points $E$ and $E'$, respectively, the combination of $C$ and $F$ consumed by the two countries if the U.S. exchanges $20F$ for $40C$ with the U.K. Explain how points $E$ and $E'$ are reached.

(a) Since the U.S. has a comparative advantage in $F$, with free trade the U.S. will specialize completely in the production of food and produce $40F$ and $0C$ (see Fig. 23-3). The U.K. will specialize completely in the production of cloth and produce $60C$ and $0F$. Thus, total world output with specialization in production is $40F$ (produced entirely in the U.S.) and $60C$ (produced entirely in the U.K.). This exceeds by $15F$ the combined output of $25F$ ($10F$ in the U.S. and $15F$ in the U.K.) produced in the absence of specialization and trade. Similarly, with specialization in production, the output of $60C$ produced entirely in the U.K. exceeds by $15C$ the output of $45C$ ($30C$ in the U.S. and $15C$ in the U.K.) before specialization and trade.

(b) In the absence of trade, the U.S. produces and consumes at point $A$ ($30C$ and $10F$) and the U.K. at point $A'$ ($15C$ and $15F$) in Fig. 23-4. With free trade possible, the U.S. specializes completely in the production of food and produces at $B$ ($40F$ and $0C$), while the U.K. specializes completely in the production of cloth and produces at $B'$ ($60C$ and $0F$). The U.S. then exchanges $20F$ for $40C$ from the U.K. and reaches point $E$ ($40C$ and $20F$) in consumption. Starting from point $B'$, the U.K. receives from the U.S. $20F$ in exchange for $40C$ and reaches point $E'$ ($20C$ and $20F$). The dashed lines are usually referred to as the trade-possibilities curves.

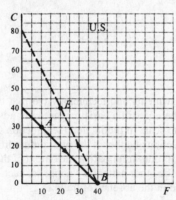
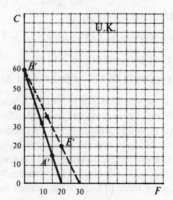

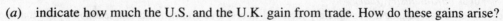

**Fig. 23-4**

**23.6.** With regard to Fig. 23-4,

(a) indicate how much the U.S. and the U.K. gain from trade. How do these gains arise?

(b) What determines the terms of trade? How does this affect the distribution of the gains from trade?

(a) The U.S. produces and consumes at point $A$ ($30C$ and $10F$) in the absence of trade and at $E$ ($40C$ and $20F$) with specialization in trade. Thus, the U.S. gains from trade are $10C$ and $10F$. On the other hand, the U.K. produces and consumes at $A'$ ($15C$ and $15F$) in the absence of trade and at $E'$ ($20C$ and $20F$)

with specialization in trade. Thus, the U.K. gains from trade are $5C$ and $5F$. The total U.S. and U.K. gains are thus $15C$ and $15F$ and equal the increases in the total outputs of food and cloth resulting from specialization in production [see Problem 23.5 (*a*)].

(*b*)  In order for both the U.S. and the U.K. to gain from trade (and thus be willing to engage in trade), the *trade* exchange ratio or terms of trade must be between the pretrade *domestic* exchange ratios. Since $20F$ are exchanged for $40C$, the trade exchange ratio is $1F = 2C$ and lies between the domestic exchange ratio of $1F = 1C$ in the U.S. and $1F = 3C$ in the U.K. before trade (see the absolute slope of the solid lines in Fig. 23-4). The smaller the U.S. demand for U.K. cloth exports and the greater the U.K. demand for U.S. food exports, the closer the *trade* exchange ratio will be to the U.K. *domestic* exchange ratio (in the absence of trade), and the greater the relative gains from trade to the U.S. and the lower the gains from trade to the U.K.

**23.7.**  Discuss what happens as nations specialize in the product of their comparative advantage and have increasing opportunity costs.

Since resources are usually not equally efficient in the production of both commodities, for each additional unit of a commodity a nation wants, it must give up more and more of the second commodity. Thus, nations generally face increasing opportunity costs or a concave or bulging-out transformation curve. As a result, as each nation specializes in the commodity of its comparative advantage, it faces increasing opportunity costs. Specialization in production then continues only up to the outputs at which the opportunity costs become equal in the two nations. This occurs before each nation has become completely specialized in production. More specifically, as the U.S. specializes in the production of food, it incurs increasing opportunity costs in food production. Similarly, as the U.K. specializes in cloth production, it incurs increasing opportunity costs in cloth production. This means *decreasing* opportunity costs in the U.K. in food production. Since the opportunity cost of food was lower in the U.S. than in the U.K. to begin with, and since it rises in the U.S. as the U.S. produces more food, and falls in the U.K. as the U.K produces less food and more cloth, an output will be reached at which the opportunity costs of $F$ will be the same in the U.S. and the U.K. At that output, specialization in production and trade will stop expanding. This is likely to occur before the U.S. has become completely specialized in food production and the U.K. in cloth production. Thus, even with trade, the U.S. will continue to produce some cloth and the U.K. will produce some of its food. (The diagrammatic exposition for the increasing opportunity cost case is more difficult and thus is left for an international economics course.)

**23.8.**  How can trade be based upon

(*a*)  increasing returns to scale,

(*b*)  differentiated products, and

(*c*)  differences in tastes between two nations?

(*a*)  Even if two nations are identical in resource endowments and technology (so that they have identical transformation curves) and have identical tastes, there is still a basis for mutually advantageous trade if the two products are subject to increasing returns to scale in production (see Section 16.6). Then it pays for each nation to specialize completely in the production of either of the two commodities, take advantage of increasing returns to scale, and exchange part of its output for part of the output of the other commodity also produced under increasing returns to scale by the other nation. By doing so, each nation will end up consuming more of both commodities than it would in the absence of trade.

(*b*)  Trade can also be based on product differentiation, whereby one nation produces and exports one variety of a product in exchange for another variety of the product from the other nation. For example, both France and Germany export and import (differentiated) automobiles to each other. This is often referred to as *intra-industry trade.*

(*c*)  Even if two nations are completely identical in resource endowments and technology (so that they have identical transformation curves) and have increasing opportunity costs (rather than increasing returns to scale or decreasing costs in production), there is still a basis for mutually advantageous trade if the two nations have different tastes. With increasing costs, identical transformation curves, and different tastes, each nation would produce a different combination of the two commodities in the absence of trade and thus incur different opportunity costs. The nation producing and consuming less of a commodity in the absence of trade will have smaller opportunity costs and a comparative advantage in the production of that commodity. The other nation will then have a comparative advantage in the production of the other commodity. The process of specialization in production and trade is then the same as described in Problem 23.7.

## OBSTACLES TO THE FLOW OF TRADE: TARIFFS AND QUOTAS

**23.9.** (*a*)  What is trade protection? An import tariff? An import quota? What are some other forms of import restrictions?

(*b*)  What important U.S. industries seek or have protection? What are some industries that do not?

(*a*)  Trade protection refers to restrictions on the imports of goods and services from abroad. These are advocated by labor and firms in some industries to protect them against foreign competition. Protection, however, results in a reduced range of commodities and higher prices for society as a whole. An import tariff is a tax on imports. This may be imposed to raise revenues (on commodities not produced in the United States, such as coffee, tea, and bananas) or for protection—usually the latter. An import quota is a restriction imposed by the government on the quantity of a good that may be imported. There are other restrictions on imports such as health regulations, safety and pollution standards, labeling and packaging regulations, and "buy American" clauses. These are often disguised methods of protection.

(*b*)  Some of the most important U.S. industries that already have and seek additional protection are the textile, automobile, and steel industries. These are the industries in which the United States has lost or is losing its comparative advantage. Some of the most important U.S. industries that do not have or need protection are the computer, aircraft, and other high-technology industries. The same is generally true for agriculture. These are the areas of U.S. comparative advantage. Tariffs have generally declined since World War II and are now on the average less than 10% on manufactured goods. Trade in agricultural commodities is still subject to many direct quantitative restrictions and other nontariff trade barriers.

**23.10.** (*a*)  Cite some of the specific arguments advanced in favor of protection.

(*b*)  Evaluate these arguments.

(*a*)  Protection is often advocated to protect domestic labor against cheap foreign labor. That is, since wages are generally higher in the United States than in other nations, without protection (so the argument goes) foreign nations can undersell the United States because of their lower wages, flood the U.S. market with imports, and depress U.S. wages. Another argument often heard in favor of protection is that it reduces domestic unemployment. That is, by restricting imports, domestic production is stimulated and the level of domestic unemployment is reduced. A third argument in favor of protection is the "infant industry" argument. This states that a newly established industry requires protection until it can grow in size and efficiency so as to be able to face foreign competition. Finally, protection is advocated in order to protect such industries as shipyards and the optical industry that are important for national defense.

(*b*)  The argument for protection against cheap foreign labor is generally invalid because it incorrectly implies that higher wages necessarily mean higher labor costs. This is not true if the higher U.S. wages are based on even higher labor productivity. Restrictions on U.S. imports to reduce U.S. unemployment is a beggar-thy-neighbor policy because it leads to higher unemployment in those nations whose exports to the United States have been restricted. As a result, these other nations are likely to retaliate and also reduce imports from the United States, and all nations lose in the end. Domestic unemployment should instead be corrected by appropriate fiscal and monetary policies. The infant-industry argument is generally invalid for the United States and other industrial nations but may be valid for poor developing nations. However, the same degree of protection can generally be better achieved by subsidies to the infant industry rather than by tariffs and quotas. Subsidies are also generally preferable to tariffs and quotas as protection to industries important for national defense.

## THE BALANCE OF PAYMENTS

**23.11.** (*a*)  What is a nation's balance of payments? What is its purpose?

(*b*)  What are the three main accounts in the balance of payments? What does each measure?

(*c*)  How are credits and debits entered into the current and capital accounts?

(a) A nation's balance of payments is a summary record of all the transactions of a nation with the rest of the world during a calendar year. Its main purpose is to inform government authorities of the nation's international position and to help them formulate monetary, fiscal, and commercial policies.

(b) The three main accounts of the balance of payments are the current account, the capital account, and the official reserve account. The current account shows the flows of goods, services, and government grants between the nation and the rest of the world. The capital account shows the flows of investments and loans between the nation and the rest of the world. The official reserve account shows the change in the nation's official (i.e., government) reserves and liabilities needed to balance the current and capital accounts.

(c) All economic transactions that lead to the United States receiving payments from abroad are entered as credits (+) in the current and capital accounts. Thus, exports of goods and services and investments and loans received from abroad (i.e., capital inflows) are entered as credits. All transactions that lead to payments to foreigners are entered as debits (−). U.S. imports of goods and services, government grants made to foreigners, and investments and loans made to foreigners (i.e., capital outflows) are entered as debits.

**23.12.** (a) How is a deficit or surplus in a nation's balance of payments measured? How is it settled? What is the function of the statistical "discrepancy"?

(b) How did the deficit in the U.S. balance of payments arise in 1992?

(a) If the sum of all the debits in the current and capital accounts exceeds the sum of all the credits in these accounts, the nation has a deficit in its balance of payments equal to the difference. This is settled out of the nation's official (i.e., government) reserves or by foreign surplus nations increasing their holdings of the deficit nation's currency. The latter form of settlement represents a future claim on the deficit nation. The opposite is true for a surplus. The function of the statistical "discrepancy" is to balance the total credits with the total debits of all three accounts taken together. For example, if the total credits in the official reserve account exceeded the sum of the total net debits in the current and capital accounts (so that the nation had a deficit), a discrepancy equal to the difference is entered at the end of the capital account *as a debit* (representing mostly unreported capital outflows).

(b) During 1992, the U.S. exports of goods and services fell short of its imports of goods and services and net government grants by $67 billion (see Table 23-2). On the other hand, capital inflows in the form of investments and loans received by the United States from abroad exceeded U.S. capital outflows in the form of U.S. investments and loans made abroad by $36 billion. This together with a (debit) discrepancy of −$12 billion left a deficit of $43 billion (−67 + 36 − 12) in the U.S. balance of payments for 1992. This was settled by foreign monetary authorities, which increased their holdings of U.S. dollars by $43 billion. They were willing to accept these dollars because the dollar is accepted as an international currency and is used to settle accounts among practically all nations of the world.

## THE FLEXIBLE-EXCHANGE-RATE SYSTEM OF ADJUSTMENT

**23.13.** (a) What gives rise to a nation's demand for a foreign currency or money? What is the shape of this demand curve? Why?

(b) What gives rise to a nation's supply of foreign currency? What is the shape of the supply curve? Why?

(c) How is the rate of exchange between the domestic and foreign currency determined under a flexible-exchange-rate system?

(a) A nation's demand for a foreign currency arises from the nation's importing goods and services from abroad, extending economic and military aid, and investing and making loans abroad. A nation's demand curve for a foreign currency is generally downsloped, indicating that the *lower* the domestic price of the foreign currency or rate of exchange, the *greater* the quantity demanded of the foreign currency. This is because imports from the foreign nation will be cheaper in terms of the domestic currency and it will be more attractive to invest abroad (see Fig. 23-2).

(b) A nation generates a supply of foreign exchange by exporting goods and services abroad and by receiving grants, investments, and loans from abroad. A nation's supply of foreign currency is generally upsloped,

## *True or False Questions*

**13.** _____ Large countries are generally more open than small countries.

**14.** _____ When each nation specializes in the production of the commodity of its comparative advantage, their combined output of both commodities increases.

**15.** _____ With constant costs, specialization in production is likely to be incomplete.

**16.** _____ A tariff is a quantitative restriction on imports.

**17.** _____ Import restrictions are required to protect the nation's labor against cheap foreign labor.

**18.** _____ Most arguments for trade restrictions are invalid.

**19.** _____ The import of a good is a credit.

**20.** _____ A capital outflow is a debit.

**21.** _____ A nation has a surplus in its balance of payments if its total credits exceed its total debits in its current and capital accounts.

**22.** _____ The United States had a deficit in its balance of payments in 1992.

**23.** _____ A deficit in a nation's balance of payments is corrected by a depreciation of its currency under a fixed-exchange-rate system.

**24.** _____ The major economic problem in industrial countries in the early 1990s was high inflation.

### *Answers to Multiple Choice and True or False Questions*

| | | | |
|---|---|---|---|
| 1. (b) | 7. (c) | 13. (T) | 19. (F) |
| 2. (b) | 8. (b) | 14. (T) | 20. (T) |
| 3. (d) | 9. (a) | 15. (F) | 21. (T) |
| 4. (c) | 10. (b) | 16. (F) | 22. (T) |
| 5. (a) | 11. (c) | 17. (F) | 23. (F) |
| 6. (d) | 12. (d) | 18. (T) | 24. (F) |

indicating that the *higher* the domestic price of the foreign currency or exchange rate, the *greater* the quantity supplied of the foreign currency. The reason for this is that the greater the amount of the domestic currency foreigners can exchange for one unit of their currency, the cheaper our exports are to them and the more attractive investments and loans to us are for foreigners (see Fig. 23-2).

(c) Under a freely flexible or floating exchange rate system, the equilibrium rate of exchange and equilibrium quantity of foreign exchange are determined at the intersection of the market demand curve and the market supply curve of the foreign currency (see Fig. 23-2).

**23.14.** (a) What happens to the equilibrium rate of exchange and to the equilibrium quantity of foreign exchange if the nation's demand for the foreign currency increases? Why?

(b) How is a deficit or a surplus in a nation's balance of payments corrected under a flexible-exchange-rate system?

(a) Given the nation's supply curve of the foreign currency, an upward shift in the nation's demand curve for the foreign currency will determine a new and higher equilibrium exchange rate and equilibrium quantity (see Fig. 23-2). An increase in the nation's demand for a foreign currency may result from a change in tastes for more imported goods and services. It may also occur if the nation increases its investments and loans abroad in the expectation of increased returns.

(b) A deficit in a nation's balance of payments means that at a given rate of exchange, there is a shortage (an excess of quantity demanded over quantity supplied) of the foreign currency. If the exchange rate is freely flexible or floating, the exchange rate will rise until the quantity demanded of the foreign currency equals the quantity supplied and the deficit is completely eliminated (see Fig. 23-2). This rise in the exchange rate means that the relative value of the domestic currency is falling or depreciating. The exact opposite occurs when there is a surplus and the nation's currency appreciates (or increases) in relative value.

## THE INTERNATIONAL MONETARY SYSTEM AND CURRENT INTERNATIONAL ECONOMIC PROBLEMS

**23.15.** (a) How is the present international economic system different from a freely-flexible-exchange-rate system? What are its disadvantages?

(b) How can a deficit or surplus in a nation's balance of payments be corrected under a fixed-exchange-rate system?

(c) When was a fixed-exchange-rate system in operation? Why did it collapse?

(a) Under the present international economic system, exchange rates are not freely flexible or completely floating because national monetary authorities intervene in foreign exchange markets (managed or dirty floating) to prevent erratic and unwanted fluctuations. As a result, deficits and surpluses are not completely or automatically eliminated. A more serious disadvantage is that a nation may attempt to keep its exchange rate artificially high in order to discourage imports and stimulate its exports. This could lead to retaliation by other nations (whose exports fall) and result in a decline in the volume of and gains from trade and a loss to all nations. What is needed is to make such a system more formal by devising acceptable rules for intervening in foreign exchange markets.

(b) Under a fixed-exchange-rate system the rate of exchange is not allowed to vary. As a result, the elimination of a deficit or surplus can only be accomplished through income and price changes or government controls on trade and payments. To do this, the deficit nation should deflate the economy (so as to discourage imports) and make sure that domestic prices rise less than in surplus nations (so as to encourage exports). On the other hand, the surplus nation should stimulate its economy in order to encourage imports and discourage its exports. If nations are unwilling to do this, a deficit can only be corrected by direct government restrictions on imports of goods and services and loans and investments from abroad.

(c) A fixed-exchange-rate system (the so-called Bretton Woods System) similar to that described above was in operation from the end of World War II until 1971. The fundamental reason for its collapse was the lack of an adequate adjustment mechanism. Nations were generally (and justifiably) unwilling to deflate and inflate their economies in order to correct a deficit or surplus in their balance of payments. On the other hand, direct controls on trade and payments restrict trade and invite retaliation. Because of the lack of an adequate adjustment mechanism, the United States incurred chronic deficits totaling over $50 billion from 1950 to 1971. Most of these were settled by foreign monetary authorities increasing their holdings of dollars. But in 1971 these authorities refused to accept more dollars at the fixed exchange rate. The dollar was then allowed to depreciate and the present system was established in 1973.

**23.16.** What are the major international economic problems facing the world today?

The major international economic problems facing the world today are:

(1) The need to reform the international monetary system or, at least, to formalize present arrangements and devise acceptable rules for intervention in foreign exchange markets.

(2) Rising trade protectionism reduces the volume and the benefits from trade and raises the danger of trade wars in which all nations lose.

(3) Excessive exchange rate fluctuations increase uncertainties and reduce the volume of foreign trade and investments.

(4) The deep poverty and lagging economic development in the world's poor nations present a potentially explosive situation.

Nevertheless, we must not exaggerate these problems and paint too bleak a picture. Since the middle 1980s, current international monetary arrangements have worked fairly well and major international economic crises have been avoided.

## Multiple Choice Questions

1. Most nations of the world are
   (a) closed economies,
   (b) open economies,
   (c) self-sufficient,
   (d) nontrading nations.

2. The production-possibilities (or transformation) curves of two nations usually differ because of
   (a) a difference in tastes between the two nations,
   (b) a difference in the availability of resources,
   (c) constant costs,
   (d) increasing costs.

3. Which of the following statements is *incorrect?*
   (a) A straight-line transformation curve indicates constant opportunity costs.
   (b) The *flatter* transformation curve for the U.S. in Fig. 23-1 indicates that the U.S. has lower opportunity costs or a comparative advantage in *food* (measured along the horizontal axis).
   (c) The *steeper* transformation curve for the U.K. in Fig. 23-1 indicates that the U.K. has a comparative advantage in *cloth* (measured along the vertical axis).
   (d) In the absence of trade, the U.S. is likely to produce only food and the U.K. only cloth.

4. Which of the following statements is *incorrect* with regard to Example 23.1 and Fig. 23-1?
   (a) In the absence of specialization in production and trade, the combined U.S. and U.K. output of food is 60.
   (b) In the absence of specialization in production and trade, the combined U.S. and U.K. output of cloth is 40.
   (c) With specialization in production and trade, the total output of food is 50.
   (d) With specialization in production and trade, the total output of cloth is 60.

5. In Example 23.1 and Fig. 23-1, trade takes place at the exchange ratio (or terms of trade) of
   (a) $1F = 1C$,
   (b) $\frac{1}{2}F = 1C$,
   (c) $2F = 1C$,
   (d) $1\frac{1}{2}F = 1C$.

6. A specific argument advanced for protection is
   (a) to protect domestic labor against cheap foreign labor,
   (b) to reduce domestic unemployment,
   (c) to protect infant industries and industries important for national defense,
   (d) all of the above.

7. Which of the following is *not* included in the current account section of the balance of payments?
   (a) The export of goods and services,
   (b) The import of goods and services,
   (c) Capital inflows,
   (d) Government grants.

8. A deficit or surplus in a nation's balance of payments is measured by subtracting all the debits from all the credits in the
   (a) current account,
   (b) current and capital accounts,
   (c) current, capital, and official reserve accounts,
   (d) capital and official reserve accounts.

9. Which of the following statements is *not* true with respect to the 1992 U.S. balance of payments?
   (a) Exports exceeded imports.
   (b) Capital inflows exceeded capital outflows.
   (c) The United States had a surplus.
   (d) The foreign official holdings of U.S. dollars increased.

10. The rate of exchange between the domestic and a foreign currency is defined as the
    (a) foreign currency price of a unit of the domestic currency,
    (b) domestic currency price of a unit of the foreign currency,
    (c) foreign currency price of gold,
    (d) domestic currency price of gold.

11. Under a freely-flexible-exchange-rate system, a deficit in a nation's balance of payments is corrected by
    (a) a decrease in the domestic currency price of the foreign currency,
    (b) an appreciation of domestic currency,
    (c) a depreciation of the domestic currency,
    (d) a depreciation of the foreign currency.

12. A serious current international economic problem is
    (a) the lack of generally acceptable rules for intervention in foreign exchange markets,
    (b) worldwide inflation,
    (c) the sharp rise in petroleum prices,
    (d) all of the above.

# Appendix A

## SAMPLE Screens From
## The Companion *Interactive Outline*

As described on the back cover, this book has a companion *Schaum's Interactive Outline* which uses Mathcad[®] and is designed to help you learn the subject matter more readily. The *Interactive Outline* uses the LIVE-MATH environment of Mathcad technical calculation software to give you on-screen access to approximately 100 representative solved problems from this book, together with summaries of key theoretical points and electronic cross-referencing and hyperlinking. The following pages reproduce a representative sample of screens from the *Interactive Outline* and will help you understand the powerful capabilities of this electronic learning tool. Compare these screens with the associated solved problems from this book (the corresponding page numbers are listed at the start of each problem) to see how one complements the other.

In the companion *Schaum's Interactive Outline*, you'll find all related text, diagrams, and equations for a particular solved problem together on your computer screen. As you can see on the following pages, all the math appears in familiar notation, including units. The format differences you may notice between the printed *Schaum's Outline* and the *Interactive Outline* are designed to encourage your interaction with the material or show you alternate ways to solve challenging problems.

As you view the following pages, keep in mind that every number, formula, and graph shown *is completely interactive when viewed on the computer screen.* You can change the starting parameters of a problem and watch as new output graphs are calculated before your eyes; you can change any equation and immediately see the effect of the numerical calculations on the solution. Every equation, graph, and number you see is available for experimentation. Each adapted solved problem becomes a "live" worksheet you can modify to solve dozens of related problems. The companion *Interactive Outline* thus will help you to learn and retain the material taught in this book and you can also use it as a working problem-solving tool.

The Mathcad icon shown on the right is printed throughout this *Schaum's Outline* to indicate which problems are found in the *Interactive Outline*.

For more information about the companion *Interactive Outline,* including system requirements, please see the back cover. On the inside back cover you'll find a list of all *Schaum's Outlines* and *Interactive Outlines* available as of the publication date of this book.

---

[®] Mathcad is a registered trademark of MathSoft, Inc.

## Changes in Aggregate Output

(Schaum's Principles of Economics, Solved Problem 4.6)

**Creating an Example Curve**

A **Keynesian aggregate supply curve** is horizontal below full employment and thereafter positively sloped.

$$full := 7 \qquad \text{full capacity output}$$

$$t := 0 .. 10$$

$$vx_t := t$$

$$vy_t := if(t < full, 1, t - (full - 1))$$

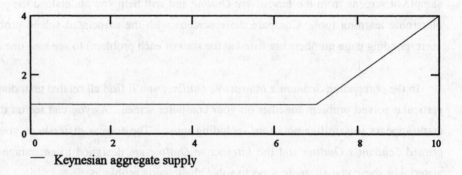

— Keynesian aggregate supply

For later interpolation, mathcad's spline function is used here to fit a line to the above data.

$$vs := lspline(vx, vy)$$

**Demand Curve Defined**

An example **aggregate demand** curve is defined below:

$$x := \begin{pmatrix} 3 \\ 4 \end{pmatrix} \qquad y := \begin{pmatrix} 1 \\ 0 \end{pmatrix}$$

$$M_d := slope(x, y) \qquad M_d = -1$$

$$b_d := intercept(x, y) \qquad b_d = 4$$

$$AD(P) := M_d \cdot P + b_d \qquad \text{a straight-line}$$

**Define a function** which solves for the equilibrium point:

$$P := 2 \qquad \text{guess}$$

$$given \qquad M \cdot P + b = interp(vs, vx, vy, P)$$

$$Eq(P, M, b, vs, vx, vy) := find(P)$$

And determine the equilibrium point as the intersection of the **keynesian aggregate supply curve** and the **aggregate demand curve**:

$$y_0 := Eq(AD(P), M_d, b_d, vs, vx, vy)$$

$$y_0 = 3$$

$$p_0 := interp(vs, vx, vy, y_0)$$

$$p_0 = 1$$

Graph the two curves together along with the equilibrium point:

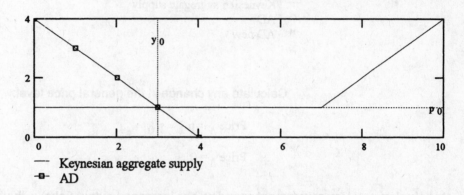

— Keynesian aggregate supply
-▫- AD

**A Change in Demand**

Increased government spending shifts the aggregate demand curve outward to $AD_{new}$.

$$AD_\Delta := 2$$

$$x := x + \begin{pmatrix} AD_\Delta \\ AD_\Delta \end{pmatrix} \qquad \text{demand is increased}$$

The line's slope remains unchanged.  Calculate the new y-intercept:

$$b_{new} := intercept(x, y)$$

$$b_{new} = 6$$

$$AD_{new}(P) := M_d \cdot P + b_{new} \qquad \text{a straight-line}$$

Calculate the new equilibrium (intersection):

$$y_1 := Eq(AD_{new}(P), M_d, b_{new}, vs, vx, vy)$$

$$y_1 = 5$$

$$p_1 := interp(vs, vx, vy, y_1)$$

$$p_1 = 1$$

**Graph the result:**

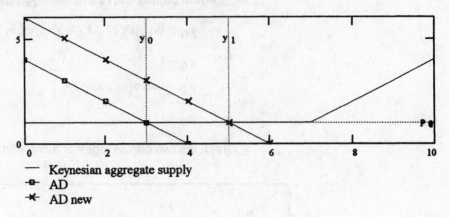

Calculate any change in the general price level:

$$Price_\Delta := p_1 - p_0$$

$$Price_\Delta = 0$$

**Conclusion**    Here government spending has increased output (jobs) without increasing the price level because the intersection of aggregate supply and aggregate demand remains in the horizontal portion of the aggregate supply curve.

**Suggestion**    Try changing the constant **full**. Increasing **full** corresponds to an increase in resources, increasing the capacity for output without an increase in the price level. Conversely, decreasing **full** may shift the horizontal portion of the supply curve resulting in an increase in the price level.

## Demand-Pull Inflation
(Schaum's Principles of Economics, Example 5.5)

**Demand-Pull Inflation**

Demonstrate how increased demand for output can result in **demand-pull** inflation.

Define an **aggregate supply curve**. In this example, the curve implies price level increase proportional to demand increase, up to full employment; thereafter, the price level increases disproportionately to increasing output. This definition uses **Mathcad's spline** function.

$$\text{full} := 4 \qquad \text{\textbf{full capacity output}}$$

$$t := 0..10$$

$$vx_t := t$$

$$vy_t := if\left[ t \leq full, 1 + \frac{t}{10}, 2^{\frac{t-(full-1)}{2}} \right]$$

$$vs := lspline(vx, vy)$$

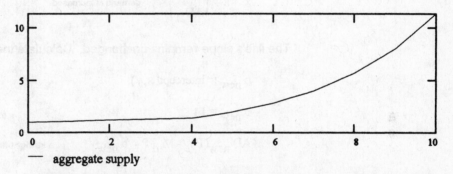

—— aggregate supply

Define a beginning **aggregate demand** curve, AD, that intercepts the aggregate supply curve at the output of full employment:

$$y_0 := full \qquad \text{\textbf{beginning supply-demand intercept}}$$

$$x := \begin{pmatrix} y_0 \\ y_0 + 1 \end{pmatrix} \qquad\qquad y := \begin{pmatrix} interp(vs, vx, vy, y_0) \\ 0 \end{pmatrix}$$

$$M_d := slope(x, y) \qquad M_d = -1.4$$

$$b_d := intercept(x, y) \qquad b_d = 7$$

$$AD(P) := M_d \cdot P + b_d \qquad \text{\textbf{a straight-line}}$$

Determine the price level at full employment's output:

$$p_0 := interp(vs, vx, vy, y_0) \qquad p_0 = 1.4$$

**Graph the two curves together along with the equilibrium point:**

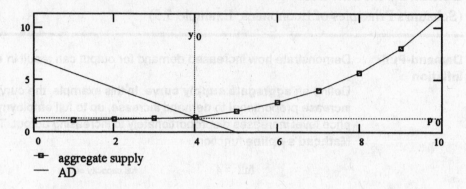

- □ aggregate supply
- — AD

**Demand Increase**

An increase in aggregate demand shifts the aggregate demand curve outward to $AD_{new}$.

$$AD_\Delta := 5$$

$$x := x + \begin{pmatrix} AD_\Delta \\ AD_\Delta \end{pmatrix} \qquad \text{demand is increased}$$

**The line's slope remains unchanged. Calculate the new y-intercept:**

$$b_{new} := intercept(x, y)$$

$$b_{new} = 14$$

$$AD_{new}(P) := M_d \cdot P + b_{new} \qquad \text{a straight-line}$$

**Define a function** which solves for the equilibrium point:

$$P := 2 \qquad \text{guess}$$

$$given \qquad M \cdot P + b = interp(vs, vx, vy, P)$$

$$Eq(P, M, b, vs, vx, vy) := find(P)$$

**Calculate the new equilibrium (intersection):**

$$y_1 := Eq(AD_{new}(P), M_d, b_{new}, vs, vx, vy)$$

$$y_1 = 7.071$$

$$p_1 := interp(vs, vx, vy, y_1)$$

$$p_1 = 4.101$$

Graph the result:

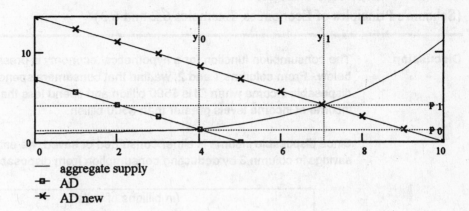

Calculate the change in the general price level resulting from the increased demand:

$$Price_\Delta := p_1 - p_0$$

$$Price_\Delta = 3$$

**Conclusion**     An increase in aggregate demand shifts the aggregate demand curve outward from AD to $AD_{new}$, which moves the equilibrium point up the aggregate supply curve; the price level increases from $p_0$ to $p_1$, and real output increases from $y_0$ to $y_1$. The AD to $AD_{new}$ increase in aggregate spending is an example of demand-pull inflation: increased aggregate spending has **"pulled up"** the price level.

**Suggestion**    Try changing $y_0$ (the **beginning supply-demand intercept**). By making $y_0$ smaller, increases in demand lead to a smaller demand-pull increase of the price level.

## The Consumption Function
(Schaum's Principles of Economics, Examples 6.2 and 6.3)

**Discussion**     The consumption function for a hypothetical economy is presented in the table below.  From columns 1 and 2, we find that consumers spend their entire disposable income when DI is $500 billion and spend less than their disposable income at income levels greater than $500 billion.

Since disposable income is either consumed or saved, we establish consumer savings in column 3 by deducting consumption from disposable income.

| (in billions of dollars) | | |
|---|---|---|
| Aggregate Disposable Income (DI) | Aggregate Consumption (C) | Aggregate Saving (S) |
| 500 | 500 | 0 |
| 550 | 540 | 10 |
| 600 | 580 | 20 |
| 650 | 620 | 30 |
| 700 | 660 | 40 |
| 750 | 700 | 50 |
| 800 | 740 | 60 |

The calculations underlying the table are presented below:

**Consumption Function**     Determine the **linear consumption function (Cf$_0$)** from the tabular data:

$$DI := \begin{bmatrix} 500 \\ 550 \\ 600 \\ 650 \\ 700 \\ 750 \\ 800 \end{bmatrix} \qquad C := \begin{bmatrix} 500 \\ 540 \\ 580 \\ 620 \\ 660 \\ 700 \\ 740 \end{bmatrix}$$

$$M_0 := slope(DI, C) \qquad\qquad M_0 = 0.8$$

$$b_0 := intercept(DI, C) \qquad\qquad b_0 = 100$$

$$Cf_0(DI) := M_0 \cdot DI + b_0 \qquad \text{a straight-line}$$

A 45 degree line which is **equidistant** from both the consumption and disposable income axes is needed.

$$M_e := 1$$                    **equidistant from both axes**

$$b_e := 0$$                    **y-intercept is zero**

$$E(DI) := M_e \cdot DI + b_e$$     **a straight-line**

**Equate the two lines and determine the only level of disposable income at which consumer spending equals disposable income (the point of intersection of the consumption line and the 45° line:**

$$x := 1$$                    **guess**

given

$$Cf_0(x) = E(x)$$

$$Intersection_0 := find(x)$$

$$Intersection_0 = 500$$

**Graph the data:**

$$i := 0, 10 .. 800$$

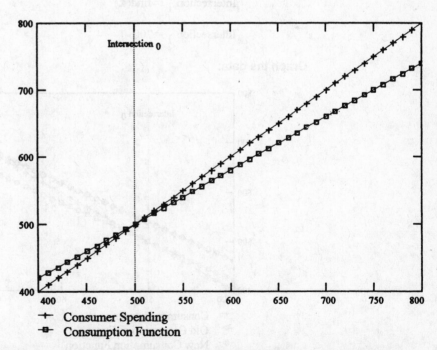

| | Consumer Spending |
|---|---|
| | Consumption Function |

**Savings**        Since the consumption line is below the 45 degree line at disposable income levels above $500 billion, it follows that consumers are not consuming their entire income and therefore are saving. Thus, **consumer saving is the distance between the consumption line and the 45 degree line at each level of disposable income.**

$$\begin{bmatrix} 0 \\ 10 \\ 20 \\ 30 \\ 40 \\ 50 \\ 60 \end{bmatrix}$$

$$S(DI) := E(DI) - Cf_0(DI) \qquad\qquad S(DI) =$$

**A Change in Optimism**

Suppose consumers become **more optimistic** and are consequently more willing to spend their disposable income. Such a trend would shift the consumption function $Cf_0$ upward to $Cf_1$.

$$M_1 := M_0 \qquad\qquad M_1 = 0.8$$

$$b_1 := b_0 + 40 \qquad\qquad b_1 = 140$$

$$Cf_1(DI) := M_1 \cdot DI + b_1 \qquad \text{still a straight-line}$$

The level at which disposable income equals spending is calculated:

$$x := 1 \qquad\qquad\qquad \text{guess}$$

given

$$Cf_1(x) = E(x)$$

$$\text{Intersection}_1 := find(x)$$

$$\text{Intersection}_1 = 700$$

Graph the data:

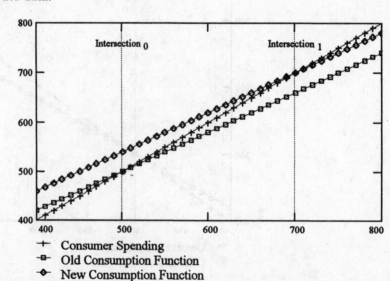

- + Consumer Spending
- □ Old Consumption Function
- ◇ New Consumption Function

## Market Supply and Demand

(Schaum's Principles of Economics, Example 2.1)

**System Parameters**

Suppose the **market demand** for **Good X** is given by the equation:

$$Q_d(P) := 1000 - 20 \cdot P$$

and **market supply** is given by the equation:

$$Q_s(P) := 500 + 30 \cdot P$$

**Problem**

(a) Find the quantity demanded and the quantity supplied when the price of **Good X** is $12. Is there a **surplus** or **shortage** in the production of **Good X**? What should happen to the price of **Good X**? (b) Find the quilibrium price for **Good X** by equating $Q_d$ and $Q_s$. (c) Prove that the price found in part (b) is an equilibrium price.

**Solutions**

The problem can be illustrated graphically over a price range of $1 to $20. $P := 1 .. 20$

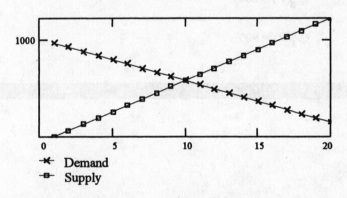

-✳- Demand
-◻- Supply

**Part (a)**

Quantity demanded and supplied are found by letting P equal $12 in the demand and supply functions above:

$$P := 12 \qquad \text{dollars}$$

$$Q_d(P) = 760 \qquad \text{quantity demanded}$$

$$Q_s(P) = 860 \qquad \text{quantity supplied}$$

At $12, the supply is greater than the demand and there is **downward pressure** on the price of **Good X**.

**Part (b)**            The equilibrium price for **Good X** is found by equating Qd and Qs and
                        finding P with a *Mathcad solve block*.

given

$$Q_d(P) = Q_s(P)$$

$$P := find(P)$$

$$P = 10$$          **The quantity demanded equals the supply then the price is $10.**

**Part (c)**            At equilibrium, the quantity demanded must equal the quantity supplied.
                        Substituting the $10 equilibrium price into the market demand and market
                        supply functions, both yield 800 units.

$$P = 10$$

$$Q_d(P) = 800$$

$$Q_s(P) = 800$$

## Liquidity of Debt: Discounted Price of a Note
(Schaum's Principles of Economics, Solved Problem 9.3)

**Problem**

Suppose Saver A lends **$100,000** to Corporation Z for two years; the debt contract stipulates that Corporation Z must pay an annual **6%** rate of interest on the $100,000 borrowed and repay the sum borrowed at the end of the second year.

Suppose that one year later, Saver A needs cash and wishes to sell Corporation Z's note in the secondary market; assume market **rates have risen from 6% to 7%.**

$$\text{par\_value} := 100000$$

$$i_0 := 6 \cdot \% \qquad i_1 := 7 \cdot \%$$

$$n := 1$$

Investors will not pay $100,000 for this debt instrument in the secondary market since the debt contract provides only a 6% interest payment.

Saver A, however, may sell this note to Saver B for a discounted price. The discounted price will be such that the Saver B will realize the market rate of 7% on Corporation Z's debt instrument:

$$n \cdot \left( \frac{\text{par\_value} \cdot i_0 + \text{par\_value} - \text{new\_value}}{\text{new\_value}} \right) = n \cdot i_1$$

Solving for the discounted price, notice that the time remaining until maturity, **n**, becomes irrelevant:

$$\text{new\_value} := \frac{- \left( \text{par\_value} \cdot i_0 + \text{par\_value} \right)}{\left( -1 - i_1 \right)}$$

And simplifying, note that the new price becomes a function of the **ratio of the interest rate and the market rate:**

$$\text{new\_value} := \text{par\_value} \cdot \frac{\left(1 + i_0\right)}{\left(1 + i_1\right)}$$

$$\text{new\_value} = 99065.42$$

---

## Profit Maximization for a Monopolist

(Schaum's Principles of Economics, Examples 18.3)

---

**Discussion**   The profit-maximizing or best level of output for the monopolist is given at the output
at which marginal return (MR) is equal to marginal cost (MC). The profit-maximizing
unit price (P) is then determined from the demand curve. Depending on the level of
average cost (AC) at this output, the monopolist can have profits, break even, or
minimize the short-run total losses.

The table below lists price (P), total revenue (TR), and total cost (TC) for various
levels of production (Q). Marginal return (MR) and marginal cost (MC) are calculated
below.  As long as **MR** exceeds **MC**, the monopolist will expand output and sales
because doing so adds more to **TR** than to **TC** and profits rise. The opposite is true
when **MR** is less than **MC**. Thus total profits are maximized when **MR = MC**.

| P ($) | Q | TR ($) | TC ($) |
|-------|---|--------|--------|
| 8 | 0 | 0 | 6 |
| 7 | 1 | 7 | 8 |
| 6 | 2 | 12 | 9 |
| 5 | 3 | 15 | 12 |
| 4 | 4 | 16 | 20 |
| 3 | 5 | 15 | 35 |

Vary C to affect total cost:   $C := 0$

**Discussion**   Appropriate curves are fitted to the data, the production / sales quantity for
maximium profit is determined, and the optimal unit price as well as total profit is
calculated.

Select the data from the table:

$P := \text{submatrix}(\text{Table}, 0, 5, 0, 0)$

$Q := \text{submatrix}(\text{Table}, 0, 5, 1, 1)$

$TR := \text{submatrix}(\text{Table}, 0, 5, 2, 2)$

$TC := \text{submatrix}(\text{Table}, 0, 5, 3, 3)$

**Define Curve** A 3rd order polynomial will be sufficient to describe all the needed curves:

$$F(x) := \begin{bmatrix} x^3 \\ x^2 \\ x \\ 1 \end{bmatrix}$$

**Fit Curves to Data**

Fit curves to total profit (TP) and unit price (P), and graph:

$$i := 0 .. 5$$

$$TP_i := TR_i - TC_i$$

$$S_{TP} := \text{linfit}(Q, TP, F) \qquad TP(x) := F(x) \cdot S_{TP} \qquad \text{Total profits}$$

$$S_P := \text{linfit}(Q, P, F) \qquad P(x) := F(x) \cdot S_P \qquad \text{Demand}$$

$$i := 0, .1 .. 5$$

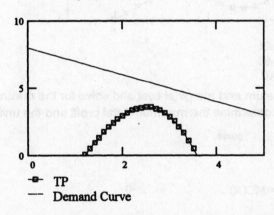

- □ TP
- — Demand Curve

Fit curves to marginal return (MR), marginal cost (MC), and average cost (AC):

$$i := 1 .. 5$$

$$MR_i := TR_i - TR_{i-1} \qquad\qquad MR := \text{submatrix}(MR, 1, 5, 0, 0)$$

$$MC_i := TC_i - TC_{i-1} \qquad\qquad MC := \text{submatrix}(MC, 1, 5, 0, 0)$$

$$AC_i := \frac{TC_i}{Q_i} \qquad\qquad AC := \text{submatrix}(AC, 1, 5, 0, 0)$$

$$Q := \text{submatrix}(Q, 1, 5, 0, 0) \qquad \text{Adjust origin of quantity for curves below.}$$

$$S_{AC} := \text{linfit}(Q, AC, F) \qquad AC(x) := F(x) \cdot S_{AC} \qquad \text{Average cost}$$

**Adjust Q for MR and MC**      $Q := Q - \dfrac{1}{2}$

$S_{MR} := \text{linfit}(Q, MR, F)$      $MR(x) := F(x) \cdot S_{MR}$      **Marginal return**

$S_{MC} := \text{linfit}(Q, MC, F)$      $MC(x) := F(x) \cdot S_{MC}$      **Marginal cost**

$i := 0, .25 .. 5$

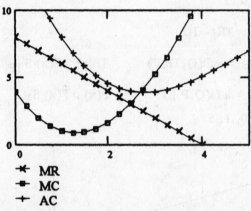

- ✳ MR
- ▪ MC
- + AC

**Results**      Equate marginal return and marginal cost and solve for the maximum profit quantity. With that quantity, determine the maximum total profit and the unit price.

$x := 5$      **guess**

**given**

$MR(x) = MC(x)$      $x > 0$

$Q_{max} := \text{find}(x)$      $Q_{max} = 2.485$      **quantity of maximum profit**

$TP_{max} := TP(Q_{max})$      $TP_{max} = 3.593$      **maximum total profit**

$P_{max} := P(Q_{max})$      $P_{max} = 5.515$      **unit price at maximum profit**

**Suggestion**      Increase C and thus increase the total cost of production. Note that as you raise expenses equally for all quantities, the quantity at which profit is maximized remains unchanged. Average costs rise until they exceed the sale price as given by the demand curve.

# INDEX